REVIEWERS LOVE *Here Be Dragons:*

"If American novelist Horatio Alger had heard the story of Peter C. Newman, he would have put his pen down, knowing real life had eclipsed imagination." — *Globe and Mail*

"Newman tells the story of how Margaret Trudeau asked him whether she should accept an invitation to mud-wrestle in the nude at a Tokyo night club. If Margaret's inclination shocks you, wait until you read about Trudeau himself cavorting in the Newmans' living room with a gorgeous female companion." — *Calgary Sun*

"To my astonishment and against all my expectations, I was entranced. Newman has written a reflective biography, candid and revealing to the point of self-laceration." — Graham Fraser, *Toronto Star*

"This is one big, honkin' autobiography, a sort of literary pre-emptive strike. Peter Newman transforms Canadian political writing into a blood sport." — Erik Floren, *Edmonton Sun*

"Even at more than 700 pages, a fast read: brisk, humorous, astute and brimming with interest.... Newman's laconic, laid-back anecdotal memoir is a must-read." — Nancy Schiefer, *London Free Press*

"Reading Newman, the adjective that comes to mind is prurient, as he piles on the details of Barbara Amiel's antics and appetites: Why did Conrad marry Barbara? 'For one, she was his intellectual soul mate; for another, she introduced him to oral sex.'" — Christie Blatchford, *Globe and Mail*

"Some might think it is demeaning to oral sex to associate it with Conrad Black." — Joseph Roberts, *Common Ground* magazine

"It is a mesmerizing story of one man's search for himself and for love. It is simply compelling reading. Newman is a superb sailor, and he takes his title from the notation on ancient maps to indicate 'where monsters dwell'— and there are a great many in this book, most of which he either slays or now accepts."
— Roy MacGregor, *Globe and Mail*

"Newman has once again served up a sensational smorgasbord of stories that will make a perfect gift for political junkies, business history beavers, or anyone who simply loves unconventional journalism from one of Canada's greats."
— Brian Flemming, Halifax *Daily News*

"The writing is pure Peter C. with flashes of brilliance, dollops of wit and dashes of sharply shared clarity that has, over these many years, become Newman's signature. It's difficult for me to imagine a more clearly written and honestly shared autobiography."
— Linda Richards, *January Magazine*

"What made Newman so successful as a journalist and writer was his honesty. He wasn't afraid to describe what he saw. And that made some of his subjects reluctant to spend time with him. 'If I were them, I wouldn't talk to me,' he says."
— Jeffrey Simpson, Halifax *Chronicle-Herald*

"Newman earned national fame as the most lethal Ottawa columnist in Canadian history. As a superb sleuth and beguiling interviewer, he winkled out one amazing story after another. Not since George Brown has a Canadian journalist wielded such direct power!"
— David Frum, *National Post*

"He certainly has left nothing out. Honour is due. Thank you, Peter."   – Ian MacDonald, Montreal *Gazette*

"If you enter this large book, there will be times when you have to set it down in order to laugh properly. It is that entertaining. He finds love in the end, which is not surprising, since he also found it at the beginning and in the middle."
                                   – Allan Chambers, *Edmonton Journal*

"Newman's description of the nocturnal sexual shenanigans after lights out at Upper Canada College will likely cause most observers of the Canadian Establishment to break out in a cold sweat. . . . Of the lions that once roamed the Canadian literary landscape, with names like Berton, Davies and McClelland, the fiercest was Newman."   – Robert J. Wiersema, *Quill & Quire*

"The author of 22 books that peered so perceptively into the cabinet rooms of government and the boardrooms of Canada's major corporations has now told us more than we ever dared know about the bedroom of the beleaguered Conrad Black and Barbara Amiel."   – Paul Gessell, *Kingston Whig-Standard*

"With the same unsparing stiletto style that has marked his best-selling books, Peter Newman looks at his own life and times in this riveting autobiography."
                                   – Yvonne Crittenden, *Windsor Star*

"Somewhere in the midst of this rollicking good read, you realize Newman is in many ways a character larger than many of those he has written about. He was privy to the secret lives of the rich and famous and he bars no holds in spilling both their secrets and his. Written in Newman's copyrighted erudite style, you'll gallop through all 700 pages."   – Paul Jackson, *Calgary Sun*

"Canada made Newman, and in some ways, Newman made Canada. His autobiography is a fine testament to that marriage."
— Morley Walker, *Winnipeg Free Press*

"Newman's life story is 'bigger than Bill Clinton's and has more sex.'"
— *Toronto Star*

"He was the only prominent editor, maybe the only prominent person of any type, who had the voices on one side of the socio-economic chasm and the ears of those on the other."
— George Fetherling, *New Brunswick Reader*

"There are many other authors and journalists selling the same ideas from the same point of view. Newman has trumped them all because he has the phenomenal ability to become absorbed in his subjects and absorbed in its retelling. *Here Be Dragons* goes way beyond Newman's memoirs. It is the best front-row narrative yet of the Trudeau age which, like it or not, still dominates Canadian politics."
— Lorne Gunter, *Edmonton Journal*

"Peter's success is due in no small part to his ability to accomplish the ultimate journalists' parlour trick: to insinuate himself into an insider's position of power, even as he has never lost his perspective as a self-described outsider."
— Anthony Wilson-Smith, *Maclean's*

"What has the chattering classes boggled over their cocktail parties is Peter Newman's candour. He prints out the names of five of his lovers, including a Miss Canada, then reveals that he had a love affair over 20 years with one, Barbara McDougall, who among other things was Canada's foreign minister under Brian Mulroney. I'm not good at math, but there does seem to be an overlap."
— Allan Fotheringham, *Hamilton Spectator*

"Newman honed his insights by skewering self-important big shots by reporting their own stupid words. He understands his own romanticism and sees himself alone, but accompanied by music and the sea. He is a story teller from whom fairness and impartiality are secondary to the vivid evocation of meaning."

— Barry Cooper, *National Post*

"You have got to have some players to stay in the game. In journalism, Newman was always that. And nobody in the wings is prepared to replace him." — Philip Marchand, *Toronto Star*

"In his chapter on Lord and Lady Black, Newman shows, like the good journalist he is, that he has knowledge that no outsider could possibly get, and is as ready as ever to spill the beans. On Conrad: 'He was one of the great ham actors of our time and ought to have been cast as a James Bond villain, out to dominate the world, with a trombone choir announcing his entrances and exits.' On Barbara: 'She was the sort of woman who kept spilling out of her dresses, then blamed the dresses.'"

— Maria Tippett, Victoria *Times Colonist*

"In Newman, Canadians will find a tormented soul and a tireless iconoclast who has spent a lifetime exploring and celebrating this country. His pointed, deeply affecting memoir deserves the applause of a grateful nation."

— Andrew Cohen, *Ottawa Citizen*

"You've been married four times: you must like weddings."
"Not really. It's the honeymoons I enjoy."

— from an interview in *Maclean's*

HERE BE DRAGONS

TELLING TALES OF PEOPLE, PASSION AND POWER

PETER C. NEWMAN

Library and Archives Canada Cataloguing in Publication

Newman, Peter C., 1929-
    Here be dragons : telling tales of people, passion and power / Peter C.
Newman.

ISBN 0-7710-6792-5 (bound). – ISBN 0-7710-6796-8 (pbk.)

1. Newman, Peter C., 1929-   2. Journalists – Canada – Biography.
3. Authors, Canadian (English) – 20th century – Biography.   I. Title.

PN4913.N494A3 2004   070.92   C2004-904885-6

We acknowledge the financial support of the Government of Canada
through the Book Publishing Industry Development Program and that of
the Government of Ontario through the Ontario Media Development
Corporation's Ontario Book Initiative. We further acknowledge the support
of the Canada Council for the Arts and the Ontario Arts Council for our
publishing program.

Typeset in Bembo by M&S, Toronto
Printed and bound in Canada

A Douglas Gibson Book

This book is printed on acid-free paper that is 100% recycled,
ancient-forest friendly (100% post-consumer recycled).

McClelland & Stewart Ltd.
The Canadian Publishers
481 University Avenue
Toronto, Ontario
M5G 2E9
www.mcclelland.com

1 2 3 4 5   09 08 07 06 05

DEDICATION

During a visit to my homeland, I went to the Theresienstadt concentration camp,
north-east of Prague, where my grandparents perished.

The terminal despair they must have felt is beyond imagination.

What struck me most forcefully was the roster of victims on the camp museum's wall.

Nine other Peťa Neumanns were listed, from 10 months to age 10.

But for our family's escape I would have been on that wall of sorrow with them,

for that is my true name. Their lives were snuffed out in the innocence of childhood.

So, I dedicate this book to them.

To all the sunrises and birdsongs they missed,

the butterflies that never had a chance to kiss their outstretched hands . . .

TABLE OF CONTENTS

PROLOGUE: HERE BE DRAGONS

Everyone sees what you seem to be; few know what you are.
— Niccolò Machiavelli

I t was night, and the sand scratched my elbows. The waters of the Bay of Biscay lapped against the beach, burnished by the crystal light of the full moon. It was the late spring of 1940. Along with my father, mother, and aunt I lay on the beach at Biarritz, just north of the Pyrenees, which form France's border with Spain. The fresh breeze carried the damp air of the Atlantic Ocean, and I shivered. Every now and then, a sand crab crossed my bare legs, and I shivered some more. As a young Czech boy of eleven, I was not considered mature enough to wear long trousers. My face sought out the warmth of my mother's embrace while my body ached for sleep.

It was the dawning of the Second World War, and we were huddled at this sandy rendezvous for the final leg of our escape from a continent ablaze with terror. We had arrived that afternoon in a commandeered taxi, at the end of our fourteen-month flight from the Nazi Blitzkrieg that seemed to follow us wherever we went. Now we were waiting on the beach for a Belgian merchant ship, the *Ville de Liège*, taken over by the Czech army-in-exile. It would carry us to freedom. I heard my parents use this word, *freedom*, and wondered what it could mean when I had left behind all that I held dear: the comfortable home in Břeclav, with its swimming pool and my private zoo, my nannies and my pet deer, our holiday hops to the Austrian Alps and the Mediterranean. We had been a prosperous bourgeois Jewish family living out a golden epoch. Now we were homeless, huddled on the shore of a strange sea, dependent for our lives on the rough mercy of displaced soldiers. Once we'd had servants and silver; now we clutched a suitcase each, and had nowhere to hide.

Suddenly, the banshee wail of a Junkers Ju-87 Stuka of the Luftwaffe pierced the night air. I looked up just in time to see it diving at us out of the sky, its wing-mounted cannons spitting orange flame. Silhouetted against the fat harvest moon, the bent-winged attacker looked like an avenging raven, the harbinger of death. Its twenty-millimetre cannons kicked up pats of sand in a cornrow pattern that was fast approaching me. With a child's natural excitement, and still not fully aware that this wasn't a bad fairy tale, I stared – transfixed – up at the pilot. Planes were much slower in those days, and I vividly recall glimpsing the pilot's face as he climbed out of his run. He had turned on the cockpit light – after all, there was no one shooting at *him* – and I could see his countenance clearly through the canopy glass. He looked ordinary to me, not at all like the fabled Master Race of Hitler's demigods I had been taught to fear, and to flee. He appeared more like a small-town functionary. Not wanting to endow him with too favourable an image, I imagined that, in his former life, he had been a village tax collector. Nor did he project hatred; his disposition was placid, almost bored. To my young mind, it seemed doubly insulting to be shot at by this ordinary-looking gent, putting in some leisurely combat time before returning to his airfield and digging into his ration of steaming *wurst und sauerkraut*.

Then the pattern of bullet spurts raced closer to me, throwing sand in my face. I watched the Junkers's grey underbelly, and its swastika-emblazoned tail, as it banked around for another strafing. I could feel my father's hand on my head trying to protect me. I remember thinking: *What's all this about? What have I done to harm this* meshuge *pilot that he should want to kill me?* It may have been the impersonal act of a German being a Good Nazi, but to me, it was highly personal. I had heard my parents talking about the persecution of the Jews but was too young to understand what they meant. We came from a generation of secular Jews. I had never been in a temple, and had not been promised a bar mitzvah, so I didn't really feel Jewish. But if Adolf Hitler wanted me dead, I had to be.

The murderous raven kept strafing our small strand of beach, tucked into a clearing behind an unused dock. There were no more than a few dozen people scattered on the sand, but the pilot spent a surprising number of rounds of ammunition on us. Around me, I could hear the screams and see the crumpled heaps of the dead and wounded: fathers, mothers, and children wailing in grief for their loved ones who were lying still under what now seemed like a devil moon.

Then, as if waking abruptly from a nightmare, I realized that something had changed. I could once again hear waves gurgling on the shore. The unexpected tranquility was welcome. The Junkers had vanished and we were alone.

No longer fearful of drawing attention to themselves, the wounded were now pleading for help. The moon was behind a cloud, and in the darkness it was difficult to count how many had been hit. Waiting for local ambulances to arrive, we were confronted by a blacked-out Biarritz, apparently indifferent to the cries of the maimed and the dying. My father, who spoke the most effective French in the family, went off to search for help.

While waiting for him to return, I recalled arriving in Biarritz late that afternoon, awed by the seaside castles masquerading as hotels – mostly shuttered now, but to my youthful eyes places of great fascination and mystery. Nothing compared with the Hôtel du Palais, formerly a villa belonging to the French Empress Eugénie, where in peacetime rich mademoiselles perfected their *café-au-lait* tans around the pool or caressed flutes of chilled champagne in the regal bar in the evenings. Traces of resort living were still to be found in the art deco casino or along the Grande Plage. Here and there I could spot the odd tourist, apparently unaware of the catastrophe closing in on Biarritz, France, and all of Europe. I recall in particular one grande dame who paraded down the empty beach with a scarlet parasol held over her head by a trailing servant. Her beach dress rustled in the breeze, and I waved at her, admiring her élan. She looked surprised, decided not to feel insulted, and gave me a limp hand gesture unexpected enough to make us both smile. I watched her disappear into the setting sun until she became a mirage, swallowed by its slanting rays. I wondered where she was now, and if she realized what had just happened on the beach where she had so calmly promenaded only a few hours earlier.

My father returned just before midnight, stunned to report that not a single door, including those of the local hospital and police station, had been opened to him.

"*M'inquiète que nous ne sommes pas personnes. Ils se soucient peu de leur image,*" he reported. ("I worry that we have become nobodies. They don't care much about their reputation.") Little did any of us realize that the French would become equally enthusiastic in their Jew hunting as the Nazis. The French definition of a Jew was broader than the Germans', as it swept more widely and endangered more categories of people.[1]

Without knowing the word or fully understanding the concept, we had become refugees: Not Wanted On Voyage. But we had escaped, and that set up in my mind for the first time the idea of

---

[1] According to historians, of the 300,000 Jews who lived in France before the war, at least 74,000 were rounded up by the Nazis or French Vichy officials. Almost all perished, including 11,400 children. Maurice Papon, who was a senior police official in Bordeaux during the war and later France's budget minister in the 1970s, was finally put on trial for war crimes at the age of eighty-six. He was accused of drawing up for German authorities lists of Jews for arrest, between June 1942 and August 1944. The 1,560 people detained, many of them children, were sent to the Auschwitz extermination camp, where few survived. Papon pleaded ill health and escaped punishment.

a personal lifeline that some benevolent deity had provided to keep me safe.

Safe, but not unscathed. Here I was, having barely attained knowledge of myself as a boy instead of a baby, and some Nazi tax collector was doing his best to blow me up. It was nothing like the newsreels, where German airplanes were blasting streams of anonymous fleeing strangers. That idiot had been shooting at *me*, even though I had tried so hard to be a good, obedient boy. I do not pretend that I fully realized at the time what was happening. Still, on that moonlit dark night of my soul, I became charged with a sense of purpose. I would search for security and stability, try to find safe haven in causes to follow and heroes to worship. By enlisting myself in the service of worthy men (and later women) who I could believe in, either through my faith in them or their faith in me, I would never feel so vulnerable and threatened again.

As an unworldly boy, I had tried reaching out with love to each of the countries that sheltered me – Czechoslovakia, Italy, France – and pretended that I was a loyal Czech, Italian, Frenchman, Martian, or whatever would come next. On that beach I formed a childish resolve to disown a world I never made. I would pledge my loyalty to anyone who would accept it. This would turn out to be more difficult than ever I could imagine.

WHEN I BEGAN THIS BOOK, I felt very much like Scheherazade, who spun her tales of the Thousand and One Nights while fearing for her life – not because mine was still threatened, but because it was about to be revealed. As I reflect on the three-quarters of a century I have spent on this earth, most of it in my adopted Canada and much of it in the public arena, I realize how much my destiny has been governed by the twin forces of time and circumstance. I have been accident-prone, in the sense that my days and nights were governed by accidental events, many of them traumatic, enough of them lucky. "One cannot divine nor forecast the conditions that will make happiness," the writer Willa Cather concluded. "One only stumbles on them by chance, in a lucky hour, at the world's end, and holds fast to the days." My life floated along, like a bottle on the tide, until I realized the bottle had a message: If I could discover my rightful place in a rightful world, I would finally be safe from that murderous raven.

Nothing compares with being a refugee; you are robbed of context and you flail about, searching for self-definition. When I ultimately arrived in Canada, what I wanted was to gain a voice. To be heard. That longing has never left me. Unexpectedly, I found myself a writer, not in response to the call of any muse, but because it seemed a good way to establish that voice, whatever its message or volume. Eventually, I found not only a voice but an audience, and ultimately a following. The little Jew boy from Central Europe began to make waves. Still does.

The journey was anything but smooth. Looking back, I cannot help but cringe at my mistakes, mourn the days and hours wasted, grieve for friends and loved ones lost or alienated, regret the times I spoke when it would have been wiser to remain silent and, especially, vice versa. I kept insisting (threatening, in fact, to print it on my business cards) that "NEWMAN IS HUMAN." Nobody believed me.

Still, for each incident that caused me remorse, another inspired gratitude. For all my faults and misjudgments, I was able to lead a life at the centre of the action, and use whatever talents I inherited or possessed. I was able to experience first-hand the events of the last half of what was supposed to be Canada's century, and to interview and profile nearly all the major players involved. At the same time, I pursued my passions: the navy, the written word, journeys to countries on the edge, and sailing – not to mention women. I've had a great run, but like the bullets of Biarritz, life's arrows often missed their mark.

The voyage from Břeclav, in southern Moravia, to Burlington, in southern Ontario, where we initially settled, turned out to be a blessing. Through luck, the process of elimination, fortunate navigation, and my father's powers of persuasion, we ended up in a country that enjoyed the mandate of heaven. The great lone land that during my watch evolved from a Krieghoff landscape to an urban jungle became mine to chronicle. Through my books, I was able to corner and dissect the compelling men and women I encountered along the way. I was trying to make sense of my adopted country, my brave new world, and my evolving self. Whatever recognition I gained was incidental to this quest for understanding and the crusade to validate my still fragile sense of self and hope of belonging.

So relentless were these pursuits that they created in me what Pierre Trudeau called, in another context, "dynamic tensions," a bundle of contradictions that stoked my inner fires. I donated myself to various causes, the main one being to gain recognition for myself as the authoritative Boswell of Canada's various establishments. During the 1970s and 1980s, my four book-length studies of the country's elite, and the controversies surrounding them, qualified me as the literary arbiter of Canada's rich and famous – Robin Leach without the air-raid-volume seal honking. Yet I never felt part of that fabled universe. I was welcome to graze on Establishment pastures, but only as a barely tolerated visitor. Its members granted me unprecedented access, boasting to one another about "being Newmanized," but didn't completely trust me. Ian Sinclair, then the boisterous head of the CPR, told a friend that I had interviewed him and that he was damn sure I would quote him accurately. Asked how he could be so certain, Sinclair shot back: "Because while Newman was taping me, I was taping him!"

In the early 1970s, when the chairmen of the Big Five banks threw up their opulent skyscraper head offices on Bay Street, each one higher than its competitor's, the only exception was Royal Bank chairman Earle McLaughlin. His building didn't try to compete for number of floors, but became the most appropriate symbol of Bay Street in that its windows were coated with real gold. When it was done, McLaughlin invited me to his new office. I was appalled; he occupied the whole top floor of the building, and its opulent satin decor reminded me, as I later wrote, of a Turkish whorehouse.

When that issue of *Maclean's* came out, he phoned me. It was a brief exchange.

"Newman?" he said. "This is Earle."

"Yes, sir . . ."

"When were you last in a Turkish whorehouse?"

He hung up without waiting for an answer.

I AM OFTEN ATTACKED for not openly expressing either drooling admiration or fanged loathing for the business and political elites who provided the fodder for my books, columns, and articles. More often than not, I treated my subjects as rebels to their cause and traitors to what was best for their country. I would allow some acquisitor to drone on at length about the price of his possessions (although seldom their value), or some politician to lament interminably about how his wisdom and his patriotism were misjudged by the jealous, the bitter, and the ignorant. I then left it to my readers to judge for themselves the results of my stratagem of holding my protagonists to account with damaging self-revelations, carefully marshalled out of their own mouths. I seldom resorted to invective or sledgehammer prose; I found my purpose better served by more subtle means. My intent was to wield my pen with the delicate edge best illustrated by *New Yorker* humorist James Thurber, describing two men duelling. One of them slices through the other's neck with such a fine sword thrust that the victim is unaware of what has just happened, and urges his opponent to keep fighting. The victor sheaths his sword, shrugs, and, as he walks away, says over his shoulder: "Try sneezing."

That's my idea of a perfect character sketch, the art of writing at its finest.

There were some prominent members of the elite I could not pretend to stomach. Others (such as the late Izzy Asper, Paul Desmarais, the late Harrison McCain, Peter Munk, Izzy Sharp, and

Gerry Schwartz), I continue to admire. Conrad Black, whom I had some considerable part in inventing, became the poster boy for capitalism gone berserk. His do-it-yourself ethics brought him into terminal disrepute, and no one lamented his demise.

To successfully dissect the anatomy of corporate power requires intimate knowledge of the insiders' operational code. It also means having to masquerade as one of the anointed, which explains why I spent my dozen years mingling with Central Canada's elite, tightly encased in a three-piece suit, and did not don my Greek fisherman's cap until I had escaped to the West Coast, to seek a more authentic existence.

We non-fiction writers are like sailors, infected with the germ of distance, who can never be tamed or domesticated; only rented on occasion, but never bought. Those of us who have gained some measure of credibility practising this mad craft thrive on a pretend intimacy that spawns betrayal. However friendly an interview, however intimate the revelations, we writers remain temporary sojourners in a strange land. We follow our own agenda and thus are bound to disillusion our hosts. This does not imply misquotation or unfairness, but it very definitely implies selection. I would set out my thesis, and then choose the quotes and the facts that supported its dominant themes. With the publication of my books, this set up inevitable tensions. I grovelled to pry open the Canadian Establishment's secrets but I never told them mine.

It was easy. I never had a dynasty to lose. Besides, survivors get the last word.

IN MIDDLE AGE, I became known as "Captain Canada," an impassioned cultural nationalist who spent eleven stormy years rescuing *Maclean's*, the country's national magazine, from extinction. I gravitated to the centres of influence and power in Montreal, Ottawa, and Toronto and wrote millions of words, documenting my adopted country's political evolution, power structure, and business history. I was the much-married *bon viveur*, who (I told myself) wanted nothing more than to find a tranquil, happy home life. It was always my intention to slow down enough so that I could legitimately be called a workaholic instead of a work-obsessed control freak. I never made it.

Thousands came to know me, or at least to know of me. One of the peculiarities of becoming a celebrity in Canada, however minor, is that people are constantly coming up to remind you who you are. I remember being encircled by a curious and bubbly tourist in Vancouver who kept staring at me. She finally pointed an accusing finger and delivered her verdict: "You're somebody!" When I modestly admitted that this might be so, she blurted out: "You can't fool me. I'd know you anywhere, Mordecai."

Such exquisite inconsistencies have led naturally to profound misunderstandings about me, which I accept as the cost of leading an eccentric, unscripted life. In this book, I have set out what I really thought and felt along the way, as distinct from what others wanted me to think and presumed I was feeling. I would like to pretend that the currency of my life has been valued on a single, immutable standard, and that I always knew where I was heading. But that would be untrue. I have led my life following the twin beacons of exhilaration and curiosity, and it has been a fabulous journey. As that master of the electric psyche Friedrich Nietzsche noted: "One must have chaos in oneself, to give birth to a dancing star."

This book's title, *Here Be Dragons*, is associated in maritime tradition with early charts of the southern seas, in particular the hazardous waters below forty degrees South Latitude, where ancient cartographers used fearsome beasts – fierce dragons, hungry lions, and raging elephants – to indicate the dangers associated with uncharted seas and lands.[2] It seemed to me appropriate, not because I ever confronted such mythical winged monsters, but for other reasons. When I came to Canada as a trembling

---

[2] The sole surviving example appears on the early sixteenth-century Lenox Globe, where written over the east coast of Asia, then the edge of the known world, the Latin motto "*HIC SUNT DRACONES*" appears.

eleven-year-old, I landed in a *terra incognita* as unknown and frightening to me as any of the watery voids on the primitive maps of early explorers. More important, in my writings I determined to chart new territory by portraying political leaders and business warlords not as dishonest stumblebums or knights in shining armour, but as breathing, sweating, and often hyperventilating individuals caught in circumstances that tested their character. This was an approach that I was among the first to explore – that, and the world of feelings in print, which journalists had previously ceded to novelists and beatnik poets. Thus, *Here Be Dragons*.

Since Canada was my *terra incognita*, where I slew my share of dragons, personal and professional, the phrase seems apt. I figured that if your future can be taken away from you in one day, as mine was, you want to make sure it will never happen again. If I discovered what Canada's power barons were really up to, at least I wouldn't be taken by surprise.

In the process, I tried, not very successfully, to protect myself by maintaining two separate personae: Peter C. (it stands for Charles, not Canada, as one of my satirical friends maintains) Newman, the professional nerd who takes himself seriously as a court jester to the Establishment, amusing the powerful while simultaneously poking fun at them; and also Peter Newman, who takes himself seriously not at all, and who delights in the absurdities of life – except for agonizing over lousy book reviews.

My slightly heretical approach created a following among readers that allowed me to remain a popular *Maclean's* columnist for half a century, and to sell two million copies of my twenty-two books. June Callwood, writing in the *Globe and Mail*, kindly claimed that I had created "realism in political writing in Canada" and was "the first to write about politics as examined theatre and politicians as collapsed gods." Not to mention providing "a tapestried look at the rich men of Canada whose lives are more secret than monks' and more powerful than locomotives."

REFERRING TO A particularly tumultuous period in Hawaiian history, James A. Michener described it as "the time when the gods changed." I witnessed a transformation equally profound during my half-century of chronicling Canada's breath-taking evolution. By any standard, the upheaval in Canadian society, politics, and economy during that time has been unparalleled in our history. We have seen the dismantling of the Old Canada that recklessly squandered its values and virtues, and its replacement with a loose coalition of city-states, tied to one another under the Maple Leaf, too frequently treated as a flag of convenience, or, more often, inconvenience.

We Canadians have yet to discover any true centre of gravity, or unifying sense of purpose. There is no precedent for the accelerating velocity of contemporary events, nor is there precedent for the contradictory behaviours of the ten prime ministers who reigned from 1948 to 2004, all of whom I have known and angered by my writings. It was a time of heroic encounters that called for political giants. Yet most of the pivotal confrontations I witnessed reduced their protagonists and harmed their country. After half a century of recording its twists and turns, its debacles and pratfalls, my chilly conclusion is that Canada takes a lot of killing.

I have found writing to be an imperfect means to inadequate ends, but it does endow its practitioners with a measure of influence. My chosen profession proved an attractive option because it opened doors and did not require inherited status as the price of admission. Being a writer allowed me to be a front-line observer of the bellicose clashes of my time and yet remain a non-combatant. Being a witness was a lot more fun (and much safer) than being a participant. My books were more than a log of the sweeping changes in Canadian life during the last half of the twentieth century, they were a storyteller's attempt to tell it like it really was, instead of how it might have been, or should have been. They exposed the foibles and fables of the country's business and political elites, and recounted their march to folly.

Those of us who toil in the muck of current events share one great advantage: we know that events never unfold as predicted. News is chaotic by definition. It is what happens when men and women play the odds. History occurs at the intersection of circumstance, character, luck, and timing.

Most non-fiction writers are vulnerable romantics, the junkyard dogs of the written arts, begging for a bone yet always ready to bite their masters. Those of us who chronicle political events will temporarily align ourselves with any cause, however ragged its flag or insignificant its army. Political ideology means less to us than the shades of the puff in a pigeon's breast. Personal convictions are for the most part incidental, derived from the simple tendency to lean against every prevailing wind, be it blowing from the loosey-goosey political Left or the grumpy-mumpy political Right. We like to think of ourselves as champions of the underdogs, ready to run off on any crusade that promises to deliver justice, fair maidens, or both. Yet in reality we are literary taxidermists, attempting to preserve passions, places, and people, whose stories we magnify and sensationalize while bending facts and rationing truth. Objectivity and fairness seldom enter into it. Even the simplest recital of a social event or a political reflection during a marginally relevant debate will mirror the writer's cultural bias − or, just as likely, his upset stomach from a hurried meal downed with too many slugs of cheap vino. Yet, like doctors who maintain the fiction that they can heal, or politicians who maintain the illusion that they can govern, writers pretend to be impartial. The excuse for our errors and exaggerations is that we are writing "a rough draft of history." More rough than history.

I AM PAINFULLY AWARE of the need to set down these remembrances before they vanish beyond the rim of memory and comprehension. Given that our lives make only partial sense to us, and no sense at all to anyone else, my record has too seldom benefited from self-awareness. Like everyone else, I lived from day to day with my residual weaknesses and hidden strengths, with sweetness and loss, with renewal and exhaustion. I wish I could believe in forgiveness and redemption, in slates wiped clean, in immaculate grace and swift atonement (particularly my own). I do not. Acts have consequences. To be validated, their burden must be assimilated. Some days, my past feels like some smooth, heavy stone that cannot easily be shifted to see what lies beneath.

Lives are viewed most clearly in retrospect, as the poet Samuel Taylor Coleridge noted long ago when he described experience as "the stern light of a ship which illuminates only the track it has passed." Still, I believe that it is precisely this stern wake that sets one individual apart from another, and is thus worth analyzing and documenting. I agree with Cesar Chavez, the California fruit-pickers' labour organizer, who wrote, "When we're honest with ourselves, we must admit that our lives are all that really belong to us. So it is how we use our lives that determine what kind of men we are."

Here Be Dragons explains how I used my life, and what kind of man I am. Mine has been a solitary journey. My only constant companions were the sea, my music, and the blue iguana masquerading as my inner child. And I feel genuinely humbled by the numerous benefactors who threw me lifelines along the way. Their generosity, not always intended, created an immense debt that this book will in part repay.

The unexamined life is not worth living, as Socrates concluded, but the examined existence becomes real only when shared with others, in my case through the highly subjective act of writing. One problem is that while most biographers know too little, all autobiographers know too much. I have weeded out discussions of most of the issues, political and economic, that provided the context for my labours, since I covered that swampy territory in my books.

At the same time, I have attempted to write not just with my brain but also with my heart and my gut. I wanted to capture the fury and fear I felt when, as a little boy, I watched the Nazis invading Prague on the Ides of March, 1939. I wanted to recall the strangely comforting aroma of my mucker's wetsuit and sweaty rubber boots at the end of the night shift as a teenage underground gold miner in northern Quebec. I wanted to recreate the pervasive odour of diesel oil aboard a Royal Canadian Navy warship at sea. I wanted to portray the palpable, acrid smell of raw fear as half a dozen political leaders I came to know faced their inevitable defeat by angry voters. I wanted also to catch the ocean's salty aroma riding the shimmering waves of the Pacific under the glint of the crescent moon.

My previous books were fuelled by the energy of their protagonists. This time, I am the sole catalyst. It's a daunting prospect. I approach the task as though I were sitting around a campfire telling my tale to cub scouts or retired sanitary inspectors, knowing they will ask impossible questions. Why, Mr. Newman? Why all those big fat books, Mr. Newman? Why all the marriages? Why all that travel, why all that ambition? Why all the bother pretending you're a regular guy? Why indeed. To write a valid memoir, the author must confront difficult truths and reveal not just the facts and the plot line, but the *story* contained in a life. The most difficult issue when dredging up memories has to be the question: How do I quarry facts buried in the past in order to attain "the ring of truth," in the service of my plot?

Having survived more than seven event-filled decades, I have structured this book in consecutive intervals, each covering an aspect of my life, with pauses in between to reflect on its most ardent passions. Hindsight gives our lives structure, but in the reality of daily living everything happens at once. We chomp a hard-boiled egg in a spacious Toronto townhouse on Saturday morning and play with a thought. By Wednesday afternoon we are moving to Vancouver Island, to live on a knapsack-jammed thirty-five-foot sloop. There is no telling which seemingly trivial incidents will set our lives on radical new paths while the nightmares that bedevil our sleep vanish with the dawn. Each experience led me to another, and the angle of my bounce determined the direction of my life.

I have found it unnecessary to raise an artificial barrier between my private life and public events, as they seemed so often to have happened in tandem. For example, I have never felt it was entirely coincidental that my marriage of twelve years to Camilla Turner foundered the same week as the Meech Lake Accord collapsed, both following long and difficult negotiations. If there appear to be parallels between the stories of Newman and Canada, it is not because I claim any exalted status. It just sort of happened, more or less that way.

After such a long run, I occasionally still feel as insecure as a one-album country singer. Success and fame have always been piranhas nibbling at my nerve ends. I could never get enough of either and thus missed enjoying both. The cost of success is the absence of a balanced life; the quest for fame takes its pound of flesh in the loss of reality. The latter exacts a higher price than the former. Neither brings genuine satisfaction, and all too often I have created the conditions that have contributed to my unhappiness, so that I found myself running ever harder in the pursuit of ever more elusive goals. Rebecca West, my favourite British essayist, observed that "there is nothing rarer than a man who can be trusted never to throw away happiness, however eagerly he sometimes grasps it."

The animating current in this book has been self-revelation, its dominant tone, a wry, tentative sounding of my life so far, circumscribed by memory's limits. In writing this book, I set aside glorification of the self, the ultimate heresy of any memoir. Objectivity was neither possible nor desirable. Only the dead can be truly objective. The sole claim I make for *Here Be Dragons* is that I have written it as honestly as I could, and that I left out as much self-justification as possible. It wasn't easy.

CHAPTER ONE

CHEATING THE HOLOCAUST

*Throughout your days you will be seized by memories, memories
desperate and sweet enough to make you lose your breath, and they will
link you to the violent, tender, inexplicable land of your beginning.*
— Tennessee Williams

One of my earliest memories is of walking, as a boy,
through the woods of southern Moravia and stumbling
across a field of the white-speckled scarlet mushrooms
that I had thought existed only in fairy tales. I was overcome by a
sense of wonder. This is followed closely by the memory of watching white snow fall on black Mercedes convertibles, while Gestapo
officers rode their running boards, fearsome and grim in their
long grey overcoats. Their breath left vapour trails behind them as
though they were the horses of the Valkyrie, who rode on claps of
thunder. I was overcome by a sense of terror.

Wonder and terror have ever since intermingled as the pole stars
that have guided my life.

I was born on May 10, 1929, in Vienna. My parents actually
lived in Břeclav, Czechoslovakia, an hour's drive from the Austrian
capital, but my mother insisted on Austria because it had better
hospitals. She had already lost a baby, a girl named Elizabeth, a few
weeks after childbirth and was not prepared to take risks with me.

In the carpet pattern of Central Europe, Břeclav occupies a
patch near the centre, in the southeastern part of what was then the

province of Moravia, administered from the seat of Brno. Bohemia lay to the west, Austria to the south, and Slovakia to the east. (I am a Moravian by birth and a "bohemian" by persuasion.) Břeclav became a town in 1872, but its historical roots stretched back at least as far as the Great Moravian Empire of the ninth century. Little of this glorious past remained, apart from a few ruins and a colony of white storks that continued to nest among the centuries-old oaks that had once surrounded the town's ancient hunting chateau.

At the time of my birth, Moravia had 3.5 million inhabitants, supported by a prosperous agricultural base and industries as modern as any to be found in Europe. Three-quarters of the population was Czech and one-quarter was German, while five-sixths was Roman Catholic. And then there was the family Newman – or Neumann, as our name was then. We were Czech by nationality and mother tongue, Jewish by loosely observed religion.

Břeclav was a tough, nondescript company town, where my father happened to be the company. He owned and operated a sugar beet refinery, which was not only the town's largest employer but also its only buyer for sugar beet crops from miles around, an important product in Czechoslovakia, where it was too cold to grow sugar cane.

Our home was the equivalent of the local manor, being easily the largest and most luxurious in town. We lived the sheltered existence of privilege in interwar Europe, a way of life now entirely lost, or driven behind protective walls and tax hedges. I grew up in another time, a *belle époque* that turned into a *fin de siècle*, made to seem as exotic by the passage of time as by my particular circumstances, which were exotic by the standards of any era.

I remember the tinkling sounds of my mother's piano coming from some distant upstairs room while I wandered along halls with glistening wooden floors under oriental carpets and looked through faraway windows. Our home seemed always to smell of polish and flowers. There was never so much as an unclean ashtray or a book out of place. Our mansion was also, apart from my mother's regular piano exercises, largely silent, a silence emphasized by the fact that while I and my family spoke Czech, most of the staff spoke German, so there was little domestic chatter. Servants glided wordlessly in and out of rooms, carrying freshly starched linen sheets and meticulously buffed silver samovars. Staff looked after the cooking, the cleaning, the laundry, the shopping. Our four-storey brick home, darkened by the soot from my father's refinery, had three maids (one just to polish the silver), two gardeners, one cook, and a chauffeur/mechanic. These servants were my most familiar company, as children seldom came to visit and I had no close friendships. I would linger in the kitchen, helping the cook by grinding the morning coffee in a wooden grinder with a large brass handle. The chauffeur would allow me to "help" polish my father's car, or I would sit behind the wheel, pretending to drive. My other male role model was my maternal grandfather, Theodore, who fussed over me endlessly on his periodic visits – I soaked up his attention like a thirsty plant. And there was always, never far from my side, a nanny. My nannies were young, single women who supervised my bathing, dressing, eating, studying, and playing.

I had my own large quarters, and I was expected to spend much of my time there, indoors. The shelves of my rooms were packed with toys and games of every description, most of them gifts from my father's employees. They were seldom used, with one exception. Lacking friends, I developed a youthful affection for a stuffed dog that I named Haro. He went everywhere with me, providing the hugs and affection that I so sorely craved.

I was taken outside daily for fresh air and exercise in our expansive gardens, again watched over by nannies who saw it as their mission to prevent me from ever getting cold, wet, dirty, or having spontaneous fun. When it snowed, which was often, they bundled me in stifling clothing to the point of immobility. But I loved my outings, and my parents had spared no effort in making the walled garden a child's wonderland. I had a small blue car with an electric motor, which I could drive along the garden paths, and there was also a playhouse fitted out with a living room, a bedroom, and a bathroom. It contained child-sized furniture, and there I would invite my imaginary friends to tea. I even had a small enclosure that housed my own petting zoo, inhabited by animals such as rabbits and a pet deer.

My clothes were the fashion of the day for boys of my station. I wore short trousers or *lederhosen* as play or school clothes, but changed into a miniature tailored suit just like my father's for the evening meal. One holiday, to my acute embarrassment, my parents dressed me up as a country girl in Czech national costume. I was allowed to eat at the family table but not expected to speak, except in response to direct questions. Often, we were entertaining business or social guests, so I spent the entire meal listening or, more likely, wandering through the corridors of my imagination. Once each evening, I would be escorted into my parents' presence and they would question me about my day. These encounters were friendly but also formal. I ached to know them better.

Once or twice a month at bedtime, and always without warning, my mother or father would appear at my bedroom door and dismiss the nanny for the night, taking over the bedtime story and tucking me into my sheets. I longed for these nights more than anything, but as they occurred at random, I could never figure out how to make my parents reappear. Yet, I certainly did not feel that I was a neglected child. My parents loved me but were the products of their class and generation, which meant that they put duty and the provision of luxuries ahead of my emotional well-being. Child-rearing in those days was a form of quarantine, with most of my elders treating children as tiny, dim-witted adults not ready for life, whose future character depended on their youthful impulses being suppressed.

I attended the local public school and enjoyed my studies, but as the only rich student in an otherwise working-class town I found it difficult to make friends. I was the only child to be driven to school by a chauffeur in a limousine, my father's grey, monstrous Tatra 80. It was the most luxurious motorcar in Czech history, designed for the country's founder, President Tomas Garrigue Masaryk, and only twenty-two were ever sold. It had a six-litre, twelve-cylinder engine, generated 120 horsepower, and could reach speeds of 140 kilometres per hour. My arrival at the school gates in this spoke-wheeled locomotive, with a chauffeur to open my door, did not endear me to my classmates who had trudged to school on foot. I would try to make up for this by "sharing" (i.e., giving away) the packed lunch prepared for me daily by our cook. I never had trouble finding takers for the fancy food, but had less luck translating this into friendship. I could hardly blame them – they were intimidated by the fact that my father employed their fathers. I was not bullied or tormented, but merely left alone; the few times that I did play with children my age was when their fathers came to visit our home, and I never knew whether these boys were there only for the toys. When the son of the factory's chief engineer came over to play, he was so impressed by the array of toys on the shelves of my room that he began to jump up and down, shouting, "*Všechno dolu!*" ("Everything down!")

I was not an unhappy young scholar, but as lonely as if I lived on a deserted island. Which, in a way, I did. My childhood was a quandary. I had everything any coddled youngster could possibly want. Everything except a feeling of acceptance. Could this hunger for affection have triggered my lifelong search for eternal love; for incorruptible, quotable political heroes; for virtuous, sexy heroines; for the perfect sailboat; for some imaginary, unborn literary critic who would praise my books? That might be Psychology 101, but what the hell – it rings true to me.

Twice a year we would go on holiday, in summer to the Italian Riviera and in winter to the Austrian Alps. These excursions were planned with the logistical complexity of a military assault. A selection of servants would accompany us; so, too, it seemed, did most of our belongings. I remember my father enlisting platoons of railway porters at train stations, who would wrestle with our mountainous stack of hat boxes, standing wardrobes, steamer trunks, medicine chests, suitcases, hold-alls, and boot boxes. We were equipped for any conceivable climatic, social, or medical emergency. Yet my father always made arrangements with meticulous

care and tipped heavily, so we would be wafted coolly and efficiently from one train compartment to another, arriving at our
destination fresh and relaxed. We favoured resort hotels at the
better places, such as Bad Ischl, Gstaad, and Marienbad. Apart from
the one year that a school tutor accompanied our party, these were
my favourite times of the year. My father was an excellent skier,
and in the Alps I was trained by the best instructors; summer
months meant endless, indolent days on the beach. As we were on
holiday it meant that I got to see more of my parents.

MY FATHER, Oscar Karel Neumann, was a self-made man in an
age when they were rare: you were supposed to inherit wealth and
power instead of acquiring your own. He was born on February 3,
1885, graduated from public school at the age of seventeen, and
then went to Prague, where he entered the Commercial Academy.
He subsequently worked "in sugar" and eventually controlled ten
refineries, 36,000 acres of sugar beet farms, and a number of other
enterprises, such as breweries and liquor distilleries.

My father's success was the result of a shrewd business head,
single-minded determination, and a capacity for hard work. He
also had far-ranging interests, invested widely, and developed a
social network of national influence. In addition to his sugar
refinery, he diversified into candy manufacture – on my occasional
trips to a boiled-sugar sweets factory he ran, I imagined that he
had the best job in the world. His influence extended to the top
circles of Prague, where he was director of a national bank and
sat on the government's blue-ribbon economic advisory council,
chaired by the country's president. He was also a member of the
National Grain Monopoly and belonged to the conservative
Agrarian Party, which then held office. In short, he was the prime
power broker for southern Moravia, unrivalled for his personal
contacts and political influence.

My favourite among his circle of friends was Jan Masaryk, son of
the country's founder and later Czechoslovakia's foreign minister,

who was a frequent visitor in our home, sometimes joined by Jarmila Novotná, a vivacious lyric soprano he would accompany on our piano. He made a fuss over me and would carry me to bed on his shoulders; I was enchanted by this musical, ribald, mischievous storyteller, so different from my parents' other, more formal friends.

Father was the head of the Czech Rotary Club and played the part, generous with his friends when it came to advice, money, or time. He was a non-smoker and an occasional drinker. He had a bellow of a laugh and a gregarious nature, but he was more reserved with me. I felt he loved me because he would tell me so, but these statements were not accompanied by any cuddling or playful wrestling of the kind indulged in by other fathers.

In my dominant memories of my father he is departing or arriving in the Tatra, satchel in hand. On those occasions when he did have free time, he was out aggressively pursuing his hobbies. He loved to hunt and would leave before dawn with a shotgun or a rifle in hand, to return later with a brace of quail, a deer, or clutch of rabbits. He insisted on eating the game he shot, and many of our dinners were interrupted as some hapless guest cried out in pain, having bitten a piece of the lead shot that regularly salted our meat courses.

He was a powerful presence, one of those natural animators who carry the force of persuasion within themselves, yet seldom give the impression of exercising control over others. He loved to play bridge, to talk politics, and in pre-war Czechoslovakia to mould events to his, and his country's, advantage. In person, he was warm and charming but seldom intimate. We never discussed ideas, because I was only twenty-one when he died and had formed none. But I worship his memory, not only because he saved my life, but because he never talked about how he managed our miraculous escape. He felt that assuming such burdens is what fathers do. Of all the many men and women I have met during my seventy-five years, he is the one I most fervently wish I had come to know better.

My mother was not a traditional Jewish mother – at least not the kind who assumes that the foetus isn't fully developed until it graduates from medical school. She loved me without reservation yet with little demonstrable passion. There was something once-removed about her, as if she were saving her parenting for a future occasion that never came. Her beauty was striking, and she dressed the part. She lived to be eighty-six, and even well into her sixties would turn heads when she entered a room. But I never knew how much of her reserve arose from snobbishness, because she didn't make friends easily and seldom mixed with people she did not consider her kind.

Her maiden name was Wanda Maria Neumann, and she had been born into a rich brewing family in Olomouc, a background and breeding that was reflected in her elegant, refined manner – a distinct contrast to my father's boisterousness. Her beauty combined the sophistication of a European aristocrat with the dark sultriness of a gypsy. She had dark, passionate eyes, chestnut hair, olive skin, and a cultured, melodious voice. At the time of their marriage, my father was thirty-five years old, she was twenty-two. She was a hell of a catch.

My father had not been her first love. Determined to become a concert pianist, my mother had enrolled as a young woman at a music academy in Vienna; there, she had met a young Austrian doctor, closer to her own age, by the name of Hans Brunner. They embarked on a passionate affair built on their love of classical music and kept alive by the flame of their intellects. During his lifetime Brunner wrote more than two hundred stage plays – none of them performed, but much praised for their intricate social messages by the few who read them. He was heavy-set and physically awkward, but his charm was such that not only did my mother fall for him, so too did her sister, Erika. However, in those days the opinions of parents mattered, and Hans could not match the strength of will and social clout of my father. Wanda married my father, and Brunner emigrated to the United States.

My mother was a faithful and loving partner to my father, who loved her profoundly and showed it. She ruled over domestic matters and was a meticulous hostess, to the point of keeping records, in a series of bound notebooks, of what meals she had served to each of her guests and their preferences, so that no dish would ever be repeated. But her practicality ended with household matters; when it came to the wider world she hid behind a conspicuous other-worldliness. She belonged to that vanished breed of society ladies who reacted to stress with the expedience of swooning.

Her remaining passion she poured into music. She would often retreat to the music room for hours on end, play the piano to herself, and dream of concert halls and her days in Vienna. My parents were respectful of each other, never quarrelled in front of me, made many good friends, entertained widely, and enjoyed their grand lifestyle while it lasted. Though I sensed that theirs was more a model marriage than a passionate union, after their world came to a sudden and violent end, they proved to be brave and hardy companions during their long flight through Europe and their difficult existence as struggling farmers in Canada.

And yet – and yet, there was something lacking. I saw my parents so seldom, and our family unit was so tightly controlled, that I came to depend on my nannies for nourishment of the soul. Although I was directed to call them "*Slečna,*" or "Miss," as soon as I could get away with it I would call them "*Teťa,*" or "Auntie." They were simple farm girls who hoped to better themselves through work at the big house in town, moving on as soon as they found a better position in Brno or Prague – or a husband with a good job anywhere. For them, being my nanny was just a stepping stone, but for me, they were the chance to fill an emotional void. I would shower them with compliments and throw my arms around their necks. Sometimes, when they weren't attentive enough, I would feign an injury just to be coddled and hugged. They were patient with me and impersonally kind, but there was a line they were unwilling to cross. They would play games with me but never treat me with the unbridled affection I needed, much though I wished they would. And always, always, they would find a better job, a better town, or a better man – and leave.

My favourite nanny was a farm girl named Greta who had come to our family to earn money to support her ailing father. Unlike the others, who I suspected were putting on a show of affection, I felt that Greta really cared for me. A big, bosomy young woman with red cheeks and a lusty laugh, she was indulgent, permissive, and more of an adult friend than an authority figure. She stayed with us a year, but then her father's condition worsened and, like all the others, she departed.

I could never understand why. What had I done? I tried so hard to please them. "Be a good boy," the nannies would continually implore me. And I would try to be helpful, obedient, considerate. I seldom threw a tantrum, and when they said it was time to leave the garden and come inside, I complied without complaint. When they said it was time for bed, I put on my pyjamas. "I love you, Teťa," I would say to them, giving their necks a big squeeze. "And I love you too, Peťa," they would reply, patting my head. Automatically, politely, without conviction. I knew they didn't really mean it. But I prayed they wouldn't leave. Yet, they did. Inevitably, one crushing disappointment followed another. After a few months, usually, just long enough for me to become attached to them, I would walk past the entrance hall and, see their cardboard suitcases packed and ready by the door.

With a child's egocentricity, it never occurred to me that they were leaving for their own reasons, to pursue their own futures. Their departures left me feeling as guilty as I was bereft. I hadn't been good enough. I had surely misbehaved. But how? I felt the pang of rejection and the confusion of despair. I would rush upstairs to my bedroom and bury my face in a pillow, refusing to say goodbye to them. Then, a few days later, my mother would tell me to put on my best clothes and I would be ushered into the drawing room, where I would be introduced to the next one. Once again, I would mount an emotional offensive. This time, I swore by whatever powers I could conceive, I would be better. This time, I would get it right. This time, she wouldn't leave.

When I actually did misbehave, which was seldom, I found the consequences could become nasty very quickly. I was never more mortified than by the mishap just before the 1936 Olympics in Berlin. My father had donated a rowing scull to the Czech team, and our family was driven in the Tatra to the official launch, where the boat was christened *Wanda*, after my mother. My father, as befitted the nautical nature of the ceremony, had purchased a new white linen suit and an admiral's hat. As we sat together in the back of the Tatra under the warm summer sun, with the roof down and my mother's hat flapping in the breeze, I suddenly realized that I had forgotten my chocolate bear somewhere on the seat. My mind calculated the trajectories and I realized my father must be sitting on it. But I said nothing, hoping against hope that I was mistaken. I wasn't. My father stepped from the limousine and I could see the unmentionable brown, sticky mess on the back of his trousers, in the worst possible location for smutty innuendo.

As the ceremony progressed, the rowing team and assorted dignitaries did their best to hide their amusement. But my father soon realized something was wrong.

"Wanda?" he asked. "What are they laughing at?"

"It's your pants," she told him. "You seem to have had some kind of accident, dear."

In slow motion, I saw his hand reach behind his trousers and palpate the evidence. He brought the damning mess around and inspected it, holding it under his nose.

"Peťa?" he said. "Is this your doing?"

I confessed that it was and, to my astonishment, he slapped me. He had never hit me before, and never did again; the embarrassment had overwhelmed him.

Even now, some seventy years later, I remember with a stab of shame the one time I was caught stealing when I was six and at the tailor's being measured for a new suit. My attention was drawn to a button on the tailor's bench, navy blue with a crown-and-anchor motif. I was already bitten with the nautical bug and simply had to have that button. When I was convinced the tailor wasn't looking, I reached over and slipped it into my pocket. Soon I was home with my treasured loot, but my joy would not last long. The telephone rang, and I heard my mother mention the tailor's name. "A button? A blue button? I will check and call you back."

She came into my room. "The tailor called and said he is missing a blue button with a crown and anchor on it. He said that he saw you playing with the button and wondered whether you took it." The way she said those last two words, I knew the tailor might be willing to call it a mistake, but my mother wasn't. I produced the evidence. "But why, Peťa?" she asked. "Why?"

I can remember nearly every word of the ensuing lecture. We had a Reputation and people would Talk. I had brought Shame on our House. The tailor was Like Us and that was no way to treat a Jew. Or Anyone Else, for that matter. The tailor is Poor and we are Rich. Had I no Conscience? She had not raised her Only Son to be a Common Thief who would Rot in Jail. One thing was certain – I knew how it felt to be Caught, and I never wanted to feel that way again.

Life, I also learned, could bring undeserved rewards as swiftly and unexpectedly as it brought deserved punishments. For weeks leading up to my ninth birthday, my parents forbade me to play in the garden. I didn't really mind. Deer make lousy pets, anyway; they get big and grow horns. But as my birthday falls in May, I was feeling housebound, eager to enjoy the spring weather. On the day of the festivities, I was led into the garden, my mother covering my eyes with her hands. She removed them, and I saw my present – a swimming pool. Such a luxury was nearly unheard of in rural Czechoslovakia at the time. Even the President didn't have a swimming pool. I was overwhelmed with the gift and my parents' generosity.

As things turned out, I would enjoy only one season in my pool before a dream-like sequence of events brought our privileged lives crashing down around us.

WE CALLED WHERE WE LIVED MORAVIA, but the Germans claimed it as part of the Sudetenland, and that was a problem. Pre-war Czechoslovakia was an envied pearl in the heart of central Europe. Since the end of the First World War, while Germany had struggled through economic catastrophe, inflation, currency devaluation, and what it saw as the humiliating terms of surrender, neighbouring Czechoslovakia had prospered as the most successful capitalist democracy in central Europe, ranking as the world's tenth-strongest economic power.

The country's 2,500 castles were testament to a long and bloody history that included an interlude during the fourteenth century when Prague ruled the Holy Roman Empire, making it the centre of the world. But the haughty Hapsburg dynasty took control and eventually folded Czechoslovakia into the Austro-Hungarian Empire. Independence was regained three hundred years later under Tomas Masaryk, a Charles University ethics professor who became the country's first president and philosopher-king. Masaryk attempted to establish an enlightened, fair, and multicultural republic. He largely succeeded, but could not satisfy the demands of the three million Germans within the country's boundaries, who had been the ruling class during the period of Austrian domination. They lived in the Sudetenland, a territory that covered the Czech border regions, including my home town of Břeclav – which they ominously began referring to by its German name, Lundenburg. Břeclav was a loyal Czech enclave in a suddenly militant Germanic sea.

My father was a politically committed nationalist, a "true Czech," as such men were called. Ever since Hitler had tricked his way into becoming German chancellor on January 30, 1933, my father had followed his progress (and his brazen, violent anti-Semitism) with mounting dread. We were secular Jews who did not deny our Jewishness, but neither did we participate in its rituals. Unlike the Jews of Poland, with their broad-rimmed hats and sidelocks, or the Russian Jews who became revolutionaries,

Czech Jews like us were among the most assimilated, not to mention cultivated and cultured, in pre-war Europe. Our Judaism was more an ethnic identity than a sustaining faith.

To my father's thinking, Hitler's evil intentions were confirmed by his annexation of Austria on March 12, 1938. Our family had a large wooden radio cabinet, where my father would listen to the nightly news broadcasts. I often joined him, and although none of the news reports made much sense to me, I have a clear memory of being frightened by Hitler's voice – he was always hysterically angry. My parents' anxiety mounted as they heard reports of Nazi storm troopers vandalizing Jewish homes and businesses in Austria. At first, the Jews were simply humiliated – forced to clean the road surface of Vienna's Ringstrasse with toothbrushes, for instance – but later there were reports of them being rounded up and deported. These atrocities were happening a mere fifty kilometres away, in the city of my birth. I felt frightened, and, for the first time that I remember, burst into my parents' bedroom, desperately needing to be cuddled and reassured.

My father refused to consider any thought of leaving Břeclav, so confident was he in the strength of our armed forces and the goodwill of our allies. The Czech army had thirty-five divisions and could mobilize a million men under arms. It had two thousand kilometres of fortifications dug into the mountains that ringed our national frontiers, an impenetrable defence that could hold off the Nazi Wehrmacht. They were so closely interlocked, my father boasted, a rabbit couldn't get through them without being spotted. Our air force had 1,500 aircraft, my father said, easily a match for the Luftwaffe. As for our allies, Czech security was guaranteed under the Locarno Pact. French forces had promised to defend Czechoslovakia against foreign invasion, and Russia had agreed to follow. My father told me not to worry about this madman, Hitler.

As we listened throughout the summer months, the Nazi dictator's speeches took on an ominous new dimension. He began openly to support the demands of Germans living in the Sudetenland. By September, he had called for them to demand self-rule.

My mother, along with most of Europe, felt that war was inevitable, but still my father waited, confident in our allies. He remained fixed to the radio reports, shouting encouragement, and later disdain, as Hitler summoned Britain's prime minister, Neville Chamberlain, to Munich. French president Edouard Daladier was invited to the conference, and Benito Mussolini represented Italy, but it did not bode well that neither Czechoslovakia (whose fate hung in the balance) nor Russia, our most powerful ally, was invited. "Chamberlain!" my father would snort. "A mayor of Birmingham, and out of his depth even then! And Daladier! A baker's son who should never have left the kitchen." My father's sense of outrage was fuelled when Chamberlain remarked, as he set off for the conference: "How horrible, fantastic, incredible that we should be digging trenches and trying on gas masks here, because of a quarrel in a far away country between people of whom we know nothing." Meeting in the Bavarian capital on September 30, England and France capitulated to Hitler's demands and signed the Munich Pact. The deal allowed Hitler to occupy the Sudetenland immediately, in exchange for promises of a later plebiscite, which was never held. As the terms were announced, for the first and only time in my life, I saw my father weep. Our allies had betrayed us, and our proud armed forces would not even be given the chance to defend their country. Once the Germans were past our mountain defences, my father knew, they would never leave.

When Chamberlain arrived back in London, he waved that treacherous Munich Pact over his head and announced that he had guaranteed "peace in our time." But Winston Churchill, then a backbench MP, was much more prophetic: "You were given a choice between war and dishonour," he berated Chamberlain. "You chose dishonour, and you *will* have war." Abandoned by our allies, Czechoslovakia had no choice but to surrender, and our country's president, Eduard Beneš, resigned.

My father understood that the storm troopers and pogroms were mere days, perhaps hours, away. He collected himself and called the family together in the salon.

"It is over for us here," he said, fighting back the tears. "Now, we must flee." I found this news difficult to comprehend. Flee? Where? "Prague." When? "Tonight! We cannot be found here." Turning to my mother, he explained: "Look, you know that I am part of the Beneš government that the Germans are trying to overthrow, and they want the factory. They will come here first." Turning to me, he instructed, "Go, Peťa. Now! Pack some things in a bag. Take no more than you can carry in one case."

I heard my mother catch her breath, but she neither wavered nor fainted. Instead, she placed a calming hand on my shoulder.

"But *Tati*," I demanded, "when are we coming back?"

"We may never come back."

"Never?"

Our world was crumbling around us, but my parents were resolute and, I realize now, incredibly strong.

"Peťa," my mother said, "now is the time to be brave."

But I did not feel brave. I felt confused and lost. I could think of only one last question.

"*Maminko*," I asked, "can I take Haro with us?"

WE SPENT OUR LAST NIGHT in Břeclav crouched at the bottom of my emptied swimming pool, as my father considered this to be protection against air raids. We could hear the drone of Nazi aircraft in the distance, but no bombs fell. At first light, we left for Prague, which lay beyond the Sudetenland territories granted to the Germans. We could drive there in the Tatra and stay with my grandparents.

Our chauffeur, crying as he drove the limousine for the last time with the family in the back and our meagre luggage in the trunk, took us the distance to Prague. The car was the property of the factory, and he would be driving it back after depositing us. My father instructed him to garage the vehicle pending our "return." They both knew there would be no return, but the driver promised to follow his instructions. When we reached our destination in Prague, he knelt down to my level and promised to take good care of the Tatra for me. He tousled my hair and told me to be a good boy. Then he stood, saluted my father, and drove off in the long grey limousine. We never saw him or the car again.

We stayed in my grandparents' comfortable apartment, which suited me fine, since my grandfather pampered and played with me. Our family there consisted of three grandparents and my mother's sister, Erika. Relations were somewhat frosty between Erika and my mother. Erika, considered the less-attractive sister, had always lived in my mother's shadow and she had never married, but she proved to be an indulgent and kind aunt. Prague was to offer only a temporary respite, however. Hitler, who had always intended to annex Bohemia and the remaining part of Moravia (with its powerful Skoda armaments works), was merely annoyed by the delay imposed by the Munich Pact. Through his agents, he interfered with the Czech government and fomented discord in the streets, stirring up the Slovak and Ruthene minorities. My father was hardly ever at home, as he spent each day visiting embassies, searching for a country that would grant us sanctuary by issuing a visa.

My mother received each new report of gangs marauding in the streets or of anti-Semitic violence with tears, and became preoccupied with "the gas." Poison gas had been a haunting feature of the "Great War," as it was then called, and she expected that Hitler would use it on Prague. She eventually persuaded my father to buy the family gas masks – bulky and probably useless Japanese-made contraptions that only heightened our sense of anxiety. I couldn't get mine to stay on my nose and soon gave it away to a younger boy who didn't have one. It was a mark of our innocence that we could imagine no wartime atrocity more awful than poison gas.

On March 14, 1939, Hitler summoned the new Czech president to Berlin and informed him that, unless all of Czechoslovakia was surrendered to him, he would bomb Prague and destroy it. Our country's humiliation was complete. On the following morning, the ides of March, I perched on the windowsill in my grandfather's flat, awaiting the Nazi invasion. Hitler had proclaimed that his troops would arrive in the capital at 9:00 a.m., and with typical German punctuality they did. Through radio broadcasts, we had been warned that resistance would be "*zertreten*" ("crushed"). But there was nothing stopping me from watching the invasion, so my grandfather and I walked over to the Old City and stood in the snow.

I had never expected an invasion to be so silent. The streets were as still as the hush of a cathedral. We felt suspended in a wintry nightmare. My memories of the invasion as it began are not of voices, but of the distant sound of horses snorting in the cold air and leather soles crunching in the snow, the rumble of diesel engines and the drone of approaching aircraft. Then, suddenly, at the stroke of 9:00, they were upon us.

Grey shapes formed in grey smog. The mist that rises from the Vltava River had mingled with the smoke from burning coal then used to heat buildings, leaving the streets covered in a dirty beige shroud. The shapes took form. I saw their field-grey leather winter coats, grey steel helmets, glistening rifle barrels, and black boots stamping a menacing tattoo that grew louder as they came out of the mist. The first wave was young and cocky, fodder for the resistance that never came. Their eyes scanned the cobblestone alleyways twisting through the Old City, half expecting the rapturous welcome that had greeted their occupation of Vienna. Then came the clatter of vehicles on the stones: grey motorcycles with machine guns mounted on their sidecars, mobile gun carriers, and armoured half-track tanks.

A child ran into the street, bringing the devil's parade to a brief halt. His mother ran after him, brandishing her fist in the face of a Nazi driver and shouting in the Bohemian dialect: "You stupid oxen! Go back where you came from. Nobody wants you here!" She bundled up her child and returned to the crowd, greeted by a wave of applause. Another woman stepped forward to shout at a canvas-covered truck carrying soldiers, "*Co si prejete?*" ("What do you want?"). No one answered her. A brave youth tossed a snowball at a hawk-nosed Nazi riding in the turret of a tank; the German humourlessly trained his machine gun on the boy, but did not open fire.

Next came the clop of hooves as the cavalry appeared. These were the older, battle-hardened officers, their grey capes covering the flanks of their black horses. Bringing up the rear were the shock troops, the Gestapo among them, blond and unsmiling, riding their massive Mercedes cabriolets.

By noon, the Germans had seized the city's strategic choke points: the Ruzyně airfield, the war ministry, and Hradčany Castle, residence of the heads of state. The German agents who had infiltrated Prague by the thousands in the preceding weeks now lined the streets for Josef Goebbels's propaganda cameras, cheering the invading brutes and pretending to be "peace-loving Czech peoples." At the same time, a hastily erected Nazi street kitchen was handing out hot soup to "starving Czechs" (in reality, well-rehearsed Germans) for the benefit of newsreel cameras. Some three thousand German youths had enrolled in Charles University the previous semester; they now appeared in the Brownshirt uniforms, marshalling crowds and "restoring order out of anarchy."

What the cameras did not show was the spontaneous procession of Prague's real citizens to Vaclavské Namĕsti (St. Wenceslas Square), the city's and the country's spiritual heart, which sloped down from the statue of its patron saint. The square's traditional hot sausage stands were shuttered that day; people could not bring themselves to think of munching *horké párky*. Instead, following a nonexistent cue from an invisible conductor, the Czechs assembled on that history-rich place spontaneously broke into their national anthem: "Kde Domov Můj?" ("Where Is My Home?").

The routine of life had abruptly halted. In the marketplace at Uhelný Trh, women sat among their stalls of goose-liver pâté, pork hocks, and fresh unsalted butter, quietly sobbing. The only restaurants open did business under duress, serving self-congratulatory German officers their victory meals. Ambulances screamed across the city — a great mystery, as there had been no armed resistance.

Czech humour soon contrived an explanation: they were carrying German officers sick from all the cream cakes they had devoured.

As a nine-year-old, I was vaguely envious of these Nazi supermen and played with the idea that it might be more fun to be one of them – purposeful and triumphant – while my fellow Czechs were so lost and cowed. But something inside me knew that this could never be, and knew also that these grey ghosts had stolen my home and my country. All was lost in the first twenty-four hours. That same evening, Hitler arrived in Prague, slept in the royal castle, and gloated over his new dominion. Though he was a vegetarian and a teetotaller, he nibbled Prague ham and drained a glass of Pilsner, boasting to his retinue that Czechoslovakia had ceased to exist. He was right. My home country was no more.

MY FAMILY HELD an emergency council. It was agreed that my parents and I, along with Erika, would try to escape from Czechoslovakia. My grandparents, blessed by innocence and age, felt they would be safe from the Nazi barbarians and decided to stay behind. The decision cost them their lives: they later perished in the concentration camps. The day after the invasion, storm troopers had begun rounding up intellectuals, resisters, journalists, and "antisocial elements" – such as innocent but influential Jews. My father left early in the morning and did not return until late at night, once again trudging the streets, pounding on embassy doors in a frantic search for asylum. While applying at the Canadian immigration office for a visa (an otherwise futile bid, as the Canadian government at the time practised a disgraceful zero-admittance policy toward Jews fleeing Nazi persecution),[1] chance threw us a lifeline.

---

[1] In their definitive study of Canada's anti-Semitic policy during the Second World War, *None is Too Many: Canada and the Jews of Europe 1933–1948*, authors Irving Abella and Harold Troper document that when Frederick Charles Blair, director of the federal immigration branch, was asked how many Jews should be allowed into the country during the ravages of the Holocaust, he replied:

My father happened to meet a Canadian Pacific Railway land agent named L.J. Hornat. He argued his case and they struck a deal. Hornat would provide a document depicting Oscar Neumann as an experienced farmer, which would qualify him for a Canadian entrance visa. In exchange, my father would buy a farm from the CPR using some money he had salted away in England.

That night, my father triumphantly returned to our little flat with a smile on his face, some papers in his pockets, and a coil of Moravian sausage in his hand.

"I have the most wonderful news!" he said. "We are going to Canada!"

"Canada!" Everyone cried. "Canada!" Then we fell silent. The truth was, we knew next to nothing about Canada, other than that it was on the other side of the moon, a frozen land filled with Eskimos, ice, and snow. It didn't sound promising.

"Yes!" my father said. "We are going to Canada, and just listen to this –" He paused for effect. "We are going to be *barley farmers!*"

My mother swooned.

Once she roused herself, father attempted to generate some enthusiasm by showing us the document that Hornat had typed up for the Canadian authorities on CPR letterhead. The document made no mention of my father's career as an industrialist, or his political influence. Instead, it portrayed him as being of hardy peasant stock.

"'This man has lived on a farm at Lodenice, near Brno, and has won a barley-growing contest,'" my father read. This was not exactly an untruth, although the closest my father had come to growing the barley was signing the cheques for the farmers who did. "'He is a robust type of man,'" he smiled at that part, "'and is

---

"None is too many." He kept his word. The authors record that between 1940 and 1945 there were only a handful of exceptions to this shameful policy of exclusion – fewer than a dozen families in total, ours among them. "One fact transcends all others," they wrote, "the Jews of Europe were not so much trapped in a whirlwind of systematic mass murder, as abandoned to it."

not only a theoretician but also a practical farmer. He and his family have been baptized Catholics —'"

"What?" my mother cried.

"I'll get to that later," my father said. He continued reading: "'. . . baptized Catholics. He is, one can see, a thoroughly capable man, able to make his way in the world, and would be an acquisition to any country.'"

He looked for our reaction.

"Baptized Catholics?" my mother trembled in disbelief.

"A mere formality, my dear. Oh, yes — and there is one other hitch. We have no transit visas. We have to somehow make it through Europe on our own. So? What do you think?"

"I think," my mother said, "it is time we saw our priest." And she laughed. The idea suddenly seemed to amuse her greatly.

On May 8, the Neumann family presented itself to Father Leo Mojsis, a Catholic priest in the Bohemian parish of St. Margarita, in Prague's Brevnov district. With a Charles University medical professor named Josef Saidl as my godfather, I was welcomed into the Faith. The ceremony cost our family five crowns, making it the religious equivalent of a Las Vegas wedding. I could not take my eyes off the priest — all raven black and glowering. He was the only person present who seemed to understand what was really going on, and his name — Czech for "Moses" — was comforting to a Jew about to commit apostasy.

"In the name of the Father, the Son, and the Holy Ghost," he intoned, and all I could think was: *Ghosts? Now we have ghosts?* I looked around the dark corners of the church and shivered; I was ready to bolt out of there.

The priest looked down at me and his face softened. "It means the Holy Spirit," he said. "The little bit of God that is always with you. Just like your guardian angel. Here, my son. I want you to have this." He produced a small plaster-of-Paris angel, with red robes and golden wings, and gave it to me. "To watch over you," he explained.

I thanked him with genuine appreciation, and put the angel in my pocket. It followed us across Europe, and it has followed me ever since. As I write these memoirs, the angel is still on my desk, maintaining its watchful vigil.

I didn't feel any less Jewish for being a Catholic, or any less Catholic for being a Jew. It was just a thing we did, and it probably didn't bother God. As we left the church, my father slapped his fedora on his head, and had the last word in Yiddish. "*Das is alles meshuge*," he said, "It's all craziness."

WE LEARNED THAT EVENING that our home in Břeclav had been taken over for a Nazi officers' club. My mother wept. To cheer her spirits, my father took her to the Prague National Theatre for a performance of Bedrich Smetana's *Má Vlast* (*My Country*), which was followed by a fifteen-minute standing ovation, with the conductor kissing the score and holding it out to the audience. Its performance was immediately banned.

Meanwhile, the noose was tightening around us. The Prague list of Jews was placed directly under Berlin's jurisdiction, and random arrests became the order of the day. A temporary concentration camp had been set up near Prague, and a man named Adolf Eichmann, head of the Gestapo's Jewish section, arrived in town to personally implement the harsh anti-Semitic edicts he had invoked in Vienna.[2]

To reach Canada, we had to get to England, which we could only do from France, and the best opportunity to cross into France seemed to be from Italy. My father reasoned that as a German ally,

---

[2] Eichmann was an Austrian Nazi who rose to become the chief architect of the "Final Solution," promoting the use of gas chambers in extermination camps to eliminate six million Jews during the Holocaust. He fled to Argentina after the war ended but was captured by Israeli agents fifteen years later and returned to Israel, where he was hanged. His last words were, "To sum it all up, I have to say that I regret nothing." The philosopher Hannah Arendt coined the term "the banality of evil" to describe him, adding: "The trouble with Eichmann was precisely that so many were like him, and that the many were neither perverted nor sadistic, that they were, and still are, terribly and terrifyingly normal."

Italy would have the least strict entry requirements from Prague. In the confusing days following the invasion, he was able to obtain exit visas from the German authorities on the condition that he first sign away all rights to his property and refineries in Břeclav. On July 6, we left for the Italian frontier by train. As Jews, we were restricted as to how much cash we were allowed to take with us. My resourceful mother hid a hefty cache of jewels in her hat box, while my father handed me a small album of stamps to carry in my pocket. He did not tell me their value, because he was afraid that I would be too obviously nervous going through customs. In fact, the stamps were rare treasures, representing a significant portion of my family's remaining wealth. I was not particularly interested in stamps, and just before our train left the station I noticed another boy my age playing with a cap pistol. Now, *that* was something that would be really useful. I traded him my stamp album for the pistol, and happily spent the journey drawing a bead on the German train guards.

As we approached the frontier, my father turned to me with a comforting smile. "And where is your stamp collection, Peťa?" he asked.

"I gave it away, Papa. But look what I got in trade!"

My father's face blanched. "And with whom did you trade it away?" he asked.

"Another boy."

"And where is this other boy?"

"He was at the train station in Prague."

"I see."

My father was silent for a long while, as he no doubt pondered the vagaries of life. I don't think he ever forgave me, and I don't blame him.

THE NEXT EIGHTEEN MONTHS were a tumble of arrivals and departures, a scramble for visas, a flight from fear. One by one, my mother's jewels disappeared to finance our exodus. Each time, the ritual was the same. My father would explain that he needed money again, usually to bribe some corrupt official. With exaggerated slowness and increasing heaviness of spirit, my mother would drag out her little hat box and remove the smallest item remaining. "More," my father would say. "We need more." She would add another piece of jewellery to his outstretched hand, and he would bolt from our hotel room like a thief, to disappear among the diamond merchants of the Jewish ghettoes. A few hours later he would return, with small bundles of paper currency. "Is that all?" my mother would ask. "It's not so much." Our resources were dwindling, and our days were numbered. Unless we could get to Canada before the money ran out, all would be lost.

Our Italian entry visa was valid only until August 15. We settled in Venice, perhaps because of its long history of tolerance toward Jews. The Venetian city fathers had allowed Jews to settle there since 1516, requiring them to live in the Cannareggio district's Ghetto Nuovo (the world's first "ghetto," from which the word derived), where they were locked in their neighbourhood at night and had to follow social and economic restrictions, but otherwise enjoyed religious freedom and could build synagogues. We stayed first at a hotel along the Grand Canal, but it proved too expensive, so we moved to the Lido, one of the floating city's adjacent islands. We lived in a small *pensione* off Gran Viale Santa Maria Elizabetta, the main shopping street, near the Lido proper, a strand of beach where I spent many happy hours. One day I was allowed to tour the visiting Italian naval cruiser, the *Raimondo Montecuccoli*. The Italian navy might not have been the world's most finely honed fighting machine, but whatever its sailors lacked in firepower they made up for in panache. Their uniforms were the crispest and smartest I have ever seen on board a naval ship, which is saying a lot. The ship itself was cared for with lavish attention to detail, and it sported some stylish touches, such as teak trim to the handrails. *One day*, I vowed to myself, *I, too, will be a naval officer.*

Every Sunday night, after our family meal, my father would make his way to the Santa Lucia rail station to catch the overnight train to Rome. He would spend the entire week sitting in the ante-room of the French embassy, in an effort to obtain a visa for us. Once in France, he knew, we could catch a boat to England, with-draw the money he had deposited there, and purchase our passage to Canada. But every Friday he would be home, empty-handed, having spent the better part of the latest jewellery heist in a futile effort to bribe some French official into granting us the required document. Time was swiftly running out; the Feast of the Assump-tion on the fifteenth of the month would mark the end of our legal stay in Italy. After that, we would be fugitives, subject to immedi-ate deportation to Czechoslovakia and certain death.

On August 12, three days short of the deadline, an envelope inexplicably arrived from Paris, containing special entry visas for France. We made our dash to freedom, part of the human tide des-perately seeking French sanctuary.

We were in the French capital three weeks later, on the evening of September 3, when Hitler's Blitzkrieg forces thundered across Poland, prompting England and France to declare war. My father listened to the broadcast from the radio in the hotel lobby. That night, the lights went out in Paris, and civilians were ordered to flee the city. Instead, my father volunteered to join the French army. Being fifty-four years of age, he was never called up, but it was a brave gesture.

Europe was on fire. Everyone's motto was "*Sauve qui peut*," which translates as "Let those who can save themselves." Finding our-selves unable to escape France, with no civilian travel available to England, we moved south to Nice, where I was enrolled in L'Ecole Sasserno, a private Catholic boys' school, and painfully began to learn French. Once again, that temporary nest proved too expen-sive, and we moved next to Néris-les-Bains, the site of ancient Roman baths, not far from Vichy. There we stayed for most of nine months. I attended a municipal grammar school, and, by the end of the first semester, could speak the language, ranking eighteenth in a class of twenty-three. We lived quietly in our tranquil French village, while my father (dressed in his closest approximation to the outfit of a Canadian barley farmer) went calling on Canada's beleaguered embassy in Paris to grasp the chance of gaining official admission.

Everything changed on May 17, 1940, when Hitler's war machine invaded France, crushing all resistance. Within a week, the Nazis had smashed their way to the English Channel and were encircling Paris. The French capital surrendered without a fight on June 14 – but once again, a lifeline had appeared. We had been in Paris just two days earlier to finally receive "*Visa Numero* 316, Valid for Travelling to Canada," accompanied by the scribbled notation: "CPR agricultural family. London's approval received over phone." The wonderful Mr. Hornat had come through.

We had still to get out of Paris, then out of France. Humiliated beyond endurance, France's prime minister, Paul Reynaud, had resigned, and his Third Republic administration had fled southwest to Bordeaux on the Bay of Biscay. This would be the last major French city to fall, and it became the destination for the human river flowing out of Paris. We joined the current, to become part of the fleeing mobs of refugees that Nazi fighter pilots used for target practice while returning from more serious missions. Retreating across the bountiful fields of rural France in the heat of a glorious summer gone mad, just ahead of Hitler's tanks, we prayed to whatever deity we could conjure up to rescue us from this doomed continent.

When we reached Bordeaux, we found a city possessed by demons. Refugees from Holland, Belgium, and France had overrun its limited facilities. Hotels were sold out twice over, some renting their beds on a shift basis. Normally a city of 300,000, Bordeaux's population had ballooned overnight thanks to the arrival of more than a million hysterical refugees.

Every café along the Rue Ste.-Catherine, Place St.-Pierre, and the Rue de la Rousselle (once the centre of the salt fish trade) was crammed with sweating exiles, talking in low voices, circulating the same rumours spread by the same hotel doormen looking for tips, nursing red wine and absinthe while nervously looking over their shoulders for the Nazi motorcycle scouts they feared might arrive at any moment. The talk was mostly about Hendaye, a border village in the Pyrenees. Hendaye's main attraction was a narrow bridge over the rushing Bidassoa River that provided access to Spain. That country was ruled by the fascist dictator Francisco Franco, who provided no haven to refugees. But neighbouring Portugal was neutral, and did welcome exiles, providing they held visas to their final destinations – and these were honoured at the Hendaye border post. The catch was that Lisbon did not accept Jews, but this edict was ignored by the Portuguese consul general in Bordeaux, Aristides de Sousa-Mendes, a devout Catholic with an enlightened attitude who had decided to help the frightened refugees as a humanitarian gesture. He personally issued transit visas to an estimated ten thousand Jews.[3]

Rumours were flying that the Nazis had already reached Bordeaux's suburbs. We had to move fast, before the Germans sealed off all the Atlantic seaports. In one final, desperate effort, the family split up, with each of us holding a place in one of the long queues outside the various diplomatic offices. I was positioned outside the British consulate, where we seemed to have the least chance, but which did represent Canada's interests in Bordeaux. My parents were lined up at the Spanish offices, while my aunt was part of the mob trying to reach the benevolent Portuguese consul.

I overheard a conversation between two French women standing in line behind me. One of them mentioned that the Czech army-in-exile, which had fought the Nazis across France, had commandeered a merchant ship in nearby Biarritz for their planned dash to England the following morning. I ran through the streets

---

[3] The Portuguese government recalled de Sousa-Mendes within two weeks of this magnificent initiative. Even on his way out of the country, he signed the passports of every Jew waiting at the border. Back in Lisbon, he was fired from the diplomatic corps and, after drifting from one occupation to another, died, poor and ignored, in 1954, a forgotten saint.

to tell my parents this exciting news. The crowds of exiles were becoming increasingly frantic at the sound of approaching German guns, like animals preparing to bolt from a forest fire but not sure which way to run. But when I reached the Spanish consulate my parents were not there. They had given up on Spain and were on the way to pick me up at the British queue, so we could all converge on Portugal. When they arrived at the British consulate, I was nowhere to be found. My mother, true to form, fainted.

They retraced their steps through the streets, alive with other panic-stricken people, and found me. We quickly realized we could do nothing about the opportunity I had overheard without our passports, then being held by my Aunt Erika. We no longer required a Portuguese visa, but we did need an entry visa to Great Britain, and urgently. We raced over to the Portuguese consulate, where by sheer chance we spotted her from the street in the lengthy line snaking to the consul's third-floor office. She happened to be standing beside an open window. We yelled for her to throw us the passports and rushed back to the British consulate, where a kind vice-consul issued us United Kingdom transit visas, writing in the margin, where the duty stamp is usually affixed: "Gratis. No time to charge fee in emergency."

My father hailed a taxi and asked the surprised driver how much it would cost to rent the vehicle for the rest of the day. The driver named a price, my father paid it, and within a few hours of my hearing the rumour we were rolling down the coastal highway toward Biarritz. We easily found the ragtag remnants of the Czech army and the tattered freighter they had commandeered, the *Ville de Liège*, a Belgian ship under charter to an American grapefruit company. Their commanding officer recognized my father, and we were granted permission to join his evacuating troops. But the ship was anchored offshore and we couldn't be ferried aboard until early the following morning.

We survived the nocturnal machine-gunning on the beach and embarked with relief on the early tide aboard the *Ville de Liège*, which, as it turned out, was the last major vessel to leave France and safely reach England. Later ships were either detained in port or dive-bombed by the Nazis. We were spared only because our vessel had an American flag aboard, which we tied firmly to the stern. The United States was not yet at war with Germany and the Luftwaffe pilots who spotted us didn't want to provoke an international incident.[4]

Every night we steamed without running lights to confuse any attackers, and eventually reached Liverpool. Many of the four hundred escaping pilots on board our ship eventually formed their own squadrons in the Royal Air Force and fought with distinction during the Battle of Britain. I loved that crossing, being the only kid on a ship with daredevil pilots recounting their exploits.

As soon as we landed at Liverpool, we were shipped to a London suburb and thrown into the British equivalent of a concentration camp. The British government suspected that our group might be harbouring German spies, and I vividly recall Scotland Yard agents walking among us, picking out six individuals for further questioning. Two of them were later frogmarched out of the place in irons. The rest of us were placed in barracks with no privacy and awful food. I was just grateful that our family was allowed to remain together.

Our brief time in London was highlighted by the Blitz, when the Luftwaffe launched deadly nighttime air raids against the city. The Germans believed that British morale would crack within days, but it only served to steel Londoners' resistance. On most nights, especially those with a full moon, or "bombers' moon" as it was called, the air-raid sirens sounded and we slept in a nearby underground Tube station that provided shelter against the bombs. Safe we might have been, but comfortable we were not, and I will never forget the overpowering stench of urine. The city streets smelled of burst sewage lines, wet plaster, and burned wires; the bombed-out buildings stood out like stone lace etchings against

---

[4] Later, as a fervent Canadian nationalist, I mentioned in my speeches that, despite my aversion to U.S. imperialism, I owed my life to the American flag.

the fiery sky. What impressed me most were the air raid shelters for animals in Hyde Park.

My father obtained our British exit permits (in addition to one visa to enter, the British required another to leave – they don't call it the "genius of British bureaucracy" for nothing), which carried the warning: "No Return to the United Kingdom." We left from Liverpool on September 21, 1940, aboard the seven-thousand-ton Furness Line's Royal Mail Ship *Nova Scotia*, part of a thirty-four-ship convoy that included four naval escorts. With the convoy's commodore aboard, we were designated as the lead ship in the centre column, which also made us the most vulnerable to U-boat attacks. At night we followed a zigzag pattern to avoid torpedoes. I was in my element, on board yet another ship. We never removed our clothing or life jackets and passed our nights in the first-class lounge, so that we were close to the lifeboats. At twilight or dawn, the peak times for torpedo attacks, we stayed in the lifeboats themselves. The precautions were justified. Four days out, our convoy was attacked by a U-boat wolf pack at dawn.[5]

There was no warning: one moment I was sitting quietly in the lifeboat with my mother and father in our bulky Mae West life preservers; the next there came the screaming sound of torn metal, and the sight of fire and smoke rising from three ships in succession off our port bow. I clung to the gunwale and watched with fascinated horror. I could see merchant seamen slipping off the nearest of the wounded vessel's decks, falling to certain death in the oil-slicked waters. The ship listed and its stern lifted from the surface; smoke and fire were blowing from its portholes. There was a series of secondary explosions as bulkheads gave way; then, in the space of a few seconds, the fatally wounded vessel slipped below the waves. When the smoke cleared, I could see the blackened heads of the survivors bobbing in the water, screaming for help. Then they

---

[5] One of the convoy's escorts, HMCS *Ottawa*, was skippered by Captain E.R. Mainguy, who would be my first admiral when I joined the Royal Canadian Navy.

too fell silent. Our escorts sounded sirens and criss-crossed the cold waters around us, dropping depth charges in a futile bid to strike one of the U-boats, which had fled as silently as they had arrived.

The following dawn, the U-boats struck again. This time, the ships were closer and the flames lit the waters around our boats like a crimson sunrise. Our crew tried desperately to launch lifeboats in time to rescue survivors, but another three ships were lost with nearly all hands.[6]

Our last evening at sea, I stayed up to watch the stars, and get a sneak preview of the Canada we were approaching, that distant and mysterious land we had been fleeing toward for the past fourteen months. What would our farm be like? Would I meet an Eskimo? At some point I drifted off, and upon being roused in the morning I was told that the coast of Nova Scotia was off our port bow. I rushed forward for a look and was surprised to find the trees were green and the soil was brown – I had expected the land to be permanently covered in snow.

We landed in Halifax at Pier 21, where we were tagged like cattle and herded into large cages. The labels identified us by nationality, date of arrival, and ultimate destination, while the cages sorted us according to language group. Undoubtedly it all made sense to some Ottawa bureaucrat, but to a Jewish refugee, it was not the welcome we had expected. We were exhilarated to be on Canadian soil at last, but at the same time were grieving for our lost friends, family, and homeland. We were also anxious about having to pull off the deceit of pretending to be farmers, and worried whether we could actually survive by living off the land. This brief period of detention magnified our anxieties a thousandfold, reminding us of the regimentation and persecution we thought that we had left behind in Europe. But our worries eased once our papers were cleared and an immigration inspector waved us to the pier's annex, where we were welcomed by volunteers

---

[6] I am indebted to John D. Haikings of Annapolis Royal, Nova Scotia, for sharing with me his records and memories of this particular convoy.

from the Jewish Immigrant Aid Society and fed a Fig Newton each. Nothing has ever tasted better.

It was September, yet unseasonably hot. Newsreels had portrayed Canada as "the land of eternal snow," so before leaving England we had outfitted ourselves with fur coats, made from fluffy and slightly pungent British rabbits. Boiling hot and overdressed, we decided before boarding the Canadian Pacific immigrant train to Montreal to celebrate at the coffee shop of the nearby Nova Scotian Hotel. First, I had to visit the basement bathroom, where I was confronted by a pay toilet. You had to drop a dime into the slot before the door would open. I didn't have any Canadian money and didn't know the language well enough to ask for help. Luckily the gap under the door was high enough for me to slide under, but as soon as I did, I imagined that I would be caught and deported.

Back in the coffee shop, our family was talking animatedly in Czech, discussing our future plans and wondering what to order, since none of us understood a single word of the menu. Our waiter appeared and offered advice to us in perfect Czech; he had arrived a few boats back.

What a curious place, where you had to pay to go to the bathroom, but the waiters spoke Czech. Then it suddenly hit me: this was my new home. There was no going back. This country was going to shape the rest of my life.

CHAPTER TWO

CIRCLE JERKS, SNOBBERY, AND THE LASH

The only time I recall sex being mentioned at Upper Canada College was when our housemaster, Jimmy Biggar, confided in us that "it is a proven fact that all well-educated people are virgins when they get married." Fool that I was, I believed him. If only he had taken the trouble to explain that sex isn't pre-marital — when you don't intend to marry the lady.

We owed our escape from the Nazis to the CPR's land-marketing scheme, which required us to stay on a farm for five years. Rather than pretend that we could master some wild, virgin acreage on the Prairies, we settled on purchasing through the company a fifteen-acre fruit and vegetable spread at Freeman, Ontario, about an hour south of Toronto. Freeman in its entirety consisted of a post office, a railway station, a general store, an Imperial Oil gas station, and Clan's Coffee Shop. The farm's irrigation system and high-quality loam produced two crops a year, but it was hard work. We often rose at 4:00 a.m. to sell our produce at Hamilton market, which inaugurated my life-long habit of rising early.

"Every act of immigration," observed the Canadian psychiatrist Vivian Rakoff, an immigrant himself, "is like suffering a brain stroke. One has to learn to walk again, to talk again, to move around the world again, and probably most difficult of all, to re-establish a sense of community." That wasn't difficult for me because at my age I was adaptable and longing to connect with the

New World. It was harder for my aunt, who went off on her own to McMaster University. Although she held a doctorate in chemistry, and instructors were needed in wartime, she encountered a glass ceiling against female professors. Later, in desperation, she retreated to another skill. As a young girl she had learned to use a sewing machine to make beautiful little doilies. Now, she became part of a sweatshop operation turning out girdles on a piecework basis. She eventually moved to Toronto, where she became a social worker and helped to launch the Meals on Wheels program for housebound seniors. Her only solace was classical music; she often accompanied my mother on her violin. She did not make friends easily, but when she died of brain cancer, Toronto's Jewish community grieved and saluted her passing.

My mother, who in Czechoslovakia had never visited a kitchen except to consult a chef, also found it difficult to adjust. She still defined her life by what she had left behind, and never totally accepted the fact that we no longer belonged to the *erste gesellschaft*, or high society.

My father never lost his optimism and set out to conquer his two deficiencies: an inability to drive from the front seat (farmers couldn't afford chauffeurs), and his tortured rendition of the English language. Neither effort was totally successful. An ancient Model T Ford came with the farm and he set out to practise driving it on the area's back roads, often having to be towed home. In those days, the money-making business of issuing drivers' licences was farmed out to shopkeepers who voted for the provincial party in power. The nearest examiner happened to be a tailor on Hamilton's York Street. My father failed his driving test every time he tried it, until he ordered a new suit from the tailor shop and miraculously passed with flying colours. He never had a serious accident but treated the succession of automobiles we had as bumper cars. When he drove to visit Ernest and Tidy Neubauer, our closest friends, who lived on a neighbouring farm, they would watch my father come up their driveway and lay bets on whether his car would hit the tree on the right or the lamppost on the left. He never quite made it in between.[1]

My father did make progress with his English, so that within six months of our arrival he was asked to speak about Czechoslovakia to Hamilton's Rotary Club, whose members gave him a standing ovation. We knew no Canadians except these Rotarians, who adopted us as a project and assigned each other to come and visit us at our farm to teach us Canadian ways. Their kindness in making us feel welcome was genuine and comforting when we needed it most. For the first time, we lived as a true family; I didn't feel part of a tableau, as I had in Břeclav. We were together in a real world and had miraculously survived an impossible journey. It made us appreciate life and each other. We had little money but plenty of time, and we spent it together.

I was too preoccupied with my own insecurities to fully realize how remarkable it was for my mother and father to take so readily to running a tiny fruit and vegetable farm. We did have a hired man – or, to be precise, a series of hired men – but my parents worked from dawn to dusk, weeding, cultivating, picking, and packing our fruits and vegetables, with a cheerfulness and companionship they had seldom exhibited in their former lives. The winters were slow, but tool maintenance and taking care of our two plough horses (Joe and Bob), chickens, and pets kept us busy. We had a cat called Misha that insisted on showing us every mouse

---

[1] Originally from Hungary, Ernest Neubauer had studied in Vienna to become a symphony orchestra conductor. There weren't enough orchestras to go around, so he became a doctor instead, but never forgot his first love. He spent every spare moment in his music room reading from the scores on his pretend conductor's podium, conducting his large collection of classical records. Occasional errors had been recorded, which made Ernest furious. Tapping his stick on his music stand, he would yell at the musicians that they were playing in the wrong key, too fast, too slow, or whatever. But the music never stopped. We spent many happy hours together. I still see his widow, Tidy, now in her magnificent nineties, who lives at her home on Hamilton Mountain and makes the best Wiener Schnitzel in the universe.

she caught in the barn, preferably at mealtimes, and a dog called Toby who was a Heinz 57 Varieties mutt. Saturday afternoons were my mother's weekly highlight. The Metropolitan Opera House in New York City broadcast its matinee performances over the CBC, and I was deputized to listen in at the end of the program, when they announced the next week's offering. My mother (and my aunt, when she was visiting us from Hamilton) would spend hours guessing what the coming features would be. Since I knew nothing about opera, I could give them no clues. My father spent his time worrying about the progress of the war, learning most of his English from Lorne Greene, who read the CBC's newscasts at the time.

But not all was rosy. Early in 1945, we received word through the International Red Cross that both sets of my grandparents had been taken to the notorious concentration camp in Theresienstadt, near Prague, where they perished. My mother never really recovered from this news. It was beyond comprehension why these elderly innocents would be so ruthlessly killed, or how a society as seemingly cultured as Germany's could spawn the monsters who did it. Why had the world not risen up in revulsion against this mass murder, or, failing that, at least offered sanctuary to its intended victims?

In Canada, we were also feeling the sting of anti–Semitism, though at immeasurably lower intensity. Immigrants in rural Canada were scarce in those days. We were generally made to feel like outcasts, and we were never invited into a Canadian home. To protect ourselves from prejudice, we didn't use our own name on the farm truck, preferring the anonymous: "DEPENDABLE FRUIT GROWERS." One exception was a local fundamentalist Christian sect, which invited me to its Sunday school. It was the first time I realized that religion could be fun, because as far as I could figure out, the worshippers came mainly to clap, sing, and shout "HALLELUJAH!" The preacher enjoyed himself the most, boogying to the music like an early Blues Brother. I learned to sing (badly) some of their hymns, and whenever we had European visitors, my parents would march me out so that I could warble, "The Best Book to Read Is the

Bible," complete with holy-roller intonations, such as pronouncing Jesus as *JAYzus*. The other exception to our social isolation was the Royal Canadian Sea Cadet Corps, Iron Duke Division, which recruited me as a drummer.

Most of my cultural education took place during the Saturday matinees at the Hume (later Roxy) movie theatre in Burlington, where I followed the exploits of Hopalong Cassidy and his dishevelled sidekick, California. (We looked down on Roy Rogers, because he sang like a wuss.) I eventually attended Burlington High School, which (rightly) expelled me because I regularly goofed off and bicycled to Hamilton to watch John Wayne war movies during school hours. I also briefly attended Ashbury College in Ottawa and Hillfield School in Hamilton, but could not claim to be a star pupil. Having attended eight schools that taught in four languages by my early teens, I was badly in need of some educational purpose and stability. Unlikely as it seemed, this would come in the form of Canada's most prestigious private school.

I ARRIVED AT TORONTO'S Upper Canada College on September 4, 1943, a chilly, raining, autumnal day. The trees were taking on a russet glow against the landscape, a latent colour waiting for the departure of green. Some leaves had already fallen, clogging the gutters with brown mush, the better to match my mood.

Unlike most students attending a posh boarding school for the first time, I had not departed the crowded metropolis for a tree-lined campus in the countryside, but the reverse. I had left the tranquil rural setting of the farm and its familiar routines for the racing heart of a strange city. That morning at the train station, I had bid a teary-eyed farewell to my parents, trying to put on a brave face for my father, who had sacrificed much so that I could take this journey.

"Peťa . . ." he began to say in parting, but turned away.

My mother tenderly patted the kerchief in the breast pocket of my "good-as-new" suit. She pressed a parcel into my hands. It was

a white plastic radio, ordered on the cheap from the Eaton's catalogue, but I was thrilled. My own radio. I suppose today the equivalent gift would be a laptop with an Internet account. That little
radio was to become my link to the outside world, my mentor, my
secret best friend.

My life's journey had begun. The moment was so fraught with
meaning that as the train started to move I felt everyone must be
looking at me. But nobody was. Around me, bored commuters
read newspapers and stared out the window, drugged by narcotic
routine. I wish that I could say how, as a bright-eyed youngster
setting forth into a strange new world, I faced the future with
determination and sprouting ambition – or at least with some
dread. But all I felt at the time was a numb sense of being very
alone, a feeling I would not shake for years – if ever.

The loamy fields of Brant County soon gave way to urban
buildup, and before I knew it the train whistled into Toronto's
Union Station. I've never forgotten emerging from the platform
and walking out into the arrival area set aside for travellers being
welcomed by their Toronto families. I jealously glanced around,
pretending to myself that someone would run up and hug me, but
soon found myself instead fumbling with the strange custom of
buying a streetcar ticket and making my way to Avenue Road and
St. Clair, the location of my new boarding school.

I was a fourteen-year-old Jewish refugee with faulty English, at
an age when I desperately wanted nothing more than to fit in with
my peers. But walking through the iron gates into the schoolyard,
I sensed that was not going to happen. The sober buildings projected the frigid air of a religious compound, heightened by the
tall tower with inaccurate clocks on its compass points, which I
soon learned was known as the four-faced liar.

Upper Canada College in 1943 was still very much a prep
school for Establishment offspring, all of them boys, most of them
destined to take over the levers of Canadian industry, government,
and finance. None was burdened with hand-me-down suits or
fractured syntax. Some – such as Conrad Black, David Thomson,

Ted Rogers, and Hal Jackman (not all in my year, though our paths would often cross later in life) – were deposited and picked up at the front steps by chauffeur-driven limousines, just as I had been in Europe. Meanwhile, I had stepped from my chauffeur-driven city tram, feet aching from tight new shoes, hoping no one would look too closely at my "tooled leather" suitcase, which showed cardboard through one of its battered edges. Bewildered, I strode up to the main stone staircase, being careful to tread lightly on my left shoe, which still squeaked, and presented myself in my best broken English to the hall porter:

"Hallow. I am New-man."

The porter, who wore ribbons from some distant war, raised a bushy eyebrow at me, taking in my dated Harris tweed suit and, I was sure, the cardboard trim of my luggage, and replied:

"New *boy*, you mean."

"No, New*man*. Peter Newman. You are please expecting me?"

"Oh, I see. All right." The porter smiled. We had shared a small joke and I felt better. He consulted a clipboard. "You're in Seaton's House," he said at last. "I'll take your bag and you can follow me."

As we strode across the quadrangle, the porter delivered a summary of the important rules and customs: "The school is divided into houses, with only two, Wedd's and Seaton's, for boarders," he told me. "The House will be your parent, and your new parent does not want you leaving the school grounds. Your parent does not want you consorting with the opposite sex. Your parent prohibits drinking alcohol or smoking at any time, on or off school grounds. Your parent expects you to wear the school uniform and to uphold the good name of the college. You will treat your parent with respect. Got all that?"

He didn't wait for a reply before delivering his punchline: "Break these rules and your parent will cane your backside until the flesh hangs from it in bloody strips."

I stared at him blankly. Had I survived that dive-bombing at Biarritz for this? Maybe my English just wasn't good enough to comprehend his warning. Maybe he was joking? I was to learn the hard way that he wasn't.

"Here is Seaton's House," he said, as we arrived at my new parent's home. "Breakfast is at oh-seven-hundred. Better go early while there's still something to eat."

I thanked him as he handed my bag back to me.

"Oh, by the way, as a new boy, you'll be fagged," he added, referring to the private school system modelled on the master-servant relationship of an army officer and his batman. "You'll be assigned to a senior boy and you will have to do anything he asks. You'll polish his shoes, run his errands, and make his bed. Disobey and you'll be given 'doubles,' which means running around the school on the double. Disobey him twice, you run the circuit twice. Don't even think of disobeying a third time. But if you don't blot your copybook and keep your nose clean, you'll find it's not so bad."

I hadn't yet enough fluency with the language to grasp his idiom, but I was determined to keep my nose spotless. And how did one blot a copybook?

Seaton's had been named after Sir John Colborne (later Lord Seaton), who founded the college in 1829 when he was lieutenant-governor of Upper Canada. Once inside the house, I was hit by an odour that would become all too familiar: the smell of stale socks and over-bleached sheets. Dormitory assignments were posted on the notice board – I was in a second-storey room with four other boys, all of them first-years like myself.

I found my quarters unoccupied. Amid strange surroundings, all I could manage was to unpack my few belongings and sit on my bed, awaiting further instructions. I forced myself to remember why I had been enrolled here, what my father had forfeited to send me to this place, the expectations placed upon me to succeed, the chance it represented to make something of myself.

Before it had been suggested that I attend Upper Canada College, I had never been exposed to the North American idea that "exclusive" meant requiring nothing more (or less) than buckets of cash. I had been raised to believe that an "exclusive" education implied some kind of scholastic merit. But I was to discover that this institution did not excel either in great teachers or school spirit. What UCC offered, that no other school in Canada could, were the twin requirements for success in the North American business world: a well-stuffed Rolodex and an unstuffed mind. Above all else, UCC had the feel of a private club. Most of my fellow students were the spawn of wealthy WASP parents who were too preoccupied making money to bother with their sons' educations, too alienated from their kids to care, or just plain happy to place the snotty little buggers into an institution that would beat some sense into them.

By contrast, I was Jewish, foreign, and *nouveau-pauvre*. But I was blessed with a caring father, so concerned about his only son's future that he paid a considerable portion of the bloated UCC boarding fees despite his own newly restricted circumstances. (A portion of my schooling was paid out of the UCC wartime scholarship fund, for which I was then, and remain today, properly grateful.) He knew that I would never lose my accent if I continued living at home, where we spoke mostly Czech and German. So he was throwing me into the ultimate immersion course: the WASP piranha pool of Upper Canada College.

My reverie, sitting on my bed, was interrupted by the bounding appearance of Doug Fisher, a fellow first-year who would become my best friend. "Hello, what's this?" he puzzled, as he entered the dormitory. "A new boy!"

Doug had the habit of answering his own questions. Despite being much more outgoing than I, he also appeared self-contained and as solid as the Canadian Shield that had raised him. I took to him immediately. To my relief, my foreignness didn't seem to bother him in the least. "I guess you could say I'm a stranger here myself," he confessed. "I'm from Val D'Or. That's in northern Quebec. It means 'Valley of Gold' – pretty grand name for a bush mining town. My dad's the doctor there, owns the hospital at nearby

Bourlamaque. He says I need some big-city spit and polish, so he sent me here. Come on, dinner's up. We have to get there early –"

"While dere is someding still to eat," I finished.

The day's worries faded into insignificance. I had found a friend. Most of the rest of the UCC boys have run together in my memory like some Greek chorus, but Doug (and later Peter Grant) stood alone as boon companions.

UCC AND I WERE NOT A PERFECT FIT. As the writer Ted Allan would later observe of me in the *Winnipeg Free Press*, "His almost vaudevillian eastern European accent and swarthy appearance were considered a low comedy counterpoint to the laconic sangfroid and nasal honk which characterized his schoolmates' fledgling mid–Atlantic personalities. He wasn't privy to the elusive signals that bespeak shared experience. He was a DP, a Jew, clearly unsuited for the concentric circles of Canadian power. He was to those people what he remains to them today, an outsider."

Certainly I felt the loneliness of an outsider, especially when the other students teased me mercilessly whenever I trotted out my bare-bones English. At dinner my first night, I was asked by one of these unctuous bullyboys if I wanted a second helping of dessert.

"No, danks," I blurted out. "I am quite fed up."

The table broke into belly-pumping laughter. The "danks" was a combination of the German *danke* and the fact that, like most European immigrants, I couldn't get my tongue around the diphthong. The "fed up" may have been incorrectly expressed, but it was accurately aimed. I was being offered a refill of a cold tapioca-and-raisins dessert deservedly known as "fish eyes in glue."

Faced with the combined horrors of college food and public ridicule, I grew determined at that moment to master the language. My mixture of Czech, German, French, and basic English had to go if I were to blend in with this crowd. Amazingly, the humiliation galvanized me to such an extent that I lost my accent in six weeks flat. I discovered that (unlike French, which I had so lately learned) English is a highly pragmatic language; there exists no Academie Française to preserve its purity. To this day, my written and spoken English are not the same. While I feel comfortable writing, my spoken English continues to feel like a second language. Especially when I read from my works, I often sound as though I am reciting the operating instructions from some complicated Japanese electronic toy manual. (Batteries not included.)

My first day at the college had not exhausted its store of surprises. That night, back in my room, someone casually suggested a "circle jerk" to celebrate the new term. I soon got used to participating in this ritual. Luckily, we remained the young gentlemen we were supposed to be – the accelerating activity remained under the sandpaper covers of our sheets.

When the routine custom had been completed, I retired at last to the sanctuary of my new radio. I had removed its dial light to hide its presence from the house masters who regularly patrolled our rooms, all too often at crucial moments during our under-the-sheets fumbling. The little receiver came equipped with earphones, which I slipped over my head. Rapt, I listened long into the night. The dulcet tones of a CBC broadcaster filled my hearing, loud, clear, and understandable. Here, at last, was a companion lacking entirely in snobbery who would not make fun of my accent, and who would patiently lead me through the traps and snares of my new language. That radio became one of my most formative influences. Happily, I let the college slip away and became lost in reverie, alone at last, at one with my inner self.

I was desperate to learn my new home country's language, history, and culture. Luckily for me, this was the golden age of CBC radio drama (especially Andrew Allan's *Stage* series), both documentary and theatrical. I overdosed on these nightly offerings, not fully understanding them, but getting used to the cadence of the language, and to the identities of Canada's villains and heroes.

The real fun began after midnight, when the airwaves throbbed with the excitement of remote pickups from the American networks, bringing in the big band sounds from the ballrooms that then ringed every large North American city. Having been raised on the tedious metronome of classical music, the big bands' open-ended melodies and daring time signatures opened the way for me into the culture that I was so determined to join. My nocturnal menu of CBC documentaries, news, and current affairs programming gave me a better education than UCC. When I finally fell asleep after hours of listening, I would dream without much differentiation about John A. Macdonald and Benny Goodman, Wilfrid Laurier and Tommy Dorsey, Mackenzie King and Woody Herman, with the certainty that this would always be my country and my music.

One night, I picked up a Mutual Broadcasting Company remote broadcast from the Rendezvous Ballroom in Balboa Beach, California, and heard Stan Kenton for the first time. His music poured out of my little radio like a hailstorm. I was smitten. I had never heard anything like his musical energy, evocative melodies, and driving rhythms. They opened up a wider, wilder world of possibilities. I might have been confined by college, class, and tongue, but here was a music that spoke to me of freedom and inventiveness. I was supposed to worship my heritage by loving Mozart; instead, jazz had set me free. I was hooked with a devotion that would last a lifetime.

MY MOST VIVID RECOLLECTION OF UCC is of its teachers. Most of them were helpful and normal, especially my favourites, Norman Sharp and Pop Law. But the exceptions ran the spectrum from crackpots to sadists. I was never sexually molested, but we were certainly aware that several students repeatedly suffered such indignities, though it only became clear in retrospect how common an experience that was. Some teachers were merely nerds, like Freddie Mallet, who taught chemistry in a laboratory setting. He would begin each semester's classes by earnestly admonishing us to "not play with the apparatus in our drawers." To our teenage minds, this was an open invitation to endless snickering, but he never seemed to catch on.

What I could never figure out, then or now, was why Upper Canada College regarded physical punishment as such an essential part of secondary education. What was so desirable about getting whipped? And I don't mean a light slap on the wrists. For every infraction, real and imagined, teachers caned our bare bottoms with malicious delight. There was a distinctly savage undertow of sexually charged sadism to these beatings, which, while perverse, were accepted as normal by students and faculty alike.

Among the brutes who delivered this punishment, Wedd's assistant housemaster, I.K. Shearer, was the most notorious. A lanky Englishman who taught French, he caned students for no apparent reason other than his own enjoyment. His beatings had a ritual quality that I will scarce forget. Once when I was targeted for a beating for some minor bit of boyish excess, Shearer sent me – as he did all his victims – to his office, which resembled the interior set of some dark Gothic thriller. Once there, he presented me with dice.

"Roll 'em," he said.

I complied.

"Six," he wheezed, clearly delighted. "That means six of the best. Bad luck."

As though I weren't terrified enough, he then led me by the ear to his "special cupboard." He opened it to reveal a collection of whips worthy of a medieval torture chamber. By this time he could barely contain his excitement and, savouring every moment, described their properties. "This one," he said, caressing a slender reed, "is the whippy one. It gives you a little more snap, but it doesn't have quite the same weight. Now this one, it really gives you a crack, but I can't swing it as hard because it doesn't have a whip to it."

I found myself performing the dreadful calculation of weight versus whip, an awful choice for a child. I hesitantly chose the lighter model. After half a dozen hard strokes from I.K. (something I was to experience several times) I couldn't sit comfortably for a week. Seldom was this caning delivered for anything more serious than a childish prank; the punishment exceeded the crime and the hurt was more than physical. It is a testament to UCC's prevailing mentality that the Marquis de Shearer hung on to his sadistic tenure for thirty years before he was abruptly dismissed, long after I left.

The self-proclaimed champion victim of UCC's lashing era was John Gartshore, who calculated that during his three years at the college's upper school he was caned 1.14 times a week. Conrad Black claims that the only distinction he earned at UCC was being declared runner-up for the 1955 "Zebra" award for the most frequently beaten boy in the junior locker room. "One of the more enthusiastic flagellators," he recalled, "was Laurier LaPierre (the political commentator and senator), who later publicly declared his homosexual activities. It became possible to imagine some of the socio-economic and psychological displacements that must have motivated this penniless young French-Canadian socialist to assault so violently the comfortable derrieres of Upper Canada scions." Another character, a master known as "Daddy" Darnell, would hurl a wet boxing glove at inattentive pupils, then reel it back on a string. He was finally fired and became the janitor in a Toronto apartment building. The practice of caning was outlawed in 1975.

Far outnumbering the floggers were the college's eccentrics. One of the more legendary, immortalized by Robertson Davies (UCC 1928–32) in the novel *Fifth Business*, was Dickey Potter. Shell-shocked in the First World War, he used to climb the water pipes in his classroom and teach from a precarious perch near the ceiling, his academic gown hanging off his narrow shoulders. Not even unexpected visits to his classroom by the headmaster, who casually talked to him while Dickey was perched in mid-air, could get him down.

The resident eccentric during my time at UCC was Owen "Buzz" Classey, who taught French and had, during his youth, been H.G. Wells's private secretary. He took no part in college activities and inhabited a set of rundown attic chambers that he turned into his fiefdom. Once settled in his classroom, we would await his dramatic entrance. It was heralded by a faraway hunter's cry: "WERRRRRRRK, you bums!" The chant was repeated with increasing volume as he approached and finally entered. "WERRRRRRK!, Werrrk! Werrrrk, you bums!" he would coo to himself, as much as to us, as he circled the classroom on tiptoes.

He certainly made learning French an adventure, though the only directive I recall him issuing was to read *Maria Chapdelaine* in the original French. "Take her to bed every night," he advised. A stringy, wrinkled gnome with liver spots and a Charlie Chaplin moustache, he was nicknamed "Buzz" because of his faulty hearing aid, which seldom stopped buzzing. He had to keep punching himself in the head to clear the noise. He neither heard nor responded to most of our questions, but he was armed with some sort of back-of-the-head radar. Spotting an inattentive student, he would cuff the idler with a textbook unmercifully hard. My fellow Old Boy, the author Jim Bacque, recalled how one boy had his head slammed on the desk by Classey until blood came out his ears.

Because of my wartime foray to France, I spoke the language – unlike most UCC boys, who were expected to study French but never actually to learn it. As a result, Classey treated me as if I had been assigned to his classroom as a spy by some malevolent foreign power. He would sneak up behind me to see if I were drafting a secret dispatch to my controller. As soon as I spotted him he would waltz away, muttering to himself in French about *la Résistance*. I didn't have the nerve, but my classmate William Kilbourn, who later graduated from the universities of Toronto, Oxford, and Harvard to become a popular historian, decided to test Buzz's hearing. He brought his mouth organ to class and played France's national anthem, "La Marseillaise." Classey paid not the slightest attention until Kilbourn strayed into a Glenn Miller tune. Buzz immediately swooped down on him and stopped the concert.[2]

---

[2] "We loved Buzz," Kilbourn confessed in his memoirs. "He was the ultimate anarchist, and seemed to be a parody of everything that the school stood for. If the place made you miserable, he was an ally, however distant. Although I never

A very different character was J.M.B.P. "Jock" de Marbois, who was loosely connected to the Modern Languages and Geography departments, though he spent an inordinate amount of effort trying to teach the boys polo, planting them aboard a wooden horse he had built. (We never had the heart to tell him he was flogging a dead horse.) A kindly but distant presence who taught while sitting cross-legged on his desk, he'd been born on the island of Mauritius in the Indian Ocean and had married the Countess Tatiana Vladamorovna, whose father had commanded the Imperial Horse Guards in Russia when the last czar was deposed. De Marbois had been hunted across post-revolutionary Russia with a price on his head, and during his subsequent exile it was said that he became fluent in twenty languages.[3] He undoubtedly makes an appearance in another Robertson Davies novel, *The Cunning Man*, where he appears as "Jock" Daubigny, a much-travelled teacher at "Colborne College." Davies writes of the character's mysterious service in three navies and even speaks of his experience with cannibalism.

Eventually, de Marbois had settled down to a naval career, but it wasn't certain in which navy he had actually served, since he had been made a Commander, order of the British Empire, as well as being awarded the Légion d'Honneur by France and the Legion of Merit by the United States. He'd held the exalted rank of commodore in both the Canadian and Royal navies, and during the Second World War had headed the Naval Intelligence branch in Ottawa. Why he taught at Upper Canada College was never clear to him or us, but he told wonderful stories, and I adored his dash, his elegant manner, and his swashbuckling tales. He encouraged in

---

attempted a conversation with him, any more than you would expect to have an intimate dialogue with the March Hare or the Cheshire cat, I believe that he recognized I had been unhappy at UCC, and treated me, in his remote way, as a kindred spirit."

[3] It was rumoured that during his travels he had eaten human flesh among the savages of Tierra del Fuego. I later wooed his lovely daughter Natalie, but she would neither confirm nor deny the story.

me the improbable dream of someday becoming a naval officer, an ambition that later prompted me to serve in the Royal Canadian Navy and its reserves for forty years.

The most feared presence at the college was its principal, Lorne "Butch" McKenzie, whose appointment in 1943 was regarded as a wartime expediency, pleasing neither the college's governors, the boys, nor McKenzie himself, who declared that he was unsuitable for the job. He was right. A mathematician by calling and a sadist by temperament, he felt much more at home teaching binomial theory and calculus than setting an example of rational and inspired leadership. He was a terror to his students, displeased with their efforts, and possessed of a hair-trigger temper that threw him, as Kilbourn later recalled, into a kind of "divine frenzy."

I was exposed to one of his more extreme forms of tyranny in math class. "Newman!" he shouted, adding the names of five other boys. We were called to the blackboard and ordered to write trig-onometry formulae with our right hands, while simultaneously wiping them off with a chalk brush in our left. We eyed each other balefully and gave it our best effort. Oddly enough, he found no complaint and sent us back to our desks. The next six were called to the blackboard. "This time," he said, "do it faster." This was repeated, with each wave of students going through this exercise at an ever more rapid pace, until it turned into madness. Boys were jotting down formulae at a maniacal speed while brushing wildly at the board. As the game became more intense, Butch became more displeased, eventually turning his back to the blackboard.

"I can tell by the ticking of your chalk, boy, whether you've got it right," he told one exasperated student as he threw him out of class. That boy was lucky. McKenzie treated the other stragglers to a taste of his whip, which he kept soaking in alcohol behind his principal's desk. You knew this would be no ordinary caning, but a violation of the Geneva Convention.

MY GOOD FRIEND Doug Fisher's father arranged a summer job for me in one of Val D'Or, Quebec's working gold mines. Strong for my age, I worked three summers at Bevcourt Gold Mines, owned by the Jowsey family, who had brought several mineral properties into production. Bevcourt was a discovery shaft, which meant that we were paid double wages in lieu of safety rules, a welcome trade-off for a kid helping to earn his tuition. I financed the balance of my UCC bills in eight weeks, working from 7:00 a.m. to 6:00 p.m., six days a week. It was a tough gig. The first year, as joe-boy, I cleaned debris, prepared excavations, drove the company truck into town for mail and dynamite, and wooed my first serious girlfriend, the mining engineer's lively daughter, Diane Lloyd. She was an eye-opener for me, beautiful yet unpretentious, natural and caring. We only kissed, but it was a merry awakening.

The last two summers I was moved underground as an assistant mucker, the lowest job in the mine. This involved removing the rock dislodged by the dynamite planted in drill holes by the previous shift. The ore, sometimes containing unexploded powder, had to be loaded on steel trolley cars. These often derailed, which required jimmying them back into position with steel bars. It was hot, difficult, wet, and dangerous work, for which I was paid the princely sum of $5.60 per eight-hour shift, from which $1.50 was deducted for company meals, leaving me with a net gain of $4.10 a day. Many of the veteran miners suffered from silicosis of the lungs. That deadly illness and poor ventilation meant a brief life span. I can still hear them coughing themselves to sleep at night in our rundown bunkhouse on nearby Lake Wyeth, which boasted neither electricity nor running water.

To the brawny Ukrainian and Swedish miners, a private school kid from Toronto who had never worked before might as well have been from outer space. But once they realized I could take a joke and was willing to pull my share of the loads, they were kind and protective of me. We might have had a boss above ground, but once inside the shaft we were all equal, in the sense that we had to look after one another's safety.

Working in the mine, I learned that every sound has its meaning. A silent shaft is dangerous. A healthy mine breathes, murmurs, creaks, and shifts. Ranked among my most wondrous memories is coming up to the surface at the end of a night shift at 3:00 a.m., swallowing that first gulp of fresh air and glimpsing the polar moon. Ranked among the most terrifying is my memory of the August afternoon when I emerged from the shaft to find the surrounding clearing filled with animals: the sure sign of an approaching forest fire. Even before smoke obliterated the horizon, and before the food began to taste smoky, the animals simply appeared, no longer afraid of man. Somebody said that the telephones had gone dead; the fire must have burned a pole somewhere along the line. By instinct all of us headed straight for the dynamite shack to bury the explosives. The fire was closing in, as the distant crackling became more audible and trees could be heard falling. Still the animals poured into the clearing. Their hides scorched, they joined a tightening circle. The bears were the last to panic, while the deer stood paralyzed with fear. I found it strange that, having been felled by generations of hunters, the forest creatures sought security in human presence.

Two bushwhackers, their rogue tree-cutting operation halted by the flames, suddenly appeared out of the forest. They advised us to abandon the mine, inviting us to follow them to a river, ten miles to the north. Nobody moved. I asked one of my fellow muckers why we didn't hide in the mine.

"No, boy." He shook his head. "That's sure death. The fire sucks the oxygen right out of the shaft. You'd suffocate." A Department of Lands and Forests plane circled the mine and dropped water pumps. They were left where they fell. There was no water for them to pump. Night and day become indistinguishable as the smoke hid the sun. Only rain could douse this fire. Eventually, and just in time, it did.

The daily grind of performing tough physical labour in a hazardous setting, where others depended on me and I on them, taught me more about real life than Upper Canada College ever could. After that summer job, for the first time, I saw the college for what it was and became determined to live by more liberating standards. The North was a part of the country I had never imagined, a land without horizons, limits, or the petty concerns of city life. It was while working in the mine shaft that I first learned to differentiate between real life and its hoity-toity imitations. The miners, who had nothing to give except their muscle, were not only decent and unpretentious but, being mostly immigrants themselves, recognized me as a fellow bohunk – one lucky enough to be getting an education. Their attitude was far more generous than that of the college boys, who personified WASP self-complacency, rooted in their excessive sense of ancestry, parochialism, and inflated egos.

UPPER CANADA COLLEGE imprisoned its students and teachers alike in a tidy, taut world that had little connection to the sloppy liberating realities of life on the outside. Because its impact was felt in the formative, early years, the values instilled by the college tended to be overpowering. Attending UCC was life's high point for many of the unindicted co-conspirators who shared my floor at Seaton's. What I thought of as a luxurious gulag was, to many of them, the emotional zenith of their lives. Intense friendships were cemented, and individual pinnacles were reached on UCC's playing fields. No influence was more cohesive, no bonds more lasting than those made at the college, because that was where a lifetime of behaviour patterns were set. Youthful impressions, absorbed through willing pores, determined future priorities, presumptions, and prejudices.

Looking back on the college's environment, I realize that what it instilled, in those of us willing to absorb the message, was less an education than a way of life. Common patterns of forbearance and indulgence, shared attitudes and manners, idioms of speech and even measured limb movements were passed from one generation of students to the next. In the process they developed what I can only describe as a mid-Atlantic accent, one that tended to lift vowels and slur final consonants. The end result was the dilution of Canadian English with a mild Oxbridge accent, like the tang of an expensive perfume.

That's what education at UCC was all about. Most of its students led protected lives; to them, sugar rationing was the ultimate war atrocity. They were devoted to perfecting the subtleties of common purpose that identified members of the Canadian Establishment to one another, learning the elusive signals that bespoke shared experiences and common values. Try as I might, I could never master any of these signs and signals, which was the real reason I felt so much an outsider. It wasn't my (vanishing) accent, my religion, my inability to play any sport more demanding than tiddlywinks, my big nose, or my foreignness that made me feel so out of place. Even in my dazed psychological state, I recognized that I simply wasn't one of them, that I would always be set apart from these people. How could I identify with those musty portraits of ancestors that lined the halls of their grandfathers' studies at the Rosedale or Westmount mansions where they spent their boyhoods? How could I ever hope to reproduce those languid summers at Auntie's gabled cottage near Murray Bay or St. Andrews-by-the-Sea? How would I know anything about the way roses bloomed at the country places on lakes St. Joseph or Memphrémagog, especially during the season of Deirdre's coming-out party? Hell, I was spending my summers shovelling muck into steel trolleys a thousand feet underground, chaperoned by Mike, the big Bohunk from nowhere, who had saved my arm from being crushed. And I was ecstatic to be there.

A giant step removed from its British equivalents (which one critic described as producing a race of languid duchesses and intrepid deer stalkers), Upper Canada College attempted to propagate the notion that social privilege existed on this side of the Atlantic, and that rebellion against it, however fleeting the temptation, was ultimately self-defeating. It was an imported creed, but the strictness with which it was applied was very real. The college's dominant philosophy was reflected in the famed dictum of Eton College headmaster Michael McCrum: "I am prepared to give the boys more liberties, provided they do not take them."

ALTHOUGH I AM AVERSE TO all sports, I actually became the member of a junior soccer team in 1947, because participation in some form of sport was compulsory. For reasons too vague to recall, I was moved up as a spare on the intercollegiate team, which must have been a powerhouse without me, as we won one game 19–0. Luckily, I was never called on to play.

Because bottoms do eventually get worn out and caning ceases to be a deterrent, if it ever was, an essential disciplinary element at UCC was the cadet battalion. The compulsory weekly drills, persnickety annual inspections, and formal Battalion Balls were integral elements of the curriculum.[4] For once, I took advantage of the college's offering, thanks to the clock tower.

At the time, the clock tower was the students' preferred bolt-hole. Teachers seldom ventured to its upper reaches, because there were no elevators, and nothing much was supposed to be happening up there. This meant freedom. One of the uppermost cubby-holes was home to the College Radio Club, where interested hobbyists built crystal sets for about fifteen dollars each, which picked up scratchy signals that could be listened to over earphones. This intrigued me. I joined, and in my second year was voted in as the club's president – my first and only elected office. I quickly discovered that the smoke in my club didn't all come from soldering irons. The club's popularity was based less on the desire of electronic geniuses to invent new ways of capturing the airwaves than on the needs of guys who recognized it as a good place to smoke,

---

[4] It was a source of endless pride that for two days in 1866 the UCC boys' battalion happened to be the only military force left to defend Toronto against the Fenian raids from south of the border, and thus became the sole Canadian cadet corps to earn battle colours, although they didn't actually see action.

which was taboo throughout the school. My presidential mandate, as the dumb immigrant boy who didn't know any better, was to let them do it, which I did.

Next door to the Radio Club in the tower was a room where drummers from the battalion practised their noisy art. I realized what brought this band of brothers together was not the love of music but rather their hatred of marching aimlessly around a playing field lugging heavy Ross .303 rifles, originally designed for the Boer War. It was much more fun to play an instrument, especially the drums, which after my brief Sea Cadet experience, I thought would be easy to master. That turned out not to be true, and the competition was fierce, but eventually I was promoted to sergeant and lead drummer, which meant that the whole damn battalion marched to the step I played solo on my snare.[5] Our specialties included "The Thunderer" and "The Old Oaken Bucket."

The highlight of my time at UCC was leading the battalion through the annual inspection review. Resplendent in our red sashes, with our brass buttons gleaming, our puttees neatly wrapped, and our boots brought to a hot-spoon shine, the battalion cut an impressive figure as we began the precision drill in front of an admiring crowd of parents and official military visitors. For the first several minutes, I tapped out the routine four-four measure on my snare, but then some kind of Kenton-inspired imp took over my sticks. I played a jazz paradiddle that put a little extra zip in the cadets' step. I followed with some rim shots and shuffles and, sure enough, the parade responded with a soft-shoe boogie. For several bars, I jazzed things up, infuriating the band major, who glared daggers at me. But I had put some life into the troops, who knew I was disobeying orders – and getting away with it.

That was a rare bit of fun. The worst part of life at UCC was the isolation, especially on weekends. As boarders, we were allowed

---

[5] I occasionally accompanied Michael Snow, the jazz pianist, artist, and filmmaker, then a UCC student. He later joined Ken Dean's Hot Seven, which played a piece called "Blues in the Clock Tower."

out only on Saturday afternoons, which those of us who were, or appeared to be, of legal age spent at the Casino, a sleazy downtown burlesque theatre, gaping at nearly naked women. On Sunday mornings, we had to attend service at Christ Church Anglican church in Deer Park. Apart from that, the only escape was when we were granted a couple of long weekends for home visits each term. Unable to afford the fare home, I mostly stayed alone in the college dormitory. Of course I was lonely, but I also became self-reliant. I wrote letters to my parents, disguising my solitude as a time to study and get ahead, which I rarely did. (My grades were totally unremarkable, but I made sure that I passed each of my four years. It was the only way out of there.)

It was an absurd, eunuch's existence. I had no chance to learn how to approach women at a time in life when I should have been learning to deal with them as friends and companions. Instead, they became unattainable, mysterious, and untouchable creatures. I could not imagine that they experienced desires not so different from my own.[6]

When teachers mentioned the opposite sex, which was as seldom as possible, they referred to them, with an unkindly grimace, as "*girrrrrrrls,*" pronouncing the word as if it were Gaelic for "mortification of the flesh." In sharp contrast, our mantra as teenagers went something like, "If you don't think about sex every five minutes, your mind is wandering." The "nice girls" took piano lessons, dressed in pleated skirts, and wore training bras under their starched blouses. They were not the ones who populated our erotic fantasies. It was difficult to recall the sensual essence of women when our only contact was with the college matrons. But my, were we uninformed. We thought "oral sex" meant talking a good game.

The only time I recall sex being mentioned was when our housemaster, Jimmy Biggar, confided in us that "it is a proven fact that all well-educated people are virgins when they get married."

---

[6] Almost alone among Canada's private schools, UCC to this day remains resistant to coeducation. But at least the staff nurse now distributes condoms.

Fool that I was, I believed him. If only he had taken the trouble to explain that sex isn't pre-marital – when you don't intend to marry the lady.

I happened to participate in the last of the college's infamous "pyjama parades," one of the more curious manifestations of our sexual frustrations. The parade was an annual event until it was stopped by the local Forest Hill police. In accordance with tradition one spring night at 3:00 a.m., a pyjama-clad gang of us, led by James Douglas (later a star of the Stratford Festival), sneaked out to nearby Bishop Strachan, our sister school. There, we gathered on the lawn of its residence, shouting inducements. The girls knew we were coming and had rolls of toilet paper ready, which they unrolled and threw at us with appropriate abusive comments. Vulgar yells were exchanged, expressing more frustration than anger. Other than that, nothing much happened – except that the police carted Douglas and a few fellow conspirators away and kept them overnight. Thankfully, there were too many of us to spank.

THROUGHOUT MY TIME AT UCC I was imbued, to the very marrow of my being, with the notion that duty and responsibility were the highest virtues. Nobody ever mentioned spontaneity and joy. Anyone who has studied Canadian history will quickly recognize in that dour approach the Lowland Scottish catechism that endowed English-speaking Canada with its Presbyterian ethic. The idea that duty and work take precedence over exuberance and creativity, and that one must be close with one's money and emotions – these were the joyless creeds that pervaded Anglo-Canadian life for the first two-thirds of the twentieth century. There was a time when such virtues were honoured (mostly in their breach) by Canada's first robber barons, so it was fitting that they were passed on to their offspring at UCC. Their Establishment fathers might have attended church every Sunday, but their weekday business ethics were closer to that of Caribbean pirates, waving legal briefs heavy in precedent instead of blood-encrusted cutlasses. Since my time at UCC, it has become the most adaptable, not the best connected, who control Canada's economy. But when I attended the college, and for many years afterwards, what mattered most was the latticework of connections formed at the school.

The career path for the sons of the Canadian rich was as plodding and predetermined as the Stations of the Cross. After three or four years at Upper Canada, interspersed with summers at Taylor Statten camps in Muskoka, there came the obligatory jaunt through Europe on a mini grand tour. This usually consisted of a brief look at the Prado in Madrid, a leisurely stroll around Florence, and lightning visits to the discreet bordellos off the Champs Élysées in Paris. After that, it was straight to the trading desk at Wood Gundy, A.E. Ames (the only underwriter on Bay Street with carpeted washrooms), or the family firm. Canada's dominant clans perpetuated themselves through inbreeding and fellowship. At the time, the members of this protected enclave flourished without straining their brains or muscles, except for bouts of bridge at the Toronto Club or doubles at the Lawn and Tennis.[7] While fourth-generation *"girrrrls"* opened antique shops, the boys who had brains became surgeons, while those not so equipped went into brokerages or banks. The success of these inheritors depended on the generation to which they belonged. To the founders of family firms, business was everything; to their children, it was a challenge; to their grandchildren, a property to be sold or pissed away. After that, it became a quarrel.

UCC's well-groomed image as the West Point of the Canadian Establishment has since become strained. In my day I certainly met

---

[7] Patrick Crean, who later became a book publisher, told James FitzGerald, author of *Old Boys: The Powerful Legacy of Upper Canada College*: "The sense of being superior didn't really come from the masters. It was almost like there was a powerful psychic energy field we absorbed every day, walking into the prayer hall. But the overwhelming impression I have is that most UCC guys were either traumatized in varying degrees or became lobotomized servants of the system. Many of them just tunneled their way through life and ceased to think critically of themselves or the world, if they ever did."

a sprinkling of Eatons[8] and the offspring of many of the families I would later write about. In retrospect, it seems obvious that I formed a set of attitudes, not entirely kindly, toward the Canadian elite, later reflected in my studies of the Canadian Establishment. Most of the school's graduates, if they bothered to read my books, undoubtedly considered them a rude intrusion into their collective privacy. While I was at the school, they suspected that I was not one of them; my subsequent books and articles proved it.

But such a simplistic conclusion doesn't ring true. Any lasting influences are subtler to convey. For one thing, I left UCC with only a vague impression of my fellow students. I kept an emotional distance as a kind of defence mechanism and focused on my own thoughts and music. Certainly, I felt the loneliness of an outsider, but I didn't blame the boys for that, and bore them no sense of bitterness. Still, my stay at Upper Canada College served to familiarize me with the Establishment's quirks. For one thing, it made me aware that such a distinct breed existed in what was supposed to be an egalitarian society. My Canadian Establishment books were only groundbreaking in that I was the first journalist to write about the country's elite in any serious context. Probably, I was the most appropriate person to do so, because I could never regard them with the envy or veneration of an uninformed stranger. When interviewing some smug and smarmy corporate bigwig in later years, I would recall that the last time I'd seen him, he had been getting fagged at UCC, cleaning a toilet with a toothbrush, or rubbing his behind from its exposure to I.K. Shearer's rude ministrations. It was hard to work up much awe.

Upper Canada College prepared me for a world that no longer existed, if indeed it ever had. Unlike a surprising number of alumni, who continued to treat their time at the college as the

---

[8] George Galt, the master who tried to teach John Craig Eaton grammar, recalled that the young inheritor couldn't differentiate between *there* and *their*, finally deciding to spell both as *thair*. He later flunked out of Harvard, before helping to run his family business into the ground.

high-water mark of their circumscribed lives, my real life still lay ahead. The days of black-gowned masters with canes in their desks, the rustling of the rhododendrons, the smell of oxblood leather chairs in the common room, the bullying prefects, and that cold glass of morning milk that reeked of saltpetre – such memories awaken little nostalgia in me, and even less affection. I longed to see one senior student brave enough to grow a *Viva Zapata!* moustache, but never did.

I did, however, learn a few useful things. I learned how to speak English with a Canadian accent. I seized on the idea that I could become a naval officer. I learned to play drums and went loco when I first heard the sounds of the Stan Kenton Orchestra. All that and something else. Because the school stretched my potential at an early age, whether it had intended to or not, it pushed me to the invaluable discovery that the harshest limits we have to overcome in life are those that are self-imposed.

Ambivalence is certainly what I feel about my years at Upper Canada College, the highly touted finishing school that damn near finished me. Despite its many good points, it robbed me of my rites of passage. At a time in life when my hormones were raging, my curiosity was unquenchable, and my desire to learn ranged beyond school texts, I was confined to sterile quarters, detained and hobbled in the heart of a great city. When I graduated, I felt as though I were being released from a freak show cast by Federico Fellini.

WASP Like Me

~∰⊘

Toronto in the fifties was a Calvinist Tehran. The mullahs wore
dark suits and belonged to Protestant denominations, making sure
that nobody dared toboggan in High Park on Sundays.

When I graduated from Upper Canada College into the
Toronto of the 1950s, I began the decade as an unemployed twenty-one-year-old virgin; I ended it as a
twice-married father and acclaimed author. Everything that happened in between was driven by that era of exuberance and repres-
sion, freedom and constraint, innocence and guilt.

My family's five-year agricultural commitment was over and
my parents had moved to Toronto, which regarded itself as a colonial bastion of English manners and WASP morality. The year we
arrived, schoolchildren celebrated the end of the war in Europe by
standing at attention, waving miniature Union Jacks, and listening
to a broadcast of King George VI declaring victory. "Canada was
settled by Englishmen who felt they were doing their duty to
England," wrote the essayist Ted Rushton. "Immigrants looking
for personal advantage went to the United States."

By the age of eighteen I had already been a Jew, a Catholic, and
a Holy Roller. So I now decided to become a WASP and join the

majority.[1] It was a wise decision. Nearly all of my successes in the years ahead would take place within WASP institutions: the Royal Canadian Navy, the University of Toronto, the *Financial Post*, *Maclean's*, the Royal Canadian Yacht Club, McClelland & Stewart, the Ottawa Press Gallery, Penguin Books, and my marriages.

Canada was on a roll and I wanted to join the mainstream. Most Canadians truly believed that the second half of the twentieth century would belong to them. The 1958 Royal Commission on Canada's Economic Prospects assured a lucky nation that its standard of living would continue to be the world's highest. For the first time in their muted history, Canadians felt wildly hopeful, convinced that their large and magical land was the new Camelot. Of course, they were still an agrarian, poorly educated lot, which helped to explain their optimism. Fully a quarter of the nation's houses lacked indoor plumbing and half of Canadian adults had not completed ninth grade. Yet the country's future was guaranteed by a national resources boom forecast to last forever, making Canadians the luckiest and (on a per-capita basis) the richest people on earth. The resultant tax revenues guaranteed there would be no problems that governments could not attempt to solve. A universal old-age pension was introduced, replacing the hated means test, a humiliating procedure where recipients had to prove that they were poor and in need. Unemployment Insurance took the fear out of being jobless, while the newly formed Canadian Labour Congress tried to ensure that everyone would be treated fairly at work. The charity wards of hospitals disappeared under a new insurance scheme, the forerunner of Medicare. Disease and poverty, so the promises went, would soon be legislated out of existence.

---

[1] I also toyed with the idea of becoming an agnostic, but they don't have holidays. The term WASP (White Anglo-Saxon Protestant) is used here to mean someone who is part of the long-dominant Anglo majority tradition, regardless of origin or religious belief. There were, of course, sub-species among this group and finer points of prejudice to be learned.

"Miracle" drugs like penicillin and the polio vaccine were made available to all, while the baby bonus was intended to make sure no child need go hungry.

Their material needs satisfied, Canadians began to reach for a culture that would flow from their own, rather than imported, sources. For the first time, they became self-confident enough to appreciate eccentricity. In their most famous cultural oddball, the piano virtuoso Glenn Gould, they gained not only a musical master but a professional character, prone to making such off-the-wall remarks as, "Mozart died too late rather than too early." Gould's status was confirmed during his professional debut in 1957 when George Szell, conductor of the Cleveland Symphony Orchestra, declared: "That nut's a genius!"

At the other extreme of the cultural scale, this was the decade when Canadian television was born. Furniture was rearranged to accommodate the square monstrosity and its rabbit ears, while families moved their meals from dining areas into living rooms. The shift marked, as worried commentators warned us, "the death of conversation." Sports came to the small screen in 1952, when Foster Hewitt broadcast his signature greeting, "Hello, Canada!" and ushered in a half-century of play-by-plays, while Maple Leafs owner Conn Smythe had set the tone of the game long before by saying of the team's opponents: "You can't beat them on the ice if you can't beat them in the alley."

Mostly, Canadians watched and memorized the punchlines of hit shows from the United States like *I Love Lucy* ("Lucy, you got a lot 'splaining to do!"), *Burns & Allen* (Gracie: "They laughed at Joan of Arc, but she went right ahead and built it."), *The Aldrich Family* ("Coming, Mother!"), and *Dragnet* ("Just the facts, ma'am"). Canada began to be absorbed by American pop culture as never before and couldn't get enough of it. It was not immediately apparent to me how much television had opened the floodgates to a cultural conquest that I would spend much of my adult life trying to resist. As Tom Wolfe would observe decades later, the introduction of television had the effect of moving the U.S. border two hundred miles north. Elvis Presley's 1957 Canadian tour, boosted by his TV appearances, served as the psychological dividing line between the staid, post-war forties and the psychedelic sixties. Between those two convulsive periods, the fifties was an interlude of prosperity, naïveté, and smugness. The perfect time for a young journalist to hone his craft.

Canadian cities began to stab towers into the sky; urban sprawl cascaded over natural boundaries to smother orchards and farm-lands. "Green" was still a colour, not a way of life, much less a political party. In their working and personal lives, most Canadians preferred security and conformity over individualism or self-expression, though a few nonconformists opted for personal liberty, joining the beat generation of Jack Kerouac, the American vaga-bond whose *On The Road* dropped like a bomb in 1957 into the buttoned-down minds of the picture-perfect suburbs. I was no suburban vagabond and, despite my love of jazz, neither was I a beatnik. I did not fancy Zen Buddhism, and when a young woman pressed a copy of Allen Ginsberg's *Howl* on me in 1956 it left me cold. Sandals and beads were for French film stars showing off their boobs at Cannes, but not for me. As soon as I could afford it and was out looking for a job, I dressed in the white-collar livery of WASPdom: grey-flannel suit with narrow lapels and cuffed trousers, white shirt with button-down collar and neutral necktie secured with a Windsor knot, black Oxfords with parallel laces and a mirror shine. If you were not in the trades, anything other than a dark suit was cause enough for committal to an asylum. The degree of con-formity is hard to imagine. The streets of downtown Toronto resembled a convention of the Men in Black.

Life in the Canada of the fifties had its dark, repressed side, but it was also characterized by a certain kind of Wonderbread depend-ability. The sensibilities forged in that oasis of a decade would influence Canada's evolution for a generation or more, maintaining the nation as a quiet backwater, in contrast to the cultural torrents flowing south of the border. Canadians would have been proud to read U.S. novelist John Updike's take on their country two decades later, after his own had been soiled by race riots and a costly foreign war: "Clean straight streets; cities whose cores are not blighted but innocently bustling. Anglo-Saxon faces, British once removed, striding long-legged and un-terrorized out of a dim thin past into a future as likely as any. Empty territories rich in minerals; stately imperial government buildings; parks where one need not fear being mugged." The fifties dream, realized.

TORONTO WAS THEN BICULTURAL: English and Irish, except for the bankers, who were Scottish. Since I couldn't claim squatters' rights in any of these groups, I tacitly understood that I could never grow up to be a firefighter, police officer, or political ward-heeler. Jobs were plentiful, but you rarely qualified for promotion as a francophone, "coloured" (any colour was accepted, to paraphrase Henry Ford, as long as it was white), female, or an immigrant with a detectable accent. Male WASPs reigned supreme, perpetuating their insular, tea-and-crinoline society. I would like to report that I dug in and resisted the WASP dominance and proudly proclaimed my individuality, my ethnic background, and my Semitic roots. But I did not. I tried desperately to act like a WASP, to think like a WASP, to dress like a WASP. If I had thought I could get away with it, I would have worn a kilt.[2]

Despite my burgeoning love of Canada, I never subscribed to the notion that my adopted land was a "benign cultural mosaic" in contrast to America's "harsh melting pot." The nation's ethnic structure had been set in place during the first decade of the twentieth century, as nearly a million Europeans chose the western plains to make their last, best stand. It was the perfect arrangement: Toronto-based WASPs appropriated the proceeds of the resulting booms in food processing, construction, and manufacturing, while

---

[2] My official induction into WASP ranks took place on April 28, 1949 in the County Court, Judicial District of York, when our family name was legally changed from "Neumann" to "Newman."

the homesteaders (mostly no-name "Bohunks") performed the back-breaking labour involved. In return, immigrants were allowed to maintain their way of life, as long as their cultures posed no greater threat to WASP hegemony than folk dancing at Dominion Day ceremonies on Parliament Hill.

My family hoped I would come to my senses and enter a proper bourgeois profession for an enterprising Jewish boy, like running a business, practising law, or flipping real estate. "Real estate" was to my generation what "plastics" represented to Benjamin Braddock, the Dustin Hoffman character in *The Graduate*. Our fathers were continually leaning over to shout: "Land! You're a *schmuck* unless you own land!" The prevailing wisdom was that "they're not making any more of it, you know." I couldn't comprehend why such a vast country should harbour such anxieties about the land running out; besides, I had no head for numbers and lacked the compulsion to be rich. I knew that none of these commercial pursuits would give scope to my emerging creative flair. My parents suffered in silence, accepting my chosen path of becoming, as Malcolm Perry of the Vancouver *Sun* would eventually describe me, "an ink-stained heavy."

Toronto in the fifties was a Calvinist Tehran. The mullahs wore dark suits and belonged to Protestant denominations, making sure that nobody dared toboggan in High Park on Sundays.[3] It is difficult to exaggerate how thoroughly Toronto was a WASP beehive, sometimes known as "Little Belfast." The chief civic event of the year was the Orangemen's Parade on the twelfth of July, held to celebrate the victory of the Protestant king, William III, over the Catholic king, James II, at the 1690 Battle of the Boyne in Ireland. The parade, which at its height stretched for eleven miles and took four hours to pass, included a large body of well-oiled officers of

---

[3] Even this was an improvement over the Toronto of the 1930s, when City Council posted police constables with stopwatches in the wings of the Royal Alexandra Theatre, primed to bring down the curtain if the embrace between stars Lynn Fontanne and Alfred Lunt lasted more than twenty seconds.

Toronto's Finest shouting, "God bless King Billy and St. George!" and "Remember the Boyne!" while being led around the streets by a drunken guy on a white horse. The flutes and drums played "Lilliburlero," otherwise known as "Protestant Boys." There were Union Jacks everywhere, and the white ladies, carefully segregated at the back of the parade, looked splendid in their white dresses, white hats, white gloves, and white shoes. Thus did Culture and History collide in mid-fifties Toronto.

I recall watching one parade go by, ruminating that except for the grey overcoats these people weren't that different from the shock troops who invaded Prague in 1939. Not that they were evil, but like the Nazis they wanted to impose their creed and their ethnic exclusivity on a country that thrived on more diverse streams of thought and behaviour. To a man, the Orange brigade was fiercely anti-Catholic, anti-French, anti-foreign, anti-Jewish, and anti-fun. As such, they were a perfect reflection of the city. When my mother applied for a job at a millinery shop making small Sunday hats for large Protestant ladies, the owner, Rose Broderson, reassured her in a letter that it was "a Gentile estab-lishment." (May Rose rest in peace, still blithely unaware of the Semite agent she allowed into her house of hats.) My mother quit soon afterwards to become a saleslady at Holt Renfrew, another WASP stronghold. There was only one non-British international restaurant in Toronto at the time, a smoke-filled Hungarian joint called Czardas.

Most Jews either passed themselves off as lapsed Unitarians or stayed in the faith, where they were marginalized as members of a mysterious, pushy cult, their dismissal justified by the belief they had "killed Christ." (I always reckoned Italian movie direc-tors were responsible, not to mention Mel Gibson much later.) I chose to opt out of my own ethnic roots. Am I ashamed to admit it? Not at all. My only experience of the richness of my religious and ethnic heritage was the time it had nearly got me killed. Much better and safer to watch the Orangemen's Parade while blending in with my off-the-rack Eaton's suits that camouflaged my "European" looks.

I enjoyed Toronto's Scottish Diaspora most of all. There was something decidedly Judaic about their adaptability, their networking and clan instincts, their sense of loyalty, the determination to maintain their identity, and their dedication to hard work. They shared an almost rabbinical obsession with using pursed lips as instruments of righteousness. The two cultures diverged, though, in their approach to humour and exuberance, qualities that the Scottish catechism eschewed because it maintained that only a fixed dose of piety could be exchanged for a sprinkling of grace. In contrast, every Jew knew that laughter and passion were the only paths to survival.

My favourite illustration of the combination of Scottish spirit and Jewish chutzpah occurred during a Toronto Establishment party I attended at the home of Gordon Gray, then chairman of A.E. LePage. Toronto-Dominion Bank chairman Dick Thomson and his wife Heather showed up in full Scottish regalia, piped in by a 48th Highlander. For some reason the guests started to tease Murray Koffler, a Jewish elder and chairman of Shoppers Drug Mart, sarcastically suggesting that he should attempt a Highland sword dance, which seemed a most unlikely prospect. Koffler appeared highly reluctant, then walked over to Thomson, hesitantly borrowed his dagger and sword, and, accompanied by the piper, faultlessly performed the intricate steps, ending with a slight bow to his startled audience. Later, when I asked Koffler how he knew the steps, he winked and confessed that as a young man he had been a Highlander cadet, but left when he realized promotions were not in his future.

My other favourite WASP was John White (I swear) Hughes Bassett, who in the 1950s dominated Toronto like a mythological Titan, running its hockey team, football team, its most exciting newspaper and most popular television station. He was so compelling because he overcame his natural WASP prejudices and was, for example, an enthusiastic booster of Israeli independence. In recognition of his contributions, the Toronto Jewish community's exclusive Primrose Club, then just as adamantly anti-WASP as the Toronto Club was anti–Semitic, made an exception and invited him to join. When his name went up on the Primrose notice board as a prospective member, Bassett scribbled beside it the anonymous warning: "You know what happens when you let one in!" and laughed uproariously as he watched members read his little message, wisely nodding to themselves as they walked away.

Toronto's WASP hegemony was finally broken in 1983 when two Jews (Sydney Hermant and Eddie Goodman) became the chairmen, successively, of the Royal Ontario Museum, then the city's defining WASP institution. Toronto has since become an ethnically varied community, with so many nationalities on display that the surviving WASPs have been reduced to a visible minority and roast beef has become an ethnic dish.

I enrolled at the University of Toronto and recall my university days dimly as a grey time of apprenticeship, lacking any unifying generational experience. We were the Class of '51, the kids who came along after the war but before the Cultural Revolution. We were the sober, silent, crewcut generation, dragging ourselves through library aisles looking for textbooks. We published few journals, shared few causes, left no marks. We grew up separately, unaware of each other. We received our insights unquestioned from our professors, and regurgitated them at exam time as if by rote. If we thought of Canada at all it was as an accidental backdrop, the butt of self-deprecating jokes.

Like the country, the U of T was on a roll. Its faculty included such giants as communications gurus Marshall McLuhan and Edmund Carpenter, historians Donald Creighton and Harold Innes, political scientist Frank Underhill, and above all, the literary critic, Bible scholar, and William Blake devotee Northrop Frye, who began his lectures with typical humour: "Where Canadians got the monotone honk you're listening to now, I don't know," he would say. "Probably from the Canada goose."[4]

My first year was spent off campus, at a hastily transformed munitions factory in Ajax, twenty-five miles east of the city. The downtown campus was overcrowded with veterans taking advantage of government-subsidized higher education. As a result, 7,300 returning servicemen took their engineering courses in Ajax. I joined them. After my summers working underground, I had decided to become a mining engineer, attending classes on the three thousand acre site of the former munitions factory. We were driven to classes in converted tractor-trailers that we nicknamed "Green Dragons." The advantage of being at Ajax was that there was nothing to do but study; the disadvantage was that female students made up a measly 0.4 per cent of the student body. To fill the gap, busloads of single female Bell Telephone operators were occasionally bused in to spend the evening, but I didn't take advantage of the opportunity to convince one to stay the night. If I couldn't be a WASP, at least I could be a virgin, two states of mind that I equated because I naïvely believed that unmarried sex was not a WASP-sanctioned pastime.

To fill my evenings I became the Ajax correspondent for the *Varsity*, the student newspaper, whose editors referred to the *Globe and Mail* as "Toronto's other morning paper." I passed my first year and returned to the mine for the summer. But a mishap in the pits, when a friend was almost blown to bits by dynamite, persuaded me to opt for a safer career. A vocational guidance counsellor ran a few tests and declared that I was fit for only one occupation. "Become a meteorologist, my boy," he advised. His reasons remain a mystery,

---

[4] Frye was a remarkable teacher who unforgettably explained James Joyce's concept of epiphany. He recalled staying in a motel north of Toronto when he opened the curtains and saw two branches laden with icicles on either side of the window, silhouetted against a field of snow. On one branch sat a bright red cardinal, on the other a blue jay. "If I could have died then, I would have died a happy man," he said.

but my parents believed my head was in the clouds too much already. Instead I enrolled in a general arts course at the downtown campus, where the female students turned out to be just as unavailable to a bashful virgin as they had been out in the sticks.

At my father's urging I decided to take a master's degree in commerce, specializing in economics. A friendly lecturer took me aside after marking my essay a C-minus to console me that it had been well written, if off topic. He said I would never make it in business and suggested I stop wasting my time (and his) on the intricacies of accounting.[5] I was at a loss to know what to do. I spent most of my time reading at the wood-panelled Hart House library, seldom attending lectures but granting myself a self-directed course in North American literature, systematically working my way through the shelves. Reading the masters was the best education I could have received as a writer.

I devoured anything I could get my hands on: the whole canon of Canadian writers as well as a large part of the growing body of American and British authors. At the time, the status of Canadian writers ranked somewhere between taxidermists and rat exterminators. Their works – often concerning the mating habits of beavers, the memoirs of forlorn women braving life on the frontier, or the history of the North-West Mounted Police – were relegated to a section labelled "CANADIANA" at the back of the library, quite a festive word for such a dreary collection. "CANADIANA" was located between other sluggish sections such as "CALLIGRAPHY" and "CANNIBALISM," ensuring that readers seldom ventured into those nether regions. Groping through those dark shelves, I managed to read all of Hugh MacLennan, Donald Creighton, and Bruce Hutchison, even if my sense of national identity was not yet fully developed.

Meanwhile, I also shamelessly consumed American and British writers. In terms of fiction, in those years I was most influenced

[5] Joe Hrabovsky, a recent Hungarian immigrant who had been an accountant in his homeland, wrote my accounting exam while I wrote his essays.

by Ernest Hemingway's *The Old Man and the Sea*, his 1952 portrayal of the fisherman Santiago's great heart and determination.
I was impressed by Hemingway's minimalist prose, but, having
convinced myself that I could never match it, I opted for a more
colourful style of writing. Norman Mailer's 1948 novel *The
Naked and the Dead*, written by a war-seasoned veteran of twenty-
five years of age, triggered my lifelong appreciation of this consummate rogue's evocative talent. I was mightily moved by
African-American author and jazz musician Ralph Ellison's
Invisible Man, his 1952 novel drawn from his experience of race
relations in America, which vaguely echoed my own situation.
Aldous Huxley was another hero to be worshipped. Although
much of his work, such as *Antic Hay* and *Brave New World*, was
actually written in the 1920s and '30s, it gained a fresh audience
in the disaffected 1950s.

It was also in these years that I learned about narrative non-
fiction, the radical idea that a non-fiction book can, and should,
read like a novel. Normal Mailer's Pulitzer Prize—winning account
of the 1967 peace march on Washington, *Armies of the Night*,
remains to me the defining example of personalized "new journalism." Another book that doubtless forged my future interests
was Anthony Sampson's *Anatomy of Britain*, with its perceptive dissection of class and society. "In Britain," he wrote, "the segregated
world of public schools crops up in all kinds of institutions: A
boy can pass from Eton to the Guards to the Middle Temple to
Parliament and still retain the same male world of leather armchairs, teak tables and nicknames. They need never deal closely
with other kinds of people, and some never do." I was hooked. The
novels of the Lebanese-American writer Vance Bourjaily, such as
The End of My Life, *Hound of the Earth*, and *The Violated*, viewed
reality in fresh dimensions, but it was his autobiographical *Confessions of A Spent Youth* that really grabbed me — he caught the
immigrant's experience better than any other writer. Philip Wylie's
essays, such as those published in *Generation of Vipers*, were as
mind-blowing as they were mind-broadening.

I wrote many poems but published only one. In 1949, the literary journal *Acta Victoriana*, whose editorial adviser was Northrop Frye, judged my effort to have "a Blakean sense of revelation, lively diction and adjectival energy." It later won second prize in *The Varsity*'s annual poetry contest – a great encouragement, as it was my first published work.

Other than this fillip, my university stint was a dumb slog, unrelieved by romance, enlightenment, or joy. My grades were unremarkable. I did well in palaeontology and poorly in psychology, suggesting I understood fossils better than people. I only remember two events from all those years. In Europe, Czechoslovakia's occupiers had switched from the Nazis to the Communists, replacing one set of thugs with another. There was a Communist Club at the university, and a group of us began taking out memberships until we had a majority. At the annual general meeting, we put forward two motions: the first, to donate all of the club's funds to the Red Cross; the second, to dissolve the Communist Club. They both passed. It was my first and only hostile takeover. The other memorable event was booking Montreal's Johnny Holmes Orchestra for our graduation dance. It was a swinging success, since his sidemen included a piano virtuoso named Oscar Peterson and the incredible Maynard Ferguson on high trumpet.

I kept busy earning extra money with the naval reserves, an important part of my extracurricular life at university and beyond (which I describe in detail elsewhere). Money was also to be made working night shift at the post office, and a group of us went down to the Union Station main branch to sort letters during the Christmas rush. There were no postal codes then, so we had to memorize thousands of locations. "You and your friends are sorting too damn fast," I was warned by a veteran union postie, who left no doubt that we might get hurt if we didn't slow down. We did, and parted as friends of the permanent crews. The following Christmas, I switched to Eaton's Toytown in the main Queen Street store. I was assistant to the in-house magician, the Mauritian-born illusionist John Giordmaine. He introduced me as "the young conjurer from the land of Frankenstein!" but was very careful to let me demonstrate only the simple, cheap tricks. Weary mothers left their kids to see the show while they continued shopping. After watching me perform some disappearing trick for the tenth time, the children would raise a singsong: "I saw you! I saw you!" This would not be my career.

MY MAIN CONCERN IN THE 1950S was sex, or, to be precise, its absence. I spent most evenings – not to mention mornings, afternoons, and midnights – worrying about girls. The biggest worry being, when would I get one? "Going steady" was the popular craze. This, it seemed to me, was a useless intermediate stage, like purgatory, but it would have been a welcome development if it had helped me get to "first" or "second" base. In those days, getting to "first base" was a kiss; "second base" was a grope; "third base" was oral satisfaction; and a "home run" was intercourse. To hit a home run was usually out of the question before marriage. Couples prized virginity because it was somehow equated with future faithfulness.[6]

This perception was challenged in 1953, when Dr. Alfred Kinsey's report on female sexuality confirmed that fully half of women had experienced pre-marital sex, while a quarter of married women had committed adultery. I had no idea where I could find Dr. Kinsey's women. There were no sexual self-help manuals then, no "adult" magazines in the corner stores. By contrast, frowning pharmacists gave you the third-degree in response to a whispered request for "safes." *Playboy* hit the newsstands in that same year with a nude Marilyn Monroe as its first centrefold, but the magazine didn't become available in Canada until four

---

[6] Tom Wolfe much later described love's radically altered baseball game for singles in the year 2000: "'First base' meant deep kissing . . ." he wrote, "'second base' meant oral sex; third base meant going all the way; and home plate meant learning each other's names. Getting to home plate *was* relatively rare, however."

years later. Its message of urbane sophistication and sexual freedom remained as remote to me as membership in the Toronto Club. "Spanish fly" and "blue movies" existed only in the popular imagination. "Call girls" and lesbians (always described as "man-hating") populated some of the racier dime novels, but the call girls weren't listed in the Yellow Pages. There were strippers, but they didn't get naked – even their nipples were covered by "pasties," and women display more flesh today on any European beach. Gays were afraid to move openly among polite society. "The Pill" was a popular seasickness remedy. Before I was married, stepping out on Saturday nights, I put Brylcreem on my hair and kept a "rubber johnny" in my wallet, just in case. I knew what I was chasing but really didn't know what to do if I caught one.

Courtship consisted mainly of dancing cheek to cheek under an excessive amount of bunting and embracing through multi-layered skirts at park pavilions, or at school gymnasiums and draughty suburban dance halls. It was the height of *savoir faire* to carry a mickey of booze in a brown paper bag in your hip pocket, and *de rigueur* to spike the fruit punch. Girls wore daring summer dresses an inch above the knee and copied the vamp posturing of Hollywood movie stars such as Ava Gardner, Lana Turner, and Rita Hayworth. The more risqué among them attempted to mimic the brooding sexuality of Veronica Lake, of the waist-length tresses.

Unfortunately for me, being a serious-minded reader didn't win you a game of backseat bingo, whereas being brawny and "dreamy" left you "made in the shade." The guys tried to strut like Marlon Brando in *On the Waterfront* or swagger like Gary Cooper in *High Noon*. I attempted both, but only managed a Don Knotts portrayal of Hopalong Cassidy.

For girls, being sexy included adopting a husky voice and chain-smoking like Lauren Bacall in *To Have and Have Not* ("You know how to whistle, don't you, Steve? You just put your lips together and blow"). Sex for most of them consisted of kissing with a little tongue. Few were willing to go any farther, in case they were considered "tramps." I longed to meet one. I did have a few close calls.

I went for private dance lessons to the home of a delicious "older" lady, who wanted to do more than dance, rubbing up against me in a way that didn't feel like the tango. I was too bashful to follow her lead.

While I was working up in the mines, a few of the guys took me to the local whorehouse, but that wasn't the way I wanted to launch my love life. In the fifties, boys sublimated their frustrations with well-fingered "French postcards" imported by older brothers who had visited Paris and smuggled them back, along with banned copies of Henry Miller's *Sexus* and D.H. Lawrence's *Lady Chatterley's Lover*. Not to mention *Tender Was My Flesh*, by Winifred Drake. It was a dry season.

My problem was that I suffered from a Madonna-Whore complex, likely the result of being raised by intimate nannies and a distant mother. I visualized women as either saints deserving their own basilicas or would-be finalists on the Dixie mud-wrestling circuit. I seldom saw them as human beings with the same flaws and desires as my own. I knew nothing about women – their anatomy, their thought processes, how to approach them, or how to woo them into submission.[7] One of my early challenges was to puzzle out exactly what my friend Frank had meant when he'd told me that he'd dumped the latest of his many female conquests because "she had two left tits." That diagnosis haunted me for years. Still does.

As a fledgling WASP, I longed for a freckle-faced blonde and found one in the person of Kathleen Briggs of Burlington. She was the quintessential shiksa, the WASP princess. Her face was half concealed by the Gothic arch of her golden hair, she had dimpled cheeks, was as thin as a hologram, and wore pearls the size of jaw-breakers. What a dream. She even came to one of my Toronto

---

[7] I had heard wild tales about a female "pleasure centre," which, it was rumoured, would render any woman insane with desire – if only it could be found. From what I'd been told, I figured that it was best to go into action with a flashlight, a compass, and a couple of trained Navy SEALs.

parties. We dated just long enough for both of us to realize we were meant for others. During my first year in Toronto I went out with thirty-six girls, all but one a certified WASP. Three dozen at-bats and a strikeout every time.

INTO THIS LONELY VOID walked Patricia Mary McKee of Carrickfergus, County Antrim, Northern Ireland. This was no ersatz colonial WASP but the genuine article, direct from a part of the world where being a White Anglo-Saxon *Protestant*, or an Anglo-Celtic one, was standard issue, and a war cry. The whole deal was a set-up, with its roots in the Old Country. Richard Morawetz, a former Prague industrialist who was the unofficial head of Toronto's Czech community, had known my father in Czechoslovakia. He had fled the country early enough to keep his fortune intact; with it he'd purchased Carhartt Canada, makers of coveralls and welding clothes. He knew that I was a penniless university student with few opportunities to socialize, so he invited me often to parties at his Forest Hill mansion, where I befriended his son, John, whose wife Maureen was Patricia's sister. The Irish colleen's sojourn extended into a long-term stay, as she moved into the home of John and Maureen. With her being a stranger to town and somewhat underfoot, I wasn't surprised to get a call from John at my apartment one evening toward the end of 1949. "Peter? I need a favour. Maureen's sister has been here for weeks and doesn't know anybody. We're having a family party on the weekend and you're invited. You'll be introduced, so chat her up a bit, take her out on the town, try to show her a good time. It'll be no hardship, believe me."

He was right about that. As the cocktail glasses clinked one Saturday night at the Morawetzes, I found myself charmed by this Irish lass and her musical brogue, her elegant Old World manner-isms, and above all, her sweet dimples. The McKee family owned Belfast's largest construction company and she had been well raised, although I later discovered that her father had been an abusive alcoholic who mistreated his family. Perhaps some vestige of this affected Pat's attitude toward men, although I was unaware of it at the time.

In short order, Pat had told me – with a twinkle in her eye – that she did not want to return to Ireland, but wished instead to follow her sister to Canada, permanently. "Oh, but it's not so well for a young woman to be in the world on her own," she added, just in case I was entirely thick.

I felt John's paw on my shoulder as he pulled the two of us together. "But you're not, now, are you, Pat?" he said, with a wink in my direction that would have been obvious to a blind man. "Peter here is just the man to show you around."

We had nothing in common but loneliness, but that and good manners were enough. Pat was a pleasant companion, an undemanding person who laughed at my fumbled attempts at humour and thrilled at every little kindness I showed her. The Morawetzes were delighted at our budding relationship, and it was an added bonus that it seemed to cement ties with a family I respected so highly. We drove around Toronto and I showed her the sights and restaurants as though I owned them all. I had no idea what real love felt like, but what I felt was good enough, and better than feeling lonesome.

I began to date Pat to the exclusion of other women; when my father learned of this, he was highly displeased. "Peťa," he wrote, in the first of many letters I received from him while I was in Halifax on naval manoeuvres one summer. "You are only twenty-one years old and you don't have the means to support a family. You should not be getting so serious so soon. Remember, I was thirty-five when I married your mother. Play the field and enjoy yourself. You have plenty of time to think of marriage." He had me there – I was about as financially solvent as Zambia. But it was not until the two of them met face to face that he revealed his real reasons. "She's not right for you," he said bluntly afterwards. "You have nothing in common. She's a nice girl, and she will make some man a nice wife – but that man is not you. You're too young to know what you want. This is your first girlfriend and you think it's the real thing. It's not, it's puppy love. If you marry her, you will regret it."

He was trying to protect me from myself, but for no other reason than rebellion I decided to prove the old man wrong. How could he know what was best for me? My father's intervention had the opposite of its desired effect, and I began to look at Pat as marriage material. I avoided discussing her with my father but instead chatted about Pat with my mother, who had a soft spot for her from the beginning and would continue to regard her with fondness the rest of her life. "Such a brave girl, to come to Canada like that," she would say. Possibly, she admired Pat for following her heart, whereas my mother had followed her parents' advice. My mother and I conspired against my father's wishes in the pursuit of Pat's hand.

My father died abruptly in August 1950, of a heart attack at the age of sixty-five, while on holiday with my mother in North Conway, New Hampshire. We had grown somewhat closer since our arrival in Canada, a process made easier because I was – except where Pat was concerned – entirely lacking in rebellion. I had tried to please him and draw close to him but had never quite crossed the distance that had separated us in Břeclav. "He was the best of men," I said at his funeral. "He saved our lives, and in the process we got to know one another. It was a privilege to be his son." But that didn't come close to expressing what I felt. He was the sort of man who found it difficult to express any sort of emotion (a trait I inherited), and this separated him not only from me, but also from my mother. After his death, I realized it was wrong to have valued our family life for its benign, unruffled calm. There might not have been anger but neither was there passion. I resolved to live my life differently, to follow my heart and live out my emotions.

My father's unexpected death would have driven me closer to matrimony in any case, but it was followed by another loss for me that guaranteed a trip to the altar. Within weeks, my mother's lover from the 1920s in Vienna, Dr. Hans Brunner, paid a visit. He had become a professor of medicine at the University of Chicago but had never married, as he remained faithful to the memory of my mother. As soon as he heard of my father's death he appeared on her doorstep, offering condolences that soon turned into kisses. He wooed her with walks on Centre Island, which then boasted a hotel and fancy restaurant. My mother was so impractical that when my father died she did not even know how to write a cheque. She was bereft, realized she needed a man to manage things, and doubtless still harboured feelings for Hans. She quickly decided to marry him and move to Newark, New Jersey, where he had a home.

Within the space of six months I had lost both my parents. I had no other family and few close friends. Finding my world suddenly a very empty place, I proposed to Pat on bended knee and she promptly accepted.

My best friend at the time was Norman Bell, a fellow naval reserve officer and later a Harvard sociology professor. When I told him the news of our engagement he insisted we go for a drink.

"To Pat, eh?" he said, lifting his glass.

"Yes, to Pat," I replied, lifting mine.

"So, what's the sex like?"

The question floored me. Pat and I had never had sex. Not with anyone else and not with each other. There was no passion to our union. I thought this was normal for couples. As for our virginity, I felt that saving oneself for the wedding night was what good WASPs did. Norm, who was to be my best man, couldn't believe it.

"Haven't slept with her?" he said, when I explained the situation. "What's the matter, she won't give in?"

I told him that I hadn't really pressed the matter. I had always behaved like a perfect gentleman, I said, not realizing how silly I sounded.

Norm spent some time looking into his glass. "Look, Peter," he said, "I can see buying a horse without riding it. But I can't understand why you would buy a horse you haven't even *tried* to ride."

Soon I was wrapped up, as was everyone, in the wedding preparations and never gave the pending nuptials much serious contemplation. I was getting married, hurrah, hurrah! Three cheers for me! But as we were waiting in the vestibule to walk into the Rosedale United Church for the ceremony in May 1951, Norm took me aside.

"Look at me," he said, gripping my shoulders. "You don't want to do this."

"Yes, I do," I said. "I want to get married."

"No, you don't. You just don't want to be alone, and that's another matter altogether. Now listen. There's a window over there. It's not too high off the ground. Jump. Now! Get the hell out of here. I'll go into the church and make excuses for you. It'll be all right, these things happen. You'll never regret it if you jump, but if you go in there and get hitched, you'll be sorry the rest of your life. Now, go man, go. JUMP!"

"I can't," I said, trying to hide my temptation.

"Why not?"

"Because I'm getting married."

"*Arrggh!*" Norm spun about, pressing his temples with his hands. "Okay. You get married. But you'll be sorry." (Gentle Reader, if the best man at your wedding ever advises you to jump through a window rather than go through with the ceremony, jump.)

For our honeymoon we shuffled off to the romantic hot spot of Buffalo, New York, and checked into the Statler Hotel. Following a wedding feast at Leonardo's spaghetti joint, we returned to our suite for the long-anticipated consummation. Pat disappeared into the bathroom "to make myself comfortable" while I put on my pyjamas and lay on the bed puffing my pipe, trying to look suave and worldly.

When she returned to the bedroom, I gasped: her hair was in a net and there was Noxzema night cream slathered all over her face. Her body was shrouded in some kind of Bedouin tent that wouldn't even bring a blush to the cheeks of a Taliban. She drew the covers over herself and I hovered over the white paste, trying to find a spot to kiss. I had never smelled Noxzema before, but it was a scent I would recall the rest of my life. We somehow managed The Act, after which Pat rolled over and turned off the light.

The morning after, I celebrated our wedding night by sneaking down to the hotel lobby to linger over the Sunday *New York Times*. And nothing in the rest of the honeymoon ever matched the crazed excitement of that first night.

We returned home to settle in a tiny house at Applewood Acres, a Toronto suburb of houses with such numbing, cookie-cutter similarity that if you forgot your house number you needed to call the police for assistance. I soon began the long journey away from myself that was the hallmark of my marriage. I joined the local congregation of the United Church, because Pat was a member, and we attended every Sunday. I never quite figured out what was going on there. I knew what Jews believed, and I knew what Catholics believed, but I never quite figured out which God the compromise Church of Canada represented. After attending a few months of Sundays, I felt that I should open prayer with, "Dear Father, Mother, Son, Spirit, Guiding Light, Holy Essence, Small Voice, Big Guy In The Sky: How *you* doin'?"

Pat soon became pregnant, a condition she would maintain for most of our marriage. But she had difficulties in carrying to term, and suffered stillbirths with three baby boys. I attended three funeral services for the tiny tykes, all by myself, weeping uncontrollably for the sons I never had. Pat was confined for all of her pregnancies after the first one, and the long periods of isolation, along with the sadness of losing our babies, caused her to fall into a protracted unhappiness for which she seemed to regard me as the cause. It was a disappointing time for both of us. I escaped into work; Pat just grieved. I started to feel that I was only valued for my reproductive capacity, which had now been called into question. I was otherwise an alien in her world, her suburb, her church, the confining canvas of her existence. I had got what I wanted, and it wasn't what I wanted. Our marriage shifted from being passionless to being frosty. Disappointed at home, I began to look for satisfaction at the office.

CHAPTER FOUR

MY FLAME OF POWER

*From now on, I would sacrifice almost anything and anyone
to the unquenchable fires raging inside me.*

My father's death and my marriage meant that I had to leave university and work. I had read a manual on job-seeking, which claimed that the best way to impress a potential employer with your sense of purpose was to wear a hat, specifically a fedora. I followed the advice, but at every interview a secretary would take away my coat and hat, which I took as the reason I never got an offer. Finally, I heard that there was a vacancy at the *Financial Post* and wrestled the secretary for my fedora, placing it on the desk squarely in front of Ronald Alexander McEachern, the *Post*'s intimidating editor-in-chief. We talked for a few minutes about my interrupted degree and my European background, until he could stand it no longer.

"What the hell," he demanded, "is that silly hat doing on my desk?" When I explained why I had placed it there, he snorted like a Polish motorcycle. *This could go either way*, I thought to myself. Then he burst out laughing and gave me the job. It paid $186 a month and was the lowest editorial position available. "You can start by summarizing the annual reports of every Canadian company for the brief write-ups we carry in the paper," he said.

"It will teach you exactly who's who and what's what in Canadian business." The job was repetitive and dull, but I did learn the detailed infrastructure of the corporate world. I quickly noticed how the same few names kept turning up under various guises – this was the genesis of my *Canadian Establishment* series.

My mentor and immediate boss was the felicitously named James Joyce, a past president of the Granite Club who later became chairman of the Ontario Development Corporation. He was a bachelor and a strange duck. He seemed to know everything about stocks and bonds, but couldn't operate a typewriter, was blind in one eye, deaf in both ears, and dictated all his stories to a succession of pretty secretaries, who sat next to him or occasionally on his knee. The most talented journalists in the place were Ron Williams, a former air force navigator who became the country's leading labour reporter, and Vic Koby, who could write anything about anybody and make it sing. Chuck Mile was the kindly managing editor who helped us cope with Ron McEachern's temper and quixotic demands. Gordon Smith wrote the editorials and, as he put it, kept himself in great physical shape so he could "outlive McEachern and piss on his grave."[1]

The *Financial Post*, which was then Canada's only reliable business paper, was entirely McEachern's creation. He reigned supreme from 1942 to 1964, a brilliant, grumpy, flamboyant enigma who worked in a darkened office under a single desk lamp, scribbling his commands with an old-fashioned fountain pen in green ink on sheets of yellow paper, ending with a scrawled "R.A.M." He was physically tiny, wore large horn-rimmed glasses, chain-smoked, and, instead of small talk, punctuated his comments with sighs, snorts, sniffs, and grunts. He had earned a doctorate in medieval history, financing his studies by playing the Wurlitzer between

---

[1] At the time, no women were considered suitable to write about business, and when the *Post* broke that barrier by appointing Bea Riddell as a reporter, her byline was B.W. Riddell. When her gender was revealed, a dozen readers cancelled their subscriptions.

movies at Shea's Theatre and the organ at the chapel in Knox College. Weddings were his specialty; his top score was seven ceremonies in one day. He had spent most of 1932 in Germany, learning the language and keeping his Nazi pursuers at bay, once escaping from a Hitler-inspired beer hall riot by jumping through the window of a ladies' washroom. Beginning in journalism as the music critic for the *Toronto Star*, he'd benefited from the civilian manpower shortage of the Second World War and somehow talked himself into the editorship of the *Post*.

McEachern was considered impossible to work for, but he taught me to approach business writing through the character of the people doing the actual trading, acting under enormous pressures, often with qualms, sometime with guts. "We're in show business," he reminded me. "Business news is a basic human interest story. We have to put on a show every week to hold readers and get new ones, to entertain as we inform." He demanded what he called "hard writing," which meant first-hand research. He could be brutal. He sent one piece back to me with the notation, "This isn't the fucking story. This is shit. Dig deeper." And he was right. His instincts were almost infallible. The staff reacted to such tough love with distinctly un-Canadian violence. News editor Cy Bassett once threw a typewriter at his door; Ron Williams chased him around his desk, threatening violence; and insurance editor Don McLean promised to beat him silly in a grudge boxing bout. I just hunkered down and realized I was being paid to attend the best journalism school in the country.

Slowly, with much trial and many errors, I developed the beginnings of a writing style, adopting the literary techniques discovered in the many novels I had read and attempted in the poems I had written while at university. There was nothing startling in any of this, except that I was the first to apply such an approach to Canadian business journalism. McEachern helped broaden my horizons and my use of language. To describe a drive-in movie theatre then showing a Hollywood tearjerker, I wrote: "There wasn't a dry windshield in the place." My series on Canadian private schools began with Mark Twain's memorable quip: "Cauliflower is nothing but cabbage with a private school education." A feature on dance studios led off: "Do you steer your partner around the dance floor like a bicycle?" When I was assigned a story about Texas hair restorers operating out of Montreal, I concluded that "the only thing that stops falling hair is the floor." I tried my little trotters at everything: stories on dog food, motels, mobile homes, and summer camps – none of it great journalism, but much of it fun to read. Mainly I introduced the irreverence to business reporting it so badly needed. McEachern expressed his growing confidence by giving me a front-page column, "The Signs and Portents," and assigning me a tour of Europe. In my spare time, I became Canadian correspondent for several U.S. magazines, including *Trains*, *Vend*, and briefly *Forbes*, to help pay the bills.

I was financially strapped but never asked for a raise, although I learned later that Vic Koby had gone to see McEachern without my knowledge. "This is none of my business, but I think it's yours," he told him. "Newman is dreadfully short of money. He's so depressed, he's going to quit. If there's anything you can do for him, you can save a good man for the paper." McEachern harrumphed a couple of times, and then replied, with more insight than generosity: "It wouldn't matter what I paid Newman. He'd still be depressed." Actually, I was more worried about my faltering marriage than about money, but he did raise my pay a little, and transferred me to the Montreal bureau.

Montreal was still the country's most dynamic city, and St. James Street was the Wall Street of Canada. It was vibrant, romantic, and colourful, open to every indulgence forbidden to Toronto WASPs. The city seemed crammed with elegant women who dined at the Ritz (lunch in the Oak Room, tea in the Palm Court, drinks in the Maritime Bar, dinner at the Oval Room) and projected a sensuality that would have been illegal in Toronto. The city's leading stripper was Lili St. Cyr, who was from Minneapolis and spoke not a word of French (she actually *would* have been illegal in Toronto). Her act at the Gayety climaxed (as did the audience) with her being jilted by an imaginary lover. Standing at an open stage window, she took off her clothes in the hope of bringing him back while threatening to jump. Patrons would yell: "Don't jump, Lili! Don't jump!" which incited her to disrobe even further. You had to be there.

There was an active red-light district on Berger Street, and when the ethics of Anna Beauchamp, the liveliest of its madams, were questioned in court, she shot back: "We always close on Good Fridays!" *City Unique*, William Weintraub's account of these lawless years, tells of enterprising whorehouse operators who had special doors to broom closets equipped with padlocks so that police could report that they had visited the offending premises and padlocked the doors.

It was a time in the province when both Church and State owed their undivided loyalty to Premier Maurice Duplessis, who manipulated the folk memory of the Conquest to maintain himself in undisputed power for most of two decades. His laws severely restricted freedom of the press and gender equality. While husbands could demand a divorce on the grounds of a wife's infidelity, wives could legally leave their husbands only if they "committed adultery with a concubine kept on the family premises." This was unlikely, even for Montreal at its most uninhibited.

Our office at the corner of Peel and St. Catherine streets was at the centre of the action.[2] For the first time, I felt the reality of Canadian history as I met Montrealers whose great-grandfathers had traded beaver pelts, built the railways, dredged the rivers, and exploited Canada's hinterland. In this francophone city, the English-speaking elite remained in charge, living out their careers with a sense of imperviousness that Dickens would have found

---

[2] My *Financial Post* associate, Gordon Minnes, and I tried to find a way of dealing with a small ethical problem. Most Quebec-based companies included a ten- or twenty-dollar bill in their annual reports, presumably to help us feel favourably disposed to their contents. We couldn't return the cash, because nobody admitted to sending it. So we took each other to lunch.

contemporary. Most members of the resident Anglo elite were equal-opportunity bigots, keeping both Jews and French-Canadians out of key corporate directorships, McGill University, the chartered banks (even at the cashier level), the private clubs, and the Montreal Stock Exchange.

I made it my business to confront their most racist characters. Caryl Nicholas Charles Hardinge, the Fourth Viscount Hardinge of Lahore, was close to a living caricature. He belonged to that hard-bitten generation and class of bigots who spoke English to any French person they met, insisting they could be understood if they only spoke *louder*. Neither was Hardinge impressed by Sir Edward Peacock, then one of Canada's legendary merchant bankers. "No good in the stock market game," was his verdict, "too much of a gentleman." Whenever I interviewed the viscount (whose British title dated back to 1846), he had the disconcerting habit of speaking through his lunch, literally spitting out his words. After every encounter over a meal, I had to send my suit to the cleaners. He had come to Canada in 1926 as an aide to Canada's governor general, the Earl of Willingdon, and later became chairman of Greenshields, the Montreal investment dealer. His view of the French-Canadian problem was simplicity itself: "Grossly exaggerated, I think. What?" I filed these and other interviews to the *Post*, but they were seldom published.

By way of contrast, I was also the first Canadian journalist to interview Hal Banks, the combative head of the Seafarers International Union, brought up from the United States to defeat the homegrown but Communist-led Canadian Seamen's Union. He assumed that all he had to do was dictate what he wanted to see published in the paper. Still, it was a scoop, and the article's quotes were used both for and against him when he was tried for beating up a Canadian sea captain in 1964 and deported. "You know what?" he told me as we wrapped up. "If I don't like this story, you might not like your face when my guys are finished with it. Got that?"

I hung out at Louis Melzack's Classic Books, the start of what was to be a great chain, the Orange Julep off Decarie Boulevard, the

Aux Delices Café, and the jazz joints behind the Windsor Hotel, but seldom participated in the wide-open life of the city. I commuted nightly to Dorval, where Pat and I had an apartment and, being a faithful married man, I usually left downtown by 6:00 p.m.

By the end of 1955, there had been a shuffle at head office, and I was transferred back to Toronto as the *Post*'s production editor, which meant that I put out the paper at the printing plant every week and handled most of the feature and news assignments. It was a big jump, but the fun had gone out of it. I had meanwhile been freelancing articles to *Maclean's*, and in 1957 was invited to join the staff as its first business editor. My leave-taking from the *Post* to its sister publication in the Maclean-Hunter empire was memorable. We all had large wastebaskets near our desks that quickly filled up with the day's discarded newspapers. I smoked a pipe, which I would always empty into the receptacle, until one day the whole thing caught fire. It was a Tuesday afternoon, right on deadline, and everyone was too busy to do anything about it. As the flames grew higher, one of the investment editors moved his files so they wouldn't be engulfed and went back to work. Editorial secretary Donna Murray poured what was left in her teacup into the inferno and then phoned building maintenance, who told her they might look into the problem later. The flames were getting so hot that I had to leave my desk and edit copy standing up. Finally, a reporter named Eric Richter grabbed a fire extinguisher and doused the flames. If the incident had been filmed, it would have been a slow-motion study of imbecilic lassitude in the face of obvious danger. When it came time for me to leave a few weeks later, during the presentation ceremony in the newsroom I remarked: "In all honesty, I can say that I'm the only person ever to leave a permanent mark on the *Financial Post*." Then I pointed to the charred spot on the floor, where the wastebasket had been. Ron McEachern laughed harder than anybody.

Maclean's was a leap into a higher dimension. At the time, joining the magazine's staff even at a low rung was considered to be answering Canadian journalism's highest calling. The publication had shaped the country's collective imagination since its first appearance in 1905. It was woven into the dreams and memories of the country, having pulled together a national audience long before TV and network radio. Canadians grew up with it; at a time when the country was a random scattering of isolated communities, *Maclean's* served as a vital, if fragile, platform from which the nation could speak to itself.

This was never truer than during the tenure of Ralph Allen, the magazine's editor when I joined. I worked for him most of a decade. We belonged to different generations, came from different backgrounds, and had different personalities. And although I did not presume to tell him so or to count myself among his friends, I adored the man. I never encountered anyone I could so implicitly trust and unabashedly revere. "He was the fairest-minded man I've ever met," wrote Peter Gzowski, who joined *Maclean's* about the same time as I did. "There was no side to him. Because he was so straight with you he made you straight about yourself." He neither looked nor behaved like the idol we made him out to be. He was, in fact, an ill-tempered, freckled, fat, mouth-breathing redhead, whose idea of hell was a literary cocktail party; to him the personification of evil was any public relations man who wandered onto the editorial floor.

Ralph's special quality could be summed up in the unique confidence he inspired. He had no patience with ideology or cant, and he was a true Canadian in that he made up his beliefs as he went along. But certain of his convictions were not negotiable, chief among them being the integrity of his magazine and his compulsive sense of fair play. When I flew to Washington to interview Jimmy Hoffa, the head of the Teamsters Union then about to launch a membership drive in Canada, I came back with a great shot of him testifying before Robert Kennedy's senate committee, holding his hand over the microphone so that no one could hear what he was whispering to his lawyer. Ralph vetoed my suggestion that we publish the photograph to accompany my profile because it didn't give Hoffa an even break. There was a streak of puritanism in him that detested the tendency among journalists to rob people of their privacy.

It was not that Ralph singled me out for special treatment, but his detailed comments on my writing attempts added up to a graduate course in the art of non-fiction. My completed assignments went up the line, first to articles editor Ian Sclanders, a dour but talented Maritimer; then to managing editor Pierre Berton, whose daily energy output could light a city; and finally, to Ralph. All three scribbled marginal comments on the manuscript I had considered perfect. Their knack was not to prove that they were better writers than me (which they were), but to take the side of the reader and force me to clarify my message. *Who he? Use your brains. Irrelevant. Rework. Awkward. Run it through your typewriter again.* These were typical comments. From those critiques and rewrites (seventeen was the record) emerged my style.

Ralph Allen hailed from Oxbow, deep in the heart of south-eastern Saskatchewan, where his father was the CPR's station master. He became a fabulously original war correspondent and top sports writer, although his best writing went mainly into his own novels, which were autobiographical only in the sense that each had one character vainly standing up for reason in a mad world. He found joy in his books, and after he finished his last one, *Peace River Country*, he phoned me to say that it was "damned good." When a book of mine was published, he sent me a note that I treasured: "Writing a book has always struck me as a very close parallel to going to war – a great place to have been; and a great place to be back from." When he died prematurely from throat cancer in 1966, Christina McCall wrote: "Ralph Allen was a good man. When I met him first I was very young, and I thought there were lots of good men, and that my world would be full of them. But now that I am not so young, I know two things: that there are not many good men and that I am forever lucky and forever different because I knew one." Amen.

During my second year at the magazine, Ralph decided to do something about our impossibly long lead time, which dictated that copy would be published thirteen weeks after it was written. He persuaded the printing plant to complete one form with more recent, late-breaking news that would be printed fast, on yellow paper, and wrapped around the magazine. These "Yellow Pages" would give writers a still-ridiculous, but more benign, lead time of two weeks. I was placed in charge of the project, and it was an exciting development, as it meant I was editing a small magazine within a magazine. It also proved to be exhausting, since in my spare time I was freelancing for a half-dozen American magazines.

The most memorable episode of that assignment was when I almost slept through it. "Peter was put in charge of this last-minute effort which required a great deal of stamina, energy and smarts," Pierre Berton, who was managing editor, later recalled. "He came to me one morning, the day he was supposed to put out the Yellow Pages, and told me: 'Look, Pierre, I took the wrong pill. I don't know if I can stay awake long enough to get the pages out.' He would take two different colours, a blue pill was a booster, the other, yellow one, which he usually took at night, put him to sleep, and he had taken the sleeping pill. I went in to see Ralph Allen and I said, 'Newman took a sleeping pill.' And Allen said, 'I don't care what he's taken, but the son of a bitch better get the Yellow Pages out whether he's asleep or not, or out he goes.'"[3]

At this time I was also offered a plum job with *Time* magazine in New York. After being flown down for several interviews, I was asked to fill the second-highest rung on the Canadian edition.[4] I turned them down. Instead of forgetting about me, *Time* made two other offers. A friend of mine then on their staff told me later that they interpreted my repeated refusals as proof that I was some

[3] At the time most of *Maclean's* editorial staff used to lunch at Old Angelo's, a nearby Italian joint. Occasionally our meals were disrupted by an itinerant painter, who they shooed away. I thought his charcoal drawings were marvellous but didn't have the nerve to buy one. I later found out his name was Fred Varley.

[4] As a test, I wrote the *Time* story on Billy Graham's first Canadian Crusade for Christ, held at Toronto's Exhibition grounds. The number of converts on the

kind of "Lefty." Similar nibbles from *Business Week*, *Forbes*, and the *Wall Street Journal* were also rebuffed, but I did get a lot of junkets to New York that year.

MEETING CHRISTINA MCCALL was the highlight of my early years at *Maclean's*. Despite our growing disenchantment, Pat and I remained married. On the surface, we were doing fine. Pat got a good job at the Toronto General Hospital, where she was making decent pay as an electro-encephalograph operator. On weekends she rode horses, even once participating at Toronto's Royal Agricultural Winter Fair. She was a good cook of traditional Irish dishes and we often had our small circle of friends for dinner; at Christmas we went to the large Morawetz party, where I was welcomed as an in-law; and in the summer months we holidayed for two weeks with my mother and Hans. But outside of those moments, we spent hardly any time at all together. I worked very late, usually until ten o'clock, and to relax when I got home I played my drums, to the accompaniment of Stan Kenton records, until it was time to go to bed and face the Noxzema. On most weekends and many holidays I was out with the navy, in pursuit of a promotion. Pat continued to express her chronic unhappiness, and I could do little but agree with her. We discussed openly the fact that our marriage was not working and began to talk about the possibility of a separation.

Then I met Christina. She was an honours graduate in English literature from the University of Toronto, on the staff of *Maclean's* as an editorial assistant. I was bowled over – long black hair, the eyes of a nightingale, a zaftig figure, and smooth, alabaster skin.

---

first night was unprecedented, but the collection plates came back with nothing but small change. When Billy asked me why, I told him that, even when they are saving their souls, Canadians want to be sure it was tax deductible. The next night he announced that donations were deductible and the money rolled in. On his way backstage, Billy whispered to me: "Bless you, brother . . ."

Even in her twenties, and before she had written her major works, Christina was marked as a special person.

When we met, I had just found a calling (instead of a job), the comfort zone of becoming a writer, and Christina understood that world because she was a part of it, as Pat could never be. She was a natural writer, the way some fortunate singers are blessed with perfect pitch. More than that, like our common mentor Ralph Allen, she lived by a code of ethics as strict as his, and lived and loved *Maclean's* as much as I did. She had first arrived at the magazine in July 1952, at the age of seventeen, having just graduated from high school, and working to earn her university tuition. "What happened to me that morning," she later recalled, "was that I fell in love – with magazines in general and *Maclean's* in particular. With the smell of glue and the sight of page proofs, with the layouts on the art department wall, with the cover paintings hung in offices and the schedule sheets clipped to beaver-boards. But most of all, with the kind of people who were running that magazine, with the ideas they projected and with the *élan* with which they lived. To hell with Tyrone Power and boys in thick shoulder pads and football sweaters. These were Writers, glamorous men of wit and grace that went out and got stories and came in and wrote well, who wore outrageously casual clothes, told outrageously boastful anecdotes and displayed outrageously iconoclastic attitudes towards established values."

She returned to the magazine following graduation and rapidly moved up through fact-checking, research, and writing. When we met, I recognized her charms and talent and also that there was not – and I have a very sensitive nose – the faintest whiff of Noxzema about her. She had attributes that Pat lacked: a lust for life, literature, learning, and an appreciation of Peter C. Newman. Part of what threw us together was the corporate culture. As two of the magazine's rising young stars, it was almost expected that we would either get along famously or feud famously. As it turned out, we were both passionate about great writing and great journalism, hoping to combine the two; we talked endlessly about Ralph Allen and our career aspirations; we read the same books and were both consumed by the prevailing political issue of the day, Canadian nationalism. Working at *Maclean's* was a heady, glamorous experience for us, and I found the electric hours flew by in her presence, unlike the metronome existence of my home life. As I saw more of her, I noticed she dated many handsome men, but seldom more than once. I resolved to extricate myself from my unhappy marriage as decently as possible, confess my growing feelings to Christina, and, if she felt the same way, terminate my future with Pat.

I took the first step, and found to my delight that Christina might reciprocate my feelings when the time was right. Over the next few weeks, I confessed to Pat that I was no longer happy in our marriage (without mentioning Christina, as we had not embarked on any intimacies) and said that we should consider a separation. She seemed to agree, until I arrived home one night to find (to our mutual surprise) that she was pregnant yet again. I felt conflicting emotions – delighted at the prospect of becoming a father but disappointed that the mother wouldn't be Christina. I promised Pat that I would remain in the household until the child either miscarried or was born; after that I could promise nothing.

I was more miserable than ever at home, yet my career was about to take its first stag's leap. I had been turning out a blizzard of articles on Canada's economic boom, the encroachment of American investment, the liberalization of Canada-U.S. trade, the falling value of the Canadian dollar, and, increasingly, profiles of top Canadian businessmen. They turned out to be a mysterious bunch, and it occurred to me that no book had been written about these sub-Arctic moguls since Charles Vining's *BIGWIGS: Canadians Wise and Otherwise*, published in 1935. When I was invited to lunch by R.A. Browne, the Canadian branch head of the British-based publishing firm of Longmans, Green, he proposed that I do exactly that. He offered the princely advance of $500 and I accepted on the spot. Three years later, on my twenty-ninth birthday, I delivered my first book. It was an 80,000-word manuscript consisting of a dozen loosely connected profiles, bound between a portentous epilogue and a pretentious prologue. "Power is for princes," trumpeted the opening sentence of *Flame of Power*. Meanwhile, as the ensuing chapters made painfully clear, the guys I was writing about would have to do.

The fawning prose of the jacket copy (written by me) touted how Peter C. Newman "had always been intrigued with the power wielded by that small golden group whose acquisitive itch has catapulted them beyond the prosaic strivings of ordinary men." That was the beginning of the notion that there existed a power elite in Canada, though I didn't realize that chronicling its anatomy would become my obsession fifteen years later. "Man has always been alive to the itching in his palm," I wrote. "But only a few remarkable Canadians have evolved their acquisitive impulses into economic influence so immense that it grew beyond their control, like a forest fire that feeds on itself." As if this weren't enough, I added: "They stabbed the hump of mine head frames against the brumal blankness of the North and erected the angular silhouettes of factories across the urban twilight." Purple? It was aubergine. *Brumal?* I still don't know what it means. In preparing these memoirs I finally looked it up: it's a synonym for wintry, derived from the Latin "*brevis*," for "short," indicating the shortened days. I probably saw it in a thesaurus and enjoyed its pretension. It never occurred to me as a young writer to use words that people, including me, could understand.

Of the dozen powerful businessmen I featured, two remain fresh in my memory. Sir Herbert Holt had never before been profiled, although he came closer than any tycoon before or since to wielding power on a scale that determined Canada's fiscal direction. During his ascendancy in the first three decades of the twentieth century, he gained control of three hundred companies on four continents, including Holt Renfrew (named after its founding furrier, John H. Holt, who died in 1915). He also controlled shipyards, international utilities, a forest empire that produced 10 per cent of the world's newsprint, hotels, streetcar systems, railways, and, although he seldom saw a movie, he founded the Famous Players theatre chain. He controlled the Royal Bank of Canada, headed what was then the world's largest corporation, Hydro-Electric Securities Ltd., and in 1928, when Canada's total paper currency in circulation was worth $300 million, directed assets worth $3 billion. Earlier in his career, he had been the engineer in charge of punching the original CPR tracks through the Rockies, and later built a railway across the Peruvian Andes, which he first surveyed on muleback. During the First World War, he designed the transportation network that supplied the troops who halted the Kaiser's decisive thrust across France – a feat that earned him his knighthood.

Holt looked to be the personification of capitalism run amok. Three inches over six feet tall, he walked with the heavy gait of a tugboat skipper, flexing his knees to compensate for the roll of an imagined ship. His face resembled a scrubbed Irish potato with pinched, garter-blue eyes. He preferred gloomy suits and starched white shirts with stiff wing collars, encircled by rainy-day neckties that gave him the austere look of a Presbyterian minister conducting a funeral service. He had no intimates and few diversions. At age seventy-six, he had suddenly decided to climb a mountain. His first attempt ended with a fall down a precipice that left him partially paralyzed. Two years later, he joined the Montreal Light Aeroplane Club and learned to fly. He died on September 28, 1941, at the age of eighty-six, from the shock of stepping into an overheated bath. The International League baseball game at Montreal's Delorimier Stadium was interrupted at the bottom of the fifth inning by the scratchy voice of the announcer issuing a news bulletin: "Sir Herbert Holt is dead." The crowd hushed, exchanged whispers, then cheered.

My problems with trying to write about Holt were that he was dead, that there existed no archive of his life, and that even his contemporaries could remember little about him except that he had been a first-class son of a bitch. He aroused such loathing that he was the target of several assassination attempts during his lifetime, and would occasionally walk to his office inside a moving phalanx of four bodyguards with cocked shotguns.

Instead of giving up, I learned my first lesson of authorship: never overlook the obvious. The few yellowed clippings about Sir Herbert in the Montreal *Gazette* library included obscure references to a man called Sévère Godin, who had served as Holt's private secretary for thirty-eight years. I felt like an archaeologist digging at a site without reliable maps. The odds of Godin being traceable – never mind alive, active, and willing to talk to me fifteen years after Holt's death – seemed to be zero. On a hunch, I looked him up in the phone book, a source that most journalists disdain because it is far too obvious to maintain the profession's mystique. There he was, his office listed in one of the chateau-style towers along fabled St. James Street in Montreal's financial district, which once boasted more millionaires per city block than Monaco.

Not wishing to risk the chance that he wouldn't talk to me, I barged in on M. Godin one morning unannounced. To my youthful eyes, he was easily a hundred years old. Scattering excuses (in French) for my abrupt entry, I looked around the gloomy office and its vintage furniture. It appeared to be a stage set for an old-fashioned robber baron's hideaway, including a brass spittoon. There was a scar on the mahogany desk from the attempt by a deranged stockbroker to kill Sir Herbert. The office was as inert as a mausoleum.

Godin said nothing. He sat crouched behind the massive desk, as though he could somehow rid himself of my presence by keeping very, very still. I broke the extended silence by explaining with baroque politeness that I had come to seek his advice on how to approach the daunting task of writing about Sir Herbert Holt. He leaned forward, clasped his hands as if in prayer, and kept staring at me. His mummified face peered at me above his high wing collar, similar to those worn by Sir Herbert. I sensed that he was thinking: *Should I trust this* maudit Anglais, *or should my memories die with me?*

Perhaps it was the three-piece suit I wore that day as part of my fumbling attempt at formality. I felt a mixture of respect for this ghost of another era and fear that he was actually an artifact, part of the fancy woodwork, unable to speak even if he felt so inclined. What probably prompted him to break his vow of silence was the slow realization that in the whole wide world only he and I cared to remember that Sir Herbert Holt had ever existed. Although self-evidently young and inexperienced, I had unwittingly presented Godin with the opportunity, perhaps his last, to validate his life as the great man's spear-carrier. Whatever the reason, he shrugged, muttered a few incantations to the great man's spirit, and nodded his assent. I had my story.

My other memorable encounter was with Lionel Avard Forsyth, the combative head of Nova Scotia's Dominion Steel & Coal Corporation (DOSCO) during the 1950s. His watermelon figure on a five-foot frame was nearly as wide as it was tall. That he spilled over two airline seats did little to detract from his image as a bloated capitalist. But as I peeled back his layers of experience, I discovered that he had worked the decks aboard a square-rigged schooner, played second base on a professional baseball team, surveyed a railway in Cuba, driven a Boston streetcar to put himself through Harvard, and at one point had become a professor of Romance languages. He had also performed the unprecedented legal feat of arguing (and winning) three cases before Britain's Privy Council – a particularly neat trick as he had never attended law school. As well as running Cape Breton's coal mines and steel mills, he was a breeder of prize-winning Jersey cattle and a minor but accomplished poet.

Forsyth's greatest attribute was that he never took himself seriously. He had a delightful habit, when making speeches to snoozing after-dinner business audiences, of shaking them awake by suddenly shouting: "*Who put the Benzedrine in Mrs. Murphy's Ovaltine?*"

No other journalist had examined Forsyth's background, assuming that he was just another dreary, overweight businessman. That was my second important lesson: never assume that business executives are as dull as they appear. They couldn't be.

The characters who populated my book, while rich and powerful, suffered from a common malady best described by the Indian philosopher Rabindranath Tagore: "I thought that my invincible power would hold the world captive, leaving me in a freedom undisturbed. Thus night and day I worked at the chains, with huge fires and cruel hard strokes. When at last the work was done, I found that it held me in its grip."

The most important benefit of my first book was that I discovered the pleasures of writing. After being captive to the limitations of space and time inherent in newspaper and magazine journalism, I had broken free. I had discovered the most precious of indulgences, the opportunity to express my love of language. My critics would later note that I grew to love the language too much (if not too well), becoming a menace with my galloping metaphors and other convoluted manifestations of the written word. But having learned English late in my childhood, I longed to manipulate my newfound skill, to experiment with the sensuality of words, allowing emotionally charged descriptions to flow through my fingers onto the keyboard of my faithful Hermes typewriter.

FLAME OF POWER HIT THE BOOKSTORES in the early autumn of 1959, and nothing happened. Well, almost nothing. One of my profiles was a critical look at Edward Plunkett (E.P.) Taylor, then Canada's symbol of capitalist greed, who was regularly attacked by the political Left as "E(xcess) P(rofits) Taylor, The Mad Miser of Millions." Speeding across the country in his black Packard sedan, equipped with Canada's first mobile office, he acquired thirty breweries that he turned into the world's largest beer monopoly, manufacturing suds worth $1 million a day. In one of my milder sallies, I described him, with a touch of heresy uncommon for the time, as "a genuine robber baron who didn't even pretend to have a conscience."

Asked by a *Toronto Star* reporter for his reaction to my cheeky chapter, Taylor uttered a verdict that caught the ambivalence of everything I've written since. "Well," he harrumphed, "we all know that Newman is a goddamn Communist. But I'm not taking him off my Christmas card list just yet."

My perfect epitaph.

Two weeks after publication, my slim volume went into orbit. The rocket that launched it was a review by William Arthur Deacon, a former Winnipeg lawyer and lapsed Methodist who had been the *Globe and Mail*'s literary editor since 1928. "Fun and surprise, humour and adventure are the qualities that Peter C. Newman has abstracted from the lives of eleven Canadian tycoons to make his book as hilarious as it is informative," he began. Then the review became even more glowing, which modesty (not my strong suit) forbids me to repeat. Another boost arrived with the book's selection (along with Yousuf Karsh's *Portraits of Greatness*) by the Readers Club of Canada and a rave review in *Time* magazine, which concluded that I had done my best to show that millionaires were "mostly men only a mother or wife could really love."

The *Wall Street Journal*, which seldom reviewed books published only in Canada, devoted an editorial page column to *Flame of Power*, claiming that "it transcends current political–economic tempests." *Toronto Telegram* columnist Nancy Phillips best expressed the press consensus. "Frankly," she wrote, "I was disappointed to find he wasn't the insufferable young man I'd expected. He's simply an astute dreamer, that rare combination which seems to antagonize both the practical and impractical members of our society."

The most balanced assessment came years later in a profile of me written by Elspeth Cameron in *Saturday Night* magazine. "Unlike the dull business reporting of the day, his book used all the standard techniques of the he-man adventure story: character (usually heroic, tough and colourful), action (based on struggle and the rise to power), dialogue (extended metaphor and the symbolic use of settings). He turned the humdrum world of buying and selling into the stirring saga of a nation. But Newman foundered badly in his window-dressing introduction and epilogue. Where did Newman stand in relation to the economic issues he raised?" Fair comment. Cameron astutely postulated that the creative drive of capitalist manoeuvring resembled my struggle with English, my "determination to manipulate language into a powerful conveyor of meaning."

By mid November, the book's measly first print run of three thousand copies was sold out. Longmans produced a gift certificate that allowed readers first crack at the next five printings that followed. Nearly fifty thousand copies sold. In the end, E.P. Taylor did have a point – the most thoughtful critique of *Flame of Power* appeared in the March–April 1960 issue of the *Canadian Marxist Review*.

Any writer's first book is the most important because it either whets or dampens his literary appetite. I remember carrying my first copy in my briefcase for weeks, taking frequent peeks at it, in case it had somehow disappeared and the whole thing was a dream. The French dramatist Eugene Ionesco accurately noted that instant success turns a writer into a praise addict: "If nobody talks about me for a couple of months, I have withdrawal symptoms, though I know it is stupid to be hooked on fame." It becomes a drug, terminally unsettling to mental balance, a price I would willingly pay for the rest of my life. Without being aware of the exact moment of transition, I became one of Ionesco's case hisories, held fast in the grip of the psychic chains created by an early success, demanding to be fed. From now on, I would sacrifice almost anything and anyone to the unquenchable fires raging inside me.

SUCCESS IN MY PROFESSIONAL LIFE was accompanied by the final collapse of my marriage. *Maclean's* had been without an Ottawa bureau chief, as Blair Fraser was on a round-the-world assignment; in his place, Ralph decided to send me to cover the capital in 1957. John Diefenbaker was about to come into office, an event that would dominate my life for the next several years. I bought a house on Mountbatten Avenue and settled in, with my drums in the basement. I finally had to confront the fact there was nothing remaining in my marriage. I had committed the classic error described by Stephen Leacock: "Many a man in love with a dimple makes the mistake of marrying the whole girl."

Pat had given birth to a beautiful daughter, Laureen, but we had grown so far apart as a couple that there was no remedy except divorce. I felt I had lived up to my part of the bargain and had seen her through the pregnancy, but could not now contemplate the thought of playing "happy family" when the only emotions between us were regret and recrimination. My life had moved on, I felt, and so had hers. I screwed up my courage and made the call, asking Pat for a legal separation as a prelude to a divorce. I then called Christina. If I were free, I asked her, would she marry me? She answered eagerly in the affirmative.

I was not prepared for the social censure that followed. I never saw the Morawetzes again, and my mother would have fainted if she hadn't been so angry with me. "But to be sixty and to look back on a marriage with Pat – an unexciting, unshared forty years – would for me be more sad than I could bear," I wrote to her. She disagreed and never approved of my decision or forgave me for abandoning my young family. She kept in close touch with Pat and Laureen, while refusing to acknowledge the existence of Christina. I felt such scorn from our circle of friends that I avoided visiting Toronto as much as possible for the next twelve years, and such a poisonous state of affairs brewed up between Pat and me that I missed seeing my daughter grow up, which became a lifetime's gnawing, painful regret.

With poor legal advice and the guilt of my separation hanging heavily over me, I signed a document that bound me to pay Pat half of my salary until either of us died, with built-in cost-of-living increases, the only exception being in the event of her remarriage. Although she was only twenty-eight and a fully qualified medical technician, she quit her job and never worked again. She spent the rest of her life with Hugh Foster, a wealthy Toronto magistrate, but for the obvious reason they never married, and I paid alimony for forty cursing years. I could not decide which I regretted more:

signing such a numbskull divorce settlement or failing to heed my father's advice – or, more likely, both.

Yet one outcome was positive. My alimony agreement might have been financially disastrous, but it gave me more impetus to work than ambition alone could ignite. My career had taken off and I had become what I had so long desired: a published author. I finally felt freed to see what my future would be with Christina, who held out the promise of being my ideal mate. I had paid the price and could now start a life of my choosing. For the first time in many years, when I banged my drums to the rhythmic extravaganzas of Stan Kenton, I played with soul.

CHAPTER FIVE

STORMING OTTAWA'S BARRICADES

~✧~

"Journalists are like Germans," a politician once complained.
"They're either at your feet or at your throat.
At the feet to get information, at the throat when writing it up."
This became my standard operating procedure.

I vividly recall the frigid cabin of the Trans-Canada Airlines Vickers Viscount turboprop as it made its way to a bumpy landing in Ottawa. It was the early winter of 1957, and the pilots who flew for TCA seemed afflicted with some bush pilot mentality that regarded the passenger cabin as a waste of good heat. I was flying in from Toronto, a cock-o'-the-walk reporter on a "luxury" flight charged to my *Maclean's* expense account. We rolled up to the Ottawa airport terminal, little more than a paved runway beside an operations shed with some yellow snowplows parked about. It was a cold, wet day that soon would be turning dark. The air was clouded by a frozen mist, the dreaded "snow fog" of Ottawa winters that pierces straight to the bone. I grabbed my bag from the indecorous heap on the tarmac, pulled my coat more tightly around me, and hailed a Red Line cab to my hotel.

The gloomy arrival suited my mood. My personal life was in tatters. I was still married to Pat, but wanted to wed Christina, and was about to experience a financial debacle as a result of my ruinous divorce agreement. My family and closest friends felt I was, at worst, a villain for leaving my marriage, at best, a careless buffoon. Although Christina had promised her hand in marriage, the obstacles seemed daunting in the extreme. I was isolated and guilt-ridden, anxious about the future and confused about the present. I decided to use this interlude as the perfect time to infiltrate every nook and cranny of Ottawa, to become as determined a reporter as had ever hit this bucolic capital. I was in love, and in lust, with Christina, but respected her wishes not to live together before marriage. The waiting period would seem interminable. While my nights were filled with longing for her company, I devoted my days to carving out a professional niche for myself.

The taxi driver was a political anthropologist: as we drove through Ottawa's forbidding outskirts, he pointed out the various departmental buildings left behind by successive administrations as concrete monuments to, and the only evidence of, their passing. These buildings were relentlessly sombre and repetitive, unrelieved by pleasing adornment or a warming human touch.

I caught my breath as we proceeded slowly through the mist into the city. As we drove along the Rideau Canal, I imagined myself a player in Ingmar Bergman's film *The Seventh Seal.* "I want knowledge!" one of the doomed characters moans, "Not faith, but knowledge! I want God to stretch His hand toward me, to speak to me . . ." I felt sorely in need of direction and comforted myself with another line remembered from the film: "We are ruled by Fate, which has no answers, only appointments."

The taxi pulled up at the Bytown Inn, a modest bed-and-breakfast that masqueraded as a grander hotel, much like a retired gentlewoman living slightly beyond her means. It kept the British custom of running a rooming house for the convenience of its owners, not the guests. The bed linens were embroidered, but the mattress had long ago fallen into a permanent slump. One bedroom wall was decorated with amateur paintings of the Gatineau Hills in autumn. I unpacked my suitcase and set off to explore my new environs.

I boarded one of the rickety streetcars that ran along tracks sunk into the middle of Ottawa's major avenues. It was the evening rush hour and I got my first good look at my new neighbours. At least, I tried to get a good look – Ottawa folks spend six months of the year buried under a towering pile of parkas, galoshes, mukluks, fur-lined gauntlets, toques, fur hats, and cashmere scarves. They were so bundled against the weather it was difficult to tell the men from the women. Ottawa is the second-coldest national capital on earth, exceeded as a harsh-weather posting in the diplomatic world only by Ulaanbaatar in Mongolia. From the streetcar window it was not hard to find the Parliament Buildings, since municipal restrictions kept downtown buildings below 132 feet, the height of the Peace Tower. I stepped down from the tram and got my first taste of the merciless "Wellington Wind."

I often wondered in later years how much that wind and Canada's political culture were linked. In a peculiar twist of Canadian political geography, the wind is at its worst, its most bitter, biting, and bone-chilling dastardliness, as it reaches Parliament Hill at the top of Wellington Street. The winter winds come rushing down across the frigid rocks of the Canadian Shield and in from the heaving North Atlantic. They are super-chilled as they race down the icy Gatineau and Ottawa rivers and the Rideau Canal. As a finishing touch, they are whipped into gale-force fury by the vortex tunnel of Wellington Street. By the time the Wellington Wind reaches the House of Commons, the Senate, the Prime Minister's Office, and the Parliamentary Press Gallery – in short, the nerve centres of Canada – it is an evil, malicious force that sucks air out of lungs and brings conversation to a numbing halt.

I fixed my eyes on the main doors under the Peace Tower and sprinted for cover. Inside, I found myself in the hall of honour, where, conscious of the solemnity of the occasion, I told a commissionaire that I needed accreditation to the Press Gallery. He was sitting on one of those old wooden swivel chairs once used by railway telegraphers, and I noticed beside him a brass spittoon.

After considering the situation, he leaned forward and picked up the heavy black handset of the old-fashioned telephone and spoke with the Commons operator.

"Put me through to the Press Gallery."

He gave me a long once-over as he waited for the connection.

"Bob? Commissionaire, Peace Tower. The new *Maclean's* guy just showed up. Yeah, Blair told me. What's that? Okay." He put down the receiver. "Go on up," he said, jerking his thumb in the direction of elevators. "Third floor at the back."

Such was the accreditation process.

As I was later to learn, the studied informality of Parliament's workings was the result of an intricate system of allegiances, favours, and obligations that dominated the lives of non-elected workers on the Hill. All of it was completely off the books, under the watchful eye of the sergeant-at-arms, an official appointed by the government who was in theory responsible for security and the buildings' services but in fact was the *capo* of the Hill. If Yvette in the third-floor cafeteria was having it off with Bruno the messenger, he had better hear about it. If an MP's office needed a new sofa, better see him. There were two ways to get things done on Parliament Hill, the official way and the sergeant-at-arms's way, and his way was better.

I made my way up the carved-brass elevators to the third floor and then to the rear of the building along marble-lined corridors. And there it was – the Parliamentary Press Gallery, the Crown Jewel of Canadian Political Journalism.

My chin dropped. The Crown Jewel of Canadian Political Journalism was a dump – a slovenly combination of fire trap, speakeasy, and rumour mill, with all the charm of a derelict attic complete with an odd pair of galoshes and abandoned straw hats. Desks and piles of papers had spilled out to choke the surrounding public corridors. Inside was a maze of cubicles, a complex warren built out of surplus furniture and piles of old newspapers. Teletype machines jammed the passageways and the few open spaces were cluttered with filing cabinets and empty beer cartons stuffed with old *Hansard*s. Only the upright Remington typewriters looked as though they got any use.

This was home base to the five dozen journalists who covered the nation's business, although the number to be reckoned with was much smaller and included Norman DePoe, Marjorie Nichols, Charlie Lynch, Arthur Blakely, George Bain, Michael Barkway, Grant Dexter, Hy Solomon, and *Ottawa Journal* publisher Grattan O'Leary, who made the rest of us seem witless. The others too often strayed to the illegal bar and gambling lounge that was the gallery's saving grace.

For such a high-density zone, the gallery was oddly quiet. There was a slow-motion quality to the place. It had a whorehouse rhythm of much preening and chatter interspersed with brief periods of furious activity. When I arrived no news was breaking, so the clerks were tidying up, popping news releases into wooden pigeonholes, while scribes in various states of grooming decay hunched in their swivel chairs, here and there, reading carbons of each other's news stories. The clerks in charge were Bob Carisse and Georges Gagné, who helpfully pointed out the *Maclean's* cubicle and explained the basic layout. They showed me a small storage room near the clerks' desk where I became acquainted with the "blind pig" or illicit bar. Put thirty-five cents in the Coke machine, and out would pop a pint of Molson's finest: slip fifty cents to the clerks and they would pour a mixed drink; for three dollars, a bottle of rye, rum, or gin could be made to appear. My conducted tour ended at the gallery's far end, which some long-forgotten innocent had filled with reference books and comfortable leather chairs, so that members could peruse previous parliamentary debates at leisure. This was known as the "Reading Room," and the sentiments behind it were truly grand. Over a fireplace at the back a rhyming couplet had been inscribed in the oak transom:

For words, like falling drops of ink,
Can make hundreds, perhaps thousands, think.

It always struck me as questionable poetry, and worse circulation, but the intention was noble.

The afternoon gin rummy games were harmless affairs, with stakes limited to a penny a point. "When the *Ottawa Citizen*'s Norman Campbell is on a roll you'll hear him bellowing 'jiggy jig, jiggy jig,'" someone told me. "But be careful, he's a sullen loser." According to legend, one young ministerial aide, when dealt a perfect hand, was afraid to lay it down, intimidated by Campbell's wild temper. The evening sessions of high-stakes "stuke" (a western form of blackjack) were more serious. They continued long into the night, with "chits" (IOUs) recognized as legal tender. Mike Starr, the Oshawa MP who later became Labour minister in the Diefenbaker government, was a particularly wild, undisciplined gambler. He'd roar "*Pour banquo!*" and bet against the pot with nothing much in his hand, often losing an entire week's pay on the turn of a card. When he became a regular after the 1958 election, Tory backbencher Jack Horner claimed a corner seat, where he would peek at his down card, squint at the pot of several hundred dollars, and then bet a quarter. This would drive Starr ballistic. "Jesus, Horner!" he would scream. "You've got fifteen thousand head of fucking cattle filling their fucking bellies on as many fucking acres, and all you can bet is one fucking quarter?"

This was my cultural indoctrination to the Valhalla of Canadian political journalism. As I got to know them better, I realized that most of the gallery members were failed romantics who were spending the wrong years in the faith. They had become stenographers instead of investigators, agreeing on the story "line," operating as a captive Rat Pack. Their idea of journalistic fairness was to remain scrupulously passive, reporting most stories not as they happened but as they were presented. Prisoners of their slovenly habits, they felt invulnerable and unconcerned about the accelerating seismic changes in the country. With some notable exceptions, they considered themselves a league of gentlemen. They were dedicated mainly to not being struck off the guest lists for the prime ministers' annual garden parties and to staying on the "A" roster of invitations for diplomatic parties.

The best advice I ever heard about Ottawa came from the unidentified veteran who briefed Roy MacGregor, its best young journalist, when he arrived in the summer of 1978: "The only way to work Ottawa is to approach each story as if you've just arrived in town that morning, and write each story as if you're leaving town that night."

I WAS TWENTY-EIGHT YEARS OLD and had arrived in Ottawa just before John Diefenbaker, the Prairie populist, came to power. I left eleven years later at thirty-nine, just after Pierre Trudeau, the Philosopher King, began to disillusion his disciples. Between those two waypoints, I became a political junkie, one of those deluded characters consumed entirely by life within earshot of the Peace Tower's bells. I came to believe the entire nation hung on every word that emerged from the capital. The lure of politics is how it makes itself seem so important and everything else unimportant. It is a mental disorder common to ruling orders that become too far removed from their subjects – just as in the Vatican, say, where prelates believe the entire Catholic world follows their every intrigue. I came to see the Hill as a cloistered monastery. Very little of what occurred beyond its precincts was of interest to anyone behind its walls; its residents spent enormous amounts of time arguing angels on pinheads. Ours was a closed community, its contacts with the real world almost accidental.

For those of us caught up in it, it was also an exalted existence. Ottawa constantly reminded itself of its importance. Every piece of information came stamped as "Immediate," "Urgent," "Confidential," or "Secret." An army of functionaries served every need. At the snap of a finger, you could get the printers to work up a stack of crisply printed letterheads. You could ask librarians to pore over ancient records to determine the number of Orders-in-Council issued in 1907, or send a liveried page into the Commons chamber with an urgent message for an elected member, rushed to its destination in a leather-bound dispatch box. Never mind that the message might be an invitation to a pub crawl in Hull. In Ottawa, it was – and remains – every bit as critical to *look* important as it is to *be* important, because either one will achieve the goal, which is to *feel* important.

Backbenchers from all parties, whether from Esquimault or Antigonish, quickly learned that their positions had about the same heft and glamour as that of the manager of a small real estate branch office. The commute to work could be three thousand miles and still the local MP was held responsible back home for every sparrow that fell from the sky. Every now and then elected members were required to come to the aid of the party with a vote or speech that could as easily have been delivered by a trained seal.

Everything was done to counter this feeling of powerlessness with the perquisites of power. Members were given entry to the Parliamentary Dining Room and its white-linen, white-glove service at soup kitchen prices. They had access to the Parliamentary Library, to ministers of the Crown, to the party leaders; they were awarded free flights, hefty expense accounts, and princely pensions that kicked in after six years of service. The rites and routines of Ottawa conspired to have excessive self-absorption meet inflated self-importance.

Immigrants want nothing more desperately than to ingratiate themselves into the core of their adopted country, having previously been consigned to its fringes. The immigrant's journey is from the periphery to the centre, whether in business, the arts, or politics. I had arrived from Europe less than two decades earlier, speaking not a word of English and knowing not a single Canadian, except for a passing acquaintance with a waiter at the Nova Scotia Hotel in Halifax who promptly forgot my name.

Yet here I was, embarked on an assignment at the very marrow of Canadian politics. If I wanted to walk the corridors of power, I had only to open my office door and stroll down one. It did wonders for my bruised ego and offered emotional escape, if not respite. An Ottawa gig in those days was a guaranteed inflater of status and it brought an instant improvement in the way I viewed my situation. I threw myself into my work and pushed my personal worries out of mind.

Looking back, I can see that, despite my crumbling private life, I had just embarked on the greatest adventure of my professional career. In Ottawa, I took my first steps through the complex maze that led to the nexus of the Canadian power elite. Ottawa is where I consolidated my literary reputation and became known to my peers. It was where I infiltrated the political Establishment and used my insider status to pry open doors to the hushed, elegant reception rooms of the privately rich and powerful.[1]

Ultimately, Ottawa was a place that allowed a Jewish refugee to write biographies of prime ministers, savage in their intent and execution. I was disparaged in return, and yet I got away with it. No wonder I became a Canadian nationalist. It could not have happened anywhere else.

I QUICKLY REALIZED THAT the press gallery and its don't-rock-the-boat approach represented its members' mainstream mentality. There were many worthy journalists who rose above the rest, but the fact remained that this was another place I didn't fit in. I couldn't pretend to be "one of the boys." I had begun to pride myself on being a loner, and this seemed to be a good place to develop that skill and demonstrate the advantage of hunting for news and

---

[1] A useful vehicle for wheel-greasing in Ottawa was the embassy dinner, held at the ambassador's official residence in Rockcliffe according to a simple but unvarying agenda – cocktails, dinner, chat, and everyone out by midnight. As a newcomer, I found that these events placed me in professional hands for an introduction around the essential Ottawa. I quickly learned to rank the embassies: France for the best food; France and Italy for the wine (although the Germans, Japanese, and the Holy See had surprising cellars); and the Irish for rousing talk. The Americans were wary hosts, but knew everything and everyone worth knowing. They thought they ran the country, and they did.

views on my lonesome. "Newman," columnist Douglas Fisher noted in print, "was like a prowling bird dog." The key to success was sweat equity – hard work, tracking down facts (and rumours) diligently so that when I interviewed the Cabinet minister concerned, I knew almost as much about the subject as he did, and could fake the rest.

The original Houses of Parliament at Westminster had the "central lobby" in a corridor alongside the debating chamber, where elected MPs could meet the press and public by invitation. Hence, a "lobby correspondent" was the archaic term for a parliamentary journalist, and hired guns seeking to influence legislation were still known as "lobbyists." In my time, the practice was followed in Ottawa, where ministers briefed journalists in the Commons lobby in a very relaxed setting. As no words were recorded on tape or camera, the "scrum" in those days often meant a small group of reporters sprawled on sofas faithfully taking dictation. I was the first print member of the Gallery to use a tape recorder, a German-made reel-to-reel model; it weighed a ton, but it could pick up a fart from a fly on the Commons ceiling. My colleagues eyed the contraption suspiciously, but it endowed me with advantages. The politicians I interviewed talked to me with confidence because they knew that if my quotes were inaccurate they could demand to hear the tape; at the same time, they couldn't later deny what they had said. The scene changed after 1959, when the first radio reporters were allowed into the gallery and recording became commonplace. Today, all reporters tape the words of politicians, but at the time my innovation was resented. Other reporters felt that tape-recording their words would cause ministers to become more formal and cautious, and I was the recipient of angry glares. When the radio reporters came on the scene, old-style print journalists attempted to sabotage their rivals' recordings with hand-clickers played like castanets, to spoil their broadcasts. Soon after that, television arrived in the imposing presence of the CBC's ace newsman, Norman DePoe.

The National Press Club of Ottawa was then located above Jack Snow Jewellers on Sparks Street, where DePoe's legend loomed as large as it did over the national airwaves. DePoe would rise from an evening's intake of gin and tonic and make an unsteady passage to the street. The CBC maintained a remote studio on the top floor of the Chateau Laurier Hotel, little more than a boomerang's throw away. DePoe would hail a Blue Line cab for the short hop to the hotel and find his way through his booze haze to the elevator. The remote studio had no technician, only a button that was pressed to activate the hookup, and DePoe could manage this no matter what his condition. Then he went live to the nation – always careful to wedge his bum against the corner of a desk to guard against falling over. His commentaries were unfailingly superb.

It took a few years after the arrival of broadcast media for the press corps to perfect the running to ground of MPs as they emerged from the Commons to get a few words on tape or film. At first, these were chaotic jumbles that deserved the epithet "scrum." For sheer sport, nothing could match the unruliness of these early gangbangs, in which I happily participated. They remain a brief but unforgettable part of parliamentary lore, a series of free-for-alls reminiscent of the Pamplona bull runs. Reporters staked out their strategic positions, like prostitutes taking up their favoured doorways. At the sight of prey they would leap forward, causing the politician to make a zigzagging run for it, like a quarterback trying to avoid being sacked. It usually ended in a tangled clump of bodies, cameras, and boom mikes at the base of the stairs; the rule of thumb was that the larger the tangle, the bigger the crisis. Bending over clutches of cobra-shaped microphones that they believed (rightly) were poised to bite them, the besieged politicians had the opportunity to be spontaneous and say something real. They seldom did. Their most dangerous remark was some convoluted version of "No comment," which reminded me of Chancellor Bismarck's classic retort "Never believe anything in politics, until it has been officially denied."

The scrums eventually evolved into more-or-less civilized forums, to avoid the frequent injuries suffered by press and politicians stumbling downstairs or being knocked about by equipment.

In return for being unmolested, politicians agreed to answer a few questions at a microphone set up in the lobby. It is a toss of the coin whether that actually improved the quality or truthfulness of the words being said, but it at least allowed Canadians to see and hear their elected officials in the flesh.

My main advantage was that the Ottawa editor for *Maclean's*, Blair Fraser, had chosen me to be his assistant while he went touring the world. I earned my spurs in political coverage by filling in for him, and was later appointed the magazine's Ottawa-based national editor. The closest Canadian counterpart to Washington's legendary commentator Walter Lippman, Fraser was more Establishment in his manner than in his writing. Unfairly dismissed as a Liberal Party mouthpiece, his most intimate contacts were among Ottawa's public servants, whose policy objectives he shared. He was extraordinarily generous in passing on his knowledge and contacts to me, though we eventually split over our opinions of John Diefenbaker. He recognized him as a political charlatan; I saw him as a folk hero.

Fraser also introduced me into the Rideau Club, the very private men's bastion across Wellington Street, where members enjoyed a Full Monty view of the Parliament Buildings for an annual fee of $150. The club's plush decor was complemented by the hush of privilege and members who moved (and in many cases looked) as if they had been preserved in aspic. At the time, the club treated Jews and women with equal disdain, refusing membership to both. I declared my religion as being a Fraser acolyte, and that did the trick. In 1964, Fraser led a move that saw five prominent Ottawa Jews admitted to the club, including Louis Rasminsky, governor of the Bank of Canada. Women were officially sanctioned in 1979.[2]

---

[2] Seven months later, the club caught fire and burned to the ground. I hate to think how many members connected the two events. The club was reborn in a downtown high-rise, and the fire provided Ottawa press lore with one of its cleverest lines. Sprawled out on the parliamentary lawn and watching the club burn, CTV's Ottawa bureau chief Craig Oliver quipped: "At last – an Ottawa story I can understand!"

The last time I visited the Rideau Club in the late 1990s, the maître d' (instead of the surly superannuated army majors I remembered) was Almaz Belay, a stunning Whitney Houston look-alike from Eritrea, on the Red Sea.

If Toronto had struck me as a city that failed to keep up with the times, Ottawa was a city that didn't care what time it was. On its internal clock, it was still 1867. I was told of the infamy perpetrated by the Public Works Department on the Parliament Hill statue of Queen Victoria, who had chosen Ottawa as Canada's compromise capital. Two male lions crouched at the foot of her throne, cast in all of their bulging masculine splendour. Following a complaint from an outraged female citizen, workmen with acetylene torches removed the objects of outrage. It all confirmed the verdict of the British travel essayist Jan Morris, who summed up Ottawa as existing in "a kind of extraterritorial limbo."

My life in Ottawa gradually improved. The rundown bungalow on Mountbatten Avenue at least had a basement where I could install my drum set, and I promptly began lunching at the Rideau Club with friends and contacts. I soon managed to interview the three men who dominated the nation's capital: Prime Minister Louis St. Laurent, Trade minister C.D. Howe, and mandarin-in-chief Norman Robertson.

At that point, St. Laurent (known as "Uncle Louis" because of his avuncular manner) was seventy-five. He had recently weathered a brutal, overly scheduled tour of India, plus the debilitating Pipeline Debate that had served as the litmus test of the Liberals' inborn arrogance. I had been warned that his mind functioned like a short-wave radio with a weak battery, tuning in and out of his surroundings. Since I wasn't up on the issues of the day, I decided to concentrate on his remarkable biculturalism. A few politicians were bilingual in those days, but hardly anyone was bicultural.[3] A child of Quebec's Eastern Townships, he had a French father and

---

[3] This was long before same-sex marriage legislation, when ambitious politicians realized it also paid to be bisexual.

Irish mother. "I didn't know at first that there were two languages in Canada," he told me. "I just thought there was one way to speak to my father, and another to talk to my mother." I looked at him in disbelief. He was a gaunt gentleman with a pearl stick pin in his funereal neck tie, his face a mask of disengaged wisdom, his eyes reflecting the stunned, glassy stare of an ancient mariner who had seen too many albatrosses. "Don't you see?" he said with a measure of exasperation, not realizing that I admired him just for still breathing. "Even now, I dream in either English or French, depending on the subject. Civil law *en français*, and common law *en anglais*." That resonated with me, because I felt that I became a true Canadian only when I started dreaming in English instead of Czech. Although I was a political neophyte, I realized at the end of our brief chat that there was no way the ghostly St. Laurent could win the impending election. Uncle Louis was a dead man walking.

My attitude when I called on Clarence Decatur Howe, by then near the end of his own remarkable run, was one of mixed curiosity and reverence, as though visiting the Golden Buddha of some remote shrine for the very first time. More than anyone else, he had been responsible for Canada's wartime economic transformation, its post-war recovery, and its modern industrial economy. He was legendary for his "dollar-a-year men," recruited from the top ranks of the private sector and poached from all levels of public service to run the war effort in 1940. Under his watch, Canada had been transformed from a rural colonial backwater into a modern urban economy that ranked as the world's third-largest trading nation. Raised in Boston and a graduate of MIT, Howe was a transplant to Port Arthur, Ontario, where he owned a major engineering firm that built most of the Great Lakes grain elevators. He entered politics in 1935 as an instant Liberal.

I had arranged an interview for no other reason than that I wanted to meet him, but was surprised to find him in an untidy cubicle in one of the temporary buildings left over from the war. This was probably his final press interview. "You have ten minutes," his secretary cautioned me, in a hushed, proprietary whisper. I emerged two hours later. Howe was into his seventieth year and some of the thunder had gone out of him, but he was just as blunt and forceful as I had expected.

I told him a story I had heard from E.P. Taylor about his first day on the job in Ottawa as one of the dollar-a-year men. Taylor walked into the cramped office of Henry Borden, until recently a Toronto lawyer. Borden gestured for Taylor to sit down and continued his conversation with the sales manager, as it turned out, of North American Aviation Inc. in California.

"Yes! Yes!" Borden was shouting into the mouthpiece of the old-fashioned upright telephone. "Yes, we damn well need those trainers. Yes, we have our own air force to train and Britain very nicely sent us theirs. I am offering cash on the barrelhead . . .

"I *am* aware that the Neutrality Act does not allow you to ferry or freight warplanes into an Allied country. We're not asking you to do that. Deliver the planes to North Dakota, right on the boundary line. Taxi 'em right up to the border, yup. Stand back and let our fellows on the Canadian side throw ropes across . . . Yes, *ropes*! Just attach them to the undercarriages and we'll pull them into Canada. Got that?

"Thanks. It's a pleasure doing business with you."

I asked if that was how business got done in wartime Ottawa and Howe nodded in smiling agreement. I wanted to know how he had decided individuals' duties.

"I never assigned duties, only responsibilities," he replied stiffly. But something in my innocence of Ottawa ways must have touched him, because he then outlined in detail how he had pulled together the contingent of volunteers who had mobilized the country's economy. Howe told me in some detail of recruiting the thousand men (and one woman, John Turner's mother, Phyllis, who worked with the Tariff Board). We talked the afternoon away, the lion in winter and the puppy news hound. Right there, in that messy little office, "Howe's Boys," as they were called, had become the founding elite of what I would much later delineate in half a dozen books as the Canadian Establishment.

Near the end of C.D.'s monologue, I committed a major error of tact. "Why did you say, 'What's a million?'" I asked, referring to the minister's nickname.

"Never did, young man," he barked, signalling the end of the interview. "If you're going to be successful around here, check the words you use. Don't ask such a silly question until you look up what I really said. It's right there in *Hansard* for November 19, back in 1945. Good day, Mr. Newman."

Chastened, I returned to the gallery and looked up the *Hansard* of the day in question. Howe had been referring to a debate on the 1945 budget estimates. His exact words were: "I dare say my honourable friend could cut a million dollars from this amount; but a million dollars from the war appropriations bill would not be a very important matter." The bill called for expenditures of $1.36 billion, so he had a point. It was Opposition MP John Diefenbaker who translated the comment into, "We may save a million dollars, but what of that?" And later abbreviated it to "What's a million?", a nickname that had stuck to Howe's shoe for the rest of his life. I had learned two valuable lessons: never to raise insults around sensitive egos unless I was sure the interview was already over; and never to assume anything was true just because everyone believed it.

I later secured an audience with Norman Robertson, the under-secretary of state for External Affairs and overlord of Ottawa's old boys' club. He had dominated his department and the public service for two decades and was said to be the only Canadian negotiator who fully understood the Columbia River Treaty. An imposing presence in his black three-piece suit and the last pair of spats in captivity, Robertson behaved as though he had accidentally found himself dwelling in this sub-Arctic Bloomsbury-on-the-Rideau. His accent was mid-Atlantic (east of the Azores), spiked with the softly arched diction of an Oxford University graduate. You could smell the Carr's Water Biscuits on the man.

This was in the bear pit of the Cold War so I politely requested a *tour d'horizon* (leaning on my early bilingualism) of the situation in Europe. Robertson was as brilliantly evasive as I expected, his

recital peppered with parenthetical innuendos and buried quali-
fiers, but the tipoff came as he wound down his little lecture. "We
are inclined to the view," he mused, his hands in roof formation,
in front of his face, "that it is too early to presume which Soviet
satellite will be the first to implode: the Hungarians, Poles, Czechs,
East Germans . . . whomever." There it was. The more colloquial
"whoever" or even "whatever" would never do. This kind of
mannered diction was an essential Ottawa touchstone. Any misfit
most Canadians would have labelled "a fruitcake" Robertson
would call "a bit eccentric." His most biting reproach was to hang
offending underlings with the old UCC verdict that they had
"blotted their copybook." His great strength, I was told, was
"ironing things out."

The East Block where Robertson worked was a neo-Gothic
Victorian stone pile on Parliament Hill, which then housed all of
External Affairs as well as the Prime Minister's and Privy Council
offices. My memory of the place is of a forest of hat racks festooned
with fedoras. It reeked of decisions being taken by secretive functionaries, expert at calibrating compassion against expediency. I
mused that prior to going to bed, these super-brains probably
recited passages from John Maynard Keynes's *General Theory of
Employment, Interest, and Money*, which one of them, Bob Bryce,
had actually brought across the Atlantic.

Fuelled by the resentment of having been patronized by their
British mentors, the mandarins became the agents of Canada's
decolonization. These former Rhodes Scholars wielded the shears
that cut Westminster's apron strings by negotiating Canada's jurisdictional devolution from the Mother Country. This post-war
period comprised our impressive "middle power" years, when we
exercised a positive and surprisingly significant influence on
world affairs, especially in the founding of the United Nations, the
North Atlantic Treaty Organization, the Bretton Woods Accord,
the International Monetary Fund, and the World Bank. My brief
encounters with Norman Robertson and closer ties with his colleagues confirmed my initial impression that they were brilliant,

honest, diligent, cordial, cultivated, and unpretentious. But they also inflicted more damage to Canada's long-term future than any invading army. In the process of removing British imperialism's grip, they turned Canada into a client state of the White House, which eventually left us open to the tender mercies of the U.S. military-industrial complex. It was during their watch that Canadians moved directly from being bastard Englishmen to becoming bastardized Americans. We never had the chance to behave as truculent Canadians in the interval, able to claim our own space and cultural independence.

The missing element among the mandarins I got to know (except for a blessed few) was a passion for anything more important than their predilection for minor French cheeses. Their reaction to being told any unexpected news, whether a distant declaration of war or the tale of some benighted assistant deputy who had blabbed Privy Council secrets to a stripper across the Ottawa River in Hull, was a mumbled, "So I've heard . . ." They behaved like water bugs scurrying across the Dead Sea, borne by its prevailing winds but never getting wet. They bonded while comparing fly-casting techniques at the private Five Lakes Fishing Club in the Gatineau Hills, or enjoying doubles at the Rockcliffe Tennis Club.

"I played tennis regularly in a foursome that included 'Mike' [Lester B.] Pearson, the department's minister; Arnold Heeney, his deputy; and Terry McDermot, a former headmaster of Upper Canada College, then the department's chief of personnel," I was told by Tony Griffin, a senior External officer who later became one of my favourite sailing companions. "These games were the greatest fun, with continuous badinage. A return of service that passed Pearson at the net, for example, was known as the Guatemala shot, meaning that this sort of sally could lead to a diplomatic posting to Guatemala City."

The mandarins claimed loyalty to whatever party was in office, but the staying power of the Liberal Party was such that it inevitably endowed them with common cause. (Between 1940 and 1957, eight senior public servants became Liberal Cabinet ministers.) Among themselves, most of Ottawa's mandarins referred to John Diefenbaker's half-dozen years in power as "The Duration," as if they had come safely through a long and painful siege. The Prince Albert politician returned the compliment by blasting away at "the invisible incognitos, the dictators who dominate Canada." During his six years as prime minister, Diefenbaker consulted Robertson precisely twice.[4]

What I found so fascinating about these worthy anachronisms was that they operated as an organized power structure, sharing bonds of service. Their instinctive ability to negotiate a workable compromise on any issue (where to have dinner, or how to react to De Gaulle's *force de frappe*) was due in part to common schooling. Eleven of the mandarins who counted had attended Oxford (eight on Rhodes Scholarships); another eight had graduated from Harvard, which was Oxford's North American branch plant. Though concentrated in External Affairs and Finance, they were dispersed round the city and to outsiders appeared to have few connecting links. Their thought process, however, was firmly wired into one perambulating brain: that of Norman Robertson, who liked to toy with his oysters at the Rideau Club's daily lunches round the communal table in the left-hand corner of the main dining room. Somehow they communicated with one another faster and more effectively than any computer network yet invented.

By the time I arrived in Ottawa, the mandarins were still powerful but on the verge of becoming an endangered species. The fate of that proud elite was sealed when their *beau ideal*, Lester Pearson, resigned as prime minister in 1968. He was the last and most successful of their number, and his departure signalled an end point to their dominance as definitively as the fall of the Berlin Wall, many years later, terminated the once-exalted status of

---

[4] One of Robertson's legacies is that in 1950 he hired a young constitutional lawyer from Montreal as an adviser to the Privy Council Office. His name was Pierre Elliott Trudeau.

Cold War spies. The spooks and the mandarins shared certain articles of faith: the concealment of emotions, the art of being unassuming, and the sanctity of keeping secrets.[5]

As I rose to leave Norman Robertson's office, I understood why he was the ultimate Ottawa Man: he symbolized the essential division between power and influence. They intersected in his office, and he exercised both. Watching him weigh his answers to my questions, I realized why the public service mandarins almost always had their way. Canada's MPs suffered from superficial views strongly held; they were ideological acrobats, willing to square almost any political circle, allowing their pragmatic approach (defined as "where the votes are") to decide where they stood on any policy. This made them easy to manipulate. The mandarins knew how the game was played. *Yes, Minister* existed as a placating, somewhat patronizing phrase and attitude long before it became the title of a British sitcom. The Canadian mandarins were well practised in pretending to support their elected masters while carrying the day. The politicians never had a chance. The bureaucrats' strength was in the networks they used to bring about their intended political effect. Lord Acton wrote: "Power tends to corrupt and absolute power corrupts absolutely." In Ottawa I learned another version: that power connects and absolute power connects absolutely.[6]

BY 1959, MY DIVORCE had gone through. Christina had moved to Ottawa. That autumn we were married at city hall, with two

---

[5] John Le Carré, who wrote their bible, once explained that "a secret is something that is revealed to one person at a time," which sums up the standard information flow in bureaucratic Ottawa.

[6] When journalist Brian McKenna asked Jean Drapeau, who knew a thing or two about the subject, whether he agreed that "power corrupts, and absolute power corrupts absolutely," the authoritarian Montreal mayor hesitated a moment, then replied: "That is true. But not absolutely."

friends, Bill Stevenson and Frank Fingland, acting as our witnesses, and spent a magical weekend honeymoon at La Sapinière in the Laurentian Mountains. We felt exuberantly joyful after our long wait, gradually began to find friends, and dug in, determined to make Ottawa our permanent home.

Christina had been raised in a strict Presbyterian home in North Toronto with a stern father, a Freemason who worked for the city, and a spunky and spirited mother. She graduated with honours in English from Victoria College at the University of Toronto, which brought her under the influence of Northrop Frye, who became one of her idols. Over the next four years, she worked her way up the *Maclean's* editorial chain to researching and writing articles, later moving over in the Maclean-Hunter family to become an assistant editor of *Chatelaine* when it was in its glory under the editorship of Doris Anderson.

With Christina I discovered love for the first time, and compatibility with a woman that I had never dreamed possible: in our work, books, music, complementary outlooks, and temperament. She was smart, beautiful, and longed for the same kind of life I did. She had hated it as much as I that we met when I was married. And was equally torn by this state of affairs, as she made clear in a letter she wrote to my mother on the eve of our wedding:

> I wish that we'd met under different circumstances and I hate this role I'm playing of being the other woman in the ugly triangle. It's completely alien to my nature and I have no arguments to justify it – except that I sincerely believe Peter will be happier with me, and that he will be much better off living in an environment of understanding. We want the same kind of quiet, serene life and we think we can live it better together.
>
> This doesn't mean that I think we will have an easy, carefree existence. We will have a great many worries, more than most people. For one thing, we will have financial troubles from the beginning. But a much greater worry is that I know

Peter will not be completely at rest until Pat remarries. I'm sure I seem to her to be completely thoughtless and she couldn't possibly understand my feelings, but I do worry for her terribly and wish most fervently that this bad time will be over for her and that she will be able to begin a new life with another man more congenial to her nature. But despite my feeling sorry for her – and for all of us – it still seems to me to be much, much better for them to be separated than to live an increasingly unhappy life together. I may be rationalizing my part in this situation by saying that it seems to me the really tragic act took place when they made the mistake of marrying each other.

After moving to Ottawa to be with me, Christina started writing for *Chatelaine* and *Saturday Night*, her prose lighting up both magazines, while I began thinking about another book. Within three years, my second book would launch us into the role of a new power couple on the literary and political scene. Nothing in our marriage would ever be so sweet as those early years when we were just Peter and Chris, a couple who enjoyed sharing our time together above all else, while quietly making progress through Ottawa and loving the city, our time, and our lives.

We started to host a few small parties for friends and to circulate in what passed for the capital's social scene. Heading the list were the senior federal bureaucrat couple Sylvia and Bernie Ostry, the children of Russian immigrants who were then the city's reigning distinguished power wielders. The Ottawa season was climaxed and highlighted by their annual autumn house party, known as Ostry National Day, and we were always there. We had arrived in pre-Radwanski Ottawa, when Madame Burger's, across the river in Hull, was the only restaurant of note, though La Touraine on Elgin Street and the alcoves in the Chateau Laurier's Canadian Grill were the places to be seen for power lunches. In those days Prime Minister St. Laurent lived at the Roxborough Apartments, and his wife brought jars of preserves from Quebec City, storing them under their bed. Every morning, the prime minister walked to the East Block, alone and unguarded, tipping his fedora to anyone who recognized him.

We quickly added "Ottawa night life" to our list of local oxymorons, which included "parliamentary debates," "affordable housing," "civil service," and "informed sources." The only decent after-hours restaurants were Nate's Delicatessen for Montreal smoked meat and the Cathay House for Chinese. When Bobbie Simpson, a former Ottawa Rough Rider, opened the town's first nightclub above a restaurant he bought from Paul Anka's father, it closed within six months for lack of customers. Since there was no National Arts Centre, major entertainment events were presented on a makeshift stage set up in the gymnasium of Glebe Collegiate, and later at the Capitol movie house. We felt like hillbillies in Hickory Hollow.

Having come to maturity in Toronto, Christina and I found Ottawa a confining place, but we began to adapt to our environment, boating on the Rideau Canal in the summers, attending political functions (except prime ministerial garden parties), and forging a circle of close friends – but working most of the time, increasingly as a team. We edited one another's stories, debated their structural strengths, used each other's contacts, and realized how great a working as well as emotional partnership we had created. It was a busy, happy time. Lucky us.

DURING MY DOZEN HECTIC YEARS on the Ottawa beat, I filed nearly two million words, first for *Maclean's*, later as Ottawa editor of the *Toronto Star*, and ultimately for my own syndicate. Despite my best efforts to remain fair and accurate (if not entirely objective), I was regularly accused of being a partisan hack, loyal to one political party or another.

Not so. I was strictly neutral. I attacked everybody.

Having voted at one time or another for every political movement except Social Credit and the Canadian Levitation Party, I found myself searching not so much for a compatible ideology as for a style of politics that was open and free from cant. That proved to be an impossible dream. Try as I might, I could never discover any meaningful differences between Grits and Tories, the country's governing parties. It seemed to me that they both behaved as organized appetites for power, using temporary alliances of regional and economic interests to frame the issues around which elections could be fought and won – or lost.[7] Perhaps the most useful party breakdown was provided by Roy MacGregor, in response to some survey or another trying to paint the Press Gallery as being either Too Left in its thinking, or Too Right. The average member of the Press Gallery, MacGregor perceptively concluded, was: "Conservative in his soul, Liberal in print, and NDP at the bar."

Watching the Liberals in action for nearly half a century, I concluded that their philosophy was simplicity itself: to govern Canada by striking the most marketable balance between elitism and egalitarianism – a sedate form of populism with an extended shelf life. For them, Ottawa was a company town, and they owned the franchise. Liberals instinctively reacted with an almost gravitational pull to the notion that the political ideal was to do as little as possible, and as much as necessary. They followed the advice laid down by Keith Davey, the backroom "rainmaker" who invented the modern Liberal Party: "in politics, perception is reality." The

---

[7] The only fundamental division between them that I spotted was that Liberals tended to fish from rented rowboats, while Tories preferred casting off docks, letting the fish come to them. Conservatives also favoured sleeping in twin beds, while Grits preferred doubles, which explained why there were more Liberals.

Another reason why there were more Liberals was that they had few qualms about counting the ballots of dead voters. It was Mike Pearson who tipped me off to that bizarre practice when I saw him shortly after he had returned to Ottawa from campaigning in Newfoundland. "It was a cool afternoon," he told me. Premier "Joey Smallwood and I we were being driven in the back of an open car through the streets of St. John's, waving to the people. When we went through a cemetery, I put my hands in my coat pockets to keep warm, but Joey nudged me, and said, 'No, Mike. Keep waving. This is our best district.'"

party's leaders saw themselves as natural heirs of the haughty attitude that once characterized the divine right of kings, harbouring
the petulant assumption that they alone knew what was good for
Canadians, and that it was plain dumb to vote for any other party,
except as occasional comic relief.

It's a paradox, but it seems to me that Canadian political parties
have tended to define themselves by their enemies. When Tories
and Grits squinted at their opponents across the green Commons
carpet, they recognized themselves. Both realized (but never admitted) that their styles of governing amounted to an exercise in
synchronized swimming. The NDP, in contrast, despised bloated
capitalists, even if that vanishing breed was doing a pretty good
job of eliminating itself. Similarly, Reformers and their ilk drew
their strength from openly hating gun control advocates, gays,
vegetarians, pea-soupers, cappuccino drinkers, people who didn't
take Hallmark greeting cards seriously, and months containing the
letter, "R."

The longer I stayed in Ottawa, the less attention I paid to political labels. My favourite instance of how little party differences
counted was the day Prime Minister Pierre Trudeau named Eugene
Forsey, former research director for the Canadian Labour Congress
and a socialist firebrand, to the Senate. Asked on which side of the
Red Chamber he would sit, Forsey calmly explained: "It's because
I am a Sir John A. Macdonald Conservative that I will sit in the
Senate as a Trudeau Liberal." When I heard him say that, I was
stunned, but nobody else considered his partisan calisthenics in any
way unusual. The day ideology died in Canada was September 29,
2003, when the NDP issued a press release announcing that its commissioned focus groups had opted overwhelmingly that Jack Layton
keep his moustache. When the only political party that could claim
a vestige of underlying philosophy felt it was necessary to test
public opinion before deciding whether its new leader should
shave his upper lip, it was time the razor was applied elsewhere.

While close-up exposure did not attract me to any partisan
viewpoint, living and working around the Hill, meeting Canadians

from coast to coast to coast, and seeing the remarkably civil manner in which we dispose of our public business made me more than ever a nationalist. As this feeling grew from a hobby into a crusade, I began trying to persuade Canadians that they weren't put on this earth merely to outlast cold winters. Ours might be a putty culture, but it was well worth preserving.

The world needs putty cultures. Part of Canada's strength is that we don't take ourselves too seriously. Both Republican and Democratic national conventions in the United States leave observers in no doubt that they have checked into a blinking Las Vegas casino of politics. The action is high-stakes, fast-paced, and hard-core. Their politicos are true believers, convinced that the choice of their president will chart the course of history, destiny, and divine revelation.

A Canadian political convention is every bit as boring as those three words suggest. At best, the delegates hope their work might result in a paved road out to their subdivision, or a quarter-point drop in the mortgage rate. The hottest place to be is the nearest Denny's, White Spot, or piano bar after midnight. Somewhere in the hidden depths of the convention centre, the leadership candidates will be hosting entertainment suites. In the United States, fortunes are paid to get into these VIP areas to cut a quick deal with the candidate; in Canada, delegates search out the leadership hopefuls because the word is around that they're handing out free booze. The rule of thumb about covering these gabfests was that Conservatives attend because they want to debate policy; Liberals because they want government contracts; NDPers because they want to get laid; reformers (and their heirs) to munch free Kentucky Fried Chicken.

Non-partisan, convinced of the goodness of my country but not of the people who ran it, out to drum up a readership and uninterested in following the herd mentality, I became a Martin Luther style of rebel. Although he turned out to be the founder of the Protestant faith, Luther did not begin as an anti-Catholic. He was put off his feed by the Church's imperfect disciples and ecclesiastical abuses, which undermined its authority. Similarly, I was never as vicious as with politicians whose ineptitude, stupidity, dishonesty, even pragmatism threatened the perfectibility of the Canada of my dreams.

AS MY REPUTATION and audience grew, I found it easier to gain access to the hard-to-reach politicians. I had one decided advantage over my competitors in the Press Gallery, where I went to get my mail but seldom hung out. Not having to file daily (even at the *Star* I wrote only three columns a week), I had the luxury of picking subjects that piqued my interest and conducting in-depth research (that is, asking dumb questions) while probing the current administration's soft underbelly (that is, finding well-informed leaks). I kept away from the traditional sources mined by my gallery colleagues, who expended most of their energies buttering up Cabinet ministers, ambitious MPs, and their press aides. They would, for example, work these contacts to try and reconstruct what went on inside the weekly party caucuses, which were barred to the press. I very soon discovered an alternate source for the same inside data, simply by tapping into senators. They were full-fledged caucus members, but nobody bothered to interrogate them. Feeling ignored, they were delighted to see me, and leaked like the *Titanic*. Better informed were the bright young assistants to ministers and those inside the PMO. They didn't belong to the Rideau Club or go canoeing with Blair Fraser, but they did feel ardently that the political process wasn't allowing the more enlightened policy options to bubble up, and they wanted an outlet for their thoughts and theories. They became my sherpas, guides to the shifting winds at Ottawa's political summit, and sources of my most interesting scoops. To my delight, discretion was not their long suit. Less approachable but always decorative were the upwardly nubile young women who hung around ministers' offices, usually as press secretaries.

Nearly everyone I met in partisan politics was enraged by "the power of the press," complaining that the media were biased against them, and that journalists were public mischief-makers and attention-seekers who suffered from excessive vanity, if not delusions of grandeur. (A reasonable point of view, I always felt.) But it was another thing to suggest that the press did not provide a useful service. The bureaucracy, when it stymied new ideas, often stopped a bad idea from getting through. The press gallery worked the same way; because it got so many things so wrong so often, there was less public panic when it got the odd thing right. The real purpose of the press was to throw as many stories as possible into the air, in the hopes that at least a few would stick, like Ottawa snow.

There was in the press itself a sort of tribal mentality that amounted to an agreement that everyone had it pretty good and there was no point rocking the boat. Their status on the Hill protected them from most hardships and hazards, save one: being recalled by head office. There was also more competition between newspapers and radio stations at that time, which provided a never-ending cycle of deadlines that had to be met. The result was a bureaucratic mindset of covering your ass. Most reporters shared the same objective: get it fast, but get it right – "right" meaning the same story as everyone else. That way no one had their news sense questioned, and everyone was happy and home in time for dinner. This bred a cynical sense of black humour, as expressed in various maxims about the nature of political coverage in the nation's capital:

- Any Ottawa news story more than six weeks old is news all over again.
- If you want to allege an MP is a pig fucker you don't have to produce the pig. You just have to get him to deny it.
- Any story you don't have to retract is a great story.
- In any situation where estimates are used (casualties, crowds, etc.) the largest estimate is the most accurate.

- You don't have to speak French. If it's important enough, they'll say it in English.
- A "source" is someone at the Press Club bar. An "informed source" is someone at the Press Club bar who has talked to someone *not* at the Press Club bar.
- An "informed source familiar with the minister's thinking" is the minister.
- A story on polls is only news when it confirms what the editors want to hear.
- The only times anyone in Ottawa ever talks is when they are trying to take credit, shift blame, or hide something.

What we did exercise, on those rare days when we got lucky, was influence in creating the climate of public opinion. "The Fourth Estate," if there is such a beast, responds in direct relation to the treatment it receives. Approached with respect and touches of humour, most journalists respond in kind; shunned as alien elements within the body politic, they become precisely that. Many a politician has made the mistake of trying to befriend them, when what they want is respect. Reporters are insecure, not lonely.

Trudeau showed his contempt for journalists by spraying them with gravel spewed from the tires of his gull-wing Mercedes, but under their bluster they liked it, because at least he was showing them the respect given an adversary. When Brian Mulroney wanted to ingratiate his way into the Press Gallery's affections in his early years, he tried to buy its members off with signed photos and bits of ribald bonhomie. It not only didn't work, it backfired.

Throughout my time in Ottawa, politicians pretended to trust me, though I knew they were really courting my readership. I gained the cachet of being an insider, and I did everything possible to encourage this myth in order to broaden my access. "Who sups with the Devil needs a long spoon," goes the proverb, so while I sought to dine with the powerful, I was careful to use long-handled cutlery. As Hugo Young, the late and lamented political essayist for the British paper the *Guardian*, wrote in his final book, *Supping with the Devils*: "If we purport to be telling it like it is, we can't avoid talking to politicians. They own the truths we like to think we're reporting. The line they're spinning is at least half the story, and the columnist has the advantage of being able to expose the spin and deride it. But he must sup with the devils constantly. Though writing, I contend, as an outsider, he must discover as an insider."[8]

The cardinal rule of Ottawa is simple: power is measured by proximity to power. I was an ardent, quiet nationalist, proud of my country and desperate to maintain its independence. I saw my value increase when I winkled out information different from the daily diet, and became a determined mercenary in my pursuit of the scoop and the truth – whenever possible, simultaneously. "Journalists are like Germans," a politician once complained. "They're either at your feet or at your throat. At the feet to get information, at the throat when writing it up." This became my standard operating procedure. I liked to think that Ottawa was about the contest of ideas; I learned it was a market bazaar where vanity and influence pursued obligations and favours. At least I never went so far as to subscribe to the prescription of Malcolm Muggeridge, the British iconoclast who spent some time in Canada. When I asked him to define his vision of the perfect government, he considered the idea for a few seconds, then replied with a wink: "I've got it: an oligarchy, tempered by assassination."

THE LEAST USEFUL SOURCE of news in Ottawa was the most public display of its function, the proceedings of the House of

---

[8] Truth in the political context is a slippery commodity best defined by the veteran *ABC News* Washington correspondent Sam Donaldson, in the wake of the Monica Lewinsky affair: "Bill Clinton's problem was that when he swore to tell the truth, the whole truth, and nothing but the truth, he thought it meant he was supposed to tell three different stories."

Commons, the only Canadian institution run by its inmates. I found there was something anaesthetizing about attending the daily Question Period, which started late enough to allow everyone time for a long lunch, yet early enough to get them home for dinner. Reporters would wander over from the Press Club bar or down from the Parliamentary Dining Room and take their seats in the actual press "gallery" from which the name derived. Below them the backbenchers would arrive first, slouching into the Commons with the enthusiasm of jaded priests performing the final Mass of the day, with the prime minister the last to take his seat. A nod to the galleries, and the show would begin.

The art of looking good in Question Period changed after television entered the Commons in 1977. I was there on that day, and MPs of all stripes were visibly transformed. Most of them sat stiff as boards, especially those in the "cheerleading section" directly behind and beside the leader. Many had preened for the day and were careful to check their personal grooming and direction of the camera angles before they rose to speak. In those days MPs were not allowed to read from notes and extempore oration was the order of the day. Impressive speakers were those who could fill the chamber with booming indignation and reach the visitors in the distant Strangers' Gallery with over-the-top histrionics and dramatic gestures. On television, this made them look like certifiable maniacs, so MPs learned to play more subtly to the cameras. Indignant outrage is now emoted through smouldering brows, cool competence through the set of necktie, collar, and kerchief. The daily duel is about as unscripted as Japanese kabuki theatre.

The introduction of new technologies did result in one comic episode. Defence minister Paul Hellyer's executive assistant Bill Lee was seated in the gallery one afternoon, bored stiff; to amuse himself, he pulled out a three-foot-long telescopic ballpoint pen, which resembled a walkie-talkie aerial, and began to mutter into it. Another Liberal on the government benches, Marcel Prud'homme, had a similar pen of his own, and extended it, pretending to answer back. The suspicious Tories spotted this byplay and cried foul. At their dinner-hour caucus, they prepared an official protest against the "electronic spy device" being used by the Grits. In the evening session, Conservative House Leader Gordon Churchill rose to his feet to lodge the protest, just as he noticed that two of his own party's MPs had been given similar trick pens by Lee. He sank back into his seat, bewildered and speechless, as the three MPs and Lee jabbered like naughty ten-year-olds into their pens for the rest of the sitting.

Question Period has since become a risk-free affair, unless the Cabinet ministers chosen to respond are so careless as to forget to read their briefing notes, or so over-refreshed as to be unable to make them out. Even this does not fully explain the day in 1996 when Diane Marleau, then the minister of Health under Jean Chrétien, was asked why Canadians felt so deeply about Medicare. "Oh, if I knew that, I could tell you a lot about it," she burbled. "Could I! I guess it's probably for many reasons. But you know, there are all kinds of considerations. There are lots of things happening. For me, I'm not sure. I'm not going to give you a direct answer, because I really don't know . . ."

Though disillusioned by the goings-on in the Commons, I was enthralled by the Parliament Buildings themselves. I would return at night, when the daily hustle was over, to prowl the corridors. When I turned on the lights at the abandoned Press Gallery, I could see cockroaches scurrying away from half-eaten sandwiches and ketchup-soaked french fries; often the light would disturb the slumber of an inebriated or maritally challenged scribe. I would hang around for an hour or two, reading the *Hansard* "blues," reporting that day's events.

My steps echoed along the marble floors and granite walls as I paced the sepulchral emptiness of the corridors, surrounded by oil portraits and bronze busts of long-forgotten faces. More than once, I heard the echo of footsteps when there had been no originating sound. Some frustrated ghost, I would conclude. An MP who died in office before his private member's bill had been read? An independent member consigned to the purgatory of trying to get the Speaker's attention? The stately building unquestionably hosted ghosts. Sometimes I would meet one.

These otherworldly encounters would take place in the outer reaches of its highest corridors, somewhere beyond cleaning supplies and frozen meat storage, where the nooks and crannies were assigned as offices to the most obscure MPs in the Commons and the most easily ignored members of the Senate. It was as close as you could get to living in a cardboard box and still have a parliamentary address.

At the sound of my footsteps, some night owl would stick his head into the corridor:

"Who's that out there?"

"Newman," I would say. "*Maclean's*."

"*Maclean's*, eh? Well it just so happens, *Maclean's*, that I have an open bottle in my office. So come in, before you get hit by a pigeon."

And that was how I received my *real* education in Canadian government. The MPs and senators would spill forth their lifetimes of experience. I came to see them as the Ottawa equivalent of those crones who used to knit at the foot of the guillotine during the French Revolution: say what you will about them, they knew much about public executions. In the same way, Parliament Hill's elderly habitués briefed me on how to read the entrails prophesying political downfalls. The way to approach them was through the photographs on their walls. Politicians don't have any taste for art, but they know the value of a photo gallery. The pictures given pride of place showed the office-holder in close and friendly proximity to a PIP (Politically Important Person). A photo of them shaking hands was even better, particularly with a U.S. president (major bag) or someone vaguely foreign-looking. Kids in wheelchairs, or nakedly starving, could be used in a pinch for a grip-and-grab snap while holding a fat foreign aid cheque. There was a story behind every picture, and asking to hear them taught me more about political Ottawa than a dozen textbooks.[9]

It was during just such a midnight encounter with an old Liberal pol that I first heard the confident prediction that the Grits were going to lose the 1957 general election. To most members of the governing party, this was rank heresy. They had been in power since 1935. Every building in Ottawa had a Liberal encrustation that had been growing for twenty-two uninterrupted years. An entire Canadian generation had reached maturity knowing little else; nothing in the federal government had changed, except that the bodies kept acquiring new faces. Most Ottawa observers believed that the Conservative candidates preparing to go to the polls behind their new leader, John Diefenbaker, faced the same prospects as the British cavalry charge of the Light Brigade. But my midnight briefings had convinced me otherwise.

That night I walked home through the downcast grey of early morning. The winter air rolled in cold from the flanks of the Ottawa and Gatineau rivers, and the birch limbs chattered with ice. Sunrise would come soon enough. A few months, and it would be spring. Life had a predictable air. By the time the snow had melted,

---

[9] My knowledge of Ottawa became a profitable commodity when best-selling novelist Arthur Hailey hired me in 1962 as his researcher for *In High Places*, his best-known political thriller. He gave me 5 percent of his royalties from the book in return for providing the background of how a typical prime minister might react to the offer of an Act of Union by the American president. It was too far ahead of its time to be one of his smash hits, but it did go through twenty printings, and paid for one of my boats. I remember driving up and down the (then) gravel road to Rideau Hall where one of its scenes took place so that I could describe to Arthur what kind of sound car tires made on the driveway to the viceregal residence.

While in Ottawa, I also became interested in television, and co-wrote several CBC series, including the eight-part *Tenth Decade* (about the Diefenbaker-Pearson wars), *Style is the Man Himself* (about Pierre Trudeau), and *The Days Before Yesterday* (on Canadian history). All produced by my boating buddy Cam Graham, who later did the TV version of *The Canadian Establishment*.

and the 1957 election campaign was underway, Ottawa's nervous system would realize that the unthinkable was happening. The Barbarian was at the gate; the Huns had unsheathed their steel. The sclerotic national capital was about to hiss and pop with more sparks than Dr. Frankenstein's laboratory. The name of the lightning bolt was John George Diefenbaker.

CHAPTER SIX

THE MAKING OF A RENEGADE

I'd like to claim that the remarkable success of
Renegade in Power *changed me not a bit, that
I remained the unassuming, unpretentious, charmingly clumsy,
generic no-name writer I was meant to be. But I can't.*

O n February 14, 1962, I signed a contract with Jack
McClelland to write my second book, originally to be
called *The Tory Tornado*, about John Diefenbaker's emotional conquest of a generation and how his administration eventually imploded. I received an advance of $1,000. The Diefenbaker
government's fall on April 22, 1963, created a buzz for the project,
later retitled *Renegade in Power: The Diefenbaker Years*. This was the
book that kicked my career into that rarefied mega-seller category
that is the dream of every author. Equally important, it brought
Jack McClelland into my life. He would be my publisher for the
next twenty years, my friend and literary mentor for life. We published eight books together and sold 800,000 copies.

McClelland has been called "the prince of publishers" and "the
sweetheart of publishers." He was both: he was royalty and he was
loved. A naval hero, he commanded Motor Torpedo Boat 797 in
some of the riskiest CQBs (close-quarter battles) of the Second
World War. "Have you been sailing all your life?" the recruiting
officer asked him when he signed up. "No," he replied. "Just since
I was five."

In his biography of McClelland, James King accurately describes our initial partnership: "From the outset the sometimes reclusive Newman saw himself as a far different kind of author from Pierre Berton and Farley Mowat. He was insecure, afraid to put a wrong foot forward in public. He was also by nature a troublemaker, a journalist who was not afraid to confront the famous and powerful and to display their feet of clay. Newman was often discouraged by the task of taking on Diefenbaker." Indeed, I was on the point of giving up several times, but Jack would come to Ottawa four or five times a year and we'd have dinner at the Chateau Laurier. He would make me feel that this daunting project was worth it, and I'd go back to my typewriter with renewed vigour.

I had made up my mind to write a different kind of political book, sensing how technology had changed public expectations. Almost all political journalism of the day was dry and verbose; I believed that television had given the public a sense of place and detail that should also be reflected in my prose. If TV showed crowds, then I would describe not just that they were there, but how they behaved, why they were there, and how they felt. Although this approach has since become the standard form of political journalism, at the time it was untried and unwelcome – at least in this country. I decided that I would attempt to write contemporary history as novels that happened to be true, or as true as I could make them. The intersection of personality and circumstance, not friendship or ideology, would fuel the narrative; it would be the work of a storyteller bound by facts, eager to utilize the compelling fictional techniques that keep readers turning pages into the night.

In Theodore H. White's just-published epic *The Making of the President*, about how John F. Kennedy had won America's highest office, I found my model in reverse. *Renegade* would chronicle *The Unmaking of the Prime Minister*. I was fortunate in my timing. The gore and the glory that the politician from Prince Albert, Saskatchewan, introduced to Canadian politics had turned a dull topic into a spectator sport, and I was there to reconstruct his astounding rise and even more astonishing fall. His had truly been a leadership cult without leadership.

The title change was my own, though we played around with *Maverick in Power*, and a few other possibilities. Use of the word "renegade" became one of the book's most potent selling points (and trigger for the anger of most Tory politicians, who condemned the book without getting past the jacket), but I felt it was justified. Diefenbaker was a renegade[1] in the sense that he opposed the basic tenets of Canadian conservatism: encouraging individual responsibility, and nurturing the British connection. By the end of Diefenbaker's time in office, federal welfare payments had doubled; and when he resigned, *The Times* of London wrote in a leading editorial that "fewer tears were shed than over the upset of any major Commonwealth figure since Oliver Cromwell." He was also a renegade in the Robin Hood sense, of taking from the rich (Central Canada) and giving to the poor (Western Canada and the Atlantic provinces). Finally, I dubbed him a renegade because he was a traitor to his own cause: he interpreted the voters' splendid acclaim of him in 1957 and 1958 as adequate proof of his greatness, and once in office betrayed the trust they had placed in him.

In a sense, I had been researching the book since my arrival in Ottawa five years earlier, writing countless columns and articles on this most enigmatic of Canadian politicians. By the time my manuscript was completed, I had interviewed nearly a thousand friends, critics, and observers, in fact just about anyone who might share their Diefenbaker insights with me. I had enough material to fill six books, but in a habit that became the modus operandi for all of my subsequent volumes, I organized my research by a series of consecutive cuts, reducing my files to manageable size. The final version ran to only 160,000 words. This was after the last of my five drafts eliminated 50,000 words, since I couldn't undeniably

---

[1] *Renegade*, from the same root as *renege*, means someone who abandons one set of principles for another – a legitimate term for the Chief, who abandoned Conservatism for Diefenbakerism.

source all of my data and was determined to prevent the Tories from finding any hook upon which to hang my lynching noose. I checked and double-sourced everything I wrote – but the Diefenbaker Cabinet was divided into so many factions, with each trying to justify its actions, that it took repeated corroboration before I felt safe in using any anecdote or repeating any "fact."[2]

I still had to stretch the conventions of journalism to make a point. For example, I was well aware that most of the participants on both sides of the 1963 plot to overthrow the prime minister were seldom sober. How to prove it? Easy. I persuaded a friendly member of the parliamentary custodial staff to give me the stats on ice consumption in the Commons during the height of the crises. Ice cubes delivered daily went up at least 30 per cent, to 3,800 pounds, during the attempted coup. Point made.

I knew I had overdosed on my research when, during a trip to Prince Albert, I went to have what was left of my hair cut by Diefenbaker's favourite barber, Frank Dixon at McKim's Barber Shop. I had hoped for some ultimate pearl of wisdom, but his entire contribution consisted of: "Well, John's always treated me right," and a lousy haircut.

Working almost around the clock to complete a book and keep my day job as political columnist, I became a cloistered monk for six exhausting months. My copy was carefully vetted, a chapter at a time, by Martin Lynch, then the assistant news editor of the *Globe and Mail*, who rode herd on most of my books, and my volunteer academic adviser, the learned Paul Fox at the University of Toronto's political economy department. The most important contribution to the manuscript was the editing and occasional rewriting by Christina. Not only did she possess killer political instincts, but her sensibilities honed my style and redefined the

---

[2] I was pleased to see that when the first academic study of the Diefenbaker period was published in 1995, *Rogue Tory* by Professor Denis Smith, who had access to the former prime minister's private papers, none of my major facts or suppositions (including the title) was challenged.

literary voice I had been seeking. I wrote the last paragraph of the final chapter on August 29, 1963, and the book went to press at midnight the same day. Jack McClelland broke publishing records by having it in the stores by the end of October.

I REALIZED THAT TO UNDERSTAND Diefenbaker the man, I needed to comprehend the region that had given birth to his brand of politics. One of my mentors in this was Dr. Merrill Menzies, the Saskatchewan-born London School of Economics graduate who had written a forty-page memorandum that provided the theoretical basis for Diefenbaker's "vision of the North." Lowell Murray, the son of a Cape Breton miner who became senior adviser to half a dozen of the country's most influential Conservative politicians, was another. A man of conscience, he wanted the truth to get out, and he agreed to keep a journal for me (as did several others) detailing daily events, especially during the *coup d'état* of 1963. My arrangement with the journal-keepers was simple: they would record everything they saw and heard, but not pass along the notes until whatever crisis I was writing about had been resolved. That way, I could exclusively reconstruct the details in my book without affecting the outcome by publishing premature leaks.

Allister Grosart, the voluble national director of the Progressive Conservative Party of Canada, was another valuable source. My monthly afternoon-long debriefing sessions with him were highly educational. Grosart's thesis was that "government is nothing more than a series of occasions," and he staged more than a few. One of his early tricks was to decorate the platforms on which major Tory functions were held with flagpoles fabricated from aluminum pipes. Hidden under the floor were two household vacuum cleaners blowing in reverse, which were turned on when the first notes of the British and Canadian national anthems rang out. This would snap the flags to attention, as if blown by an outdoor breeze. Later, bits of chaff and confetti were added – pretty simple effects by today's standards, but they mightily impressed the delegates inside the hall. Grosart was Ottawa's original spin doctor. One of his typical tricks: during the final hectic week of the 1957 election campaign, Louis St. Laurent testily charged that most of the Tory candidates were running not as Conservatives but as Diefenbakerists. Grosart had the speech mimeographed on plain white paper and sent it in unmarked envelopes to every Liberal constituency organization in the country. The Liberal candidates assumed they were receiving instructions from party headquarters, and dutifully repeated the line set down by their leader. The *samizdat* was faithfully reproduced and sent along through the party machine. It was, in effect, supportive of the Diefenbaker election theme: that it was not the same old Tory party, but something very different – the Diefenbaker Party – which was exactly the message Grosart wanted to broadcast.

Working from party headquarters lodged in a decrepit three-storey brownstone on Laurier Avenue East, formerly one of Ottawa's better-known bordellos, Grosart ran a primitive set-up, with Flora Macdonald and Patrick MacAdam (both of whom would figure prominently in the Mulroney years) providing the administrative support. I made it a habit to pop over to Grosart's office. At that time, few journalists had figured out how much influence such backroom boys exercised, but I found him to be the closest thing to an alter ego Diefenbaker ever had. He would patiently drag me through the fine points of the Chief's mental process, depending on the silky-tongued blarney that was his birthright to explain the inexplicable. The son of a Dublin preacher, he had been an investigative journalist, a Baptist sermonizer, the Canadian promoter for *Gone With The Wind*, an army machine gun instructor, a Tin Pan Alley song plugger (still collecting royalties from "When My Baby Smiles at Me"), a military historian, "Mr. Adventure" on CBC Radio, and a long list of other odds and sods, including the ghost writer of the biography of Count Freddie de Marigny, the accused killer of expatriate Canadian millionaire Sir Harry Oakes in the Bahamas. He faded away into the Senate after the disastrous 1962 campaign but never wavered in his loyalty to the

Chief. Interestingly, when *Renegade* was published and he was asked to comment, he winked and casually cited only one factual error in its more than four hundred pages: that during the 1962 campaign he was hospitalized for a peptic ulcer, not a bleeding ulcer as I had claimed.

If *Renegade* had a literary godfather, it was LeRoy Abraham Faibish, a Romanian Jew who grew up on a farm in Shaunavon, Saskatchewan, and went on to graduate in philosophy from Queen's University. He was officially the executive assistant to Agriculture minister Alvin Hamilton. In fact, Roy Faibish was the government's only resident intellectual. A knowing sparrow of a man, he was intensely loyal to the Chief but was the only operative inside the Tory tent with the *cojones* to contradict him and deliver unpopular tidings. After *Renegade* was published, Diefenbaker pulled Faibish aside and whispered, in a conspiratorial hush:

"You know, his name isn't Newman – it's *Noyman!*"

Evidently, "*Noyman*" was some kind of Prairie code for "Jewish." To which Faibish replied, to his eternal credit: "What the hell does it matter if his name is Mickey Mouse? What the hell does it matter? What's your point?" He knew exactly what point the Mighty Chief – defender of ethnic underdogs – was making. Dief fell silent, the quip having gone over less well than it might have in Prince Albert. Nothing more was said, but because of this outburst Faibish was forever distrusted as the most likely "mole" in the Diefenbaker organization. For once, they were right.

Faibish operated along broader lines of reference than all of the other Tories combined, being equally conversant in Chinese history, social anthropology, Marxist theory, Jewish folklore, and high finance. His favourite thinkers were Franz Kafka, Albert Camus, Arthur Koestler, Patrick Watson, Alvin Hamilton, and the Bulgarian-born Nobel laureate Elias Canetti. He genuinely believed in Diefenbaker's brand of politics and provided me with a logical framework for what, coming out of the leader's mouth, sounded like a carelessly served smorgasbord. Even if Roy made up aspects of Dief's ideology as he went along, at least, between the two of us, we endowed him with a credible, Left-of-Centre political philosophy. It was Roy's dream that Diefenbaker reorient the Conservative Party so that it would be attacked from the Right for being too socialist, and from the Left for not being socialist enough. We had a thousand conversations, always on the run, with Faibish impatiently explaining some subtlety of government strategy, or rationalizing Diefenbaker's latest pratfall. Every page of *Renegade* bears his imprint, not because his briefings were that detailed, but because his insights allowed me to understand Diefenbaker's character and made me appreciate the tragedy of his downfall. Later, Faibish was as close to Trudeau as he had been to Diefenbaker, and even closer to Brian Mulroney, who wanted him as his chief of staff. Roy went on to the CBC, helping to produce *Inquiry* and the legendary *This Hour Has Seven Days*, served time on the CRTC,[3] and spent the last two decades of his life in London.

While overseas, Faibish lived in a luxurious, reconverted maisonette on Westgate Terrace, overlooking Redcliffe Square, with his wife, Barbara, upstairs from the actor Hugh Grant. He also kept a country retreat in Northern Ireland. He sent me incredible e-mails, such as this one: "Hitler once said that 'the Jew has invented conscience,' I would add that the Jew is the memory of history." One of his last visitors, before he died of a heart attack at seventy-two in 2001, was the cellist virtuoso Mayda Narvey, who wrote in her diary: "There were memories of his childhood in Saskatchewan, the immigrant Jewish farmers and cattle dealers living side-by-side with patriotic Germans. The story of how at the age of seven he was strung up in a cloth sack by two young anti-Semites leads us into his connection with John Diefenbaker, the lawyer who took his case."

Armed with such valuable sources and a youthful overconfidence that allowed me to believe I could rewrite the template of political

---

[3] He was forced to resign from the CRTC after Liberal MP Simma Holt complained that he had told her to shove the anti-CBC button she was wearing "up her ass." Faibish admitted only to a "vigorous conversation."

journalism, I set to work. I described how Dief actually spoke and recorded for posterity the jaw-dropping clangers that fell from his lips. When he said, "In the event this eventuality should be eventuated," I quoted him word for word. When he postulated the historical incongruity that Cromwell had said, "Do something to assure this Canadian legislation must pass!" I pointed out that Cromwell had died two hundred years before Canada was born.

I thought *somebody* should reveal that the prime minister's words couldn't be taken at face value. It is possible that he believed his own blarney when he repeated it often enough, but Dief could stuff more additives into a story than Player's can cram into its cigarettes. Returning from a triumphant speech to the United Nations, he could not resist the urge to add spin to his account, since it might snare some ethnic votes. Speaking to the Montreal Ukrainian Centre some time later, he recalled: "So I said to Mr. Khrushchev, 'Give the *Yew-Kah-Rain-Ians* the vote!' Then he got mad, and that's where he took off one of his shoes – *you remember!*" It was a great story and it won him enthusiastic applause. But there was one small hitch – it couldn't possibly be true. The famous shoe-pounding incident happened sixteen days *after* the Chief's speech, when Diefenbaker was safe at home in Prince Albert.

I would call him out for mistruths, but I resolved to part from the convention of the day and not bother to record every word Dief ever said. Instead I saw my role as a camera; I attempted to replicate the experience of an event. This was the only hope I had of capturing the essence of Dief, whose words were secondary to the spiritual experience of hearing the prophetic cadence with which he enunciated them. Paying attention to the response of the crowd led to some gems. When Dief solemnly told a friendly Prince Albert crowd during the 1962 campaign that hearing his first name again was "something money can't buy," I recorded the skeptical response of a woman beside me: "What else did he think I'd call him, after forty years?"

This was not my only departure from the journalistic norms of the day. At a time when politicians were treated with the reverence afforded demigods, I used phrases such as "a mental lightweight, a perpetual playboy, an amiable goon" to describe his Cabinet ministers – in the case cited, George Hees. "A lovable hayseed" was my description of Alvin Hamilton. I spilled the beans about a Quebec minister who relieved himself, after a drinking binge, into a potted palm at Montreal's Dorval Airport. "Even this might have been forgiven, but for two facts. First, he insisted on pulling his pants down instead of merely unzipping them; and second, he was accompanied at the time by the editor and a photographer of one of the largest Quebec dailies."

Canadians had not seen their political masters savaged in print in quite this manner before. They lapped it up.

"IT'S A RUNAWAY! It's a runaway!" shrieked a hysterical female voice down my Ottawa office telephone line. I recognized the excited tone of Steve Rankin, the publicity director for McClelland & Stewart. I couldn't figure out what she was banging on about. A runaway car?

"Steve," I tried to calm her. "What's a runaway?"

"*Renegade!*" she shouted. "It's jumping off the shelves! Bookstores can't keep it in stock. They've never seen anything like it. Jack's ordered another press run. The phones are going crazy. Everybody wants a piece of you. I'm telling you, IT'S A GODDAMN RUNAWAY!"

I should have been delighted. Instead, my mouth went dry and my knees turned to jelly. I reacted not with joy but with guilt. I had only wanted to play with the genre a bit, place a different spin on things. I wrote about body language and sights and sounds and ambience. I had never done a news story in my life. I was the colour guy. The feature man. The scene-setter. What did I know?

Having dealt over much of my writing life with successful men who have achieved far more than they expected (or ever felt they deserved), I can confirm that many of them believe they are charlatans about to be exposed and humiliated. I could relate to this contrary impulse. That also explained my seventeen rewrites and ten galley proofs. I was an obsessive fiddler with my prose – all the better, I secretly felt, to delay that inevitable day when I would be unmasked. Rivers of self-doubt told me it was acceptable to seek acclaim, but far too risky to actually have it. "Okay, *schmuck*," I told myself, trying to calm down. "I didn't mean it. I was just scribbling away, I never thought it would be taken seriously." I was terrified that I was being set up for the big fall.

Despite my solid WASP credentials as the Ottawa representative of *Maclean's* and the proud pony in the literary stable of a Scottish-Irish publisher, I still felt like a woebegone European Jew caught eating a ham sandwich. I had expected *Renegade* to cause a small stir in Ottawa bookstores, perhaps even inspire an invitation or two to speak to a ladies' reading club in the suburbs. Never this. I spent my working life in dogged pursuit of recognition and the ear of the reading public, so I cannot deny that I wanted fame. But my first taste of it left me terrified. It was a healthy response, but it was not to last.

The book launch, held at Toronto's Park Plaza Hotel, was a typical McClelland extravaganza, attended by most of the usual literati. Modestly assuming that Christina and I would be central to the event, we stood around waiting to be introduced, or asked to comment. I even had a short speech of appropriate elegance and gratitude in my pocket. Everybody kept talking and drinking, then drinking and talking, with the odd nod in our direction. We finally decided to leave when the party had clearly fallen into disarray. This was not a literary sendoff; it was a drunken brawl. As we made our exit, we passed by Jack and one of his pals, the artist Harold Town, who were trying to hang one another with their neckties. They didn't notice us leaving.

On October 29, 1963, three days before its official publication, the *Toronto Telegram* published a banner front-page, four-column news story by L.M. McKechnie: "A cruelly truthful book published this week threatens John Diefenbaker's bid for political resurrection. It will haunt his every move to persuade the electorate of his fitness for office. But it is no partisan political indictment but an honest journalist's painstaking assessment." Two inside pages had been cleared to carry the details of *Renegade*'s message.

At this point I was becoming seriously concerned that John Diefenbaker's reaction to the book might well be violent. "Not to worry, Peter," Jack reassured me. "If the worst happens, we'll publish your book posthumously." The annual Tory party meeting was to take place soon in Ottawa, and the ever-thoughtful Jack told me that he intended to hire a professional wrestler, dress him up as a hotel bellhop, and have him page me throughout the convention. The theory seemed to be that I would by then be so hated by the Conservatives that at the very mention of my name they would take a poke at the bellhop. How this was supposed to sell books escaped me.

I didn't really need much help. No Canadian book published up to that point had sold so many copies so fast: well over 100,000 in its various editions. The pace was slowed only by the speed of McClelland & Stewart's presses, which completed six pre-Christmas printings. Booksellers told me that people just kept coming into their stores to buy "The Book" – no title, author, nothing – and the clerks would automatically hand them *Renegade*.

I made fifteen appearances on the CBC, including debates with Conservative minister Alvin Hamilton and Conservative senator Grattan O'Leary, whom I accused (unjustly) of having been invented by Diefenbaker. I ignored their partisan criticisms – in fact, I was learning rapidly to treat criticism only as a slight. Bobbs-Merrill, an Indianapolis publishing house, brought out an American edition, which prompted the *New York Times* reviewer to comment that it was "a clinical, almost psychiatric, analysis of the complex and devious character of the most controversial figure in Canadian politics." *Newsweek* noted that *Renegade* was "selling faster than *Lolita* or *Lady Chatterley's Lover* ever did." Brian Flemming, the Halifax savant who later became a senior associate of Pierre Trudeau, reminisced: "Getting *Renegade* was tough because I was then in England. I read it in one sitting, and thought it was a defining moment in Canadian publishing. Once digested, my copy was passed among fellow Canadian students, and created the same excitement as my Paris-bought copy of Henry Miller's *Tropic of Cancer*." Douglas Fisher, the important Ottawa columnist, tagged the book as having "the raciness of a Raymond Chandler novel." Readers found it shocking – and exhilarating – that I "wrote in public the way everyone in Ottawa talked in private," in the words of Robert Fulford, then with *Maclean's* and later the esteemed editor of *Saturday Night*. "His frankness changed Canadian journalism. He invented the book as a weapon. In 1963, it was something of a revolution. By the time *Renegade in Power* finished its run on the bestseller lists, the era in journalism exemplified by Blair Fraser was over and the Newman era had begun."

The kudos kept coming. Peter Desbarats, later dean of the graduate school of journalism at the University of Western Ontario, noted that my book had "set a standard in literary assassination for an entire generation of Canadian journalists." The most elegant comment came from Hugh MacLennan, the Canadian novelist and social commentator, then in temporary exile in Grenoble, France: "This is certainly the most remarkable biography I have ever read of any Canadian," he wrote to me in a private letter. "It could not possibly have succeeded – and this succeeds totally – if it had been approached in a conventional way. All through the book I detected what might be called a surgeon's pity for his patient. It took enormous courage to write and I can imagine you have had a great deal of repercussion since. The art and clarity, the completeness and the cohesion of the portrait, give *Renegade*, at least to me, the great internal authority of a work of art."[4]

It was heady stuff, and like all heady stuff, it made mine bigger. I had taken a calculated risk and it had paid off, but there is no creature blinder than the man who takes full credit for his success. That same urban, educated, relocated populace that had voted for

---

[4] *Renegade* quickly became mandatory reading for doctoral students in Canadian history and was reissued in the Carleton University Library series.

– and later massacred – Dief was a prime audience for my style of journalism, which reflected their own suspicion and impatience with the man. I had many helpers to reach my goal. Had the book flopped, of course, I would have looked to them for the cause of its failure. But now, I refused to look for the cause of its success farther than my bathroom mirror.

Diefenbaker himself, asked about *Renegade* at every press conference, alternated between complaint and denial. One day he would harrumph: "I haven't read it yet." The next, he would report: "In the first eight pages I found, I think it was sixteen mistakes."

In fact, he had not only read my book and annotated almost every page, he actually had six hardcover copies in his private library at his house in Rockcliffe. The collection was spotted by Michael McCafferty, his special assistant, who recalled the occasion very clearly: "I had pulled out the copy that had his notes on it, and he asked if I had read it. I told him that it was part of our political science course at university. Diefenbaker geared himself up into high dudgeon, and said: 'Well, I've never read it.' Yet there was his handwriting all over it. He must have gone through it a hundred times."

Although he suffered at the hands of a largely hostile Press Gallery, none had gone so far as to describe his speaking style or the homespun nature of the people who came out to show him support. I had treated him – a shock for politicians at the time – as a fallible human rather than as an untouchable deity. In retaliation, he took great delight in mispronouncing my name as "*Kneeman*," or more frequently as "*Noyman*." He called me, in public, the "Bouncing Czech" and in private, "that Viennese Jew." In the Diefenbaker Centre at the University of Saskatchewan in Saskatoon, where the former prime minister's correspondence is kept, there is a note in his own handwriting (its authenticity verified by the resident archivist) which reads:

Then there is Newman. Here is the literary scavenger of the trash baskets on parliament hill. He is in close contact with the Liberal hierarchy and gets his briefings from them as that what he should publish. False Propaganda. Vicious. Cruel Stories. Carricatures [*sic*]. He is an innately evil person who seems intent on tearing other people to pieces. Seems honourable people have no protection from his mind and pen. He makes his fortune in doing so. NOTE: He is an import from VIENNA!

A seventeen-page critique of the book by two of his staff members is also in the files. But the worst charge they came up with was that "Newman and McClelland want to sell books." (Guilty as charged!) At one point, Diefenbaker asked loyalist Gordon Churchill to call Roy Faibish onto the carpet. He knew that Faibish had been one of my best sources and told him: "This is terrible. This book reveals information that otherwise would not be in the public domain." Roy replied: "Yes, but do you find it malevolent?" Churchill said: "That is not the point. I sure as hell find it destructive."

The only factual error publicly cited at the time was reported by a minor Cabinet minister named Walter Dinsdale. I had described him as "a gentle slump of a man who relaxed by playing second cornet with the Salvation Army's Ottawa Citadel Corps." Not so, thundered his press release. He played *first* cornet. Ever the gentleman, I corrected his rank in subsequent editions. The Dief-appointed associate minister of National Defence, Pierre Sévigny, told Dale Thompson, a McGill University political scientist, who in turn told me, that *Renegade* was "a sensational piece of work designed to catch the headlines in order to make a fast buck, which is a typical Jewish trick." Then Sévigny added incongruously: "Of course, Newman is just like all those goddamn Anglo-Saxons, they just don't understand anything about Quebec."

Jack Horner, the most physical of the Tory brothers from Alberta, threatened to "tear off Newman's writing arm," which was an act of courtesy, coming from him. He had previously told Dick Bell, a Tory Cabinet minister who had dared express doubts about the

Chief, that he was going to maim him, strangle him, and then turn him into a pretzel.[5]

The book suffered the worst drubbing in the small dailies in the small towns that were, and would forever be, Diefenbaker country. The *Aurora Banner* ran a stirring editorial urging their readers not to waste the $7.50 being charged for my book, when for the same price they could get two cases of beer. The *Simcoe Reformer* limited its critique to the book being "too heavy"; they meant by weight, with the editor confessing the only way he could read it was to prop it on a chair in front of him. The Orillia *Packet & Times* let go with all guns blazing, and a sentence even longer than any of mine: "It should be born [*sic*] in mind that the author is one of the wave of shallow, glib young men which has engulfed the agency, publishing and broadcasting world, along with their inevitable pipe or beard, the leftist outlook and callow viewpoint, an air of intellectual detachment and patronizing indulgence is an invariable part of these fellows' stock in trade, and it is probably to this last affectation that we owe Mr. Newman's belittling title." The strangest notice was a front-page retraction in the *Flin Flon Miner*: "Yesterday the *Miner* carried a story about a writer who assayed Mr. Diefenbaker as a *Renegade in Power*. We feel that using that story was not in good taste and wish to disassociate ourselves from it. No one has asked us to make a retraction. But we feel better having done so." I got the same reaction in person whenever I ventured west of Wawa. At a book signing at an Eaton's store (it had an apostrophe

---

[5] A true-blue Tory backbencher from Crowfoot, Alberta (before he crossed the floor and became a Liberal), Jack Horner supplemented his MP's income by selling made-to-measure western outfits from his parliamentary office, measuring customers and sending out for mail-order suits. He ended up as chairman of the CNR. It seems to be a Conservative trait to handle press relations the Cosa Nostra way. Bill Fox, while Brian Mulroney's press secretary, arrived on the doorstep of Jim Munson, the *Toronto Star*'s Washington correspondent, the day an unfavourable article under his byline had appeared. When his wife said he wasn't at home, Fox passed on a message: "Tell him from me that I'm going to tear his lungs out."

then) in Winnipeg, an angry lady came up to me and chastised: "I know John by his first name! This is a terrible thing you've done! I'll never shop at Eaton's again!" (No wonder they went bust.)

And then there was the Senior Citizens' League. I never did find out who they were, but they certainly knew where they stood. I quote only a brief, non-repetitive excerpt from their press release:

We, having many Members in every District in Canada, soon arranged to gather conclusions and ideas from across the country, and with hardly one exception, all Members agree that no groundhog would be so low and degraded as to build his own cesspool and then crawl into it for the purpose of raking up muck and to try to throw into another person's face unless they were either demented entirely, or was moulding some hatred for some selfish, personal reason. It is quite certain the real reason Mr. Newman has his bloody knife into John Diefenbaker is because he is the only person that has done anything worthwhile towards helping we Senior Citizens. Any person that takes anything seriously out of the filth and the lies that his depraved mind has put into book form, is playing with devilish fire, as Hitler did in years past.[6]

---

[6] One reason Dief commanded such loyalty among seniors was his shameless worship of the monarchy, which knew no bounds. After Mrs. Diefenbaker served her chicken salad to Princess Margaret at Harrington Lake, the Chief was so chuffed by the royal approval of his wife's cooking that he released her favourite recipe:

Mrs. Diefenbaker's Chicken Salad
10 cups chicken cooked and diced (2½ cups)
10 tsp lemon juice (2½ tsp)
5 cups diced celery (1¼ cups)
2½ cups seedless grapes (⅔ cup)
10 hard-cooked eggs (3)
3 cups blanched almonds (¾ cup)
2½ cups of mayonnaise (⅔ cup)

Reduced amounts in brackets will make 8 servings of about ¾ cup each.

(I put them down as neutral.)

I was a commercial success and had won the esteem of my peers, but it came as a great relief to have my suspicions of Diefenbaker confirmed by some of those closest to him. About six months after the publication of *Renegade*, I received a phone call in Ottawa from John Cuelenaere. He was the longest-serving of Dief's law partners in Prince Albert, and I approached our meeting feeling defensive. He turned out to be a tall, elegant man armed with a cane.

"That stuff you wrote about John. You got it all wrong," he said.

I nodded humbly, and was preparing a rebuttal when he added: "Why, you said that he defended clients whether they could afford him or not, because he was that anxious to see justice done. That's *bullroar*, sir! The people who retained him knew two things: first, that he would probably get them off because he would ignore the evidence and make an emotional appeal to the jury; and second, that if they did retain him, they had better pay their bill fast or he would foreclose their farms." (Bingo.)

I'D LIKE TO CLAIM that the remarkable success of *Renegade* changed me not a bit, that I remained the unassuming, unpretentious, charmingly clumsy, generic no-name writer I was meant to be. But I can't. My name aroused quick reactions in strangers, and I lapped it up. There is nothing that compares to being recognized as you walk down the street or being greeted with overinflated enthusiasm at restaurants. Early acclaim had its advantages, and I cannot deny that I enjoyed it, but I don't recommend it. Fame and ambition are companions, like Falstaff, in tow long after their amusement has expired. They are creations that enslave their master, and I ended up serving them, no matter the cost.

There were even deeper forces at work than a young literary success impressed by his genius, allowing his newfound celebrity status to go to his head. There was a feral power behind the energy and venom I had summoned for the book. For me, it was personal. Dief had not let down his country or party, he had let *me* down —

and I took it hard. He was the first of many heroes I would put on a pedestal, only to detonate it beneath their feet.

I had originally greeted Diefenbaker with hosannas and presented him to my readers as the solution to every national woe. It was an impossible expectation, but I expected it all the same. I was bound to be disappointed, and I turned against him later. I did the same with Trudeau and Mulroney, both of whom I considered personal friends and political saviours before the inevitable crash of expectations. The same, curiously – or perhaps not so curiously – was true in my personal relations. A pattern had established itself: initial fixation and an elated sense of promise, followed by dashed hopes and a crashing sense of disappointment. I never got through to the other side of this process, a realistic appraisal of the individual and what they could do for me or my country. This failure came from an inability to shake my perpetual sense of threat. If the heroes and heroines I selected were all that could keep me safe, then failure on their part was interpreted as a personal catastrophe.

Among those who have taken up pen to chronicle the great game of Canadian politics, few have done so with more perception than Dalton Camp. By the time my book came out, we had known each other for a decade, through three election campaigns, and I respected him enormously. "What I fear most is orthodoxy," he once told me, a maxim he followed in a lifetime of electioneering, spin-doctoring, and writing his columns and books. I wrote him some months after publication of *Renegade*, complaining that I was being attacked from some powerful and unexpected quarters. "Canada," I intoned, "is not an easy country in which to be a patriot."

Camp responded with merciless insight in a letter I still have, which I cannot read without pangs of recognition and remorse. What did I expect? Mega book sales, overnight fame, *and* the love of a grateful nation? Was I trying to be a famous writer or a famous patriot? He explained that Canada is not a land of patriots, but of loyalists – and there is a wide difference between the two: "Allegiance is the requisite of every oath of public office, and loyalty the

shim in the hand of every politician, grand vizier, battalion commander, sales manager, headmaster and prefect in the land. It is
our native ethic, the ultimate virtue to which we subscribed even
as we fled the rabble of the first American patriots, or expelled the
Acadians, or sent our sons to war." Yes, I had exposed the "quirks,
foibles, and eccentricities" of the high and mighty for the first time
in Canada. Yes, the public had bought my book in droves. But had
I ever considered that there might be consequences, that some
people might be *offended* by what they read? If I wanted to be
loved, Dalton effectively said, I should feed the readers saccharine.
But if I wanted to be respected, I had to give it straight and learn
to take my lumps like a big boy.

The complaints of those small-town papers suddenly made
sense; so did the wide berth given to me by previously friendly
Tories in the corridors of power. Camp had been spot-on – if I
wanted to take sides or even express a strong point of view, I would
lose the affection of some people whose opinion mattered to me.
My determination to reach an elevated perch on the journalism
tree would exact a personal toll. Decades later, Camp would write,
with his gift of insight: "Newman's fame soon became his notoriety: the true victim of *Renegade in Power* was not Diefenbaker,
but Newman."

Truer words were never writ. The success of the book was the
beginning of the end for Peter Newman and the end of the beginning for Peter C. Newman. The self-styled media creation was
born. I created it; I chose it; but in the end, it was *not* me. Yet that
was the coin which paid for my passage from the world of nor-
malcy to the world where everybody knows your name.

"I know that part of our past was good, unusually good, and
that you did love me as much as you were able for a very long
time," Christina was to write me years later, long after our marriage had ended: "But when I go over that past in my mind for
perhaps the hundredth time, it seems to me now from this great
distance that the change came in 1963–64, in the aftermath of the
publication of *Renegade*. From that time on, the tendency already

in you to make a fiction out of yourself began to distance you from reality. . . . The intense fame became too much for you and gradually took more and more of your real self, until you were left as nothing much but a terrified ambition – and I am not using that as a rhetorical device. This showed in your work, of course . . . but where it showed most was in your life."

CHAPTER SEVEN

THE LAST ROUNDUP

Given the odds against his victory, John Diefenbaker should have campaigned in a straitjacket. But he loved every minute of it. And so did I.

O f all my experience as a political journalist, the 1965 election that followed publication of *Renegade* is the one forever etched in my mind as a pivotal event. I may well be the last journalist still writing who witnessed that mystical campaign riding the back of a train. I watched it develop from its baleful start in Halifax to its climax in the howling halls of the Great Plains. That western part of Canada was never an off-spring of what Donald Creighton called "the Empire of the St. Lawrence," but a proud land on its own. Its people, who swarmed the platforms to welcome the Diefenbaker train, wanted one thing understood, plain and simple: they were nobody's country cousins, now or ever.

I soaked up the atmosphere of those rural way stations and grabbed the chance to immerse myself in Canada's political heart-land. The campaign was staged in 1965, when Canadians were beginning to lose their link with the land. The country's acceler-ating urbanization had mostly destroyed the connection between identity and landscape. Instead of being the defining element of our lives, our sense of place had been reduced to a mere backdrop to events. But not aboard the Diefenbaker train. We *were* the event. In many instances we were the last passenger train, all four cars, ever to snake through the sparsely settled terrain, stopping at settlements that would never again play a part in national elections.

When I decided to include this chapter in my memoirs I deliberately adapted my original dispatches from that epic journey. They alone caught the immediacy of those never-to-be-repeated, heart-tugging moments. At Yarbo, Raymore, Watrous, Biggar, Wadena, Mortlach, Morse, Maple Creek, Taber, Fort Macleod, Claresholm, Nanton, Vulcan, Barons, Three Hills, Findlater, Aylesbury, Lumsden, and Gull Lake – these, not in that order, were some of the main way stations.

The election itself was less a campaign than a guerrilla war, fought with unreliable troops and eccentric lieutenants. The Canadian Prairies became a land for Diefenbaker to flee across, every whistle stop a destination, a momentary reprieve from the partisan fury that had erupted among urban voters who no longer responded to his call. At some point early in the campaign, Dief transformed himself into a figment of his own imagination. He ignored his dismal prospects and baptized himself the personification of the national will. This was no more harmful than any deluded individual who believes himself to be Napoleon or Jesus, except that clinical case histories like that don't usually run for national office (George W. Bush being the possible exception). Given the odds against his victory, Diefenbaker should have campaigned in a straitjacket. But he loved every minute of it. And so did I.

While his political rivals were comfortably lodged in jet planes, issuing press releases as they flew from one airport to the next, "the Man from Prince Albert" was jolting into small towns at twenty-minute intervals aboard his chartered train, pushing its punishing way across the country. His advisers had warned him that such a campaign would prove disastrous, because in the age of the airplane and automobile, railway stations no longer figured in most Canadians' lives. But Diefenbaker wanted to see his people one last time. To him, the tracks were not rusting ribbons of steel but umbilical cords to his past. If the train stations were there mainly for their symbolic value, well, so was he. The hoot of the locomotive in the night had been the classic summons to adventure in the days when he was young, and he was bound to relive that time of his life and the lives of his followers.

As I climbed into my narrow berth, I was caught up in the mantra of wheels over track through the prairie night: "I THINK I can . . . I THINK I can . . . I THOUGHT I could . . . I THOUGHT I could . . ." I looked out my window and saw the rising moon cast a pale light across the empty land, staying awake far into the night, watching the lonely farmyard lights flickering like fireflies in the distance and the cozy huddle of passing villages. I had known Diefenbaker as a politician like no other – I had, in fact, written the book – but this would be the first land-bound passage I would take with him of such extended duration and poignancy. It was his fifth national campaign, and my disenchantment with Diefenbaker was by then complete, but I felt only admiration for his odyssey from these steppes to the nation's highest office. Each day, I rose at dawn to a pewter sky, which soon turned to a crisp autumnal light.

Even by the standards of the mid 1960s, it was an incredibly primitive operation. The brakeman riding the rear caboose could communicate with the conductor or locomotive engineer only through hand or lantern signals. The only way the press could stay in touch with their home office was to send telegrams along the way; these were plucked from the moving train with pincer-like gizmos held out by local telegraph operators.

Everyone sensed that a clear Liberal sweep was in the offing, so the press car was filled with second-tier reporters, more often sent to cover royal visits or to interview the widows of the victims of axe murderers. Diefenbaker had been reduced to a curiosity. The press car resounded to the Chief's high oratory as the radio correspondents played and edited their tapes. "What was that?" some print reporter would shout. "Play that again." The news reporters on a daily cycle were neither required nor allowed to stray far beyond a faithful reporting of Dief's speeches; by the end of the campaign, many could lip-synch his oratory word for word. Meanwhile, another reporter shouted "Cheat!" at the card table, while still another inquired loudly as to the likelihood of getting another bottle of booze from the porter. It was life inside a sound chamber, wrapped in a time capsule, contained in a madhouse. In such an environment, gossip and rumour spread quickly. Typical was the tale told by Ron Collister, a *Toronto Telegram* newsman who would pick the most gullible-looking person he could find at each station.

"See that whistle?" he would say, pointing at the locomotive.

"Uh, yep."

"That's not the *real* whistle. That's the high-frequency whistle. It's pitched so high that only dogs and reporters can hear it."

"Well, I'll be . . ." Whether they believed him or not, they were too polite to mention. (What Collister didn't realize was that since most of the locals equated journalists with canines, the story made perfect sense.)

I enjoyed special standing as "the guy who wrote *Renegade*," but tended to remain aloof from the usual fun and games. I always found it difficult to blend in with "the boys," and this voyage had an emotional element for me that I wanted to savour alone. It was closing a chapter for both the Chief and me, and I wanted to absorb all the drama of the occasion. Still, being somewhat removed from the daily grind made me a target for the rumour mill, and the tale was soon doing the rounds that Diefenbaker was about to kick me off the train. The story got back to the *Toronto Star*, and in response its editors arranged a charter plane that, if Dief carried through with his threat, would buzz every whistle stop, so my coverage could continue. Hearing this, I spread a counter-rumour – the Chief planned to kick me off the train personally, while it was *moving*. It was impossible to believe, of course, but the press gang would look at me with relief whenever I made an appearance. I was never sure whether they were nervous that Dief would follow through on his threat, or whether they wanted to be sure they hadn't missed out on a good colour piece, if he proceeded to carry it out.

The press car was filled with the noise of tapping typewriters, the tinkling of ice cubes, and the slap of cards on Formica tables, covered by the enormous din of conventioneers on a getaway. "C'mon, Newman," they would shout at me. "Stay for a game." I would meekly shake my head and lug my German tape recorder into plain sight. "Tapes," I would explain. "Transcribing my tapes." This gave rise to another rumour – that I was being leaked all the good stuff – but in fact the voice I was transcribing was my own. Throughout the day, I would whisper into my microphone what I saw and experienced: the sight of townspeople lining up on the station platform, squinting in the sun to catch sight of the Chief's approaching train; the coffee-talk; the dazzled reactions of station masters, heroes for a day.

In his private car, Diefenbaker dictated and signed three hundred letters a day to well-wishers along his route. Between whistle stops, particularly late in the day, fatigue would dissolve his face into deep creases and lines. The greatest campaigner Canada had ever known was showing his age. One night, I was in his carriage to clarify something or other, and he appeared in his bathrobe. He spoke to me while shuffling around with hunched shoulders, dodging and ducking like a prizefighter preparing for the ring.

THE CAMPAIGN HAD started in Halifax, where the omens had not been good. Our motorcade from the train station to his first speech at the Queen Elizabeth High School auditorium was escorted by a lone motorcycle cop, and a fat one at that. Always anxious to identify with his locale, Diefenbaker must have felt particularly desperate. "Had it not been for the trade winds between here and Newfoundland," he declared with a straight face, "my great-great-grandmother would have been born in Halifax."[1] The geographic nonsense did not matter, as those who came to see him were by then such die-hard Diefenbakerists that he could have

---

[1] Trade winds generally blow westward between the subtropics and the Equator.

said his ancestors arrived on favourable intergalactic winds from the star Betelgeuse and nobody would have noticed. A grizzled veteran with a handlebar moustache drooping at one end, waving a Union Jack, told me his name was George Fader, that he was eighty-four years old and had come all the way from Truro to glimpse Diefenbaker. Was that a hardship? "Praise God, no," he replied. "I've lived to see him." It dawned on me that recording the story of this campaign would be less about the politician than about his people.

Dief had to make a token appearance in Quebec, the province he never understood and which now treated him as an alien from another planet. He gamely tried a few words of French in Matapedia, where five off-duty trainmen and three stray dogs turned out to meet him. At Rimouski, seven lonely Tories were waiting on the platform. Diefenbaker didn't recognize the local candidate, though it turned out to be one of his former MPs, Gerard Ouellet. At Amqui, I happened to be standing beside Dief when he was introduced to a M. Legris, who in turn presented his son, standing beside him. "*C'est mon fils*," he said, proudly.

Diefenbaker smiled and extended his hand. "*Bonjour, Mon-sewer Mon-feece*," he said. *Hostie!*

Rather than doing the sensible thing, which might have been pretending they were a mass suicide cult, the few Tories in Quebec tried to improve the Chief's optics by loading a car on his train with supporters from Montreal. They dismounted at each stop to swell the welcoming crowds, and then climbed back on board for the next gig. But they eventually got bored and infiltrated the press car for free drinks, where they soon gave the game away.

It wasn't until the Diefenbaker train hit the Prairies that the campaign really started. At each waypoint, the station platform was filled with a (genuine) crowd bearing placards aloft, carrying their handwritten campaign slogan: "HE CARED ENOUGH TO COME." Nothing else mattered. Diefenbaker cared and he had come. Pearson, who was firing salvos of canned Liberal propaganda from his chartered jet, hadn't come and, by implication, didn't care.

What's more, if he did come he wouldn't understand. It was a political gimmick,[2] but to those of us who were there, it rang true.

The Chief moved like a legend over the land. Everywhere his train stopped, clusters of people would seek the sight of him under the slanting autumn sun. Men with fingers hooked into their broad belts gazed at the former prime minister, their wind-creased faces showing a warm glow of recognition. The wind fluttered the hair of the women as they shyly shook his hand to extend a mute blessing, occasionally performing a rusty curtsy. I walked through them and looked back at Dief, framed by the impatient train and a crowd that wanted him to stay at least another hour, and realized I was witnessing a unique tableau of gratitude and anger. The locals who turned out at these soon-to-be-abandoned waypoints had shown up because Diefenbaker reminded them of the time when they had been at the forefront of Canadian civilization. For that they were grateful, but there was anger as well. Theirs was the politics of resentment. For a while the Chief had offered hope – a hope, his people now realized, that would vanish with him.

Their fathers had turned the virgin sod and planted wheat fields, fed the eastern multitudes, and fought the good fight in two European wars. In return they had been pushed aside by a world they never made and seldom visited; they had seen their influence and legacy lost to the moneyed, urban East. They retreated into the hard nut of patient optimism that made their humour drier than the soil after a season's drought and their spirits more resilient than stinkweed. They had survived blizzard, locust, hail, and freight rates, but they knew they could not survive Dief's departure – there were no other Chiefs in line.

Our cynical journalistic impulse to jeer in these bucolic backwaters was quickly blunted on the stone of the people's authentic emotions. They were joyful that "John" had come, that was true, but also grieving that it would be for the last time. The hands shaken on platforms were work-worn, hard hands that connected people

---

[2] First used by Nelson Rockefeller in the 1964 Oregon presidential primaries.

to their mother soil. I met aging cowboys straight out of old-fashioned Hollywood Westerns, who used words like "varmints" to describe the infant-eating bankers who foreclose on loans. I met the Daisy Mae types, their fresh allure untainted by sophistication, and frequently wished that I were a cowboy. I talked to their canny mothers, who could lay their eyes on me and in the work of a minute have me figured out, as they liked to say, "six ways from Sunday." There was no spin out there. It got to the point where Tory organizer Hugh Arscott could accurately predict the size of the day's crowds by the dust on the road – if it was dry enough to harvest, the numbers would be down. Neither the Chief nor the Second Coming would ever get in the way of bringing in a crop, and Dief would not have it any other way.

Diefenbaker's rapport with his people was not built solely on remembering their names, shaking their hands, or reciting comforting homilies. It was mystical and it was palpable when he stood silently on the station platforms, looking into men's eyes and women's feelings, seeming to share their worries and fear of the future. He could do little now to improve their lot, but it was the contact – the sight of him – they wanted, and that was enough.

He was comfortable among them, at his playful best as he called out to some old-timers in Melville, Saskatchewan: "When did you get here?"

The oldest among them proudly replied that he had arrived in 1903.

"*When* in '03?" Diefenbaker retorted.

"September, I recall . . ."

A gleeful Diefenbaker shot back: "We came in *August!*"

At Morse, local musicians serenaded him with an unsteady version of "The Thunderer." I couldn't file my copy because the telegrapher was playing drums in the civic band; all I could do was hang around the caboose, watching. As the train pulled out, the band struck up "God Be with You until We Meet Again." I hopped on board the departing train and saw, for the only time in my life, John Diefenbaker in tears.

Later in Swift Current, Saskatchewan (known to residents as "Speedy Creek"), two dozen blue-gowned ladies from some church choir swayed in time to the music from the back of a flatbed truck. When they broke into an emotional rendition of "Land of Hope and Glory," Diefenbaker's sound baritone voice joined the chorus. It was my turn for tears.[3]

At Duck Lake, he told a cluster of adoring supporters: "They say I've made mistakes. But they were mistakes of the heart." Somewhere along the route, an old man sat by the tracks in the fading light, holding up a crudely lettered sign as the train rolled past: "JOHN, YOU'LL NEVER DIE."

He spoke mostly from the back of the train over a great megaphone, his beloved wife, Olive, beside him, and never said anything much except that he was sure glad to be there. It was a communion that no other politician could comprehend, much less replicate. In such company, with my background and high profile, I stood out like an evil creature from Hades. It was important for me to bird-dog Diefenbaker as closely as possible to pick up the small details so essential to my style of writing, and we had more than a few "elevator moments" where he either looked right through me, shot me a look with the venom of a snake's tongue, or just gazed at me while cursing under his breath. But he never upbraided me publicly and he allowed me to stay on the train. What I wrote was no longer important to him; he had come to be with his folk, and nothing else mattered.

In Taber, we enjoyed a boil-up of the sweetest fall corn in Christendom. The Chief told a hush of schoolchildren: "I only wish that I could come back when you're my age to see the kind of Canada that you'll see. So dream your dreams; keep them and pursue them."

---

[3] The oddest musical accompaniment to the campaign was played by a group calling itself The Cotton Pickers in Prince Albert. They opened with a Hawaiian luau tune and went on to play polkas.

In support of my nascent theory that kookiness increases in direct relation to the proximity of the Pacific Ocean, it was in the foothills town of Fort Macleod, Alberta, that I heard a pensioner whisper in the Chief's ear: "That Pearson is a devil! He wants to give away the Crowsnest Mountain to Quebec!" That terse prediction sent me out to walk the land and relax a bit. It was a wet day, and I remembered classical composer Igor Stravinsky's comment that "the smell of Russian earth is different." The smell of damp Prairie soil at harvest time is different too, I thought. Stravinsky also said that "such things are impossible to forget," and I have never lost the nurturing scent of that good black loam. The story of a country emerges slowly from its landscape, through dinosaur bones, arrowheads, and the memories of what once moved. Dief, I knew, would not be forgotten in his own land. Then I heard the whistle calling us mad dogs – and canines, too – and quickly returned to the train. We moved north then, across the Alberta badlands.

At Stettler, two raggedy kids were proudly waving a huge, hand-lettered cardboard sign: "DIEF FOR CHEIF."

By the time we hit Calgary and Edmonton, his campaign was on fire. We were being escorted in style, with three sleek outriders on each side of the Chief's car and saluting police officers waving us through intersections.

WHAT ENDOWED THE WHISTLE-STOP tour with its thin ration of substance was Diefenbaker's nightly oratory at high schools, Legion halls, and community centres. His speeches were reminiscent of old-time tent revival meetings, where the language of exhortation took the place of logical discourse. As Diefenbaker rose each night, his manner was at first halting, his voice muted, as though gathering strength, unwilling to expend his remaining energy. The crowd would hush to catch his words. Once his listeners had committed their attention, his voice would take on an infectious rhythm, clipped consonants alternating with long open vowels, the Biblical cadence of a fired-up evangelist, harvesting souls for the Lord. The left hand would hold back his ever-present imaginary lawyer's robes, while his right hand swooped down in accusatory chops. The whole man swayed to the melody of his words, giving physical expression to his outrage. After attending dozens of these rural pageants, I realized they were not political events at all, but a shared celebration of faith. Diefenbaker reminded his listeners of a simpler time when people lived in one house all their lives, with one woman, one God, and one hairstyle. He invoked a time when people did a little business so they could socialize, instead of the other way around; when they still entertained themselves with games of cribbage and "500," and the wives cooked hot cross buns on Sundays.

He would take on a highly formal and tragic tone while reciting the woes of the Liberal government, like some gruff ship's captain performing a burial at sea. The next instant, with the energy born of gloating, he would call down hellfire on the wicked Grits. When the moment demanded, he would invent words ("Those crimesters who support the Liberal Party"), mangle his metaphors ("I never look a gift horse in the eye!"), and clang together head-shaking non sequiturs: ("I owe you all so much! Why do I continue in public life?").

The dullest part of every speech was his recitation of Tory election pledges. Diefenbaker didn't understand (and probably hadn't read) his own policy platform. One Tory scheme promised that up to five hundred dollars could be deducted from federal taxes to help pay municipal levies – but only for those living in owner-occupied houses. In Winnipeg, he baffled his audience by referring to the scheme as being limited to "home-occupied houses." In Medicine Hat, he declared that "only home-owning owners" would qualify. In Simcoe, Ontario, he said the scheme was limited to "home-owning occupied houses." When I phoned Campaign chairman Eddie Goodman at Tory campaign headquarters in Ottawa for an explanation, he quipped: "We'll give you an answer when we think of one."

Once a week Goodman and his crew of youthful advisers would hold a late-night session at the Chateau Laurier Hotel to discuss their tactics, including campaign slogans. Jim Johnson, a young economist I had once worked with at *The Financial Post*, who was advising the campaign, came up with a slogan that not only tapped into most Canadians' feelings about the leader, but turned it into an honest appeal for votes: "GIVE THE OLD BUGGER ANOTHER CHANCE!" It didn't make the cut. Another time, when it looked as though Diefenbaker might have a winning chance, Goodman looked around at his crew of helpers, most of whom had opposed the Man from Prince Albert at some time in the past, and told them: "If Dief wins, there is going to be the biggest political bloodbath this country has ever seen – and much of that blood is now running in the veins of those in this hotel room." The remark was greeted with shrieks of laughter, and the assembled company began to plot how they would react on election night following a Diefenbaker victory. It was agreed that Goodman would go on national television and apologize to the people of Canada for having played such a monstrous practical joke on them. He would declare, "You weren't supposed to vote for us," then the entire Tory headquarters crew would join hands and leap off the roof of the Chateau Laurier.

AFTER WITNESSING a great deal of open adulation, I got a glimpse of another side of John Diefenbaker's place in the public mind when we left the train to campaign on Vancouver Island. We were both waiting for the same elevator in the lobby of the Empress Hotel in Victoria. The Chief was going up to rest for the next day's exertions, while I was preparing to write an account of his disastrous performance earlier that evening at the local armoury.

But the lift was a long time coming, and we both turned as a giggle of girls passed us on their way to a dance. The Chief tensed a little and half extended his hand to them in greeting. The girls paid him no attention and he slowly drew it back. He was the best-known and the most controversial politician in the land, fighting his most exciting campaign. Yet none of the young faces registered the slightest flicker of recognition. We looked at one another. For one revealing moment, I saw a man struck by the terrifying realization that the new generation was immune to his political magic. To them, he was just another old guy, and if they knew him at all, it was as a duffer out of the history books, possibly that one who drove in the Last Spike. Dief had been born when Queen Victoria was on the throne. This was the Swinging Sixties, when The Pill was not something you took for headaches and "drugs" were not what your doctor gave you. He was trying to remain relevant in a spinning world of moon shots and mass protest. As he stood there, uncomfortable and unrecognized, John Diefenbaker looked a million years old, and I felt sorry for him.

The elevator arrived and the old Dief reasserted himself. "How do you do?" he said, holding out his hand to the startled, smiling, middle-aged operator.

I knew at that moment that Dief was terminally out of touch with the new generation of Canadians. He had originally made a pitch to the impatient, ethnic youth of the West and promised them a nation where they could carve out a Northern Frontier and join it as equal citizens. His crusade had started with a speech in Winnipeg seven years earlier, when young women swooned as though he were a Beatle. Now in Victoria he didn't warrant a second look. The good people of the plains would always be his, but he had lost the younger urban generation elsewhere.

The leader had picked up a canary somewhere along the way, and spent hours trying to coax the bird to sing. He was convinced it would be a good omen if the bird whistled, but the canary just sat there, and the two of them cocked their bird-like heads at one another. The bird never did sing, but on the morning of November 4 in Saskatoon, the train's steward, Fred Tomlinson, did a passable canary imitation while the Chief's back was turned. Diefenbaker was delighted and became quite excited. "Did you hear that? The canary whistled! It whistled, I tell you! Things are looking *up*!"

He was never told the truth: that every other omen pointed in the opposite direction. Mass movements like Diefenbaker's will always wane in popularity once they overtake the events or circumstances that gave them birth. Diefenbaker's time had run its course. The cities had all the votes. Toronto alone elected more MPs than all of Alberta. The whistle stops hadn't turned the tide. By the end of the campaign, he seemed to be moving by numbers, the energy drained out of him. He looked like a drooping Madame Tussaud's wax figure, in which the paraffin has run.

When we reached Diefenbaker's home riding of Prince Albert two days before polling day, a foot or two of snow lay on the ground. It was not the same country where the election had started, in either mood or weather. We were moved into the Marlboro Hotel while the official party remained aboard CNR Car 97 at the railway station.[4]

That Sunday evening before the vote, I went for a walk through Prince Albert. The town was deserted, lines of street lights setting off the evergreens that marched in dark and serried stillness toward the northern horizon. I must have come too close to one of the "home-occupied houses" because a dog barked, setting off a chain reaction of yelping pups up the street. I walked by the old

---

[4] We had been rehearsing campaign songs all the way across the country and during a Saturday night's alcoholic daze decided that our musical talents were too precious not to be immortalized. Paul Champagne, the campaign's wagon master, arranged for Lumby Productions to come up from Saskatoon and record the performance. We commandeered a local radio station studio and spent Sunday cutting a record: LPLP 120, which still exists, with Susan Dexter on piano, CNR porter Fred Tomlinson on guitar, and me on drums. We called ourselves The Press Corps and Fugue Society and let go with eight numbers, including "East Block Blues," "The Resurrection Chorus," and "Grit Jiggin' Ground." Since we never played together again, we were justified in boasting that we had never sounded better.

Lincoln Hotel and went across Central Avenue, past the two-storey Toronto-Dominion Bank building, prominently proclaiming: "Diefenbaker, Cuelenaere & Hall, Law Offices." The town had been an important fur trade depot, and the Hudson's Bay Company sheds were still there. (I would return to the region twenty years later to research my history of the Hudson's Bay Company, which had once owned all of that spread out real estate.) Encouraged by the clarity of thought brought on by a bottle of vintage Baby Duck, I pledged that I would someday write a tribute worthy of the men and women I had seen and met on this incredible campaign.

The election results poured in the next day. Considering the circumstances, the vote was a triumph for the Old Chief. He held the Liberals to a minority government. Outside Quebec, he won fourteen more seats than the Liberals. All of his western whistle stops had gone solidly Tory, but only one Conservative (Lincoln Alexander) survived in the fifty constituencies of Canada's largest cities. It was clear that Dief was Yesterday's Man and would have to go, whether he wanted to or not.

Tomorrow's Man would eventually arrive in the form of a hip, young, bilingual (able to shrug in either language), bachelor lawyer from Montreal, in sandals and Roman curls. Pierre Trudeau would become the Prime Minister of Peace and Love, while Dief had represented Fire and Brimstone. Trudeau would be the better prime minister, but Dief remained unrivalled on the campaign trail. He was the mass-media politician who could still touch people in church halls. His powers of oration and his ability to generate a cult of personality were never matched, but he over-stayed his welcome and had to go.

FORTY YEARS AFTER he stepped into obscurity, Diefenbaker continues to command affection. The younger generation love him because he was so camp, so cool. His style is still gently mocked. An older generation remembers that he articulated a vision of Canada every bit as legitimate as Pierre Trudeau's. He extended human rights and the electoral franchise. If he failed to bring westerners, Natives, ethnics, and immigrants (including the *Yew-Kah-Rain-Ians*) into the warm parlour of Confederation, at least he made them more comfortable on the porch. And he did it all with smoke and mirrors. He believed in no destiny but his own. He was our Wizard, and he treated Canada as his Land of Oz. He conned us into believing him, and when the Land of Dief failed to materialize, why, he just went back to the polls and conned us again.

We never held it against him. We loved being taken. He gave us a 92.5-cent dollar and we called it the "Diefenbuck" – oh, what a lovely joke! When the threat of nuclear conflict was at its worst, we called his fallout shelter in Carp, Ontario, the "Diefenbunker" – oh, what a lovely war!

There is a part in everyone who remembers him that secretly wants him back. In what can only be described as a lighthearted lark in 1974, Bob Bossin, leader and banjo player for the folk group Stringband, composed a song called "Dief Will Be the Chief Again." He sent a tape to CBC Radio's *As It Happens*, then going through one of its periodic Diefenbaker retrospectives, desperate for anything fresh. The following night the song was reviewed on the program – by Dief himself.

"Barn-burner, isn't it, sir?" asked host Alan Maitland.

Silence.

"Well, Mr. Diefenbaker?" asked Barbara Frum.

"As a connoisseur of good music," Dief replied, "I am simply delighted."

The song had a devoted cult following in this country and was number one at CKBI Radio in Prince Albert.

Our affection for Dief has grown posthumously, out of a national reluctance to say anything nice about politicians until they are long dead and buried. The image of his rattling jowls and Marie Antoinette curls, courtesy of Duncan Macpherson's cartoons, remains indelible in the Canadian psyche. The most popular television advertisement in recent years had a young man reprising a variation of Dief's "I am a Canadian" speech. Bob Robertson and Linda Cullen of *Double Exposure* performed a Canadian comedy classic when they marked the hundredth anniversary of Dief's birth with a skit about a call-in radio show from beyond the grave, "Diefenbaker Live on Newsworld."

DIEF: You, madam, remind me of a skunk that I once ran across while stumping my constituency in Prince Albert. That pesky skunk and I found ourselves blocking each other's path. And there was the most odious smell in the air, and I simply yelled "SHOO!" and it was gone.

CALLER: Well, what does that have to do with . . .?

DIEF: SHOO!

"Diefenbaker" surfaced again as a half-breed Arctic white wolf, the canine companion of RCMP Constable Benton Fraser (Paul Gross) in the hit television comedy-drama *Due South*. The dog was bad-tempered, stubborn, and able to lip-read in Inuktitut. The ultra-cool Canadian rock group The Rheostatics released an album in 1996, *Music Inspired by the Group of Seven*, which included a sample and remix of Dief reading the Second World War poem "High Flight." He is the subject of thirty-six books, the most recent of which, *Diefenbaker for the Defence*, was published in 1999. The placards held by the tracks in his last campaign as party leader were right: "JOHN, YOU'LL NEVER DIE."

I JOINED THE CHIEF for his last personal campaign in May 1979, flying to Prince Albert, Saskatchewan. Dief was well in decline by then. What I did not realize, until much later, was that the former prime minister was experiencing a serious health crisis. In the previous two years, he had become obsessed with planning his funeral, and he was delighted when his special assistant, Michael McCafferty, suggested that his unrepentant remains be moved by train, recalling the historic journey of Abraham Lincoln's coffin from Washington, D.C., to Springfield, Illinois. "After that," recalled Bunny Pound, his former secretary, "he was always talking about the damn funeral train, who would be on it, where it should stop, and constantly revising his list of pallbearers. He would scream with laughter when he thought about it."

During this campaign for his final re-election as MP, Diefenbaker accepted only one non-partisan speaking engagement, to the Saskatchewan Nurses Association, when the campaign was just getting underway. He regaled them with the usual anecdotes, but then he got stuck. "I appointed the first French-Canadian governor general," he boasted, but he couldn't remember Georges Vanier's name. "For the first time in Canadian history!" he emphasized, obviously searching his memory for that elusive moniker. Finally he thought he had it: "Yes," he thundered, "the first Canadian governor general: Dwight Eisenhower!" No one in the audience seemed to notice his memory lapse, but soon afterwards he experienced one of his seizures.

"He suffered a seizure on Good Friday in the 1979 campaign," McCafferty confided to me, long after the Chief was dead. "We were in the Baptist church. I could see his eyes starting to roll and I just sensed it was going to happen. I knew this was going to be a serious situation and sure enough it was. I got him back to the hotel and that night we had a real bad situation in terms of the campaign. We cooked up a story about him having the flu, though at that time his seizure was so bad that he actually had a minor stroke.

"The poor man," McCafferty sadly reminisced. "When he had these seizures, he didn't know where he was or who he was. On that Saturday morning after Good Friday, he was calling me 'Big Boy,' his nickname for his friend Max Carment that he'd used when they were growing up together."

McCafferty recalled for me the sad tableau:

"Where are we?" Dief asked, surfacing from his fit of grand mal epilepsy.

"We're in Prince Albert, sir."

"What are we doing here? How did we get here?"

"Well, we flew."

Dief looked puzzled and wanted to know, "Why are we here?"

"We're here for the election, sir."

Dief looked startled; his loyal aide was shocked by what he said next: "Did King dissolve the House?

"Pardon me, sir?"

"Did Mackenzie King dissolve the House? And where is Edna [Edna Mae Brower, his first wife]?"

McCafferty stood by Dief's bed with tears rolling down his face. He held the old Chief's hand. "Sir . . . this is 1979."

"I could just see the shock in his face . . ." he later told me.

THERE WAS A MANIC, almost irrational edge to Dief that became more worrisome with his passing years. As it turned out, Canadians were not only in the dark about his physical frailty, but also only vaguely aware of the mental imbalances that accompanied it.

The novelist Hugh MacLennan, whom I had then yet to meet, wrote me following publication of *Renegade*. It was a startling letter, which came close to being a psychoanalysis of the Chief as he referred to a recent encounter with him:

> The more he sought to protect himself by will, by authoritarianism, by Biblical quotations, by false camaraderie, the more Diefenbaker stripped his soul. His was the most tormented, unresolved Oedipus complex I have ever encountered in an important man. He was driven by it all his life, as so many millions of us are, and underneath he lived in a kind of terror. Something of this, I suppose, was at the root of his charismatic appeal. More people pitied him, despite what they may have said against him, than he could ever guess. And underneath was the uneasy feeling he created in the nation, the unlocking of similar aspects of the personality within millions, which endowed him a kind of unconscious

admiration because so many of us felt, intuitively, that if he failed catastrophically, we failed with him. Along with this went something else: the collapse of the easy theory of the divinely inspired hick which died in the States during the 1920s and never existed at all in Eastern Canada.

Diefenbaker had haunted MacLennan since the summer of 1958, when he, along with *Maclean's* writer Barbara Moon, had interviewed the prime minister at his official residence. "Later that day, I became physically sick; I literally threw up," the novelist wrote me. "This was clearly because of some uncanny power the man had of animal communication. I remember saying to somebody then that if I had within me the conflicts that raged in Diefenbaker, I would be torn apart inside forty-eight hours." MacLennan also revealed an exchange that took place that day but couldn't be used publicly. Under the terms of the interview, it was stricken from the record.

Barbara Moon asked the prime minister: "But Mr. Prime Minister, as you describe your father, aren't you making him appear a little forbidding?" Diefenbaker leaped to his feet with his face contorted, and snarled: "That question doesn't exist! Enough of this! You psychologists shall not leave here wresting from me the secrets you have come to discover." MacLennan confided in me: "I swear, this was the most naked thing I ever encountered in a sober man in all my life."

The debate of over Diefenbaker's psychological state seldom surfaced during his lifetime, and even posthumously it remained the sole purview of academics. Following a lengthy interview with the Chief in the mid 1970s, Professor Jack Granatstein, the York University historian, recalled: "I regret to say that I left his office convinced that I had been in the presence of evil for the first and only time in my life." The University of Toronto's Michael Bliss took that notion even further, writing about his "palpable touch of madness" and quoting unnamed colleagues of the Chief who "claimed that his last will should be declared void because he had

not been mentally competent when he drew it up." He also reproduced a conversation between Ontario premier Leslie Frost, who
said of Diefenbaker to Conservative organizer Eddie Goodman in
1961: "Sometimes I really do believe he's crazy." To which Eddie
responded: "Why only sometimes?"

I never subscribed to such sensational rumours, believing myself
unfit to judge the mental state of others. But I did often wonder
at his periodic paranoia and loss of self-control. I am convinced
that John Diefenbaker, especially in his later years, was a victim of
a severe case of epilepsy, which, combined with his medications,
might have affected his behaviour. My source for this conclusion
was mainly Michael McCafferty, the Saskatchewan political science
graduate who was his special assistant for the last three years of his
life. One of his jobs was to give Dief his regular doses of Dilantin
and Divalproex, medications prescribed by his personal physician,
Dr. J.C. Samis, to control his epileptic symptoms.[5] The high doses
of these medications "would have explained a lot of his erratic
behaviour, like constantly flying into rages," McCafferty told me.
"The seizures got more and more frequent toward his death. It
took an awful toll on him. He would rip the whole room apart.
I was amazed at his strength. Of course at the time, there was a
conspiracy of silence and I firmly believed in it myself out of
loyalty; that we were never to ever tell anybody. But I was petrified
that his seizures might happen any time, even in the House of
Commons. Amazingly enough, they didn't."

DESPITE HIS FRAILTY, he could still bring down thunder with his
oratory. The day before the vote (which he won with a 4,200
majority), Diefenbaker spoke at a Legion hall near Prince Albert.
I squeezed into the last row at the last minute, hiding behind a

---

[5] One study of the symptoms treated by Divalproex describes them as "motor
hyperactivity, reduced need for sleep, flights of ideas, grandiosity, poor judgment, aggressiveness and hostility." Enough said.

rhino-sized Legionnaire, hoping not to be noticed, in case I riled the Chief unnecessarily. All went well as he launched into his vintage harangue.

Suddenly, he stopped cold. I could feel his eyes drilling into me.

"There *he* is," he triumphantly announced, to the audience's puzzlement.

"There he is!" he repeated, pointing at me, without mentioning my crime or my name.

"THERE HE IS . . .

"THAT HIRELING OF LIBERALISM . . .

"WHO WRITES PSEUDO-BIOGRAPHIES . . .

"FOR MONETARY GAIN!!!"

In a flash, the audience connected the two of us and realized who I was. The finely coiffed Baptist matron sitting beside me became so agitated she popped her hairpins. The legionnaires broke into heckles and jeers aimed in my direction. I hooted and hollered along with the best of them. Who was I to quibble, even if only the last part of his accusation was true?

I had arranged to meet Peter Lougheed later that day at his hotel room in Prince Albert. The Alberta premier was in town to give Dief's campaign a boost, and I wanted to interview him about his jurisdictional wars with Ottawa. When I arrived in the premier's suite that evening, there was John Diefenbaker holding court.

We looked at one another like vanquished knights, too spent to feel anger or regret.

"You spoke well today," I sputtered. I sensed this would be my last chance to clear the air between us and I searched for the right words. "I've attacked you, but I've never stopped respecting your courage or admiring your spirit. You are a great man, sir."

He looked at me, but said nothing. There was nothing left to say.

Three months later, he was dead.

DIEFENBAKER DIED FOURTEEN years after his last national campaign. On August 22, 1979, he was laid to rest by the side of his second wife, Olive, on a grassy knoll overlooking the South Saskatchewan River at the University of Saskatchewan campus in Saskatoon. His papers and archives are stored at the nearby Diefenbaker Centre and a human rights institution that operates in his name. He was an inveterate pack rat: his archive comprises three million documents. A bronze plaque at the graveside marks his resting place with a brief tribute. It is a peaceful spot, with the lazy river making its stately progress north and the prairie winds rustling softly through the willows.

John Diefenbaker and I were opponents, certainly, but respectful ones. His casual anti-Semitism and petty-minded streaks could be pardoned; his failure to translate his vision into reality once in office could not. I owed him, not only for inspiring in me the confidence to believe I could go anywhere and do anything despite my ethnic background. He also gave my pen the raw materials it needed for getting me there. He was a shooting star that flashed across the sky, then fell back to earth in the silent heart of the country, whence he came.

CHAPTER EIGHT

BUMBLING TO BABYLON

~卿⊙

*His dedication to civility and decency
made Mike Pearson behave as if he would rather
be himself than be a great prime minister.
His tragedy was that he could not be both.*

As prime minister, John Diefenbaker always kept the red
NORAD hotline telephone on prominent display in his
East Block office. "Why, I can get the American president
at any time!" he would boast to visitors. After Lester Bowles
"Mike" Pearson took office in the spring of 1963, he removed the
emergency instrument from its prominent location and hid it
carelessly behind a curtain. When it suddenly began to ring one
winter morning during Cold War tensions, he couldn't find it. He
had been interrupted in mid-conversation with his External
Affairs minister Paul Martin, and the two men began chasing each
other around the room like a pair of Keystone Kops. "My God,
Mike," gasped Martin, as they failed to locate the source of the
sound. "Do you realize this could mean war?"

"They can't start a war," puffed the optimistic Pearson, "if we
don't answer the phone." As it turned out, the caller was a confused
Bell subscriber who wanted to speak to "Charlie" and had mistak-
enly dialled the most highly classified number in the country.

That little vignette summed up the stewardship of Mike Pearson,
Canada's ace diplomat, who wore a dented political crown uneasily

from April 1963 to April 1968. To this day, he is revered as having been unfailingly civil, engagingly friendly, and likeably unpretentious. Up close, however, his government had a different hue. Despite being groomed by a long career in the elite foreign service, Pearson was chronically ill prepared for power and despite its many accomplishments, the daily record of his government was a series of mishaps that threatened to blunder into farce.

Speaking of farce, I was the first to publish the NORAD hotline incident. I approached Pearson later, who confirmed my account's veracity, so I asked him whether he had ever actually used the emergency telephone. "Certainly," he replied, and even remembered the date. "On April 21, 1967, I was being driven to my summer residence on Harrington Lake when the car struck a rock and broke its transmission. I used the phone to call for a tow truck. I had to go through the American military, at a time they were urging us to spend more on national defence. They weren't impressed, but did forward my message to a garage in Aylmer."[1]

"Our Mike" had a deserved reputation for unassuming sincerity. The problem, as the impish Tory senator Grattan O'Leary liked to point out, was that "no one can be sure from day to day what he's going to be sincere about." Instead of offering leadership, Pearson presided over Canada as if he were still president of the General Assembly of the United Nations, with the provinces sitting in as member states. In 1965 alone, he staged 125 federal-provincial

---

[1] That was before the Harrington road had been paved, when it was little more than a treacherous logging access road. In those pre-security days, there was no fence around the prime minister's country retreat, no locked gates, and no RCMP security detail. Hikers and backpackers often knocked on the PM's door to ask for directions and were never turned away.

When he first settled into the Harrington Lake lodge, Pearson was told that his predecessor had caught a four-and-a-half-pound trout, which really upset him because he couldn't beat that record. He finally tracked down a local farmer who assured him that Diefenbaker had indeed hooked a fish that size, but never managed to land it in his boat. That allowed Pearson to enjoy life at the cottage. The two leaders never stopped competing.

conferences. His motto was the avoidance of catastrophe through the negotiation of a last-minute compromise. "We'll jump off that bridge when we come to it," he would reassure his nervous aides, while studiously leading from the rear.

His Cabinet, initially hailed as an assembly of the country's brightest talents, was soon racked by scandal. Half a dozen of his ministers and their aides were forced to resign – instead of peace, order, and good government, Pearson's time in office was characterized by blitzkrieg, bedlam, and bad government. Obviously, it was a fabulous time to be an Ottawa journalist.

Pearson had earned the sobriquet of "Honest Broker" on the international scene, with a Nobel Peace Prize to prove it, having introduced the idea of international peacekeeping forces during the 1956 Suez crisis. As prime minister, he bolstered Canada's position as a "middle power" and sent Canadian armed forces under UN command to put out regional brush fires in the Gaza Strip, India–Pakistan, and Cyprus.[2] It was ironic that he failed to keep the peace on his home turf. Despite his reputation on the world stage, his untidy and ethically challenged administration left him cast as King Rat in a low-budget gangster film. No episode sullied his government more than the case of Lucien Rivard, a Mafioso who had managed a gambling den in pre-Castro Cuba

---

[2] Unable to figure out whether we were the least of the great powers or the greatest of the small powers, we decided in the smug afterglow of the Second World War to become something called a "middle power." We sent contingents of peacekeeping soldiers into trouble spots under United Nations auspices, where they would be shot at, mauled, and manhandled, but not permitted to return fire or retaliate in any way. It was perfect casting. Out of that dazzling display of diffidence grew our reputation as international "good guys." It also meant that Canadian passports became a valuable commodity; having one identified its bearer as essentially harmless. Several of the most senior Soviet spymasters (including such major players as Robert Soblen, Colonel Rudolph Abel, and Gordon Lonsdale, who obtained the plans of Britain's nuclear submarines) operated on Canadian passports. Many modern spy masters continue this proud tradition.

and later became a ringleader in the North American heroin trade. Rivard was arrested in Canada during the summer of 1964 and sent to Bordeaux jail near Montreal. The United States petitioned for his immediate extradition to stand trial as a Mafia kingpin. Instead, at least four of the Liberal government's most influential ministerial assistants, including Guy Rouleau, Pearson's own parliamentary secretary, lobbied the government relentlessly to grant Rivard bail – in other words, to spring him.

Before that could happen, Rivard sprang himself – with a little help from his friends. Late one March afternoon, with the outside temperature well above freezing, Rivard was allowed to leave Bordeaux's main enclosure to water the outdoor skating rink, even though it was already melting and overflowing its edges. He used the water hose to slide down the prison wall and disappeared into the night. Such hanky-panky was meat and drink to Opposition leader John Diefenbaker, who referred to Rivard first as "a destroyer of men's souls," which quickly escalated into "that inhuman beast, walking around with seventy pounds of heroin, enough to degenerate almost a whole generation." Finally (and inexplicably), Dief linked the gangster directly to Pearson by demanding at an election rally in Fort William: "Where was the prime minister when they threw the bodies into the lime pits?"[3]

The Pearson record included several impressive accomplishments – a national health insurance scheme, a national pension plan, the restriction of capital punishment to murderers of police officers and prison guards, a made-in-Canada flag – but these were in danger of being overshadowed by the many scandals. Things got so bad that at one annual Press Gallery dinner, Pearson began his speech by raising his right hand. It was encased in a black Cosa Nostra glove, and it brought the house down.

---

[3] The Grits exacted their revenge on Erik Nielsen, the Conservatives' Yukon MP, who acted as his party's prosecuting attorney. His taxes were audited so often that he was forced to spend most of his time over the frozen tundra, flying a bush plane to earn the money he allegedly owed National Revenue.

Among my best sources were members of the diplomatic corps – intelligent, sophisticated, world-weary, and frustrated by the irrelevance of their sub-Arctic postings – who had nothing better to do than stay well informed about Ottawa's political shenanigans. Tony Lovink, the ambassador for the Netherlands and dean of Ottawa's diplomatic corps, summed it up for me over jellied consommé at the Rideau Club. "Pearson delegates too much authority without imposing the required discipline," he observed. "He has lost control of his Cabinet. Canada is the only ship of state that leaks from the top."

It was true, and I was at the receiving end of the tap. I published so many leaks in my column that Pearson opened a Cabinet meeting by reading aloud from one of my columns, which quoted, verbatim, remarks made in a previous closed session. This despite the confidentiality of Cabinet deliberations, kept sacrosanct by custom and by law. "I am fed up with reading about this government's intimate deliberations before they're cold on my tongue," he cautioned. "I implore you not to talk to Newman, not to allow your assistants to talk to Newman, and not even to talk to your wives who might conceivably talk to Newman." (A full account of this meeting, of course, had reached me before the day was out, as did the makeup and instructions of the special caucus committee on secrecy set up by Pearson.)

Walter Gordon, one of his government's most senior privy councillors who was my friend but not my source, remarked with a straight face that it might be a kindness to give me a chair. "It must be pretty uncomfortable for Peter to be crouched under the table while the Cabinet's in session," he said, then burst into laughter as two ministers actually glanced surreptitiously under the table to see if I were really down there. Pearson was not amused. "If this leaks out," he warned, "I'll fire you all." His harangue was faithfully reported in my *Star* column two days later.

I never enjoyed plying my mad craft more than I did during the Porous Pearson Period. "The politicians pay attention to Newman," wrote the magazine journalist June Callwood in *Saturday Night*.

"On a Saturday last October, he wrote a column on the disgruntlement in Liberal ranks, saying the bloom was off the regime. The following Monday, Pearson went around the Cabinet table to ask: 'Is Newman right? Are we through? Am I through?' 'Oh no, Mike, certainly not,' his ministers responded as one. 'Newman is a doom crier. He went after Dief, now he's going after you.' That Wednesday, the new Gallup poll appeared showing, of course, a 7 per cent drop in Liberal support." She generously characterized me as "The Hill's relentless seeker after political Progress and Truth, and therefore prone to high-mindedness, fits of gloom, and a certain intolerance of human frailties."

MY REPUTATION HAD BEEN SECURED with the runaway sales of *Renegade*, but if I possessed a "certain intolerance of human frailties," I was most harshly intolerant of my own. Having tasted the first fruits of success, I hungered after the full banquet of recognition, money, access, and influence. I whipped myself into ever-greater efforts, and in 1964 I switched from being Ottawa editor of *Maclean's* to resident columnist for the *Toronto Star*. The move was prompted by an offer from my hero and mentor, Ralph Allen, who had left *Maclean's* to become managing editor of the *Star*. The move expanded my exposure exponentially through the *Star*'s syndicate of thirty Canadian dailies, including the largest in every province, with a combined circulation of 2.5 million readers. Whatever my influence, I had the numbers. No Ottawa commentator, before or since, has enjoyed such a massive readership. My closest competitors were Charles Lynch of the Southam chain, with a circulation of 630,000, and the Fisher-Crowe *Telegram* syndicate, with 300,000 readers. It was my good fortune that just as I had reached such a wide audience, Ottawa had become an abattoir of political reputations. I became chief chronicler of the carnage, secure in the knowledge that the worse the government, the better the copy.

More by default than design – the capital's social scene then lacking animators – Christina and I became one of *the* Ottawa power couples. We hosted a whirlwind of parties that were popular because they were refreshingly lacking in formalities, agendas, or airs of any kind. Our invitation list was drawn up on the basis of who was interesting rather than who was important, and as a result the conversation flowed like wine, the ideas bubbled like champagne, and the food – ordered from Boushey's Delicatessen – vanished like the dew. Christina was a skilled and gracious hostess who revelled in bringing people together and having her home the centre of activity. She enjoyed being the focus of attention and was always impeccably turned out in the latest fashions, purchased on her frequent visits to Holt Renfrew in Toronto and Montreal, there being few decent boutiques in Ottawa at that time.[4]

Christina, of course, continued to write, later noting: "Because of the restrictions on the subjects that women were thought capable of writing then, commentary on cabinet decisions of consequence, particularly when they had to do with economics, or international affairs were thought to be beyond our scope." She wrote on all those subjects, as well as definitive profiles of Maryon Pearson and Olive Diefenbaker, but mostly, she helped me write *The Distemper of Our Times*, a popular history of the Pearson hiccup. Her editing was every writer's dream because she possessed a sixth sense for the right phrase. She once described her role as being my "researcher and editor, an extra pair of eyes and ears." She was all that and much more, encouraging me in expressing my feelings about events and people.

We were the first English-speaking journalists to entertain Pierre Trudeau, who had recently been elected as a Liberal in Mount Royal and appointed as Pearson's minister of Justice. At that time he was squiring Madeleine Gobeil, a spirited Gallic soulmate he had met while she was an undergraduate at the University of Montreal.

---

[4] In one of her articles, Christina disdained the typical fashion sense of an Ottawa spouse as trying for "that little-brown-hen look: shiny clean undyed hair, cashmere sweater, string of pearls, black silk dress, white kid gloves, old beaver coat – maybe a small, tatty mink stole."

They spent fourteen years in an intimate, romantic *entente cordiale*, with Pierre never quite promising a more permanent commitment, while not entirely dismissing the possibility, either. I recall one particular evening when they came to visit us and could hardly keep their hands off one another, rolling on our living-room carpet and embracing as if they both meant business.[5]

A sampling of the letters that Christina wrote to my mother during these years (which I inherited after she died in 1986) gives some indication of how deeply we were implicated in our work and the attendant whirl at social functions, and how subtly this had shifted our priorities:

- I think Peter should really take at least a week's rest. When he's feeling well, he just never stops working.
- Colorado [the NORAD headquarters at Colorado Springs] was lovely – like a summer resort – I had an eight-hour interview with an Air Marshall and we were guests of honour at his home. I also had some good interviews at the Pentagon. Nothing else new. Working like mad.
- On Friday we're invited to three things – two cocktail parties and one dinner – all of which we ought to attend.
- I think what's wrong with Peter is mostly exhaustion. He never gets enough rest, or more important, recreation and I hope he's going to take more time off.
- We have just finished our hectic journey across the Prairies and are now in Vancouver, in a charming hotel. We have five days off (during which time Peter has to write three columns, but still it is better than nothing). Peter is also going to interview the B.C. Premier and speak to a university students' group.

---

[5] When Trudeau decided to marry Margaret Sinclair in 1971, he didn't have the nerve to tell Madeleine and asked his friend Gérard Pelletier to deliver the news. Gobeil left Canada for Paris, completed her doctorate at the Sorbonne, and took a senior position at UNESCO, but the two frequently met as friends after Margaret and Pierre divorced.

- The invitation list is now up to eighty and I'm convinced that no more than sixty-five people can possibly be fitted into our house.
- Peter promises to be altogether more civilized, relaxed, unharried, and amusing — at least that is what he said yesterday, but five minutes ago he phoned up with an idea for a new book to be published in 1970. I couldn't decide whether to swear, hang up the phone, yell, or what, so I just laughed weakly.
- Peter's nerves are very bad, he is losing weight again and nothing much seems to help.
- I was going to write you yesterday but felt so exhausted after going to meet the Queen Mum that I had to spend most of the day lying down. It was disappointing that she wasn't more gorgeous, but I suppose it was more important that she was so nice.
- Last night we were at the Pearsons' for a cocktail party and had a very good time. Tomorrow there is a party for Karsh, the photographer, who has a new wife and a new book, both of which he seems to be displaying at that time. We are beginning to feel that we should perhaps give another big cocktail party.
- The success of the book [*Renegade in Power*] goes on phenomenally and Peter is very happy. A nice sidelight is the money, which should help us get a house.
- Peter is taking tomorrow off as a relaxing measure; he gets so tired he is speechless in the evenings and has to sit on the sofa before dragging himself off to bed.
- It's not just the work, but the invitations — we now have to go out this Friday, have the big party Saturday, go to cocktails at the British Embassy on Monday, and to Toronto on Tuesday.

We realized all too late that our feverish pace as careerists and socialites had planted the seeds of our ultimate separation. Our dreamy conversations about literature and journalism had become a distant memory; we talked less and less often about our intimate thoughts and desires, and more and more often about the politics and society around us. I had a gnawing sense of guilt that we shared so little private time, but my pangs of conscience went unresolved.

I was busier than ever and working from sunup to sundown in a hot lather. In addition to my syndicated column, I had a television series to write, regular commentaries to provide for the CBC, and speeches to prepare and deliver. Vancouver impresario Perry Goldsmith had just launched Contemporary Communications, an agency for public speakers, and I was his star billing. I would hop a jet to such destinations as Edmonton or Charlottetown about every other weekend, make a public appearance, and return home a day or so later with an extra $5,000 in my bank account. It was easy money, but it carved deeply into our personal time. It got to the point where we stored up our married life in reserve for the few weeks' boating holiday each year in the Thousand Islands of the St. Lawrence. By then, the bumps and grinds of daily living had often bruised us to the point where Christina would retreat into one of her darker moods, while I was remote and preoccupied with my next tactical career move.

We were slowly drifting apart, but neither of us paused to consider or complain — we were having head-spinning fun and we both enjoyed the limelight. Christina longed to rise on the social ladder as much as I did. She also had a burning and understandable desire for her considerable writing talent to be recognized, an abhorrence of plainness, and a dread of the ordinary. Mingling with what passed for high society convinced us we were "making it," even if we were not exactly sure which "it" we wanted to "make." The dynamic between us shifted, gradually at first, almost imperceptibly; then noticeably; and eventually, dramatically. That process took a full decade to marinate, from publication of *Renegade* to just before my first book on the Establishment.

WHILE PEARSON QUIETLY BLUNDERED AWAY in the background, the rest of Canada had joined the social revolution of the sixties. Pearson was hopelessly out of touch with the spirit of the times: instead of tie-dyes, he wore bow ties; instead of "mod," his style was "plod." To his way of looking at things, "dropping acid"

was an accidental spill in a laboratory; "pot" was a cooking implement; and a "trip" was an annual vacation. "This generation," proclaimed Marshall McLuhan, its chief prophet, "lives mystically and
in depth." This description did not apply to Mike Pearson.

Pearson's administrative style harkened back to the politics of
benign bureaucratic despotism that had dominated the country
since its inception. It was no accident that nine former senior
bureaucrats (himself included) were sworn into his first Cabinet,
and that they held five of the seven most powerful positions. The
one time his government was caught out by an unexpected Opposition vote, Pearson was in the middle of a bridge game at the luxurious Jamaican villa of his pal, Senator Hartland de Montarville
Molson. From the day he assumed power, Pearson set out to
confirm his elitist credentials. As soon as he was sworn into office,
he rushed off to London for a meeting with Harold Macmillan
and the British Cabinet (half of whom he knew by their first
names), then hopped over to Paris for a *tête-à-tête* with his buddy,
the American ambassador "Chip" Bohlen. Then it was on to
Washington for tea with his confidant, Dean Acheson, the great
guru of America's post-war diplomacy, and a side visit to join
"Scotty" Reston of the *New York Times* and his wife Sally for cocktails. Days later, he visited President John F. Kennedy at his
Hyannisport compound, where he matched his knowledge of
baseball scores with White House aide Dave Powers. When he
tripped up Powers on some 1926 southpaw's earned-run average,
Kennedy said, "He'll do." And the two leaders agreed to install
nuclear weapons on Canadian soil.

IT WAS BACK TO THE FUTURE, as Pearson restored Ottawa to its
position as an Establishment haven after the Diefenbaker years.
Pearson and Dief had been born within two years of each other at
the tail end of the nineteenth century to rural Ontario families,
but they had nothing else in common. Where one relied on political instinct, the other valued in-group logic; where one sought

out new and radical solutions, the other sought safety in the tried-and-tested approach to power. Where one challenged credulity, the other invited cynicism. Pearson displayed the befuddled uncertainties of a slightly embarrassed chemistry professor searching for a misplaced formula. Diefenbaker plunged on, worshipping the frescoes painted by his imagination. During the curious decade when this odd couple ran our affairs, the two men expected the worst of each other and were seldom disappointed. Diefenbaker so hated Pearson that he even phrased his questions to draw out his opponent's lisp, by using words such as "pusillanimous" that he knew the Liberal leader could not wrap his tongue around.

Their contradictory views of the country were amply displayed on May 24, 1967, when fifteen thousand angry farmers converged on Parliament. It was one final convulsion of Canada's once-great agrarian community. These were Diefenbaker's People, the same crowds I had encountered on his whistle-stop campaigns across the West. I walked among them as they milled about the manicured lawns of Parliament Hill, recognizing the John Deere baseball caps stained with axle grease and the faded fedoras with the ragged red feathers stuck in their brims. Their mood was very different from the last time I had seen them, when they had still enjoyed a sense of place in their country. Now they felt not only dispossessed, but forgotten. Their land was no longer the touchstone it had been. The ribbon of rail that had once connected them to mainstream Canada had turned out not to be hard steel after all, but a reminder of abandoned dreams and hands shaken on railway platforms, also now abandoned.

They had come by car, truck, and even tractor to the national capital, a bewildered, motley assembly hungering for some small sign of empathy or understanding. All that happened was that the Mountie barricades went up. Pearson was in charge now; he ordered the parliamentary doors slammed in their faces and never appeared before them or acknowledged their presence. They deserved better, much better than that — at least a nod of recognition, the tip of a hat. But the doors remained resolutely shuttered.

As the farmers slowly, wistfully, dispersed into the Ottawa night, I felt ashamed of my country.

A STUDY IN CONTRADICTIONS, Pearson took bold risks, such as his inspired struggle to give Canada its own distinctive flag; at other times he was far too careful, as in his constant dilly-dallying on constitutional reform. Alone among Canada's ego-driven, power-hungry prime ministers, he saw his function strictly as a catalyst, an agent of change who resolves issues without being altered in the process. "You must draw limits in your commitment," he once told me, "or you become uncivilized."[6]

Civility was Pearson's mantra, conditioned in him by the fondly remembered era of "quiet diplomacy." After an unlucky first job as a sausage-stuffer in a Hamilton meat-packing plant, he joined the External Affairs Department in 1928, but was almost turned down on the grounds that Vincent Massey, one of his examiners and then Canada's ambassador to the United States, decided there was "something curiously loose-jointed and sloppy about his makeup."

He had risen to become the personification of Canada's brief flowering as a post-war middle power, growing up at a time when political leaders could occupy high office without giving much thought to the voters.[7] There was a convenient myth afloat in Ottawa during his time in office that Pearson was some kind of captive hero. His friends and supporters visualized him as a man

---

[6] His self-deprecating humour helped relieve the stress of his office. His favourite story was about the cavalry officer who crawled into a frontier fort with three arrows buried in his back, and was asked if it hurt. "Only when I laugh," he gasped. "My job," Pearson quipped, "only hurts when I don't."

[7] That attitude was most visible on election night in 1965, when it became obvious that he was not going to win what Pearson had so smugly demanded from the voters: "a comfortable majority." Keith Davey, the campaign manager, lamented: "We let you down . . ." Pearson, taken aback by such an admission of weakness, shook his head: "Oh no, Keith," he replied, "*the country let us down.*" There it was, proof positive of the Grits' genetic strain of political arrogance.

who, instead of acting in line with his innate decency, allowed a retinue of self-interested, streetwise advisers to subvert his finer instincts and blunt his effectiveness. "Mike is not being himself," they would reassure each other.

That was absolute rot. The way prime ministerial decisions are taken ultimately remains impenetrable, but Pearson was never a prisoner of his advisers; they were not only his instruments but his creations, and they remained influential in national politics only because Pearson decided it. Taking office one day before his sixty-sixth birthday, with most of his attitudes set in concrete, I found Pearson easy to caricature but impossible to paint. His pleasant personality was overshadowed by the elusive and contradictory character of the man.

While there was much disagreement about his qualities as a prime minister, few defended his inability to run effective campaigns against John Diefenbaker, who could do nothing else. During the four bitter elections they contested, the Liberal leader started out with a majority of popular support that was his to lose, then lost it. He eroded his vote by 7 percentage points (almost to the decimal point) during each six-week campaign and on election day snatched defeat from the jaws of victory. I was in his campaign cavalcade in Toronto during May 1962, when a traffic light halted us in front of the Scott Mission that provided free meals for the homeless. Four hundred hungry men were lined up in front of the building, staring at Pearson's white convertible stopped alongside. They started to wave, and somebody shouted: "Come on in, Mike, the soup's fine!" Although he had been crossing the country declaring that unemployment was Canada's greatest problem, Pearson remained glued to his seat. His handlers began to tug at him, pleading that he should mingle and say a few words – there was, after all, a caravan of journalists present, hungering for a photo op. "No," he said. "I will not exploit their misery for political gain." (Good for him, but not great for his vote count.)

Similarly, in the 1963 campaign, his organizers had worked hard to mount a successful kickoff in London, Ontario, traditionally

poor territory for the Liberals. They succeeded so well that they
not only filled the city's largest arena, they were left with an overflow of two thousand supporters shuffling outside. When Pearson
drove up, David Greenspan, a Toronto lawyer who headed the local
organization drive, pushed his way toward the limousine, shoved
his head though the car window, and shouted: "Mr. Pearson! These
people outside can't get in. They've been waiting in the cold for
two hours. Here's a bullhorn. You must say something to them."
Pearson shrank back with an emphatic shake of his head. "I can't
do that." Finally, Gordon Edick, then the Ontario Liberal Party's
assistant director, physically barred Pearson's way into the arena
until he had grasped the bullhorn to mutter an awkward acknowledgement of the crowd's enthusiasm.

His lack of passion confirmed him in the public mind as a curiously disengaged politician who would not be brought to bay by
the urgencies of the moment. In an age of image politics, Pearson
seldom projected any sense of personal commitment. And yet –
despite his unblemished record of appointing party bagmen and
hacks to the Senate – his sponsorship of medicare, pensions, bilingualism, and the flag were acts both courageous and necessary. He
demonstrated the strength of his political principles, but his weakness was an inability to transfer principles into electoral success or
an effective grip on power.[8]

To assess Pearson on his own turf, I spent part of one election
campaign touring his home riding of Algoma East in northern
Ontario. His constituents didn't know quite what do with their
distinguished MP. At one of his meetings, I heard the briefest political introduction on record by a poll captain: "I've been asked to

---

[8] Asked by the prime minister how she thought the government's bilingual
program was faring, Secretary of State Judy LaMarsh, just back from a western
tour promoting the policy, replied: "Well, Mike, all I can tell you is that the
other day at a rally in Red Deer, where I was promoting the teaching of French,
a woman got up and shouted: 'If English was good enough for Jesus, it's good
enough for me!'"

introduce Mr. Pearson, who has been asked to speak to us. I have. He will." My favourite Pearson cheerleader was a moppet of a kid, around whose neck someone had hung an "I LIKE MIKE!" placard. Uncertain about his instructions, he kept yelling: "I LIKE MILK! I LIKE MILK!" At the end of that meeting an elderly woman tottered up to Pearson, held his hand, and sweetly chirped: "God bless you, John Diefenbaker." I shared the reaction of Maryon Pearson to the day's events. Her husband ended the meeting by asking: "Now, is there anything else anybody wants to bring up?" She sarcastically whispered, loudly enough to be overheard: "Yes. The last five cups of coffee."

"UNLIKE THE AMERICANS, we do not salute our flag," the former Liberal Cabinet minister Mitchell Sharp wrote in his memoirs. "In fact, we got along for a century without one." The flag issue had been quietly shelved by every Canadian government since Confederation as being too divisive to permit legislative action. In fact, the Canadian Red Ensign was not properly a national flag at all. It was a "jack," or naval flag, its blue version flown from the stern of warships. It bore the Union Jack in the upper left-hand corner and the Canadian coat of arms in the lower right field. It had first been authorized for use on Canadian ships by the British Admiralty in 1892, and had gradually acquired general acceptance. An Order-in-Council issued in 1924 had permitted its use at Canadian diplomatic offices abroad, which was where the debate had ended until Pearson revived the issue in 1964.

Pearson had been alarmed by the rise of the Quiet Revolution in Quebec, and had been warned by his 1963 Royal Commission on Bilingualism and Biculturalism that Canada needed to reshape its institutions and symbols to include French Canadians, or serious trouble would result. He decreed that a national flag which carried the combined crosses of St. Andrew (Scotland), St. George (England), and St. Patrick (Ireland) was no longer acceptable as a national symbol. He braved a raucous six-month debate in Parliament to bring in the Maple Leaf flag, a struggle that marked his finest hour.

Ironically, although most bedrock Anglo-Saxons regarded Pearson's abandonment of the Red Ensign as an unacceptable concession to Quebec, most opinion leaders in French Canada saw it strictly as an internal wrangle between English-Canadian nationalists and British imperialists. "Quebec doesn't give a tinker's damn about the new flag, it's a matter of complete indifference," commented Pierre Trudeau, then a law professor at the University of Montreal. But the new flag proved to be as immediately popular in Quebec as elsewhere, and it gave the federalist cause in the province a much-needed symbol to counter the provincial ensign, which still carried the colonial vestige of four fleurs-de-lis, representing the kingdom of France.

The flag debate raged through 308 speeches in the House of Commons, led by the implacable resistance of John Diefenbaker. The Prince Albert politician, an unabashed admirer of the British monarchy, emerged as the staunchest defender of the status quo. His campaign against the flag recalled his 1962 speech at Macdowall, Saskatchewan: "I want to make Canada all Canadian and all British" – whatever that meant. In his ridicule of the new flag, he verged on the ridiculous himself, such as when he suggested its white background would be lost against the snows of winter; or that Canadian schoolchildren would confuse it with the flag of Peru, which bore a similar design. "Why does the government insist that the Christian crosses, the spiritual elements, be removed from our flag?" Diefenbaker thundered. He blathered on about how the new flag would treat "all the milestones of our past greatness as irrelevancies," but in fact, it was the Chief who had become irrelevant to a modern, secular Canada.

Other Tory speeches ranged from the hilarious – Russell MacEwan from Pictou, Nova Scotia, demonstrated his enlightened attitude to Quebec by singing "Alouette!" – to the bizarre, as when Jack Bigg, an ex-RCMP officer and the Tory backbencher for Athabaska, Alberta, managed to bring Joan of Arc into the debate. "They took Joan's flag down," he lamented. "They put her lily banner in the dirt, and she was only a woman. But what a glorious woman she was. She put her lily banner out in front and never looked back, and with her small army swept the ranks clear. She put the rightful heir on the throne of France. Then the king of France ratted on her, and you know the rest. Now she's a saint. Which of those opposite, in their male pride, will stand up and say that they think the lily banner of France and the cross of St. George should be laid in the dirt?" (Nobody owned up.)

To such ideological nonsense, Pearson offered a simple and sensible answer: "Am I supposed to be forgetting my British past because I look forward to my Canadian future?" he asked. "This is the flag of the future, but it does not dishonour the past." For once, he was in touch with the mood of the new Canadian generation. Schoolchildren by the thousands sent their proposals for the flag to the Prime Minister's Office; meanwhile, the initial Pearson design (consisting of a "white field charged with three red maple leaves conjoined on a single stem, with blue borders") was eagerly copied by Toronto nightclub strippers, who adopted the spirit of the new ensign by jiggling on stage covered only by three strategically placed patriotic maple leaves. Even Leonard Cohen got into the act, suggesting that Canada adopt *four* Maple Leaf designs, one for each season – a small green leaf for spring, a larger green leaf for summer, a red leaf for autumn, and a "white outline" of a leaf against a white background, for winter.

Early on the morning of February 15, 1965, the day of the official flag-raising ceremony, I followed Public Works clerk Paul Poirier a hundred feet up a ship's ladder to the summit of the Peace Tower. I wanted to describe the view as he unfurled the new national flag, hand-sewn by a fellow Public Works employee. At precisely noon, with a cool sun breaking through the clouds, the muffled sound of a twenty-one-gun salute could be heard. Moments later, a theatrical gust of wind gave the first flutter of life to the new ensign. Diefenbaker took out a white handkerchief and ostentatiously dabbed his eyes for the benefit of the television cameras. Queen's University political science professor A.R.M. Lower best summed up the public's reaction: "Being Canadians, they do not express themselves in words, they hide resolutely away any gesture or grunt that might conceivably betray emotion, but the sharp observer gets the signals all the same. There is nothing in this of turning backs on a hated past, nothing suggesting that old ties were irksome. The point is simply that the country is growing up, coming to see itself as an entity, taking the interest in itself that any organism, to be healthy, must. Each time the average citizen looks at the new flag, he unconsciously says to himself 'That's me!'"[9]

The flag unleashed a new and contemporary spirit of Canadian nationalism, within the context of a larger international community, which was the lasting legacy of the Pearson years. Two years later, this spirit was confirmed when a cannonade of fireworks marked the opening of Expo 67. The shells burst in a multi-coloured tattoo over the St. Lawrence River, launching the most impressive monument to Lester Pearson's internationalism and Canada's national pride. It was on his watch that the world's fair, Canada's first, was sponsored, built, and managed. At the very moment when the governor general declared Expo 67 officially open, I was standing in front of the United States pavilion, a

---

[9] The problem with the Maple Leaf as a national symbol is that half the country has no maple trees, and while there are nearly a hundred varieties around the world, thirteen of them native to North America, none are exclusive to Canada. The Alberta poet/novelist Leona Gom described the typical reaction of northern Alberta youngsters, asked by their teacher to draw the new flag. One of the pupils asks, "How come we never seen one?"

"We all gasp, crayons cringing over maple leafs, but teacher looks not mad but something else, she looks out the window at the thick hair of poplar and spruce braided across the sky, and she says, 'You're right. It doesn't grow here,' and we wait, there must be something more, but she only says, finish your colouring, and outside the wind accuses the unknown forest."

Buckminster Fuller–designed geodesic dome, shimmering and soaring in the sun like an aviary fit for eagles. Beside me, a young Expo hostess, done up in white leather and powder-blue uniform, shrieked her pleasure: "*C'est merveilleux!*" And it was marvellous, all of it. It was a wow of a fair, a painted celebration of Canada's first century, a pop-fest of miniskirts and mega-themes. If Canadian nationalism was born on the killing fields of Flanders, it came of age on the pulsating grounds of the Expo world's fair. I was overwhelmed by the feeling that if this was possible, that if my frigid, self-obsessed country of twenty million people could put on this kind of spectacle, we could do almost anything.

My most unexpected surprise was the United Kingdom pavilion, so stodgy on the outside, so witty within, a celebration of the history of the English-speaking peoples presented with unexpected flair and self-deprecating humour. In the middle of industrial marvels, depictions of literary giants, and historical pageants, there was an untidy line of bushes with burrs and tangled weeds and singing birds and a sign that proclaimed: "Is there under heaven a more glorious and refreshing object than an impregnable hedge?"

On the monorail that ringed the grounds and provided a breathtaking look at the fair's marvels, people were poking each other and saying, "Look at Greece!" "Look at Cuba!" "Look at Czechoslovakia!" "Look at France!" – taking pleasure in every nation's accomplishments. For one short and magical summer, the Iron Curtain was drawn back, and racial and class divisions were erased. It was an event to remember for a lifetime. I came to the fair a nationalist, full of pride in my adopted Canada. I left a humanist, full of hope for all mankind. It was a sentiment that reverberated across the land; we all felt that Canada had reclaimed its sense of promise, and its role in the brave new world that beckoned. In hindsight, we were perhaps naïve, but the emotional impact of Expo would define my image of Canada – and the shape of Canadian politics – for decades to come.

IN SOME CURIOUS FASHION, it often seems that my personal life is reflected in the mood of national events, and Canada's Centennial year was no exception. It was also a vintage time at home. Christina and I had moved into a stone-built house on Opeongo Drive by Dow's Lake, which was part of the National Capital Commission's Driveway system that curves through the most attractive parts of Ottawa. It was an idyllic neighbourhood, meticulous in its upkeep and preservation. The street had no billboards, no mailboxes, no telephone poles, no commercial premises of any kind. Milk carts and bread wagons were permitted to make their deliveries only between the hours of midnight and 6:00 a.m. Garbage trucks were forbidden and residents carried their refuse out to back alleys. There was no street parking, unless you were hosting a wedding reception, in which case you could submit a complicated appeal to federal authorities who would reluctantly issue a permit for six cars to park in front of your house. Section 19 of the civic regulations provided "six months' imprisonment for anyone apprehended carrying a torpedo along The Driveway" – only the fear of which prevented me from launching one in the direction of the Parliament Buildings.

In the summer of 1964 we were blessed by the arrival of a daughter, Jennifer Ashley. We had planned on having a child and were delighted with the addition to our family. For me, it also eased the pangs of missed fatherhood following my divorce from Pat; for us as a couple, it meant more time together with a renewed sense of commitment. Chris and I would spend hours foolishly looking at our daughter, neither of us able to get over the feeling that she was a miracle. Like all new parents, we were overly anxious – when we attended *la shin-dig annuelle* at the French embassy to celebrate Bastille Day, Christina phoned home three times in four hours to check with Glenna Hall, our babysitter. As the months passed, my daughter only grew in interest and delight. We had a nightly bedtime ritual: she would sprinkle a flower box with her toy watering can, rock precisely seventeen times on her teeter-totter, then bid night-night to the birdies and the flowers.

In the mornings I would climb into bed with her and we would pretend to be paddling down the Rideau Canal. It was magic.

RENEGADE IN POWER HAD DOCUMENTED the Diefenbaker years as an inevitable disaster, like a latter-day *Titanic* sinking with brass bands playing, flag (Union Jack, of course) flying, and the captain shouting hysterical orders to crewmen who had long since abandoned ship. *The Distemper of Our Times*, my history of the Pearson years, proved a much more complicated assignment. The Pearson voyage, in comparison, seemed more like the journey of some peeling, once-proud tramp steamer, its engines wheezing as it lurched from port to port with the lackadaisical skipper making up his schedule as he went along.

Chief among my sources for the book was Keith Davey, who had been recruited from the Toronto advertising world by Pearson as national director of the Liberal Party, and who later served in a similar role for both Pierre Trudeau and John Turner. When he came to Ottawa in 1961, he set about rebuilding the rusty Liberal Party machinery across the country, cog by cog, instilling it with purpose, enthusiasm, and something resembling the New Frontier spirit of John Kennedy. A hunched, handsome Eagle Scout in politics, he was the most widely liked presence in that cold capital city. He also leaked like a sieve. A few times a month, we would lunch together at the Granada Café, a greasy spoon around the corner from the Liberal Party's headquarters on Cooper Street, sharing hot meat sandwiches while he would give me the inside dope on what was going on. Although he carried a button pinned inside his wallet that read "STIFLE YOURSELF," he seldom did. He revealed his plan to modernize the Liberal campaign machine by importing President Kennedy's private pollster, Lou Harris, to help run the 1962 campaign. I used that controversial fact in a subsequent column, but we remained good friends. In contrast with the Tory backroom crowd, who approached reporters as warily as they would a nest of rattlesnakes, the Liberal coterie actually seemed to enjoy encounters with members of the press, whom they regarded as persuadable, if not downright friendly. Along with Davey, these included Dorothy Petrie (who later became his wife), Jerry Grafstein, Tom Kent, Dick O'Hagan, John Roberts, and Jim Coutts, all of whom provided the human dimension that made the Liberal Party bearable, and ultimately powerful.[10]

Alberta-born and Harvard-educated, Coutts acted as Pearson's appointment secretary but was privy to Ottawa's secrets of the deep. He told anybody who asked about my book that it would have been a pamphlet without the assistance of Mike McCabe and Maurice Sauvé. He was half right. A professional economist and amateur hellraiser, Sauvé was an impatient and passionate reformer dedicated to introducing democracy and accountability to the Quebec wing of the party. That made him unacceptable among most of Pearson's Old Guard Quebec lieutenants, who kept getting caught in embarrassing scandals. Maurice became a friend but seldom a source, because he took his Privy Council oath seriously and refused to share Cabinet secrets. Mike McCabe, executive assistant to Finance minister Mitchell Sharp, became my most valuable contact. "Chaos is a concept I love," he would say, to explain his affinity for Liberal farce and misrule. An academic disciple of Marshall McLuhan, he had an appetite for power, a disregard for protocol, and the ability to elevate the mundane with his enthusiasm and imagination. Despite our close relationship, he felt I never understood the intrinsically anarchistic nature of Pearson's government. "You kept writing about conspiracies and secret plans," he told me years later, "while I kept telling you that mostly Pearson ruled by accident, or the kind of moving osmosis by

---

[10] It was Keith Davey who introduced me to professional hockey. On February 20, 1979, he invited me to a Toronto Maple Leafs home game against the Philadelphia Flyers. Having never been to such an event, I arrived wearing fur-lined boots, several sweaters, and a heavy duffel coat, carrying a blanket, thinking the arena must be cold. The game consisted mainly of players wrestling on the ice, and I never went again.

which the Liberals tend to govern. And I remember you answering: 'Well, that wouldn't make much of a column.' You sort of reminded me of Winston Churchill's post-war dictum: 'I expect history to treat me kindly. I intend to write it.'"

As well as these essential tattlers, I was privy to the whisperings of Ottawa's senior mandarins and obtained several top-secret documents, published in *Distemper*'s dozen appendices. When interviewed about my book for the *Ottawa Citizen*, Judy LaMarsh, the most lively and outspoken of Pearson's Cabinet ministers, remarked: "If Peter Newman were a minister of the Crown he would be breaking the Official Secrets Act. It's obvious that some of my former colleagues must have. After I was through in Parliament, I burned my official documents in my garden. When I opened Newman's book, there they were staring out at me." This was not said in jest. My publication of the secret papers almost landed me in jail. Professor Jack Granatstein, a tough academic historian, who usually used my books for target practice, declared that *Distemper*'s "appendices alone are worth the price of the book," adding that I was "almost certainly" in breach of the Official Secrets Act.[11] As well as the actual texts of a series of diplomatic notes exchanged between Ottawa and Washington over the Canadianization of the Mercantile Bank, which were the sharpest protests ever exchanged by the two countries, I published a private and highly confidential letter dated December 4, 1964, in which Pearson had attempted to blackmail Diefenbaker. The Liberal leader threatened the Chief with exposure over how the Tory leader had allowed a potential breach of security to go unpunished during the grubby Munsinger affair. Gerda Munsinger, a Munich-born prostitute,

---

[11] Among Granatstein's many books was one he authored on the hundred most influential Canadians since Confederation, in which I ranked at number twenty-eight, just ahead of Northern Dancer, the successful racehorse. I was always grateful to the professor, not for my inclusion, but for the rank in which he placed me. I would hate to have gone through eternity just *behind* that prolific stud.

had been carrying on a dalliance with Diefenbaker's associate minister of Defence, Pierre Sévigny. "The Munsinger case has given me grave concern," wrote Pearson. "It affects the security of the country. The Minister of Justice brought the matter to your attention, yet no action was taken." This was all true, but Diefenbaker pointed out that when he had called Sévigny on the carpet, his minister had a unique and credible defence. "There was no security breach involved," Sévigny told the Chief, adding, "She was just a wonderful fuck." This rendered the Baptist PM speechless for the first time that anyone could recall. (Sévigny later confessed to Diefenbaker biographer John Munro that he "would fuck Gerda again tomorrow," if he could.)

In a memorandum to Cabinet dated December 15, 1968, the RCMP agreed to investigate my publication of these secret documents as a possible offence under the Criminal Code. I faced a five-year jail term if convicted. My fate was discussed in a Cabinet meeting four days later. According to the official minutes of the meeting (which I obtained, old habits dying hard): "Some ministers said that there was nothing to fear from such an investigation of Newman and much to be gained by way of a warning to others not to publish classified material." Pierre Trudeau, who was by then responsible for RCMP activities, saved my butt by insisting that if anyone was to be charged, it ought to be the people who gave me the documents. (I never determined whether his intervention was the result of a courageous determination to champion freedom of the press, or his memory of rolling around on my living-room floor.)

No one was the wiser about the identity of my informants when *Distemper of Our Times: Canadian Politics in Transition, 1963–1968* came out and repeated the success of *Renegade*. Fuelled by the promotional wizardry of Scott McIntyre, then with McClelland & Stewart, sales were about as high, reviews about as good, and pre-publication orders beat all previous records. Mel Hurtig, then running Edmonton's best bookstore, reported that sales of *Distemper* were running at 4.3 per minute. In a review for *The Canadian*

Forum, then the country's most lively Left-wing publication, Professor Thomas Hockin declared: "Newman is the political therapist to a nation. And nothing second-hand about it. It's the ugly mirror of Dorian Gray in full regalia. Sure, the Liberals don't like it much. All the more reassuring to the rest of us." That comment was prompted by Lester Pearson's verdict on my book, which he described as a "lucrative, key-hole striptease contribution, if not to history, at least to the gossip of our times, which rely so much on second-hand pulsations from the psychiatrist's couch." The most surprising review was a five-thousand-word barnburner in the *St. John's Telegram* by Farley Mowat: "*Renegade* was not just a *tour de force*, it was a warning shot across our bows. The broadside was still to follow. *Distemper of Our Times* is that broadside. I confidently assert that with his new book Newman will instigate a revolution which will explode our smothering apathy toward Canadian politics and politicians, brutally shaking them loose from their insulated indifference to people and to reality." The *New York Times* greeted the American edition (published by Alfred A. Knopf) as confirming my reputation as "guardian of the best set of leaks in Ottawa."

The praise was welcome, but I never considered the impact of the wounds I had inflicted on my political victims until I read Bruce Hutchison's review of *Distemper*:

Of the politicians' horror at his approach Mr. Newman remains sublimely unconscious, or totally indifferent. For in manner he is as mild and friendly a man as ever skinned a skunk or slit a political throat, always with such delicate surgery that the victim hardly feels it until the surgeon has left town. He talks in a soft, disarming whisper, with a boyish smile. But once he finds the nearest typewriter his shrill voice, in print, sounds like an electronic bullhorn in a narrow cave. Oddly enough, he never realizes how much he is hurting the politicians, who seldom complain lest they invite a second blast. To him all this is just part of the game and in his strange innocence he wonders why anyone should be distressed. Actually, he is more distressed than his victims because he judges them unworthy of the nation that he loves. To the hungry, penniless Czechoslovakian boy, Canada must have looked like a transcontinental candy shop. To the mature man it has become a cathedral of solemn worship, the shrine of his private Canadian Dream.

For the first time since Dalton Camp wrote his reaction to *Renegade*, I realized how much of a writer's character can be discerned through his prose by a perceptive reader. Hutchison's understanding of my evolving character possessed a surgical precision.

IT WAS A CREDIT TO PEARSON'S personal grace that he surrendered office in the winter of 1967, calling for a leadership convention the following April. It was time to make way for a different kind of participatory politics represented by Pierre Elliott Trudeau. Pearson worked behind the scenes to let the party's power-brokers know he was well disposed toward Pierre (while Mitchell Sharp steered support in public), which guaranteed him the leadership.

My rush to judgment of Lester Pearson's record abides. His tenure proved that, even with the best of intentions, Canada remains devilishly difficult to govern.[12] Once again – not for the first time, and certainly not for the last – I had welcomed a change of leadership with unrealistically high expectations. Perhaps the compromises of politics in the real world would always gut my Utopian dreams. But that was no reason to abandon them, or to accept mediocrity. At the core of Pearson's disappointing performance was that his dedication to civility and decency made him behave as if he would rather be himself than a great prime minister. His tragedy was that he could not be both.

---

[12] One of Pearson's less attractive habits was that he tended to disperse the blame for mistakes to his underlings. "He was always quick to lay down his friends for his life," quipped Pat MacAdam, the Tory backroom strategist.

John Diefenbaker's blood feud survived Pearson's death from cancer, on December 27, 1972. Pearson's closed casket lay in state in Parliament's Hall of Honour, where thousands came to mourn his passing. Among those who paid their last respects was Sean O'Sullivan, who was first a Tory MP, then the Chief's loyal assistant, and later a Catholic priest. He reported to Diefenbaker on the scene of shuffling mourners paying their hushed reverence. Dief grew increasingly agitated, until O'Sullivan mentioned the detail that the casket was closed.

"You've seen my funeral plans, and you know it will be different for me," the Old Chief cackled. "*My* casket will be open!"

"Do you know, sir, why Mr. Pearson's casket had to be closed?" asked O'Sullivan. "In addition to the cancer, he developed jaundice at the end, and this caused a lot of discoloration."

Diefenbaker could hardly contain himself. "This is it," he enthused, almost dancing with joy. "I knew it had to be something . . ."

While an astonished O'Sullivan listened in, Dief telephoned his wife. "Olive!" he crowed. "He was as green as a beet!"

When she asked what he was talking about, he replied: "Pearson. He's as *green as a beet!*"

O'Sullivan's disquiet grew as the Tory leader dialled number after number, passing on his bizarre news to cronies across the country. Although O'Sullivan had never known jaundice to turn anyone green, nor had he ever seen a green beet, this did not deter the Chief from reiterating his garish description. O'Sullivan quietly slipped from the office, leaving Diefenbaker to his unbecoming jig on Pearson's grave.

Mike Pearson left instructions to be buried in an inconspicuous cemetery near Wakefield, Quebec, where he had bought a burial plot in 1948 for ten dollars, along with his old friends and fellow public servants Hume Wrong and Norman Robertson. His final resting place is a fitting testament to his modesty and simple patriotism. In autumn, the graveyard is filled with drifting red maple leaves.

MY GRANDPARENTS: Theodore and Pauline Neumann. (Her father had been mayor of Warsaw.) They were murdered by the Nazis at the concentration camp in Theresienstadt.

MY PARENTS: Oscar Karel and Wanda Maria Neumann. She studied to be a concert pianist; he ran pre-war Czechoslovakia's largest sugar beet refinery. (All photos Newman family collection)

GROWING UP SPOILED: My favourite rocking
horse; first sailor suit; and dreaming of my future.

ESCAPING TO CANADA: After settling on a fifteen-acre vegetable farm in Freeman, near Hamilton, Ontario, I attended Upper Canada College in Toronto (where I was the lead drummer in U.C.C.'s battalion band) and earned part of my tuition as a gold miner in northern Quebec.

MY FIRST WIFE: Patricia McKee, the Irish colleen with the dimple:
few happy days, or nights.

COVERING THE WAR IN LAOS (1961): The only guy with a suit in the jungle. (*Maclean's*)

MY ENDURING MENTOR: Ralph Allen, editor of *Maclean's* 1950–1959. (*Maclean's*)

MAKING WAVES: Interviewing the Rt. Hon. John Diefenbaker for my controversial biography *Renegade in Power*. A *Toronto Star* cartoon by Duncan MacPherson shows Mr. Diefenbaker in disguise trying to borrow the book from the Parliamentary Library – having claimed that he had not read it, but the first chapter had sixteen errors. (*Toronto Star*)

"I'M SORRY, IT'S OUT— MR. DIEFENBAKER."

CHRISTINA McCALL:
She became my second wife
in 1959. We were married
for seventeen years and it
was mainly her influence
that moved my prose from
reporting about facts to
writing about feelings.

THE TWO LIBERALS IN MY LIFE: Mike Pearson, the flawed achiever, and
Pierre Trudeau, the gunslinger with an icicle for a heart.

CHAPTER NINE

PASSIONS: MY DOUBLE LIFE IN THE ROYAL CANADIAN NAVY

Peace is brief.
As fragile and transitory
as apple blossoms in the spring.
– Barbara Tuchman

The French novelist Victor Hugo described the nets strung across the River Seine at Saint-Cloud, designed to catch the bodies of Parisians who drowned themselves, as a missing link with posterity. Even on the best of golden summer days, that same melancholy mood permeates Pearl Harbor. The Day of Infamy, when the bombs and torpedoes of Japanese Zeros shattered the sitting-duck American fleet, lives on in this place.

Clearly visible just below the waves are the battleships USS *Utah* and USS *Arizona*. Their American ensigns float at full mast since they remain in commission as tombs for the thousands of sailors killed on December 7, 1941. At 7:55 a.m. on that fateful day, nearly two hundred torpedo planes, bombers, and fighters from six Japanese aircraft carriers descended on the U.S. Pacific fleet, engulfing it in flames within fifteen minutes. In the midst of the turquoise ocean in which the battleships were sunk, the ships' hulls have coloured the water above them battleship-grey, an appropriate hue for a mausoleum. Their hulls are mute testament to a history that can be neither altered nor enhanced.

Now, I have come to this historic venue on a mission. It is August 15, 1988, and I am dressed in my summer whites as a commander in Canada's naval reserves (the same rank as James Bond, and of Prince Charles when he married Lady Diana, I comfort myself). My assignment is to deliver a message to Admiral Ronald Hays, commander-in-chief of the U.S. Pacific Command (CINGPAC) who hails from Urania, deep in the heart of Louisiana, and still speaks with a soft southern twang. He is a forty-year naval veteran who holds military sway over half of the earth's surface, from the East African coast to the Pacific shore of the Americas. His is the world's most powerful naval command, with more than a quarter of a million sailors quartered in 220 fighting ships.

On the other hand, I represent the western alliance's puniest navy – Canada's Maritime Command, a tinpot fleet supported by a nation that, in per-capita military expenditures, lags behind such awesome players on the world stage as Madagascar, Togo, and the Seychelles. Canada spends $12 billion a year on defence, which sounds like a lot until it is expressed as a fraction of GDP – about 1 per cent. In NATO, that puts us just ahead of Luxembourg, whose armed forces consist of seven hundred plumed and puffed-out toy soldiers who pretend to be guarding the royal palace.

No wonder that my business – to persuade this grand admiral that in the future his fleet ought to manoeuvre more frequently with ours – is quickly concluded. He allows that this is a fine idea, sounding like a champion heavyweight boxer who has just swatted a pesky mosquito, and sends me off to see Vice-Admiral Duke Hernandez, commander of the Third Fleet, which would be more directly involved in any such Canadian caper. Keeping watch over fifty million square miles of ocean in the eastern Pacific, the Third Fleet consists of 80 ships, 1,200 aircraft, and more than 200,000 sailors and marines.

A former naval aviator who rose to command aircraft carriers, Hernandez is quartered aboard the battle cruiser USS *Coronado*. The flagship bristles with so many missiles she looks like a floating pin cushion. The admiral boasts three post-graduate degrees in international affairs and proves to be a lively debater, who, unfortunately, is well-enough briefed to dismiss anyone representing Canada's naval service as not being on a serious wavelength. After a polite interval of about ten minutes, he gets up and, trying to keep the condescension out of his voice, asks, "Can I do anything else for you?"

I suspect this is more a dismissal than a kindness, but decide to take advantage of the offer. "Yes, sir," I say as I jump to my feet. "As a matter of fact, you can. I've seen every movie and read every book about Pearl Harbor, but I've never been here before. Could I have a tour?"

"No problem," he replies, as he rings for his flag lieutenant to relay my request.

"Can't be done, sir," replies his smooth-bore assistant. "Our visitors' boat is being repaired and won't be ready for a week."

"No problem," repeats the admiral. (When you have military control over half of the earth's surface, nothing is a problem.) "Take *my* barge."

Now, this is a serious proposition. Admirals' barges are elegant vessels, used by them to inspect their fleets. They are luxurious vintage motorboats, easily identified by the flag of horizontal red and white stripes displayed on the bow, indicating that they take precedence over all other naval vessels within their jurisdictions. The following morning, wearing my yellowing summer whites, I climb aboard this admiral's barge, a spiffy, fifty-five-foot, broad-beamed example of wooden-boat workmanship at its finest. It is manned by two seamen standing on the stern in gleaming whites, who execute an elaborate ballet with their boat hooks after I return their salutes.

In charge is a seasoned coxswain, his chest expanded by a rainbow of ribbons, who, in an alcohol-cured voice, leaves little doubt that he feels humiliated by the lowly status of his cargo. Why has his admiral inflicted this visiting fireman on him? Has he not devoted his life to the double eagle? Has he not served long enough to avoid such a routine chore? I notice that the coxswain walks with a pronounced starboard list, as though permanently leaning into a western squall. His mood does not improve when I congratulate him on his nautical tilt. "Makes you look like a real seadog," I josh. He glares at me but says nothing.

After we pay appropriate homage to the USS *Arizona*'s drowned crew, the coxswain pointedly suggests, "How about going back now, sir."

"Oh, no," I counter. "Let's go for a spin to the outer harbour." So we drift due east through the lazy afternoon while I savour the sun and a Diet Pepsi. Suddenly, I notice the coxswain freeze in his position at the wheel. He asks me to hide in the cabin, a request I ignore. Then I recognize the problem. Heading straight toward us is a long, grey line of the most impressive battle wagons I have ever seen. The Third Fleet of the United States Navy is coming home from the sea and is about to enter its home port. I feel as if a street of skyscrapers is coming right at me and sense dozens of high-powered binoculars being aimed at the admiral's barge by people trying to read my rank and my business.

At this point, the coxswain is madly waving his arms across his face to indicate that the admiral is not aboard and everybody should relax. But Hernandez is not a relaxed admiral and he often stages surprise inspections. So the incoming captains are not about to take a chance. As the flotilla approaches us, I can hear ships' whistles blowing, see salute flags being raised, and spot officers and crew racing to line up impressively on the port side of their ships' superstructures, ready to salute their admiral. The coxswain and I look at one another. We shrug. There is only one thing to do. Naval decorum demands that a salute be held until it is returned. So I climb aboard the barge's saluting platform and, like a pope presuming worship, execute a smart salute as each man-o'-war steams by, flags aflutter, whistles blaring.

As they pass the barge, the captains' reactions are mostly puzzled looks and shaking heads, with the exception of one grizzled skipper who slaps his forehead and stomps off his bridge.

And that's how I brought the United States Navy's Third Fleet into Pearl Harbor.

THAT WAS ONE SMALL INCIDENT in the double life I led during more than four decades: as a pushy journalist and an undercover naval officer, in love with both professions and determined not to betray the integrity of either. It was a tough gig. At least once a week, after my work day, I would disappear into a nearby closet and, like Superman, change into my uniform and peaked officer's cap to attend to naval matters. No one ever saw me, except driving around Toronto, alone in my car; more than once at inter-sections pedestrians would spot my cap (similar to those worn by cabbies in those days), climb into my back seat, and order me to take them to the races, or some such. I was occasionally tempted to deliver them to their destinations and mint a little extra cash but never did.

I enlisted in the Royal Canadian Navy as an ordinary seaman on October 21, 1947, three months after graduating from Upper Canada College. In a sense, it was inevitable that I join the navy. Ever since my earliest breath, I had been fascinated by the sea, by tales of seafaring, and by the great fleets and warships of the world. Perhaps it was the result of a sheltered upbringing, which naturally caused my mind to seek farther horizons – and in my youth, wan-dering led to the sea, not to the air lanes of the sky.

The first book I read in English was C.S. Forester's swashbuck-ling tale of Napoleonic adventure *Beat to Quarters*, featuring Captain Horatio Hornblower of the Royal Navy. (In Forester's later "prequels," he was demoted to Mr. Midshipman Hornblower.) I devoured it, plunging into the scents and colours of the faraway Nicaraguan coast, feeling betrayed by the mad captain El Supremo and enchanted by Lady Barbara. The other novels followed, and I was soon captured off the Spanish coast in *A Ship of the Line* only to escape home to England in *Flying Colours*. I resolved to be just like Hornblower: compassionate, courageous, quick-witted – and, above all, a consummate Royal Navy man. Growing up in land-locked Ontario, I relished tales of square-rigged adventures, and in later years, I joined the Royal Navy for the cinematic exploits of *Lieut. Daring, R.N.*, or enlisted in the Royal Canadian Navy to hunt U-boats with Randolph Scott aboard *Corvette K-225*.

This love of naval literature has never left me. When it was published in 1951, I was profoundly influenced by Nicholas Monsarrat's *The Cruel Sea*, the classic tale of war in the North Atlantic. As a navy man, how could I not be transfixed by its opening lines: "This is the story – the long and true story – of one ocean, two ships, and about one hundred and fifty men"? I read the tale of the corvettes HMS *Compass Rose* and *Saltash*, and their cat-and-mouse games with wolf packs of U-boats, while I was myself on the North Atlantic in a warship.

There were two other reasons for joining the navy besides my love of the sea. I doubted that I could ever afford a boat of my own, so my chances of feeling the ocean swell under my feet would have to be at government expense. On top of which, I somehow felt that I would be a certified Canadian only when I walked down the street in naval uniform with the "CANADA" badges on my shoulders. Not surprisingly, then, I found myself at the navy recruiting table for undergraduates at the University of Toronto signing the requisite forms, and a short while later I was sworn in as one of nine thousand volunteer members of the University Naval Training Division (UNTD), which flourished for a quarter of a century during the height of the Cold War.

My proudest moment was the day I first put on my sailor suit. It was the standard sailor's square rig, dating back to the time of Nelson. To my delight, there on both shoulder flashes was the word "CANADA," as I had expected. Only seven years before, I had stumbled ashore in Halifax, and now I was returning to the same port, a certified Canadian, officially stamped as such, ready to help defend my new homeland.

I found that when I went on my first training course in Halifax it was easy to fit in with my fellow recruits. We were bonded by a mutual ignorance of all things nautical – many of my comrades in arms had come to the sea from the Prairies, and none of my battalion experience from school turned out to be transferable. What we learned had little to do with war. We were taught the naval code of conduct, knot-tying, Morse code, weather forecasting, navigation, sailing, semaphore, how to march to exhaustion, how to survive early-morning calisthenics, and how to salute as if we meant it. In the evenings we became adept at wooing the lively girls of Halifax. It really is true that girls love a man in uniform. Besides, it didn't hurt that they believed us all to be gentlemen from good homes. I conducted my amorous pursuits at private sailing clubs on the northwest arm of Halifax Harbour, although many cadets braved the rougher seaman's bars along Upper Water Street. Our efforts were for naught, since nearly all the girls were good Catholics, and in those days good Catholic girls *didn't*. Along the way, we grew up. We became a band of brothers, proud of our service, which voiced and practised a very un-Canadian love of country that stayed with us the rest of our lives. At a time when domestic travel was still a luxury, we met and bonded with young Canadians of our own age and education from every province, including Quebec, awakening to the fact that there was a land out there – and a people – worth knowing.

When the UNTD was breech-birthed during the final phase of the Second World War, it was a late addition to such similar training schemes as the Reserve Officers Training Corps (ROTC), founded by the Canadian army in 1921, and the University Air Training Plan (UATP), established by the air force in 1939. Incredibly, our service's official name was originally the Canadian University Naval Training Service. For most of its founding year no one seemed to realize the embarrassment that lay in its initials.

As members of the UNTD, we got off lightly, inevitably known as the "Untidies." But even if the regulars, whom we derisively called "Pusser types,"[1] made fun of us, being a UNTD in the 1950s and 1960s was a rare and valuable experience. Most days of the year we were campus cats, trying our best to baffle the professors who marked our tests and essays. But one night a week, we changed into uniform to drill at the nearest of forty naval reserve divisions, buildings far from the oceans known as "stone frigates." In those days, the Royal Canadian Navy, which during the Second World War had grown into the free world's fourth-largest fleet, was still a fifty-two-ship armada that made a difference. Every summer, we boarded trains to either Halifax or Victoria to earn our sea time, which often meant trips to Bermuda or Hawaii.

My first venture was aboard the minesweeper HMCS *Portage*, at nine hundred tons one of the smallest of the RCN's training ships, bound for St. George's in Bermuda – or, more accurately, for The Pirates' Den, then the island's most notorious hangout. As ordinary seamen we slept in hammocks, and my most vivid memory was the early-morning wake-up call, with an iron-lunged petty officer blowing his bosun's pipe and bellowing: "Wakey, Wakey! RISE AND SHINE! Drop your cocks and grab your socks!" (I sometimes got it the wrong way around.) There was no respite for us greenhorns. The training was relentless and the sea was cruel. On the return journey, I was assigned as port lookout on the open side of the bridge just as we were edging into a minor hurricane.

---

[1] The term comes from Pusser's Navy Rum, an essential ingredient in the daily portion of grog issued to Jack Tars until 1970. The name "Pusser" is a corruption of the word *purser*, the naval officer responsible for a ship's stores, including rum. For more than three hundred years, the navy handed out grog (one part raw rum diluted by two parts water) to most ratings daily, which proved to be a handy antidote to the mostly inedible food rations. (As we downed our rum, our favourite toast reflected the sailors' most fervent prayer: "To our wives and sweethearts – may they never meet.") This practice made us superior to the U.S. Navy, which allowed nothing stronger than iced tea on its warships. One time in Halifax, tied up next to the mighty USS *Missouri*, as we were answering our "Up Spirits" call, we heard the battleship's crew being hailed: "Now hear this – All hands to the fantail for chocolate ice cream!"

As the little ship ploughed into waves many times its height, they upended her into nearly vertical positions; the bow then slammed down like a machete. I prayed that the hull's steel plates had not been riveted into place by the lowest bidder. On calmer days, I cleaned heads (toilets)[2] and flats (passageways), never comprehending how a ship could get so dirty in the middle of a heaving ocean.

When I took over as helmsman, the officer of the watch glanced back at the ship's wake and remarked that it reminded him of a "snake with hiccups." (Why didn't he become a writer?) I learned that the wisest regular aboard any navy ship is the three-badge able-bodied seaman, his badges indicating lengthy service without promotion: "Thirteen years of undetected crime," as one of them described it to me.

Two years later, I shipped out aboard HMCS *Iroquois*, a Tribal-class destroyer, on her way to Charlottetown. The training, conducted by Executive Officer Peter Godwin Chance, Pierre Simard, and his assistant Jake Howard (who later became a distinguished Bay Street lawyer), was the toughest and the most useful we experienced. I was not a star pupil. One night off the coast of Prince Edward Island I was on anchor watch, which meant spending most of the night on the bridge making sure that we didn't drift ashore. One of the bearings I had to check was a lighthouse emitting flashing red signals. Unfortunately, I mistook the tail light of a car going through a grove of trees along the coastal highway for the flashing red light of the lighthouse. I transposed the speed of that moving object to the ship and rushed down to inform our navigator that we were drifting at twenty knots. I hid in the chain locker for the next two days.

By the spring of 1949, I had become a cadet, one rank below a Royal Navy midshipman. This pleased me, as in my imagination Mr. Midshipman Hornblower had almost become Mr. Midshipman Newman. The only difference between our uniforms was that

---

[2] So called because latrines were formerly kept in the "beakhead," or the space in the ship forward of the forecastle.

our gunnery kit didn't have the midshipman's three buttons on the cuff, which were put there to prevent snotty-nosed young officers from wiping their noses on their sleeves. My $30 monthly allowance was increased to $170. The following summer, in July 1950, I volunteered for the Korean War. The previous month, North Korea, backed by Chinese Communists, had invaded South Korea in force, triggering a conflict that would last three years and cost more than a million lives. Canada's initial response was to lend naval support to the United Nations coalition defending South Korea. Three destroyers, the *Cayuga*, *Athabaskan*, and *Sioux*, were sent to Korean waters under UN command, but there were no takers for reserve cadet volunteers. I decided to leave the executive branch for something more interesting.

I knew that I wanted to write, so I requested a transfer to the only two branches that had anything to do with the written word: Naval Intelligence and Naval Information. There, I came under the influence of my first important mentor, Captain William Strange. A native of British Honduras, Captain Strange had written novels, drilled for oil in Trinidad, taught at a British private school, and acted as a tutor to the children of the pasha of Egypt. After emigrating to Canada in 1929, he became a popular literary critic and a prize-winning CBC radio play producer. He spent most of the Second World War in charge of Naval Information, and when I arrived on his doorstep in 1950, he became the first adult to take me seriously. By giving me responsible writing assignments and allowing me to interact with naval officers at every level, including Rear-Admiral Rollo Mainguy (then in charge of the Atlantic fleet), he instilled in me my first dollop of self-confidence. I grew to greatly admire both him and his wonderful architect wife, Jean, who survives him in their post-retirement home at Lake Chapala, near Guadalajara in central Mexico.

All this effort came under the heading of trying to make the grade, so that at the end of four years, along with my degree, I would be promoted to sub-lieutenant in the Royal Canadian Navy (Reserve). To earn my commission, I first had to pass muster at a sombre selection board. Only 22 per cent of the candidates made the final cut. For some reason that annoyed me then and disturbed me a lot more afterward, the standard method for determining whether aspiring cadets were keeping up with current events was for selection board chairmen to inquire whether they regularly read the Canadian edition of *Time*. It was hardly an ideal test for those about to offer their lives in the cause of Canadian nationhood, I figured, and adamantly denied ever having opened *Time*,[3] or even knowing what it was.

After receiving my commission in 1951, I returned to Captain Strange's directorate in Ottawa and slowly began to dovetail my naval and civilian careers. As I moved up in journalism and the navy (I was promoted to commander in 1980), there emerged a unique confluence of interests. The navy wanted someone with journalistic credentials and a basic knowledge of naval matters to document its fatal failings, hoping to provoke some national pride – and naval spending – among politicians. At the same time, editors loved such scandalous revelations. To avoid any conflict of interest, I requested that my naval pay be stopped, and spent most of four decades merrily attacking the navy with its blessing. My dispatches revealed, among other flaws, such bizarre situations as:

- At one point, three of the destroyers that were counted as part of our NATO contribution were laid up permanently at dockside so they could be cannibalized for spare parts to keep their sister ships afloat.
- Another member of our official NATO fleet, the grandly named HMCS *Crusader* – which had seen action in Korea – was in such dire straits that whole areas of its plating had rusted out and you

---

[3] I know of only one cadet who beat the system. When Robert Perry, later managing editor of the *Financial Post* and at the time the youthful stringer for *Time* in Winnipeg, was asked the inevitable question, he drew himself ramrod stiff and replied: "Sir, in Winnipeg, I *am* *Time* magazine." He not only got his stripe, he was given command of a training ship one summer on the Great Lakes.

could walk through its watertight bulkheads. It found its final rusting place at a Cape Breton junkyard.

- The supply replenishment vessel HMCS *Protecteur*, part of our contribution to the first Gulf War against Iraq, was not fitted out for combat at all, except for being painted battleship grey. The only reason an antiquated three-inch gun was mounted on its bow was not to shoot at anyone, but so that as a warship the *Protecteur* would enjoy priority at diesel re-fuelling pumps.

- The naval training vessel HMCS *Porte St. Jean*, which had the distinction of being condemned as unseaworthy on its maiden voyage, similarly armed itself when its skipper went into a Canadian Tire store and bought enough material to build a wooden "gun-like" structure around a narrow-gauge open sewer pipe, painted grey. He then ran up two empty bleach bottles on his mast to simulate the style of fire-direction electronics to make his tub look more like a warship.

- The ultimate insult to Canada's navy was the private-sector purchase of four $800,000 submarines (complete with ballast tanks and battery-driven motors) to take shoppers, twenty-four at a time, on underwater tours of an artificial pond created at the West Edmonton Mall. This meant that the shopping centre had a larger and more modern fleet of subs than the navy, which at that time had only three, 1960s-era boats that were eventually replaced by obsolete British submarines, all of which leaked.

- The stories about Sea King helicopters, which are between thirty-four and forty years old and require thirty hours of maintenance for each hour in the air, are legion. But one Sea King set a record for slow flight in the spring of 2002, when it took three weeks to reach Halifax from Vancouver because of the number of landings for emergency repairs.

- As late as 1985, most of our destroyers were using navigation and communications equipment operated by vacuum tubes instead of microchips. When I asked one commanding officer where he was able to find replacements, he told me they were still being made by a factory in Poland but were now difficult to obtain (this was during the Cold War).

• When the twenty-year-old destroyer HMCS *Athabaskan* was being armed to participate in the 1990 Gulf War, its only anti-aircraft weapon was a pair of Second World War–vintage Bofors guns that had to be borrowed from the Maritime Museum in Halifax.

A story, told in Halifax wardrooms in the 1990s, had an eager officer exclaim, "We attack at dawn!" To which his straight man asked, "Why at dawn?" The reply was: "That way, if we don't succeed, we won't have wasted the whole day."

The horror stories were not confined to the navy. I wrote about army cadets training in New Brunswick during the 1960s without enough rifles to go around, so that many had to carry broomsticks pretending they were weapons. My favourite moment of the day was when one cadet pointed his broom at another and triumphantly announced: "Bang, bang, you're dead." To which his intended victim replied: "No, I'm not. I'm a tank!"[4]

Such stories were fun to write, and I like to think that a few political consciences were pricked, but I'm not sure. Our insulting approach to national defence, after all, has a long tradition. In the 1930s, when one of the Calgary cavalry regiments switched from horses to tanks, it had to simulate the newfangled vehicles by using burlap-covered frames mounted on motorcycles – until they were replaced by Chevrolets clad in sheet metal.

MY DOUBLE LIFE as a navy shill and independent journalist would have been more difficult to reconcile were it not for these horror

---

[4] For some reason, these stories always remind me of former Washington Mayor Marion Barry's boast: "Outside of the killings, we have one of the lowest crime rates in the country."

stories. To my mind, it was easier to justify using my naval contacts as a journalistic source when the end result was not a glorious puff-piece about the all-seeing wisdom of the naval brass, but yet another embarrassing revelation about their equipment inadequacies.

Still, I freely admit that by pointing out these deficiencies I was playing into the navy's agenda of goading its political masters into spending more on appropriations.

The case has never been convincingly made that Canada's military spending should reflect its role; rather, its role depends on the amount of military spending available. Military requirements are unpredictable by their very nature, the only certainty being that there will, come any crisis, be demands that exceed the amount set aside for it. Peacetime governments can either spend as little as possible, risking the possibility of being unable to respond to crises as they arise; or spend more than necessary, to be in a state of readiness for any unexpected emergency. In the past thirty years or so, Canadian politicians have consistently chosen the former course, with the result that we have been pathetically unable to meet our obligations to the world community. To mention just one example, the anticipated "peace dividend" at the end of the Cold War has disappeared in a miasma of Gulf conflicts, Balkan strife, ethnic cleansings, and terrorist activity. I enthusiastically agreed with Jean Chrétien when he declined Canadian military involvement in the second war against Iraq on the grounds that the case for war had never been convincingly made. But I do think Canada has a necessary role to play in peacekeeping duties and the enforcement of UN sanctions. It was a source of personal embarrassment to me as a journalist, and professional embarrassment as a naval officer, when Canada was forced to scrounge through naval museums to arm its warships for duty in the Persian Gulf.

In any case, I made no effort to hide my conflict of interest, if any such conflict could be said to exist when I believed in both my causes so fervently and felt that I served them well. On the contrary, I proudly wore my naval uniform, realizing that I was the butt of jokes, both privately and in print, for being some kind of bathtub admiral. I likely received as many jabs for my dress blues as I did for my ever-present Greek fisherman's cap, another fashion icon that I wear out of my affection for the sea. Those who criticized me for not excusing myself from commenting on military affairs misunderstood my relationship to Canada and journalism. Most of my peers were raised during a period of anti-militarism. The influence of the Vietnam protests was felt north of the border, and for many of my colleagues, all military matters were framed by the image of Kent State students placing flowers in the barrels of National Guardsmen's rifles.

I had joined the Canadian navy with much less ambivalence about the military than either my journalistic colleagues or the country at large. For me, the role of the armed forces was simple – to protect the Canadian people and their sovereignty, however those interests were defined by the politicians in Ottawa. I had experienced first-hand what aid and comfort can be found from a military intent on offering assistance, rather than destruction.

Was this attitude in conflict with my role as a journalist? To suggest this is to pretend that journalists must exist in a state of detachment from their society, like monks sealed in a cloister. That was never my style of journalism, and there are many historical precedents that support my approach. The pantheon of journalists is filled with those who were committed to causes or served under arms, which experience enlightened rather than corrupted their writing. George Orwell was a declared democratic socialist who volunteered with the Republican Army during the Spanish Civil War; the resulting book, *Homage to Catalonia*, is considered the finest example of reporting on that conflict. No one has suggested that his portrayal of that war was any less vivid or accurate because of his beliefs or service as a soldier – instead, the opposite is true. Ernest Hemingway was a war reporter in Spain and in the Second World War, yet no one suggested that his declared sympathies, expressed in works like *For Whom The Bell Tolls*, conflicted with his role as a journalist. On the contrary, his fame as a politically committed novelist underscored his understanding of the human dimension of war and added to the quality of his reporting. There is perhaps no more illustrious precedent to my double life, however, than that of the young Winston Churchill. After leaving the Royal Military College at Sandhurst, Churchill entered the 4th Queen's Own Hussars and was sent first to action in Cuba, where he reported as an officer on the Cuban War of Independence for the *Daily Graphic* in London. In 1896, he saw service both as soldier and reporter with the Malakand field force in India; his resulting book launched both careers, as journalist and celebrated warrior. He later volunteered for Kitchener's expeditionary force to the Nile, where he once again performed the dual role of soldier and correspondent. His book *The River War* is still considered one of the best accounts of life under fire. Reporting as a civilian on the Boer War for the *Morning Post* of London, he could not resist entering the fighting and won fame for his part in rescuing an ambushed armoured train and escaping from a Boer prison camp.

I never felt it was the duty of journalists either to promote or to oppose; they must simply tell the truth as they find it. If my experience of the navy helped me to uncover more truths than others, then that was my good fortune. Did my loyalty to flag, naval colours, or brothers- and sisters-in-arms influence my writing? Undoubtedly. It informed my writing, made me more aware of the issues, and more determined to write about them. Did it cause me to bend the truth in any way? Not to my knowledge. That wasn't necessary, since my beliefs as a journalist and my obligations as a navy man enjoyed a happy coincidence. I wanted, and still want, the best for the Canadian navy. I will never apologize for that.

THE FUTURE OF THE CANADIAN NAVY depends on rediscovering its pride and purpose. The navy also faces problems formulating a defensive role that will allow it to remain independent of American initiatives.

Historically, one dilemma has been our past dependence on Britain's Royal Navy. The Royal Canadian Navy I joined was populated largely by graduates of the Royal Navy's training college on Whale Island, at Portsmouth. At the start of the Second World War, Chief of Naval Staff Percy Nelles actually recommended that the RCN be placed under British control, and one of his post-war successors, Vice-Admiral Harold Grant, refused to allow anyone to wear a "CANADA" shoulder flash because "it looks like hell on a uniform." (In fact, apart from the "C" on a sailor's cap tally and the shoulder flashes, there was absolutely no difference between the Royal Canadian Navy uniforms and those of the Royal Navy until 1950.) I recall young Canadian "subbies" joining the Royal Navy for training seminars and returning home with plummy English accents (calling their native land "*Canadahr*"), wearing silk handkerchiefs up their left sleeves, and looking down on us colonials.

In the winter of 1982, I was invited to visit the Royal Navy's hallowed base at Portsmouth and had a chance to see for myself what the RN mystique was all about. I arrived early for my appointment with Admiral Sir James Henry Fuller Eberle, commander-in-chief of the Home Fleet, so I toured Horatio Nelson's HMS *Victory*, permanently on view in Portsmouth Harbour. She is an impressive sight, a 104-gun, first-rate ship of the line, built in 1765 and still the oldest commissioned warship in the world, being the flagship of the Second Sea Lord and the commander-in-chief, Naval Home Command. Afterwards, I was invited for "a quick bite" at the Old Naval Academy. In the wardroom, I found myself surrounded by real naval officers, and it hit me that our green-garbage-bag uniforms (the legacy of the misconceived unification policy of Pearson's defence minister, Paul Hellyer) had robbed us of our professional identities. (I had myself been mistaken for the co-pilot of an obscure Venezuelan airline during my departure from Toronto airport.) As for the "quick bite," I will say only that it lived up to the English reputation for serving the world's worst food on the world's finest china. After our meal, we were served pudding, and I was horrified to see staring up at me from my bowl a dish all too familiar from UCC, the ubiquitous "fish-eyes-in-glue." The whole meal was bearable only when washed down with liberal glasses of sherry – the primary reason, I surmised, why the English eat at all.

Leaving the portals of the Old Naval Academy, I noticed a small sign: "Established 1729." That, I realized, was four generations before Nelson's 1805 victory over Napoleon's fleet at Trafalgar, when his famous flag signal from the poop deck of the *Victory*, "England expects that every man will do his duty," would resound through naval tradition – and I suddenly felt the full weight of the RN's heritage. I realized what Jan Morris, the British essayist, had meant when she wrote: "It was the Navy which had made Britain great, guaranteeing the island immunity and giving its people the freedom of imperial action; in return the Navy received a loyalty given no other department of State. A generation of British children grew up with the names of British battleships on the ribbons of their sailor hats, and a whole culture was created around the images of the Royal Navy. The service itself assumed an anthropomorphic character – hard-drinking but always alert, eccentric but superbly professional, breezy, naughty, posh, kindly, Nelsonically ready to disobey an order in a good cause, or blow any number of deserving foreigners out of the water."[5]

I was finally ushered in to meet Sir James Eberle, who looked exactly like a storybook admiral. His office was complete with a fireplace that didn't work, a threadbare carpet, and untidy memorabilia commemorating a career that had most recently included a term as NATO's commander-in-chief, East Atlantic. It seemed entirely appropriate that he should be a master of the Britannia

---

[5] The sultan of Morocco, after touring a visiting a Royal Navy battleship in the 1880s, was asked what had impressed him most – the sixteen-inch turret guns, the eight thousand horsepower engines, the two torpedo boats carried on board, or perhaps the electric light throughout. "The captain's face," he replied.

Beagles Club and president of the Royal Navy's Lawn Tennis Association. His cabin felt as if Nelson's mistress, Lady Emma Hamilton, might walk in any minute. As a lowly commander, I was at once mesmerized by the gold on his sleeve rank – one broad stripe and four thin ones. *My God*, I thought to myself, *one more stripe and he'll be king!*

The admiral was due to see me for an hour. Ninety minutes later we parted, after I had been a privileged audience of one for his overview of world affairs. He then dispatched me for a more political briefing to the Foreign and Commonwealth Office on King Charles Street in London's SW1, a nineteenth-century Italianate sprawl that resembled a Graham Greene version of a rundown Caribbean island's seat of government, with its white-washed corridors, sleepy guards, ceiling fans, and half-empty offices serving as a reminder of the British Empire's vanished colonies. From there, I went to the Admiralty Office in Whitehall for a quick call on the First Sea Lord of the admiralty. A sign near the entrance informed me that the building was on "Black Alert," which meant there were no terrorists expected that day – just a mendicant Canadian journalist in naval disguise, trying not to confuse the truth with the facts.

Sir Henry Leach, the First Sea Lord, entertained me like an Oxford don as he sipped a cup of tea and munched on water bis-cuits. He had a bulldog chin, kept a terrier, and looked every inch the British admiral, but I found Sir Henry surprisingly business-like. He confided that the problems of an all-volunteer force were catching up with the U.S. Navy; its training manuals had recently been rewritten for comprehension at a grade-five level. As I was about to leave, the admiral leaned back into his red leather chair and asked me to guess the level of damage U.S. nuclear submarines could inflict in the event that a Soviet first strike managed to wipe out the West's land-based retaliatory capacity. When I confessed my ignorance, he replied: "They could launch a nuclear weapon, each one three times the strength of the Hiroshima bomb, at the Russian mainland – every thirty seconds for twenty-four hours."

The admiral's terrier shook his head in disbelief. So did I. It was a chilling interview.

My experience made me appreciate Royal Navy tradition, but did nothing to dilute my Canadian sentiment. By the mid 1980s I started to give pro-naval speeches and was elected for two terms as head of the Maritime Defence Association of Canada, a publicly funded lobby group. I was appointed senior staff officer to three chiefs of reserves, including Rear-Admiral Wally Fox-Decent, a witty professor of political studies at the University of Manitoba, who became my champion. It was he who recommended me for promotion to captain, probably the only Jew to attain that rank in a navy still dominated by sea-going WASPs.

I ran afoul of Canadian military thinking only once. In 1983, I took on the freelance assignment of writing a position paper for the Business Council on National Issues, the big-business lobby group run by Ottawa's self-appointed prime-minister-in-waiting, Tom d'Aquino. The BCNI had rightly surmised that my report would recommend higher defence spending. But just then Canada was being pressured by the Pentagon to test the guidance systems of their terrain-guided cruise missiles, and that far I would not go. "Few of the technicalities about the cruise are understood by the general public," I wrote, "but Canadians have a way of smelling a rat." It seemed to me that the Canadian government was being set up by the Pentagon to test not, as was claimed, weapons for the defence of Europe, but offensive, first-strike nuclear missiles aimed at the destruction of Russian cities.

This was no petty issue. The American military had ordered twelve thousand of the missiles, each armed with a two-hundred-kiloton nuclear warhead, at a cost of $29 billion. We were supposed to test their launching capabilities from American bombers flying over the Mackenzie Basin of northern Alberta. By agreeing to these tests, the Trudeau government maintained, we would be meeting our commitments to NATO and might prompt the Soviets to take disarmament more seriously. Trudeau permitted the tests amidst overwhelming public opposition, yet his arguments for testing the cruise were fatally flawed. These were strategic, not tactical, weapons that threatened to unbalance the already precarious arms limitation talks.

As soon as d'Aquino read my report, he asked me to omit my criticism of the cruise testing. When I refused, he arranged a dinner meeting with former Tory leader Robert Stanfield, who was supposed to change my mind. We spent a pleasant evening discussing Duke Ellington's music, but I held my ground. The BCNI refused to publish my study, switching the assignment to George Bell, a retired general. I later used the report as a skeleton outline for *True North, Not Strong and Free: Defending the Peaceable Kingdom in the Nuclear Age*, which Bruce Hutchison called my "most important book." Everywhere I went during my promotional tour, serving members of the forces in ill-fitting civvies approached and whispered: "Keep it up. You're writing what we're not allowed to say."[6]

SPENDING MUCH OF FOUR DECADES in the navy had a profound effect on my life. There was certainly nothing heroic or even particularly patriotic about it. I became an ardent advocate for a cause that I believed in, and I have no regrets. The Canadian navy prided itself on being "the silent service," yet it deserved to be heard. Most Canadians live out of sight and sound of the ocean and can't begin to comprehend why we need a peacetime naval service. "Allow us to fulfil our burning desire to be significant in what we do," pleaded Vice-Admiral Chuck Thomas, the best of the postwar naval chiefs, when he resigned on an issue of principle. No one

---

[6] I was also active in obtaining and helping to raise funds for the *Sackville*, Canada's last corvette, now tied up at the Maritime Museum in Halifax. One of the other contenders was the *Christina*, a corvette purchased and converted for $4 million by Aristotle Onassis, the Greek shipping tycoon. The onetime warship featured a lounge that had barstools covered by a white whale's foreskin, prompting the owner to tell Greta Garbo, when she was his guest: "Madame, you are now sitting on the largest penis in the world."

paid any attention. Ever since Trudeau's stretch in office, Ottawa has regarded national defence as a bothersome afterthought. Trudeau himself once told me that it was his fourteenth priority, just after convicts and hog subsidies.

The Senior Service did so much with so little for so long that the politicians eventually believed it could do anything with nothing forever. That hopeful proposition broke down at the end of the second war against Iraq, when the navy admitted that it didn't have the funds remaining for fuel to keep its ships at sea, had exhausted its sea-going personnel to the point that they couldn't take on new assignments, was withdrawing from its permanent berth as part of the NATO standing naval force, and basically was going on a year's holiday, probably the first navy in history to do so.

Navies, like armies and air forces, mirror the character of the societies they are sworn to defend. In the final analysis, our survival depends on the will we can muster to protect our institutions, and that in turn depends on how much we learn to value them.

If I managed to stir up a little dirt in the defence of one of the more valuable of those institutions and woke up a few politicians to the disgrace that has become our navy, my mission was accomplished. I enjoyed the *Beau Geste* civility and touch of romance involved in being a naval officer. I became part of a lost generation that lived for their ships and their shipmates. Leafing through the photograph albums of my time in the service, I see the familiar faces of the crewcut lifers, caught up in the formalities of their careers. In their faces there is not a glimmer of duplicity, only the glint of accusation. Why, they are demanding, has the idea that Canada "expects every man to do his duty" become part of a vanished culture? Why could they not have been properly equipped for the tasks they were asked to perform? Like the statues of bypassed saints in the cathedrals of post-revolutionary France, they represent a banished heritage, a way of life outside the Canadian mainstream. And nothing will bring it back.

CHAPTER TEN

MY STAR WARS

*The Toronto Star's editorial team behaved
like a troupe of muzzled dancing bears
following the lead of their keeper,
who wasn't a jovial accordion player
but an uptight puppet master.*

While reporting from Parliament on the vagaries of the Diefenbaker-Pearson years, I maintained an uneasy *entente cordiale* with the American embassy. Then situated directly across Wellington Street from the Parliament Buildings – keeping an eye on the natives – the embassy was staffed by a platoon of brushcut operatives who didn't know quite what to make of me. On the one hand, I was known to be a Stan Kenton freak – in other words, a slave to American culture. Yet I was not regarded as a Yankee-lover, since I kept writing weird stories about how Canadians ought to throw off the yoke of U.S. imperialism and repatriate their economy, the sooner the better. At the time, this placed me one notch above UFO-spotters on the credibility scale, and as a result the embassy staff treated me with a wary bonhomie. If there was an embassy list of influential characters on the Ottawa scene, I would have rated somewhere between harmless eccentric and interesting kook, as the token (read *tame*) Canadian nationalist.

The succession of press attachés who were assigned to deal with me considered my support of economic nationalism an innocuous pastime, like collecting butterflies or having an interest in philately.

They were relentlessly good-natured and never once threatened (as they might now, since George W. Bush has turned their mighty Republic into Flintstone Country) to take away my rights to cross the world's longest undefended border at will.

These professional embassy flacks had hairy forearms, dressed and talked like Secret Service agents, and had transferable Christian and family names, such as Hathaway Johnson, Foster Brimstone, or Jeremiah Dean. My favourite among the bunch was a Mormon from Utah, who went by the name of Brigham Young or something similar. He had a loud, belly-pumping laugh, a shameless line in corn-pone humour (he would refer to the Mormon Tabernacle as "Norman's Bar and Tackle"), and he called me "Pilgrim." We were on friendly terms and he often steered visiting American reporters in my direction. These encounters typically began with a phone call from the embassy: "Howdy, Pilgrim. How's tricks? I need a favour – got this here newshound, ace reporter, top-drawer fella. He's coming into town for a big takeout on Our Neighbours to the North, longest undefended border, all that jazz. Give Uncle Sam a hand and fill 'im in? You'll like 'im. He's an in-depth kinda guy."

This happened more than once; the visitors ran to type, and I was always disappointed. I would be expecting a cross between Norman Mailer and Joseph Pulitzer, but what would arrive instead, an hour late and obviously the worse for wear, was a hardened old hand from the *St. Louis Post-Dispatch*, near the end of his shelf life, baffled by the lassitude of our lifestyle, impatient with the size of our snowdrifts, and frustrated by his inability to find a focus for his "big takeout." (There is, after all, only so much you can do with an undefended border, even if you are an in-depth kinda guy.) The one I remember best was as pretentious as he was uninformed. Sitting across from me at our embassy-sponsored lunch, he decided to demonstrate how well briefed he was by ordering a cocktail in French: "*Un Jacques Daniel dooble, sill-voo-play, maize avec pas de glass.*" Having made the effort, he muttered the explanation, "Why drown good bourbon in water, eh, Mr. Pilgrim?"

I patiently explained that I wasn't Peter C. Pilgrim, that this was only the code name used by the embassy, and gave him a shot of Parisian French: *"Je n'ai eu aucune idée que vous étiez complètement bilingue!"*

"You bet, pal," he responded, "and that goes double for me!"

After the initial pleasantries, he got to the point: "What is it with you Canadians? Why don't you like Americans? We love you guys. And where would you be without us? So what's the big deal, Pete? Don't tell me you're trying to be some kind of a frozen Cuba Libre?"

I could tell that no matter how sincere this itinerant luminary's intentions might be, and no matter how passionately I pleaded my cause, most of what I said would end up on the cutting-room floor. Still, I obligingly mumbled my nationalist set piece, pointing out that Canada as a nation was in danger of drowning in American dollars, American culture, American know-how, and the American dream. As my interrogator's eyes glazed over to the point of dozing off, I turned up the volume and told him that we Canadians resented the hell out of being brought to our knees by accidental conquerors out to crush our balls and rape our patrimony – or some such meaningless, if rebellious, cry from the heart.

Sooner rather than later the junketing visitor would go away, looking more perplexed than informed, and when his takeout finally appeared, my nationalistic rumble would be reduced to two paragraphs. It was the kind of token treatment that native witch doctors received in the old documentaries about Africa, gyrating around the fire in a necklace made of lion's teeth, spouting mumbo-jumbo and invoking the ju-ju spirits to frighten away the great white American hunters.

Times change; shift happens. The embassy stopped calling me; those in-depth guys were steered elsewhere to report on more benign expressions of nationalism. These became harder to find, as I gradually found myself less a lone voice of rebellion and more a moderate voice in a rising chorus of anti-American sentiment. My attitude – resenting Yankee influence and longing at least to *feel* a sense of independence – which had once seemed foreign to the Canadian cast of mind, had gradually become part of the national fabric.

That longing has never left me. Nationalism is the one political crusade I never tire of pursuing. Like most Canadians of my age and persuasion, for me it was born as a response to the war in Vietnam, the traumatic assassinations of the Kennedy brothers and Martin Luther King, and the violence of the American civil rights struggle. Surely, I felt, Canada was different; surely, we were more peaceable, more reasonable, more *civilized*. My sense of nationalism has since matured into something more modest and yet more enduring: an acknowledgement that my country's future, for all its faults, is not the same as the Manifest Destiny pursued by those zealots south of the forty-ninth parallel. Whether the American empire flexes its might by sending helicopter gunships over Baghdad or corporate raiders with bad comb-overs into Canadian boardrooms makes little difference. It is all part of their mission to consummate their God-given duty to convert the world to the American Way. That's a sentiment foreign to Canadians. We coddle no presumptions of destiny, manifest or even municipal. The Americans revere their War of Independence and worship their constitution as though it were Divine Writ; Canadians are content to believe that our country was born through immaculate conception, that we just sort of simmered up, an incongruous mixture of the defeated from foreign wars and those caught up in mercantile extravagances, hung out to dry in the long wash of history.

When I first began writing and thinking about the American takeover of my adopted homeland, it was a sometime thing. Significant Canadian corporations disappeared as their head offices moved southward, but Canada's basic economic infrastructure seemed to remain inviolate. It was only with the collapse of the Berlin Wall and the end of the Cold War in 1989 that the United States was transformed from an ambitious supermarket into a hyper-power, more militaristic than any since the Romans and more financially powerful than any since the British Empire at its peak. Never before had our planet been so directly wired into a single power source, and Canada — what was left of it — became the bargain basement for American trophy-hunters.

I was among the first Canadian journalists to attack the Yanks' winner-take-all strategy, which called for nice guys (read *innocente Canadese*) to finish last. I refused to recognize their takeover as a natural evolution of the trend to globalization that was sweeping the world. I took it personally. (Hell, when I'm sailing, I take *wind shifts* personally.) I have always felt that the popular metaphor of U.S.-Canada relations — an American elephant sleeping in the same bed with a Canadian mouse — gave us an undeservedly high profile. I see Canada as a flea trapped in the impervious hide of a rhinoceros; it can bite as much as it likes, but the rhino won't notice. Two-thirds of the world's top multinationals are American, most of them richer than most countries. Eight of the world's largest high-tech conglomerates live Stateside, as do the leading enterprises in such essential, post-industrial categories as financial services, biotechnology, media, entertainment, genetics, software design, and Internet. As for military technology, the United States has achieved a status unrivalled in history.

With no checks on its power or limits to its exponential growth, the sheer scale of U.S. domination has helped the cause of Canadian nationalism go mainstream. When I first began to promote the nationalist cause, it was largely the purview of the radical young, and activist intellectuals. Its appeal eventually touched an increasing number of old-line liberal internationalists, who still controlled the country's political establishment. A self-governing colony might be a contradiction in terms, but this had been Canada's pathetic status throughout most of its history, beholden first to London, then to Washington. In exchange for our borrowed American affluence, we sold our way of life to the highest bidders. In our northern naïveté, we had no inkling that by allowing the Americans to develop our natural resources and grab our most profitable companies we were permitting them to pollute our environment, direct our trade unions, deluge our media, drown our bookstores, dominate our magazine racks, control our movie houses, and flood our school texts with American ideas and values. We were in real danger of forgetting who we are and why we are here.

We ran the risk of becoming an American afterthought. If the Americans thought of us at all, it was as an attic in their mansion: a storage space taken for granted and only of concern if it became the source of strange noises or cold draughts. For our own part, we became guilty of treating our country as a vestibule: a giant waiting room where our best and brightest could linger until admitted to the glittering ballroom of American accomplishment. As Robert Fulford aptly commented, his generation "grew up believing that, if we were very good and very smart, we would someday graduate from Canada."[1]

Despite our mildly nationalistic impulses, the highest mark of approval across every Canadian field of endeavour came from south of the border: Nancy bought it on Fifth Avenue; Sam graduated from Harvard; Diane had her hysterectomy at the Mayo Clinic; we got our tans in Palm Beach; the *New York Times* loved my book – those were the meaningful accolades. We were the country cousins awed by the southern sophisticates. We understood perfectly what British novelist Anthony Burgess meant when he wrote: "John Kenneth Galbraith and Marshall McLuhan are the two greatest Canadians the United States has produced." In the fall of 1970, I drove down to Galbraith's farm at Newfane, Vermont, where he did most of his writing. During a long, leisurely afternoon's conversation, I asked him about his brand of nationalism. "Well," he said, unfolding his six-foot, eight-inch frame, "I was brought up in southwestern Ontario, where we were taught that Canadian patriotism should not withstand anything

[1] Between 1851 and 1951, Canada's population grew from two to eighteen million; during that period, seven million new immigrants arrived, while six million Canadians fled south.

more than a five-dollar-a-month wage differential. Anything more than that, and you went to Detroit."[2]

One of the most puzzling aspects of our uneven kinship – at least as viewed from Washington – was that while Canadian venture capitalists, industrialists, mayors, and premiers competed fiercely to lure American investment, when the U.S. dollars actually arrived, we would rear back and accuse the Yanks of trying to take us over. When I asked Mike Pearson about this paradox, he responded with a telling anecdote.

U.S. Secretary of State John Foster Dulles had flown up to Ottawa to discuss that very issue with Pearson, who was then our secretary of state for External Affairs. At a private Rideau Club dinner hosted by the American ambassador, just the sort of occasion at which he was at his civilized best, Pearson decided to deliver a brief but pointed lecture: "During the 1930s, while I was third secretary at the Canadian High Commission in London, a particularly horrendous murder took place in Hyde Park," he recalled. "A young woman had been murdered and mutilated, but not raped. *The Times* of London, that great newspaper, concluded its report of this outrage with the observation that the girl had been 'decapitated and dismembered, but not interfered with.'" Pearson then leaned forward and delivered his punchline: "Foster, that's the way we Canadians feel about you Americans. Decapitate us if you will. Dismember us if you must. Just don't interfere with us!"

Pearson believed that by being America's neighbour and natural ally we were, in a sense, hostages to Washington's good intentions. Of course, that was long ago, in the days when the White House still cared about being viewed as having benign intentions and

---

[2] At the end of our interview I shyly asked Galbraith about his reputation for arrogance: "As you may know," he replied, completely unfazed, "there are two forms of arrogance: that of ignorant people who pretend to know more than they do, and that of experts in their field, who really know what they're talking about. Fortunately, I belong to the latter group."

wielding a sense of moral virtue to match its military might, instead of confusing power with goodness. America's self-appointed imperialist writ, first enunciated by Thomas Paine in 1776, "The cause of America is in great measure the cause of all mankind," reached its zenith under Bush the Younger, who declared: "The liberty we prize is not America's gift to the world; it is God's gift to humanity."[3]

Living under such a massive umbrella of American interests, Canada has become an increasingly difficult country in which to nurture patriotic impulses. This was brought home to me most dramatically on January 28, 1991, when I was guest speaker at a Vancouver meeting of the Texas Society of Certified Public Accountants. Prior to my speech there was an awards ceremony, where the Lone Star state's best number-crunchers were honoured with plaques. As each winner was invited to the dais, I realized that I knew more about the history of their hometowns than Canada's counterparts: Laredo, Abilene, Galveston, El Paso, and Amarillo all recalled films I had seen, songs I had heard, and cowpokes whose exploits I had cheered during Saturday matinees. (And the list did not even include *Debbie Does Dallas*, which didn't become part of my education until much later in life.)

That small incident reinforced philosopher Bruce Powe's observation that each Canadian mind comprises two distinct and separate consciousnesses: one fully immersed in Canadian culture, entertainment and public life; the other fully immersed in American media, celebrity, and history. "We all carry this little

---

[3] In my favourite "Dubya" story, he and Dick Cheney are spending their first day in the presidential office and decide to take a break for lunch. When the White House waitress asks the vice-president what he'd like to eat, Cheney orders roast beef. She then turns to the President: "And you, sir?"

"I'll have a Quickie," Bush answers, and is astonished when the waitress stomps off, muttering, "I thought those days were over when Mr. Clinton left."

Bush turns to Cheney: "What was all that about?"

"Well, George, it's actually pronounced *quiche*."

American around inside us," he wrote. "It can't be helped. But in some areas, we've let him take the reins."

Americans wear their hearts, and their flag, on their sleeve. In the Canada I love, even the mildest display of open affection for one's home country is seen as an eccentric curiosity, if not a dangerous aberration. Americans are the eternal honeymooners, proclaiming their love from the rooftops; we are the long-married couple, expressing an ocean of sentiment in a shy smile. It is one of our quiet strengths. While appearing on Rafe Mair's open-line radio show in Vancouver, I once declared flat out: "I love Canada." The switchboard lit up like a birthday cake and the first caller, breathing aggressively, demanded that I explain myself. "You say you love Canada," she snorted. "Well, tell us, Mr. Smart-Apple Newman, why are you being so anti-American? Eh?"

I had said nothing to which Uncle Sam could have taken the slightest exception, I had simply expressed my gratitude for the country that had taken me in when I was escaping from Nazi-occupied Europe. I loved Canada then with the unaffected passion of a child, and that passion is with me still. There is nothing ideological or philosophical about this emotion. It is love, pure and simple, and like every man I see it as my mission in life to protect and cherish what I love the most, and see nothing wrong with proclaiming my love in public.[4]

Determining the line where love of country ends and fear of Yankee domination begins has become increasingly difficult. I have always maintained that I am *not* anti-American, that all I wish is for Canada to recapture sufficient control of its destiny to pursue its own, instead of imported, values. However much there is to admire in the American ethic, it is not ours. The closest anyone has

---

[4] Swayed by the same emotion, I once declared in a Winnipeg speech: "I physically love Canada!" The satirical weekly magazine *Frank* could not resist the temptation to reproduce my remark, adding the tag line: "I'd give a nickel to see that!"

come to describing our complex relationship with the United States was the former federal Social Credit leader Robert Thompson, master of the mangled metaphor, who declared: "The Americans are our best friends, whether we like it or not."

This was brought home to me during a chat I once had with Jacques Maisonrouge, then the head of IBM's European and Asian operations. I had been carrying on in my usual tiresome way about the importance of the U.S.-Canada border. His eyes searched the ceiling, until he could stand it no longer. "The fact is," he said, "that for us the boundaries that separate one nation from another are no more real than the Equator. They're just lines on a map. The world outside our parent company's home office is no longer viewed as a series of disconnected customer opportunities, but as the extension of a single marketplace." There is no doubt Maisonrouge was describing the brave new world we now occupy, but for me "globalization" will remain not an aspiration, but a call to arms.

Canadian nationalism has remained a cause in search of a leader, a crusade more often debated than joined. The outstanding exception to this rule was Walter Lockhart Gordon, the Liberal Party's Man of La Mancha, who flourished briefly under Mike Pearson's sponsorship in the mid 1960s. A true-blue Toronto accountant, he was one of those rare figures in Canadian public life who traded in ideas and principles, instead of power and status. His theories had about them the charcoal haziness of Picasso sketches, leaving too much of his intentions to the beholder's imagination. He was by nature a reformer and not a rebel. Equally quixotic was Mel Hurtig, the Edmonton publisher who was brave enough to lead his National Party to oblivion in the 1993 federal election. Revolutions are authenticated by radical shifts in national consciousness, and that requires the radicalism of a Che Guevara and the daring of a Giuseppe Garibaldi. Hurtig and Gordon were neither, but at least they focused the debate, eschewing what George Orwell called "the smelly little orthodoxies of politics" for the sake of reclaiming the country. Hurtig had the long-term advantage of being able to transpose his passions into exciting prose, and his books on the subject are monuments to the cause and his commitment, while Gordon's dry tracts read like manuals on beekeeping.

Gordon's first budget as minister of Finance, introduced in June 1963, disintegrated like a cake left out in the rain. Nearly all of his impractical repatriation measures had to be withdrawn; the Opposition demanded his head; the Press Gallery was baying for his resignation; and even his own colleagues were muttering that he had to go. I arranged for an interview with this man at the eye of the storm. As I settled in a chair across from the Regency writing desk he had brought with him to Ottawa, I uncomfortably put forward an all-embracing question. "Well, Walter," I asked. "What happened?"

Gordon glanced up blandly from his papers and replied with deceptive innocence, "What happened about *what*?"

As the conversation proceeded, I realized that his air of detachment was not a mask for despair. Gordon would survive the ordeal, as would his ideals of economic self-determination. I liked him, admired him, and felt his sorrow. As Finance minister he often had to visit Washington, but he insisted there be no official welcoming party at the airport. While other Cabinet ministers would be delayed by the formalities of a receiving line, Gordon would hop off the aircraft with an overnight case in hand, unattended and carefree. He was one of the few politicians I met who abhorred pretence of any kind, was motivated by sterling principles instead of expediency, and never disappointed me.

IT WAS WALTER GORDON'S INFLUENCE that helped decide my next career move. By the time Mike Pearson was getting ready to resign as prime minister, Christina and I were debating our own options. We were both exhausted by twelve years of the Ottawa social and professional grind, and agreed that a change of jobs and location might benefit our marriage and ourselves. Thanks to the success of my books and columns, I had been invited to take senior writing jobs at *Time*, *Business Week*, the *Wall Street Journal*, and the

Montreal Daily Star, in addition to the editorships of the Vancouver *Sun* and the *Winnipeg Free Press*. These were flattering opportunities, but none of these slots tempted me in the least – I was after a platform where I could preach my nationalistic convictions. Beland Honderich, publisher of Canada's largest newspaper, the *Toronto Star*, was prompted by Walter Gordon to consider me as a candidate for the position of editor-in-chief. Honderich had earned a reputation for using editors for target practice, but I figured I had survived hard cases before, such as the Nazi dive bomber bent on a similar mission. What mattered to me was that the *Star* was the house organ of Canadian nationalism, and as its editor, I would be in a position to advance my crusade. My Ottawa column was capably taken over by Anthony Westell.

That crusade was launched in earnest on February 3, 1970, when I had lunch in the ornate Victoria Room of Toronto's King Edward Hotel with Walter Gordon and Abe Rotstein, the University of Toronto professor of political economy who had provided Canadian nationalism with its philosophical underpinnings. After lamenting that no one seemed to care about the issue that had brought us together, we decided to establish the Committee for an Independent Canada (CIC) to lobby Ottawa for political action. We knew that to be taken seriously, we had to demonstrate that the repatriation of our economy had a broad following in the country, so we set about collecting 100,000 names on a petition demanding a halt to the growth of foreign ownership. After forming a steering committee of 120 leading Canadians to plot our strategy, we managed to get 170,000 signatures and put the issue on the national political agenda. In the year that followed, I spoke at what seemed like every Canadian church basement and Rotary Club luncheon, pushing the cause of economic nationalism.[5] With

---

[5] I also became a visiting professor in the political science department of Hamilton's McMaster University, which at that time was staffed entirely by imported American academics. The kids mobbed my classroom, especially when I promised to abolish exams and to host interesting guest lecturers.

Claude Ryan, I wrote the CIC's charter and constitution, while Jack McClelland, Mel Hurtig, and Eddie Goodman took over as joint chairmen. We had ten thousand members spread across forty chapters and became responsible for, among other ventures, the creation of the Foreign Investment Review Agency and the domestic programming regulations governing the Canadian Radio-Television and Telecommunications Commission.

I ABANDONED OTTAWA in 1969, the way a once-loyal soldier deserts a retreating army. Christina and I loved our professional lives in the capital, made permanent friends, and believed that we had been ardent witnesses to the best years of what Ottawa had to offer. But we never had enough time for ourselves, for our daughter, and for the kind of leisurely companionship we had hoped to enjoy. I thought that by moving to a new job in Toronto we could expand our time together as a couple and as a family. At the same time, after a dozen years of blasting politicians for not living up to my bloated expectations, I was hesitant to go through one more cycle of disillusionment. Pierre Trudeau, who had just succeeded Pearson, had been a friend, as were many members of his inner circle. I knew that if I remained in Ottawa, I would soon be criticizing Lucky Pierre and his disciples, many of whom I genuinely admired.

As I drove around Ottawa on a fond farewell tour, I retraced the route I had taken from the airport on first arriving in 1957, and realized again that the city has no long-term memory and no enduring loyalties. Only Ottawa's buildings survive as monuments to each successive administration's failure to cut costs and reduce bureaucracies. Those who stay beyond their allotted time find their names prefixed by "the former," which broadcasts the fact they are several steps removed from the power sources that count. They no longer belong to that clubby yet furtive atmosphere that pervades political Ottawa. Though they might once have had a devil-may-care approach to politics, convinced that it was a game, not a religion, once they've been excommunicated (*i.e.*, their phones stopped ringing), they are not so sure.

Filled with a sense of constantly renewed curiosity, I had gone tapping my way along Ottawa's corridors of power like a blind man trying to make sense of the noise and the darkness. I had chronicled how three prime ministers had stumbled, and watched as federal power had diminished. The twin levers of Keynesian control by which Ottawa had once steered the economy – interest rates and taxation – were effective only inside a closed system. But the system had gone global. Stéphane Dion, the Quebec political scientist and later twice a Liberal Cabinet minister, got it right when he concluded that "Canada is a country that works in practice, but not in theory." Most of the great issues were exhausted, not through the catharsis of solutions but due to the absence of decisive action. The essential middle ground between smugness and despair had grown dangerously narrow; there was little accommodation between the people's militant demands and the system's moderate possibilities. The cynics could justifiably claim that George Bernard Shaw's devastating prediction had come true: "If people can not have what they believe in, they must believe in what they have."

That could also be said about the Parliamentary Press Gallery, though its standards had improved dramatically since I had first crossed its messy threshold. The Watergate scandal had transformed political journalists into national idols. Reporters viewed themselves not as Bob Woodward and Carl Bernstein, the two hardworking *Washington Post* reporters who had broken the story, but as Robert Redford and Dustin Hoffman, the stars who played them in the glamorous movie adaptation of their book. A second, more serious fallout was that post-Watergate politicians were routinely presumed guilty until proven innocent. The game had changed and I hadn't the taste for its new rules. But then, I had always been an outsider in the gallery, with little respect for the rules.

This sense of antipathy was mutual. Every departing member of the Press Gallery is traditionally given a souvenir pewter mug with their name and years of service engraved on it. The fact that I was never "mugged" was proof positive that my peers felt I had not played by the rules of their game. They were right, and their slight made me proud. I was leaving as I had arrived, a political agnostic, determined to travel my own path. In the process, I had learned that Canada takes a lot of killing and I shouldn't expect politicians to be magicians. I also left Ottawa with the conviction that however unrealistic my expectations might be, and however little hope there was that elected officials could live up to them, to abandon those aspirations would diminish me, not them.

The year I left Ottawa, the capital was blessed with a new National Arts Centre, which transformed the city's cultural life. It took George Radwanski, some decades later, to publicize the fact that the capital has also gained fancy and expensive restaurants. What hasn't changed, and probably never will, is Ottawa's isolation from the country it governs and the mainstream concerns of its people. Ottawa's comfortable elites still refer, with painful condescension, to "ordinary Canadians" – a group defined as everybody else but them: all those simple souls, destined never to gain access to their closed world. I kept urging the capital's insiders to celebrate Canada Day by getting out of their stuffy Ottawa offices and hitting the road, away from the country of the mind and out into the real world: to taste the bite of salt air and watch the waves breaking against the cliffs of Conception Bay in Newfoundland, or pounding the beach at Bull Harbour on the northern tip of Vancouver Island; to ride the rivers that cascade into the St. Lawrence; to hike toward heaven in the Rocky Mountains, live in a tent for a couple of nights, and touch the damp earth of a summer dawn after a long rain. All to no avail.

But some things have changed, and none more so than the federal bureaucracy. By the end of the 1960s, the Ottawa elite had become fragmented, no longer speaking with one mind, one voice, or one attitude. Its community of purpose, which had once been transmitted by osmosis as much as by memos, had broken apart. The communal table at the Rideau Club had become just a place to have a mediocre lunch. The imprimatur of people like Norman Robertson didn't count for much any more, because there weren't enough people like Norman Robertson remaining in pivotal positions. Instead of an in-group defining policy options and bringing politicians to heel, directives followed no predictable paths, and were often the result of vertical approaches made directly to deputy ministers or one of the *machers* in the Privy Council Office. The leisurely, ambulatory brains that had once set the capital's pace were being replaced by a group of livelier, noisier, earthier men, and an increasing number of women. The guard was changing.

A minor incident occurred just as I was leaving. Norman Robertson, whom I had interviewed when I had first arrived on the scene a dozen years earlier, decided to retire. He had spent the preceding six months trying to shoot down a Treasury Board memorandum proposing that an outside team of management consultants be hired to boost the External Affairs Department's administrative efficiency. Robertson had always felt that public service was a privilege and efficiency had nothing to do with it. He saw no need for the mechanical advice of these "smart boys," as he called them. On the last day of his thirty-five-year stewardship, he took the offending directive out of his in-basket and reluctantly endorsed it with his scribbled approval. Then, as one last gesture of distaste for the new order sweeping the cozy world he had helped to create, he scratched under his signature the words: "I capitulate."

I WALKED INTO my new third-floor office in the Toronto Star Building at 80 King Street West on February 1, 1969, to begin my stint as editor-in-chief. I was thirty-nine years old, spoiling for the chance to make my imprint on Toronto and the newspaper world. My first thought was how proud my father would have been, had he lived to see the moment. The *Star* had been his favourite paper. I had achieved nothing during his lifetime except to marry Pat, over his pleading objections.

What greeted me was an empty office at least twice the size of the prime minister's; standing at one end and looking toward the other, I thought I could detect the earth's curvature. It was bare, apart from a desk the size of a ping-pong table and a bouquet of roses, into which was tucked a welcoming card from Beland Honderich, better known by his nickname, "Bee" – as in "Busy Bee."[6] I looked around my cold, unadorned surroundings and inexplicably began to feel like a nervous bride. The office and the job had been vacant since Bee had moved up to publisher in 1966. In that time he had transformed the *Star* into a good, if not great populist paper, selling more than four million copies per week. In the process, Honderich had employed some of Canada's best and brightest journalists, including Ralph Allen, Pierre Berton, Nathan Cohen, Kildare Dobbs, George Fetherling, Bob Fulford, Mark Gayn, Ron Haggart, and Bob Reguly.[7] Among the *Star*'s alumni was Ernest Hemingway, who had worked there as a reporter for three years in the 1920s under Honderich's predecessor and compared his stint to "serving in the Prussian Army under a bad general."

I thought of updating Papa Hemingway's metaphor during my orientation session with Bee. By the end of it, I knew that I had just been briefed by the paper's *real* editor-in-chief. He told me that despite the glamorous-sounding title, my authority would be limited to the editorial and op-ed pages. While I would be expected to influence the entire paper, its day-to-day news operations would remain the bailiwick of managing editor Martin Goodman. This was a sensible and practical working arrangement,

---

[6] Honderich's nickname harks back to his youth when he was hired as a stringer covering sports for the *Kitchener-Waterloo Record*. He was paid by the inch for his copy. To top up his pay he started a local baseball team, then wrote about their games. Thus his reputation as a "busy bee."

[7] When he first heard about my appointment, Val Sears, the paper's lively London bureau chief, sent me a telegram: "WHAT AN INSPIRED IDEA. INGRATIATING LETTER FOLLOWS."

except that as editor-in-chief I was rightly perceived as being responsible for every item and every typo in each of the day's five editions. I was able to confirm my title by glancing at it, on top of the list of editors published daily on the *Star*'s masthead, but I knew that I would always have the second-to-last word. The division of editorial power would haunt my tenure. To get along with Bee, I would have to behave like the bride in Germaine Greer's parable about old-fashioned marriages, with the husband assuring the wife: "If you do exactly what I want, dear, we'll have a really good time."[8]

My only caller on that first day in my office was the Israeli ambassador, happy to welcome the *Star*'s first Jewish editor. And by the way, he inquired, what time was I planning to leave for Jerusalem to write something nice about the Holy Land? *Any day now*, I thought to myself. The Middle East seemed peaceful and safe compared to what was promised at 80 King Street West. When I returned home to Christina and Ashley that evening in our rented house on Farnham Avenue, I wrote in my journal: "As the new *Star* editor, I must diminish internal dissent so that I don't need to expend time and energy on office politics. The essential way to gain credibility for the paper will be to allow its writers to express differing conceptions and perceptions of events, not merely those of its publisher."

Yeah, right . . .

MY DAYS STARTED AT 6:00 a.m., when I arrived to finalize the editorial page that had been mostly written the previous afternoon. Since I had spent the preceding dozen years as a columnist,

---

[8] I stayed away from the advertising department, except once. A Toronto furniture dealer had been running full-page ads every Saturday, claiming in screaming type that he was about to declare bankruptcy and was selling his stock at huge discounts. After six months of these weekly alarms, I phoned and told him to stop because he was hurting not only his credibility but ours. He was furious. "What are you trying to do?" he yelled down the telephone line. "Put me out of business?!"

never having to worry about anyone's opinions except my own, I found it frustrating to spend time fussing over each day's editorials, which had to reflect the *Star's* institutional views. I comforted myself with the apt description of the process by the *Globe's* George Bain, who compared writing editorials to "wetting your pants while wearing a dark serge suit – nobody notices and it leaves you with a warm feeling." That was true enough, but I liked to think of the editorial page as the soul of the paper and thus deserving of my best efforts.

The climax of each morning was my session with Bee, trying to gain his approval for the day's output. I found him to be a formidable character. He was one of those people who made you feel guilty even if you hadn't done anything wrong. As soon as I walked through his office door I would begin feeling that my tie must be crooked, and had difficulty preventing myself from fingering it. I thought of him as being surrounded by a magnetic field that heightened his sensibilities, a kind of human seismograph able to detect the motives of others on an internal Richter scale. He had a liturgical face with skin like pleated armour, and a smile as broad and fixed as the front grille of a Mercedes-Benz saloon. His unnatural stiffness was magnified by his impeccable three-piece suits, which appeared to be starched. When the *Star's* head office was moved to 1 Yonge Street on the Toronto waterfront, the joke making the rounds was that this was so that Bee could have a place to park his U-Boat.

We seldom had any problem agreeing on basic principles. I enjoyed the fact that Honderich believed, as I did, that politics was fuelled not by the exercise of power or the expenditure of money but by the quest for ideas. The comedian Dave Broadfoot once labelled the *Star* "a small-L conservative paper" – and he was right on the mark. The paper's liberalism flowed from its founding spirit, "Holy Joe" Atkinson. As early as 1909, Atkinson had advocated social justice, the equitable distribution of wealth, state support for the disadvantaged, and a proud, independent Canada, urging Ottawa to "kick the Yankee poachers out of Hudson Bay."

Those were Honderich's core beliefs – and mine. The *Star* had wrongly been accused of being a captive voice of the Liberal Party. On the contrary, we often questioned the party's policies and ethics, and we supported John Robarts's Conservatives in Ontario, as well as endorsing the NDP governments in Manitoba and British Columbia. It was over the details that Bee and I came apart. I had introduced the idea of editorials illustrated by photographs or Irma Coucill's masterful charcoal sketches, but Bee had a pedantic insistence on accompanying them with explanatory cutlines. When I ran an illustration of Gina Lollobrigida, the Italian film star, standing beside a male dwarf, he told me to add ("left") and ("right") identifications, because that was one of his rules. I reckoned any reader unable to distinguish between the two unaided ought to be reading the paper in Braille.

Among his many quirks, he hated italic fonts and sexy movie titles. When a Yonge Street cinema wanted to run an ad for *The Making of a Prostitute*, he insisted it be changed to *The Making of a (FOR TITLE CALL 531-1315)*, while *How To Make Love to a Virgin* became *How To Love A Virgin*, and so on. Two- or three-tiered headings had to be self-contained in each line within the space of fifteen characters, which was a bitch to write. Such petty meddling drove the paper's morale into the dumpster. Bee went through twelve managing editors in twenty-four years.[9] Michael Posner once wrote that Honderich "drove editors the way Andretti drove race cars – to the edge of possibility and beyond, before trading them in for a new model." Instead of concentrating on the quality of their work, *Star* reporters and editors were far more concerned with getting it past "The Beast," as Honderich was known in the newsroom. He was there every morning, making up the front page, deciding every headline, and supervising the positioning of

---

[9] Jocko Thomas, the *Star*'s veteran police reporter, swore that during his sixty years on the paper it had forty-five city editors. He would name them in order on nights when he had trouble falling asleep, since he felt they weren't that different from sheep.

each story. Somewhere deep inside Beland Honderich there was a small, unsmiling universe, and that formed the tough, take-no-prisoners core that made the man so difficult. I noticed *Star* editors and reporters watching him, trying to read his mind and head off the inevitable, "I don't want to interfere, but . . ." The *Toronto Star*'s editorial team behaved like a troupe of muzzled dancing bears following the lead of their keeper, who wasn't a jovial accordion player but an uptight puppet master.

When Anastas Mikoyan, deputy premier of the USSR, asked one of his Kremlin mentors how best to deal with Josef Stalin, he was told: "When Stalin says dance, a wise man dances." We weren't wise and Beland Honderich wasn't Josef Stalin, but we did our share of waltzing. The *Star*'s publisher surrounded himself with capable assistants whose mission it was to fulfill their purposes in his overall plan. Nothing unusual in that arrangement; it was Darwinian Management 101. He expressed absolute certainty, anchored in the very marrow of his being, about what he *didn't* want. Unfortunately, his feelings about what he *did* want were less clear. Frequently they stopped at the point of knowing that it wasn't what some hapless underling had just stayed up all night to finish. In responding to his catechism, nobody had the privilege of being wrong once in a while. And to be right, you had to remember his phobias, likes, dislikes, past preferences, and current prejudices. "We were not journalists, we were courtiers, and that is a difficult way to run a newspaper," noted Walter Stewart, who worked there for a time. Sometimes it got silly. At one point, Bee had been looking at sample covers of the *Star*'s weekly television magazine and picked out a photograph of a rising young starlet who happened to be wearing a striking red dress. The word went out that all magazine covers from then on had to include something red, and long after Honderich had forgotten all about the incident, staff photographers still carried red jackets and red dresses in their cars in which their subjects were photographed.

To call Bee a mulish perfectionist would be an understatement; to call him a frustrated idealist would be closer to the mark; but to label him a robot plugged into the *Star*'s perpetual readership surveys would probably be most accurate. The paper's editorial staff was convinced that Bee was just a fussy SOB dedicated to trying their patience. That was true of his idiosyncratic demands, but a lot less true of his substantive editing and choice of editorial content. The profile of our readership surveys dictated his selections. This was brought home to me when I suggested that we beef up the financial section to compete with the *Globe and Mail*. "Do you know who we write the business section for?" he asked. I took a wild guess and answered something like, *d'oh*, could it be business people? "No," he said, "it is edited for dentists' wives in Etobicoke." That was a valuable lesson.

As the weeks and months dropped away, my department gelled into a productive unit, a paper within a paper that was more than a megaphone for its publisher. My talented crew included John Macfarlane, Bill Cameron, David Lewis Stein, Bernadette Sulgit, Martin Dewey, and Bob Neilsen. I also introduced to the *Star*'s editorial page such writers as Margaret Laurence, Al Purdy, Hugh MacLennan, Mavor Moore, Harold Town, Irving Layton, Morley Callaghan, and Ernest Hemingway, whose *Star* columns we republished. Our department was "the only toe-hold of humanity in the paper," according to the novelist and TV host Bill Cameron.

Our most dramatic disagreement with the publisher was a fight over construction of the $200-million Spadina Expressway, which in 1970 and 1971 was a defining issue for the future of the city. The editorial board unanimously objected to the expressway, which we felt would transform Toronto into a northern version of Los Angeles. Regardless, Honderich refused to publish our call for an immediate halt to its construction. I persuaded him to give our side of the issue another hearing, and for a busy week we prepared a meticulously argued 235-page brief urging an independent feasibility study of the proposed expansion. To his credit, Honderich was swayed to accept our position. It was a first.

As I got to know Bee better, I grew to respect him, but I also realized that it was his obsession with neatness that provided his primary motivation. I began to wonder if we were ideologically compatible, as I had thought, or if he merely tolerated me because I was a clear-desk operator, as he was. On January 7, 1971, he sent an eleven-page memo to the news departments, spelling out strict new regulations to eliminate office litter and desktop clutter. His edict prohibited calendars, takeout menus, personal photos, pens, pencils, files, and notes — *nothing* was allowed on desktops after office hours. Anything found was confiscated and destroyed. The entertainment department's wastebaskets were moved beyond reach of the reporters' typewriters because Bee claimed they spoiled the orderly arrangement of the furniture. Honderich might not have presided over the world's greatest newspaper, but it was the world's tidiest.

My favourite character on the editorial board was Duncan Macpherson, the most brilliant editorial cartoonist then in captivity and the most difficult employee since Fletcher Christian sailed on board the *Bounty*. He would usually appear three minutes before his daily deadline to have me approve his drawing. Miraculously, we were never sued, although Duncan's acid-tipped quill struck at people where they were most vulnerable — their vanity. He was feared and loathed by politicians, who would call me to remonstrate in the strongest terms whenever they were caricatured. I took these complaints with a bushel of salt, knowing that a few days later their executive assistants would be on the phone, furtively asking if I could provide a copy of "that dreadful cartoon" for their bosses.

Duncan's diabolical creations must have sprung from the same inner demons that drove him to drink. Bartenders were constantly on the telephone, imploring me to rescue him from some watering hole or another. The front door of the Toronto Press Club at the time could be opened only by pressing a buzzer. One evening, after a prolonged buzz, a very drunk Duncan fell through the door, with a policeman hanging on to one leg. He shook off his boot in the clutches of the pursuing cop, who was left on the far side of the door as it slammed between them. Macpherson ran through the club and fled by the back door into the adjoining King George

Hotel. There, he whizzed through the lobby, dashed onto York Street, and entered the Berkeley Hotel, where he took off his other shoe (in his alcoholic daze he figured he couldn't be identified that way), entered the hotel restaurant, ordered a plate of spaghetti, and promptly fell asleep in it. These and other exploits caused him eventually to be banned for life *three times* by the Toronto Press Club. But he kept turning up, and the club finally did the only honourable thing: they made him an honorary life member.

Duncan legends abound. He decided to bypass Toronto's high rents by living aboard an old tug, which he moored in the harbour. When the local maritime police arrived to inform him that this was illegal, he repelled the boarders by pelting them with chunks of coal.

One trick he could never master was removing a tablecloth from under a fully set table. But that didn't stop him from practising. One evening, drunk enough to feel confident, he approached the Russian ambassador to Canada who sat with his two body-guards at Barberian's restaurant. The table was laden with steaks, red wine, and all the trimmings. As Duncan approached, the goons reached for their armpits, but the ambassador assured them that he was a friendly acquaintance. They all sat down just in time for Macpherson to demonstrate his trick – and land the entire dinner on the ambassador's lap. Restraining the artillery proved harder this time, but the dripping ambassador managed it, and Duncan crept away, chastened until the next time.

On another occasion, the cartoonist was meeting someone at Winston's, then Toronto's premier restaurant. The restaurant insisted on adherence to its dress code and wouldn't allow Duncan, who was wearing his usual Salvation Army discards over a sweat-shirt, to enter. Luckily he had a grease pencil with him, went to the bathroom, sketched a shirt and tie around his neck, then waltzed in, unimpeded.

MY CAREER AT THE *STAR* came crashing down in the first month of 1971. It all began with an innocuous memo from Bee, asking me to "find something nice to say in the paper about Mayor Garnet Williams of the new town of Vaughan." I had no problem with that, realizing that this concerned the *Star*'s application for rezoning the land on which it intended to build its new $421-million offset printing plant. I had already attended a private meeting with Ontario Municipal Affairs minister Darcy McKeough on the issue and had persuaded him to expedite the requested approval. I had also talked to Ontario Municipal Board chairman J.A. Kennedy, who had provided me with information essential to our application, which I'd then passed on to the *Star*'s lawyers. All that remained was to say "something nice" about Mayor Williams. That was the stumbling block. Try as I might, I could find nothing nice to say about the man. On the contrary, our files revealed that on every important issue, Mayor Williams had opposed the *Star*'s editorial policy.

On January 6, 1971, I sent Honderich a tightly reasoned four-page memo. "In the past you have imbued me with the idea that only the public interest should govern the contents of the *Star*," I wrote. "Since you have swept aside the essential difference between self-interest and public interest, I am conscience-bound to inform you that I cannot publish the editorial you have requested. If we were now to offer gratuitous praise of Mr. Williams we would run the risk of creating the impression that we were trying to use the editorial page to bring pressure on local government in a matter that serves only the financial interests of this newspaper." I went on to point out that my stand had received the unanimous (if unsought) support of the *Star*'s editorial board, and added: "You will no doubt interpret this as an act of disloyalty. It is not. It is an act of conscience which I hope you can respect."

I received no reply, but found myself the butt of Beland's legendary "mushroom treatment" – kept isolated in the dark, showered with manure, then canned. Authority he had delegated to me was silently revoked. It was time to move on. I resigned without making public my reasons. Of the many supportive letters I received, Duncan Macpherson's stands out: "The *Star* is losing the best talent they ever had when you leave. Apart from the ideas you instituted, it's the first time I've read the paper and felt a human and common interest in its main editorial thrust."

I had not found enough room to manoeuvre inside Honderich's despotic empire. I could easily have stayed; the sun would still have risen over Toronto if I had written a brief squib on the merits of that suburban mayor whose name I barely remember. But if the earth didn't move, I felt it shudder, and that was enough. I knew that if I compromised on that one small issue, I would join what Robert Fulford described as "several guys who used to run the editorial page and are now stacked up like cordwood outside Honderich's office." Rather than be added to the woodpile, I went for the chop.

CHAPTER ELEVEN

PASSIONS: JOURNEYS

How I Discovered Swedish Girls,
Moshe Dayan, and Italian Porn Stars

—❦—

A place belongs to whoever claims it most ardently. That's why I spent a good deal of my energy proclaiming Canada as my turf.

Still, at least once a year, I would pack my bags and roam the world, sizing up the most interesting countries and situations of the moment. These were more than the peripatetic wanderings of a footloose journalist. In some sense, they were journeys in search of emotional relief.

The deeper I worked my way into Canada's fabric in my pursuit of Home and Hero, the more restless I became. It was as though the country wasn't creative or inventive enough to contain the passions and aspirations I placed upon it. In the process, my latest political hero would turn out to be merely human, falling short of the epic proportions I had constructed for him or her. It was not unlike – in fact, it was exactly similar to – the process of discovery, excitement, and disillusionment I felt in my personal relationships. Like Canada's economic and political animators of the moment, the women in my life at any given point failed to quell my inner turmoil.

Both forms of discontent arose from the same source: a search for something I could find only inside myself. But it took me a lifetime to arrive at that emotional destination. In the meantime, I filled the void with annual escapes into the anonymity of airport waiting lounges and flights to exotic destinations, interspersed with talkative taxi drivers who followed me like unwanted Sancho Panzas on every journey. I don't regret any of these personal expeditions, and some of them count among my most vivid memories. In fact, it was vividness more than understanding that I sought in these escapes, a trait I share with many journalists.

I REMEMBER AS THOUGH IT HAPPENED YESTERDAY my visit to Steinstucken, a tiny village of forty-five houses, politically part of West Berlin but floating 1.2 kilometres inside the eastern German Democratic Republic. I was one of few journalists to visit this bizarre manifestation of the Cold War, surrounded by its own Berlin Wall. I spent a day there, chatting up the locals at the village pub, Gasthoff Zum Taubeschlag, squashed under the flaking portico of a converted barn once used by homing pigeons.

I spent most of my time sipping Botzow beer and trying not to be driven mad by the jukebox that played endless versions of "Mama, tzie die hot pants an." Finally, I got a chance to talk to the pub's owner and Steinstucken's unofficial mayor, Heinz Pieper. His deeply chiselled, kindly, simian face twisted in painful memory as he told me the story of an East German border guard named Willi Marzahn, who had jumped over the Wall and, screaming a desperate request for asylum, knocked on every door in the village. Fearing reprisals, the good burghers of Steinstucken shut him out, allowing the Communist police patrol to take him away to be shot. "I like to see the people across the other side," Pieper mused, looking out the pub's window at the watchtowers leaning into the little inn's protective zone of light. "I used to know them. It's only a few hundred metres from here. But it's another world now."

It was evening when I decided to leave Steinstucken. Light

snow was falling, and a dark purple streak against the stark silhouette of the Wall was all that remained of the day. A man entered the inn, ushering in a rush of cold air. "The new guards seem quite friendly," he said with a tentative shrug, as if he were confiding a belief in ghosts. A rusty Mercedes was parked outside, squatting there like a cashiered cavalry horse. Heinz Pieper bade me goodbye. "*Alles bleibt beim alten . . .*" he said. ("Everything remains as it was . . .")

I often visited Berlin, the epicentre of the Cold War, in the postwar years, and vividly recall President John F. Kennedy declaring his allegiance to the city's brave spirit with the shout: "*Ich bin ein Berliner!*" (What might he have said, I often pondered, had he chosen to visit Hamburg or Frankfurt instead?)

Another of my favourite ports of call to test the Cold War's temperature was NATO headquarters in Belgium. Here, in one of the drowsier suburbs of Brussels, men whose blue-veined hands and liver spots betrayed their wartime vintage controlled the nuclear balance of terror that kept the peace. Collectively, they resembled a convention of pernickety stamp collectors, but their hobbit-like appearance was deceiving. Across the bitter years and howling winters of the Cold War, they kept the faith and stood the watch on the Rhine.

Military postures always "writhe," in the memorable phrase of British Labour MP Aneurin Bevan, "on the twin hooks of conscience and expediency." But even if western Europe's youth were in the streets rioting against them, the NATO brass managed to hold the alliance together for more than four harsh decades, granting Europe its longest interlude of peace. The Brussels inhabited by these men was more a city of reactive mood than one with its own atmosphere, as the diplomatic temperature between Washington and Moscow determined each day's agenda. The admirals, generals, ambassadors, and factotums filed their assessments of the prospects for peace, which grew ever grimmer with each after-hours martini. But I was there often enough to realize that even if NATO was as outdated as the Maginot Line, at least it functioned as a deterrent.

Such probes abroad must have had some impact on my mental outlook, as I was drawn so often to the Cold War's proxy theatres of operation: southeast Asia, Israel, and the occupied countries of eastern Europe, especially Czechoslovakia. How much were members of my generation shaped by this precarious state of peace-without-war and war-without-peace? How much of my own psychological projections were modelled on the Cold War policy of pursuing vital national interests through foreign proxies? More than I liked to imagine. There can be no doubt my journeys were part of my larger search for Home and Hero: somewhere, in these foreign fields of conflict, there must have been people who had found their secure and rational place in a toxic, irrational universe. The Cold War was an apt metaphor for my character, forged in the last great hot war and ever since embedded in ice. Was I searching, like John Le Carré's spymaster George Smiley, for a sense of personal retribution and vindication in the ideological gamesmanship of the age? It didn't take much experience in these places to realize that both sides were living an illusion, fighting a Looking-Glass War. (Sadly, I could never feel myself part of the James Bond ethic. For one thing, when I shut my eyes while making love, I never thought of England – only Lake Ontario on a choppy day.)

As for Canada, its role as a proxy to American interests has left us more secure, but stripped us of our soul. We chose neither Swedish-style independence nor Israeli defiance, and instead ended up with the comforts of the mistress's boudoir: comfortable, yet screwed.

Of course, I visited the United States often, including one brief but memorable flash call on Los Angeles. The taxi that whisked me from LAX was driven by an unemployed Hollywood actor (as are they all), determined to strike up what he imagined to be probing small talk. Deciding to give his sincerity its morning workout, in the event I might be vaguely connected with The Industry, he asked what I did for a living. When I told him I was with *Maclean's*, there was a blank look, and then a big smile as his

Okie shrewdness kicked into gear. "Oh, yeah." He nodded, know-ingly. "Great toothpaste!"

I later tramped around Malibu, the gilded playpen of the stars, where luxurious beach houses sprout like miniature Versailles, and machismo lifestyles rule the roost. I noted that Malibu, at that time, was unique: it had not only no blacks, but no brunettes.

Of greater import was a visit to Iran at the end of the 1970s, just as Mohammad Reza Shah Pahlavi was about to be deposed. I hap-pened to be invited to a Canadian embassy reception in Teheran, attended by Dr. Ali Amini, a patrician scholar and reformer who had served as the country's last democratically elected prime min-ister. At the time, he was attempting to quell a populace so close to revolution that the Shah dared to drive through the streets of his own capital city only at a speedy one hundred kilometres per hour, along routes cleared of other traffic by police. When I asked the prime minister to arrange an appointment with the Shah, he laughed and said that would be impossible. His Imperial Majesty never gave interviews. But he agreed to take him a letter from me, in the hope that the Shah might answer one question: Why didn't he hasten democracy in Iran by becoming a Swedish-style consti-tutional monarch, who reigns but doesn't rule?

To my astonishment, an answer eventually arrived: "When the Iranians learn to behave like the Swedes," his Imperial Majesty wrote, "then I will behave like the King of Sweden." Not bad.

The indelible impressions left by pre-revolutionary Iran were of its horrifying contrasts. At the Canadian diplomatic party I attended, Persian beauties garbed in Dior and Balenciaga sipped Cointreau and swapped anecdotes about the Paris opera season. After stepping out into the moon-washed night, bound for my hotel not a mile away, I passed through a bazaar with beggars in filthy burnooses and hawkers who carried their wares on their backs, surrounded by throngs of children with open sores.

As I wrote at the time, "The world may be on the verge of reli-gious wars reminiscent of the Dark Ages of the Crusades. The fires of Islam are burning with such hatred for the Americans, and at least by geographical proximity, against us. Because we in North America have been in the vanguard of introducing Western materialism to the Muslim world, a clash in cultures that has been far more traumatic to the closed societies of Islam, even than the colonialism that preceded it. To the true believer, any cultural dilution of Islam amounts to annihilation. How are you going to keep them chewing herbs down on the oasis, once they've tasted a Big Mac?" Perhaps I was not overly politically correct, but – writing this in 1979 – I was more prescient than I knew.

AT THE HEIGHT OF THE COLD WAR in the early 1980s, I was invited to lecture at the Institute of U.S. and Canadian Studies in Moscow, which had recently published a Russian translation of *The Canadian Establishment*. The preface to the Soviet edition was written by Leon Bagramov, a former Ottawa correspondent for the Moscow newspaper *Selskaya Zhizn*, who was later to become a ranking party apparatchik. "*The Canadian Establishment*," he wrote, "provides another illustration of the Marxist thesis that the capitalist state is a mere committee governing the affairs of the entire bourgeois society. And this illustration is drawn by the hand of a master." I only wish Canadian reviewers had been so alert and perceptive.

In effect, the Russians had bought publishing rights to *The Canadian Establishment* in exchange for ten thousand *matryoshkas*, or nesting dolls. I say this not with bitterness, but as a fact. The Soviet ruble was not a freely convertible currency at the time, so my royalties were good only for purchases at government export shops, stacked with not much except those damned wooden dolls. I should add that the hardcover edition of my book sold for only one ruble, the equivalent of $1.50. But that wasn't what bothered me. The translators had reduced my 480-page epic into a 356-page stocking-stuffer, and of course I had no idea what was edited out.

The Soviet publishing industry had at least one gimmick that ought to be adopted in Canada. As a reward for being good (or bad) enough to be noticed, authors were paid for each published review of their works. My book was selling extraordinarily well, despite a report in the Novosti Press Agency that began with the ominous warning: "Newman is clearly not a Marxist . . ." Damn. Exposed again.

For reasons that made sense at the time (perhaps the Aeroflot safety record, perhaps some romantic impulse), I decided not to fly to Moscow for the conference. I would instead recreate the fabled voyage of Lenin in 1917 prior to the start of the October Revolution, and arrive in Moscow by train from Helsinki. Lenin, of course, made the voyage in a sealed, armoured train with an entourage of twenty-seven Bolsheviks, but for me half a century later it was still a strange and forbidding journey, where I and my fellow travellers were barely sustained by a greasy soup made entirely of boiled cabbage and cholesterol, served three times a day in the train's carriages. What I remember most about that surrealistic voyage was crossing the border from Finland into Russia.

A few hours out of Helsinki, the train pulled into Vainikkala, a little border village on the southern toe of the Finnish Republic. Local border guards came aboard, not looking at passports but boisterously wishing us goodbye and good luck. This seemed strange, as the Finns do not enjoy a reputation for giddy small talk.

During the halt we stepped into a frigid night in the dead of winter, and soon I was sipping delicious bean soup while trying to work up my appetite to tackle a reindeer-tongue sandwich, which was the only selection at the station's bar. Like most of Finland, the station reeked of wood sap. Saved by the all-aboard call, and feeling like a self-conscious extra in a remake of *Doctor Zhivago*, I climbed back unto the Helsinki-Moscow Express. It chugged a few miles past the frontier – and stopped. Through ice-marbled windows I noticed that the surrounding trees had been razed to the ground. We were stranded in a no man's land, overlaid by whorls of barbed wire stretching between watchtowers elevated on pine stilts.

Above me I heard the clatter of hobnailed boots as guards paced the roofs of the coaches, searching for stowaways. On the ground, nearly obscured by the locomotive's billowing steam, a tubby sergeant was being tugged along by the leash of a snarling German shepherd that was sniffing the bottom edges of the carriages. It struck me as absurd – who would want to sneak *into* the Soviet Union? I was tempted to dismiss the whole exercise as a spoof. But then the Soviet border guards in their sea-green uniforms marched onto the train. They appeared pitiless, reminding me of *The Old King* by French Fauvist painter Georges Rouault (cruel mouth etched like a scar, dead eyes, and bloodless cheeks). They proceeded to examine our documents and search our luggage.

I was on edge, trying to keep my eyes off the suitcase full of disco records I was smuggling in to give to critics of the regime, since selling these forbidden items was one of the few ways they had of making money. To be caught with my contraband cargo and imprisoned in some remote Siberian gulag was a fate I dared not contemplate, especially since I suspected I would be tortured by having to listen to all those disco tunes. I had packed the LPs in a separate suitcase, deliberately placed at the top of the luggage rack on the premise that no one would search for smuggled goods stored in plain view. I was right, and the guard rifled through my other luggage but left the disco alone.

As we puffed away from that wretched steppe, I spotted a pair of weathered boots abandoned by the train tracks in the snow, left there in obvious haste. I shuddered at their significance. The image of those godforsaken boots stayed with me during my Russian sojourn.

ANOTHER FLASHPOINT I reported from was Laos. It was not the obvious killing field that Vietnam and Cambodia turned out to be. But for reasons that no one clearly understands to this day, the Americans treated Laos (or "*Lay-oss*," as they pronounced it) as a strategic "bulwark against Communism," eventually dropping more than two million tons of bombs on the tiny mountain kingdom, the most concentrated firebombing in the history of warfare. Most of the bombers took off from Long Tieng, the secret CIA jungle city that appeared on no maps. At the height of the bombings, Long Tieng handled more traffic than Chicago's O'Hare Airport.

On the ground, the contest was between Communist Pathet Lao forces in the north and the American-supported Royal Laotian Army in the south, which on paper had sixty thousand men under arms, compared with less than half that number fielded by their jungle-based opponents. In one of their signature engagements, however, when the Communists fired a few noisy rounds from eighty-five-millimetre Russian cannon in their direction, the Royal Laotian infantrymen not only threw away their rifles but took off their boots so they could retreat faster.

On my visit in 1961 I quickly discovered that the best-informed foreign diplomat in Vientiane, the scruffy little capital city, was the Australian embassy's military adviser, a man with the improbable name of Colonel Bing Crosby. Running through the history of the country's various coups, he happened to mention the name of a Laotian admiral.

"What?" I exclaimed. "How can they have an admiral when they don't have a navy?"

"Oh, but they do," he replied.

"More than admirals, navies need ships and ships need water," I pointed out. "Laos is landlocked. There aren't even any sizable lakes."

"True. But the Mekong River runs through much of the southern part of the country. Why don't you take a day and inspect the Royal Laotian Navy?"

As a navy man, this intrigued me, so next day I persuaded a taxi driver to brave the land mines and take me to view the world's most bizarre naval fleet, which I would be the first foreign correspondent to inspect. I had imagined that no fighting unit could be less impressive than the Royal Laotian Army, but I was wrong. The Royal Laotian Navy, commanded by Prince Sinthanarong (a cousin of the king), boasted a fleet-in-being (according to the authoritative *Jane's Fighting Ships*) of twenty-three ships in reserve and five vessels in commission. The reserve fleet, as I found out when I reached its resting place, consisted entirely of rusting hulks irregularly parked on the banks of the Mekong River. The only activity aboard these relics came from the chickens that roosted on the abandoned vessels' decks. The keeper of this beached flotilla confided, with considerable pride, that the main function of the Royal Laotian Navy was supplying eggs to the Royal Laotian Army.

He was too modest. Nearby, swinging off rusted anchor chains, was the navy's true-blue fleet still in commission, flying the national flag, no less. It consisted of five rotting wooden transports, painted warship grey, all lacking engines and guns. The navy's only operational warship was a thirty-foot, iron-hulled monstrosity, built in 1904 and powered by a wood-burning furnace. It was this vessel that had participated in the Laotian navy's most daring (and only) maritime engagement, having shelled some shore installations during one military dustup. Its deck-mounted artillery gun scored no hits. Worse, the navy happened to be on the losing side of that particular coup and the ship had been promptly placed in "reserve," where it was now quietly disintegrating.

All of this was music to my ears. At last I had found a navy more inadequately equipped than my own.

AS I HAD NEVER BEEN A STRIDENT ZIONIST, I had not, for my own purposes, visited the Jewish homeland, but I did so for the *Star* in 1969. To my way of thinking, Israel had always been the answer for those "other" Jews, who had no ready-made country, like Canada, to accept them. That all changed between June 5 and 10, 1967, with the Six-Day War, which turned out to be a stunning victory for the Israelis. It was during the tense post-war period that I met the man who had commanded the triumphant armies.

When Israel's legendary defence minister, Major General Moshe Dayan, slouched through the open vestibule of the Yarden Hotel in Tel Aviv, all conversation ceased. He was dressed in army fatigues, without insignia, and had just flown in by helicopter from the marketplace at Deir el Balah, where terrorist hand grenades had killed two farmers. Involuntarily, I looked at his eye patch. But it was Dayan's good eye that reached out and hypnotized me in its unblinking stare, seeming to demand: "What have you done for Israel lately?"

At fifty-two, he was trim and fit in his fatigues and had just presided over the second successful war of his career. Before that, he had fought with the British army in the Second World War (losing an eye in battle in 1941), and prior to that he had been a member of the Haganah, or Jewish militia, in the 1930s. We spent an hour lunching together, and as I watched and listened, Israel's hero-general reminded me of Pierre Elliott Trudeau. It seemed an absurd comparison. One was a professional soldier whose desert warfare strategy had made military history, the other an intellectual who had never fought for his country. Yet the similarities persisted. Dayan and Trudeau were about the same height, equally bald, nearly the same age. Most important of all, I felt that indefinable quality at work that allowed both men to create space around themselves, preventing either friend or foe from touching them. Such a response fostered their individual legends, the romantic remoteness that set them apart from lesser, ordinary men. They shared impatience with routine encounters, desperate boredom with protocol, and unconcern for the moods and feelings of others. There was even some resemblance in their mannerisms, though Dayan somehow managed to shrug with his good eye instead of his shoulders. They both grew up among cultural minorities but operated outside the tradition of their backgrounds. Dayan was a very non-Jewish kind of Israeli, just as Trudeau was a very non-French-Canadian kind of Québécois.

It was pointless to stretch the comparison too far (for one thing, Dayan was much more passionate about his country than Trudeau was about his), but as I sat listening to Dayan and thinking about Trudeau, I remembered what Dayan's novelist daughter, Yael, had written about her father: "He is a lonely man who holds the key to his soul in his own hand, and he himself directs the traffic of people and ideas trying to reach him." The description fit Pierre Trudeau perfectly.

Just as Trudeau became most agitated when discussing the value of the French fact in Canada's future, Dayan's animation grew as he discussed his heritage. "A Jew," he said, "is a very specific human being, different from others by religion, language, history, and philosophy. And the problem for us is to maintain that uniqueness. I have more in common with the Jews in Miami Beach than with the Arabs in the next village." He talked with great compassion about war, about survival, and when I asked him why Israelis were such good soldiers, he replied: "They are not good soldiers. They are good fighters. They are very bad at parades and that sort of thing."

When I asked Dayan how he would rank the Canadian army, to my astonishment, he replied, "If I had to choose a non-Israeli army to fight with, it would be the Canadians, because they are all volunteers. Of course, I wouldn't want to spend my evenings with them. For that, I would choose the Italian commandoes."

We finished our meal of goose liver and grilled St. Peter fish, with Dayan explaining how peace might come because nothing was impossible in the Middle East. ("Twenty years ago, nobody thought Israel was possible.") Suddenly he grew restless; something was up. When I'd come in, I had paid no attention to the restaurant's other patrons. Now a man wearing an orange rugby shirt, who had been inconspicuously seated nearby, whispered something to Dayan in Hebrew. The minister got up, shook my hand, and vanished. So did everyone else. The patrons had all been members of his security detail.

On my last day in Israel, I drove to the shrine at Yad Vashem, not far from Bethlehem. A low, rectangular building fashioned of hewn basalt boulders, this is the national memorial to the six million Jews exterminated by the Nazis. An eternal flame flickered from a jagged bronze cup, casting shadows on the mosaic floor where, in sombre letters, are inscribed the names of Adolf Hitler's twenty-one death camps.

Genocide on the scale consecrated in this grey and grisly place leaves the visitor without emotional or moral recourse, frigid with sorrow, relieved to step outside under the life-giving sun. Yet it was here that I felt in touch, at last, with the essence of Israel. Yad Vashem has a model of the Warsaw sewers where the last ghetto survivors held out for a few extra days. Walking through these ghastly relics, I became acutely aware of why the Israelis so passionately believe that the survival of Judaism is essential to human history, and why they are its keepers. At the same time, in my own small way, I realized why being Jewish was so important – why otherwise would six million people have been killed for it?

"Dark recollections crowd in on us whenever we think about the implications of defeat," I was told by former Foreign minister Abba Eban. "The issue is not military occupation, but physical massacre. After all, much in Jewish history is too terrible to be believed. But nothing is too terrible to have happened." The Jews live in a society suspended between the European background they don't wish to jettison and the Arab culture they don't want to adopt. In the long sweep of history, the little democracy cannot survive as a western outpost on a sea of Arab hostility. Leaving Israel, I felt as though I was stepping off a schooner speeding under full canvas into a rip tide.

THERE ARE CERTAIN CORNERS of the planet that manage to escape the trials and tribulations that consume the rest of us. Of all my travels, I found the country most dedicated to this noble task was Sweden. I decided to see this Scandinavian paradise for myself, to write about this unusual land of the midnight sun. What follows borrows the text of one of my despatches:

My first impression of Swedes was their obsessive devotion to cleanliness and order, overlaid with a deafening silence, which set them apart from other Europeans, and even Canadians. Swedish silence was more than the absence of sound. It was a tumultuous stillness, deafening in its intensity. Trains, buses, and streetcars filled with speechless people rumbled through the avenues of Stockholm like wheeled coffins. Masses of shoppers walked along the cities' retail districts in absolute silence, the only noise they made being the tromp of feet. There were few street noises: no clatter of trade, no shouting parents, no cries of playing children. Brooding individualists racked by introspection, most Swedes practised silence as a religion.

That is, until they got drunk, when they tended to burst forth in loud, mournful songs. There may be happy Swedish drinking songs but if so, I never heard one. For the most part, the themes of Swedish alehouse ditties were that we are born, we suffer, and we die — so we might as well drink. Public drunkenness was so widespread and so out of keeping with the overall climate of tidiness that it seemed an aberration. It was, of course, the flip side of social inhibition. It was only under the spirit of alcohol that one had permission to be loud, emotional, and gregarious.

The Swedes are a nation of spectacle-wipers. Ask them a question and they, figuratively or literally, pause to wipe their spectacles before answering. Conversations are a series of pauses interrupted by words. In a typical anecdote, a Swedish emigrant to America returns home after thirty years and invites his childhood friend to the local inn for schnapps. After an hour of drinking, they still have not spoken and the visitor finally asks, "So, how's everything?" His friend groans, "Hell, I thought we were having a drink, not making a lot of conversation."

The Swedes have abolished poverty, defeated unemployment, wiped out slums, banished ignorance, liberated sexuality, and built the world's highest standard of living on the twin foundations of capitalist enterprise and socialist redistribution. On top of which, they are pretty good at playing ice hockey. There is just one troubling paradox about the place: so great is the psychic drain of living in Paradise that the Swedes also lead the world in killing themselves. Sweden is a country with a national bipolar disorder caused by the seasonal swings between the long, dark, introspective winters and the brief, bright, outgoing summers.

Its forests are to Swedes what winter is to Canadians: the defining element of their lives. Only 7 per cent of Sweden's land mass is arable, and only 1 per cent is settled, while the forests and woodlands of aspen, beech, pine, birch, and fir still cover 68 per cent of the territory. In the minds of Swedes, the forest occupies an even larger territory. In the psychic landscape it is always quiet, dark, and deep – and there is forever a danger of wolves. But the dark forests of the mind have also imbued the Swedes with a spiritual loneliness they call "*ensamhet*," a word that literally means "alone man," but which incorporates all of the English words for solitude, lonesomeness, oneness.

At the same time, few Swedes are burdened by Victorian sexual morality, and they recognize that love, however fleeting, is the best way to deal with the curse of loneliness. Schoolchildren are taught that sex doesn't come naturally but requires plenty of practice, like any other sport. Sexual equality long ago reached the bedrooms of this nation. A survey by Professor Nils Gustavsson of the Sociological Institute in Stockholm found that 57 per cent of the boys polled had experienced sexual intercourse for the first time because the girl insisted upon it, and 26 per cent of the boys claimed the girls "forced them into it." Statistics lie. With soft felt slouch hats and tendrils of blond hair framing elegant cheekbones, their figures and faces assembled like bone china, Swedish women must be the world's loveliest.

For a visitor, the most striking aspect of this laissez-faire attitude toward sex (perhaps because it is the most public) is the attitude toward erotica. Shops openly sell every style of pornography, from the earthiest to the most philosophical. At one of the porno shops near Stockholm's main railway station, the German tourists, smoking suggestively phallic cigars, march into the shop with purpose. They have discovered sex and are determined to conquer it with Aryan efficiency. The English visitors are curious but yellow, as if sex were a duty, like cooking, so one might as well try to make it interesting. Americans snicker to themselves, confusing a visit to a Swedish porn shop with a sexual spree.

THE CREWCUT MADE HIM LOOK LIKE the second-string coach of a Midwest football team, but the darting blue eyes and sensitive rabbit's nose marked him as an intensely political animal. I was having lunch with Olof Palme in Stockholm's parliamentary cafeteria, a sleek structure with aluminium ceilings, brown carpets, and birch-panelled walls. The prime minister of Sweden was Europe's youngest, most radical, and least formal head of government. Discreetly chewing gum and swinging his legs over an armchair, he talked softly about his brand of politics and the social utopia he hoped to achieve.

He told me that he had been radicalized by the ten months he had spent hitchhiking through thirty-four U.S. states during the late 1940s. "It was the poverty surrounded by the affluence I saw on the journey that first inspired my deep commitment to socialism," he said. "I'm against wet-finger politics – testing public opinion before you do anything. Without an ideological consciousness and a real will behind practical politics, you only have accommodation from one day to the next."

An ostentatious rebel in a country of conformists, Palme made a brief screen appearance in the mildly pornographic movie *I Am Curious (Yellow)* and later, as minister of Education, joined Hanoi's ambassador to Moscow in a march on the American embassy in Stockholm to protest the Vietnam War. Palme's message was that society can be altered without revolution and that the political leaders of democracies must commit themselves to such peaceful transformations. "The Swedish example," he said, "is interesting for only one reason: it shows that social progress is possible through somewhat boring, bureaucratic action."

Then he got serious. "I hear you like sailing," he said – obviously, his press officer had done his research. "I've lined up a trip for you this weekend with a friend of mine, up the archipelago."

The prime minister kept his word and Ola Wittergren, head of the Swedish Sailing Squadron, invited me to spend the weekend on his boat, the *Dione*, a sixteen-ton yawl. Along with his hospitable family, we sailed out to Sandhamn, an idyllic island in Sweden's outer archipelago which hosted the main outstation of the Royal Swedish Yacht Club.

That evening, after much schnapps and singing of sad songs like "The Glitter Is Not the Sea," I sat in the stern of the *Dione* listening to the suckle of water under the hull, the clatter of loose halyards on the mast, and the occasional splash of gentle waves, savouring my brief but intense experience of Sweden.

Not long after we met, Olof Palme was gunned down while walking home from a restaurant in Stockholm. Sweden continues to be a prosperous welfare state, and its legendary women are still forcing unfortunate young men to have sex.

ONE COUNTRY I HAVE NEVER WRITTEN ABOUT is Italy, though during most of my European sojourns I would sneak there for weekends and brief holidays, mesmerized by a way of life that was exactly the opposite of Canada's. Unlike Canadians, who spend their lives deferring to authority, the Italians have nothing but blithe disregard for authority of any kind, whether it takes the form of government pronouncements, official edicts, appeals by authorities, swimming-pool regulations, papal bulls, or laws in general.

The signs on the *vaporetti*, the water buses that ply Venice's Grand Canal, carry a simple message: "*È pericoloso sporgersi.*" ("It is perilous to lean out.") Not *forbidden*, but *perilous*. The risk, once declared, is up to you. In Canada, the sign would declare it an offence to lean out, without giving any reason why; in Italy, the state provides fair warning, but no prohibition. The little "steamers," as their name implies (though nowadays they spout noxious diesel fumes) slam, bang, and scrape against every "bus stop" along the canal. They would neatly remove the body parts of anyone careless enough to leave them dangling over the side. But this seldom, if ever, happens.

The warning of "peril" ensures this, while nicely capturing a dominant strain in the Italian character: it may indeed be dangerous to lean out, but the choice is up to each passenger, and must not be imposed by some unseen, higher power.

Italians do not regard the state as the guardian of public trust but as a corruptible instrument to be resisted and exploited. Think of an Italian political theorist and you think of Niccolò Machiavelli; think of a Canadian and you come up with Preston Manning. That's the difference. Italian cynicism, while refreshing for mental health, has nonetheless badly corroded the legitimacy of national institutions. Even Benito Mussolini's wartime fascist dictatorship was tempered by most Italians with a passive disobedience of its laws. Il Duce knew what he was talking about when he complained: "It is not so much difficult to rule Italy, as it is useless."

Italians regard existence as a daily contest of wits and tend not to trust each other because they never trust themselves. ("To trust is good," claims one Neapolitan proverb. "Not to trust is better.") The one safe haven, the one allegiance, the one duty is to family. Only mamma can be trusted. Among authority figures, only the influence of a powerful padrone – preferably one related by blood – can ensure fair treatment. Everyone else forms a loose series of constantly shifting alliances and conspiracies based on the mutual self-interest of the moment. The implicit deal with the state that Canadians call citizenship is considered by Italians to be *un contratto con il diavolo*, a deal with the devil, especially when it involves paying taxes. Tax evasion is not only common in Italy, it is the national sport; participation is compulsory. More than one-quarter of the economy functions underground, or "black," with no receipts or vouchers to track its progress. Even Prime Minister Silvio Berlusconi has declared that "when taxes are too high it is morally acceptable to evade them."

Credit cards are accepted in Italy, but the machines are, curiously, nearly always "broken." "That will be cash, *signore*. And we seem to be out of receipts. Here, let me write something on this napkin." Only in Italy does a special branch of the "tax police" patrol the streets, vainly attempting to make sure shoppers are issued receipts. In fact, it is a criminal offence for shoppers to discard their receipts, or *scontrone*, within 200 metres of the premises, in case they are needed for inspection – another futile measure in the battle against unreported sales that reduce taxes.

Italians distrust the state but love state-generated statistics, such as the factual nuggets that there are precisely 850,312 wild dogs in the country (usually barking at night outside your hotel window) and that only 78.2 per cent of Italians make love in bed. Another 14.2 per cent do it in cars (although not, apparently, in the Fiat 500, or *cinquecento*, as a Roman judge once famously ruled an impregnation could not possibly have occurred in the ever-present Italian bubble car) and only 0.5 per cent on stairs, most of which are fashioned out of cold marble. Marble is 0.8 degrees Celsius cooler than the ambient temperature, which presumably makes it more agreeable to lovemaking than the back seat of a *cinquecento*.

The feeble governments based on the countless fragile political coalitions that have tried to govern the country since the Second World War serve the Italian purpose perfectly. Italian society deregulates itself. Nobody observes its rules and regulations, even those who impose them. It is impossible to exist otherwise, for in Italy everything that is not forbidden is regulated. Some rules are just too silly to warrant attention. Every beach contains posted regulations that cover every aspect of shoreline behaviour, from the eating of ice creams to the square metres of sand rented with each deck chair. No one pays the slightest attention. The cathedral at Vigevano, southwest of Milan, even posts a sign at the entrance forbidding worshippers to ride bicycles in church aisles.

In general, traffic is considered part of the laissez-faire sector and vehicles move rapidly without benefit of recognized lanes, signals, or speed limits. I quickly discovered that pedestrians must rely on their agility to dive out of the way of onrushing cars. Drivers kept shaking their fists at me, and I wasn't sure whether it was because they nearly hit me or because they missed. Such mayhem might be acceptable if it were accompanied by good humour and sportsmanship, but it's not, and the *carabinieri* (the national police) are the worst offenders. They are also the world's least-respected police force, with an allegedly strict IQ maximum for new recruits. Italian joke: Why do *carabinieri* have red stripes down their pants? To help them find their pockets.

Italian ethics have changed in proportion to the decline of the Vatican's powers of moral suasion. Although Pope John Paul II, during his eternal term, has vigorously condemned contraception, divorce, and abortion, they became accepted facts of life in Italy, as they are elsewhere. Italy has the lowest birth rate in Europe and one of the highest abortion rates.

Italian women are easy to pick out by their pouting expressions, which suggest drama-filled assignations in palatial villas and mysterious sexual secrets. They are not all beautiful, but they project a sense of risk that makes them appear striking. Italian women are vibrant and Italian men are exhausted because the women are always reaching for that electric moment. They toss their hair with great emphasis, as if to dislodge nesting birds, and walk with a determined stride that somehow manages to pucker their dresses in strategic places. And the men dress with even more vanity than the women. The resulting tension of sexual challenge is palpable everywhere and contributes much to Italian *brio*. "We are a Catholic country," I was told by Umberto Colombo, a Roman intellectual, "and we have yet to absorb the Protestant ethic. We sin. We repent. Then, we sin again."

The relaxation of individual and social morals is fairly new, but the Italian emphasis on sex as the essential life force is as old as the Etruscan marbles. Sex is to Italian life what snow is to Canadian winters – it falls everywhere, so thick you have to shovel your way through it. Italian law still lets offenders off in the mitigating circumstances of a "crime of passion." Men still whistle at passing women, who respond with stinging comments about the size of their testicles. The Italian beach, whither millions flee each August, resembles a catwalk of bronzed flesh. And the Italian army still has a regulation that any soldier whose testicles are shot off in combat receives considerably more compensation than he would for losing an arm or a leg. *Naturalmente!!*

Italians love *spettacolo*, the spectacle, the show – the tendency to turn every window display, political rally, village fete, business deal, family gathering, or birthday party into a major theatrical event. It is inconceivable for Italian family members to meet without *fare una festa*, making a party, the long and exaggerated round of hugs, kisses, and compliments that is the compulsory form of greeting. Italians are born actors who adore the stage and, above all, the costumes. One example of their exaggerated sense of style was the Italian crew's deportment during the 1987 America's Cup races at Fremantle, Australia. Although they ended up a poor eleventh in a thirteen-boat contest, each crew member of the Aga Khan–sponsored Italian syndicate blew into town sporting a 290-piece Gucci wardrobe – and that was only for onshore occasions. Appearances are everything; achievement is nothing. Penniless Neapolitan aristocrats, when forced to sell off their private carriages, kept back for themselves the doors emblazoned with their family crests, so they could be mounted onto rented coaches hired to attend the next masked ball.

At heart, every Italian male is an intellectual genius, a masterful lover, and above all a successful entrepreneur. I arrived in the country determined to discover its ultimate entrepreneur and eventually found him in Milan. He had been searching for that magical niche that would earn him a fortune for the least amount of effort, and had found it. What Italians value, more than life itself, are tickets to soccer playoffs. While attending a match of AC Milan, our hero noticed that every perch was taken, *except those in the handicapped section*. The next day, he was in the profitable business of renting wheelchairs outside the stadium gates. Another genius, a Florentine artist, has made a killing for years turning out wizened art objects for African museums whose genuine relics have deteriorated beyond repair. Sicilian real estate operators have diversified into purchasing toll roads, with the appropriate enforcers in plentiful supply. In Rome, a former gigolo runs an Institute of Amatory Arts, enjoying a long waiting list.

Italy's most successful entrepreneur is Giorgio Armani, the king of Italian designers. Dapper and white-haired, he invited me into his spacious and minimalist villa in central Milan. He turned out to be a pleasant, unimposing gentleman who struck me as the most sensible, least temperamental Italian I had met. *La moda Italia*, he told me, "takes into consideration what the consumer can wear – as opposed to the French, who are more interested in shocking and making statements."

Italian capitalists are nothing if not uninhibited, displaying the peacock feathers of their self-belief in a manner that would be considered criminally ostentatious in WASP circles. I managed to interview Ravenna billionaire Raul Gardini just as he acquired Montedison, Italy's second-largest industrial group. We met at his $8-million neo-Gothic palazzo on Venice's Grand Canal. I was escorted there aboard one of his luxurious mahogany motor launches, manned by sailors in cute Gucci naval uniforms. The effect was not unlike being in a David LaChapelle photograph.

Gardini was one tough don, the kind of Italian prince to whom Niccolò Machiavelli might have whispered the wily advice, "Claim everything, concede nothing, and if defeated, allege fraud." He had a pianist's fingers – long, slender, and strong – and spoke in a voice cured by grappa and cigars. His peregrine eyes could kill, and when we began our interview, they were aimed directly at me. I cringed at the realization that, as far as he was concerned, he was talking to a nobody from a frozen, unimportant country. He was right. I wondered who would get the axe for scheduling my interview. I was equally astonished to be there. I had applied to his office for an appointment as a mere formality, not expecting to get it: during that particular week, with his grab of Montedison, Gardini was Europe's most sought-after interview subject. Expecting some Italian hotshot TV commentator, instead he was cornered by a roving editor from "Canada's National Magazine," and he was not relishing the occasion one bit. Neither was I.

I posed my standard ice-breaking question for just such situations: "So, how do you divide your time these days?"

This did not significantly advance the dialogue. Gardini pretended to ponder my question, frowned, sighed, and then fixed me with an even fiercer dagger glare. It seemed to be his default facial expression, this bird-of-prey look. I squirmed and offered my best, patented, Canadian shit-eating grin.

If I wasn't comfortable, the surroundings were. The windows overlooking the Grand Canal were framed in *pietra serena*, stone ground smooth by moving river waters. The spacious receiving room boasted Renaissance frescoes and Florentine stone pilasters. A walk-in fireplace occupied most of one wall and the furniture appeared to be straight out of a Merchant Ivory film set.

At last, Gardini gave me the benefit of his wisdom. "We entrepreneurs," he said, "have become the connective tissue – the nervous system – of the New Europe. A common European currency is inevitable. It will be the entrepreneurs themselves who will become so able in manipulating currencies that they will force the Common Market bureaucrats in Brussels to make it official." (His prophecy about the Common Market – now called the European Community – and the currency, the Euro, proved to be entirely accurate.) Then he was heading for the door and was gone.

A few months later, he was dead, having shot himself rather than face trial for fraud and corruption. How sad. I never did find out how he divided his time.

If the rise, fall, and spectacular scandals of Italy's high-flying entrepreneurs offer the Italian newspaper-reading public endless entertainment, their equally accident-prone counterparts in political life provide the nation with conversational grist. This, for Italians, is better value-for-taxes than expecting good government. Like Albertans and the weather, if Italians don't like their government they just have to wait a while. Post-war Italian governments have been notoriously fractious and short-lived, with few coalitions lasting more than a year. Yet Italian democracy has proved extremely durable and vigorous. In part, this paradox is explained by the clumsy Italian constitution, which establishes a consensus-based confederation that is even younger and less flexible than Canada's.

Italy is governed by a rota of the same "grey men" constantly shifting their chairs, while the democratic institutions remain stable. All of which makes Italian political life more varied and colourful than Canada's. One simple reason is that the country exists in a never-ending election campaign. The still night air of an Italian piazza is shattered by the scratchy voice of a truck-mounted megaphone, inviting strollers out for their evening *passaggio* to vote one way or another. Anarchist political slogans are scrawled across every vacant wall. After all, Italy is the country that gave us both graffiti and propaganda — the latter short for Sacra Congregatio de Propaganda Fide, or the Sacred Congregation for Propagating the Faith. Gore Vidal, the American expatriate who has spent most of his writing life in an extraordinary villa on the cliffs above the Gulf of Salerno at Ravello, once remarked that the country's political parties seldom have programs: "They are a flag, a liturgy, the sound of a trombone practising in the night."

It seemed to me that if there was one politician with a clear idea of where he stood it would be Achille Occhetto, head of the then-powerful Communist Party. Going to interview Occhetto, I had to pass through bulletproof glass doors and corridors lined with portraits of Lenin, Marx, Engels, and various other patron saints of Italian Communist orthodoxy. But there turned out to be very little of the orthodox about Signore Occhetto. At least, he was not about to wash his dirty Lenin in public.

When I asked the then most powerful Communist in western Europe if he expected Italy would withdraw from the North Atlantic Treaty Organization, he looked at me as if I were deranged. "Of course Italy should stay in NATO," he shot back.

"Any change of alliances would be a mistake. What is peculiar to our party is that we aim for a transformation of Italian society, fully respecting democratic principles. We are trying to forge an alliance of the Left, based not on ideological confrontation but on common support for specific policies." What a downer. "Based not on ideological confrontation"? What kind of Red talk was that? The most conservative politician I had found in Italy turned out to be a Commie. (Of course in Italy politics, as everything, is a matter of style over commitment. The real difference between communist and fascist is that the *communisti* wear round-toed shoes, the *fascisti*'s have points.)

The oddest political movement I discovered was the Radical Party, a band of pranksters whose greatest success was electing as a member of Parliament for Lazio the hard-core porn star Ilona Staller, known as "Cicciolina." Being an elected deputy meant that she was free to pursue her art without fear of obscenity charges, since Italian legislators are immune from criminal prosecution. Designed to protect members of Parliament from trumped-up conspiracies, this legal loophole has instead protected many politicians, including sitting prime ministers, from facing charges of corruption. But never before had the immunity laws been put to such popular effect. La Cicciolina's election campaign consisted of her baring her ample breasts at every whistle stop while espousing a doctrine of free love. Some flag. Some trombones.

THE LAST TIME I WAS IN PRAGUE I was a little boy, holding my grandfather's hand, watching the Nazis invading my country. My mother, father, aunt, and I left shortly afterwards for Canada, but we never heard from my grandparents again. Late in 1943, we received telegrams from the Red Cross, advising us of their deaths, with no details. We later learned that after being abducted in Prague they had been transported by the Gestapo to the concentration camp at Theresienstadt.

Thirty years later I returned to Czechoslovakia, knowing there were ghosts waiting there. I took a bus to Theresienstadt to see for myself where my grandparents had died, having learned that in this camp were enacted some of the most tragic scenes of all the grotesqueries in the Nazi cabinet of horrors.

Concentration camps were not a Nazi invention. They were started by the British during the Boer War to "concentrate" their South African prisoners in one place, but these British camps became so crowded that many prisoners died from neglect, disease, and hunger. Of the 140,000 Jews sent to Theresienstadt, 87,000 were shipped to Auschwitz and other death camps for extermination, while 34,000 others died in the camp of malnutrition, maltreatment, and typhoid fever. Of the 15,000 children who entered its gates, fewer than 100 survived. As I read the names on its Wall of Remembrance, I noticed there were several other Peťa Neumanns. They were just my age, but not so lucky.[1]

Named after the Austrian empress Maria Theresa, Theresienstadt was turned into a "model" concentration camp in 1944. This was done to impress the Danish representatives of the Red Cross, who inspected its facilities and reported to the world at large that, contrary to rumours, German concentration camps were actually gated holiday campgrounds filled with people pursuing culture, sport, and the rearing of happy, singing children. All true – for that one day. Food rations suddenly increased before the Danish visit, children were given haircuts and clean clothes, fifty amateurs sang Verdi's *Requiem*, while children performed the opera *Brundibar*. Young women were paraded by, singing as they raked the flower beds specially planted for the occasion. White-gloved bakers unloaded loaves of bread; the streets were lined with false libraries,

---

[1] Our tour guide had been a prisoner. He told us that he had been one of five young men aged 18-23 on a train to the camp. One threw out a note to let his parents know that he was still alive. It was intercepted. Because they wouldn't confess who wrote the note, two of the boys (including our guide) were forced to stay up all night building a scaffold. The next morning they were forced to watch while the other three were hanged.

phony banks, and pretend kindergartens. The Germans also shot a film of this singular event, which was widely used for propaganda purposes. As soon as the Red Cross inspectors – who had asked not a single question – departed, almost everyone involved in the film was rounded up and packed into freight-train carriages to Auschwitz, labelled "SB" for "*Sonders Behandlung*" – which meant, in effect, "Gassing without selection."

Walking around Theresienstadt, I kept searching for words to fit the atrocity. It was an exercise in futility; no rational context exists for what happened there. It is a rank place to this day; even the air seemed to have been sucked out, so that breathing was difficult. I recall seeing a sunken pit or reservoir surrounded by a balcony – an innocent sight, until I asked my guide its purpose. "The Germans would choose a dozen or more of the fittest prisoners, lead them to the pit, and give them wooden clubs," my guide explained. "They were told to murder one another, as only the final survivor would be allowed to live." And the balcony? "That's where the guards' wives used to sit knitting, while they watched the massacre below."

What I remember most clearly is that no birds sang in the trees that surround Theresienstadt's cemeteries. In the summer there are no butterflies.

CHAPTER TWELVE

THE GUNSLINGER

Pierre Trudeau was an emotional cripple with a sliver of ice in his heart.

Octber 22, 1970: Rumours of war were being passed around Ottawa like after-dinner mints. Christina and I were attending a drawn-out cocktail party at the home of Trade minister Jean-Luc Pépin, a prime target of the Front de Libération du Québec since he was one of the province's most outspoken federalists. In his professorial way, Pépin was going on about the mayhem raging in his home province. "Revolutions are all the same," he was saying, though most of his guests were too nervous to listen. "Acts against the old order are invariably preceded by the disintegration of inward allegiances. The images of kings topple before their thrones."

"Well, yeah, I suppose – but what about Mike, here?" asked John Munro, one of Trudeau's better ministers, voicing the concern we were all feeling. Mike was an army private from Bell Island, in Conception Bay, Newfoundland, who had been assigned to guard the Pépins' household against the forces of evil stalking the trimmed hedges of Rockcliffe.

It was Day 17 of the FLQ's war against Canada and our first line of defence was Trooper Mike, who stumbled only occasionally as he alternated between alcoholic hiccups and puzzled glances into the darkness beyond the living-room window. It was raining and Pépin, a fatherly type, had invited the soldier into the house to warm up and have a hot toddy or two. After asking our host to "Cut de sweet stuff, gimme de rum," our Screech Commando was feeling no pain. He was stomping around the living room, haphazardly aiming his loaded Isuzu or whatever it was, and we were positioning ourselves near pieces of furniture to duck behind. "I's de boy to squash dem crazy Frogs," he volunteered, which caught the attention of Jean-Luc, among others. When conversation stopped, he took this as a signal to fill up his ten minutes of fame with Newfie humour.

"De boys up in Gander," he confided, "want Quebec to separate, just so's we kin drive to Toronto in half the time." He accompanied the punchline with an emphatic wave of his James Bond-ish automatic rifle. It was a test. If we laughed too hard, he might think we were laughing at him and get mad. If we didn't, he would tell another joke. Somebody saved the situation by turning up the television set just as Montreal's police chief came on, looking sweaty and dishevelled.

"We're raiding blind," he confessed. "We've run out of leads."

For some silly reason I kept repeating to myself Social Credit leader Bob Thompson's recent malapropism: "If this thing starts to snowball, it will catch fire right across the country." The snowball had become an avalanche. Canada was in a state of unhinged frenzy. The mantra of TV news directors ("If it bleeds, it leads") had become the national script: the whole damn country was bleeding.

Someone changed the television channel to catch the CBC national evening news and called for quiet. The stern voice of Knowlton Nash filled the room, attempting to strike a tone somewhere between authoritative and calm, barely disguising his underlying panic. A communiqué from the Front de Libération du Québec claimed that two more kidnappings were under way. The Canadian army, swarming over Montreal in full force and battle dress, had turned the city into an armed camp. Another forty Montrealers, we learned, had been rounded up and jailed. The

Commons was raucously debating the risk posed by unnamed col-
laborators coming to the aid of unindicted conspirators. It was
Canada's first experience with domestic terrorism. We felt spooked
and betrayed. Didn't these unshaven revolutionaries realize this
was Canada, for goodness sake? We don't do revolutions. The
tumult was deafening, but none of us knew how much of what
we were hearing was real and how much was hysteria. All we knew
was that it was too much to absorb.

Seventeen days had passed since British trade commissioner
James Cross had been kidnapped by the FLQ, the first such political crime in Canadian history. It was twelve days since Quebec
Labour minister Pierre Laporte had been snatched by another cell
of the FLQ from the lawn of his home in suburban St. Lambert,
while playing touch football with his sons. It was nine days since
Pierre Trudeau had assured his place in history and in the hearts of
Canadian federalists: when asked how far he would go to defeat
the FLQ, even at the cost of their civil rights, he'd shot back, "Just
watch me!" His cheeky defiance was for show; his brute strength
was for real. But watch him we did, to the exclusion of all else.

It was seven days since, at the urgent behest of Quebec premier
Robert Bourassa and Montreal mayor Jean Drapeau, seven battalions of Canadian soldiers had rolled into the city to re-establish
the rule of law. It was six days since Jean Marchand, the Trudeau
government's senior Quebec minister, had warned a frightened
Parliament that the FLQ had three thousand trained members, with
machine guns, bombs, and dynamite, ready to blow up downtown
Montreal. "They have infiltrated every strategic position, every
place where important decisions are taken," he warned. It was a
week since the prime minister had invoked the War Measures Act,
never before enacted in peacetime. By noon on October 16, some
465 men and women suspected of being friendly to the FLQ had
been arrested without warrants or charges. It was five days since
the corpse of Pierre Laporte, strangled with the chain of his own
crucifix, had been found dead, stuffed into the trunk of a green

Chevy abandoned in a parking lot at the St. Hubert airport. Quebec Justice minister Jérôme Choquette had labelled the insurrection "a pre-revolutionary situation." With events escalated into the surreal it was difficult to believe that Canada wasn't heading for anarchy, or worse.

"Look at those eyes," I had remarked to Christina as we'd watched Trudeau's address to the nation, invoking the War Measures Act. "They're as barren as potholes." I could see her eyes gazing upward at hearing yet another one of my ditzy metaphors. She knew I would soon be rhapsodizing about his skull-formed face and his resemblance to a Buddhist monk in mufti.

Watching him declare a state of civil war, which he called an "apprehended insurrection," I was remembering the Trudeau I had seen in action two years previously. It was on June 24, only hours before the 1968 election, at Montreal's Lafontaine Park. The once-quiet Quebec revolution was gathering violent momentum. Trudeau was on the reviewing stand for the annual St. Jean Baptiste parade when furious protestors suddenly rushed toward him, shouting obscenities, hurling rocks and bottles. He stood his ground, the definition of grace under pressure, angrily waving off would-be bodyguards trying to shield him while the dignitaries who minutes before had surrounded him scattered for cover. The night was lit by a burning police car (twelve were overturned); beside me a cop on horseback reared up, preparing to charge back into the shrieking mob. "*C'est une garce!*" ("It's a bitch!") he said to no one in particular, then rode off, indiscriminately beating the rioters with his truncheon.

Claude Ryan was there that night, a gaunt, lonely figure in his light-grey windbreaker and battered fedora. "Have you ever seen anything like this?" I asked him.

"Not here," he said. "We had some bad times during the conscription crisis but nothing, nothing like this. You can not subdue revolutionary fervour with force. *C'est les situations sociales et économiques qui alimentent l'activité terroriste.* Social ills cause terrorist acts."

Back at the Pépins' we were preparing to leave when somebody told me I was on the FLQ's assassination list. "But don't worry," He winked. "You're way behind Paul Desmarais and they'll never get him." Since I had briefly been a Catholic, I crossed myself. You never know.[1] Christina and I were the first to leave the party. The last time we saw Mike, the warrior from the Rock, he had been sent out into the rain and was carefully drawing a bead on the moon, laughing softly to himself.

The following day, we were urgently summoned to the East Block office of Marc Lalonde, the PM's principal secretary. Lalonde was as tough as nine generations of scrub farming on Île Perrot, off the southwestern tip of Île de Montréal, could make him. "I'm a Norman farmer," he loved to say. "It's like being from Missouri." He had come up through the militant Action Catholique movement, understood his people, and was Trudeau's closest adviser. We had known him since he'd first come to Ottawa under Pearson and admired his appreciation of Quebec politics, which was both visceral and cerebral. We trusted him. Thin, bald, hawk-like in appearance, he bade us sit across his messy desk from him. He smiled with funereal solemnity, in a way that underscored that this was no smiling matter, then proceeded to give us his grim reading of the deteriorating situation.

"Peter . . . Christina . . ." he began, "I have called you here to discuss a matter of the utmost seriousness, but first I must warn you that I will deny this conversation ever took place."

We looked at each other and nodded. Reassured, Lalonde continued. "We believe that a group of prominent Québécois is plotting to replace the province's duly elected government," he said gravely. "The conspirators include René Lévesque, Jacques Parizeau, Marcel Pepin, and Claude Ryan. This move toward a

[1] My name was indeed on the FLQ list when it was published. At the time, Paul Desmarais, chairman of Power Corporation, the largest agglomeration of private economic power in French Canada, was hunting pheasant on Île aux Ruaux in the St. Lawrence. The feds escorted him to safety aboard a landing craft manned by troops from Quebec City.

parallel power must be stopped." He let the magnitude of the thought sink in for a moment.

"Not Ryan," Christina and I chimed in unison. "He is a man of conscience, dedicated to collective survival, not personal power. Besides, how do you know so much about the plot's members, their plans and intentions?"

"Because we know the ringleaders," he replied coolly. "We have been looking over their shoulders, you might say."

"Why are you telling us this? What do you expect us to do with such speculative information?" Christina demanded.

That brought him up short. "There is nothing speculative about this. It is true. I would surmise . . . that is to say . . . it would be prudent if certain individuals — certain individuals in the media — were made aware of the whole story . . ."

He looked up from his desk and flashed his sweetest smile, then repeated, "Of course, I cannot officially confirm anything for you."

Lalonde went on for most of an hour, trying not only to relieve our doubts but also hinting that it was our patriotic duty to disseminate news of this alarming development. We had known one another long enough that I could tell him he was full of it without calling him a liar, and I did so now, adding that I would give no credence to such a bizarre theory unless it was confirmed by Trudeau himself. "Not a problem," he answered right back. "He will call you. Where are you staying?"

Lalonde said *adieu*, closed his eyes, hunched over, and, with the seriousness of Galileo defending his theory of the universe, mumbled, "Pray for us." Chris and I looked at one another in disbelief. Our host was not impressed. "I don't suppose you people pray, anyway," he snorted, excommunicating us on the spot, as wormy Ontario Anglo Saxon Protestants, or in my case, a reasonable facsimile thereof.

We were barely back in our hotel room when the phone rang. It was Trudeau. With the insurrection yet to be apprehended, I hadn't really expected that the PM would bother taking the time to phone out-of-town journalists.

"Peter?" he asked, rolling out the word in his trademark serpentine inflection. "Marc tells me that he had a very interesting conversation with you and Christina today. And how is your lovely wife?"

"She's fine," I replied, respectfully, though trying to keep a cool distance. "But she is confused and worried, as I am. Look, Pierre, you know what Marc told us. Is there anything to it? You once explained to me that revolutions may devour humanity, but it's tyranny that generates violence. Claude Ryan might be part of the revolution, but he's no tyrant."

"Tyranny has many agents," he replied, sounding annoyingly Pierre-like.

There was a long pause, as though he was conferring with someone, or reading a note. "Yes, Peter," he replied at last. "I can confirm it. There is a conspiracy afoot. The ringleaders are Lévesque, Parizeau, and Ryan, among others. This move toward a parallel power must be stopped."

"Even if Ryan is organizing a political group," I objected, "it's only to give Bourassa some backbone. It hardly amounts to *un coup de main . . .*"

"Unelected power is not moved by benign motives," he replied with an edge of annoyance. I realized his patience was running out. "Look," he said, sounding exasperated, "what Marc told you and Christina is true: the plot to overthrow the government is real."

"With respect, how can you be so sure?"

"I acted on information I've been accumulating since I was three years old."

In other words, "Buzz off *Anglais.*"

He added that I couldn't quote him or even mention that we had talked. (I am doing so now, for the first time, long after his death.)

"But Pierre, perhaps in this case what you lacked in evidence, you have made up from conviction . . ."

The line had gone dead.

I turned to Christina, waiting with a worried look of expectation. "Pierre says it's true," I told her. "It's a coup."

She fell back into the sofa and shook her head incredulously. "This is Canada," she said. "I can't believe it. This is Canada."

We decided that while we weren't really sure what was true and what was convenient for the government to spread, either way we had the story of the decade.

OTTAWA'S SOCIAL EVENT of the year was scheduled for the following evening: the annual reception given by the super-bureaucrats Bernard and Sylvia Ostry at Five Oaks, their splendid mansion on the Quebec-Ontario border, the epicentre of Ottawa's power structure. Their living room was where decisions were debated, influence paraded, special favours refused and granted. Christina and I had become regulars at these shindigs. We had been there when Trudeau was Justice minister and allowed a visiting rock group to light up their weird cigarettes, though he didn't join them. But this gathering was different. Half the Trudeau Cabinet ministers were present, as were the key (as opposed to just the senior) deputies, earnestly whispering to one another in the corners of the large reception room, all the while watched over by their armed guards. I spotted a sobered-up Mike from the Pépin household and gave him a playful poke in the shoulder. He didn't shoot me.

The gossip was mainly about "Bou-Bou," the favoured nickname for Premier Robert Bourassa, who, it was said, had lost his balls and was at permanent panic stations, barricaded into the twentieth floor of Montreal's Queen Elizabeth Hotel. But his predicament was overtaken by the rumour of a "provisional government plot," which nobody would confirm or deny but which was certainly floating out there as the conversational truffle of the hour. I distinctly remember Alex Pelletier, a film producer and the wife of Gérard Pelletier, Trudeau's secretary of state, telling anybody who would listen, "Claude Ryan is out to take over the government, and has to be put down." It was stated as a fact instead of conjecture, but few were buying her version of events. Christina and I realized that our scoop was more perishable than we had imagined.

What many in this stodgy gathering wanted to hear was that their boy Pierre was about to put down those Gallic rebs with their dirty beards and raised fists, while at the same time protecting the realm from windy intellectuals like Claude Ryan and the terror of his convoluted editorials. Paul Desmarais was there, looking unperturbed, but packing a revolver, it was whispered. Charlie Lynch came over and confided to me that his doctor wouldn't allow him to eat any more soft cheeses because they contained more cholesterol than hard brands like cheddar and Emmental. "That makes good sense," I told him; Charlie was always on top of the news. Sylvia Ostry zoomed by, looking dazzling and dazzled, as chief animator of this pre-Waterloo gala, echoing with the sound of revelry.

At one point several of us were standing around the exquisitely maintained garden, which included underwater heating pipes so that Sylvia and Bernard could view a green patch of grass year-round. We were idly watching the guttering flicker of a stout, dripless candle when suddenly it went out. We swung around in panic, searching the night for some evil wind that might have extinguished the flame. "You know," remarked the scholarly looking gent beside me, done up with a beard and beret, "we're just catching up to recent history. Che Guevara was beatified as the role model of the young; in his over-the-cliff *Soul on Ice*, Eldridge Cleaver urged blacks to rape white women; that mixed-up geezer Herbert Marcuse became the guru of rebellions on the campuses; at home, Quebec youths heeded the revolutionary musings of our own firebrand, Pierre Vallières. Revolution is in the air. We can't escape it."

"No wonder the young are revolting," observed an elegant Westmount society import, slumming in Ottawa for the occasion, adding under her refined breath, "and some of them truly *are* revolting."

Just then an executive assistant I knew ran out of the house to announce he had been told "on good authority by one of Bou-Bou's bully boys" that this weekend five hundred of Quebec's leading citizens would be assassinated. "But don't tell anybody!" he called over his shoulder, and moved on.

We returned indoors where the armed troopers were busy examining Bernard Ostry's vintage books and vintage liquor. Christina and I had to keep quiet about our recent conversations but realized it was time to skedaddle.

BY SUNDAY NOON, I was back in my editor's chair at the *Toronto Star* and had contacted Robert McKenzie, our experienced Quebec City correspondent, to check out the story. He talked to Ryan and reported back on Claude's – and his own – disbelief that we would even consider publishing such a bizarre rumour. Our Montreal editor agreed, but added that I should listen to what the mayor was going to say when the ballots had been counted. I had forgotten that this was the day of the Montreal municipal election. Jean Drapeau, whose family home had earlier been destroyed by FLQ bombs, won by a margin of 92 per cent. At his victory press conference he surprised his supporters (and me) by thanking them for "resisting, not only known revolutionary attacks but also attempts to set up a provisional government that was to preside over the transfer of constitutional powers to a revolutionary regime."

Suddenly, I had confirmation of the story, not only from the prime minister of Canada in private, but from the mayor of Montreal in public.

I still wasn't convinced. I wrote the article very gingerly, emphasizing that "the factor which finally drove the Trudeau Government to invoke the War Measures Act was that they had become convinced a plan existed to replace the Government" – that it was the Trudeau administration (not *moi*) which "believed that a group of influential Quebeckers had set out to supplant the legitimately elected provincial administration." In other words, I took care to make it clear that I was reporting what I had been told, without subscribing to the notion myself. This was a distinction quickly lost on my peers, my colleagues, and my readers. They either wanted to believe that the provisional government story was true, or that I was deliberately spreading a falsehood, or both.

I mentioned no names of suspected conspirators, since I couldn't bring myself to believe that Claude Ryan could align himself with such an inflammatory abuse of power. I knew him well. We had connected the moment we met, several years earlier. Since then I had often called on him at the cobblestoned end of Rue Notre Dame and spent many enjoyable hours discussing Quebec's prospects in his bare cell of an office. There was no soft side to him. His face had the aesthetic strength of wisdom born through suffering, with hooded eyes and a nose sharpened as if to probe his visitors' intentions. He was the rational voice and resident saint of Quebec's Quiet Revolution, and I implicitly trusted him. Not that long ago, we had spent a day in my *Star* office (where I was now completing my article) drafting the manifesto of the Committee for an Independent Canada, which he would later co-chair. The more often we talked, the more I admired and trusted him.

I phoned Ryan and left a message: "Claude, you probably know the story I've heard. I'm writing it. Can you give me an unqualified denial?"

Beland Honderich had meanwhile come into the office. The decision as to whether or not to publish my piece would be made at the very top. The publisher had in turn brought in Jake Howard, a leading Toronto libel lawyer (who happened to have been my training officer aboard HMCS *Iroquois*). I was in Bee's office when he telephoned Ryan: "Claude, what do you say about this story being circulated about you?"

"For God's sake, Bee, tell me what things you are going to circulate." Ryan was becoming increasingly agitated. "We're not in Hitler's Germany, you know. We're in Canada."

Honderich summarized my story, then added: "We are going to publish the story, but with no names in it."

"That's not my concept of journalism," Ryan replied harshly. "As a matter of principle, I repudiate this kind of journalism, very, very strongly."

When I asked Howard whether I could include Ryan's denial, which I had by then received on my message machine, he pointed out that the mention of any name might leave us open to accusations of sedition, against which we would have no defence. I agreed to publish the six-paragraph piece, but Honderich ruled that it should remain anonymous, because so many people had worked on it, so it was slugged "From Our Ottawa Bureau." I was wrong not to insist that it go out under my name. Our Ottawa Bureau journalists quickly denied authorship, telling callers that I had been in town asking questions and that it was undoubtedly my handiwork.

The story took on a life of its own. To his surprise, *Telegram* columnist Douglas Fisher found "an unidentified but reliable" source who confirmed my story, and went even further: "Why don't you have some faith in us? Surely you must know we wouldn't have taken such an extraordinary step unless the threat was very, very serious. We learned from unimpeachable sources that such a takeover was planned. Really big people involved. Trudeau is the last man in this country to panic. We moved on the War Measures Act because it was that or chaos." Half a dozen other papers published my version of events; even the reliable Pierre O'Neil of *La Presse* labelled the facts as *"incroyables mais apparemment vrais"* ("unbelievable but apparently true"). Most other reporters decided to kill the messenger. I had seldom been the target of such malice. The *Telegram* labelled my story "grotesque"; the CBC's Larry Zolf called it a "plant"; the *Globe* ridiculed my "fantasy born of hysteria"; and the Montreal *Gazette* pointed out that it "defied belief."

What I didn't know at the time was that all of these critiques were entirely accurate.

I later learned that the original source of the provisional government rumour was none other than Claude Ryan himself. On October 11, the day after Laporte's kidnapping, Robert Bourassa had begun to lose his grip on events and on his ability to respond. Ryan called an emergency editorial board meeting to discuss ways of strengthening the premier's backbone and his government's clout. The controversial alternative-government option had indeed been discussed and just as quickly rejected – all within the context, not of setting up a parallel government, but of enlisting community leaders to strengthen Bourassa's slipping hold on power. During a conversation the same day with Lucien Saulnier, chairman of the Montreal's executive committee, Ryan mentioned the idea of a provisional government as a last resort if the kidnappings continued and Bourassa's deteriorating control of the situation presented a danger to the rule of law. "Then," he said, "and only then, there surely wouldn't be much choice but to set up a unity government, made up of the best elements." He feared that unless order was restored, Ottawa might place Quebec under some form of stewardship, which he wouldn't put past Trudeau. Saulnier passed Ryan's comments on to Lalonde, who reported them to the PM. Somewhere along the line, *Le Devoir*'s editorial board blue-sky discussion was transformed into an intended coup.

Eight days after I first heard it the story was finally shot down by its most illustrious source: Pierre Elliott Trudeau. At an Ottawa press conference on October 31, he casually confirmed that the feds had indeed been "looking over the shoulders" of the "conspirators" who were intending to form a "provisional regime." He went on to remark that there had never been any hard evidence that the group was going to carry out its intentions. He dismissed my report in the *Star* as being based on "rumours and unconfirmed speculations" and later told the House of Commons: "It has not been the government but rather the Opposition and the Press Gallery that have been launching these rumours."

Zut alors! They were his rumours. Not mine.

I felt angry and cheated by Trudeau's revisionist version of events. I hadn't been in Ottawa for a dozen years without becoming inured to the fact that prime ministers lie; it comes with the territory. I had made my reputation writing stories about political chicanery but had seldom before become its victim.

Then the penny began to drop. If the prime minister could reverse himself so casually, then the entire scenario had been a meticulously concocted lie, with Christina and me the unwitting accomplices in the feds' attempt to discredit Ryan. There had never been a plot, just Claude's musings during a gut-wrenching crisis. But when we had talked to Lalonde and Trudeau on October 23, they had not differentiated between what they knew to be true and what they wished to be true. *Le Devoir*'s publisher had always been a threat to their vision of the province as a federal preserve, for Ryan was Quebec's voice of conscience, a role that Trudeau could no longer claim as exclusively his own.

IN THE PUBLIC'S MIND, the imposition of the War Measures Act and the call-up of troops to restore order in Montreal and guard Ottawa's politicians were cause and effect of the same phenomenon. In fact, there was no connection. On October 15, when Drapeau and Bourassa demanded the presence of Canada's armed forces in the city and the province, they were merely citing relevant provisions of the National Defence Act, which requires Ottawa to grant such requests almost automatically. In retrospect, Trudeau might have overreacted by calling up 7,500 soldiers to combat the violent acts of a dozen revolutionaries. The armed might mobilized by the prime minister was awesome. (In those days, Canada could still assemble an army with meaningful firepower.) To put the call-up in perspective: seven battalions were assigned to Montreal, while nine battalions were involved in the 1942 raid on Dieppe, among the largest of Canada's armed interventions during the Second World War.

Another link usually cited in any reconstruction of the crisis was that the imposition of the War Measures Act was a desperate response to Laporte's execution. Not so. That legal escalation was formally requested by Quebec's premier at 3:00 a.m. on Friday, October 16, and granted an hour later. Laporte's assassination was announced by the FLQ a full twenty-four hours after that, and his body was not found until late the following day.

The first hint that all was not what it seemed here was an obscure paragraph in an obscure memoir by Donald Jamieson, the Trudeau government's Transport minister. He interpreted Trudeau's headlong rush into proclaiming the War Measures Act not as a specific measure to combat any "apprehended insurrection" (which is what the act cited as the only appropriate *casus belli*) but rather as a political move to shore up the prime minister's obsession with defanging Quebec's separatists. Unlike the troop mobilization, Ottawa did not have to accede to the province's request for imposition of the War Measures Act. Several senior ministers, including Jamieson, John Turner, Joe Greene, and Mitchell Sharp, were strongly opposed, since the act had never been activated except in wartime, and in this case there existed lesser, equally effective options. Jamieson suggested that a Cabinet committee be struck to demonstrate why the draconian measure had been necessary. To his surprise, Trudeau did not take up the idea. "Subsequent events made his reason for non-response very plain," Jamieson wrote. "It was his growing awareness that very little in the way of concrete evidence was going to turn up. I and others in cabinet were quite uneasy over this turn of events." He predicted that critics of the measure would realize "we had acted for political reasons or from something less than simon-pure motives." Exactly.

Guided by York University historian Reg Whitaker, I delved into the documents available under the Freedom of Information Act and found the minutes of a confidential briefing presented to Trudeau two days before the invocation of the War Measures Act. Unlike most police officers faced by persistent politicians, William Higgitt, the commissioner of the Royal Canadian Mounted Police, proved to be very tough, very precise, and equally persistent. Asked repeatedly how the provision would assist his police work, Higgitt's studied reply was recorded in the meeting's unemotional minutes: "The Commissioner said he saw no necessary action being prevented by existing laws. He said that a broad sweep and preventive detention of suspects was not likely to lead to the abductors and that he could therefore not recommend the use of special powers." For good measure, Higgitt warned that Quebec "wanted action for the sake of action" and that this "ought not to be allowed to overrule calmer reaction at the federal level." Higgitt was called back to brief the Cabinet after the feds' dragnet had haphazardly imprisoned 465 suspects. He told the ministers that this draconian measure had produced "nothing of consequence." Near the end of this second briefing (which Trudeau did not attend) the RCMP commissioner was asked bluntly whether he had evidence that any kind of insurrection was being planned. "Not really," he replied, "there is no such evidence." Shortly afterwards, during a private session with British Foreign secretary Sir Alec Douglas-Home in London, External Affairs secretary Mitchell Sharp confessed that, indeed, "there was no evidence of an extensive and co-ordinated FLQ conspiracy."

Out of this and other evidence, I easily conclude that Trudeau invoked the War Measures Act as a partisan weapon to intimidate Quebec's separatists for his own political purposes. The only apprehended insurrection the PM had going for him was the puny parallel government rumour in my story, which was not an insurrection, nor had it been apprehended, since it never got started.

What most likely happened followed the merry-go-round mentality of any Ottawa conspiracy when its members are attempting to justify, or hide, dubious actions. Lalonde heard from Saulnier that Ryan had been musing about a provisional government. Somewhere along the line, the version was torqued out of all recognition. The feds had to find a way of disseminating the story to their power network, which in turn would persuade the country's mainstream media to believe it was true. The fact that the information was disseminated only within a closed loop gave the story much higher cachet. First they got the mayor of Montreal believing it, then the Cabinet, then the Newmans and other chosen mouthpieces, and soon, enough of "the people who matter" were spreading the rumour as if it were true – even if its originators didn't entirely believe it.[2]

As the disturbing facts of that episode unfolded, I became determined that I would treat Lucky Pierre as just another political gunslinger, and not as the phantom of my opera. The gunslinger image seemed apt. He might just as easily have been one of those fabled cowboys who flourished briefly across the American West in the mid-nineteenth century. The code they lived by found resonance in Trudeau's politics, because the mark of the gunslingers was their courage of the early morning and the rawhide toughness of their quest. But they also viewed their lives as a series of throwaway gestures, as did Pierre. Like the best of the vintage frontier vigilantes, he was a loner who risked everything in the shootouts of electoral politics. But unlike most of the gunslingers, he did not end his career being scraped off some barroom floor. Instead he turned himself into a self-appointed posse of one in charge of reforming Canada's constitution – and no man (or Supreme Court) could stand in his way.

IN THE EARLY 1960S, long before he came to Ottawa, I spent many an entrancing hour visiting Trudeau in his bare cubicle at the University of Montreal's Institute for Public Law, where he taught and made trouble for Maurice Duplessis, then premier of

---

[2] How long this version of events survived was illustrated on February 10, 2004, when Claude Ryan died of stomach cancer, and in his *Globe and Mail* obituary Rhéal Séguin described the *Le Devoir* publisher's role in the FLQ crisis of 1970 this way: "At one point, fearing that the Bourassa regime was on the verge of collapsing, Ryan and others secretly set up a parallel government."

Quebec. He was an imposing presence even then, having earned degrees in law, economics, and political science from universities in Montreal, London, Paris, and Cambridge, Massachusetts. He fed my taste for irreverence, telling me the story of how he was arrested in 1952 at a Moscow economic conference for throwing snowballs at a statue of Joseph Stalin. He got off by explaining that whenever he went to Ottawa, he threw snowballs at the statue of Sir Wilfrid Laurier.

His ideas certainly weren't revolutionary; they were rigidly anti-nationalist. He told me that separatism in Quebec would never triumph because it could not transform itself into a broadly based popular movement. Instead, it had become what Trudeau called "a bourgeois revolution – the uprising of people who were afraid they wouldn't have enough important jobs in the society of tomorrow. They thought that only an independent Quebec would solve their problem, because they would be its new elite and wouldn't have to share power and jobs with outsiders." Trudeau's persuasive technique (this was the first time I was exposed to it) was derived from the Jesuit principle of not imposing your views on others but of letting people find their own way to your beliefs. I could sense even then that he was much more preoccupied with government than with society, less interested in social change than in stability and continuity, more committed to the legal concepts of Canada's federation than any adventurous attempt to fashion an independent nationhood.

What was fresh and intriguing about him, even before he entered politics, was his style: the turtleneck sweaters, the eloquent shrugs, his two Mercedes, any number of stunning girlfriends, and the lingo he used, impressive in both official languages, non-academic but highly evocative of an original mind. When he arrived in Ottawa as an MP in 1965, I was one of the few English journalists he knew. We met for monthly lunches (I always paid the bill) in the parliamentary restaurant. His agenda was to probe my knowledge of the national press corps – who not to trust and who not to trust absolutely; mine was to gather news leaks, first about the Quebec caucus, and then later about the Justice department, which he took over less than two years after his arrival.

The prevalent topic of corridor gossip at the time was finding a candidate who could lead the Liberal Party to victory, Mike Pearson having exhausted himself and his mandate. We had Trudeau to our house several times, most memorably when Beland Honderich asked us to invite the Liberal leadership candidates to a cocktail party so he could look them over. They all came to do their *Star* turn in the presence of the paper's influential publisher, flaunting their bon mots and pledging themselves to follow the paper's diktats. Christina later recalled watching Trudeau, who was standing alone in the hall, observing his rivals suck the editorial teat, carefully sipping his sherry. After remarking that the guest of honour seemed to be fully occupied, he slipped away into the night. "I was left trying to decipher the emotion reflected in his glittering blue eyes when he took in the antics of the office seekers," she wrote in *Saturday Night*. "Probably he was being 'coldly intelligent,' an attitude he assumes as often as is humanly possible. Reason would tell him there was nothing to be gained at that party, and reason would soon prove right. Trudeau's predilection for denying feelings in favour of reason was his one constant."

I was the first to place Trudeau's name publicly into contention in my Ottawa column, recognizing in him a desirable antidote to the Diefenbaker-Pearson feud, which had been polluting our politics for most of a decade. "During his brief but exciting tenure in the Justice portfolio Trudeau has established himself as a child of his times," I wrote. "His candour, his intellectual curiosity, his championing of social reforms have suddenly thrust him into inevitable contention. Trudeau could be unbeatable."

The idea was widely dismissed as a bad joke. The denizens of Ottawa's Rideau Club poked one another in the ribs as they told and retold the story about how Trudeau had turned up on a Saturday morning at the Privy Council Office dressed in desert boots and a boiler suit. He was minister of Justice at that time, but the commissionaire on duty, convinced he was a plumber with a garbled work order, had turned him away. Whenever his name was casually mentioned in the early speculative talk about leadership candidates, the subject of his hairdo inevitably came up: "How could anybody who combs his hair forward into bangs be a Canadian prime minister?" Ottawa was still a nineteenth-century town with Sunday School values and politicians who thought it was daring to use an adverb. Few could be bothered to parse Trudeau's thoughts, or even try. In the bleak chill of December 1967, just after Lester Pearson announced his resignation, Trudeau's victory seemed far from inevitable; in fact, it was scarcely credible. To most Liberals, he was an untested outsider, a heretical presence not easily encompassed by the party's collective mentality.

IN RETROSPECT, Trudeau's conquest of the Liberal Party appeared to be predestined to glory, with the other leadership contenders serving merely as spear-carriers in the dramatic elevation of a once and future king. But it wasn't like that at all. He won mainly because his competitors lost their nerve. During the first eight months in the Justice portfolio he made little public impact, except as an odd character given to eccentric pursuits. Diefenbaker attacked him because instinct told him this Grit was a serious threat, but not being certain why, Dief merely lambasted him for wearing a yellow ascot into the House of Commons.

As Justice minister, Trudeau tabled his controversial amendments to the Criminal Code that legalized abortion and homosexual acts between consenting adults. "I want to separate sin from crime," he explained. "You may have to ask forgiveness for your sins from God, but not from the minister of Justice." Then he added his famous kicker: "There's no place for the state in the bedrooms of the nation." This was hardly a startling proposition, but it had a disproportionate impact on a nation whose citizens had been numbed by generations of politicians limiting their discourse to obtusely discussing the gross national product or debating the sleep-inducing minutiae of federal-provincial relations. The first serious politician to jump on the Trudeau bandwagon was Newfoundland's premier, Joey Smallwood: "Why, there aren't four or five men in the country who can express themselves in English like this man and here I was, using my meat axe like a clumsy elephant with arthritis and he tells me he wished he could express himself as clearly."

Trudeau was rapidly becoming known for his shrugs, wisecracks, dance steps, and swan dives. There was about everything he did a subtle, indefinable intensity, a suggestion of pent-up power and hidden dimensions that fascinated the nation's TV viewers, impressed the Liberal delegates, and frightened the other, unhip contenders.

Riding a chartered jet and wearing his signature leather coat, Trudeau went campaigning for the leadership crown. His every appearance produced standing ovations. In Victoria, where the monarchy was still a significant issue, local Liberals questioned Trudeau on a topic he had previously dismissed as irrelevant. He won the crowd over with a shrug and the comment: "I was in Saskatoon last night and crowned a very lovely queen, so I feel very warm toward the monarchy." At every one of his sessions I could sense the moment his audience switched from being merely titillated to joining his cause. They came prepared to be fascinated, even scandalized by a wild man in sandals spouting socialist slogans. Instead, they found an immaculate, demure professor delivering proposals that sounded exciting but would not have been out of place in any Canadian Manufacturers' Association brief. English Canadians liked his conservative, hard line on Quebec; coming from a French Canadian, it was even sweeter to their ears. Unable to classify him as a man of either the Right or Left, his audiences chose to regard him as a man of the future. "Trudeau won because, if Expo 67 had been a person, that person would have been Trudeau," wisely observed Richard Gwyn in the *Toronto Star*.

During that leadership campaign, which proved more exhilarating than the election campaign that followed, I witnessed the man's transformation. Having grown up in a home that swam with money but was short on nurturing, Trudeau realized early on that reason trumped emotion. But in middle age he decided on a Faustian bargain: to thwart the gathering storm of separatism, he would surrender his treasured privacy and become a politician. It was a brave gambit because he was taking a chance on the maturity of Canadians. He was staking his future on an intuitive conviction that after a lifetime of nineteenth-century leaders, voters were no longer searching for a father figure but felt ready for a leading man, a postmodern, existential hero: himself.

And I was there at the creation. When the flying caravan hit Ottawa, I found myself standing beside a middle-aged couple, listening in on their chatter, as Trudeau made his way down the receiving line toward them.

"What if I faint when I see him?" the wife, flushed with excitement, asked her huge block of a sideburned husband.

He cut her in two with a look of dismissive disgust: "Ahh, don't be silly, Mabel, he's just another goddamn politician."

Then suddenly Trudeau was there, facing the husband. He said nothing but gave him a long, hard look, shook hands with that comradely gesture (one hand on elbow, the other in a firm arm-grip) used by politicians for a simultaneous hello and farewell. Then he shrugged, smiled, and moved on. The man stood there, and then quietly started to cry. He hugged his wife, then they moved away, arm in arm. A connection had been made. Watching that silent exchange, I knew the race was over. When he entered that room, he stole its oxygen. We had ourselves a new prime minister and a new politics.

THE LEADERSHIP CONVENTION that followed in the new Civic Centre was the most exhilarating political event of my time in Ottawa. It was the first convention totally dominated by television. TV screens can accommodate only one image at a time, tending to give every event equal significance, and from the moment Trudeau entered the race, the electronic media intuitively chose him as the winner. Throughout the convention, eight camera crews bathed him in the revealing beams of handheld klieg lights, endowing his presence with an incandescent glow that turned him into a star. He carried his own halo with him, shedding light as he drifted through the crowds. In turn, he provided the cameras with dramatic action. When he arrived by train in Ottawa, teenaged girls seeded his path with wedding rice, squealing in delight as he approached. I was at the station, watching the crowd surge forward like an ocean wave, gathering strength as it rolled toward him and finally bursting through the police barriers as people gasped for the sight of him. Later in the evening, at a jammed dance in the Chaudière Golf and Country Club, Joey Smallwood elbowed his way to the bandstand and, in his usual understated way, declared, "Pierre is better than medicare – the lame have only to touch his garments to walk again."

On the convention's opening day, Paul Hellyer's troops goose-stepped into the arena, his band blaring a march tune, red-and-white straw hats waving in time. Then came John Turner looking resolutely confident, surrounded by stomping, cheering, big-wheels-on-campus, the middle-aged young. Paul Martin the Elder gloomed by, raising his arms in a premature victory salute, calling out thirty first-name greetings a minute, displaying his conviction that ideologies and issues are minor diversions from the real business of politics: the handshake. Bob Winters waltzed in to the strains of "Walking in a Winters Wonderland." All these carefully planned demonstrations were suddenly made to look old-fashioned and contrived when Trudeau, as Frank Walker, editor of the *Montreal Star*, put it, "crept in like Jesus Christ," slipping unheralded into his seat followed by a scatter of homemade banners, held aloft by his moon maidens.

As the crowd roared at the sight of him, the other contenders grew rigid with nerves. They clustered with their advisers, trying to divine the source of Trudeau's magic, suspicious that he had some special trick they could master. They sent emissaries to observe him, talk to him, touch him. But the couriers come back as puzzled as ever, variously reporting that it had to be his looks, his youth, his money, his radicalism, or his reputation as an intellectual. But Turner was younger, Winters handsomer, Kierans more radical, Hellyer richer, and Martin had more academic degrees.

Trudeau maintained his inner repose, refusing to lend himself to the gravitational pull of the convention. And the more he held back, the more the crowd wanted a piece of him. "I made him get a haircut!" boasted an excited assistant. The stock of forty thousand Trudeau buttons ran out; ten thousand more were ordered. Only hours after Winters's organization issued green buttons that read "It's Winterstime," the Trudeau girls produced tags that simply replied, "It's Spring!" Throughout the convention, radiant young women wearing the Trudeau campaign's Buddhist-orange mini-skirts lit up the convention, dazzling the delegates. Gentle and graceful, with faces like flowers, they were fondled by a thousand eyes. (It was rumoured that their den mother guided their activities through a transmitter in her bra. The rumour was true.)

On the evening of the main event, the proceedings began with Paul Martin marching toward the stage at the head of an enormous bugle corps band. An old pro to the end, he delivered a "do-not-reject-this-man" speech about himself, concluding with the sound bite: "Democracy is not a system where truths are implemented by philosopher-kings." Take that, Pierre-baby. Next up was Bob Winters, a self-charmed big-businessman who flatly declared there was no poverty in Canada, just people who didn't work hard enough. The touch of Back Bay Boston in his voice gave him an edge, but he displayed all the charisma of a colouring book executive. He made a few remarks in pre-Berlitz French, ending with the ringing declaration that only mediocrity is satisfied with itself. (And Bob Winters was the most satisfied man in the hall.)

The mood changed abruptly as Joe Greene ambled up to the stand, picked up a hand microphone, and delivered, without a note, the finest speech of the evening. Folksy as a fox and purposefully awkward as Abe Lincoln, he displayed dollops of cracker-barrel wisdom but lacked the essential party power base. He praised farmers, wiped his brow country-style, went back to his seat and hugged his kids. Paul Hellyer marched up to the platform next, looking like a cavalry captain in Kaiser Wilhelm's army. He delivered a too-perfect checklist of solutions that chilled the soul. His cheering section was led by Judy LaMarsh in a pair of knee-high white boots and ninety-year-old Senator Arthur Roebuck in a wing collar, both incongruously waving straw boaters as they boogied through the building. Hellyer's aides later estimated his speech cost him at least 150 votes.

The wail of half the unemployed bagpipers in Canada heralded Allan MacEachen, who entered looking hot and nervous, constantly examining his watch in a manner uncomfortably like that of the sweating film publicist in the Humphrey Bogart film *The Barefoot Contessa*. From the very beginning his campaign had about it a melancholy air of futility. This was the authentic voice of the party's Left wing, giving the most strongly felt and easily the most boring speech of the evening.

Eric Kierans then took his turn, preceded by the engineering students' band from Queen's University. He couldn't control his kids, so he laughed with them, and they laughed back. He asked the delegates to vote with their consciences, then described where he stood on the seminal issues, saying, "We must bend all our policies to preserve the gentleness that is in our society." He promised courage, and the audience felt abashed in its recognition of it in him. Although I was publicly backing Trudeau, because I thought he would be best for Canada, Kierans was my personal choice. He alone combined superior intellect with a profound sense of humanity. "Pierre has denied that each time he makes a remark, he does so with the infallibility of a pope," Kierans told me during a coffee break. "Since he has rejected the purple, that puts me down somewhere among the assistant curates. But even assistant curates can think, and that's what I propose to do."

John Turner delivered a great speech. His c.v. made him sound like a storybook prime minister, but somehow these strands didn't add up to a convincing whole. For all his lithe vitality (he once described his one-time dancing partner, Princess Margaret, as "an interesting chick"), he had, during the five years he had spent in the House, gained a reputation for trying too hard and was said to be more anxious to please his elders than to demonstrate his convictions. It was an unfair verdict, but it stuck.

SUDDENLY, THE SIEGE OF photographers, reporters, and TV men around his box lifted briefly to allow Pierre Trudeau an entrance. As if pulled by a single string, his placards were silently lifted in every part of the crowded arena. Instead of applauding, the delegates let out a collective "*Aaahh*," like the salute to a daring trapeze artist doing his star turn. His demonstration had been meticulously planned but it looked spontaneous, as though the Liberal Party had already reached its consensus. Trudeau waited in the stands for precisely five minutes, then slouched toward the platform. It was not a great speech, but the delegates listened in awed silence. "As Liberals," he said, "we rely on that most unlikely bulwark against chaos – you and me, the individual citizen, the young and the old, the famous and the unknown, the Arctic nomad and the suburbanite." He confirmed his belief in the triumph of reason over passion. This was the sober, not the witty Pierre, softly blowing his own horn. At the end he just stood there, smiling, in his rounded Edwardian collar, a daffodil in his buttonhole. Beaming.

Waves of applause still swept the Civic Centre as two hundred Trudeau workers swarmed the stands, armed with computer-tabulated lists separated according to voting machines and determined to shanghai more converts. They were linked by telephones, walkie-talkies, and short-wave radios, with a secondary, backup communications system standing by in case of sabotage. Every move of nearly every delegate was monitored, and gangs of Trudeau's female persuaders were assigned to bring doubters in line. Watching the balloting, without a care in the world, Trudeau reached over, grabbed a grape from Jean Marchand, threw it up in the air, and caught it in his mouth. A nearby TV producer who missed the performance asked for a repeat, then stuck a microphone into Trudeau's face: "Let's hear the crunch, okay?"

Kierans and Martin dropped out after the first ballot and MacEachen joined Trudeau. Hellyer struggled through the pandemonium on the convention floor toward Turner, shouting, "Fight the Establishment, John!" That was a clue: the wild man from Montreal, who only a few years earlier had accused these very Liberals of "trembling with anticipation because they have seen the rouged face of power," had just co-opted the party's establishment.

Results of the second ballot pointed to Winters as the only candidate who could beat Pierre. This was the decisive moment. Had Hellyer backed Winters, Trudeau would have lost. Judy LaMarsh huddled with the Defence minister, pleading with him to make the move. "It's tough, but what the hell's the point of going down and letting that bastard be there? Come on, Paul, you're forty-four and we've still got lots of time." But Hellyer, still unable to believe that his computers were wrong, wouldn't budge. Joe Potts, a Hellyer booster from Toronto with a voice like a moose call and inextinguishable optimism, proposed an ingenious, if naive, compromise. Winters should flip a coin and, if he lost, join Hellyer against Trudeau. But Winters wouldn't buy it: "Look, Joe, damn it, I'm a front-runner. People would say I was nuts."

When the next ballot was announced there was still one more chance for Hellyer and Turner to move in behind Winters and deliver victory. Frightened, the Trudeau workers, led by Bryce Mackasey, swarmed out, rounding up delegates. The arena erupted into a frenzy. Uncommitted delegates watched the trio of could-have-beens sweating as they tried to broker a deal that wouldn't fly. Meanwhile Trudeau was reading notes from a piece of paper.

"Is that your acceptance speech?" asked an excited reporter.

"No. It's a love letter."

Mike McCabe, Mitchell Sharp's campaign manager, sidled over and told me, "If Trudeau doesn't win, the entrails of the Liberal

Party will be left all over this hall." Maryon Pearson had to be restrained from rushing onto the convention floor to wave a Trudeau banner.

As the final results were being read the wild chant – "Tru–deau, Cana–da!" – obliterated thought. Trudeau:1,203; Winters, 954; Turner, 195. It was over.

Few would later recall that the emotional tide that carried this singular man of reason to victory was no coronation. His margin was 51.1 per cent, on the fourth ballot.

I emerged from that steaming convention hall into the April night, feeling that I was walking out under the sheltering sky into a new Canada.

IT WAS A GLORIOUS SPRING morning on the Monday after the convention in that once-upon-a-time spring of 1968 when Trudeau greeted me as I stepped into his yet-to-be-furnished parliamentary office. He had promised to give me his first interview as Liberal leader, and there he was, ready to muse into my tape recorder. Recalling the times he had used my column to test public reaction to some of his more radical ideas while he was heading the Justice ministry, I said jokingly, "Hey, I'm really glad you won. Now I'll be able to obtain leaks from all the departments, not only Justice."

"Listen," Trudeau shot back, his face suddenly as hard as alabaster. "The first Cabinet leak you get, I'll have the RCMP tap your telephone."

He was of course legally correct to squash my feeble attempt at poking fun at the Privy Council oath that binds Cabinet members to secrecy. But his reaction to what was obviously a tension-relieving quip was so extreme that our little exchange has always stayed with me. It was an early-warning signal of just how quickly and completely power had changed the man who, only hours before, had been on the Ottawa Civic Centre convention floor doing the boogaloo, shrugging away his victory, and kissing swooning women under the shimmering klieg lights. But sure enough, at the first meeting of his ministers his opening sally was entirely concerned with Cabinet secrecy: "The source of any future leaks will be determined by official investigations, and while I might accept one such mistake on the part of a minister, I will not accept two. Should any of you disagree with a decision taken, you have a right, indeed the duty, to resign." Welcome to Chill City.

I was still feeling a bit shaken when I went to Ottawa's Civic Hospital to visit one of my favourite Ottawa characters, Bryce Mackasey, who had suffered a heart attack on the convention floor while forcibly harvesting delegates on Trudeau's behalf. A down-to-earth Irish roustabout who stood out among the dauphins and deacons of the Trudeau entourage, Bryce was a former boxing champion with calloused hands but un-calloused instincts. When I entered his hushed hospital room he was encased in an oxygen tent and seemed on the verge of taking his last breath. As soon as he caught sight of me, he threw back the plastic sheet and gasped, "Tell Trudeau I want Labour!"

I figured that if ever there was a sacred trust, this was it. Surely I was honour bound to relay this dying wish for a specific Cabinet post from one of the prime minister's most enthusiastic support-ers. Back in the corridor, I expressed my concern for Mackasey to the nurse on duty, remarking on how brave her patient was to temporarily abandon his life-support oxygen tank. "Oh, that Mr. Mackasey," she replied impatiently. "Every time someone comes to visit, he puts on that darn oxygen tent!" I did not relay Bryce's message, but somebody did, because Mackasey spent most of the Trudeau years shaking things up at Labour.

Magic was certainly in the air as the new Cabinet was named and the government took office. But even then people sensed Trudeau's cold-bloodedness when they saw his shabby treatment of Mike Pearson, who had recruited him into the Liberal Party over the fervent objections of his senior Quebec advisers, who considered him a dilettante troublemaker. Pearson had almost immediately promoted him to be his parliamentary secretary, and less than two years later named him to one his administration's senior portfolios, Justice. All the while he had made it clear in private conversations (which he must have known would be repeated) that Trudeau was his personal choice to be his successor. Yet once he won the crown, Trudeau forgot that Pearson existed. There is a long-standing tradition that on the final day of a prime minister's last parliamentary session, tributes are paid to his stewardship, allowing him to bid a dignified farewell. On April 23, 1968, Trudeau routinely adjourned the Commons, without granting Pearson that opportunity, leaving MPs on both sides of the House stunned by his rudeness. Not once during his time in office did Trudeau consult his predecessor on any diplomatic matters, except for the time he attacked him for having been too much influenced by the military establishment.

Dissolution of the Commons triggered the 1968 election campaign that left those of us who followed its progress shaking our heads in wonderment. This was not a country we knew, or a politics we had experienced before. Teenyboppers, their long manes of hair streaming like banners in the wind, and clutching machine-autographed pictures, followed Trudeau everywhere, swarming whenever he deigned to kiss one of them. Bemused toddlers were held up on the shoulders of their parents and admonished to "remember him," as the wave of excitement surged across the country. Press cameras clicked like plagues of crickets whenever Trudeau would alight from his prime ministerial jet, conjuring up images of Julius Caesar touring his Empire as he made his triumphant way from one shopping plaza to the next. I recall in particular flying with him into Halifax. Since the Tories were then led by former Nova Scotia premier Robert Stanfield, this was wall-to-wall Tory country. But along the route from the airport, as if by prearranged signal, people had backed the cars into their driveways, so they could flash their headlights in silent tribute to the invisible man in the leather coat, slouched inside the darkened limousine.

At the other end of the country, in Victoria, we couldn't get near him because he stood on a hill, Moses-like, overlooking a large park overflowing with a sea of mesmerized faces. Asked about the future of Liberalism, he allowed that "an exciting political party should have both blondes and brunettes." Prime ministers aren't supposed to talk like that. Whether it was because of his status as the country's most eligible swinging bachelor, or some transmission of pheromones, his effect on women was, well, obscene. "Their eyes are transfixed and they seem to be breathing through their toenails" observed Ontario MPP Elmer Sopha. "You'd think they all had asthma." It was a perfectly accurate description.

The campaign hardly qualified as a discourse out of Aristotle. In Winnipeg, to yet another screeching herd of supporters, Trudeau explained: "I do not feel myself bound by any doctrine or rigid approaches. I am a pragmatist." The crowd's response was the yell of a fellow philosopher-king: "Yeah, you tell 'em, Pierre baby!" Occasionally, he would play a game with himself, taking so many stabs at irony that the stage looked like a dartboard, but hardly anybody noticed.

On election night, with Trudeaumania at its height, he won 155 seats, which was decisive but not spectacular. He received only 45 per cent of the ballots cast. That translated into 56 seats fewer than Brian Mulroney would be accorded in 1984, his best campaign, and 14 seats fewer than Mulroney would win in 1988, his worst. Looking back on his ability to win votes (and considering that Jean Chrétien won three subsequent majorities), Trudeau's electoral record was hardly heroic. In 1972, after only four years in power, he managed to scrape through with a minority, winning only two more seats than Robert Stanfield, who, though warm and witty in private, in public came across as a kind of human Switzerland. Trudeau did gain a slim majority in 1974 with his campaign against wage and price controls, which he promptly implemented. Five years after that, he was beaten – wait for it – by Joe Clark. Nine months later, when Clark lost a confidence vote because he couldn't count, Trudeau snuck back in on the simple notion that anybody was better than "Joe Who?" In 1984, after four more years of Trudeau's ministrations, the Liberals were such an easy mark that

Brian Mulroney reduced them to their smallest parliamentary rump since Confederation.

Over all my years reporting Canadian politics, I discovered only one infallible rule: the voters are always right. In a country requiring six time zones to encompass its outrageous dimensions, it is remarkable that some valid consensus emerges from national elections. But it does. The voters were right to give John Diefenbaker an initial sweep, and equally right to sweep him out of office in the twin elections that followed. They were correct never to grant Lester Pearson a majority, and certainly justified in awarding a solid initial vote of confidence to Pierre Trudeau. But if my theory means anything – and I think it does – the voters were also reacting with an instinctive hesitation in the way they treated our Prince Charming during his nearly sixteen years in federal politics by never granting him their unrestrained confidence.

Still, no other country boasted a head of government who could practise his pirouette behind the Queen's back at Buckingham Palace, yell "*Mangez de la merde!*" at striking mail-truck drivers, date some of the world's most desirable women, marry a sexy twenty-two-year-old, then have two of their three sons born on the same day as Jesus Christ. He was our first prime minister to define himself less by words than by gestures; his body language was deafening. He moved with ballerina-like grace, the incongruent legacy of his training in the martial arts. He understood that politics was theatre and that great stage performances are cumulative. He was the dancing man. He would frug, grind, twist, disco, slide down banisters, dodge (or slug) pickets, high-dive, sky-dive, judo, ski, ride a unicycle, earn a brown belt in judo, and hop on or off platforms – some said fences.

One of his lesser known activities was deep-sea diving. "We met in late 1969 and during the next thirty years made some fifty dives together, from the high Arctic to Belize, and a 10,000-foot descent aboard a Russian research sub in the Pacific," recalled Dr. Joseph MacInnis, the Canadian underwater adventurer who was Trudeau's friend and coach. "I saw him make a 60-foot breath-hold dive when he was forty-nine, and he was hardly winded. A few days later, at his request and after some practice, we touched down at 250 feet. He loved the mystery and magic of the ocean. For a man driven by disciplined logic and rational thinking, it was something that could not be explained, only experienced. The ocean regenerated his humility. However easily he swam through it, he saw himself as a temporary visitor – one life among the countless species that occupied the largest, oldest, and least understood physical feature on the planet. He was not fearless, but he had more grace under pressure than anyone I ever met."

Trudeau's favoured relaxation was paddling his canoe through Canada's far wilderness, including the mysterious Nahanni River. "I know a man," he once wrote, referring obliquely to himself, "whose school could never teach him patriotism but who acquired that virtue when he felt in his bones the vastness of his land and the greatness of those who founded it."

He was full of surprises. I vividly recall attending an election rally in Toronto where Trudeau was unexpectedly asked a question in Italian. Without skipping a beat, he replied in what sounded to me like perfect Italian (and was actually Italian with a Milanese accent, because he knew that was where most of the audience was from). Then he switched back to English, and as far as I know, he never spoke Italian publicly again. If there was one gesture that caught the essence of the man, it came during a commercial flight when the stewardess offered him a glass of wine. He imperceptibly reached over to her cart, felt the bottle of Chardonnay to test its chill, and only then nodded his assent.

PIERRE MIGHT INDEED have placed reason above all else, but for six spellbound years he found himself preoccupied, at times overwhelmed, by a weapon of mass distraction under his roof who went by the name of "Maggie". She was the distracted and distracting twenty-two-year-old flower child he married in 1971, who lit up his life with mischief and love, mayhem and sorrow.

Most of what we know about their life together is derived from her books, articles, interviews, soliloquies, confessions, and public breakdowns. That's how we learned that at 2:00 a.m. one spring day in 1977 Pierre "forced" her to sign a handwritten note that excluded her from sharing in his considerable personal wealth following their separation. And how, on that occasion, he also made her return the wedding and engagement rings he had given her.

There was a time when their love was a celebrated gift – a tribute to their disparate temperaments, backgrounds, and ages. As a prime minister devoted to his brain and his privacy, Trudeau found it nearly impossible to articulate his feelings. To my knowledge, he did so only once, and that was while flying over the North Pole. In the winter of 1974, he visited the Northwest Territories, then ably administered by Stu Hodgson, a kindly extrovert who greatly admired his distinguished visitor. The two of them flew a small plane to the North Pole, where the circumference of the Earth narrows to a point. At an appropriate moment, Stu turned over the controls to the prime minister, who "flew around the world" four times.

"I told Pierre that I could patch him into Ottawa so he could say hello to Margaret from his unique perch," Hodgson later recalled, "and he got very excited. I could hear him asking the housekeeper to speak to her."

"She won't talk to me," he sobbed, turning away to hide his tears.

"Why did you marry her?" Hodgson gently asked.

"Because I love her, I truly love her," he whispered.

Later they flew over Alert, the most northern Canadian outpost, and landed at Ward Hunt Island, which is even north of that. There Trudeau erected a cairn, a stone monument to his lady-love that contained memorabilia of their wedding and the story about it written by Ed Ogle in *Time* magazine.

I don't think that Trudeau was ever angrier with a journalist than he was with me, in the spring of 1977, when *Maclean's*, under my editorship, published exclusive pictures of Margaret mixing it up with the Rolling Stones in the grittier bar scenes of Toronto and New York. The most apt comment on that episode was Stones drummer Charlie Watts's quip: "I wouldn't want *my* wife associatin' wiv us."

The day Trudeau was defeated by Joe Clark, Margaret spent the night frugging at New York's Studio 54, dancing on his political grave. "He knew of my sexual energy, and with my prime at thirty, he knew he was going to have to lock me away in the woods," she confessed to *Playgirl* magazine. "But I have so much to give that I didn't want to be locked up in the woods. And that's why our marriage broke down."

I ran into Margaret only once following their divorce. While on one of my book tours, I was invited to appear on her CJOH-TV interview show in Ottawa. Before we went on the air, she rushed into the green room, recognized me from my visits to Sussex Drive, and suggested we step next door, where we could be alone.

"Look, Peter," she said. "I need your advice. I've just been offered $10,000 to mud wrestle in the nude. They'll even fly me to Tokyo if I do it, but I said I wouldn't. Do you think I did the right thing?"

"Margaret," I should have said, "You absolutely did the right thing." Instead, I did my best imitation of a Trudeau shrug, and when we went on the air, she was still looking at me strangely.

MY DISILLUSIONMENT with the Trudeau myth began shortly after that 1968 opening-day interview in his office. At the time, he told me that he intended to implement basic reforms in Senate appointments, pledging to extend the commendable, non-partisan record he had earned as Justice minister in filling federal judgeships. Then came his first Senate elevation: Louis Giguère, a Liberal hack from Montreal with a questionable reputation who was known either as "Jiggery Bill" or "L'Aspirateur" (The Vacuum Cleaner) as a tribute to his strong-arm tactics in gathering Liberal slush funds. Trudeau had recently had an affair with Giguère's daughter, Diane. Soon after the appointment, Giguère was charged with influence-peddling in connection with the SkyShops duty-free scandal at Dorval Airport. (He was acquitted, but former NHL president Clarence Campbell was found guilty of "conspiring to give Giguère a benefit.") The seventy-three Senate appointments that followed were no better. Near the end of his time in power Trudeau set the Canadian record for a single day's orgy of senior patronage appointments: eighty-three, not counting the seventeen more he forced John Turner to make after he left office.

Never quite knowing what to make of the man, we took him on faith, and he broke it. Politics is a hard trade that normally requires half a lifetime's apprenticeship. Trudeau appeared out of nowhere to grab our attention and to seduce our well-earned skepticism, allowing us to believe that he would be different. And he *was* different, but not always better.

As an obsessive Trudeau watcher, I gradually realized that his essence was not that difficult to divine: Pierre Trudeau was an emotional cripple with a sliver of ice in his heart. His problem was that he had one, overriding obsession: to exercise his rational side. He thus tragically shortchanged himself and Canadians. As the British essayist Lytton Strachey wrote of Francis Bacon, the seventeenth-century savant, "His intelligence was fatally external. He could understand almost everything except his own heart." Compassion is a quality that cast little shadow on Trudeau's interior landscape. He behaved like some abstracted actor, coolly detaching himself from whatever was happening around him, seldom allowing other people's joys or sorrows to ravage his emotions. Yet, there are moments in every political career when mind is not enough, when passion must clamour up and make a leader more than a guest of his time.

I recall discussing that detached side of him with Gordon Fairweather (later chairman of Canada's Human Rights Commission but then a Conservative MP), a gentle soul who commanded enormous respect and affection in official Ottawa. When the Trudeaus had one of their December 25 babies, Fairweather was delighted. In a burst of bonhomie, he went down to his local post office in central New Brunswick on Boxing Day to send a congratulatory wire. The telegrapher, a true-blue Tory, said she didn't want to transmit the message, and tried to get Fairweather to give up on it. He wouldn't, but he found the whole episode amusing, a vignette of his riding's strong political passions.

When the House session opened in January, he went up to Trudeau at the usual Speaker's cocktail party to tell him what had happened, thinking the PM might find the story amusing. Trudeau simply stared back at him, bored, and finally dismissed the thoughtful MP with the curt comment: "Oh, I never saw it. There were so many hundreds of them we decided not to be bothered." Fairweather told me that he felt not so much hurt, but as if he had been punched in the chest, hard.

The longer I watched him, the more I realized that Trudeau was practising a version of de Gaullism which held that a leader's prestige grows in direct proportion to his aloofness. Remote, austere, self-contained, the blue-ice inner core of the man remained inviolate, no matter what was troubling him or Canada. If he had planned it, he could hardly have managed to alienate his core constituencies more profoundly. By the time he was a halfway through his mandate, the labour unions were pledged to his destruction, Canadian farmers were in revolt, Bay Street was apoplectic, and more than a million unemployed spat his name out in cold fury. I vividly recall watching a burly trucker at a motel near Red Deer who had lost his forty-five cents in a Coke vending machine. He stood back and kicked the thing. Nothing happened. He shook it nearly off its hinges. No luck. Then he took a deep breath, glared at the offending contraption, and yelled, "God damn Trudeau anyway!" And walked away.

Feeling threatened by the angry voices of disorder bellowing their demands outside the safe confines of his inner circle, Trudeau cut himself off from reality, mistaking the chatter of his court (whose notion of deprivation was being exposed to bad service in one of Ottawa's declining French restaurants) for the voice of the people. His acolytes treated Outer Canada (the millions of Canadians who lived west of the Humber River or east of the St. Lawrence) as a scattering of unruly colonial outposts, and they acted as though they were afraid that someone might dump tea into Victoria or Halifax harbours. He had no problem dancing the *moozmaad* in the tents of Araby, when he visited the Middle East, but never learned how to do-si-do, and his name became a curse across the West. It was said that his National Energy Policy transferred $80 billion in wealth from Calgary to Ottawa. Farmers still haven't forgiven him for introducing the metric system.

In his tendency to stifle dissent, even within his own ranks, there was a tragic fallacy. Tolerating dissent is the essential means by which Canadian society has always come to terms with change. Trudeau and his flunkies believed that they could impose logic on events and govern the country by reshaping events to fit their own legalisms. But the events themselves — history, in other words — were not logical and never could be. They were born out of harsh realities and even harsher emotions, which could not be cut to fit the leader's wishes or intentions. Before he became prime minister, Trudeau had travelled the country on the slogan that he was looking for "new guys with new ideas." Once in office, he behaved as though he wanted "new guys with the same ideas" — the same as his own. Within months of his takeover, there wasn't a member of his entourage who could call himself an agitator, nobody with the political moxie or the gonads to remind Trudeau that he might be fallible. His was a court without a jester.

He wasn't amused when asked by CTV News to comment on a column I had written criticizing his isolation. "Yeah, yeah," he said, with all the sarcasm he could muster. "If I'd only listened to Peter Newman more, things would have been much better,"

A string of such offhand insults marked his reign, the most cynical of them being his retort "Where's Biafra?" after being asked whether Canada intended to come to the aid of the starving people there. Although I was stationed in Toronto throughout most of Trudeau's term, I frequently dropped into his office, and on one such occasion I asked him why he had made such a heartless comment when he knew Canadians were raising funds to ship emergency food rations to Biafra. He looked at me as though living in Toronto had turned me into an imbecile. Didn't I know anything about Biafra's history? Was I not aware that it was a break-away province from Nigeria, and that his government had legally recognized Nigeria, and that therefore any move to raise Biafra's diplomatic status would be interpreted in Quebec as a significant boost for the separatists? "Legally, Biafra doesn't exist," he lectured me. "To ask, 'Where is Biafra?' is tantamount to asking, 'Where is Laurentia?'" the name Quebec nationalists gave to the independ-ent state of their dreams. I realized he was right, but it was typical of the man that the ideological aspects of the situation took prece-dence over filling hungry bellies.

On that same Ottawa visit I went to see Eric Kierans; after three years he had just resigned from the government on a matter of principle. "I was always listened to with great respect, but nothing would ever happen," he complained. "You know, when the Pope gets down off the altar at St. Peter's and walks down the aisle, the one thing you're sure of is that he's going to get to the other end. You can argue and argue, but the procession always goes on its way. And that's the way is in Cabinet. We have no say."[3]

What I found to be most damaging of all was Trudeau's kinder-garten treatment of the Commons, televised daily across the country. Whenever Robert Stanfield got up to ask a question, row upon row of Liberal ministers and backbenchers would start

<hr />

[3] During that brief Ottawa sojourn I discovered, to my surprise, that, without telling me, Trudeau had put forward my name to be appointed chairman and president of the Canadian Broadcasting Corporation. A decade later, Brian Mulroney made the same offer personally by telephone. I declined both, since taking kamikaze assignments was never my forte, but was pleased to have been asked. It strengthened my suspicion that neither Liberals nor Conservatives trusted me, and they wanted me out of harm's away, mired in the thankless administration of a sprawling Crown corporation.

hooting with derisive laughter, looking not like sober men conducting the nation's business but rather like a clutch of obnoxious prefects from the upper forms of some private school, sneering at an unpopular fat boy. And in their midst sat their leader, clad in a dark suit from Savile Row, a fresh rose from the governor general's greenhouse in his lapel, and with the swagger of a dandy. Watching him I had the feeling that he was impatient with being Canadian, not certain whether he should treat politics as a game or as an entertainment. He acted as though he really believed (and so stated in the Commons on July 24, 1969) that Opposition MPs were "nobodies," a fairly risky assumption since even after the 1968 election, his best, the Opposition side of the House represented 55 per cent of Canadian voters. He pursued personal grudges, notably with the most distinguished, if still combative, member of the House, the Right Honourable John George Diefenbaker. Only weeks before the former PM's death at eight-three, the two men happened to meet.

"I'll be going to China soon," Diefenbaker casually informed Trudeau.

"You can go to China or go to hell as far as I'm concerned," Trudeau replied.

"Well, I'm going to China, but our destinations in the hereafter will not be the same . . ."

"Shit!" was Trudeau's curt retort.

As usual, Diefenbaker had the last word. "They call that man PET," he said to a friendly bystander, who later told me. "Do you know what *pet* means in French? Look it up in the dictionary. It means fart."

His weak suit was economics. The enduring mystery of the Trudeau period was that the federal debt increased by 1,000 per cent during his stewardship and the annual deficit moved from near balance to $36 billion, yet nobody could figure out what Canadians got for all that money. There were no new social nets, and most of the welfare measures for which he received credit had actually been put in place by Mike Pearson. On June 28, 1970, when Trudeau was questioned about his economic policy on the CTV program *W-5*, he replied: "I'm not really trying to govern in order to be re-elected. If the Canadian people don't like it, you know, they can lump it." For some reason his Liberal backers did not choose this as his election slogan.

In 1976, when René Lévesque's Parti Québécois triumphed over the corrupt Bourassa regime to claim power – and a mandate to withdraw from Confederation – the charismatic Quebec premier was able eventually to translate his cause into a referendum, held in the spring of 1980. The burden of the federalists' case was carried somewhat uneasily by Claude Ryan, who by then had been chosen as leader of the provincial Liberal Party, and whose preference for special status within Confederation ran counter to Trudeau's approach. It turned out to be the prime minister's finest hour. His carefully planned appearances defused the sovereignty issue. At the same time it allowed him to enlist the rest of the country in his grand strategy of pushing through his constitutional reforms. When the federal side decisively won the referendum, Trudeau turned his attention to fashioning a new constitution and a Charter of Rights and Freedoms, which dramatically changed the character of our highest court. From being mostly a sleepy chamber where appeals were heard, the Supreme Court was transformed into a crucial constitutional court whose opinions had an impact on essential policy issues. Trudeau's choice of constitutional scholar Bora Laskin as chief justice had earlier foreshadowed this changing role of the judiciary: he had been waving this idea for years, like a leper's bell, at anyone who would listen.

His constitutional plan would also allow him to enshrine language rights and finally sever Canada's umbilical cord with Mother Britain. Initially, eight of the ten provinces violently opposed the Trudeau initiative, but the Supreme Court eventually ruled that approval by a majority of the provinces was required only by custom, not by law. Through a series of intricate manoeuvres, Trudeau obtained the blessing of every province except Quebec, and on April 17, 1982, the Queen confirmed Canada's status as an independent nation – at last.

TERMINALLY COOL, PIERRE TRUDEAU took leave of his office with a rare touch of civility. More than any of his predecessors, he had made unpopular decisions and challenged the voters to like him or lump him. They did both. By the winter of 1984, the electorate was lying in wait to humble him. Trudeau had overdrawn his psychic bank account. He decided to quit because he couldn't think of a good reason to stay. The constitution was home; bilingualism was permanently in place; his peace initiative had stalled; the economy was beyond salvation. There was no fun in the nation's business any more; half the provincial premiers were acting like reactionary duds and the Tory Opposition had a respectable leader who didn't provide much good sport.

He never changed – but we did.

The difference between the Canada that greeted Pierre Trudeau and the Canada that turned its back on him sixteen years later was poignantly marked by the contrast between the warm adulation that created him and the cold fury that bade him adieu. Such a dichotomy of feeling was caught by the French essayist Jean de La Bruyère, commenting on the demise of a literary rival: "It is rumoured that Piso is dead. It is a great loss. He was a good man and deserved a longer life. He was talented, reliable, resolute and courageous, faithful and generous. Provided, of course, that he is really dead."

Trudeau had already issued his own epitaph more than ten years earlier. "I'm quite prepared to die politically, when the people think I should," he'd told me in 1969. It was just one year after he took office, but I had asked him about the permanence of his gig. "You know, politicians should be like Trappists who go around in monasteries, and the only words they can say to each other are: 'Brother, we must die one day.' I think this is true of politicians.

Brother, someday we may be beaten. If I am, what will I do? 'The world is so full of a number of things. I'm sure we should all be as happy as kings.'"

It was the final irony of his reign that only in retrospect, at the time of his death and the national grief that it inspired, was his true worth fully recognized. He had saved Confederation by facing down the Front de Libération du Québec in 1970 and winning the referendum on French Canada's future a decade later. He put us on the world's map. His acid candour, his intellectual acrobatics, his nose-thumbing at the staid traditions of his office qualified him as our first existential political hero. The man with red rose in his lapel might have been a smartass, but he was *our* smartass for most of sixteen turbulent years. We mourned his passing because he made us aware that politics at its best consists of sharing in the passions of the age. "He has been purist and pragmatist, arrogant and humble, dashing and dull, a reformer of the head but a conservative of the heart, a self-described 'solitary sort of fellow' who perfected the politics of the mob, a government leader who preached economic restraint even as the *bon vivant* he sailed the Adriatic with the Aga Khan, a man of fixed personal ways who has never lived in a house of his own – a paradox, in sum, who has provoked every emotion, except indifference." So wrote Robert Lewis, then Ottawa editor of *Maclean's*, summing up this contradictory patrician better than anyone else.

Pierre Trudeau brought out the best and the worst in us, providing a feisty counterweight to his nineteenth-century predecessors. He was an anomaly because, within official Ottawa, lucidity and frankness were in short supply, yet he was seldom willing to fudge seminal issues. His tossed-off quips and vulgarisms left us a legacy of aphorisms unmatched by any of his predecessors or successors. That delightful habit was probably best caught in a 1968 TV interview, just after he took office, when he was asked about his prime ministerial duties. "I'm not going to let this job louse up my private life," he said. "And I won't wear sandals around 24 Sussex Drive . . . I'll go barefoot."

His passing in 2000 awakened the profound suspicion in many Canadians that we had somehow let him down. His intelligence and charisma had turned his stewardship into a shining political season, even if he had made enemies, as effortlessly as he attracted disciples. His brand of gunslinger politics demanded a sophisticated public response that few Canadians found comfortable. Still, Pierre Elliott Trudeau was by long odds the most resolute leader this country ever had. His shimmering intellect cast all other pretenders in the shade. He broadened our universe by making the world his stage. Above all, no matter what he did, in office or out, he always exercised his ultimate civil liberty: the right to be himself.

When he recreated himself, one last time, into political sainthood, aboard his millennial-year funeral train from where he lay in state on Parliament Hill to his funeral in Montreal, it became the Canadian equivalent of the ceremonial barge that bore Sir Winston Churchill's remains down the River Thames in 1965, "With pomp of waters, unwithstood."

CHAPTER THIRTEEN

CAPTAIN CANADA TO THE RESCUE

—✽◎

I resolved that the new Maclean's
would reach out to the heartland,
and make echoes to stir a nation.

J oan Didion, who chronicled the psychic extravagances of the
California lifestyle, once observed that the oral history of Los
Angeles was written in piano bars: "People tell each other about
their first wives and last husbands. 'Stay funny,' they say, while listening to 'Moon River,' 'Love for Sale,' and 'Send in the Clowns.'"

In the Toronto of the 1970s, the pianist was Paul Drake, the bar
was Club 22, and the "clowns" were the hucksters who breech-
birthed a Canadian movie industry on the premises, in a corner of
the Courtyard Café, at St. Thomas and Bloor. It became the epicentre of the city's – and the country's – cultural renaissance. If
Toronto was downtown Canada, then the Courtyard was surely
uptown Toronto, a combination of the Polo Lounge in Beverly
Hills, Elaine's and Sardi's in New York (where the stars went to be
private in public), Blake's in London, and the Gaslight in Paris.

It was my hangout.

During his fourteen-year gig, Paul Drake, who later married
into Belgian royalty, became the resident shrink. We compared
notes while I was writing this book. He remembered the evening
when Christopher Plummer, celebrating the premiere of *Murder*

348

by Decree, rose unsteadily in his seat to proclaim with Shakespearean dignity, "We live in a world where celebrities hold the proxies for our identities . . ." Among his audiences Drake recalled Peter O'Toole, Katharine Hepburn, Richard Harris, Elizabeth Ashley, Gene Hackman, Jack Lemmon, George Segal, Juliet Prowse, Norman Jewison, Paul Newman, Joanne Woodward, Michael Douglas, Burt Reynolds, Loni Anderson, Elliott Gould, Mick Jagger, and Debbie Reynolds, who arrived at the Windsor Arms Hotel (which encompassed the Courtyard and Club 22) with eighty suitcases.

The Windsor Arms Hotel had been purchased in 1963 by George Minden, a philosophy and English graduate who picked his friends according to whether or not they knew when to laugh at the bassoon joke in Brahms's *Academic Festival Overture*. He sold it for $22 million in 1989 and moved to Freiburg, Switzerland. The maitre d' who took care of the collateral damage was Norbert Ackerman. "I recognized film stars discreetly without fawning all over them," he told me. "They're like people who aren't fully grown up, so you need to have a special way of dealing with them, to make decisions for them without their realizing it."

Walking into Club 22 was like visiting a zoo at feeding time. The restless rumble of macho *machers* making deals to make deals kept the place buzzing, and the buzz was always about future films, or "*fillums*," as the patrons described their art form. It was the kind of place where character was determined by the angle of your cigar. Except for some Hollywood agents who had come to explore the Great White North, Club 22's clientele was Canadian, though not typically so, because they were much too ballsy to qualify for citizenship, except retroactively.

The Toronto movie boom of the 1970s was uncannily like the Leduc oil strike of the 1940s: both were real, and spawned industries with everybody holding on to their precious piece of the action. The movies they produced portrayed truths, large and small, yet essentially Canadian. Unfortunately what the big screen demanded was alchemy, and that was in short supply. "We're going straight to cult," a frustrated Cabbagetown movie mogul announced loudly one night, then jauntily began lining up another block-buster. The movie people felt most alive when they were testing their nerves, lining up their tax shelters, waiting out the offers, swinging on a bankable star who had told them she "would kill" to be in their movie but hadn't shown up yet.

The extras in this Courtyard extravaganza were CBC types, showbiz hangers on, camp followers of all sexes, and whisky priests preening their self-appointed authority, as they toyed with the pine nuts floating in their chilled cucumber *soup de jour*. Scattered among the brown banquettes were the real doers: Bill Marshall (the only one with a private phone at his table), Bob Cooper, Robert Cohen, Jon Slan, Garth Drabinsky, David Perlmutter, George Mendeluck, Fil Fraser from Edmonton, whose *Why Shoot the Teacher* was the Canadian breakthrough film, and real estate tycoon Eddie Cogan who wasn't in the business but perpetually starred in the movie that spooled through his own imagination. Michael Levine, my legal beagle, flitted about executive producing his share of screen epics, his fees paid up front, of course. Murray "Dusty" Cohl was the accomplice in so many Canadian film deals that *Maclean's* kept printing photographs of him in his black cowboy hat with the sheriff's badge on it. He once sidled up to me, and sweetly asked: "Hey man, who do I have to lay so you stop putting my picture in your goddamn magazine?" The star of the circus was Mike McCabe, my pal from our Ottawa days, then head of the Canadian Film Development Corporation, which provided the industry's momentum and seed money. Brash, confident, done up in bushy beard and safari jacket, he turned Canada into the world's third-largest film production centre, with $150 million invested in new movies during the CFDC's top year.

The self-described starlets who sat around Club 22 waiting to be discovered were convinced that to be an actress you only had to look like one. The sexual thermostat was always set on high. Late one night I watched a Club 22 barfly posing as a producer (mussed-look haircut, peasant body shirt, and Riviera jeans) lean over a stunning brunette and conversationally ask her what she liked doing best. "Balling," she replied, assuming this was her screen test. The confused would-be-seducer backed away and the jilted bride, having flubbed her line, started to cry.

At the bottom of the movie industry's pecking order were the writers, charged with the unglamorous job of turning the wild, late-night Club 22 babble, jotted down on table napkins, into filmable scripts. "Our position," declared Frank Pierson, the visiting head of the Screen Writers Guild, "is that hopefully, someday, the industry can forget the old joke about the Polish starlet who thought she could get ahead by fucking the writer."

Not being Polish, I can't pretend that I was part of the scene, but I was there, and what I caught, like an infectious disease, was the kinetic energy and unbridled optimism afloat in the Courtyard and its piano bar. If these guys had the chutzpah to go head to head with Hollywood, I could transform the comatose monthly magazine whose editorship I had recently inherited into a profitable Canadian version of *Time*. Granted, there was no connection between the two phenomena, except one: the psychological leap to the belief that we need not remain a colony in either medium. And so it was here in Club 22 that the new *Maclean's* was conceived, with those wonderful improvisers of Canada's cult *fillums* as its godfathers.

THE 1970S WAS A very special decade. I doubt if the revolutionary Canadian magazine I had in mind could have been born in any other season. It was the only time in our history when we matched Americans in average incomes and in the willingness to live a little. It was, in a word, insolent to believe that we could replicate for Canada what Henry Luce had pioneered with *Time* in 1923, documenting on a weekly basis the triumphs of the phenomenon he had dubbed as "the American century." Yet, the spirit of Expo 67 still hung over the country, affirming a newfound maturity. At a subconscious level, Canadians were resolving their traditional self-doubts. Instead of searching for a national identity, they were putting it into practice. This unexpected leap of self-reliance freed us from long-ingrained deference to the Church, governments, and multinational corporations – not to mention movies as strictly a Hollywood commodity – producing a spirit of risk and affirmation profoundly different from our tippytoe past. It was an ideal time to launch a new venture, even in such a steam-locomotive-vintage industry as national magazines. The comforting traditions of home and hearth were turned inside out. What was changing most of all was how Canadians perceived their homeland. I was convinced that in this process *Maclean's*, Canada's self-anointed "National Magazine," could play its part. My magazine would defend the realm against French-Canadian separatists and English-Canadian continentalists, quitters all, and would shout: "Listen, there are too many of us who care about this country. We won't let Canada go!"

It seemed clear to me that Canadians, no longer self-satisfied facsimile Americans living in a Sunday school dreamscape, were now reaching out for an achey-breakey future of their own making. The Protestant work ethic, in its purest form, had become as rare as the Sunday suits that symbolized it. More important, our admiration of all things American was exhausting itself in the blazing villages of Vietnam, the dark labyrinth of the Watergate scandal, and the long overdue realization that the United States was crowding out our way of life. While the Yanks had to put up with "Tricky Dick" Nixon in the White House, we were the envy of the world for having had the nerve to elect (and re-elect) as prime minister "Lucky Pierre," a cool cat in a hot world, doing his grainy thing. If the filmmakers were the first to take advantage of that blip of national self-confidence, I would be the second. This uproarious decade of changing values and dying shibboleths was the ideal time to launch my new magazine.

AT THE END OF 1970, while I was still editor-in-chief of the *Toronto Star*, I received an unexpected message from Lloyd Hodgkinson, who had just been promoted from publisher of *Chatelaine* to the same job on *Maclean's*. We had never met. He called me at three o'clock in the afternoon of December 23, 1970, and invited me for lunch the next day. I couldn't make it because Christina and I were leaving on a holiday, so he said, "Okay. Give me ten minutes right now, but don't interrupt me for the first five."

"Sure."

"I want you to be the editor of *Maclean's*."

"I've already got an impossible job."

"Hey, you said you wouldn't interrupt. I want you to be the editor – and Christina to be the associate editor, to look after the interests of women in the magazine, which has been kicking the hell out of women for years. It's the best opportunity for a journalistic couple that's ever been presented. I've been given total authority at the magazine and I'll work with you as deep and hard as you want me to, and I'll back off when you don't. The magazine must be restructured. And I'll tell you something else: if you don't take the job, I'm going to fold it."

"That's not fair. You know I care about *Maclean's*," I objected.

"Fairness doesn't have a goddamned thing to do with it. What else can I do? If I can't get the right people to run it then I've got to fold it."

"Who else are you considering?"

"Nobody. I don't know of anybody else. I mean, there's the usual run of people who crossed my mind, but they aren't going to throw themselves into the job as if it was the most important thing in the world. You two will."

I agreed to think about it.

When we returned from our holiday, Hodgkinson came down to the *Star* and we talked for most of an afternoon. "Look," I tore into him, "there is simply no way to salvage *Maclean's*. You've had six editors in the past thirty months. The magazine has lost all credibility. It can't be saved."[1] I thought for a moment.

"Except," I continued. "Maybe, one way. Remember Ben Tre? That Vietnamese city that was bombed out of existence two years ago when Peter Arnett at AP said 'it became necessary to destroy the town in order to save it.' So, start over. Forget about trying to save the existing magazine. Start over and turn *Maclean's* into a newsmagazine, and bring it out weekly instead of monthly. That's the only solution. Even the subscribers who still buy the magazine have stopped listening to it. We have to create an echo across the country to catch their attention. And we can only do that with the urgency of news. Would Maclean Hunter put up the money, even if the odds against success were bloody awful?"

Lloyd looked at me with his one good eye (the other had been lost in a youthful accident) and simply said: "You betcha. As a matter of fact, I've been thinking the same thing, because news is the only way the magazine can gain immediacy. It has to move from features to news. But it should do both, because one weakness of newsmagazines is that they don't do enough in-depth articles."

I felt immediately compatible with Lloyd Hodgkinson, who turned out to be a real *mensch*, as concerned with editorial quality as the bottom line – which *Maclean's* did not really have at the time, since it had lost $6 million over the previous ten years. Still, I told him that Christina and I would need to think about it.

"There isn't time," he said. "The goddamn magazine would go under. You've got to start February 1." My salary was not discussed, but we both realized that I would be taking a considerable cut, which I did. When I asked Hodgkinson for assurance that management would see the magazine only after it was published, so that I would retain full editorial independence, he agreed. We had a deal.

---

[1] Things were so bad that the *Toronto Star*'s Gary Lautens was running a sweepstakes in his column to name the next editor of *Maclean's*, "something that happens as regularly as clockwork and contains enough violence to keep the public's interest," he wrote, explaining the contest.

And I had a problem.

My Ben Tre scenario called for the immediate firing of eight staff members, including all of the magazine's in-house reporters except Walter Stewart, who was a great professional shit-disturber, the kind we would badly need to spice up the new magazine, and John Macfarlane, who understood the contemporary arts, had been my entertainment and op-ed-page editor at the *Star*, and carried his own credibility in his knapsack (he later went on to publish or edit just about every magazine in the country). The departing staff writers – Jon Ruddy, Alan Edmonds, Doug Marshall, and Ian Adams – had hung out at the Nanking Tavern, quaffing beer and munching chicken livers, interrupting their routine at irregular intervals to take on *Maclean's* assignments in distant outposts like Regina, Halifax, or Vancouver, then scurrying back to the Big TO. Their profiles and takeouts were competently written (because they were seasoned professionals) but I found no authentic scent or flavour of Regina or Halifax or the West Coast in their copy. That was no way to run a national magazine. A magazine's editorial contents can never be a neutral commodity. I felt that the best way to add value was to go regional, even local. Taking the editorial budget from the Nanking Brigade to enlist genuine voices of the regions was my first and most essential assignment. I determined to assign only writers on their home turf, adding their resonance to the magazine. (In a way, it was more important to find clear thinkers than great writers; good writing, after all, comes down to clear thinking made visible.)

I took the top job with trepidation bordering on terror, knowing that it would be, to use a Ralph Allen book title, "an ordeal by fire." The magazine had exhausted its mandate, due not so much to neglect as editorial plunder. Each new editor had sacrificed its hard-won reputation by destroying his predecessor's efforts, without offering viable alternatives of his own. Readers had tuned out, advertisers dropped out, and management was ready to bail out.

Before I could turn *Maclean's* into the weekly I envisioned, I first had to fix the limping monthly. Any editorial renaissance would fail unless we could somehow attract public attention. We had to get people talking about us, capture their "share of mind," as the ad guys aptly call it. We had to publish a periodical that would enlist readers, inspire advertisers, and produce the profit that would encourage *Maclean's* owners, somewhere down the road, to invest in a weekly. In that context we were blessed by the presence of Don Campbell, the head of Maclean Hunter, who had been a wartime Lancaster bomber pilot at nineteen, learning the calculus of probabilities in terms of his lifespan, which made him the ideal CEO of a publishing house. He was determined to revive *Maclean's*, approving increases in my editorial budget from $467,000 in 1971 to nearly $5 million a dozen years later, when I left. We never had an argument, even when the magazine attacked his friends, though he occasionally spoke to me through clenched teeth.

Campbell and Hodgkinson agreed that *Maclean's* had to stand for something that would ignite a response in the readers' hearts and minds. This was essential because our most powerful competitor – television – was content to cater to dull, couch-potato appetites. If our readers felt that what we published was, however marginally, important to their lives, we might have a chance. That was the easiest part of my assignment. Christina and I were ardent Canadian nationalists. What more appropriate platform for the magazine than to crusade for Canada's independence? As well as reflecting our genuine feelings, that editorial stance had another advantage: while we could not stand up to the sheer volume and the financial muscle of American periodicals flooding into Canada, this was the one area where they could not compete with us. I resolved that the new *Maclean's* would reach out to the heartland and make echoes to stir a nation.

We had one other advantage. Watching television, which had become the nation's second-most-popular indoor sport, occupied its "share of mind" factor with fierce possessiveness. But TV also gave us a small opening. Because of the newness of the medium and the still-primitive production techniques of early public affairs programming, many viewers didn't entirely believe the news they saw on TV and still went to print for confirmation. That was where *Maclean's*, as a newsmagazine, might find its niche.

Outside the editorial area, *Maclean's* most troubling problem was the combination of its comatose advertising department and its unrealistic circulation base. On paper, the magazine had 775,000 subscribers, but this was a huge liability, not an asset. We had long ago spent the subscribers' money to keep the magazine afloat and now owed them millions of dollars in as yet unpublished issues. (The magazine was then selling for $2.00 a year; it cost $3.60 to promote and administer each subscription.) Weekly publication would require new printing presses and other investments running to millions of dollars. Lloyd and I didn't dare whisper the possibility to the Maclean Hunter board (which I joined in 1972) until we had a proven track record. Hodgkinson was well aware that we couldn't make the leap to the $20.00 subscription rate required for a weekly in one step without losing most of our readers. That was how he arrived at the idea that made the transition possible. Instead of merely raising the price of the magazine, we would gradually increase the frequency of the publication from the current twelve issues a year to eighteen, twenty-four, and so on, right up to fifty-two, making sure that at each stage the magazine was in the black. This had never been done before, but it was that intuitive leap of Lloyd's which made the venture feasible.

At the same time, the few advertisers who remained loyal to *Maclean's* took our inflated circulation base as gospel, which meant that we had to spend a fortune in gimmicky promotions (and expensive premiums) to maintain the artificial totals. The advertising industry was slipping from the control of the old hands who had grown up on *Maclean's*; now media choice was increasingly made by computers, solely on the basis of "cost per thousand," which made it difficult for magazines to compete. The few surviving ads that popped up in the magazine's pages had a decidedly "compliments of a friend" feel about them. Admittedly, magazine advertising is a hard sell; a flick of attention in the reader's mind is difficult to evaluate. Unfortunately the advertising department at

Maclean's had become an incubator for Willy Loman rejects who used their offices mainly as a place to keep warm in the winter. The sales effort was spearheaded by a roughhouse war veteran whose idea of great marketing was to phone potential advertisers and accuse them of being unpatriotic if they didn't switch their business to "Canada's National Magazine." This was about as effective as urging any average group of Canadians to sing the second verse of "O Canada." Nobody knows the words, even if they *can* carry the tune.

The most paralyzing dilemma was produced by our Jurassic lead time. Because the magazine had to be printed at Maclean Hunter facilities, where commercial jobs received priority, it went to press twelve weeks after articles were assigned, eight weeks after they were written, six weeks after they were edited, and five weeks after they were illustrated. The chances of publishing anything topical were slim. That bizarre timetable meant having to choose assignments that would somehow remain topical three months later. It all came down to how many profiles of Anne Murray you could decently publish. It was Maclean Hunter's strange accounting rules that somehow made the delay more profitable. The only time Lloyd Hodgkinson panicked was when I became so fed up with the delays that I invited Toronto-area printers to bid on the magazine with a drastically reduced lead time. Lloyd suggested with some force that I devote my time to editorial issues, but the lead time did improve along with our frequency.

I WOULD OFTEN RETURN to the office at night, shuffle through the various piles of unanswered mail and unanswerable problems, and wonder how anyone dared sit behind my ridiculous three-quarters moon rosewood desk in a downtown Toronto high-rise and pretend to influence the mind of a nation. As you might expect, in a life full of coincidences, this book is being edited and published out of that same building. I realized that I would probably be the last editor presumptuous enough to feel that the country was ours to change. But I also knew we had to take a shot at it.

I sat still and tried listening to readers with my inner ear. That meant spending as much time perusing readers' letters as our writers' manuscripts. The former were usually informed by a surer instinct for what was authentic and what was contrived. They reflected relationships, not assignments or transactions. (One assistant editor, who quite openly didn't agree with my editorial stance, once told an inquiring journalist: "You know, we get a lot of letters and we have to answer them. And if those letters are any indication of what readers want, then maybe Peter Newman is right.")[2]

During those long evenings I pondered the origins and purposes of magazines, trying to decide how we could fit in. Unlike books, in which the writer basically addresses himself to the reader as an audience of one, magazines owe their genesis to a much livelier ancestry: the Forum of Rome and the village fairs of medieval Europe, as described by Theodore H. White (author of *The Making of the President*): "The really good fairs had jugglers, magicians, dancing bears, herb doctors and storytellers. What brought the peasants back each week was to find out what was going on, trading gossip and listening to the impromptu tales. Magazines are the modern equivalent of those fairs where merchants showed their wares, while peasants watched the show, compared notes and listened to the storytellers." Easier said than done.

---

[2] The very first letter I received was from a freelance writer in rural Quebec who had spotted an albino beaver in a northern Ontario lake. Pointing out that only one in twenty-five million of the animals was born white, he wrote me that the beaver had been shunned by its brown-furred cousins and was therefore "friendly and curious with anyone taking an interest in him." This was the reason the writer wanted to call his story "I Am Curious White," telling the tale "as if the beaver himself was talking, describing his lonely life and explaining how for diversion he had turned to visiting with ducks, deer and loon who were oblivious of his colour." This was not a good omen.

On the face of it, it seemed impossible for any magazine to reflect the mood in a nation that was not a village fair but a whole subcontinent. Leafing through stacks of back issues and following the magazine's obsessive hunt for some glimmer of the Canadian identity, it was easy enough to see how *Maclean's* had influenced the collective consciousness of succeeding generations. Distributed free of charge to Canadian troops during the Second World War, it had become the kind of magazine that subscribers saved in their attics, where keepsakes were tucked away. Sitting by the glare of a single overhead bulb, they would spend rainy afternoons rummaging through back issues, coming across the tatters of pages cut out by them or their children to fill scrapbooks for grade-school projects.

In few countries did general-interest magazines exert more influence. Until the advent of communications satellites it had been impossible to distribute any one newspaper across Canada, so it had been left to national magazines, led by *Maclean's*, to provide an essential East-West link. Now the big gamble was whether we could put together a mass audience at a time when the country was splitting up into special interest enclaves, and magazines were being created to cater to them.

Under the inspired editorships of Arthur Irwin and Ralph Allen, readers came to believe that only *Maclean's* had the time, the space, and the talent to pull together the essential interpretations of a country. The magazine had been woven into the dreams and memories of Canadians.

Maclean's seemed invincible at that time. "We all thought we could do anything," June Callwood, one of its star writers, reminisced. "Pierre Berton [then managing editor] phoned me one day and said: 'We'd like a piece on the universe.'

"'The universe?' I asked, a baby on my lap, not sure I had heard right.

"'Yes, the universe,' he said, impatient that the conversation was dragging on. 'Deadline in two weeks.'"

That was vintage Pierre, who was not beyond arrogance. When he received letters from readers that truly annoyed him, he'd write back, cancelling their subscriptions.

When *Maclean's* was founded, near the sputtering start of the twentieth century, Canada was a nation of small audiences, a lonely crowd united by staunch personal values that must have seemed like God-given truths. To chronicle and authenticate the Canadian experience then must have seemed like an achievable goal. But that was long ago, and in another country.

I wrote myself a memo:

Editing a magazine depends on a mixture of assumptions and insights. It's easy enough to create false excitement by magnifying fleeting fads and promoting the prophets of joy or disaster. The real trick will be to articulate the half-formed (but no less deeply felt) intuitions of the magazine's readers, voicing the underlying themes and concerns of their lives.

Within the limits of truth and libel, my most urgent assignment will be the creation of interest, combined with a sense of prophecy and confirmation to illuminate the torrent of news, rumours, scoops, and trial balloons that will arrive in this office from an unfolding universe. Any great magazine must reflect the instincts of its editor, possessed by a sense of audience that he imposes on his staff. While I should not dictate the magazine's precise contents, I must preside over its editorial mix with a renewable sense of national priorities.

My magazine will reflect the mystical nature of the Big Country beyond Toronto's cramped horizons. (I will treat the enemies of laughter with the same abhorrence as the enemies of truth.) 'The mind supplies the idea of a nation,' wrote the French philosopher Andre Malraux, 'but what gives this idea its sentimental force is a community of dreams'. Shaping that 'community of dreams', would be *Maclean's* guiding principle.

As I pondered how to activate such an ambitious undertaking with a crippled magazine, I realized that the only truly remarkable fact about Canada was its size, and the only astounding aspect of the country's history was its survival as a nation superimposed on that massive hunk of geography. Similarly, *Maclean's* most remarkable achievement was that, like the country, it had struggled on. But that was saying a very great deal.

During those long evenings in the office, I realized that my stint at *Maclean's* would be an endurance test. I was not cut out to be a manager, yet I felt that this assignment went way beyond holding onto a job or position. The newspapers started to call me "Captain Canada," and while I knew it was a satirical dig, I had every intention of steering Her Majesty's ship *Maclean's* to safe harbour. It was the first time in my career that I felt a duty that rose above my personal ambitions.

Sitting there among the wreckage of a once great publication, I remembered something that Gunnar Myrdal, the Swedish philosopher, had written: "Often it is not more difficult but easier to cause a big change rapidly than a small change gradually." He was right. This would need a big mother of a shift, and hiring capable reporters who might evolve in their jobs would be too slow. The magazine's new authority had to take root virtually overnight. As a first step I decided to enlist the help of the country's most influential gurus, including historian Donald Creighton, novelist Hugh MacLennan, author/columnist Bruce Hutchison, communications wizard Marshall McLuhan, and Quebec editor Claude Ryan. They were all my friends (including Ryan, who had forgiven my role in the FLQ crisis once he understood what had actually happened) and I assigned them stories about Canada's future (at our usual rates, which then peaked at $250 for a 4,000-word article). They all accepted and were featured regularly in the pre-weekly magazine. Theirs were not names that moved copies off newsstands, but their books and essays were on the compulsory reading lists of every university, so that not only their message but their presence significantly helped raise our profile and credibility.

At the same time I reached out for another untapped source of Canadian talent. In my books I had boasted that I was creating a new reality in the creative non-fiction format by applying the literary devices to journalism. Why not reverse the procedure and invite poets and novelists to write for *Maclean's*? "Stories move from truths to facts, not the other way around," Lewis Lapham, the editor of *Harper's*, once wrote. "Journalists have less in common with diplomats and soothsayers than they do with vagabond poets." I contacted four dozen of the best and they accepted. To give them a context, I suggested that they write about how they visualized their Canada from where they lived and wrote. Instead of specific political or economic agendas, their offhand epiphanies and literary artistry aroused precisely the kind of impact the magazine needed, and from an unexpected quarter. They didn't restrict themselves to facts; they added attitude, mood, and feelings, endowing our pages with literary grace.

Among the first to arrive was Margaret Atwood, with her wintry eyes and corrugated hair, come to deliver her manuscript personally. A masterpiece, it described one of her reading tours in the upper reaches of the Ottawa River where she grew up, in a piece of backcountry so rural that she didn't spend a full year in school until she was eleven. It illustrated her ability to step back from herself, calibrate her emotions, acknowledge the absurdities of life, then create comedy out of hurt, or vice-versa. She went on to write several other *Maclean's* essays. But somewhere along the line we slipped up and I received a five-line letter from Alliston, Ontario, where she then lived: "There's a wonderful invention kicking around. It's called the telephone. Some magazines use it for a process called checking. That's because they like the material they publish to be as accurate as possible. Sincerely, Margaret Atwood." *Zap*.

The prize-winning poet Al Purdy took up my invitation most enthusiastically, completing a dozen stories describing the Williams Lake Rodeo, profiling René Lévesque, and then reporting on a cross-country odyssey. Purdy wrote about his experiences with

Maclean's in his autobiography, including his description of the first time we met: "An audience with Newman in that ten-acre office was like meeting an eastern potentate. For Peter was an exotic, those great overhanging bushy eyebrows like shutters over a harem. And yet he was shy. But it was a shyness that by an act of will he overcame. Forty years old then, author of best-selling political books, rich and famous, so patriotic he exuded maple syrup on the bed sheets at night. He is able to say anything at all in print, insult or compliment all the great nonentities, and a nice guy too. But he couldn't prove it, couldn't let himself go, was never at ease amongst all us lesser beings." And of his assignments he wrote: "I felt I was mapping the country, long after those early cartographers, traversing the savage land that folk artists like Stan Rogers sang about. Not mapping it the way they did, but naming things, saying I was there, adding something personal to the map's cold nomenclature of heights and distances. I hope that doesn't sound silly or trivial. But we weave ourselves and our lives around such real and yet mythical places . . ."

Suddenly our in-baskets were singing with magical prose, and we enlisted the country's best photographers (including the newly discovered Michael Foster) to illustrate their stories. The fifty or so authors who contributed to the magazine included, in no particular order: Joyce Carol Oates, Fred Bodsworth, Alden Nowlan, Adrienne Clarkson, Farley Mowat, Irving Layton, Brian Moore, Rick Salutin, Hugh Hood, George Bowering, Roderick Haig-Brown, George Jonas, Ed McCourt, Mavor Moore, Ray Smith, Jack Ludwig, Bill Howell, George Woodcock, John Hirsh, June Callwood, William Strange, Harold Horwood, Jean LeMoyne, Desmond Pacey, Dave Godfrey, Ralph Gustafson, Joy Carroll, James Reaney, Jon Whyte, Mordecai Richler, Ernest Buckler, Ronald Bates, Roloff Beny, Harry J. Boyle, Barry Broadfoot, Silver Donald Cameron, Maria Campbell, Josef Skvorecky, Eli Mandel, Kildare Dobbs, and Matt Cohen.

THE NEXT ESSENTIAL MOVE was to psychologically step outside my office environment. A mile-long compass arm rotated from our editorial offices at University and Dundas would have touched the base of just about every national medium in the country, from its radio and television networks to other national magazines, advertising agencies, syndicates, press agencies, book publishers, and various word and image packagers. The natural temptation that my predecessors had succumbed to was to produce a magazine for that circle of their cohorts and personal friends. Above all, I had to resist such an easy temptation and seek talent and sensitivities far beyond Toronto's Family Compact. My first executive decision was to mount a large map of Canada on my office wall into which I could stick coloured pins to keep track of the non-Toronto stories we had published. Within eight months we had printed or assigned 147 non-Toronto feature articles. I remember how delighted I was to hear that Anne Collins, the magazine's entertainment editor, had complained about our planning meetings: "You'd be yelled at for being too Toronto-centric, but it was very hard at the time to cover theatre, for example, and not be Toronto- or at least Ontario-centric. I'd get really fed up because an artist would be breaking through in Toronto and a story about him was shot down because he didn't have any presence in Vancouver. Newman kept saying, 'Well, there are essential arts incubators across the country, and if you don't cover them, you're out to lunch.' And I'd get a little snooty about having to think, 'How is this going to play in Calgary?'"

I decided to shake things up by hiring some unorthodox talent. My biggest catches were Don Obe and Tom Hedley. *Esquire* was then the Mecca of new-wave magazine editing, and Hedley was one of its stars. "A smart, slick, slow-spoken young fellow who somehow fostered a faint suggestion of greatness, he possessed a certain style not then common in the brown-shoed Canadian media landscape," wrote George Fetherling, the chronicler of those times. "Hedley was cool. He dressed cool, he dated cool. His stint at *Esquire* had given him a certain aura, which he wore like a cloak. He was renowned as a champion conceptualizer, a spinner and vetter of ideas, a child of McLuhan whose genre was spontaneous well-written conversation combined with a basic disdain of the medium in which he was working. He was totally disorganized, as though to suggest that paperwork and the mundane practicalities of getting out a magazine were beneath him. He and Obe hung out with painters at the original Pilot Tavern in preference to word-people. Hedley was spoken of with awe because the visual side of his brain was said to be so highly developed. He was more a designer of stories than an editor in the normal sense, people avowed; a sort of god-like journalistic being who could somehow command text, image, and design to come together, in some process more closely related to physics perhaps than to management."

Hedley had actually contacted me while I was still at the *Star* to say he was looking for a job in Canada. Once I had taken on *Maclean's* I signed him up immediately, and became as mesmerized by him as everyone else. "New York was a good place for me to go under the circumstances," he explained when I asked him why he had left Canada and why he had returned. "I went to New York feeling that Canada had been betrayed by its intellectuals (lost in their political games at the university), its artists (comforting each other with false standards of excellence), and by its journalists (their writings reflected only what was superficial about Canadian life). I was no expatriate since I hadn't been a patriot in the first place – just a certain sensibility loose with a bad haircut down there in the Citadel of Honk, running with the revolution. This made for measurable personal gains, but once the gains were measured I began to feel the loss: the loss of country." He kept his enthusiasm for Toronto well under control: "I genuinely believe that the United Empire Loyalists came here because they didn't believe in pursuing happiness. Unlike the Americans who recycle their myths and hold on to the American Dream, Canadians think of defining and redefining their myths as a corny and uninteresting exercise. The country's imaginary life is obscure."

In those early months Hedley was the vital centre of the magazine, providing the visual and intellectual excitement that examined some of those myths, prodding all of us into fresh ways of looking at our country. At the same time, he was suffering from the withdrawal symptoms of having left the centre of the magazine universe. We frequently disagreed on how far he could go without insulting our audience, but the tension seemed productive for both of us. Hedley seldom appeared in the office more than two or three times a week, usually after five o'clock (when his creditors had given up for the day, we figured), but each visit was memorable. I had vowed to get the attention of our readers; he delivered it.

He wanted to produce his own issue and I put him in charge of a special American number to mark the U.S. presidential election. This turned into a disaster because he suffered writer's block over his own article, "Mickey Mouse at 44." Even though he'd had three months to work on it, it was three weeks late, and the magazine's delivery schedule was disrupted for the first time since 1905. Hedley finally left by mutual agreement and thereafter only came in a couple of times a month to write treatments. But his brief stay had turned our heads and moved *Maclean's* into a new reality, well ahead of its time.

A typical Hedley ploy: when we suddenly discovered we had no suitable cover for the September 1971 issue, his solution was to use a picture of Sam Etcheverry, quarterback for the Montreal Alouettes, with a bubble caption of him thinking: "What's a guy like me, an American expert on an American game, doing on the cover of Canada's national magazine?" And the answering cover line: "Because, Sam Etcheverry, you're as Canadian as apple pie." That was about as far as you could get from the magazine's former static covers of old railway stations and country fall fairs. It signalled a new sensibility: you could love Canada but retain your sense of humour.[3]

---

[3] Tom Hedley departed soon afterwards for Hollywood where he became a successful screenwriter, earning $1 million for *Flashdance* alone.

It would be wrong and unfair to characterize Don Obe as Hedley's keeper, but they had a highly symbiotic and productive relationship. The combination gave the magazine its edge: people were talking about us again. A self-taught Métis who had grown up on the Six Nations Reserve near Brantford, Ontario, Obe was evenly balanced, with a chip on each shoulder. He was also the best story editor *Maclean's* ever employed, and the writers fortunate enough to work with him were spoiled for anyone else. Obe subscribed to Toronto painter Bob Markle's dictum that "most Canadian art comes out of the energy of a circle of friends," and he exposed *Maclean's* readers to new sources of enlightenment when he invited several of the country's best modern artists – including Markle, Graham Coughtry, and Gordon Rayner – to set down their perceptions in words. Markle, that "Buddha in denim," with whom I often discussed modern jazz, would remind me: "I'm a painter. My hand is equal to my brain."

Obe and I quarrelled almost constantly, because he figured that if I had access to power I must have given something away for it. But I respected him and was grateful that whatever demons were on his trail had blessed him with creativity both explosive and unique. He left the magazine periodically, once satirizing my attempts to gain editorial consensus with this resignation letter: "Please accept my resignation, effective in the usual two weeks. My decision, this time, is final and irrevocable. Now try to interpret *that* consensus." He quit several times (once because I changed the word "booze" in a story he was editing to "liquor") and kept coming back, but finally left the magazine to become editor of *The Canadian*.

The most trying freelancer we had was the slap-happy Sondra Gotlieb, whose husband, Allan, became Canadian ambassador to Washington. Somebody had convinced me that she should contribute food articles. The problem was not so much that they had to be completely rewritten but that she was so difficult to deal with, and I finally ran out of volunteers willing to edit her copy. Her final submission as our food critic was distinguished by the fact that she misspelled the word *restaurant* twenty-seven times.

One of my pressing concerns was to find a columnist inventive enough to anchor the magazine's back page, knowing that at least half of our audience read the magazine from back to front. No one came to mind, but I had been impressed with Allan Fotheringham's column in the Vancouver *Sun*, had assigned him a few articles, and had enjoyed his subtly comic heretical approach. From my frequent visits to the Pacific coast I knew it was hard to spend more than an hour at the Hotel Vancouver's Timber Club (then the favoured Establishment hangout) without hearing someone complain about the latest revelations from "that bastard Fotheringham." That meant readership and controversy, two qualities the magazine badly needed. I invited Allan to Toronto for an interview and offered him a job as Ottawa bureau chief, but he couldn't leave Vancouver for family reasons. I actually had it in mind to offer him the back page. When I called my senior editors into the office for their opinions, they were unanimous: no way could anyone write a national column from the distant shores of the Pacific Ocean. "Foth, we love you," said Walter Stewart speaking for the group, "but no friggin' way can you cover Canada from Lotus Land." I overruled the staff because I felt that he *could* do it, and besides, the issue was at the core of my determination to decentralize our coverage. I asked Fotheringham to start the following week, emphasizing that his mandate was to make Canadians laugh at themselves. He fulfilled that assignment brilliantly for the quarter-century that he graced the magazine's closing page.

When Fotheringham's first file arrived on my desk it was typical of the 1,200 that would follow. He described the inner Cabinet of Pierre Elliott Trudeau as consisting of "men who have bent and stretched the Peter Principle to unreasonable limits . . . congenital stumblers and fainthearted clots who clutter up his ministry." After that, his column turned nasty.

From this running start as a *Maclean's* contributor, he wrote as if he were on a one-man search-and-destroy mission that held no one and nothing sacred. It was his boast that he had attracted twenty-six libel cases and won all but two. (His record was three libel suits in one day on three different stories.) His brand of attack-dog-with-a-smile journalism found resonance with Canadians who had grown cynical about their politicians but couldn't find the words to express their fury. "Dr. Foth," as he called himself, made that medicine go down, and left them smiling. His targets never knew what to expect. Although he was the first journalist to publicly urge his buddy Brian Mulroney to run for the Tory leadership, he later characterized "the jaw that walks like a man" as little more than "Irish charm and bullshit." His putdown of Prime Minister Kim Campbell ("an opportunist leaping, like a mountain goat, from ledge to ledge") withstood the test of time. The only politician gutsy enough to respond in kind was Jean Chrétien. Catching sight of Allan at an Ottawa Press Gallery dinner, he exclaimed, "Ah, and there's Mr. Fuckingham!"

Even his throwaway lines were gems, such as his description of airport taxis "that emit the stale odour of musk-oxen that have gone too long without shampoo." Or his one-sentence epiphany about Grit arrogance: "The Liberal Party seeps through the underbelly of this country like a nuclear submarine in the deep."

In his private life, Fotheringham had the knack of enjoying an active social calendar while maintaining his status as an independent *agent provocateur*. Although he was outwardly gregarious, social distance was essential to his art. His personal clout was based on the accessibility of his columns. Disarmingly unpretentious, his writing style drew readers in by offering a comfortable blanket. Fotheringham's writings followed where his subjects led him. "Joan Sutton is about to publish her book, *All Men Are Not Alike*," he wrote, "a fact recently discovered by female sportswriters allowed into major league dressing rooms." Often he merely jotted down what people said, interposing his own humorous twists. The politicians he portrayed seemed to miraculously fall on their swords. My profound admiration for Allan Fotheringham was rooted in my certain knowledge that he combined a cold eye with a warm heart. He was my kind of writer.

Fotheringham wasn't the only writer to draw lawsuits at the magazine. One of my early problems was dealing with a $1.25 million libel suit launched against *Maclean's* by Vic Cotroni, named by our Ottawa freelancer Allan Phillips as a kingpin of the Mafia in Montreal. The information came from the RCMP, which unfortunately begged off testifying once the trial started. Without substantiating evidence we lost the case. Fortunately in his verdict Judge St. Germain assessed the damage to Cotroni's reputation as being worth precisely one dollar, which we gladly paid. (He was later convicted of murder and of being a crime boss.) During my time at *Maclean's* we lost only one lawsuit (for $70,000), to Garth Drabinsky, for allegedly besmirching his character. We were kept out of trouble by Julian Porter, the Establishment litigator, whose unrealized dream, he once told me, was that "with blood dripping over my left eye, I would score an overtime goal to win the Stanley Cup."

MANY ASSORTED CHARACTERS passed through *Maclean's* in my day but, to the best of my knowledge, only one psychopathic personality: Alan Walker, a weird fellow who was a capable mentor and editor yet became the magazine's most disruptive influence. A graduate of Upper Canada College, he blamed the college for taking him out of the sexual mainstream. At university, he started a hire-a-beatnik service, supplying fashionable bohemians for private parties. He then worked for Canadian Press in London where he interviewed Sean O'Casey, T.S. Eliot, and other elderly men-of-letters and at home later became editor of *The Canadian* as well as *Toronto Life*. Apart from his gun collection, he gathered nostalgia. One closet of his row house on MacPherson Avenue was stuffed with boxes of Aunt Jemima pancake mix produced before the NAACP and public opinion forced removal of the product's traditional image, a kindly old black woman in a red bandana. He also specialized in magazines showing women in latex and rubber, and he kept a Colt .45 automatic in a shoulder holster hanging from his desk chair in his apartment and a .38 Smith & Wesson revolver in his nightstand.

Unfortunately he took some of his toys to the office. For the benefit of the female groupies he was ostensibly helping with professional advice, he turned his office into a house of horrors, with an exhibit of primitive abortion tools kept in a desk drawer, a bullwhip hanging from his coat rack, and several facsimile guns. An editor of the People section had to be taken to hospital for nervous stress after he viciously mocked her writing, and he reduced a receptionist to tears by brandishing his whip.

Walker's pet victim was Ann Dowsett Johnston, the senior editor who took charge of the annual university issue. "He used to say things to me like, 'Stand over there, so I can see through your blouse,'" she told me, after I had left the magazine. "I started keeping a paper trail because of the way he treated me and other female staff members. He was sexually nauseating, thinking that if you were cute and young, maybe he could mentor you and you might be one of his groupies. In 1984, when I was seven months pregnant, he came into my office on a Tuesday night as I was working on a book review that needed rewriting, pulled out his gun and said, 'Where's the goddamn book review?'

"'It won't be ready until the morning, Alan. And don't ever point that gun at me again.'

"He lowered it and said, 'I'm not pointing it at you, I'm pointing it at your kid.'

"Next day I went in to Kevin Doyle [then the magazine's editor] and said, 'You know what, I've just had it, I've had it with the whip and the gun, and I'm going to speak out because you've got a junior receptionist and a People section editor who can't, so I'm going to take the high road, I'm the more senior woman and I'm going to take this on.' Kevin called Walker in and Alan swore it had never happened, that I had made it up, and I got hauled in for lying. Luckily I remembered that Nancy Wilson, a researcher, had been sitting beside me when Walker walked in with the gun.

So Bob Lewis [then managing editor] wanted him fired, but Kevin wouldn't hear of it. And I was characterized as a ninny and a fool.

"I found it extraordinarily disturbing to have him around, and then of course it got way worse. Amongst his friends I was painted as the demon who didn't know how to take a joke. It changed my relationship to everyone at the office, and interestingly the split was not along gender lines. Walker's judgment had been awry for a long time; he may have once been a brilliant editor, but there was a devolution that was gruesome to be part of and I was caught in it. I left for a Southam Fellowship and came back to the magazine a year later but never returned with my heart. I couldn't. I had a fabulous female lawyer who strongly advised me to take him to court when she heard the story. It was extraordinary."

This happened two years after I left, but it was entirely in character for Walker. Frances McNeely, who was assistant to Rod McQueen when he was managing editor during my term, recalled that Alan would sneak into her cubicle after she had left for the day and replace the ribbon in her IBM Selectric typewriter so he could take the old one home and unspool and carbonize it in order to read the memos that Rod was sending me. Fran recalled that at one point he took out her typewriter ribbon ten days in a row. Unfortunately I was not told about his transgressions at the time and blithely kept promoting him because he was a capable editor. He campaigned insistently to become part of the magazine's planning group, and when I invited him in, he just sat there glowering at me and never said a word – then complained that I was a dictator. Bob Lewis eventually fired Walker in 1993, after he started coming to work in his underwear, seldom sober. He died shortly afterwards.

THE FIRST ISSUE of the new *Maclean's* was published in May 1971, led off by Christina's masterful character study of John Turner, then in political exile as Pierre Trudeau's putative successor. She had become invaluable as the magazine's associate editor, tutoring many *Maclean's* contributors in finding their voices, helping them to get their thoughts and feelings down on paper. "Editorially the two of you were an incredible team," recalled John Macfarlane, who was a fellow associate editor at the time. "She was maybe the most gifted editor I ever saw; her fix notes were often better than the pieces she was working on. One felt that you kind of had to live up to Christina. . . . It was an electric environment; you never knew what was going to happen next."

A half-dozen members of the jitney editorial team, including Don Obe and Walter Stewart, turned the magazine around. By the end of the first year, the *Maclean's* deficit had been cut in half, and by the second year we were in the black, with advertising up an astounding 51 per cent. "Twelve months ago I had complete confidence in you," Lloyd Hodgkinson wrote to me in an inter-office memo. "Today, I add respect as a gentleman and a professional. What you've done for *Maclean's* is a matter of record. What we can do in the next couple of years is exciting to contemplate." What Lloyd's business department in fact accomplished in the next three years was to earn a profit of $1,140,000. We were no longer Maclean Hunter's unwanted child.

The magazine, which had once resembled a smorgasbord served up by a careless chef, had been redesigned by art directors Ralph Tibbles and John Eby, with strong, clean make-up, full-page-bleed photographs, and three legible columns of type instead of an eye-straining four. We started to publish dozens of young journalists, including Roy MacGregor, Jack Batten, Penney Kome, Bill Cameron, Erna Paris, Charlotte Gobeil, Anne Charney, Valerie Miner, Philip Marchand, John Hofsess, and Steven Langdon. Harry Bruce came in with a wonderful memoir of young lust at Mount Allison University ("Going all the way was difficult when there was nowhere to go"). Walter Stewart exposed how India exploded its first nuclear bomb with Canadian materials and technology. Michael Enright, who went on to fame and fortune at the CBC, set a high standard in all his writings; Hal Quinn could turn out a cover story on almost anything with one day's notice; and

David North, the foreign editor (a post he had previously held on a Belgian magazine) kept us plugged into hotspots in both hemispheres. When Ronald Reagan decided to flex his muscles by invading the tiny Caribbean island of Grenada, most journalists arrived aboard landing crafts with the American troops, but our Michael Posner managed to rent a small boat and came ashore on the north end of the island, ahead of the invaders, and broke the story of the Americans accidentally shelling a lunatic asylum. Ex-corporal Jack Ramsay wrote an eloquent condemnation of the Royal Canadian Mounted Police that made national headlines. We also ran a cover illustrating Canada's conversion to the metric system that showed a tailor looking confused as he used an imperial tape measure to obtain the vital statistics of a bikini-clad model. It was a dumb idea, and the pickets from Women After Rights (WAR) made sure that I learned my lesson.

Still, by the spring of 1974 we had reasserted the right to call ourselves "Canada's National Magazine." Readers' approving letters poured in, as did thirty to forty unsolicited manuscripts daily. The general reaction was summed up by McKenzie Porter, in the Toronto *Telegram*: "After a decade in the hands of smart alecks, hippies, witchdoctors, and bearded Billy goats, *Maclean's* Magazine has recovered its sanity, authority, intellect, and flair."

As the magazine and its staff expanded, my management skills became an issue – or *the* issue, if the many published stories on the topic could be believed. In fact, the adverse notices were pretty well true. My job description was to save *Maclean's*, not to be the indulgent daddy of the dysfunctional family that edited it.

I could have staffed the magazine with safe, grey people who didn't understand the lyrics of "MacArthur Park," had a cautious, bureaucratic mindset, and would simply obey orders. But that would have been spiritual and professional suicide for both me and the magazine. I wanted rebels with a cause, hang-gliders from the 1960s whose hearts belonged to Woodstock and who barely tolerated me. I was fond of individual writers and editors, but making the boys and girls feel warm and fuzzy was not my priority. I wanted to be their coach, not their father. I was always being attacked for being too dictatorial or too lax, sometimes both on the same day. People expected me to fill a void in their own lives, and so I would willingly take the fall when things went wrong. The problem with getting most of the credit was that I also received all of the blame. It was in no way a one-man show.

I wanted *Maclean's* to distinguish itself from its newsmagazine models, *Time* and *Newsweek*, in one important way. These worthy publications read as they had been written by one person, and I wanted *Maclean's* to retain its writers' individual voices. This would be no cookie-cutter operation. I fussed with details, fussed with facts, fussed with deadlines, but I seldom tinkered with style. That proved again the value of regional correspondents whose voices articulated the aspirations of their far corners of Canada.

Although we were part of the stuffy Maclean Hunter organization, we prided ourselves on being its rebellious outriders. Hardly anyone (except me) wore ties, or even owned one. Several editors rode their bicycles to work and stored them in their offices. The place was overrun by scampering dogs and crying babies. Executive editor John Gault, who epitomized the peasant couture of the place, walked around barefoot and wrote many of the magazine's story treatments sitting Buddha-style on top of his filing cabinet, while smoking up. He was the best in the business, though sometimes he went too far, as when he wrote a caption for the picture of a new model Volkswagen: "From the Folks Who Brought You World War II." For a cover story on the Trudeau divorce we ran a luminous photo taken shortly after Pierre and Margaret were married, which carried Gault's simple and moving cover line: "THE WAY THEY WERE."

"The consensus was that you couldn't manage a pop stand," Gault later told me in his reticent way. "You're a writer, for Christ's sake. Why the hell would you be any good at it? You were as good at it as I was, which was awful. We argued a lot. It was not a place of sweetness and light, it was a place where ideas actually mattered. But you did have one skill that was amazing, perhaps because you had to learn about Canada as an immigrant. When you sat down to plan the issues or to write an article, you had an audience in mind that had nothing to with the early years of your life. You knew what people wanted in the magazine, if they had the opportunity to do the asking. And you did that better than anybody. You spent a lot of years studying what made people Canadian and you absorbed it, so that you became the most Canadian of us all."[4]

In truth, I had never run anything before *Maclean's*. At the *Star* I had not progressed beyond being Beland Honderich's glorified lackey, and as a naval officer my authority was defined by the number of stripes on my sleeve. "Nobody who's running a newspaper or magazine these days can be unaware of the fact that work patterns are changing," noted Germaine Greer. "You can't say to a journalist 'Be in the office from nine to five and write me six stories.' You can only hope that somehow or other some combination of licence and leisure and hard graft will produce something for you. The whole idea of getting performance out of a man or woman in return for a fixed and just sum of money must be seen as a hallucination in the 1970s." And so it was.

Before taking over *Maclean's*, I had spent a couple of days at *Newsweek* in New York, studying the subtle intricacies of how a professional newsmagazine operates. They couldn't have been more pleasant, but I remember walking around open-mouthed. It was

---

[4] One of my clashes with Gault had to do with the cadre of part-time typists we brought into the office every Friday evening to prepare copy for the plant. In those pre-computer days they produced eight versions (using carbon paper) that were distributed to the top-line editors for a final run-through. Week after week I noticed that one of the typists just sat there, and when I asked why, it was explained to me that she couldn't type. I suggested she not return, and early the following Monday a raging Gault stormed into my office. "I hear you fired Amanda [not her real name]!" I admitted that I had, since she had been hired as a typist, and that turned out not to be one of her skills. "I know she can't type, for Christ's sake," Gault exclaimed as he slammed my door. "But she was the office pusher!"

the old 10 per cent rule with a vengeance. Their staff was exactly ten times the size of the staff we had planned, except for their entertainment department, which had twenty-four staffers compared to our intended two plus a part-timer. This was significant because both *Newsweek* and the *Maclean's* newsmagazine I was planning had the same news holes to fill: a weekly forty-five pages. The cold-blooded logic of that deadly calculus was that everyone I hired had to produce or leave. Unlike newspapers, which can fill extra space with wire copy or canned features, every page in a magazine must be original. There was no time or budget for niceties, or training. (Training was a moot point in any event, since when we finally went weekly in 1978 only one of our staff, Bob Lewis, our Ottawa editor, had any kind of extensive newsmagazine experience, as a *Time* magazine bureau chief.) I had to hire reporters from the dailies and pray they could weather the switch. Some, like Angela Ferrante, Colin MacKenzie, Bob Marshall, Kevin Doyle, Ian Brown, David Thomas, Tom Hopkins, Lawrence O'Toole, Ian Pearson, Ernest Hillen, Michael Posner, and particularly Ian Anderson, flourished. Others never caught on.

There was no margin for error. My budgets were drum tight. At the start we could afford only four coloured pictures per issue, and since the cost of paper, post office distribution, and other expenses were fixed, salaries were the only token of economy, which caused much understandable friction. On the one hand, Lloyd Hodgkinson and I were making speeches and giving interviews about how wildly successful the magazine had turned out to be; on the other hand, we were forced to pay salaries that were modest at best. The reason was that when we hailed the magazine's accomplishments, we were comparing its financial health with the previous decade of bloodletting, and most of the profits we did make had to be reinvested into the newsmagazine. There was considerable turnover, but most people left for higher-paying jobs; at one point the editor of every national magazine in the country was a recent *Maclean's* graduate. Walter Stewart left his post as managing editor several times, once to collect a $100,000 advance for a book about the proposed Pickering airport. Mel Morris, his predecessor, resigned when I changed the reference to a drunk Labour minister Bryce Mackasey at an Edmonton roast from "considerably fortified with alcohol" to his "glass constantly in hand" in an eight-line People section item. It was a touchy time.

My days were full. I would get up at 4:00 a.m. and work on my books (five of the hefty mothers were published during my *Maclean's* stewardship), be in the office by 9:00, hold a cover meeting Monday mornings, planning meetings on Tuesdays and Thursdays, plus weekly sessions with Lloyd. The rest of the day would follow, with a succession of fifteen-minute windows for office visitors, who were either interviewing me or being interviewed, and a lunch at the Courtyard with whoever was in town.

Once a month, on Wednesday mornings at 9:30 a.m., I would attend a Maclean Hunter board meeting. Most of the discussions had to do with profit targets for the office forms company, the latest rate increases of the cable TV division, the fiscal health of our country-and-western radio stations, and other mundane business matters that interested me not at all. This proved to be a challenge. Having been up since 4 a.m., I inevitably dozed off, which was not a good tactic, since this was the summit meeting of Maclean Hunter's governing council, which would soon decide if and when *Maclean's* could go weekly. At first I devised a simple technique to wake myself up. I held a thick ballpoint pen, which dropped with a great clatter once I started to snooze and my fingers relaxed, the noise returning me to wakefulness. But after a while I slept through that as well, so I arranged for my seatmate, Bill Wilder, a good friend and the former head of Wood Gundy, to kick me awake at ten-minute intervals.[5]

---

[5] The most exciting day in the boardroom was when one of our subsidiaries, Metro News, was charged with distributing obscene literature. Pete Little, one of the directors, demanded to see some samples of the offending material. A stack of *Hustlers* was brought in and took ages to circulate around the table. The hush was palpable.

To divert attention from my slumbers and plug the directors into current events, I organized a series of boardroom lunches entertaining mostly politicians, including Pierre Trudeau. The idea was that they would speak for ten minutes or so and then answer questions. This worked out well most of the time, but when Monique Bégin, the effusive, garrulous, and compassionate Liberal Health minister was our guest and gave a spirited defence of the public health care system, no one had any questions. "What's the matter with you people in Toronto?" she demanded. "You never say anything, you can't talk about issues. You look dead!" As if to prove her point, nobody replied, and she carried on regardless.

THE EVOLUTION OF *MACLEAN'S* from a derelict monthly to a lively weekly was of course the story of the people who did the work. It is impossible to recapture the passion and energy spent in that magnificent effort, but I look back on that time with a sense of wonder. Not because I was by default its chief animator, but because the dedication of the staff was so extraordinary. All too often I got the credit, not because I claimed it but because the fate of *Maclean's* had become a national cliffhanger, and visiting journalists inevitably interviewed The Guy in the Three-Piece Suit in the Corner Office.

I set up a modest internship program, which paid impressive dividends. A typical case history was Ann Dowsett Johnston, who had a summer job at a restaurant after graduating from Queen's University. She started in the research department, which I had modelled on *Time*'s, to double-check all of our writers' facts, including Michael Posner's profile of Arnold Spohr, then head of the Royal Winnipeg Ballet. "Is it true that you were once a mediocre concert pianist?" she asked Spohr on her first day on the job, reading from the manuscript. There was a long pause, then the ballet director allowed, "Well, I guess you could say that." Johnston had been on the magazine for only two and a half months when her grandfather died. She attended his funeral, which happened to fall on a Friday, the day we went to press. Despite her grief she returned to the office to help close the magazine: "I went back with some embarrassment and I know it was the wrong decision, but that's how smitten I was, and how I think we felt as a group." Her intensity wasn't that unusual.

The time and place when emotions ran the highest was during the turf wars at the scheduling meetings, when stories were assigned their space. No feudal lord ever contested his territorial imperatives with greater passion. The collegiality that ruled most other times of the week went out the window. "If anything happened to reduce your pages it was taken as a complete annihilation and a cause for all-out war," recalled Anne Collins, who joined the magazine at twenty-six in 1977. "It sounds nutty when you think back on it. But it was like being in a hugely intensive boot camp. Everybody cared passionately about every single inch of your space in the magazine, which was guarded like some kind of sacred chalice."

John Gault spent most of the days when he wasn't writing treatments listening to coworkers' tales of woe, making sure that by the time they left his office they were twice as concerned and three times as angry. Yet even he developed a soft spot: "Despite all the efforts I made initially to not get involved, I did get involved – up to my ass, up to my neck, up to my receding hairline. For the first long while I was here, I thought, 'What the hell, it's their magazine.' Then I began to feel it's mine: when somebody screwed up, I damned near took it personally."

The women on staff displayed the most creative energy, led by Angela Ferrante, a former Montreal *Gazette* investigative reporter who became an assistant managing editor. She inaugurated the *Maclean's* honour roll and the year-end polls. Her article on the Holy Shroud of Turin was a heart-stopper. Elaine Dewar, Erna Paris, Linda McQuaig, and Marci McDonald (whose book on the Americanization of Canada deserved much more attention) became the most serious book authors. Then there were Anne Collins, Mary Jannigan, Ann Dowsett Johnston, Val Ross, Rona Maynard, Carol Goar, Joanne Webb, Linda Diebel, Marni Jackson,

Marsha Boulton, Melinda McCracken, Jennifer Wells, Gillian MacKay, Susan Riley, Ann Walmsley, Suzanne Zwarun, Mary Sheppard, Cheryl Shoji, Louise Campoli, Shona McKay, Marijke Leupen, and Jane O'Hara, who formed a Band of Sisters that has never been duplicated. Judith Timson burned at a higher caloric level than her fellow female writers, whom she referred to as "The Senior Shoppers." At a *Maclean's* staff party she climbed up on a table and delivered a rant about sexual tensions in the office, mentioning the way Michael Enright's butt seemed to twitch when he prowled the corridors. She imitated it, performing a kind of upward thrust with each step while maintaining evenly held shoulders. Every woman in the place collapsed with laughter because they had also observed and noted that famous walk.

There were the usual office romances, but it was the unconsummated relationships that provided the charged atmosphere, particularly during the transitions prior to the newsmagazine. New bodies were arriving weekly, mixing into an already youthful jumble of the sexes. Except for senior editors, the majority of the staff was single and focused on career rather than biological clocks or hunter-gatherer behaviours. But there were dramatic exceptions. When some pheromone phenomenon occurred between staffers it had the effect of a hormonal jolt. Barbara Amiel, who was a columnist on the magazine for eight years, raised blood pressures just by walking down the hall in her Sonia Rykiel sweaters and Wonder Woman cinched belts. "What I found so striking was that she was so much into using feminine wiles," remarked Elaine Dewar. "I sort of kept saying to her, you don't have to put makeup on to come and see me, forget it, Barbara." Once, when Amiel, in her usual tight sweater, was trying to attract the attention of a male editor, she pushed herself tight up against the window of his office, until he got the message.

I mentored many writers, but none with greater satisfaction than Roy MacGregor, who worked for the magazine on three separate occasions. His was not an auspicious beginning. "I was on a Maclean Hunter trade paper called *Office Equipment and Methods* and wrote you a note that I wouldn't mind reviewing music, forgetting to tell you I was tone deaf," he recalled. "I wrote a review of The Who and Joan Weatherseed [our very British and very square copy editor] went through the piece and put the word 'Guess' in front of the word 'Who' every single time that I used it about their great album *Tommy*. I was mortified; you thought it was funny. Then a junior job came up and you offered it to me. I can still remember getting on that elevator that first day and of all the people to get on with, there was Tom Hedley, who had a scarf about four miles long, and Don Obe, who had his leather jacket on and was smoking on the elevator. For a kid who had dreamt of magazines it was like going backstage at a rock concert because these people were my heroes."

Roy's command of creative non-fiction became textbook perfect. In his columns, articles, and books, his subjects and his country came alive, almost as if he were painting instead of writing. One example, describing in *Maclean's* the novelist Hugh MacLennan, then in the winter of his career:

Beyond him, the hardwood forest is blackening in the setting sun, blushing with the early rumours of fall. Soon the colours of Quebec's Eastern Townships will rise to equal his own anxiety; October will come and with it the release of *Voices in Time*, his first novel in thirteen years, perhaps the last. Hugh MacLennan is leaning on a visitor's car, arms folded over the roof, his hazel eyes blocking an exit. This is a man who does not fill conversations so much as furnish them, and there will be a final polish before inspection. The voice is lilting now, not choked as it was when he dealt with his first wife's death and her later, other-world appearance to him; and the right hand has settled now, not trembling as it was when he spoke, for the first time, of his own private terror during the 1970 October Crisis. Fear then, fear again now, as he prepares for what may be the final judgment. Dismissed by the critics and badly hurt last time out, he will try again in a different age and see if, just maybe, his time has come again.

The daily round of insurmountable problems and staff revolts, both minor and major, that faced me in the office was an island of calm compared to what was shaking up my personal life. Christina had left the magazine in the spring of 1972, so that we could co-author a book on the Canadian Establishment. She continued to contribute articles and attended the weekly planning meetings, but, since she was the first of the originals to depart, her absence left a large gap. To make matters worse, almost from the first day of our book collaboration it was clear to both of us that it was a bad idea. Our views of how the Establishment ought to be examined were diametrically opposed. But it was not so much the substance of the ideological differences between Christina and me that mattered. Our disagreement made us realize that we no longer saw the world in the same way. The dynamic between us changed gradually, almost imperceptibly, then noticeably, and eventually irrevocably. That deterioration in our relationship took a full decade to marinate, from right after the publication of *Renegade* to the planning of the *Establishment* books.

Our move to Toronto had only intensified the pressures. Editing first the *Toronto Star* and then *Maclean's* required cruel workloads at the office and extra social obligations, yet I never stopped publishing a steady stream of books on the side. Once Christina had left the magazine she was in high demand as a freelancer and itching to write books of her own, and the poison that seeped into the marriage and eventually killed it had mostly to do with working together. Not a single piece of copy left our various homes during our marriage that didn't bear the imprint of shared knowledge and joint editing, but as my notoriety and output increased, I grew to depend more on her than she on me, and I received most of the credit.

The divorce, amicable as it was, took two years to take effect and I remained a bachelor for five. That was a novelty, since I had gone straight from virginity to Pat, and from Pat to Christina without a break. I now had a chance, during my mid-forties, to make up for my dateless teenage courting years. So my days were filled with words, and my nights were filled with women – well, at least until the early evenings anyway. I still got up at 4 a.m. to write and so my end-of-the-date line was, "Look, I have to be in bed by 9:30, with you or without you." To my surprise – and delight – this unsubtle declaration actually worked.

The first object of my affection was Joy Carroll, a successful novelist, once painted by Harold Town, whom I met during a junket to Berlin. Elspeth Cameron, profiling me in *Saturday Night*, claimed that on my way to Europe I met Joy and that "their rhapsody of the Rhine was to have disastrous consequences: Newman's separation and divorce from Christina." Christina fired off an immediate retort, which they published: "Alas for rhapsody, alas for romance. My separation from Newman had nothing to do with Mrs. Carroll or any other Lorelei. It had to do with a fierce disagreement Newman and I had been conducting over the writing of *The Canadian Establishment*. Long before he got on the plane to Berlin, we'd had our penultimate argument and begun to go our separate ways." Alas, that was true.

For a time I found sweet solace with the alluring Ms. Carroll, whose books were a cross between *The Forsyte Saga* and *Fanny Hill*. We spent most of a year together until I recognized that she was my transitional woman and moved on. (Asked about our relationship during one of her television interviews, Joy quipped: "It just sort of Petered out.")

It was a heady time to be a public figure, in the swinging Toronto of the 1970s, and I tripped over myself wooing the willing ladies. There were dalliances with Lisa Conway, a sensuous boutique owner; Elizabeth Cleaver, the wonderful Hungarian-born Montreal illustrator; the beautiful Linda Rosier, an advertising agency owner who worshipped both Fred Astaire and Oral Roberts; Mary Jane

Friesen, the sweetest of the sweet, and as a nod to my nationalistic streak, a former Miss Canada.

The longest and most enduring relationship was my love affair with Barbara McDougall. She had left her husband and moved to Edmonton after writing for the business section of the Vancouver *Sun* and became the financial columnist for a local TV station and an executive at Northwest Trust. This was before she entered politics and won the reputation of being the coolest cat in the Commons. She was so refreshingly different from the other women I had known that she kept me captivated for over twenty years. She should have and could have been the ideal mate, but in hindsight we were singularly career-minded and not each other's first priorities.

It was a glamorous, passionate, and memory-making time, and a much-needed rite of passage. But ultimately I became sated with the roller-coaster emotions and discovered I was a nesting creature at heart, longing for the tradition, the stability, and (what the hell, I might as well say it) quite simply the convenience of saying "Brace yourself, old girl," that comes only with the comfort of a snug marriage bed.

The steadying element at this point in my life was my daughter Ashley. We spent every weekend and every second Christmas together, with summer trips to Disneyland, the Rockies, Hollywood, and points in between. As straightforward and honest as her mother, Ashley inherited my diffident manner and, having watched the collateral damage that a life in the public eye had caused her parents, she treasured her privacy. She earned a master's degree at Queen's and joined Ontario's public service, where she met and fell in love with Christopher Monahan, a good man and a great husband. They have two delightful children, Clare and Colin, who became the bouncy focus of their lives. Ashley is a determined contrarian who successfully battled the furies that consumed her parents, and I admire her for it. My parenting has not been the most attentive, but the core of my love for her has slowly matured into a profound friendship that we both want and need. The best night of our lives together was January 9, 1980, when we first saw and heard Stan Rogers, who became our signature troubadour.

I MET CAMILLA TURNER in 1977, at the Beach Grove Golf and Country Club in Windsor, Ontario. She was a guest the night that I was being feted as Journalist of the Year by the local press club, a function that soon grew tiresome because neither of us knew anyone there. We encountered each other accidentally, both seeking privacy behind a potted palm tree, and many dates later fell in love. She was a Julie Christie look-alike with a natural beauty that required almost no tending. She had trained to be a teacher but, after a stint with the National Film Board, had become an assistant editor of the *Financial Post*; she was later promoted to managing editor of *Flare*, the fashionable-living magazine. Our attraction was strong and mutual, and we felt that we had met at a propitious moment, both of us confident that we had what it took for a good marriage, including Camilla's editorial and navigational skills. (This view was not shared by most of my friends.) Our wedding was simple, with just her family and my mother in attendance, and Ashley acting as my "best man." We were married by the Reverend Eugene Fandrich, a Unitarian preacher done up in a flaming-scarlet robe, which (if I were keeping score), introduced me to my fifth religious incarnation. The reception that followed at the Royal Canadian Yacht Club was much more elaborate, with three special friends standing up for me: my publisher, Jack McClelland; my longtime Liberal friend, Senator Keith Davey; and Brian Mulroney, the Montreal-based lawyer I had first befriended while he was a student at Laval University. Our honeymoon was brief; we sailed my boat the *Indra* into The County around Picton, Ontario, for a long weekend.

Just before my wedding to Camilla, Christina (who was about to marry the renowned political scientist Stephen Clarkson) and I exchanged letters that crossed in the mail. "For twenty years of my life I valued and loved you deeply and I know, despite the pain and disappointment that has swamped my spirit since we came apart, that you loved and valued me," she wrote. "I think of you at the wheel of your boat with that crazy cap on and have tenderness for what you were and regret for what we might have become. We were lovers for a very long time and I am glad."

"I can't let you go into your new life without one more good-luck hug," I had written her. "I know you are marrying a fine man and that makes me happy. But he is marrying the best woman he will ever know, and I hope he can give you that profound love and gift of joy which we shared for so many years before it finally eluded us."[6]

In 1976, I had purchased a partially renovated shell of a house on Admiral Road, in Toronto's Annex neighbourhood, built as a private home in 1905 and turned into a boarding house in the 1950s. I had then spent eighteen months making the house my own, hoping I would eventually share it with a compatible soul-mate. Chimneys were rebuilt, the roof re-slated, and several dump trucks full of mud were removed from the basement before a new heating system was installed on a concrete floor. Its upper floor housed a separate suite, complete with study, bedroom, bathroom, and sitting room, which would eventually be occupied by Camilla but was initially Ashley's weekend home. The second floor had a magnificent bedroom, with a fireplace, a bay window, sauna, modern kitchen, and sunroom/dining room overlooking the garden, its trees populated by prancing squirrels. My cork-lined study on the main floor opened to two living rooms. One was a comfy conversation pit, a "let's curl up and have a talk" sort of place, with bookshelves lining three walls and a fireplace for rainy days. That was where Camilla and I entertained most Sunday after-noons (out of boating season), inviting compatible and combative

---

[6] It was a minor irony that almost simultaneously with our remarriages the Toronto *Sun* voted us both, in separate polls, onto their list of the sexiest women and men in the city. Alas, we were no longer together.

guests who interested us. I had picked up most of the furniture at a model suite sale in Habitat, the avant-garde apartment complex created by Moshe Safdie during Expo 67. Its designer, Hugh Spencer, was years ahead of his time for Canada and eventually did very well in the United States. The main living room's highlight was the original staircase, oak steps gleaming, newels and balustrades glowing. Every Christmas, and on other special occasions, we entertained the entire *Maclean's* editorial staff with their husbands, wives, and lovers, which ran up to a couple of hundred fairly riotous guests. More than once, unable to dislodge the hardcore revellers, Camilla and I went to bed before the last of the staff had departed, just in time for breakfast. We enjoyed our time at the centre of Canada's journalistic universe.

BY THE FALL OF 1978 it was time to put the second and agonizing part of my Ben Tre strategy into effect. In order to become a weekly newsmagazine, the *Maclean's* that had been so lovingly invented and tended since I'd arrived in 1971 would have to die. Instead of remaining a journal that explored the country of the mind and a land of the spirits, the newsmagazine would be dealing with the harsh realities of the week's news.

Even our severest critics apparently felt that we had regained enough credibility to at least be worth attacking. But *Maclean's* remained a general-interest magazine in an age of fractured specialized audiences with declining attention spans. The only salvation was to become a newsmagazine, to give our pages a sense of urgency that would give it at least a chance to hold the reader's attention. I tried to reassure the staff that some things would survive the format shift – the natural music of good sentences; the ability to close distances; the personalizing of events; the enlightened use of the narrative form to impart the human touch – that even though we would be reporting news, each story would have the emotional effect of a well-crafted short story. But they didn't believe it, and neither did I: the essence of a newsmagazine is a form of group journalism, which, when carried to its extreme, can become the literary equivalent of painting by numbers. The format demands stylistic unity, and that cannot be achieved by preserving individual writing styles. My compromise was that we would share common sets of guidelines and starting points but maintain the personal feeling between the writers and their subjects, so that they would write as witnesses as much as commentators. My hope was that as the writers' inquiries grew more vital to them, the magazine would become more indispensable to its readers – that even if we had to become less intellectual, we need not be less sensual, and would continue to wrap the facts in the five senses.

The understandable fear was that we would emulate such *Time* magazine stylistic oddities as reverse syntax ("backwards ran the sentences until reeled the mind" as the famous parody put it), hyperactive parentheses, and portmanteau epithets. We were not about to import any of these innovations. Neither would we copy *Time*'s annoying habit of sounding omniscient and smug. Our outlook would remain a healthy mixture of compassion and skepticism. But before we did anything, we needed to drastically alter Canada's magazine publishing climate.

From my nearly twenty years of lobbying on behalf of Canadian magazines, one scene comes most vividly to mind. It took place on a brisk winter afternoon during the early 1960s in the private office of Brigadier James Roberts, deputy minister of Trade and Commerce in the Diefenbaker government. It was snowing outside as we talked and it occurred to me that snow reduced Ottawa to the quintessential Canadian small town it really was. But all of a sudden Roberts made a statement that completely changed the mood and I realized that this *was* a capital, connected in its own way to the sources of world power. What we were talking about was Roberts's recent Washington visit to discuss with the State Department Ottawa's tentative plans to change the status of the so-called Canadian edition of *Time*. Roberts, a mandarin of impeccable demeanour, ranked getting excited with wearing brown suede shoes as things one simply didn't do. But he was excited now, not about *Time* particularly, but about his country and how it was being pushed around. "You know," he told me, "I wouldn't have believed it before I went to Washington but there seems nothing, literally nothing we could suggest that would upset Washington more. I had the distinct feeling that if we touched the Canadian operations of *Time* the State Department would view it as far more serious a matter than if, for example, we sold armed tanks to Fidel Castro." Roberts's confession touched me deeply because it came from a good man who lived by quiet diplomacy, still half-believed in the American dream and was obviously horror-stricken by what he had experienced.

The American magazine lobby had been hyperactive in Ottawa since Diefenbaker had appointed a royal commission headed by Grattan O'Leary, publisher of the *Ottawa Journal*, to examine the issue. Larry Laybourne, then managing director of Time-Canada, closed his submission with a humble little bow to the commissioners and declared: "I invite the Commission to consider whether *Time* magazine in Canada is not in all essential respects a Canadian periodical." That got O'Leary's Irish temper up. He telephoned *Time* publisher Henry Luce and asked him to fly in from New York. On January 17, 1961 the mighty Luce mounted the witness stand and declared, "I may be in some disagreement with my colleagues, but you said, sir, you want me to be very plain. I do not consider *Time* a Canadian magazine."

At stake was the continued existence of *Time*'s Canadian edition, which dressed up its imported U.S. magazine with half a dozen pages of Canadian news and drained away enough advertising dollars to make an indigenous newsmagazine impossible. These "split-run" magazines made it nearly impossible for their Canadian counterparts to function profitably.

In 1976, the Trudeau government tackled the issue, disallowing tax exemptions for Canadian advertisers in *Time*. Hugh Faulkner and Francis Fox were the two Trudeau ministers who most enthusiastically supported the legislation, but it was Bud Cullen in National Revenue who made it happen. *Time* magazine's lawyers had come to see him because he was thought to be sympathetic to their cause, and during the first two hours of the meeting they made impressive headway. Then their legal adviser, a partner in the Toronto firm of Tory & Tory, summed up, warning the minister: "Do you know what they'll say in New York if you put through this legislation? They'll say that Canada has become a banana republic!"

Cullen turned red and made no reply but he could hardly wait to usher them out of his office. He called his senior staff together, repeated their threatening comment, and said: "Who do those sons of bitches think we are?" In that moment, he decided to enact the legislation that took away the special status of *Time* (and *Reader's Digest*) and made it possible to create *Maclean's* as a weekly newsmagazine.

We had been experimenting with a sixteen-page news format since 1975, with mixed success. The great advantage of this was that it enabled us to recruit Bob Lewis and Kevin Doyle to the magazine, both future managing editors and editors in chief, who gave it the energy and discipline it needed. Lewis, a masterful craftsman and inspiring leader, became the best of our Ottawa bureau chiefs, while Doyle capably handled the foreign and national desks before taking on the key job of managing editor during the changeover. I acquired an impressive array of international correspondents by phoning my friend Ray Heard, then foreign editor of London's *Observer*, pointing out that there was barely any readership overlap and asking for his list of stringers. They were added (with their permission) to our masthead, instantly making it appear as though we had an impressive network of correspondents, stretching from Reykjavik to Rio de Janeiro. Our first weekly issue carried an exclusive interview by our Tehran correspondent, Kathy Keely, with Iran's most important Shi'ite leader, the Ayatollah Schariat Madari. Shortly afterwards Mary Helen Spooner, our Bolivian stringer, was threatened with execution by Interior minister Colonel Luis Gomez for a *Maclean's* story about "the para-military thugs machine-gunning the central labour office," and I requested that our External Affairs Department intercede on her behalf. We felt like a real newsmagazine. We also broke the story of Maggie Trudeau's affair with Teddy Kennedy, which caused great consternation since he was considering a presidential bid at the time.

We hired twenty new staff members for the weekly, bringing the full complement to seventy, plus fifty-three part-time contributors. The big catches were Rod McQueen, who became business editor and Angelo Sgabellone, who reactivated the art department. I wrote a sixty-page manual setting out our intentions: "My hope is that *Maclean's* will become a national sounding board, recording in print the events that shape our history and give Canada its sense of continuity, a way of defining our collective and individual lives, fifty-two times a year." The statistics were impressive. Because of the increased frequency, our annual distribution of subscribers' copies had moved from nine million when I arrived to thirty-three million when we went weekly, which made us a force in determining the national agenda. Most important, we could print a thirty-two-page news colour form to meet a Sunday midnight deadline, only twelve hours before we went on sale at the newsstands.

Coming out of the blocks, we stumbled. Our first weekly cover, based on Pierre Trudeau's suddenly finding himself in a political trap, was a fine Roy Peterson caricature of the prime minister as a cornered rat. The cover was the only part of the magazine ruled over by the joint jurisdiction of the editor and publisher, and Lloyd Hodgkinson used his prerogative on that occasion to move the controversial Trudeau cartoon off the cover and run with Bob Lewis's story. We quickly substituted photographs of Egypt's President Anwar Sadat and Israel's Premier Menachem Begin, who were meeting that weekend at Camp David on the vital West Bank issue, which appeared close to solution. But the main story of our launch became the killed cover. John Gault resigned over the issue but nobody followed him. In fact, Walter Stewart wrote a letter to the *Globe* defending *Maclean's*, which had been attacked for kowtowing to the government that had enacted the legislation that allowed us to become a newsmagazine. As Stewart (the author of a hostile Trudeau biography) pointed out, we owed Trudeau nothing except tough-but-fair coverage, and that was exactly what he got. I sided with the staff but also recognized the right of the publisher to change covers. The crisis was resolved at a well-attended launch party the next day, when Lloyd began the ensuing press conference by unexpectedly planting a kiss on my lips. I can still feel the tickle of his moustache and I didn't go back for seconds, but the issue was effectively defused.

EDITING *MACLEAN'S* and keeping up the steady stream of books tested my stamina. To save time, I used my electric shaver while driving to the office; instead of answering my magazine mail daily, my secretary bunched the letters by subject and they were answered in three marathon dictating sessions every week; I set my wristwatch wake-up alarm during the day at fifteen-minutes intervals, so that I had an excuse to cut off overlong interviews, claiming other appointments, which was usually the case; I seldom took a phone call at home or in the office without at the same time reading a manuscript or book excerpt; even on summer weekends aboard my sailboat (where I had desk, chair, typewriter and eventually a portable fax machine) I seldom stopped beavering away at my projects.

It was a stupid, debilitating life. But the honours poured in, motivating me to ever-tighter schedules. In 1971 the CBC–TV series *The Tenth Decade*, which I had co-written, won the coveted Michener Award for Journalism, and only two years later another national documentary of mine, *The Days Before Yesterday: Struggle for Nationhood* went on the air. That year I also received the first of my seven honorary university doctorates and published *Home Country*, my personal favourite among my books. I had two other volumes on the paperback bestseller lists at the same time. I flew off to Bonn for a quickie interview with German Chancellor Willy

Brandt, which was tough because it was conducted in German and he lapsed into a local dialect I could barely comprehend. The following year I collected the President's Medal awarded by the University of Western Ontario for the magazine article of the year (on Pierre Trudeau's fall from grace). I was invited to join the Governing Council of the University of Toronto and gave a lecture to the morning assembly at Upper Canada College (without once mentioning my enviable record in the dormitory circle jerks). In the summer of 1973 I attended the wedding of Brian and Mila Mulroney in the Mount Stephen Club in Montreal. The following year Pierre Trudeau offered me the chairmanship of the Canadian Broadcasting Corporation, which I gratefully turned down.

The most unexpected call was from Encyclopaedia Britannica, announcing that I had just been chosen the 1978 recipient of their Achievement in Life Award. Since I was barely forty-eight at the time, I figured it was some kind of marketing gimmick. But sure enough they flew me to a lavish banquet at the Mid-America Club in Chicago, where I sat at the head table between my fellow honourees, the Hollywood actress Ellen Burstyn and Dr. Hans Selye, director of the Institute of Experimental Medicine at McGill University, the leading guru on the psychology of stress and another former middle European. We received fancy medals and an embossed set of encyclopedias. I capped off the decade in 1979 when I went to Ottawa with Ashley to be named an Officer of the Order of Canada, along with Donald Sutherland and Alfred Casson.

At the actual presentation of the medal, the recipient customarily exchanges a few private words with the governor general and moves on. Ed Schreyer, a former NDP premier of Manitoba, who then occupied the vice-regal office, was one of Pierre Trudeau's more surprising appointments. The last time I had seen Schreyer was in Winnipeg when he was still premier, at a lengthy and rather liquid dinner at Dubrovnik, then the city's best restaurant. Speaking off the record, Schreyer complained that he had taken a wrong turn in Canadian politics, because if he had been a Liberal, the party would have looked after him when he retired or was thrown out of office. Having just recently returned from Chicago, I tried to console him by suggesting he might sell Britannicas at Portage and Main. I hadn't seen him since, but here he was, dressed up like a Gilbert and Sullivan potentate, and I couldn't resist. "Hey, man," I whispered as he hung the coveted medal around my neck. "You did okay!" He bowed slightly to disguise his regal wink.[7]

I finally realized that the orgy of awards had got out of hand when I received a letter from His Serene Highness Prince Ernst August of Lippe (Lippe was an independent mid-European principality between 1720 and 1918), naming me one of his Chevaliers. He awarded me the Order of the Rose, its citation praising me for "the truth inherent in your written presentations, all appreciated by His Serene Highness." I tried to persuade him to become a Canadian book reviewer, but I somehow doubted if I could get the staff to call me "Chevalier Newman." I was damn sure they would never refer to me as "His Serene Highness."

BY THE WINTER OF 1982, the magazine was on a solid footing. But I was in the process of turning into exactly what I had feared I would become: an administrator. When I had arrived I'd made an informal deal with Lloyd Hodgkinson: we would both leave *Maclean's* the year after the magazine earned a net profit of at least $1 million. That had now happened. Michael Levine had meanwhile negotiated my Penguin contract for the Hudson's Bay

---

[7] The musical highlight of the decade was hosting a touring Stan Kenton for lunch at the fifty-fourth floor restaurant in the Toronto-Dominion Centre. Nobody recognized him: the bums. That weekend my band played a benefit at a banquet of the Writers' Development Trust, attended by Margaret Atwood, Pierre Berton, W.O. Mitchell, and Leonard Cohen. To my surprise, Leonard enjoyed The Bouncing Czechs but wouldn't agree to cut a record with us. I later advised him, musician to musician, that he could improve his singing if he recorded his songs at 33 rpm and played them at 45 rpm, to speed up his delivery. "We have to talk . . ." he told me, but I never heard from him again.

histories, giving me an escape hatch. It was time to hoist anchor. Lloyd left a couple of years after me.

I had my successor in place (or so I thought), having worked successfully and pleasantly with Rod McQueen. McQueen had once served as a speechwriter for Robert Stanfield, but more recently he had been a fine business editor at *Maclean's* and had evolved into a capable and dependable managing editor as well. We did have some personnel problems with the firing of half a dozen junior staff; I took full responsibility for this, but he undeservedly got the blame.

The final issue I took up with the staff was my abhorrence of unattributed quotes, which had sprung up in every section of the magazine like a plague of dandelions. My memo summed up my position: "I am firmly opposed to their use and ask that you avoid them. Canadians have a more strongly developed sense of fairness than Americans; they do not want to see public figures condemned (or praised) by critics (or admirers) not courageous enough to put their names beside their opinions. As well, without having to attach a name to the quotes they use, journalists can put their own emotions and ideas into the mouths of nonexistent unnamed sources. Neither do I believe they are necessary to good reporting. We can make the same point as strongly by using a straight expository style, which strikes me as being much more open and free of potential abuse."

My decision raised a firestorm of protest, which confirmed my suspicion that too many of our writers had resorted to making up quotes whenever they were stuck for comment, or wanted to express their own views. The fuss reminded me of how difficult (and out of character) my impersonation of "Captain Canada" had turned out to be. I also found myself becoming a commodity in the sense that anything I did (or didn't do) was news. The absurdity of it all struck me most forcefully in the public speculation about the sand in an executive sandbox I had acquired at Expo 67 and used at home as a coffee table. There were four published versions of its origin: 1) that I had flown the sand in from the garden of my home town in Czechoslovakia; 2) that I had brought it back from the Sinai Desert when I wrote my series on Israel; 3) that I had gathered it on the beaches of Dieppe in memory of the Canadian troops killed there; 4) that it was from a beach in the Bay of Quinte where I had run my yacht aground. In fact, I had bought it at a Hamilton gravel pit.

I realized that being editor of *Maclean's* had not been a hallucination exactly, but was certainly the kind of intense experience that seemed unreal in retrospect, or at least divorced from my vision of myself. When I took on the job I had a clear idea of what I wanted to do: publish the best writers and illustrators, create a good working atmosphere, pay fair wages, and in the process revive a Canadian institution that was dangerously close to expiring. The doing of it turned out to be difficult beyond anything I had imagined. It was possible to keep the ship from sinking only because a group of loyal and like-minded people invested themselves, body and soul, in the enterprise. Their names are mentioned in this chapter. While I was not the all-wise manager I had hoped to be or should have been, I believe that I gave our writers and editors more encouragement, more breathing space, and more stylistic licence than any other mass media voice in the country.

My efforts in that respect were bolstered by the enlightened attitudes of Lloyd Hodgkinson, Don Campbell, and their predecessors, Floyd Chalmers, and Messrs. Maclean and Hunter. Unlike most publishers and proprietors, they never pushed their personal agendas, which is the dominant motivation of most of their peers and the reason they're in the media instead of something that makes real money, like selling pork bellies or running video arcades. I'm still astounded that a company as enlightened as Maclean Hunter ever existed. On December 14, 1994, after the company was sold to Ted Rogers (who has so far maintained its tradition), there was a final meeting of the Maclean Hunter board to which its former members were invited. My indelible memory of that occasion is of Don Campbell, the former bomber pilot, closing the meeting, silently looking around the ornate dining room, holding on to the lectern as if it were a lifeboat, then bursting into tears.

My departure happened to coincide with the certification of a union, the Southern Ontario Newspaper Guild, at *Maclean's* which took management (myself included) by surprise. I handed in my notice at the same time, and there was inevitable speculation as to whether the two events were connected. They were not, as the text of my resignation letter to Lloyd Hodgkinson emphasized:

When you asked me to join the magazine in 1971, it was to help revive a dormant monthly publication with a staff of less than a dozen people, revenues of less than $2 million, and no great odds of survival. Now, eleven years later, *Maclean's* is a vibrant publishing entity with a full-time staff of seventy and solid profits on revenues of $30 million. Our readership is nudging 2.5 million a week and the magazine has never been financially healthier.

There will be the inevitable speculation that I have chosen this particular time to resign because of the unionization underway at *Maclean's*. I have no problem in dealing with unions, having been editor in chief of the *Toronto Star*, which has the strongest Guild in the country. My reasons for departure are not hard to discern. I have during the past couple of decades published seven books and I am currently in the process of completing my biography of Conrad Black, as well as beginning extended research for my multi-volume study of the Hudson's Bay Company. It simply isn't possible to continue the overloaded schedule of attempting to complete these projects while carrying on as editor of the magazine, especially now that I feel my original mandate has been fulfilled. I was a writer before I became an editor, and I am returning to what I enjoy doing most.

The last day in my office I found the memo I had written to myself when I first arrived and felt bemused tenderness for that naive and innocent much younger me, determined to turn *Maclean's* into a literary bullhorn that would provoke a response in the country at large. I suppose we did create an echo, faint as it was – and who could ask for more than that? I was left with shards of memories, and I was glad that I was leaving – as were most of the staff.

Valerie Chrysdale, who was editorial comptroller of the magazine and probably knew the staff better than anyone, caught *Maclean's* downside: "There was something dark about the newsmagazine format itself, a darkness and heaviness, a negativity that reared its ugly head, again and again. Probably it was due to the magazine being staffed by writers who tended to be highly introverted and weren't use to communicating with each other or even themselves. If there were problems, nobody had it out and released the tension, so that it was always there."

In the first draft of my final editorial I wrote that "sometimes the staff functioned with the precision of a crew of an attacking submarine. At other times, I wondered how I came to be presiding over Canadian journalism's most elaborate day-care centre." I was persuaded to drop that reference, but I stand behind it. Maybe I should have gone with the salute to his staff made by Graydon Carter, editor of *Vanity Fair*: "I don't run a magazine. I run an opera company." Instead, I concluded my valedictory: "It has been a joy giving magazine reporters the chance to practise a new style of uncompromising journalism – an approach to reporting that attempts to make sense of the moments that endow history with its excitement and meaning."

Jane O'Hara attacked my stewardship in the *Globe*, and a bitter chorus of "Ding, Dong, the Witch is Dead," led by Arlene Arnason, chief of the research department, was heard in the office, but there was little backlash over my departure. Angela Ferrante reminisced: "Isn't it wonderful that we cared enough to have all those rousing fights and accused each other of all sorts of horrific things, all in the name of trying to generate some good journalism?" A note came in from Elaine Dewar, who later published some epic books: "Did I ever say thank-you for giving me the opportunity to make my career and find my voice? Probably not. That's a lot to owe to anyone." Most welcome was an unsigned editorial in *La Presse*, which summed up my stewardship as having produced a magazine which "for the first time demonstrated that there was a very active and interesting English-speaking society in Canada."

Lloyd appointed not Rod McQueen but Kevin Doyle as my successor. "Under Newman," summed up Val Ross, the crack feature writer who served under both regimes, "we were like Beirut, there was warfare but it was wide open and anything could happen; under Doyle we were more like Poland. It was much more rigid, with many rules and much grayer." Later she wrote in the *Globe and Mail*: "Nine years ago, I worked for Peter C. Newman, when he was editor of *Maclean's* magazine. We were afraid of him then — he had a habit of stealthy approach that journalists found unnerving, even sinister in a boss. Yet recently, at a party that included former *Maclean's* colleagues, I found myself saying that I missed him. The colleagues, to my own astonishment, agreed. 'He had a vision of the country,' they said. 'He had an ear; he had an eye.'"

CHAPTER FOURTEEN

BLACK MAGIC

How Conrad Became a
Weapon of Mass Self-Destruction.

I was in the living room, watching Lord Black of Crossharbour slowly dying on my television set. It was mid February 2004 and I was tuned in to the court hearings in Wilmington, Delaware, that would determine his future as a press lord, mover of markets, coiner of words, and dropper of names.

As soon as I caught sight of him, shuffling past the television cameras, I knew it was game over. Watching that magnificent trickster, once known simply as Conrad, whom I had crowned as "The Establishment Man" three decades earlier in my book of the same title, I realized that he had changed. His Lordship no longer walked with that loping stride of entitlement that until so recently had marked his passage across boardrooms and croquet fields. Black loved croquet, his only sport, which he once described as being played ideally on summer evenings by the glow of Chinese lanterns, like a Monet painting with the women in their long lace dresses and the men in their wing collars, batting away.

I adjusted my TV set, even banged it with my fist, but instead of lace dresses and wing collars, all I saw was a fugitive trying to hide from himself. I had always found Black's eyes to be his most compelling physical feature. During my fifty or so interviews with him over the past three decades, I had discovered that whenever he became bored with my questions, his gaze went as blank as that of a Vegas croupier. But when I brought up something he didn't like, his eyes would glint with Cromwellian intensity. Their colour was a matter of minor dispute. "I think they're hazel. I'm not sure," he told me, immediately expanding a simple statement into pedantic historical irrelevancy. "Even Sir Neville Henderson, the British ambassador in Berlin, in his memoirs refers to Adolf Hitler's eyes as being surprisingly blue, so blue one could become quite lyrical about them if one were a woman. Hitler, of course, had brown eyes. And Henderson's embassy wasn't very successful, in any case." Black, of course, has eyes that are gunmetal grey.

Except just then, in his hour of humiliation, he seemed to have no eyes at all, just a clenched slit near the top of his face, as though he were squinting through the gun turret of a tank. While answering reporters' questions, his face loomed up on my screen, bloated, and somehow lacking its characteristic bulldog definition. I expected him to sprinkle the scene outside the courtroom with some of those tedious and protracted bon mots that, during his twenty years in England, had provoked Mary Soames's cruel quip that he had become "the biggest bore unhung." (Mary Soames comes by her wit honestly; she is Sir Winston Churchill's daughter.) Instead of witticisms, Black now merely kept repeating that "there was no evidence of any impropriety." But his voice was off pitch somehow. I realized he was too upset to filter out his condescension when talking to the reporters he had always resented. On more lucid days, he had described them as "hacks toiling through a miasma of mounting decrepitude." During a 1992 editorial strike at *Le Soleil*, his Quebec City daily, he had boldly decreed that it was "one of the great myths of the industry that you need journalists to produce a newspaper."

But on this day much larger issues were in train. The scaffolding that held up Conrad Black's good name (and credit rating) would begin to collapse during the three days of testimony. This trial in a faraway place (in the heart of America's corporate governance country) could destroy Black's mystique once and for all. Its logical fallout would most likely imprint his name on the other side of the ledger, not as a business genius but as a disgraced financier, who had a way with words.

Delaware is a state where anyone can incorporate a company overnight via the Internet for $400. But it also produced a learned and gutsy judge named Leo Strine, who proved to be Conrad's match. Watching the press lord hyperventilate as he awaited his court appearance, the title of the Hollywood blockbuster *Blackhawk Down* kept running through my mind. Hawks are magnificent birds of prey, elusive, hovering creatures that obey their own laws, and this particular hawk (like the helicopter in the film) was down for the count.

It was difficult to believe that less than half a decade earlier Black had been the proud proprietor of the world's third-largest publishing empire, with five hundred newspapers and magazines spreading his word to nearly six million daily and weekly readers, in the process earning annual revenues of $3 billion, with profits rolling in at the rate of $1 million every two days. But over the past year he had been accused by the directors of his own operating company of looting its treasury, and was soon to be accused of having been "engaged in a pattern of racketeering activities" for which a penalty of $1.2 billion was sought. Under the Racketeer Influenced and Corrupt Organization (RICO) statute – originally drawn up in 1970 to deal with such Mafia figures as Sammy "The Bull" Gravano and John Gotti, the New York Cosa Nostra kingpin – the law provides for a tripling of damages to the guilty, which was here specifically aimed at Black's alleged devil-may-care spending of corporate funds. "He used Hollinger as a cash cow to be milked of every possible drop of cash, often in a manner evidencing complete disregard for the rights of all shareholders," stated the investigation of his record, sponsored by his own board of directors. "He engaged in a wide range of criminal acts spanning many years, including mail and wire fraud, interstate transportation of stolen property and money laundering." According to the allegations contained in the motion, Black and his immediate circle had "unlawfully diverted" 72 per cent of Hollinger's net income (US$380 million) to themselves. That compared with the more reasonable management fees of 4.4 per cent of net income on the *New York Times* and 1.8 per cent on the *Washington Post*, and included such fripperies as spending $130,000 to refurbish Conrad's 1958 Silver Wraith Rolls and his wife Barbara Amiel's tip to the doorman at Bergdorf-Goodman, the luxury New York department store — both expensed to company accounts.

The sandstorm of suits and countersuits that accompanied all of these manoeuvres will put several generations of lawyers' offspring through Ivy League universities, but will achieve little else. No meeting ground was possible when a company accused its founding chairman, CEO, and controlling shareholder of misappropriation on a grand scale, and when Black simultaneously launched a countersuit against his own board for $850 million — to monetize his claim that his hand-picked directors had defamed him, making him, as he claimed, "a loathsome object." In one of the ironic twists in this case that borders on comedy, on May 14, 2004, Black launched yet another suit in Delaware to force Hollinger directors to pay the legal fees for his suit against them.

No one could emerge unscathed from this corporate stalemate made in hell. The pressure on Black grew so intense that when approached by *The Sunday Times* for a brief interview, he lost his command of obscure words and spat out, "No dice. You people have fucked me over too much already." Not one of Conrad's usual witty epigrams.

Once on the witness stand in Delaware, the Establishment Man was plainly not himself. Instead of bluster there was blubber. "I have been horribly defamed, characterized, and stigmatized as an embezzler," he pleaded. "I am trying, apart from the direct legal proceeding, to retrieve my reputation as an honest man." Hunching his shoulders against the hail of accusations, he grew hesitant when asked substantive questions. Where, one of the opposing lawyers demanded, were the documents concerning the sale of newspaper assets from Hollinger to American Publishing, one of Black's private companies? Why had that transaction not been submitted for board approval? That flip – and the many that followed – had yielded Conrad and his immediate pals a neat US$148 million, tax-free, in the form of non-compete clauses. It was the ultimate Black gambit: to collect bonuses for not competing with himself. So, where were the documents?

"I'm not sure," was all that Black could muster.

Gordon Paris, a Black appointee who had taken over the chairmanship after the Hollinger operating board fired Conrad with an unceremonious Saturday morning phone call, in court characterized his predecessor as "an unworthy schemer and bully" who had terrorized the board, at one point announcing he would fire them all if they didn't do his bidding. Rough treatment under any circumstances, but in this case bizarre, because the directors had been executing his bidding all too well. They were, after all, his *consiglieri*, the good old boys who, over the preceding two decades, had rubber-stamped his every request.

This was a male bonding movie gone terminally sour.

Under mounting pressure from minority shareholders, in May 2003 the directors had hired Richard Breeden to head an internal committee charged with investigating Black's transactions. If corporate governance in the United States has a raging bull, it is Dick Breeden, a Harvard Law School grad who had advised presidents Reagan, Bush (the smarter one), and Clinton on the issue, and later served as a tough and effective chairman of the Securities and Exchange Commission. During his tenure, 1,200 enforcement actions were successfully initiated, and he had just come off restructuring WorldCom Inc., the high-tech firm that could boast of having perpetrated the largest corporate fraud in American history. Now Breeden was describing to the Delaware courtroom what he thought Black would do if he were allowed to go through with his attempt to sell the firm's assets out from under its own operating board (and minority shareholders) to Sir David and Sir

Frederick Barclay, a pair of obsessively secretive British entrepreneurs who had built a Gothic castle on their own (tax-free) island in the English Channel. If it succeeded, the backstairs ploy would put immediate cash into His Lordship's jeans, plus the US$10 million bonus he was privately promised by the Barclays for clinching the deal. "About thirty seconds after I heard about the offer," Breeden declared under oath, "I thought that Lord Black could hide the money in Beirut or the Outer Hebrides." Breeden went on to attest to Black's version of corporate governance: "He threatened the board on many occasions. At one meeting he said that he knew where [Hollinger board member] Ray Seitz's property was in the U.K. and that he would have it taken away from him, then issued the same threat to Graham Savage [a distinguished Toronto director recently appointed by Black]. He said that he would fix their wagon good, though he didn't use those exact words."

When Breeden's initial report charged Black and his partner David Radler with receiving unauthorized and unreported non-compete payments of $32 million from Hollinger, Black refused to return the money, unlike Radler. Instead, he countersued the former SEC chairman, which might turn out to have been his most self-destructive move of all. You don't threaten Dick Breeden, who immediately escalated the legal jihad.

Judge Strine's verdict that historic day in Delaware was pure censure, leaving our hero flopping around on a hot dock like a hooked and landed barracuda. In terms of Black's pride, perhaps the most painful comment came on page 108 of the judgment, when Strine described Black's defence as "frivolous" and confessed that the press lord's evidence did not "tug at his heartstrings." The judge called Black's statements "evasive and unreliable . . . lacking the ring of truth." Concerning the sale to the Barclay brothers, the judge flatly disallowed Black's desperate manoeuvre and labelled him a deceitful bully.

Strine's condemnation, spread over 129 closely reasoned pages, lacked nothing except any hint of ambiguity. His message was brutally clear: Lord Black of Crossharbour, Thesaurus Rex, Defender of the Divine Right of Things, Master of the Non-Compete Clause, was toast. In fact, Black was fortunate that his trial took place in 2004. Delaware was the last state in the union to abolish whipping as a court-imposed punishment; its whipping posts didn't come down until 1972.

For all his wit and bravado, Conrad Black had become a weapon of mass self-destruction.

That was the day the music died for Canada's poster boy tycoon, and some of it died within me, because I was there at the creation. He wove his own legend, knitted his superego all by his lonesome, but I was his original myth-maker, the scribbler who sat with him for a decade recording all those convoluted words and labyrinthine thoughts that added up to the Legend of Conrad Black.

WE FIRST MET when he returned to Toronto from Montreal in 1974. Black was twenty-nine, had earned a law degree from Laval, had written an unusually perceptive master's thesis on Quebec premier Maurice Duplessis, and, with his partners Peter White and David Radler, had purchased the *Sherbrooke Daily Record* for $20,000. At the time I was working on my first volume of *The Canadian Establishment*, but I had mentioned him only once, in passing, as "an interesting new boy." He was socially awkward, dressed like a disc jockey at a classical music station (conservative but uncoordinated), and carried himself gingerly, as though constantly crossing ponds of freshly formed ice. He spoke a form of convoluted English I had never heard before but I assumed dated back at least to the Duke of Wellington. His wit and erudition, his rhetorical pyrotechnics, are what first attracted me to him. I was mesmerized by his encyclopaedic brain and photographic memory.

John Finlay, one of Conrad's associates, recalled a dinner they had at Toronto's York Club with Pierre Gousseland, the French-born chairman of Amax, a giant U.S. metal-extracting firm. "Conrad absolutely dazzled him," said Finlay, "by going through

France's five republics in perfectly fluent French, not just by dates but by individual ministers, their accomplishments and downfalls. This fellow just sat back and listened, spellbound. But after dinner Gousseland had to leave, and we withdrew to the club's drawing room with an Englishman who was the Amax senior vice-president of finance. When it turned out he had served aboard a Royal Navy battle cruiser, Conrad started to go through the British fleet, gun by gun, inch by inch. They were talking about a particularly tense period during the Second World War, and Conrad asked him, 'Where were you when that took place?' The Englishman said, 'August 1943? I can't remember.' So Conrad asked him, 'What ship were you serving on?' As soon as he found out it had been HMS Renown, Black shrugged and said, 'Oh well, you must have been stationed in Gibraltar.' The fellow just wilted."

Even when there were just two of us at his home or office, he would act out his answers to my questions, rising in his seat to imitate Charles de Gaulle or Napoleon Bonaparte, his favourite role models. "I have always felt," he told me at the time, "it was the compulsive element in Napoleon that drew him into greater and greater undertakings, until he was bound to fail." The foreshadowing was lost on me at the time.

Interviewing Black on and off for most of three decades, I found that his pomposity grew tiresome, so I began to play a game with myself. I kept asking him how he enjoyed air travel, expecting that one day he would describe the shuttle between Toronto and Montreal as something like "a miracle of heavier-than-air locomotion." (He didn't, mainly, I suspect, because he never flew commercially.) He reeled in his sentences as if they were hooked swordfish dancing on the surface of the sea, making up words ("dowagerish"); honing his outdated insults ("I warn you, this man is an insufferable poltroon"); and coining epigrams. Former Ontario premier David Peterson once described taking the French edition of Black's Duplessis biography on a holiday with him to brush up on his bilingualism. Although he was fluent in the language, he had to buy a French dictionary to look up Conrad's arcane choice of words, and then had to purchase an English dictionary to see what they meant.[1]

Having studied the man at close range, it seemed to me that most of Black's verbal excursions into baroque dialogue were strictly play-acting. I remember in particular having a conversation with his then wife, Shirley, when we were alone for half an hour or so while he took a phone call. She asked me why Conrad spent so much time "acting out his own script of how a great man ought to live and talk. Everything he says when he's being interviewed or at a dinner party with people of influence is quotable. But when we're alone, he's much more likely to say things like, 'Let's go and get a pizza.'" It was a revealing comment, confirming my suspicion that Conrad had missed his calling. He was one of the great ham actors of our time and ought to have been cast as a James Bond villain out to dominate the world, with a trombone choir announcing his entrances and exits. In retrospect, I realize he was attempting to create a form of immunity, digging a protective moat filled with beehives of words to guard his inner self. As an amateur historian he realized the importance of generating that quality of remoteness which sets any society's memorable figures apart from the lesser orders. When I first began to probe his psyche, the barely concealed symptoms of his neurosis were hard to miss: he described his late twenties and early thirties as having been afflicted with "diffuse, paralyzing, strangling anxiety attacks, night sweats and bouts of obsessive terror." Luckily we met after he had stopped carrying a barf bag around with him, to mitigate his fear of sudden nausea.[2]

---

[1] When Black was asked about Calgary Bishop Frederick Henry's criticism of his treatment of the *Herald*'s striking workers, he shot back: "If your jumped-up little twerp of a bishop thinks I am not a very good Catholic, I think he's a prime candidate for exorcism." Not the usual patois of the confessional.

[2] A considerable chunk of text was removed from Conrad Black's autobiography on the advice of his publisher and his lawyer, who thought that the details of his psychiatric treatment were too revealing.

Conrad began to acquire a small literary reputation when I introduced him to Jack McClelland, recommending that he turn Conrad's thesis on Duplessis into a book, which he did. He also started to squire around town some strikingly attractive women, none more exotic than Anna-Maria Marston. Born in Brazil of wealthy Italian parents and recently divorced, she was a charter member of what the *Toronto Star*'s Lynda Hurst dubbed Canada's "Concorde Crowd, who sunbathe in Cuernavaca, ski in Klosters, visit friends in Palm Beach, and wouldn't dream of not popping in to see Roloff [Beny] in Rome." The former curator of the Henry Birks collection of antique silver, Marston enjoyed a highly visible aristocratic lifestyle, maintaining that "Toronto isn't Rio, it doesn't have the same tradition of servants." (Talk about foreshadowing.)

I would like to report that I instantly recognized in Conrad the seeds of self-destruction. I didn't. What attracted me was the smell of a great yarn that would require a dedicated storyteller. I identified, perhaps subliminally, a sense of destiny in him, the potential to be a pivotal and dramatic figure when he grew up. I thought he was worth a book because the existential streak in his nature might lead him to the wilder shores of the corporate world, where he would triumph, or destroy himself.

I decided to stay in regular touch with him, first at the nondescript office he maintained at the boutique Toronto brokerage Draper Dobie, and later when he was given a desk at Dominion Securities. For most of seven years, we met every two months or so after my shift at *Maclean's* when I would debrief him about the state of the business establishment's current shenanigans and his own, increasingly bold initiatives. He would have impressed Machiavelli with his pointed attempts to soften up the players then in charge of Argus Corporation, the predecessor company to Hollinger. He prepared himself, like a heavyweight boxer in training for his prize bout.

OF THE FIFTY OR SO interview subjects I spoke to during my research for *The Establishment Man*, none was more interesting than George Montegu Black, Conrad's father. A graduate in French and English literature from the University of Manitoba, he married into the Riley family (after a six-year engagement), which placed him at the summit of Winnipeg society, his wife's father having been part of the original syndicate that financed London's *Telegraph*. He became an accountant and spent the Second World War in Ottawa, running Canadian Propellers Ltd., the only Crown corporation to show a profit. There he attracted the attention of E.P. Taylor, then the head of Argus Corporation and planning his postwar expansion into the brewing industry. Duly hired as president of Canadian Breweries, Black increased productivity by 25 per cent a year and successfully invaded the American market.

Despite his success, his relationship with Taylor grew increasingly troubled. One source of that tension was Black's prodigious dexterity with figures. He could multiply two six-digit figures in his head and instantly come up with the correct sum, down to two decimal points. At board meetings, Taylor kept testing him: "What percentage is that, George?" he would ask, and when Black snapped back with "12.36 per cent," Taylor would call in an accountant with a calculator to check the answer. It was always right. That annoyed Taylor no end, as did Black's reorganization of the company. By the mid 1950s he had so decentralized its operations and delegated so much of his own authority that he spent only from two to four o'clock in the afternoons at the office. Under his hands-off management technique, Canadian Breweries continued to prosper in North America, though the overall results were being dragged down by Taylor's territorial ambition to take his company into the hotly competitive British market (designed to earn him a peerage). During a strike, Black refused to settle. "If you don't turn around and snarl at these guys," he warned Taylor, "they'll cut you to pieces." But Taylor caved in and fired Black. From the age of forty-seven he was on his own, though he maintained his

22.4 per cent interest in Ravelston, the private holding company that controlled Argus.

Tall and ungainly (he had grown twelve inches in one year during a childhood illness), the older Black spent the last two decades of his life in his study, participating in no diversions except smoking (often two cigarettes at a time) and ringing the miniature St. Bernard's bell that summoned his Spanish butler, Fernando Aranda, who refilled his martini jug, often until dawn. He lived for his nightly seminars with Conrad, devoting his declining energies and failing eyesight, to one life-sustaining purpose: teaching his younger son the fundamentals of the market economy, and explaining how stock-value fluctuations can be exploited. He instilled in his boy an appreciation for the relevance of historical perspective, and tutored him in the art of seeing through grownup deceptions. (He even demonstrated why gambling on any scale was wrong by installing a slot machine in the living room that was fixed never to pay off.) Significantly, he steeped Conrad in the lore of Argus, so that the boy became determined to eventually take over the rich but underperforming conglomerate.

These nocturnal sessions became the most significant formative influence of Conrad's life. His friend John Fraser remembers that "childhood was a prison for him. His head was practically splitting because he was so impatient to get out into the real world." Seldom has a son's career been dedicated with such single-mindedness to having the world acknowledge the worth of his father, which eventually prompted Conrad's takeover of Argus, and his banishment of the executives who had sided against Black the elder.

"Even then," recalled Laurier LaPierre, the historian who taught Conrad at Upper Canada College, "he was like a champion runner. I sometimes watch those contestants at the Olympics and find myself fascinated by the tension as they wait to spring into the pool or onto the running tracks. Conrad was like that, except that he seemed to know precisely when the starting gun would go off. His entire sense of life revolved around the idea that through a combination of circumstance, accidents, and evolution, God was granting him this extraordinary power that he must guard well and pass on. He always felt himself to be a genuine instrument of history, with the capacity to create events."

The defining event of Black's time at Upper Canada College was the oft-told tale (revealed in print for the first time in my book) of his expulsion. Along with two accomplices he had broken into the principal's office and stolen copies of the year's final examinations, which he copied on the Argus Xerox, then sold to his fellow students. He turned a profit of $5,000 but was caught and unceremoniously asked to leave. When the plot was revealed and those who had purchased the exam papers had to write a tougher set, they planted his burning effigy on the front lawn of the Black residence and cursed him whenever he appeared. Conrad was not amused: "As I was walking out the gates a number of students who literally hours before had been begging for assistance, one of them on his knees − were now shaking their fists at me and shouting words of moralistic execration after me. I've never forgotten how cowardly and greedy people can be." Conrad's father was highly exercised by the incident, blaming the school, and basing the defence of his son on the highly dubious contention that "cheating has always been common in schools, but nobody had thought to put it on a commercial basis until Conrad came along."[3]

The event itself, and Black's reaction, were a curious foreshadowing of his destiny. At the time, he was living in a $1 million house in North York, being chauffeured to school in the family

---

[3] When Conrad and his friend John Fraser (who was at UCC with him, but had taken no part in the theft) went to the same summer camp, its motto was carved in a beam over the main dining room: "IN THE BOY IS SEEN THE MAN." Fraser recalls drawing Conrad's attention to the inscription in the context of what had just happened, but got no sign of recognition from his school chum that it might apply to him.

Cadillac and completing his homework on the way. He had no need for spending money. The exam papers caper was not primarily a money-making enterprise, nor was it meant as a protest against school discipline. He was just testing how far he could defy the odds, whether the gamble was worth the risk.

The biggest gamble was his daring 1978 takeover of Argus, multiplying the $7 million he had inherited from his family into control over corporate assets worth $8 billion, using tactics that I described as requiring "the balls of a canal horse." It took fifty pages of my book to describe the intricate details of how Black managed the deal, which came down to persuading the widows of its former owners, ladies who had been graceful Olympic figure skaters but had not the slightest idea what they were signing, as they later admitted, to support his takeover. It set a pattern. All of his significant acquisitions involved families whose great days were long gone: the Fields in Chicago, the Berrys in London, the Fairfax family in Australia, and the Southams in Canada. His empire was based on the senility of others and his own chutzpah. The positive side of his legacy is that he improved every major paper he bought, and the only one he started, the *National Post*, significantly uplifted the standards of Canadian journalism, particularly under its founding editor, Ken Whyte.

As for the others, the majority of his papers were small-town North American dailies that were run like sweatshops. The Black formula, worked out and implemented by his partner David Radler, was razor-edged. He would move into a likely property and count the newsroom desks, calculating how many reporters he could afford to fire (though he hadn't seen their faces yet) and still provide enough editorial matter to separate the ads. This resulted in small-town daily newspapers operating with Radler's legendary three-person news operation: an editor, a reporter, and a sportswriter, with the balance filled in by canned wire copy. This led to strange anomalies. For example, on February 11, 1978, when a Pacific Western Airlines jet crashed at Cranbrook, British Columbia, killing forty-three of those aboard, the Black-owned

Cranbrook *Daily Townsman* covered the tragedy mostly by using Canadian Press copy out of Toronto.

Whenever they took over a newspaper, Black and Radler would assign budgets to each department and audit their results; shift administrative functions to a central accounting office; replace obsolete presses and upgrade layouts; strike a deal with unions to cut staff positions; freeze salaries; eliminate expense accounts; centralize purchasing; and give the former owner/publisher a fancy title with no executive power. And that was it: new paper; new owner; double the profit.[4]

In the quarter-century after his Argus takeover, Black dazzled nearly everyone touched by his corporate legerdemain, a good Conrad word for taking rabbits out of apparently empty hats. No other Canadian businessman in memory had attracted so much attention. In his prime, Black exuded the aura of raw power. The young Black had a highly disquieting impact on almost everyone, even when he wasn't there. A fellow Bank of Commerce director described one executive committee meeting when Black's financial affairs were being discussed, so that he had to temporarily absent himself. "The boardroom reverberated with Conrad's absence," my informant recalled. During the autumn of 1997, when the moderator of the United Church speculated about Jesus Christ's divinity, hinting that he might not have been God, CTV's *Double Exposure* comedy team picked up the cue. "Great news," they chuckled. "Conrad's back in the running."

Black was overly infatuated with successfully tucking away ownership of the Argus group of companies (which he transformed into the even more complicated Hollinger organization). Commenting on the steel-trap grip he held over his business empire, he told a CBC-TV interviewer in the mid 1990s: "Short of

---

[4] Radler was so budget-conscious that when he was running the business side of the *Sherbrooke Daily Record* and an employee marched into his office with a list of grievances, he threw away the complaints, then charged the unhappy fellow two cents (deducted from his paycheque) for wasting a sheet of paper.

death, imprisonment, or demonstrable insanity, I'd say we were in a pretty good position."

His short list of political and business heroes illustrated his belief that history is determined not by mass movements but by the wilful acts of eccentric leaders, royal whim, and confluent intrigues. He had scant confidence in the perfectibility of man but aligned his path with authoritarian figures unafraid to proclaim the grandeur of their dreams: risk takers like him, who launched themselves against impossible odds and bet the farm. For most of his first six decades, he lived a charmed life, best caught by Michael Lewis, the American high-tech writer, who described Internet mogul Jim Clark as "the guy who always won the game of chicken because his opponents suspected he might actually enjoy a head-on collision." That was Conrad, until Dick Breeden pushed him right off the freeway.

MY VOLUME ON BLACK was published in 1982 to mostly favourable reviews, and soon overtook *Jane Fonda's Workout Book* at the top of the bestseller list. Several critics questioned my presumption in writing a full-scale biography of a thirty-seven-year-old, no matter how successful. Ken Adachi in the *Sunday Star* caught the book's flavour: "Given Newman's sardonic tone, this is a dismaying story. Black emerges as unpleasant and vulgar, manipulating other men on a plane of intuition and will power far above the reach of ordinary mortals."

The most revealing commentary was in a letter I received after publication from Conrad himself. He was not pleased. "What is particularly irritating is that it is not open season on me, but upon a largely fictitious image that you created for me," he wrote, "of a chillingly ruthless and rather conceited person, obsessed with materialism, pontificating endlessly, and viewing the world through the prism of a reactionary proprietor. In presenting a book ostensibly about me but which really tells the readers more about you and your fantasies, you have unintentionally inflicted more inconvenience upon me than you might imagine."

How could I have been so wrong?

The best part of the entire venture was its launch aboard HMCS *York*, Toronto's reserve naval division, where I served as a staff officer. The entertainment was supplied by my band, Peter Newman and his Bouncing Czechs, featuring me on drums. It was a case of Jack McClelland wanting cheap entertainment, but we gave "How High the Moon," and "Satin Doll" our best shot and improvised on "Establishment Man Blues," all the while being recorded for broadcast on the CBC's *The Journal*. We had a ball, with three parts of my life happily coming together.

HAVING ALREADY OWNED UP to inventing Conrad Black, I might as well confess that I was also chief midwife to the journalism career of his future wife and co-defendant, Barbara Amiel. In 1975, during my stint as editor of *Maclean's*, recognizing her talent, I rescued her from freelance hell and employed her as a feature writer and columnist for seven years. That was her first full-time writing job, and it provided a national launching pad for her fierce right-wing views, which I published because I believed, as she did, that freedom of expression means little unless eccentric views like hers can be aired and debated. It was due to my patronage that she moved from obscurity to prominence as the most articulate and opinionated Canadian polemicist of her generation.

I had been impressed by her freelance pieces for *Saturday Night* and occasional appearances on the CBC. While I abhorred her facile dismissal of the small-l liberalism that was my own ideological bent, I admired the nerve of her contrarian views and her penchant for ad hominem attacks. Despite my itchy fingers, I never changed a word or thought in any of her columns. She was a postfeminist polemicist for bizarre causes at a time when the word *neocon* had yet to be coined, but I thought she would introduce some badly needed controversy into the magazine's pages. Her first published article, "Let's Reinstate Debtors' Prison," set the tone. I recognized in her a classical libertarian — the sort of person who objects to such nanny-state interferences as being obligated to drive on the right side of the road, to allow human rights commissions to exist, and to pay taxes. I felt that a columnist unencumbered by conventional wisdom would provide the magazine with a counterweight to the prevailing orthodoxies of the day, and she did. Her essays found a ready if sometimes angry audience, and I never regretted the decision to hire her.

In fact, I actively defended her whenever the forces of political correctness came calling, such as the time I protected her against militant groups of irate German Canadians who demanded a retraction of her use of the word "Hun" to describe the Teutonic belligerents in two world wars. Since we had both lost family members to the Holocaust, she had my public and private support. But when I suggested that she might have avoided trouble if she had referred to them as "Sauer Krauts," she burst into tears. That was my first revelation about Ms. Amiel: she had less sense of humour than Stephen Harper – and none about herself.

While I treasured her shock value, she left me with the impression that her opinions were swallowed whole, undigested, to be defended with unsheathed claws instead of mental effort. I could never escape the feeling that, despite her claims to be a champion of unfettered freedom, she stood mainly for the greater glory of Barbara Amiel. This was an impression I shared with nearly all those who watched her scratch-and-gouge climb up the journo-celebrity ladder. "The reason she was so un-Canadian in certain ways is that she was so up front about her ambition," noted one of my senior editors at *Maclean's*, Angela Ferrante. "She was definitely not WASP. She was definitely not Establishment. She was a pusher and a grabber and an achiever – and that always throws Canadians off."

She was among the most difficult columnists *Maclean's* ever had in its stable, which takes in a lot of territory. In a pattern she was later to repeat at *The Times* of London and the *Daily Telegraph*, she was a misery for the editorial desk, a second-guesser of headline choices, a whining pest over each lost comma or adjective, and a drama queen who made a point of milking every situation for its maximum emotional impact. She was the ultimate deadline rusher, literally staggering into the office, one hand at her afflicted head, the other tremblingly clutching her manuscript, arriving on the last minute of the last hour of her due date, dropping it on her editor's desk in feigned relief.

What I didn't count on was the extent to which Barbara would use her striking appearance to further her career and how much her sensual presence would upset the office. I always knew when she was arriving because in those days the bullpen resounded with the loud *tip-tap* of typewriters, and I could hear them grow silent as she paraded through the rows of male writers to her cubicle. She was the sort of woman who kept spilling out of her dresses, then blamed the dresses. In her private life, she readily confessed that she had "run amok among many lives," but desperately wanted to be taken seriously for her professional attitude. She was often the enemy of her promise. You don't advertise your intellect by sashaying to work in thigh-high boots, a tight sweater tucked into tighter jeans held up by a heavy leather belt dripping with metal studs. She proclaimed that clothes were her "sexual armour," which didn't really justify her wardrobe, since it was a come-on instead of a deterrent.

"As a young editor there who she sort of liked but perceived as a leftie I was hardly her intimate," recalled my entertainment editor, Anne Collins, who later became publisher of Random House Canada. "Her marriage was breaking down and she was having a hard time writing. Whenever I asked her to back up her views she'd accuse me of trying to censor her. She was either a nervous wreck in a sweatsuit with lank hair and a codeine pain-killer habit, or an imperious beauty in a floor-length mink, stream-ing men behind her. I never knew which Amiel would show up in my office."

"I always liked Barbara at a very primary level," Robert Miller, one of the magazine's most talented cover-story writers, remi-nisced. "She would come into my office on a regular basis and ask for help with her leads. She would come up behind me and sort

CAPTAIN CANADA'S
FRIEND AND MASCOT
(*Maclean's*)

DEFENDING CANADA: Founding lunch of the Committee for an Independent Canada, with the Hon. Walter Gordon and Prof. Abe Rotstein. (*Toronto Star*)

Glory days at *Maclean's*. (*Maclean's*)

PETER C. NEWMAN (HOME·GROWN).

SMOKING OUT *TIME*: My fight to neutralize *Time*, which was masquerading as a Canadian magazine, made *Maclean's* possible as a weekly, and inspired this 1974 cartoon by Aislin a.k.a. Terry Mosher. (*Montreal Gazette*)

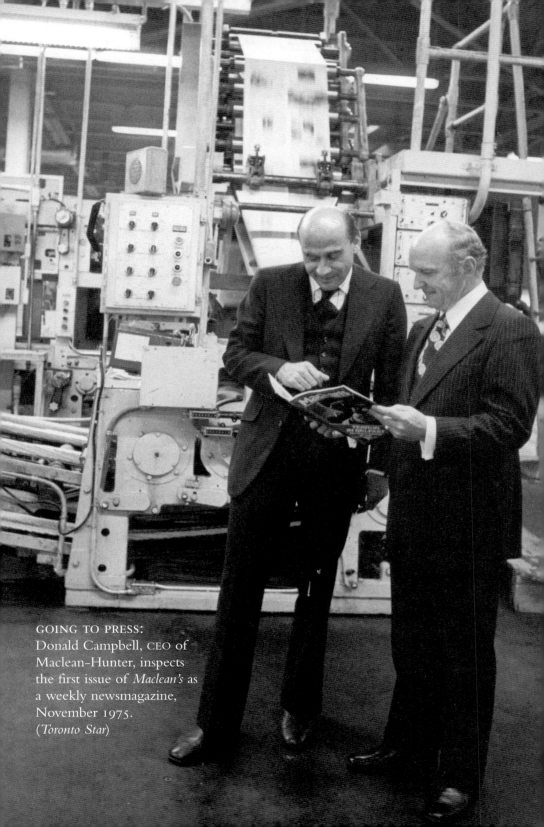

GOING TO PRESS:
Donald Campbell, CEO of
Maclean-Hunter, inspects
the first issue of *Maclean's* as
a weekly newsmagazine,
November 1975.
(*Toronto Star*)

RIDING THE WAVE: As *Maclean's* editor I arranged my office so that I looked directly at a large-scale map of Canada, meant to remind me that the country stretched beyond Toronto. For every out-of-town assignment I stuck a pin into the map. Likewise, our covers reflected the diversity of the country. (*Maclean's*)

HOT AND COLD TIMES WITH PIERRE TRUDEAU: I visit the Prime Minister's office to deliver the first copy of *Maclean's* as a newsweekly (1975). Later, in March, 1979, when his wife, Margaret, enjoys a hot weekend with the Rolling Stones, ("I wouldn't want *my* wife associatin' wiv us," said Charlie Watts) and *Maclean's* publishes exclusive pictures of the event, Monsieur Trudeau is not amused. (Donato, *Toronto Sun*)

PETER NEWMAN PLEASE!

BRIAN MULRONEY: Seen here with Mila and Jack McClelland, my publisher, at my 1977 wedding to Camilla Turner. They, along with Senator Keith Davey, stood up for me at my third wedding. Later I interviewed him in Baie Comeau the day after his 1988 election victory.

MY THIRD WIFE: The beautiful Camilla, who took my breath away. (*John Reeves*)

CHARLIE PACHTER'S PORTRAIT: Presented to me by Abe Rotstein on my fiftieth birthday, it captures my quest for new horizons. (*Charles Pachter*)

of lean over my chair, her right breast suitably settled on my left shoulder, and exhale this wonderful aroma of Jaffa orange groves. She was just a very heady, sexy person. I used to tell her, 'Barbara, we've got to stop doing this to each other. Why don't you go to the Holiday Inn across the street, take a room, have a bath and I'll be over in twenty minutes? And we won't tell the Austro-Hungarian Empire,' which was what I always called George Jonas, her husband. I liked her but never wanted to get any closer than that kind of banter, because I was a happily married man, one of perhaps four left in the whole country."

She had married George Jonas in 1973 and left him five years later, but he remained (and still is) a powerful influence on her life. I knew that because I used to have formal meetings with *Maclean's* editorial employees once a year to review their salaries and discuss their progress. Except Amiel. She insisted that her interests be represented by George, who was a poet, a motorcyclist (Yamaha 750), and a Hungarian, not necessarily in that order. All I knew about Hungarians was the joke that they would go into a revolving door behind you and come out ahead of you, and when George arrived to negotiate her pay packet it was an awesome spectacle. He would swagger into my office in full biker gear – encased in Russian-style boots and his imposing black leather from ankle to neck, gladiatorial helmet tucked under his arm. He was the world's only biker who smoked through a long, silver-tipped cigarette holder and preferred debating existentialism to comparing cam shafts. What Amiel never knew was that we were friends, would compare notes and kibitz around a bit, then, after feigning long and intense debates (because we both realized that she was waiting outside the door), would take twenty seconds to split Barbara's salary demand and my budgeted raise down the middle until the following year.

Fellow writers used to drop into my office to share her latest epigrams, like dispatches from the front. Somebody heard her confess brazenly that "Sex is no good without pain." Another report claimed that she poured eight spoons of sugar into her tea and announced, "If you want to get on, you must learn to frighten men," which she did. Senior writer Judith Timson described a memorable sunny July day in 1979, when Amiel sent the magazine's writers, celebrating a birthday, into a tizzy: "She had walked into the room, accepted a piece of birthday cake, and then promptly, before she could eat it, began retching, vomiting blood and bile into the nearest wastebasket. Typical of the Amiel curse, at least one staffer thought she had staged it." In a profile of Amiel she later wrote, Timson described the time Barbara was walking along Toronto's Bloor Street with a friend when a man passed by, smilingly acknowledging Barbara.

"Who was that?" the friend asked.

"I'm not sure," she replied, "but I think it was my first husband." (That would have been Gary Smith, whom she wooed for six years but left after seven months. Thirty years later, he still carried her picture in his wallet.)

Unlike the rest of us, Amiel felt compelled to act out her fantasies in public. Ross McLean, the iconic TV producer who had employed her at the CBC, felt "there was a studied quality in her. Every observation, every utterance, seemed to be preheated, plotted. Barbara had trouble being what she might call herself." Even in repose, she was always posing, playing the femme fatale in her own movie. While she kept insisting that it was her mind and not her body that merited attention, she was widely suspected of having acted as Mother Nature's little helper. I did my best to discourage the office cottage industry that specialized in monitoring her nose jobs (comparing minute replications of Beak One with Beak Two), but other parts of her anatomy were more prominently discussed. She airily dismissed any mention of implants with the quip, "If I used silicone, my breasts would be twice as big; I don't do things by halves." This testimony was calmly but authoritatively contradicted by one of her early suitors, who informed me, without being asked, that when he had gone out with her, "She had no British accent and no breasts."

Larry Zolf, the CBC's intellectual court jester, who went to university with Amiel, witnessed her transformation: "When I first met Barbara she was a funny, quirky Jewish lady of the Trotskyite persuasion hanging around University College at the University of Toronto. At the time, she had a well-off boyfriend reputed to have connections to organized crime. He bought her cashmere sweaters and skirts by the dozen. Then, ever so slowly, right before our very eyes, Friedrich Hayek's *The Road to Serfdom* replaced Trotsky's *Permanent Revolution*. Soon Barbara was University College's number-one conservative. Her conversion was accompanied by a nose bob and chest lift, which really made her look special."

In 1983, after I had departed *Maclean's*, Amiel left to become editor of the Toronto *Sun*, a lively tabloid that delighted in printing pictures of her. Christie Blatchford, who at the time was one of the paper's star columnists, vividly recalled the staff watching how Barbara walked from the library to her office at the other end of the newsroom in an open trench coat, under which could clearly be seen a black bustier, garter belt, and stockings. Many have speculated that Margaret Atwood immortalized Amiel by using her as the model for the opportunistic character of Zenia in *The Robber Bride*.

Amiel was a classic example of a woman whose looks made her vulnerable to false accusations. Doug Creighton, then publisher of the *Sun*, told me about an incident that occurred during a celebratory meal to announce her takeover from Peter Worthington, the paper's previous editorial director.

"On her first day as editor of the *Sun*, I took Barbara for lunch at Winston's," he recalled. "I was toasting her, telling her to be her own person, that there was nothing really scary about us, that we weren't going to go left wing or anything like that, and if there was something that she was trying to change which potentially was an embarrassment to me or the paper, she should call me. I kept telling her to just be herself and mentioned Worthington a few times."

"'Why do you keep mentioning Peter Worthington?' she asked.

"'Well, he was your predecessor, he hired you, and he trained you as editor. I'm just trying to say he's gone, that's done.'

"So she leaned back in the booth and said — just at the precise moment when everybody in the restaurant had stopped talking for a split second — 'You think I'm fucking him, don't you?'"

"'Jesus Christ, that wasn't what I was saying, but I suppose your question demands an answer, and I would say, yes.'"

"Well,' she said, 'I'm not.'

"'That's a great waste of journalistic effort,' was my reply, and I remember that the lawyer Fraser Elliott was sitting at the next table. He heard the question, but didn't hear her answer, and his eyes were just bugging out."

By 1984 Amiel had left the *Sun* and moved to London, where she married David Graham, a charming and handsome son of the Ottawa Valley, Harvard graduate, and wealthy owner of the United Kingdom's largest cable system. They tried unsuccessfully to have children, but the marriage didn't survive. The saddest scene of their breakup occurred when Barbara was living alone in a Chelsea townhouse and returned home from bicycling to find one of her ground-floor windows had been broken. Inside was a distraught Graham, his hands bleeding from the broken glass, jealously reading her diary to see who she was dating. Her new consort turned out to be Lord Weidenfeld, a talented, portly septuagenarian who is Britain's leading Jewish publisher. When Weidenfeld, not a notably attractive man, was asked what had earned him the solace of so many beautiful younger women, he unabashedly replied, "I am the Nijinsky of cunnilingus."

Then came Barbara's astonishingly rapid personal and professional climb. She wrote a column in *The Sunday Times* that became a must-read. She built a formidable reputation. But soon she began to use her columns less to express fresh ideas than to shamelessly name-drop, exorcising her last visible links with a poor childhood in St. Catharines, Ontario, to thumb her nose at her past, as if to say, "Look at me, I have arrived." I was left wondering why she no longer thought it good enough to be known for her writing and needed to become a society groupie.

At the same time, her outrageous behaviour fed the tabloids, rewarding her with instant notoriety. When Algy Cluff, chairman of *The Spectator*, invited her on a dinner date, she accepted, but warned him: "There's one thing I have to tell you: I won't be wearing any knickers." On another occasion, when a prospective date, to whom she had just been introduced, asked about the attractive belt she was wearing, Barbara took it off and waved it in his face, tauntingly announcing: "Usually, I wear *only* this." One story had her wandering around in a haze at the height of summer, in Knightsbridge near Harrods, dressed in monster sunglasses and her ankle-length mink coat. She stumbled from one liaison to another, as though offering markers against her time in some sexual purgatory of her own making. Mayfair's aristocrats tended to tolerate her ways as a bit of East Enders' mischief, while others more thoughtfully suggested she ought to donate herself to science so that her self-obsession could be preserved for posterity. Robert Fox, a perceptive London commentator, concluded that "Barbara is a lady of enthusiasms and passions, has balls the size of aircraft tyres, but I would contend is not a great journalist."

When she interviewed Germaine Greer and described her as suffering from "terminal self-absorption," the Australian feminist in turn described Amiel as having "great hobbit feet, a breakfront bosom and effusing patent insincerity."

ALONG CAME CONRAD. In summer 1992 I found myself in London and decided to drop in on Black, by then firmly entrenched as proprietor of the *Daily Telegraph*. He had sold the newspaper's impressive building on Fleet Street and become one of the first tenants of Paul Reichmann's epic Canary Wharf dreamscape, then awash in red ink. The outlying office complex was impossible to reach by public transit. To woo potential tenants, the Reichmanns operated a launch service from Charing Cross Dock on the Thames River. Posing as a would-be renter, I boarded the VIP vessel, which was equipped with soft blue sofas and turbocharged engines that allowed it to cruise at twenty-five knots. We swept through historic London, past Royal Festival Hall and under Waterloo Bridge, passed St. Paul's Cathedral, ducked under London Bridge, and came up alongside HMS *Belfast*, the last of the Royal Navy's cruisers, permanently moored on the river. Then the shore view began to deteriorate, awash with moss-covered piers, derelict barges, and rotten pilings that supported abandoned docks rarely glimpsed by tourists. Suddenly rising out of the river's mist was Canary Wharf. The day I arrived there was only one crane at work and a lonely gardener planting purple pansies. But the size of the project was breathtaking, especially since it sat in such splendid isolation. It was like running into the Taj Mahal on Baffin Island.

When I walked into his tennis-court-sized office, I found a very different Conrad Black from the one I'd known. For one thing, instead of rising energetically from his deep leather chair, he majestically decanted himself, appearing considerably thickened and considerably more majestic. There was no longer anything comfortably dishevelled about him; he was a perfect parody of a British merchant banker, bespoke by Huntsman of Savile Row. He still loved to drop names such as Kissinger's ("Had breakfast with Henry this morning, who said that the standard of statesmanship is the lowest he's seen in all his adult life"), but his remarks were offered less as boasts than as vaguely informative footnotes. In his new position as publisher of what was arguably Britain's most influential newspaper, and chief proprietor of the world's fastest-growing media empire, Black had attained a state of grace that finally allowed him to capitalize on his aura. He'd had his teeth fixed and crimped his unruly hair. The world's financial and intellectual elite now lined up to see *him*. The evolution of his theatrical personality reflected his realization that all great stage performances consist equally of reality and sorcery, and that the most difficult role is to play yourself. He had at last found the courage of his condescension and was enjoying every minute of it.

"I feel myself very fortunate," he told me, building a finger pyramid in front of his face. "I have a position perfectly suited for me that I've worked rather hard for a number of years to design. I do pretty much what I like and don't do very much that I don't like. I don't mean that in a social, hoity-toity way, but I'm personally happy with my lot. Let's not mince words: remember Bernard Shaw's description of the British grinding down those beneath them by the same measure they defer to those above. Well, it's part of the culture here that newspaper owners, and especially owners of the serious and responsible newspapers, are very deferentially treated – frankly, rather more than they deserve. But it would be hypocrisy for me to object to that, as one of its beneficiaries." He felt comfortable in the tradition of previous Canadian press barons, Lords Beaverbrook and Thomson, who had traded Canadian winters for British peerages, and fully expected to follow their example. While still in Canada, Black had considered himself a tenured anglophile, busying himself with such aristocratic irrelevancies as having his friend the Duke of Norfolk officially approve a family coat of arms.[5]

Black reminded me that he was still basing his corporate strategy on military analogies, advancing "like a platoon of men through a forest, parallel lines moving in various directions," adding, "whenever there is a breakthrough, I exploit it." His tactics had never worked more effectively than in his capture and subsequent revival of the *Daily Telegraph*, whose 1.1 million weekday circulation made it Britain's most popular broadsheet. After putting into place a superb editorial team under Andrew Knight, Max Hastings, Peregrine Worsthorne, Frank Johnson, and Charles Moore, he had halved the staff and turned the once moribund paper into a lively enterprise. Its 1991 earnings of $86 million, on revenues of $464 million, were an incredible 29 per cent higher than the $67 million he had paid to gain control of the company in 1985. Under his guidance, the *Telegraph* had increased in value by an astounding

---

[5] It consisted of an eagle and a lion holding a big blue book over a shield that featured fleurs-de-lis, sheaves of wheat, and a plumb line crossed with an anchor. His appropriate motto was "Say Not the Struggle Nought Availeth."

1,500 per cent. "We are making about a million pounds a week," he boasted, "and unlike most other businesses I've been in, it is all disposable income."

We chatted for a good two hours. I could sense that he had been rehearsing all his life to be what he had become. This great historic Empire City, he must have felt, would at last provide an appreciative audience for his stored-up knowledge, revealed in such parlour tricks as reciting in reverse order the kings and queens of England in ninety seconds; rhyming off the names and tonnages of every ship on both sides of Sir Francis Drake's 1588 confrontation with the Spanish Armada; or listing the daily casualty rates during Hitler's siege of Stalingrad. At one point, he casually showed me a personal letter from Prime Minister Thatcher, one of the last she had written from 10 Downing Street:

> Dear Conrad;
> I was enormously grateful for the support of the *Telegraph* over these last few difficult weeks, and I know what a role you personally played in ensuring that. I hope that we can now make sure that the principles and policies in which you and I both believe will be taken forward by my successor.
> Margaret

Earlier, Thatcher had confided to Lord Young, her secretary of state for Trade and Industry, that Conrad's knowledge of British history had made her "feel like a wet," implying that she was a left-wing Tory, which she wasn't. But on another occasion at 10 Downing Street, when they were discussing the trooping the colour ceremony, Black began a long-winded explanation about its history. She held up her hand and entreatingly silenced his monologue: "I know, Conrad. I know . . ."

He had moved impressively into London society's stratosphere, much to the displeasure of his then wife, Shirley, who hated all that pomp and circumstance, particularly climbing in full public view into their stretch Rolls, which Conrad insisted on ostentatiously parking outside any public functions they attended. She had even altered her name to Joanna, having been informed that if he became a lord, her name might not sound sufficiently noble. But her heart wasn't in it. She decided to divorce Black and eventually she married Brian MacDonald, the ex-priest who had been retained to convert her to Roman Catholicism when her husband made the switch. That left Conrad free and footloose in swinging London. His pontificating reached a new low when, asked about his divorce by the BBC's Sue Lawley, he announced, "It was the result of our bifurcation of interests," leaving both interviewer and audience shaking their heads.

ENTER AMIEL. She was Josephine to his Napoleon, a middle-class ethnic girl with matchless ambitions but limited hopes of entering high society, until she captivated a powerful man who would make her his empress, from which heights she could dictate fashions, organize literary salons, and influence tastes and ideas. Conversely, he was the Napoleonic tactical genius who became a bumbling nerd when confronted by an alluring woman.[6] Conrad famously declared his slavish devotion to Barbara when he described her as being "preternaturally sexy," a phrase that suggests being "beyond, or surpassing the natural."

"Preternatural" was also a charge levelled against Amiel's appearance, which, like Dorian Gray's, had grown ever more youthful with the passage of time. Nearly four years older than Conrad, she looked twenty years his junior – a miracle really, or perhaps a testament to the preservative powers of right-wing thinking.[7]

---

[6] Napoleon's devotion to Josephine was once awkwardly expressed when he sent her a message: "Home in four days. Don't wash."

[7] An alternate theory was that she regularly attended Clinique La Prairie in Clarens-Montreux, Switzerland, which offers a revolutionary revitalization program that has had remarkable success in reversing aging by injecting patients with foetal cells of sheep.

When Conrad began to woo her, Barbara was in her most kittenish, coquettish phase, living in a two-storey flat with its reception hall casually strewn with letters praising her accomplishments, and an upstairs boudoir that featured a four-poster bed with a mirrored ceiling, while her negligees hung on a rail that circled the room. Into this den stumbled Conrad, who had once confided to me that he found seduction "a Sisyphean task." In a less florid description, his pal Hal Jackman speculated that "like a lot of great and brilliant men, Conrad doesn't feel at ease with his body and his sexuality, and is therefore vulnerable to someone who can sort of zero in and take advantage of it." *Zap*.

"I had known Barbara for a long time but had never made any sort of overture," Black told me. "One fine day she invited me to the opera. I arrived early and 'set out my stall,' that's a British expression for making professions of amorous intent. She was completely flabbergasted and suggested that I see a psychiatrist. Not that she thought I was crazy but to make sure that what I was saying was indeed what I meant." Being Conrad, a man of the world but not of the boudoir, he followed her advice, and went to call on a well-known analyst on Harley Street for a forty-five-minute session. "I explained how I had set out my stall and asked his advice on whether my sensations of amorous purpose and intent ought to be pursued."[8]

Why did Conrad marry Barbara? For several reasons, according to his most intimate confidants: for one, she was his intellectual soulmate; for another, she introduced him to the delights of oral sex. According to John Fraser, "She was his peacock feather, the manifestation that he wanted to display of himself. They exulted in each other." To watch them together at the height of their renown was to witness a mesmerizing ballet of sensuality and power. She moved inside Conrad's field of force, trembling like a

---

[8] The shrink gave Conrad his blessing; and if any reader thinks I'm making this up, the transcripts of all my interviews with him are stored at the archives of McMaster University in Hamilton.

magnetic compass needle, her high spirits in harmony with his. She had his number; with her, he was reborn. Yet theirs was a vampire love: she fed on his money; he fed on her sexuality.

Years later, in a private conversation, Black confessed to me that his only serious ideological disagreements with Amiel were "over such issues as drug enforcement. She felt all drugs should be legalized and opposed gun control while I didn't. She felt that speed limits were ridiculous. While I found them inconvenient, they didn't bother me too much."[9]

Their 1992 wedding – attended by the Duchess of York, Baroness Thatcher, Lord Rothschild, Sir David Frost, and all the usual royal suspects – was followed by their honeymoon, which was a gift from Peter Munk, the gold and real estate magnate, then a Hollinger director, who told me the story.

"My original partner, David Gilmour, owned Wakaya, a luxury private resort on one of the Fiji islands which had eight exquisitely designed *bureys* [huts], one per couple, and four chefs to cater to the guests' every whim. When the blissful couple arrived at the Fiji airport, after a gruelling twenty-hour flight, Conrad headed for the local VIP lounge, which of course didn't exist, the airport being furnished mainly with a few plastic chairs and buzzing flies. It's just a big, messy room with natives hustling you to buy drinks and candies. It was over a hundred degrees, and there was no air-conditioning. Finally, Gilmour's Cessna arrived to take them to the resort but it was a bumpy ride, and all that anyone remembered of the flight was Black muttering, 'I'll kill Munk.' But then the plane landed, the newlyweds got out, and Conrad, though absolutely frazzled, spotted a familiar-looking figure leaning against a nearby palm tree.

"'That,' he said to Barbara, 'looks like a better-looking Tarzan version of Michael Heseltine!' [Conservative Trade minister and a

---

[9] On the same occasion I checked Conrad's attitude toward capital punishment, which, to my surprise, I had heard he opposed. "Yeah," he chuckled, "hanging's too good for them."

serious rival for the succession to Margaret Thatcher.] 'Well, it is,' Barbara replied, and they both felt that they were back in civilized company."

"Conrad was a sight," Gilmour later reported to Munk. "By the fourth day he looked like he totally belonged. Actually, like he owned the island. He went from totally cynical to totally happy and though he and Barbara were booked for a week, they stayed twenty-two days."

AS I LOOK BACK on my nearly thirty years of knowing Amiel, to some extent having shaped her career and followed her professional and amatory exploits, she reminds me more and more of a character in the novel *Nothing Lost* by John Gregory Dunne, a supermodel with $19 million in the bank who calls herself simply Carlyle. "In the perfection of her self-absorption, she had no sense that acts have consequences and treated the acceptance of responsibility as if it were a disease." That's Babs. Like Conrad, she felt that her place in life granted her special dispensation, claiming that, "Even the most deathless love has its credit limits, and many women overspend them." [10]

At the time Amiel married Black I was happy for them. It seemed a perfect match. Instead, their marriage detonated a frantic quest to amass luxury goods that extended beyond reason, even beyond compulsion. Their nouveau riche flamboyance, which was worthy of neither of them, reached an unimaginable scale, including the acquisition of a quartet of permanently staffed luxury homes worth $90 million. There was nothing they were prepared to deny themselves to prove that they had arrived. Barbara's pathological spending habits were not learned or inherited, but instinctive: a defence mechanism against an inbred insecurity so profound

---

[10] On a more personal level, she declared: "The more sophisticated the circles in which one moves, the more it is taken for granted that a women's promiscuity is no more a reflection on her general morality than a man's."

that it took over her life. When she told the fashion editor of *Vogue* that her extravagance knew no bounds, it was not a boast but a fact.

Everywhere Conrad and Barbara travelled, a butler and maid preceded them to assure their comfort. His salary was $130,000 plus board, and that didn't include the under-butlers, chefs, chauffeurs, housemen, footmen, and guards at each of their residences. While visiting Munk and his wife Melanie at their primitive island on Georgian Bay, the Blacks were appalled that their hosts had no servants and everyone had to do their own dishes.

In London, they became a favourite target for the city's gossip purveyors. "Amiel," wrote Stephen Glover, media critic of the *Evening Standard*, "is one of those brutes who go on the rampage, spraying bullets in all directions, before turning the gun on herself." Ewa Lewis, a columnist for the *Tatler*, twittered that "Black and Amiel have a high social cachet. Barbara makes him more known. She's glamorous and bright. Before they married he was just a chunky newspaper proprietor. They are power and glamour." Then, Lewis added her ultimate benediction: "*They are not perceived of as Canadians at all!*" (My italics.)

With Shirley/Joanna, Conrad had lived in a relatively modest house in outlying Highgate, but when Barbara swept into his life, the newlyweds moved into London's most prestigious area, purchasing a mansion near Kensington Palace, the royal residence of British sovereigns until 1760 and the home of Princess Diana. Peter Munk, who had once considered moving into what became Black's house, had inspected the premises and derisively dismissed the idea of ever living in what he called "the biggest house in London." The Blacks bought it, then purchased the house next door and combined the two into an enormous, elegant, eleven-bedroom mansion, valued at $30 million. (Although Conrad has three children by his former marriage, a prominent London socialite who toured the residence reported that it contained no children's rooms.) It featured an indoor pool and two elevators as well as a unique "environmental chamber" where the pampered Lady Black could alter not just temperatures and climates figuratively transporting herself to any part of the world (except, of course, St. Catharines).

Twice a year the Blacks entertained at legendary parties. Madame Tussaud's Waxworks come to life, the guests were not the "A" list, tending to include slightly shopworn characters such as Roger Moore and Joan Collins. But the scattering of peers (whose mobile eyebrows were their most expressive facial features) and their aristocratic-looking wives (who knew how to twist their lips into the characteristic British upper-class trout pout) made up for it. When I attended Black's receptions and parties, I sensed an unpleasant element of courtiers being summoned to account. Speech patterns altered nearly imperceptibly as Conrad drifted into the room, checking out the lay of the land over the shoulders of the people whose hands he was shaking, to spot the most prized celebs. Guests would steal glances at him, trying a little too hard to appear casual, unexpectedly making exaggerated hand gestures. It was as though they had cornered some unusual big-game specimen that had the power to rattle their teeth, and weren't quite sure how to react. What made his London entertainments so distinctly uncomfortable was that he made it painfully clear he intended to become not merely the media establishment's leader but its messiah. He declared himself instantly overqualified to join its sequestered ranks and made little attempt to disguise his intended ascendancy. The couple's most famous appearance was on July 1, 2000, when they attended an eighteenth-century-style ball at the home of Prince and Princess Michael of Kent, with Conrad done up as Cardinal Richelieu while Lady Black stayed in character, costumed as Marie Antoinette.

Just as Conrad's troubles began to mount, Barbara wrote an article in *GQ* magazine, one of the London glossies, in which she described how her personal priorities had escalated into never-never land, ignoring her husband's troubles. "For some people," she wrote, emphatically including herself, "jewellery is a defining attribute, rather like intelligence or the number of residences you have." She boasted about owning "a fantastic natural-pearl and diamond brooch," which languished in her safety deposit box because it was simply too big to wear. The contents of her several London closets became common gossip, including a dozen Hermes Birkin handbags fashioned out of unwilling crocodiles and forty jewel-handled Renaud Pellegrino evening bags. But it was her collection of Manolo Blahnik shoes that attracted the most attention. These are not boots made for walkin'. Their Spanish designer, who calls himself "a sculptor and engineer," carves each last by hand out of beech wood, "giving special thought to toe cleavage." Each of Blahnik's creations is an art object. Madonna has claimed "they last longer than sex." They sell for about a thousand pounds ($2,300) a pair, and Barbara had well over a hundred in her London house alone, some with kitten heels. ("Buckingham Palace floors don't like stilettos," she explained to the uninitiated among us.)

As it turned out, the most apt comment on this freefall hedonism came from Margaret Wente, the *Globe and Mail* columnist, who wrote: "Only a few hundred women in the world can afford to dress like Mrs. Black, and Mrs. Black may not be among them." She wasn't; but the arrangement they had was that Barbara paid for her off-the-rack purchases while the hubby sprung for her couture.

According to Dick Breeden's report, Barbara was paid US$1,141,558 between 1999 and 2003, for which there was "no legitimate basis." That included her retainer for editorial advice to the *Chicago Sun-Times*, where, it was claimed, she had not set foot for more than four years. On top of that she received more than $1 million through a company named Black-Amiel Management, while Conrad contributed $250,000 to charities in her name. On April 12, 2004, Amiel cashed in most of her options, allowing her to buy Hollinger stock worth US$3.1 million for US$2.25 million below market value. That meant she was profiting from her husband's downfall, since that's what was driving the stock price higher.

It was Amiel who harvested the most intense attention, but under her influence Conrad's pretensions ran a close second. In his Toronto Georgian mansion he preferred to meditate in the eighteenth-century cardinal's chair he kept under the rotunda of his library, a three-storey structure capped by a copper dome modelled on that of St. Peter's in Rome. The house, a mixture of *Brideshead Revisited* and Canadian Quaint, also had a fireplace with a seventeenth-century, hand-carved surround by Grinling Gibbons, the artist responsible for much of the decorative work at Blenheim Palace, Hampton Court, and St. Paul's Cathedral. At his London home, Conrad enjoyed formulating his corporate tactics seated astride Napoleon's portable campaign stool.[11]

When the Blacks decided they needed an extra female guest to fill the dinner table at one of their parties, Eleanor Mills, a twenty-six-year-old features editor of the *Telegraph*, was invited to attend. She rushed home to dress and primp, arrived excited to have been asked, and was enjoying herself when it turned out that the expected male guest had not appeared. Conrad went over to Mills and rudely told her, "Finish your drink and skedaddle." In front of the assembled guests she was escorted through the kitchen door to the servants' entrance and told to wait for a taxi. Instead, feeling humiliated and insulted, she made her own way home, but not before standing outside the Blacks' mansion, shaking her fist and giving voice to her outrage: "One day you'll be fucked and it's going to make me very happy!"[12] This tale of rudeness without provocation struck me as the low point in the Blacks' social climbing. They were so insecure that an extra dinner guest, who had cheerfully responded to their rushed invitation, had to be ejected because of some silly, unwritten rule about even numbers. That, as much as the scandals that followed, marked the beginning of the end of their run as deserving gentry. There was nothing gentrified

---

[11] This made perfect sense since neither of the chair's occupants managed to come up with a survival strategy. At one point, speculation over his obsession with collecting Napoleon memorabilia reached the point where Rosemary Millar, his London assistant, issued a press release announcing that, "The Proprietor of *The Daily Telegraph* does not own Napoleon's penis."

[12] Mills, who later became editor of the review section of *The Sunday Times*, turned out to be the stepdaughter of Tessa Jowell, the Culture minister in Tony Blair's Cabinet, which even then was considering Conrad's title.

about them, and London's fellow colonials felt ashamed to be represented by them. Another story told the same tale. When the golden couple was visiting fellow peers in the British countryside, Conrad left thirty pounds for the chambermaid. On the way home, when he discovered that Lady Black had already tipped the maid, he phoned their host and demanded the return of his gratuity.

THE BLACKS' DOWNFALL dates back to spring 1994, when Conrad engaged in a feud with Rupert Murdoch, the pragmatic proprietor of *The Times*, who had reduced his paper's cover price to overtake the *Telegraph*'s then heady circulation lead. Black reacted by pledging that he would never follow suit. To fatten his reserves he sold 12.5 million *Telegraph* shares to British institutional investors, reaping $170 million, while urging his newspaper's staff to invest in the company by buying its stock. Many followed his advice, and never forgave him for the consequences.

That social season Conrad and Barbara hosted a party for 150 glitterati at the Ritz, with guests including Princess Diana and Sir James Goldsmith (who had just been elected to the European Parliament). Two days later, on June 21, Black went back on his word and drastically reduced his paper's newsstand price to match that of *The Times*. That cut his paper's revenues by $95 million, driving *Telegraph* shares down to nearly half of their previous value. At the time, the *Telegraph*'s account was handled by Cazenove & Co., the bluest of the City's blue-blood firms, the Queen's own stockbroker, incorporated in 1828 when it helped finance the expansion of the British Empire. Cazenove's discreet and illustrious partners were so upset by Black's crude opportunism that they resigned from the firm's historical association with the *Telegraph*, publicly emphasizing the seriousness of Black's betrayal. Conrad replied with history's wordiest snort, describing the broker's actions as "scandalous and dishonourable, an orgy of self-righteous English hypocrisy. They just scuttled out the back door into the tall grass." But the British newspaper broker Hylton Philipson, of

Pall Mall Ltd., spoke for the City when he declared: "Conrad has pissed off the Establishment on this one." A senior London financier who was advising Black at the time, recalled: "I walked up to him at the end of one meeting, and said: 'You know, you'll never be able to have lunch in this town again.'" That wasn't quite true, but the incident prompted Black to move the core management of his empire to the United States, which turned out to be an essential factor in his undoing.

While money in London is mainly discreet, guarded by the merchant bankers in Threadneedle Street, who handle accounts noiselessly behind the daffodils in their window boxes, serious American financiers operate not just in another currency but on a much more grandiose scale. It's the difference between being merely rich and being independently wealthy. The Blacks definitely belonged to the former group, but behaved as though they ranked with the latter. (The rich spend their money; the wealthy live on the interest; the filthy rich make do with the interest paid on the interest.) By transferring most of their corporate activities (as opposed to their social life) to the United States, the Blacks moved into a higher league that operated on a much more costly wavelength, and according to much tougher regulations.

Conrad and Barbara established their first American beachhead on New York's exclusive Park Avenue, where they purchased two luxury condos. Peter Munk had originally suggested they buy the unit then owned by his partner, David Gilmour (which was originally designed for the actor David Niven), combining three full-floor layouts with internal staircases and massive picture windows overlooking Central Park. The Blacks decided it wasn't big enough and had Robert Noakes decorate a much larger unit for them. When Conrad phoned Rosemary "Posey" Boxer, the Canadian socialite who knew everybody, to ask for the name of a good architect, she suggested Philip Johnson, then considered among the world's best. Johnson phoned her the day after he had met the Blacks to complain about their behaviour and asked her why she had nominated him. "Well, it's a lot of money and I thought it might be fun for you," she explained. To which the world's leading architect replied, "I don't need the money, and I don't need that kind of fun."

Back when I was writing *The Establishment Man* I had visited the Blacks at their Palm Beach address, 150 Canterbury Lane, a cozy but unpretentious winter retreat, which anywhere else would have ranked as a luxurious and highly desirable abode. That wasn't good enough for Lady Black, who felt that Palm Beach was not a resort like others, but a place where wealth can be converted into pleasure at a highly favourable rate of exchange. It is the most assiduously zoned community on earth. Local bylaws forbid fast food outlets, laundromats, billboards, electric signs, aluminium siding, hippies, funeral parlours, and hospitals; the dead and dying are discreetly carted across the causeway to West Palm. Recessions and other economic phenomena happen to other people in other places. Most Palm Beach residents are the heirs or possessors of fortunes too massive, too cleverly diversified, and much too carefully husbanded to be affected by mere swings in the business cycle or, heaven forbid, SEC investigations. Social climbing is the second most popular indoor sport. The late Arthur Somers Roche, an American millionaire who spent most of his life on the golden peninsula, once appeared at an Everglades Club costume party dressed up as a social climber, with a ladder up his back. Its four rungs were lettered, in ascending order: "Common People," "People," "Nice People," and "Right People."

In Palm Beach, becoming one of the Right People depended on where and how you lived, a truism that prompted the Blacks in 1997 to buy their most luxurious dwelling yet, from John Drexel III of the Philadelphia banking family. It was a 20,000 square foot palace at 1930 South Ocean Boulevard, featuring a ceramic-tiled tunnel under the street that opened up to three hundred feet of private Atlantic beachfront. Conrad calculated that, including its $4 million elevator installation and $3 million fountain, the ten-bedroom hangout was worth a cool US$36 million. Besides, it was his turn to make a silly statement that would infuriate Hollinger's hard-pressed shareholders: "Some people are offended by the extreme opulence but I find it sort of entertaining."

Even seasoned Palm Beach veterans blanched at that clinker. Curiously, it was Barbara Amiel who had foreshadowed the future back in 1993. In a *Sunday Times* column published in November, shortly after she married Conrad, she had written: "My husband is very rich, but I am not. I don't regard my husband's money as my own. Having married very wealthy men before my current husband, I can guarantee that I parted from them leaving both their fortunes and my opinions intact. I have been a bitch all my life and did not need the authority of money to be one. My detractors were calling me a fascist bitch long before I had a penny. I am a North London Jew who has read a bit of history. That means I know this: In a century that has seen the collapse of the Austro-Hungarian, British, and Soviet empires, reversal of fortune is this rich bitch's reality. One might as well keep walking and have the family's Vuitton suitcases packed."

That was a good idea, because the orgy of her spending habits had attracted the attention of minority shareholders' groups. Their accountants costed out her closet and calculated that the wife of the chairman of a company that had shrunk to four papers from five hundred and was losing serious money could not possibly afford her self-advertised lifestyle. It was her boasts about her wardrobe, which some SEC investigators assigned to the case had learned to recite by heart, that provided the catalyst for the charges that followed. Not since the Edwardian Age had anyone so blatantly dropped their inhibitions about showing off their material possessions. It was almost as if they believed the "lower orders" would enjoy the spectacle, instead of being disgusted, while London society shuddered in embarrassment.

THE FIRST CONSEQUENCE of the Delaware court's verdict was a journalistic witch hunt in London, the place where Black was most anxious to preserve his wounded dignity. The judge had been stern and disapproving, but Black had yet to be charged with any crime. London's newspapers, however, are the most competitive on earth, and nothing sells papers faster than a fallen idol. If a minor Cabinet minister or major football star is caught in bed with a prostitute or pneumatic assistant, it becomes a screaming headline for days on end, and if that doesn't move papers, the event is escalated into a sexual threesome involving wild animals or teddy bears. The papers move like a wolf pack, closing in on their victims until a juicier target comes along. In Conrad's case, every published "exposé" of his downfall proved especially titillating, since it was inevitably accompanied by a scene-stealing portrait of the glamorous Barbara in various coquettish poses, sporting her fabled décolletage and uttering one of her snooty quotes, guaranteed to extinguish whatever sympathy remained for her beleaguered hubby.

The trigger for that style of commando coverage was a column in the highly respected *Financial Times*, where, on the day after the Delaware verdict, staff writer John Gapper tagged Black "a scoundrel" whose reputation had been "destroyed." That comment set loose the unfettered newspaper wars. From then on, Conrad was treated like a rogue elephant, a solitary beast, shunned by the herd. He had lost control of his media empire and found himself facing an inflamed press corps, enraged regulators, disillusioned directors, and exasperated shareholders – his name tainted, his future circumscribed by his past. His cachet as a corporate statesman guiding such high-octane think-tanks as Bilderberg conferences and Trilateral Commission forums seemed a dim memory. The Chicago office of the FBI had joined the SEC's continuing investigation, signalling the likelihood of criminal charges. That might at least leave Black with unlimited time to work on his next book: *A Life in Decline*, the sequel to his 1993 autobiographical doorstop *A Life in Progress*.

Capitalism is a forgiving if selfish creed. It places no limits on the making of money or how it is spent, except for three: do not break the laws of the land; do not treat your corporate treasury as your private piggy bank; and, if you do, don't advertise it.

Instead of answering the serious charge against him, which he had every chance to do at a hearing of the Securities and Exchange Commission on December 22, 2003, on the advice of his lawyers, who said that they had not had enough time to prepare, Conrad invoked the Fifth Amendment, claiming that anything he might say could be used to incriminate him. Not a great tactic, if you are trying to win public sympathy.

During this season of torment, all his energy was directed to establishing his right to be right, and everybody else to be wrong. I found his attitude reminiscent of Cornelius Vanderbilt, the most audacious of the American robber barons, who declared: "What do I care about the law? Ain't I got the power?" Apart from pirates with parrots perched on their shoulders, unbridled capitalism produced few more compelling figures than the primitive moguls whose origins date back to medieval Europe, when feudal noblemen robbed anyone crossing their estates. In modern dress they emerged as the robber barons who dominated the original exploitation of oil, steel, and banking in the United States, men such as John D. Rockefeller, Andrew Carnegie, Leland Stanford, and J.P. Morgan. These and other tycoons became extraordinarily wealthy by manipulating the economic system to their advantage, committing various misdemeanours in their climb to glory. Their trademark was to build themselves castles to live and party in, such as "Breakers," the seventy-room Newport "cottage" erected by Cornelius Vanderbilt II in Newport, Rhode Island. Theirs might have been a dated and highly dubious ethic, but Conrad Black, a hundred years later, was not shy about sharing it.

Conrad's responsibility for what appeared to be a gross misappropriation of corporate funds remained to be proven. But the fact that Hollinger's corporate audit committee, packed with his lifelong friends, had resigned en masse on November 21, 2003, demanding his departure as CEO, was a matter of record.

Their dramatic exodus had no effect. He decided to walk on alone. Yet to Black-watchers like me, that event was of signal importance. Hollinger's audit committee was billed as independent.

In fact, all but one of its members happened to be Conrad's best friends, or, more accurately, his cronies. He had picked broadcaster Doug Bassett as one of his original partners, way back in 1978. Dougie, as he was known by everyone, carried his life in his hands like a placard, waving opinions and convictions with infectious charm and terrier friendliness. The son of the media mogul John W. Bassett, he was never a heavyweight, but it felt good to have him on your side. Of his relationship with Conrad, Bassett once told me, "We're great believers in friendly hands, great believers in working together as a unit. There's great strength in that."

Former department store magnate Fred Eaton (an expert in how to total your career) had known Conrad as long and as intimately as Bassett and had been a member of the same boards. In return, Fred named Conrad to Eaton's key operations committee during the late 1970s.[13] "He's got a fair bit of panache," Eaton told me about his buddy Conrad, "and he lives like a wealthy and unabashed proprietor." More revealing was Fred's message when Black was plotting his Argus takeover and needed Eaton's support: "I don't really understand all this, but you've got my vote."

Eaton had also introduced Conrad to former U.S. secretary of state Henry Kissinger, who would turn out to be a key player in the Black comedy. Allan Gotlieb, Canada's former ambassador to the United States, was a more recent recruit to Black's inner circle, having been appointed a Hollinger director when he left diplomatic life in 1989. He had since become one of Black's most influential legal advisers. Maureen Sabia, the other audit committee member who quit, had no personal links to Black, but she was an authority on corporate governance; the addendum to her resignation spoke for (as well as to) her colleagues: "The selection criteria for directors must not be about friendship with the CEO,

---

[13] Part of the arrangement was that Conrad was allowed to buy suits, at a considerable discount, in the Pine Room of Eaton's main downtown Toronto store. Unlike other clients, Conrad expected Ilie Dumitru, the chief resident tailor, to drop into his office for fittings.

but about how the knowledge and experience of a candidate can contribute to the proper functioning of a board." The fact that the trio of his buddies unanimously recommended Black's immediate ouster as Hollinger Inc.'s chairman spoke volumes about what they had discovered. The move left Hollinger without an independent audit function, as well as gutting its corporate governance committee. "Call it an epic betrayal in the annals of Canadian business," wrote the *Toronto Star*'s ace business columnist David Olive. "That Black's friends would have turned against him was a parting that the week before would have seemed unimaginable. . . . Except for those periods when Bay Street took a sabbatical from analyzing the Black maze, has there ever been a year when some poor soul on the Street failed to earn Black's wrath by pronouncing unhappily on the opacity of Black's manoeuvrings?"

The abrupt departure of Black's former partners drew public notice to Ravelston, the mysterious holding company at the very heart of the scandal, which I had been the first to write about. Shortly after Black took over Argus, he had sold Ravelston to Hollinger, then a defunct gold mine. Most of the revenues of Hollinger had thus been diverted into Ravelston, whose stock was more than two-thirds owned by Conrad, while roughly another third was owned by his senior partner, David Radler. Through its super-shares, Ravelston owned only one-third of the equity but three-quarters of the voting control of Hollinger International, its operating arm. The complicated corporate structure, which amounted to a form of legal money laundering, had been set up by Black's predecessor, J.A. "Bud" McDougald.[14]

After Conrad acquired the majority holding in Ravelston he wrote a confidential memo to his partners, starkly revealing his motivation: "For three and a half years now we have pursued the

---

[14] Ravelston was originally named after a Scottish mansion where McDougald's great-grandfather was born in 1814. The estate's magnificent formal gardens, described in Walter Scott's novel *Waverley*, later became the playing field for the Mary Erskine School for Girls, which took over the Edinburgh property.

policy of maximizing Ravelston's underlying equity while upgrading and fine-tuning its assets to improve our ultimate return on that equity. This policy led over that time to what was probably the greatest compression of corporate dealing in Canadian history." It had indeed, exponentially increased Ravelston's value, which in turn became the main source of Black's personal income. When Black was asked why Hollinger's auditors were not permitted to inspect Ravelston's accounting records, he replied, "Because they weren't invited. What does it need to be verified for?" His attitude was best caught in *Just Rewards*, a study of Canadian business ethics by David Olive, who quoted Conrad's plaintive lament: "The only charge that anyone can level against us is one of insufficient generosity to ourselves."

Tony Fell, Bay Street's most knowledgeable and astute operator, had taken his friend Conrad aside at a party in Palm Beach thirty months before any problems had surfaced, and strongly advised him to wind up Ravelston and all of the other problematic features of the Hollinger corporate maze. "He promised he'd look into it, and then didn't do a damn thing," Fell said later. "So he's either a fool or a crook." These were warnings that any rational CEO would have rushed to obey. I concluded that Conrad's strategic survival instincts had evaporated under the Palm Beach sun, inducing a mood of indolent impregnability, multiplied by the distractions of Barbara's charms.

BELIEVING HIS LEGEND, Conrad thought he could outwit, outcharm, and if necessary out-bully anybody, anywhere. For more than two decades, his gambit succeeded, and he might have eluded the regulators. But there was one group – his minority shareholders – that he had failed to bewitch. His witticisms and pretensions carried no weight with them; they wanted a fair share of profits, and higher dividends. To them, Black was the guy who had run their company into the ground and looted its treasury. By October 30, 2003, Moody's had downgraded the company's securities to junk status, dubious about Hollinger's ability to service its debt load, and even more worried about its "questionable corporate governance practises."

However dishonest Conrad might eventually turn out to be, he was clearly operating in the wrong century. "Ultimately, Lord Black probably should not own a public company," wrote Janet McFarland in the *Globe and Mail*. "He is not cut out for it. He has said he believes corporate governance is 'a fad.' He is a throwback to another era, in which the concepts of good governance were dismissed as flowery ideas that get in the way of running a company. He's wrong about that, as activist shareholders have proved. But given Lord Black's disdain for the duty of care involved in public share ownership, he should stick to managing only his private holdings." That was a valid criticism, and it reminded me of something Black had told me on January 22, 1993, confessing how he had harvested his fortune: "We sold assets at premium values and applied them to buying stock of discounted companies, much to the irritation of some onlookers. We originally created wealth out of thin air but in a way that was perfectly licit." He never hesitated to defend greed. I still remember the chill I felt late one Thursday, right after his successful coup, sitting in his splendid Argus headquarters, when we got onto his favourite subject. "Greed," he confessed, that long ago evening, "has been severely underestimated and denigrated, unfairly so, in my opinion. It is a motive that has not failed to move me from time to time."

His critics' most damning argument concerned the Himalayan pay packets that Black had been extracting for the past two decades. His actual income was difficult to gauge because it flowed through wedding-cake layers of holding companies, all of which he personally controlled (but did not entirely own), so that it was never exactly clear how much cash he was trousering. According to Dick Breeden's initial investigation, Black and his immediate circle received salaries amounting to US$33.5 million in 2003, which compared with the combined $6.9 million paid to the top executives of the *New York Times*, *Washington Post*, and *Wall Street*

Journal, the world's largest media empires. At the time, the holdings under Black's charge had dwindled from five hundred papers to four: London's *Telegraph* and *Spectator*, the *Chicago Sun-Times*, and the *Jerusalem Post*. At the same time, his record of running Hollinger had been stunningly inept. Since 2001, Hollinger International's losses had exceeded US$550 million, while every other newspaper chain was flying high with double-digit profit ratios. (Since Hollinger International had gone public in 1994, its average annual return had been 3.2 per cent, compared with 17 per cent at the *New York Times* and 14 per cent at the *Washington Post*.) Despite such dismal results, on top of his other compensation Black was also paid most of the $38 million in management fees charged to Hollinger by Ravelston. The most peculiar items in this long roster of personal compensation were the non-compete fees that amounted to just under US$88 million, all of it tax-free. These payouts, given to Black and Radler, were meant to guarantee that they would not reappear as competitors in the publishing markets they had just abandoned.

I tried hard to make some kind of sense of these transactions but couldn't. The non-compete pattern was replicated by the Black-Radler subsidiaries named Bradford Publishing and American Publications, which bought and sold papers on their account while throwing off hefty non-compete payments. The process was memorably described by the media analyst of the *Chicago Tribune*: "Black and Radler borrowed money from Black and Radler to pay back Black and Radler for not competing with Black and Radler." The perfect perpetual money machine had finally been invented.

Sale of the former Southam empire to the Asper family, which netted the pair about $53 million in non-compete fees, was the most puzzling of all. Because of Prime Minister Jean Chrétien's objections, Conrad had angrily and noisily given up his Canadian citizenship, in order to be eligible for a British title. On the day Black sold his Southam holdings, including the *National Post*, to the Asper family for $2.3 billion, he explained the main reason for having done so: "The *National Post* requires a resident Canadian proprietor and I no longer qualify as that." Since Black himself had cited the regulation that disallowed non-Canadians from owning newspapers, why were the Aspers paying him an exorbitant fee not to start a competing paper? And why did they divert a huge share of the selling price directly into his noble jeans?[15]

Few journalists were willing to tackle Black's bizarre pay packets and exorbitant lifestyle head on because he had earned his reputation for suing at the drop of an adjective, and had in fact issued writs against fifteen offending scribes, myself included. My lawsuit was triggered by a story I had written for the November 1983 issue of *Town and Country*, when that high-gloss American society house organ published a takeout on Canada. In it I described Conrad as "the black sheep of the Canadian Establishment," which in retrospect seemed like mild praise. The letter from his lawyer, Peter Atkinson (now himself entangled in Conrad's flailing downfall), thundered on about how I had "grossly defamed his client in the most egregious fashion" (the prose style must be catching), pointing out that black sheep "stand in conspicuous and unfavourable contrast to the group." Well, duh.

In that context it was doubly significant that Hal Jackman, who had served Black faithfully since 1978 as a director, shareholder, and fellow toy-soldier collector, entered the fray. "Sooner or later, reality sets in," he told the *National Post* at the height of the 2003 crisis. "You can pull things off a couple of times, but then people start to get realistic about you, and the charisma doesn't work any more. Conrad has a need to be tempting fate all the time. I just think he has a death wish."

That was a devastating pronouncement, but entirely consistent with Jackman's private views, dating back a full decade. I interviewed him on January 7, 1992, in his viceregal office at Queen's

---

[15] I was on my tugboat off Gibson's Landing when I received an SOS from Izzy Asper, asking me to rush him a copy of *The Establishment Man* because he was contemplating doing a mega-deal with Conrad and wanted to find out more about him. He did use my book, but I forgot to ask for a non-compete fee.

Park (he was lieutenant-governor of Ontario at the time) when Black was still riding high. "Conrad's destiny is to be a poseur," he told me. "He'll be courted and wined, get invited to the White House and Buckingham Palace, and he'll enjoy it. But he'll be pushing the bounds of what you can get away with. You wonder whether he's pushing the bounds of reasonableness."

On top of all those millions pouring into Conrad's piggy bank were Hollinger's generous corporate allowances, which covered the cost of his two private jets, not to mention a car collection which at various times included a 1967 Cadillac limousine, a 1954 (as well as a 1958) Rolls-Royce Silver Wraith, a Mercedes, a Lincoln Continental, a Bentley, and a Packard in a pear tree. One of his jets was a $15-million Canadair Challenger 601, its cabin floor fashioned out of mahogany, its dark oak panelling set off by original Group of Seven paintings with softly glowing picture lights above them. The other Conrad-Barbara luxury airborne conveyance was a top of the line Gulfstream IV that had recently been refurbished for $3 million to include a luxury leather sofa with a fold-out bed and a full set of Christofle silverware. Operating this fleet cost $7 million annually, all paid by the company, including holiday hops to Bora Bora. Even this extravagant arrangement occasionally raised Barbara's ire, as she twittered, driving yet another nail into Conrad's coffin: "It's always best to have two planes because however well one plans ahead one always finds one is on the wrong continent." (That covered all the bases, just in case there was still one Conrad supporter out there tempted to defend their lifestyle.) Amiel-watchers also noted that her "I never fly commercial" declaration was carefully issued only after the Concorde had been permanently grounded.

As well as their extravagant transportation needs, Hollinger covered the annual fees ($248,580) for the Blacks' two New York condominiums and the permanent apartment suite above Chicago's Four Seasons Hotel, not to mention their entertainment bills at the best clubs and most luxurious restaurants. Millions were also paid into Holcay Holdings Ltd. in the Cayman Islands, and to another Barbados company. The Blacks' income averaged an estimated

$100 million a year. By the end of 2003, Cardinal Value Equity Partners, a Connecticut-based hedge fund and Hollinger shareholder, adopted some of Black's hyperbole in framing their charge that he had looted the company of $300 million: "A more heinous tale of self-interested avarice and deceit by a chairman and CEO toward a company and its shareholders is hard to find in the annals of corporate history."

A separate but parallel issue was Black's purchase for US$8 million of valuable Franklin Roosevelt correspondence using Hollinger treasury funds. He obviously used the material to research his massive (and excellent) biography of the former American president. Asked by the *Financial Times* why he didn't buy the papers himself, Black brazenly replied, "Eight million dollars was not something I was prepared to spend." In other words, Hollinger's minority shareholders could afford such an unusual investment more readily than he. Luckily, no one asked them. On March 13, 2003 (two years after the purchase), a committee of the Hollinger board examined the transaction without requesting an independent valuation. The only available cost estimate was a letter from Glenn Horowitz, the fortunate dealer who had sold the papers to Conrad, claiming that they were now worth $12 to $15 million, though he had bought them for $3.5 million less than a year earlier. As fiercely independent as ever, the Hollinger board not only unanimously blessed the purchase but had the nerve to record in its minutes that the acquisition had been "a corporate investment of no benefit to the Chairman." (The same minutes might also have noted that elephants fly.) Characteristically, Black dismissed his critics as being below contempt, telling London's *Sunday Times*: "We are not running a Christian Scientists' meeting here, where we all have to sing from the same hymn sheet. Anybody who complains about our financial survival can take a hike."

The Roosevelt incident proved conclusively that Hollinger's weakest link was the decorative but ineffective roster of corporate directors and advisory board members recruited by Black, mainly to boost his and Barbara's social climbing. The majority of the pooh-bahs he had gathered might have known which fork to use and how to fake their understanding of the new constitution of the European Union, but they were little more than hood ornaments and failed miserably in their sworn duty to monitor their host's corporate shenanigans. The two boards included at various times: the former Tory prime minister and Conrad's patron saint, Baroness Margaret Thatcher; Valery Giscard d'Estaing, the former French president; Richard Perle, the renowned "Prince of Darkness" who masterminded the Bush administration's regime change policy, which validated the invading of any country where apple pie wasn't the national dish. There were also half a dozen superannuated British lords (Carrington, Hanson, Hartwell, King, Rawlinson, and Swaythling), plus Sir Evelyn de Rothschild and Sir James Goldsmith, the rogue financier best known for his aphorism that when a man marries his mistress (which he did) that creates a vacancy which must be filled. Still other notables included: Gianni Agnelli, the worldly chairman of Fiat; Bob Strauss, former head of the U.S. Atomic Energy Commission; Richard Burt, former chief negotiator for strategic arms reduction with the USSR; Major-General Shlomo Gazit, former chief of Israeli military intelligence; His Eminence Cardinal Emmett Carter of Toronto, Conrad's spiritual adviser; Henry Kissinger, the deep-throated former American secretary of state; Chaim Herzog, former president of Israel; David Brinkley, the ABC news commentator; Zbigniew Brzezinski, former U.S. national security adviser; James Thomson, a former governor of Illinois; Peter Bronfman, businessman and family member; William F. Buckley of the *National Review*; and George Will, the right-wing columnist.[16]

These rarefied individuals constituted Conrad's private court, a retinue he used to dazzle visiting firemen, especially bankers

---

[16] When Conrad's empire began to unravel, Buckley and Will wrote favourable articles on Black, not bothering to identify themselves as being on his payroll. Asked by a journalist why he hadn't informed his readers, Will replied that he saw no reason to do so. "My business is my business," he barked. "Got it?"

examining his creditworthiness. While they had won distinction in their own fields, only Agnelli, who ran Fiat into the ground, was trained to read balance sheets. An auditor who dealt with the board claimed that most of them had not the slightest inkling of accounting practices. "They probably thought that EBITDA was some kind of Spanish liqueur, instead of the abbreviation for 'earnings before interest, taxes, depreciation, and amortization,'" he surmised. As a group, they lacked the energy or political will to force Black, who both charmed and intimidated them, to account for his actions. On paper, they were an awesome crew, all right, but their average age left the impression they would feel winded playing chess. At one point, three Hollinger directors were over eighty.

Black's strangest additions to his boards were Robert Campeau, who had bankrupted some of New York's best department stores; showbiz impresario Garth Drabinsky, who had been indicted on sixteen counts of fraud; and Alfred Taubman, the chairman of Sotheby's, who went to jail for price fixing. All three were appointed directors by Black after they were in serious trouble with their shareholders, the law, or both. "Like Napoleon and other of his romantic heroes, Conrad saw himself as bigger than life, confident that he could follow his own rules," Stephen Jarislowsky, the guru of Canadian corporate governance, concluded. "He can not stop living on the edge. If he asked me to serve on his board, I would want $1 billion of liability insurance to protect myself. I don't think anyone in his right mind would want to be an independent director at Hollinger."

TRACING THE CHRONOLOGY of Black's descent into a hell of his own making, I struggled with the question: Why? What was it all about, Conrad? I concluded that the arc of Black's downfall coincided with his appointment, in the autumn of 2001 (appropriately enough on Halloween), to Westminster's upper chamber, when he assumed his title, Lord Black of Crossharbour. The name came from an area of bonded warehouses within the walls of nineteenth-century London that contained the departure docks for imperial ventures, near Canary Wharf where Black had his office. Lords are expected to choose titles that identify their geographic locations. Since Canary Wharf was on the Isle of Dogs, his only other options would have been what Black called "the slightly un-euphonious" titles of Lord Canary or Lord of the Dogs.

He had always wanted to be a press lord; now he was. But he took the wrong message from that elevation. His title had less to do with merit than with position, since it was traditionally bestowed on proprietors of the Conservative *Telegraph*, having been given to Black's predecessor, Lord Hartwell, and most of his predecessors during the newspaper's 130-year history. Yet Black started acting as if, having joined a higher order of humanity, he could disregard conventional boundaries. (Hence Conrad's declaration when climbing aboard one of his private jets at the height of the crisis: "I'm not prepared to reenact the French Revolutionary renunciation of the rights of nobility.")

The British House of Lords is roughly equivalent to Canada's Senate, except that our Upper Chamber is as lively as a rock concert, compared to Westminster's dreary mausoleum. I had visited the Lords most frequently in the mid 1980s, researching my books on the Hudson's Bay Company, because many of its former governors were in attendance. I found myself in a geriatric paradise stuffed with stuffed elderly dukes, earls, barons, and bishops. They sat there, gazing vacantly at one another, whispering in mildewed tones, terrified of dying with empty appointment books. I spotted three former prime ministers: Alec Douglas-Home (Lord Home of the Hirsel), Harold Wilson (Lord Wilson of Rievaulx), and James Callaghan (Lord Callaghan of Cardiff). "In his dotage, sorry to say, makes no sense at all," somebody breathed, pointing at Wilson, nodding in a corner with a fixed grin on his face. My host was the fourth Lord Strathcona and Mount Royal, a great-grandson of the Labrador fur trader who had been associated for seventy-five years with the HBC, twenty-five of them as its governor. The current Strathcona turned out to be a tall, courtly gentleman with a great white beard and hair growing all over him, sprouting out of his collar and shirt cuffs. "I'll risk the beef," he said, as we settled into the Peers' Dining Room, a setting straight out of an Alexander Korda extravaganza, with silver serving dishes and waiters who appeared to have been carved out of Pears soap. It was not an inspiring spectacle, and I wondered why anyone with his marbles intact would want to be a lord.

Conrad had waged an unrelenting if secret campaign on behalf of his title. When he casually remarked to his old school chum Dan Coulson, then in operational charge of the *Telegraph*, that he really wasn't sure whether he wanted it, the answer came back, "Oh, come on, Conrad, you'd crawl over broken glass for it." During the time when he was up for the title, he telephoned 10 Downing Street so often that they began to make fun of him, because he sarcastically introduced himself to prime ministerial aides as "The Great Commoner." As soon as Jean Chrétien, the Canadian prime minister, heard the rumour, he notified Tony Blair that under an eighty-year-old non-binding resolution statute, Canadians were discouraged from accepting foreign titles, and the British prime minister took the exasperated Conrad's name off that season's list.[17] And Black sued Chrétien twice but couldn't find a Canadian court that would take his brief seriously. He finally renounced his Canadian citizenship with the wordy snort: "Having opposed for thirty years precisely the public policies that have caused scores of thousands of educated and talented Canadians to abandon their country every year, it is at least consistent that I should join their dispersal."

If becoming a lord made Conrad feel impregnable, he must have been barricaded into a realm of his own invention, more attuned to the hallucinations of Don Quixote than the *realpolitik* of Napoleon Bonaparte. Black had not so much been corrupted by power as by the appearance of power. One satirical theory put

---

[17] In fact, at least a dozen Canadians had been awarded British knighthoods while retaining their citizenships.

forward by Black's confidant, John Fraser, master of the University of Toronto's Massey College, is that since, under Tony Blair's populist government, most appointees to the Lords had been commoners, it would be "Conrad's first opportunity to meet ordinary people."

As I watched him that day of his induction ceremony, comfortably lodged between Baroness Thatcher and Lord Carrington, duded up in his ermine collar, crimson robe, and goofy wig, slow-marching into this hall of the living dead, I wondered, in the name of all that was holy, whether it had been worth surrendering his Canadian citizenship for such a dubious privilege.

EVERY ONCE IN A WHILE the gene pool spits out a Conrad Black. It is a tragedy for him and for Canada that he didn't live up to his potential as a model twenty-first-century entrepreneur. The last of the great press barons, as opposed to the smooth media moguls who followed, Conrad was possessed, as the American writer Michael Lewis put it, "by a clarity of vision, prompted by the purest form of greed." In his anguished progression from idol to outcast, Black suffered some telling insults. When it became obvious that he was on the way out, the price of his company's stock more than doubled – ironically, making his shares worth that much more. At the same time, while his companies were barely staying afloat, his chief rival (and one time equal) Rupert Murdoch was setting new revenue records and reporting earnings increases of 70 per cent. Black's saddest moment was his forced surrender of the *Telegraph*'s chairmanship, which had been his passport to the international status he had so dearly coveted. He had turned the once valuable title into a money-loser that was nevertheless a cash cow for him. In 2003, for example, the newspaper had to pay an extraordinarily high dividend of £55 million to Black's management company. That was £15 million more than the *Telegraph* group's pre-tax profit. When he was asked if he would ever consider giving up that prestigious franchise, he echoed the owner of Harrods department store: "To quote Mr. Al Fayed, only God will separate me from the *Telegraph*." (And He did.)

While Black had tried to sell the *Telegraph* to the Barclays without bothering with shareholder approval, once the Delaware judge disallowed that end run and Hollinger's operational arm openly solicited bids (selling the paper to the brothers for $1.6 billion), Conrad switched sides and haughtily demanded a shareholder vote. The reason for these shenanigans was Black's justified suspicion that if the paper was sold outside his personal jurisdiction the proceeds would be held in escrow to cover future litigation against him. (Still the ambitious socialite, he bolstered his case for the value of the *Telegraph* by pointing out that "the property can pave the way for the owner to dine with the Queen.") Judge Strine threw out his case, ending Black's struggle for financial survival.

Strange things began to happen. London's National Portrait Gallery, which is a movable feast of Great Britain's greatest sons and daughters, quietly removed the Blacks' portrait. The British capital's chattering classes pegged Conrad as being the reincarnation of Augustus Melmotte, the anti-hero of Anthony Trollope's epic novel *The Way We Live Now*. A mysterious financier of dubious integrity, Melmotte comes to London from the Continent in 1871. Described as "a man of Napoleonic ruthlessness," he purchases an outsize mansion in Grosvenor Square, is awarded a title, and takes up with the coquettish Lady Carbury, portrayed as being "false from head to foot." Melmotte is at first embraced by the British Establishment but later revealed to be "a horrid, big rich scoundrel," becomes bankrupt, and takes his own life. One of London's most talented journalists, who had worked for Black, condemned him for "living outside the Judeo-Christian tradition," and being instead "in the Nietzsche-Darwin mould, where no rules apply." He lost his remaining credibility at the *Telegraph* when he closed the staff canteen, drastically reduced the budget of the paper's reference library, and attempted an abortive raid on the pension plan. A former editor of the *Sunday Telegraph*, the wonderfully named Peregrine Worsthorne, accused Black of turning his papers into American and Israeli propaganda sheets, "proving himself to be a proprietor with scant respect for the financial niceties – the very opposite, in short, of a guarantor of respectability and reliability – but also imposing upon the editorial line all the inflexibility of an ideology."

Meanwhile in Canada, a Montreal academic named George Tombs, who spent several years writing a Black biography and had talked with dozens of his associates, started to get midnight calls from his interviewees. They surreptitiously begged him to let them alter their testimony, now that Conrad was under water. It was typical of Canada's psyche that Black's downfall created ill-concealed joy. "When can anyone remember one person bringing as much happiness to Canadians as Conrad Black has provided?" asked Robert Fulford in the *National Post*. "This has been a time of intense pleasure for all who detest or envy Lord Black. . . . The daily news has seldom been less than exhilarating."

What had impressed me in reconstructing his grab for Argus so many years ago was the subtlety of his tactics and the smoothness of their execution. "You've got to have the cadence just right," he told me, "and you must treat events with a certain rhythm, maintaining a kind of symmetry as if you were conducting a symphony orchestra." He had done precisely that, at every step of the struggle to win the Argus crown and in his dazzling coup to gain ownership of the *Telegraph* group.

But in devising his defence against the avalanche of charges hurled at him, he acted more like Peter Sellers than Arturo Toscanini. It was that absence of planning or strategy, anything really except stonewalling, flat denials, temper tantrums, and pratfalls, once his integrity and methods had been challenged, that I found so puzzling. He must have seen the storm approaching. Tony Fell had warned him, as had others, but he did nothing, ignoring viable options, allowing the riptide of accusations to wash over him. That left his friends, critics, and observers alike convinced that he was either dumb or guilty, and he is not stupid.

But as I talked to those closest to him and meditated about this strange construct, so flawed and yet so talented, a third and highly improbable alternative emerged. He was truly convinced that he had done nothing wrong: he believed that he was merely following the jungle ethic of unfettered capitalism, the ideological mainstay of his own upbringing and that of his chosen handmaiden. He genuinely imagined himself to be one of the anointed, immune to the mundane regulations that govern ordinary behaviour, and he felt comfortable about flouting society's conventions, since he recognized no sanctions except his own.

I recalled one long afternoon that had grown into evening, during my original interviews for *The Establishment Man*, when it came to me that he suffered from what the French call *l'orgueil* – an untranslatable desire to play God that implies its possessor is seldom wrong and never regretful. "I may make mistakes, but at the moment I can't think of any," Black cheerfully admitted that day, in a phrase that he pronounced carefully, as though rehearsing his own epitaph.

No need to prompt him now. Chances are that he will spend the rest of his life as a refugee from his media empire. Unlike Napoleon Bonaparte, who spent his dreary exiles on forlorn islands in the Mediterranean and South Atlantic, Conrad Black will suffer the ignominy of internal exile, reviled by his onetime admirers, shunned by the very capitalists whose role model he imagined himself to be.

He will feel terminally puzzled by this turn of events and blame everyone except himself. Black's nature is governed by a brash certainty that he was exempt from evil, and therefore innocent of any accusations, even before they were made or after they had been documented. Because he had so much, he thought he should have it all. Within his imperious bearing there thrived an inclination to avarice which, like Amiel's obsession with luxury, knew no bounds.

Conrad had turned himself into a latter day Citizen Kane. He looked like a young Orson Welles and behaved like an old William Randolph Hearst.

Babs and Conrad, our very own golden couple, have been disgraced. They may have millions squirrelled away to tide them over in great comfort and aplomb, but they have lost their reputation and social standing. We no longer envy them. We pity them. And that must be the most cruel punishment of all.

CHAPTER FIFTEEN

THE SPY WHO CAME INTO THE FOLD

—⁂—

Corporate power is not tangential to Canadian society.
Corporate power is Canadian society.
— Professor James Eayrs

I drove past the countrified mailbox with the "Green Meadows" sign on it, followed the colonial-style picket fence, cruised up the manicured driveway between its elegantly swaying willows, and finally caught sight of the magnificent Toronto residence of John Angus "Bud" McDougald, dean of the Canadian Establishment.

It was Tara, Georgian columns and all, right out of *Gone with the Wind*. And if there was any truth to my conjecture that the Establishment was the country's hidden but all-powerful gravitational force, a second government of sorts whose members set the politicians' boundaries, I was about to meet the *real* prime minister of Canada.

It had taken me most of 1972 to negotiate this opening gambit for a series of volumes I hoped to write, tracing the ganglia of the influential decision-makers who ran the country. When I left Ottawa to edit the *Toronto Star*, I lost politics as the subject for future books; with my determination to write about what I *felt*, I had to be on the spot, inside the arena where Canadian politics was still practised as a blood sport.

Almost accidentally, in Toronto I began to meet the heads of large corporations and the chairmen of the humongous Big Five banks, men who were secretive, puritanical, uptight, and yet, for all their arrogance, compellingly fascinating. My interest grew as I learned to discern the subtle differences between wealth and power, between influence and authority – not to mention between their reality and mine. A few of the individuals I approached became openly hostile when I outlined my intentions, some were friendly, all were circumspect. For the most part, they treated me warily but did not exclude me entirely from their confidences. Having limited their past dealings with journalists to muffled signals transmitted through their public relations flacks, they weren't sure how to treat me, since I expressed little interest in their balance sheets. Instead, I wanted to know who they really were, how they connected with one another, and, most of all, what lay behind those tiny doses of accountability they released like limp balloons at annual meetings. Apart from creating fortunes for themselves, these disciples of unbridled capitalism were dedicated to bringing profitable order out of democratic chaos. They believed in the capitalist system without any sense of sin, as the Inuit must have felt about sex before the missionaries came. I quickly realized the validity of Gore Vidal's admonition that anyone who doesn't feel paranoid about power is not in full possession of the facts.

Viewed through a working journalist's hourglass, the exercise of power is essentially a spectacle of character and circumstance in conflict, and that was what intrigued me. Quarterly corporate earnings may drive investors to ecstasy or despair, but it was the raw exercise of power that fascinated me, because it provoked the most compelling of human emotions: greed, fear, the need for conquest, the almost sexual excitement of unleashing power. Power was best defined by Lord Russell, the British mathematician-philosopher, as "the production of intended effects."

Recognizing the validity of John Porter's epic study *The Vertical Mosaic*, which showed that power resides in various elites, I did not intend to fit the Canadian Establishment into any quantitative sociological categories. The seminal revelation came over a jug of Merlot I shared in the early 1970s with University of Toronto political scientist James Eayrs, who had become one of my liveliest *Star* columnists. He reminded me that Canada's Establishment was dominated by the corporate elite because its members moved freely from function to function, sliding in and out of Liberal Cabinets, filling pivotal seats on the boards of cultural institutions, making themselves felt within the governing bodies of universities, running most of the aggregations of power in the country that counted. "Corporate power is not tangential to Canadian society," he told me. "Corporate power *is* Canadian society." This ran counter to the conviction held by most Canadians that they lived in a proudly classless society, in the sense that nearly everyone belonged to what George Orwell cleverly called "the lower-upper-middle" class.

I would prove otherwise. I would document my theory that most of our destinies were governed by a shadowy group of financial manipulators I called the Canadian Establishment. I would define and detail their origins, interconnections, rivalries, prejudices, values, strengths, mercenary motives, and operational codes. This would not be a bloodless audit of their common strains – this would be a journalist's exposé of who they were, what they did, and how they got away with it.

The deeper I tunnelled into these bastions of established authority, the more I realized there was no point trying to push my way into their company as just another UCC old boy, pretending I was one of them. They would never accept me or share their confidences if I remained the earnest Viennese Jew with a notebook, determined to invade their privacy. I would have to humour them, shatter their vows of silence by becoming their court jester.

I was not interested in becoming a clown but felt highly intrigued by the Shakespearean notion of the court jester as a streetwise bit player who gathered and delivered uncomfortable truths to the court, disguised as quips and fables. He brought news of the troubled outside world to the royal entourage, at the same time telling tales about the court's smug intrigues to those outside the castles' battlements. He was in the court, but not of it. Any reigning monarch with a pinch of wisdom realized he had little to lose by allowing a court jester into his presence; his professional ambivalence could be exploited. In her masterful profile of me in *Saturday Night*, Elspeth Cameron was the only one who caught the essence of my tightrope act: "On one side of the high wire, satire (which would alienate his subjects); on the other, hero worship (which would cloy his readers). With all the sly cunning obsequiousness of the court jester, Newman managed to flatter his courtiers and slyly nudge his audience at the same time."

I still can't believe I got away with it.

My venture almost foundered before it started. Everyone warned me that if I was serious about tracing the roots of power in Canadian society, I would somehow have to persuade "Bud" McDougald, the chairman of Argus Corporation, the country's most significant private capital pool, to take me into his confidence. That was not in the cards. Unlike his predecessor, E.P. Taylor, whose mantle he now carried, McDougald shunned public notice. Few Canadians were aware of his existence, and even those insiders who operated in his immediate orbit knew him less by sight than by reputation. McDougald had no interest in what people thought of him. He understood power, where it resides, and how to exercise it, and thus knew that discretion was good, anonymity better. He had never been interviewed before, and the last time he'd had his picture taken for the newspapers was in 1940, during a savings bond drive. He sensed that those of his would-be peers who appeared on television or in books, magazines, and newspapers did so because they were still in the process of testing the stretch of their authority. McDougald knew precisely where he belonged: at the very top. He may well have been the least visible member of Canada's business Establishment, but without question, he was its most powerful.

McDougald was the archetype of the evil tycoons the radicals loved to fanaticize about. His lifestyle, his imperial bearing, his view of public power (bad) and private prerogative (good) ran to type. He was obsessively tough and chivalrous, ultra-right-wing in his outlook, and self-confident to a degree that went beyond mere pride and prejudice and was something simpler, like terminal self-absorption. Because he had never lost at anything he'd tried, winning had become the only tolerable condition of life for him. During the half-century he spent building up his corporate holdings and personal fortune, McDougald's claim to uncommon privilege had been nurtured by the obsequiousness of the many lesser men who found comfort in deferring to his certitudes.

I wrote and telephoned McDougald asking for an interview, but received the expected brush-off. Then I managed to wheedle from a prominent Bay Street fundraiser a list of his best friends and started to invite them for lunch, explaining what I was doing, how badly I needed to interview Bud, who wouldn't talk to me, and how I was therefore going to describe his $10-billion empire as best I could on my own. This produced the expected reaction. "What $10-billion empire? Bud's lucky if it's worth $2 billion. You can't do that. It would be highly irresponsible!" Of course they were right, but I put on my best "we're all friends at the money trough" look and assured them that I had confidential documents proving the man we called "Bud" was a dark and wicked creature who knew the secrets of the deep, and bits of nonsense like that. I kept it up till my luncheon companions started looking at me funny, which was exactly what I wanted. I was well aware that as soon as they were back in their offices, they would be on the hotline to Bud: "There's this crazy guy out there, editor of Canada's biggest newspaper, and he's got these goofy theories about you he aims to publish. Sounds like a rotter or a nut. Stop him, Bud. This could turn nasty for all of us."

Nothing much happened. I would occasionally see McDougald in the distance, staring at me during some public event, but I would pay no attention and keep contentedly muttering into my nonexistent beard. Then one sunny Wednesday he called, out of the blue, inviting me to Green Meadows for "a bite" the following

Sunday, making it very clear that this was *not* for an interview, just to straighten out the facts.

His estate had formerly stretched over three hundred acres, but had been reduced to a mere nineteen in a 1969 deal with the North York City Council that permitted McDougald to maintain the only barn within city limits in return for disposing of his extra land for badly needed housing construction. The homestead consisted of a Georgian stable with attached indoor training arena for his eight resident thoroughbreds, separate cottages for the chauffeur and gardener, an Olympic-sized swimming pool, plus a luxury shed as big as a football field that I couldn't identify. But it was the gleaming mansion – large enough to require a permanent staff of six servants – with its Rhett Butler ambience and hand-crafted shutters, all there within sight of the city's apartment towers, stabbing aimlessly at the sky, that made me blink in disbelief.

He greeted me coolly, as though I had come to sell him a vacuum cleaner. Then he started to walk around me, assessing my conformation, inspecting me like a horse that he was about to reject for his fancy stable. But I was well briefed, geographically and socially, and casually pointed out (as if reciting the Stations of the Cross) nearby gentlemen farmers whose estates I had visited. He softened a little but kept his distance, as if I might bite him. That gave me a chance to have my first good look at the man. Well into his sixties, McDougald's physical appearance was surprisingly engaging. The cheek lines that stretched from his nose to the corners of his mouth formed a precise isosceles triangle. The blue-grey eyes were watchful, alert to my every move, or any signals that might betray my true intent. His grooming was beyond impeccable: the three-piece suit was fashioned by the firm of Huntsman's, one of Savile Row's most exclusive shops (and Conrad Black's bespoke tailor thirty years later). His English bench-made shoes had been carved from the hides of young alligators.

At our indoor picnic lunch, I didn't have any trouble picking the right fork because only one was offered, but when he asked about my background, I described in great and exaggerated detail our luxurious pre-war lifestyle and the size of my father's sugar factory, broadly hinting that he had been the Bud McDougald of pre-war Moravia, which was a serious misrepresentation both of my father and of Moravia. Whatever I said was enough to earn me a grand tour of the house. The front hall had a porcelain fireplace, blue-and-white wallpaper, a huge bowl of seasonal flowers on an Adam table, and a Scottish grandfather clock made by Robert Macadam of Dumfries. The sunroom was done up in white wicker with pink chintz. The pale-green-and-gold decor of the drawing room provided an elegant setting for the richness of the Queen Anne furniture; the dining room featured the inevitable Sheraton table with ecru lace mats. The walls were crammed with paintings of horses. There was a majestic canvas of McDougald in the dining room by Sir James Gunn, who had painted the official portrait of the Queen, and a striking canvas in the sitting room of his wife by Pietro Annigoni. The pantry had special cabinets for seven sets of exquisite china, including a complete Lowestoft service. The dessert silver was fashioned out of gold.

The upstairs quarters of Mrs. McDougald (whose real name was Maude but whom everyone called Jim) were dominated by pink. There was even a pink dog's dish in her pink bathroom. An intelligent and attractive presence, she had been an Olympic figure skater and a golf champion, and had ridden a motorcycle for the Red Cross during the war. Of Conrad Black's later takeover of her husband's company, which she and her sister, Doris Phillips, inherited, she later complained: "My sister and I, like absolute idiots, birdbrains, signed and signed the transfer documents. It was our stupidity, really. I don't think we can blame anyone else."

Then "Bud" asked me if I wanted to see his garage, without hinting why. This was the large shed I couldn't identify on the way in. It turned out to be a museum housing his thirty cars, and the only garage I've ever seen lit by glittering chandeliers. There were five Rolls-Royces, including a 1913 Silver Ghost that was the most valuable in captivity; a 1928 model 38-250-SS supercharged Mercedes-Benz with a custom handmade body; the 1924 Isotta

Fraschini Type B built (out of tulip wood) for the Spanish king Alfonso XIII; a 1909 Hupmobile; a 1920 Kissel Gold Bug; plus various Bentleys, Packards, Bugattis, Alfa Romeos, not to mention four custom-built Cadillacs. On the side of each vehicle, so small it was hardly visible, there had been affixed a gold shield engraved with McDougald's coat of arms and his take-no-prisoners motto: *Vincere Vel Mori* (Conquer Or Die).

I inspected the cars but watched McDougald, learning to read his silences and every twitch of his eyebrows. He was beginning to relax, and following our car tour, he told me a rambling anecdote about power and the limitless boundaries of its exercise as we sat in his sunroom, cluttered with racing trophies and Royal Family mementos.

"One day," he recalled, "I was coming back from London on a Pan American plane – my wife and I were on it – when Bishop Fulton J. Sheen got on and sat near us. It was an old Stratocruiser, and we were about an hour out and were supposed to go to Shannon first, when the pilot announced we were going to have to change course and fly to Reykjavik, Iceland. He said we were going to run into some pretty rough weather, and we'd better tighten our seat belts. It was the worst trip I was ever on. You could see the old wings just flapping.

"My wife said to me, 'Give me fifty dollars, quick.'

"I said, 'What do you want fifty dollars for? Here I am, all strapped in.'

"'Well, give me a hundred dollars, then.'

"'What do you want a hundred dollars for?'

"'There's Bishop Sheen. I want to give it to him so he'll pray for us.'

"'Don't worry about him,' I said, 'he's full out now. What's good for the bishop will be all right for us . . .'

"We landed in Iceland about midnight. It was broad daylight. It was an American base [Keflavik] and all those GIs came down to the plane to see Sheen, and I thought, now there's a fellow, if he wanted to twist that power, what damage he could do.

"A few weeks later I was having lunch with Cardinal Spellman in New York and Sheen happened to be there. When I was introduced to him he said, 'Oh, you're the fellow who wouldn't let your wife give me that hundred dollars. I'm mentioning it on my program tonight,' and he did. But I couldn't help thinking about the power that man had at that time; it was fantastic."

He was relaxed now. At some point during our chatter I had quoted to him the accurate Argus asset and profit figures "just to straighten out the facts." In fact, he owned only 275 shares of Argus. But he was the majority shareholder in Ravelston Corporation, which exercised control over the entire conglomerate. (The same arrangement as in Conrad Black's day.)

His manner of speaking was lulling, without highs or lows: the most recent visit to his Toronto house by Prince Philip; the rose-cultivating skills of his head gardener; the socialist tendencies of Pierre Elliott Trudeau; his triumphs at the British racetracks; the new Massey-Ferguson plant being built in Poland; the real reason the Packard Motor Car Company went bust: the advice he gave President Eisenhower about dealing with the Russians; the broken valve on the propane tank that heated his swimming pool – all discussed in the same monotone. There was little sense of irony in his makeup. He told me that he had never taken a drink, never smoked or eaten sweets, hadn't had a cavity for thirty years. That was about as philosophical as he got.

He loved the insider's world he had created for himself, but never really felt comfortable with the changing ethics of the society in which he had prospered. He would have felt much more at home within the strictly defined hierarchies of the seventeenth-century England of Thomas Hobbes, who saw life "as a perpetuall and restless desire of power after power that ceaseth only in Death."

The harsher side of McDougald's nature was tempered by a Henry Jamesian sense of the urbane, a faith in proper etiquette, the restriction of passion, respect for privacy and the proper order of things. As we talked into the afternoon, I detected an unexpected facet of his character. In the face of all his power and riches, there was a cast of sadness in Bud McDougald's world. Although he had set himself above the constraints of ordinary lives, happiness had not visibly followed. He seemed dimly aware of some loss to which he could not put a name. Somehow the anticipated satisfactions kept eluding him; more success didn't bring anything he couldn't have had before – except perhaps the absence of fear. "I admire guts more than anything else in other people," he said, holding me, suddenly, in his steely gaze. "There are so many people you can trip up because you can outsmart them. Not because you're smart, but because they're afraid." Without either of us confirming it, I knew my secret was out: he had figured out the trick I had used to obtain access to his presence, and he admired me for it, because I hadn't been afraid.

He winked. I shrugged. We had reached an understanding. *The Canadian Establishment* was born.

McDougald had grown up in his father's Rosedale mansion and sporadically attended Upper Canada College but was best remembered for being "asked to leave" the college after tying the rear axle of the principal's Model T to a tree branch, so that when he got in and started up his wheels spun in the air. The extent of Bud's fortune was difficult to estimate. The combination of his personal stock holdings and his position as chairman and president of Argus gave him direct control over such dominant corporations as Dominion Stores, Massey-Ferguson, Hollinger Mines, Domtar, and Standard Broadcasting. "We're proprietors," he said of the Argus setup, "and that's where I got the reputation for being tough. When you own something you can say what you mean and not be afraid of losing your job."

I received the best indication of his income from Percy Finlay, a Hollinger director who had grown weary of McDougald's endless lamentations about the iniquities of the federal government. "Bud, why do you think you have the right to complain so much about this country?" he had asked him one day in the Toronto

Club, surrounded by the big-money men sipping their Macallans. McDougald didn't even glance around before he gave his answer. "Because," he said, "I'm the only man in this room who has paid personal income tax of more than a million dollars every year for the past sixteen years." Bud believed that his high tax bill automatically granted him a roving commission to criticize governmental activities. But he was never tempted to run for Parliament, dismissing the idea "because of the sort of people you have to meet, all that terrible going to strawberry festivals and the like." He considered all politicians suspect by definition, and when I asked him to name one exception, he couldn't. Finally, after torturous effort and the running down of long lists of possible candidates, he allowed that perhaps Abraham Lincoln wasn't all that bad. Then a look of pure mischief came over his face: "Of course, I like John Wilkes Booth even better."

What I found most interesting about McDougald was that he had used his indigenous power base to build up remarkable circles of influence in Britain and the United States. He had little trouble masquerading as an Englishman or American. He told me about the time he was having tea with his friend Sir Harmar Nicholls, a British MP, on the terrace of Westminster, when two Labour members came by, took one look at McDougald in his morning coat, and, assuming he was a new Tory backbencher, tried to enlist him in a scheme to tear down St. Paul's Cathedral for a housing project. McDougald became so vehement in defence of the British traditions represented by St. Paul's that the Labourites abandoned the idea on the spot.

While in London, McDougald stayed at the ultra-luxurious Claridge's Hotel in a special suite with bay windows angled to allow him an unobstructed view of his Phantom VI Rolls-Royce parked on the street below, so that he could signal the chauffeur when he was on his way down. The oversized limousine was decorated in royal colours and lent to the Queen for ceremonial occasions. He knew the Royal Family well enough that on his 1967 visit to Toronto Prince Philip chose to stay with him, as did

Princess Anne and her husband, Captain Mark Phillips, when they came to open the Royal Agricultural Winter Fair in 1974.[1]

The American headquarters of McDougald's empire was an eighteen-bathroom Mediterranean-style villa on Palm Beach's Ocean Boulevard (near Conrad Black's future mansion), which he bought from one of the du Pont heirs in 1960. While in Palm Beach, Bud entertained at the Bath and Tennis Club, which had the only swimming pool in the world that maintained a bylaw against the display of bellybuttons, and the Everglades Club, which not only didn't allow Jewish members, but banned Jewish guests as well. (Conrad belongs; Barbara doesn't.)

Our only disagreement came when my book was done and McDougald asked to see a draft of my chapter about him. I told him that I never showed anyone anything I had written before publication and that he could be no exception. He rose from his desk, expressed some not very complimentary thoughts about me, hinted heavily that for him to purchase Maclean Hunter might be worth the trouble of shutting me up, and finally calmed down when he recognized that my position was not negotiable.

After the book appeared, he would occasionally invite me to drop into his Argus office, to sip Richmello Instant Coffee and munch Dominion Store vanilla cookies, speculating on the state of the world, discussing how fast the country was going down the drain, and tabulating who was moving up or down in the Canadian corporate power game. Our meetings continued into the fall of

---

[1] Murray Koffler, then chairman of Shoppers Drug Mart and unofficial head of Toronto's Jewish community, knew the royal couple was there, but McDougald, who didn't even pretend that some of his best friends were Jews, refused to invite him to a reception he had organized to keep the regal presences within his social orbit. Not for a minute put off by that cold shoulder, Koffler walked through the back door leading to the McDougalds' kitchen, told the cook he was a friend of the family, and strode into the living room. Catching sight of Koffler, the Princess rushed right over to welcome him, much to Bud's dismay. (Murray and his wife, Marvelle, had been the only Canadians invited to Mark and Anne's wedding.)

1977, just before he left Canada for the last time, when he decided we should visit the Toronto Club together "to show the flag a little." The club was his private fiefdom. He headed the admissions committee and confessed to me that it was the only kind of committee he would ever join: a committee of one, himself. Our visit was a memorable occasion. McDougald was ushered in like royalty through a private door, scattering small comments to favoured members as if they were papal benedictions. Those he missed came over to his table (reserved for him whether he was in town or not) to seek his approbation. But he wasn't happy with what he saw. "My God, it looks like a convention of plumbers in here," he complained. "People are actually coming into the Toronto Club wearing wooden shoes!"

That reminded me of another criterion McDougald had used in determining the club's membership. He would never allow anyone to join who wore white or diamond-patterned socks. His wife told me of an occasion when a man's socks had ruined his career. "They were looking for quite a top executive for one of the Argus companies, and they had tried everybody," she recalled. "Finally, this chap seemed as if he were going to be simply perfect. Some of the other executives had met and interviewed him, and the poor fellow came into our living room, hitched up his trouser legs and sat down, showing his white socks. My husband turned to the others and just said, 'Out . . . Useless.'"[2]

After he left for the season in Palm Beach, McDougald kept calling, telling me at least one new story about himself. My favourite concerned a large ranch he had acquired in Florida, which had housed a private zoo. Under the terms of his purchase, the animals were to be removed, but he discovered that the alligators had been left behind, dozing in the sun. McDougald demanded to know why. The former owner informed him that it was because

---

[2] A quarter-century after McDougald's death, veteran Toronto Club members still pay homage to his memory, nodding reverentially as they pass his special table, the only one with armchairs.

she had read in my book about his preference for alligator shoes. He blamed me for his having to bear the expense of removing the animals himself, since he didn't wish to disappoint the previous landlord about the accuracy of my research.

We all hate to get older, but it was typical of McDougald that he would try to do something about it. During the final two years of his life, he engaged in a battle of documents with the archives of the 48th Highlanders, attempting to prove that he really was two years younger than his recorded age, vaguely maintaining that he had faked his birth date in order to enlist when he was a youngster. The few friends who were aware of the ploy realized it was part of his half-serious attempt to extend his term as a director of the Canadian Imperial Bank of Commerce past the compulsory retirement age of seventy.

During our last conversation before he left Toronto, I asked about the provisions he had for succession at Argus, since he was childless.

"*If*, as and when I croak . . ." he started to reply.

The unfinished phrase hung between us. I ventured to ask, "How do you mean, '*If*?'"

He looked at me for a long, revealing moment, as if staring into the camera of history. Then he shrugged, raised his eyebrows, and waved his hand in a gesture of dismissal that seemed to indicate that both of us were well aware of the complexities of human existence, and what was the point in adding to them.

McDougald died in 1978, one day short of his seventieth birthday. His strength of will found one posthumous expression. When reviewing the arrangements for his burial, his wife realized that Bud would have been appalled by the length of the hair on the sextet of young professional attendants supplied by Rosar-Morrison, the funeral directors. She telephoned the firm and told them that her late husband wanted them to get their hair cut. They did.

I remember Bud McDougald with mixed emotions. While I didn't share his view of the world, at least he had temporarily allowed me into his, as my entry point into Canada's Establishment.

His passing removed from the corporate scene one of its few memorable characters. The digital computer men who succeeded him managed their affairs more efficiently (except Conrad Black, who used Bud's corporate conjuring tricks but had none of his subtlety) but they lacked his grandeur, chivalry, and ultimate conceit. He was the last of his kind, and I was glad to have known him.[3]

THE MASSIVE OAK DOOR to the elegant apartment tower near Upper Canada College was guarded by two rumpled, unjacketed doormen. They looked very out of place and very Canadian there amongst the Jacobean chairs, Oriental rugs, and dark tiled floors, scattering cigarette ashes over all that chaste splendour, getting ready to pull out their portable radio for the showdown between the Philadelphia Flyers and Toronto Maple Leafs.

Christina and I were there to visit Neil McKinnon, the recently deposed chairman of the Canadian Imperial Bank of Commerce (CIBC), who lived one floor below the penthouse, with a panoramic view across the city that seemed eternally enchanting, no matter what the hour or the season. He was a small man, tanned, with freckles on his forehead, who tended to wear grey, summer-weight suits, slightly too large for him in the shoulders, with ties – black and grey prints – too narrow for the fashion. He looked neutral somehow, like a Swiss ambassador to the Principality of Monaco. The apartment was large and comfortable, filled with floating pink silks, *matelassé* grey sofas, and the de rigueur Sheraton dining-table set with hand-embroidered placemats, crystal, and some kind of silver ding-dong in the middle. McKinnon moved among these comforts like a very powerful man with all the accoutrements of

---

[3] Black was deferential to McDougald while he was alive and able to determine the future of Argus, but posthumously Conrad had nothing but contempt for him: "The whole Argus empire was a façade," he told me. "Quite apart from all this mythology of Bud being the great arbiter of the Canadian corporate elite, his companies were incompetently run and on a one-way trip to the receiver."

big money but none of the ease. Even though he operated in circles of supreme influence he had never quite shaken off the air of a chartered accountant from Cobalt, Ontario, where he went to work for the Bank of Commerce when he was only fourteen. McKinnon rose to become for seventeen years Canada's top banker, only to be relieved of his power by a directors' rebellion late in 1973.

I assigned myself the difficult task of reconstructing the only *coup d'etat* in the history of Canadian banking. If I could somehow capture that unique event, it would endow my initial volume with an authentic – and very rare – example of civil war within the Canadian Establishment. To make the point stick, I would need to gain access to the minutes of the board meetings where the ouster took place. This presented a triple-tiered problem: all board meetings of publicly traded companies were secret (even to court jesters), none more so than the monthly gatherings of bank directors, and within the banking community the minutes of the CIBC were treated with the stealth usually accorded state documents carried in briefcases chained to couriers' wrists.

I knew McKinnon well enough to realize there would never be another banker like him. Unlike his fellow practitioners, who exercised their leverage as an expression of their institutions' collective wills, McKinnon regarded his position as a cockpit of personal power. His self-confidence was due in large measure to his airy dismissal of what had been the surest strength of most Canadian bankers at that time: success by inadvertence. Sustained by three decades of continuous economic growth, their loan decisions stood more than a reasonable chance of being vindicated. McKinnon had a kind of sixth sense about banking. He could parse the prospect's balance sheets in minutes and size up the credit risks involved. He knew how to inject a multiplier into his deals so that the return on large loans wouldn't be limited to the basic principal and interest; how to trade off his clients' strengths against their weaknesses; just how far to float a new venture and when to sever its credit lifeline.

When Christina and I tried to question him about his dethronement as CIBC chairman, he refused to discuss the details. But it must have scared the hell out of him, made him feel vulnerable when he'd thought he would never be vulnerable again. After all, when you've done everything he'd achieved, with chauffeured limousines at his call and private aircraft flying him to board meetings in Philadelphia, Buenos Aires, and Hong Kong; and above all, when you've exercised that headiest of banking powers, the supreme right to veto or approve loans for millions of dollars – when you've done all that and done it exquisitely well for most of twenty years, you think you've armoured yourself against anything life can throw at you. But it turned out that he had not armoured himself against hurt, and this explained his look of wounded perplexity.

Neil McKinnon's problem was that he understood power better than he understood talent. When it came to dealing with the executives who worked for him, he used his intelligence as a weapon instead of as a security blanket, under which they might share his confidences. Impatient with subordinates who wanted reasons and assurances, he made most of the big decisions himself. "Neil ran the Commerce as if he were a giant amaranthine plant, a kind of flower that allows no vegetation to flourish in its vicinity," one of Toronto's more botanically minded financiers confided to me. "He could not tolerate crown princes. He would bring good people forward then cut them down." He went through four presidents, including the most promising young executive in the bank, with whom he shared a mistress. Page Wadsworth, his eventual successor, was appointed president twice, but none of this made much difference because McKinnon ran the bank anyway. Whenever he went on trips overseas he would lock his office door, leaving no one with access to important bank documents.

What came into play was an Establishment consensus, never really expressed but forming just the same, that McKinnon had misjudged the mechanics of running a big bank in the modern age. Although he was not aware of it, by the spring of 1971 his iron hold was being questioned among the only group that possessed the countervailing force to bring him down – the bank's own board. At the time, the Commerce had fifty-seven directors, and I knew about a dozen of the main participants in the putsch. From them I was able to piece together a shaky and incomplete outline of what had happened. I called Bud McDougald, who was a veteran Commerce director, to see if he could arrange an appointment with the ex-chairman for me – but he couldn't because he had been one of the rebels.

Then I did something I've never done before or since. I had a few undiluted vodkas, sat down at my typewriter, and wrote a pretend chapter on McKinnon's overthrow. It was full of gaps. When I didn't know exactly what had happened in the boardroom, I made it up. Yet I larded in enough substantive leaks from friendly directors to cause some serious collateral damage (to the bank and to my reputation) if it were ever to be published in that form. I then sent my draft to the ousted chairman by courier, pointing out that, since I had incomplete information, I had no choice but to publish the enclosed manuscript.

I waited for the phone to ring. It did. It was McKinnon. "Get over here," he barked, without even introducing himself. When I saw him in his office, he didn't tell me much, but he did invite Christina and me for dinner that evening.

When we had finished the meal, during which the chatter had been about everything except what was on our minds, McKinnon abruptly stood up, and said, "I've got to take my dog for a walk. Why don't you relax in the library? I'll be a while." We walked into his library, and there was the motherlode. Laid out in chronological order on a desk were the bank board's minutes and internal memoranda, with the essential events marked by yellow grease pencil, so I could follow the plot. I had my story.

It turned out that McKinnon, as he saw it, had been fighting for the fiscal integrity of his bank. A month before the directors voted to reduce his authority, McKinnon had warned that the Commerce's liquidity ratio was too low in relation to outstanding loans. Even the dry prose of the board's minutes couldn't disguise the emotional tone of McKinnon's plea: he had spent most of the Depression of the 1930s in the bank's credit department, and the last time there had been similarly excessive loan ratios was in 1929, just before the Great Crash. Then, on a Sunday night in March 1973, for the first time in its history, the Commerce "went to the window." This was an ultra-secret bailout that granted chartered banks short-term Bank of Canada funds whenever their loans temporarily overtook their assets. The bank's solvency was never in question, but its request was such a serious matter that the Bank of Canada was prompted to send a letter requesting an accounting of its liquidity prospects. To McKinnon this was the ultimate affront, but also the vindication of his concerns. A few days later, he was told that with board approval, Commerce loans officers were out signing up a lot of high-risk, high-profit prospects. "After nearly forty-eight years' service with this institution, of which more than twenty-five years have been spent in positions of most serious responsibility during which the Bank has shown the greatest growth in its history, I do not propose to sit here and watch the financial position of the Bank deteriorate into a totally unmanageable situation," he wrote the directors. But it was too late. He was voted out of office.[4]

By the time Neil McKinnon returned from walking his dog it was after ten and my tape recorder was full of notes from the secret board documents. No one mentioned our little excursion into the library but Christina suggested we call it a night, and within seconds we were out of there.

---

[4] Walking by one of the bank's executive offices, on his way to the fateful board meeting at which he was voted out of office, McKinnon noticed the dissenting directors, along with some of the bank's executives, gathering to toast their coming victory. They were noisy and happy, behaving with high good spirits, as if a siege had been lifted. He walked in and stood there, dead still at the doorway, and stared at them. The revellers fell silent. Then the about-to-be-deposed chairman turned to leave and shot back over his shoulder a memorable farewell: "I just wanted to see what a room full of sons of bitches looks like."

As he was helping me on with my coat, the cashiered chairman of Canada's second-largest bank looked me straight in the eye, and asked, with pretend sweetness: "Tell me, Mr. Newman, do you use this technique very often?"

"No." I grinned back. "Do you?"

THE MCKINNON VISIT turned out to be our last joint venture. Christina had decided that she should leave *Maclean's* so that we could start on *The Canadian Establishment*, which we were planning to write as co-authors, with her concentrating on politics and me writing about business. It hadn't worked. Her approach was much more ideological and opinionated, condemning our elites for their colonial mentality and jungle ethics. I was more interested in laying out the anatomy of the economy's power structure, documenting its incestuous relationships, but instead of condemning it as an axis of evil, allowing readers to make that judgment. This was not done because I was devoid of feelings or opinions, but because in all my writings I had the strong conviction that the best way to involve my readers' emotions was to let *them* decide how they felt – allowing them to determine whether these elitist studs were candidates for beatification or the guillotine.

Our final split was over the approach of the *Establishment* book, but it came to a head during an unconnected dinner at the home of Dick Malone, then publisher of the *Globe and Mail*. A former army brigadier who was on the scene for the liberation of Paris, he lived in the past, so much so that when one evening he kept discussing "the war" I assumed that he had been talking about the Second World War, which was his favourite. But his references made no sense to me, and it turned out he was talking about England's fifteenth-century War of the Roses.

The Brigadier had known Churchill, regularly shopped in Jermyn Street, still drank Madeira after dinner, lived in a Tudor-style house in Toronto's posh Forest Hill area, and was interested in all things British, having met various minor baronets at Blandings

Castle or some manor house. On October 12, 1974, he invited us to come over for dinner because our mutual friend, the Victoria writer Bruce Hutchison, was in town, and knowing we had just come from Ottawa, they wanted to hear the inside story of Trudeau's latest exploits. Malone rolled his cigar and asked me to give the two of them a rundown. I explained that I had been to the capital on a specific mission (trying to get the Liberals to alter Canada's magazine legislation so that *Maclean's* could go weekly) and hadn't reconnoitered the current political situation, but that Christina had, and she might brief them. She did so, brilliantly. At the end of her recital, Malone turned to me, puffed his cigar, and muttered, "Well, that was very interesting, Peter." I hadn't said a word. For a moment, we were both speechless. I pointed out as politely as I could that it was Christina, not me, they ought to be thanking, but it went right over their heads. We skedaddled out of there, but at that moment we both knew the marriage was over.[5]

We had unwittingly, even against our separate wills, set ourselves in competition, and thus become rivals and antagonists. We had enjoyed so many good years, had done so much, created great lives – I look back and fervently wish we could have maintained the miracle of the love we found, and sustained a marriage that ought to have endured. Christina was a wonderfully honest and loving woman, who gave me more of herself than I deserved. Perhaps the vision we held of each other was too perfect. Perhaps I exploited her talents too blatantly for us to remain equal partners, so that while there might still have been love between us, there was no longer truth, and so, sadly, we had to part.

In the end, we divorced over religious differences: I thought I was God, and she didn't. She haunts me still.

---

[5] It was sadly reminiscent of an incident that John Gregory Dunne, the Los Angeles screenwriter and novelist, described in one of his books. A Hollywood producer had come to see him and his wife, the immensely talented Joan Didion, and treated her, as Dunne put it, "as an honourary guy who took notes."

ON MY OWN, I found that what had started out as a vague idea had become an obsession. I wrote six books dissecting Canada's Establishment and spent more than a decade pursuing its adherents. Holding down demanding full-time jobs during the research and writing of these books, I found myself in a frenzied decade of incessant work. I had always woken up early and done my best writing in the early mornings, when my mind was fresh and the phones didn't ring, but now I had to regiment my time, start promptly at 4:00 a.m., and write until I was due in the office at 9:30. The books (coming in at more than 200,000 words each) were topical and so had to be written in a frenzy over eight months (between January and August) prior to fall publication. Eventually I became so exhausted that I could get myself up in the morning only by wearing two wrist alarms, set fifteen minutes apart: the first to jar me out of my deep sleep, the second to get me up.

The idea of there being a dominant elite was hardly original, but I identified their names and stations, their interconnections, habits and habitats, their successes and failures, and tallied their sustaining extravagances. My studies documented the power networks that ran the country, providing half a dozen snapshots of the Canadian elite in transition from the pseudo-aristocracy I had detailed in my first volume (*The Canadian Establishment: The Old Order Dynasties*) to the ascendant meritocracy I described in my last (*Titans: How the New Canadian Establishment Seized Power*). The quote that I had taped on my computer while I wrote the series was from Scott Symons, the radical novelist who became Canada's least expendable exile: "Every nation needs an elite of some kind, or we are stuck with eternal mediocrity as a national fate. And every effort to construe such an Establishment is invidious, hurtful, challenging, delicious . . . and necessary."

I had first become intrigued by the notion of a resident Canadian elite one sunny afternoon during my stay in Ottawa, when I walked out of the Parliament Buildings through the Senate door and encountered Senator Norman McLeod Paterson, the prosperous Fort William grain merchant who owned 109 grain elevators and the largest fleet of ships on the Great Lakes. One foot on the running board of his tug-sized Rolls-Royce, he was having his picture taken, bellowing orders at the cameraman, and glaring at me for disrupting the shot.

"Are you part of the Canadian Establishment?" I asked, not quite knowing what I was asking or what he might reply. He was a big, bloated man, showing his years, with a red face that contorted in anger. "What do you mean, we're rich old men?" he fumed. He then jumped into the car and roared away, almost running over me in his fury. I couldn't figure out why my casual question had caused such consternation from an individual who not only was an arrogant capitalist but acted and looked like the caricature of one. I would learn.

My thesis was no woolly writer's invention. The Establishment was the hidden hand behind the hidden hand that organized means of production, decided who got what and when. Their exercise of self-anointed authority was subtle, yet without appeal. Because of its outsized geography, Canada had no single, monolithic Establishment. Instead it formed overlapping rings of power shaped like the Olympic symbol, orbiting around various capital pools and regional power barons. That overlap formed a confederacy of regional Establishments, loosely knit yet tightly interlocked. The significance of this phenomenon was easily summed up: That how an Establishment organized itself determined how the nation pursued its objectives. That in order to fully understand Canadian society it was not enough to dissect its politics, listen to its music, view its paintings, read its literature, and cheer for its hockey teams. That equal attention had to be paid to the thousand men (and, sadly, too few women) who formed a non-elected government operating beyond the reach of public knowledge and accountability, and who determined trends – political, cultural, and economic – skewing them sharply in their own favour. That members of this *junta* (linked more closely to one another than to their country) formed a psychological entity, based on their common values, common enemies, and common interests.

Jack Clyne, the chief justice of British Columbia, cleared up a mystery for me when he explained: "Money doesn't bring happiness, but often the pursuit of money does." No Canadian was more money-minded than Roy Thomson, the skinflint proprietor of *The Times* of London and the original beneficiary of the North Sea oil bonanza. In 1972, when his friend Max Bell, the Calgary publisher, lay dying of a brain tumour, Thomson came to visit him. "Roy," said Max, "I'm worth millions, but I'd give everything I own for good health." Thomson shook his head in horror and counselled him, "Don't do that, Max. Offer half."

The Establishment loyalists I interviewed led one-dimensional lives; business was their religion. Their laughter had little frivolity. Even sex was usually by appointment. Whether they used power or abused it was determined by what they could get away with. They pretended that real power was political, practised by elected politicians, and that what they exercised was responsibility. (Said in a resonant, sincere voice.) That claim reminded me of watching a Teamsters vice-president testifying to a U.S. congressional inquiry, who was asked whether he would describe his organization as being powerful within the trucking industry. After a puzzled look, trying to decide whether this was a serious question, the bull-throated Teamster replied: "Lissen, Senator, being powerful is like being a lady. If you gotta say you are, you probably ain't."

MY INITIAL VOLUME was the hardest to write because I wasn't sure whether my approach was valid or whether I could obtain access to enough interesting people to make a book about them worth reading. In six years of tough slogging, I taped 678 interviews, most of them with reticent and reluctant individuals who had never talked to a journalist before about anything except their companies' quarterly earnings. It was a particularly difficult season to be recording their thoughts on my tape recorder, since during much of that time the Watergate investigation was grinding on in Washington and the contents of the Nixon Tapes, on which the

American president had confided his most revealing idiocies, were in the daily headlines.

My strangest interview was with Montreal's Joseph Kruger II, the third-generation ruler of his family's newsprint empire, then the fifth largest in North America. He was so paranoid about publicity of any kind that he kept grabbing my tape recorder, pushing the rewind button, and trying to wipe out anything interesting he might have said, which amounted to repeating that he had nothing to say to me. All I discovered was the rather useless fact that his father lived in a thirteenth-century castle near Dublin called Rathaldron and was master of the Meath Fox Hunt. Brian Flemming, the Trudeau aide who later became a Halifax political columnist, expressed a common reaction to my project: "Because he pulls no punches, the miracle is that Newman keeps convincing these enormous egos to keep talking into his tape recorder."

It *was* a miracle. All I know is that if I had been them, I wouldn't have talked to me.

My main advantage was that I am naturally deferential in person (if not behind my computer) and temperamentally unobtrusive. I usually look sleepy and about to expire because I have maintained a killing work schedule most of my adult life to keep up my alimony payments. If I've learned anything, it is that being unassuming and acting helpless gets you almost anything in this country. "There are two Peter C. Newmans," Natalie Veiner Freeman (who later married Senator Jack Austin) wrote in *City Woman* magazine. "There is the social Newman – slouching conspicuously and self-consciously in and out-of rooms, eyes focused somewhere between the door and the farthest wall. Shy, tired he often falls asleep sitting straight up in his chair. He has no small talk, dropping his voice and swallowing the ends of sentences on the rare occasions when he tries. He is so subdued he lulls people into giving candid interviews. But hand him a piece of paper and a typewriter and there's an instant Clark Kent/Superman personality switch (enemies would say Jekyll/Hyde). Writing transforms him; it is the key that unlocks the passage to an underground consciousness that is deep with insight."

My idea was to write what were almost self-portraits, and for that I needed lengthy interviews. I had to draw out my subjects by first gathering enough inside information to make them think I knew much more about them than I actually did. Acquiring the necessary ammunition required cross-interviewing. I would come to Vancouver, for instance, and meet Peter Brown, the combative but perceptive head of Canarim Investments, and spend half my time asking him about Sam Belzberg, Jimmy Pattison, Edgar Kaiser, Nelson Skalbania, Bob Lee, and the other big hitters. Then I would run to Bob Lee's office (and the others') to interview them about Peter Brown, and so on. They often revealed intimate details about their rivals' bank balances, motivations, takeover targets, and mistresses. Unvarnished truth about themselves was not a common currency.

Truth in this arena can be a negotiable quality. On December 20, 1996, I flew to Toronto from Hopkins Landing in British Columbia, and found myself wading through the Eaton Centre, swimming against the crowd, on my way to interview its namesake: Fred Eaton, titular head of the retailing empire and unofficial dean of Canada's Establishment. As I turned toward the family's private offices, two young women passed by, done up in the radical-chic style of a few decades back, complete with Che Guevara combat fatigues, Frye boots, and expensively mussed hair. I threw them a salute and they gave me that eyeballs-rolled-to-ceiling look reserved for out-of-town wharf rats loose in the big city. When I arrived, Fred was out. I should have known. It was five days before Christmas and he was doing his Establishment thing: cruising the stores, magnanimously wishing his underpaid, non-unionized staff carefree holidays.

Once he returned, he conducted me around the office, showing off a scale model of *Defender*, the stunning forty-seven-foot Day Sailer designed for him by the naval architect Mark Ellis. It seemed like an appropriate moment to mention the rumours swirling around Bay Street that Eaton's was in big trouble, that its bankers were fed up with the stores' pathetic cash flow and were planning to foreclose, that the Eaton empire was about to collapse.

"No, no," he protested. "Why would you think that? There are always stories about us, that we're being sold or something. Nothing to it."

I realized only later that, as he might have put it, he was "misspeaking himself," which he ought to have learned to avoid as part of his toilet training. Fully a month before our interview, on November 21 (as revealed in court documents), Eaton's traditional lenders had turned down the family's request for a 50 per cent increase in their unsecured loan. At the beginning of the same week that I met with Fred, the family was on the brink of insolvency. Two months later, the once powerful clan filed for bankruptcy protection. Court documents contained a phrase that shook the Canadian Establishment to its elegant roots: "The applicants are insolvent."

To offset this barrage of disinformation, I was fortunate to have access throughout my project to a trio of invaluable intelligence agents. They knew everybody worth knowing and freely (if anonymously) shared their information with me. As prominent society women they were privy to the significant whispers; their sympathetic personalities attracted many confidences. First, the whip-smart Liz Tory, whose husband John was the surrogate CEO of Ken Thomson's amazing empire, was Toronto's busiest and most sought after social animator. Her real advantage was that she used that position to bring people down to earth, being the most realistic and forthright "lady who lunches." Someday I shall replay our tapes and issue a CD of Liz Tory's Greatest Hits. Posey Chisholm (born Rosemary Fennell, but with more identities than the Scarlet Pimpernel) was one of a kind, whether entertaining at her Venetian *palazzo* or her New York penthouse. In one of his rare understatements, Allan Fotheringham once called her "the most amazing woman in the world." She would pace her thirty-second-floor downtown Toronto apartment and spill everybody's secrets, looking as innocent as a freshly picked rose. The third, Barbara Frum, was my guardian angel in that she listened to my exploits, then talked me down from making a dumb, premature assessment about some power-crazy yokel who was about to be hung out to dry by the Ontario Securities Commission. *Maclean's* published her obituary under the heading "A death in the family," and that was how I felt about her premature passing at fifty-four in the spring of 1992. She was a *grande dame* and a great dame, and I miss her so.

From the start I intended to write about the Establishment crowd as though they were sports stars, telling tales of their exploits, the equivalents of winning or losing their Stanley Cups, sitting out their penalties, and the time they slugged the opposing team's left-winger into oblivion. That was easy because the level of introspection of most corporate honchos and hockey greats was about the same. (For reasons completely mysterious to me, nothing so gives the illusion of intelligence as the possession of large sums of money. There is no connection.) My profiles revolved not around numbers in their balance sheets, but about harried individuals struggling with their consciences, their rivals, government regulators, and tax assessors. I found it puzzling that until I ventured into this virgin territory, the business of business was considered either too irrelevant or too boring to merit literary attention. Even in F. Scott Fitzgerald's *The Great Gatsby* and Arthur Miller's *Death of a Salesman*, the best works about American business, neither Jay Gatsby nor Willy Loman was portrayed actually at work. The notion that compelling heroes and villains could be created in corporate boardrooms, or that takeovers and mergers were a blood sport with profound social and cultural consequences, had yet to be explored, at least in Canada. As federal politics became increasingly dumbed down, my attempts to turn Big Business into Big Stories found increasing acceptance.

Hunting down my subjects brought me close to the line between reporting and stalking. Most of them gave in when I pointed out, with all the cloying sincerity I could muster, that I would of course have to write about them anyway, so why not talk to me? Only two major Establishment figures eluded my net: Fred Mannix and K.C. Irving. Almost equally unreachable was Eric Harvie, the mysterious, mega-rich Calgary oilman who had purchased the CPR's expiring oil rights – including those to the Leduc sections where Imperial Oil struck its gusher in 1947. He agreed to meet with me a few months before he died in 1975, only because so many of his friends had (at my behest) pestered him till he did. But he was damned if he was going to give me an interview. As usual I had briefed myself on his remarkable life and even managed to obtain his First World War service record. He turned out to be a lean figure with close-cropped hair, a handkerchief up his left sleeve and a vicious-looking cane that he tapped lightly against the floor, as if keeping time to some private drummer.

"Now," I kicked off the interview, "when you were with the 15th Light Horse Regiment in the trenches at the Somme, and were getting ready to go over the top and face the entrenched Germans across the no man's land, did your whole life flash before you?" He considered my question for a minute or two, looking inconsolable, then gave me his considered answer, which in its entirety consisted of: "Yep." And that was how the entire interview went, except for those occasions when he said: "Nope."

The Mannix family was a much harder case. Fred, the founder of its considerable fortune, was so close-mouthed that his public relations adviser, David Wood, had his pay docked every time the name of the company appeared in print. His son Ron, who inherited the mantle, had a similar approach to publicity. But after intervention by my friend, the former Alberta premier Peter Lougheed, I received a letter from Mannix's lawyer, setting out nine conditions under which he would agree to be interviewed. I instantly accepted them all and received a written confirmation from the young Mannix agreeing to see me. Then he unexpectedly told me to go to hell and cancelled the meeting. He remains the prickliest member of the Oil Patch, which isolated him among that league of honourable gentlemen. Until wiretapping or breaking and entry were legalized, I was stuck.

K.C. Irving, who then owned New Brunswick, not only refused my entreaties but regularly cursed me for the description I published of him in my first volume: "A tearless Presbyterian who doesn't drink, smoke or swear, K.C. Irving is ruthless and unfeeling in pursuit of dollars to the point of denying farmers the right to salvage firewood from the loose logs left at river edges after the spring log drives of his forestry companies." Irving had a weird idea of democracy. When he noticed a decline in traffic on one of his bus routes, he was told that his raising ticket prices had led people to organize car pools. He went to see premier John McNair and demanded that he immediately outlaw car pools. The startled premier pointed out as diplomatically as he could that this was outside his jurisdiction. But Irving never forgave him. In the next election he backed his opponent, throwing McNair out of office.

When his former daughter-in-law, Joanie Carlisle-Irving, asked K.C. what he thought of me, Irving replied, "Newman said I was a tearless Presbyterian. I'd like to know what Godless denomination he belongs to that permits him to bear false witness against his neighbour."

THESE PROFESSIONAL ANNOYANCES were upsetting but didn't spoil the book's reception, though the Establishment itself remained highly skeptical of my efforts. Some of its Toronto members, for example, put enough pressure on the bookshop at the Art Gallery of Ontario to cancel its advance order. In Vancouver, an Establishment architect named Allan Weisman told an enquiring reporter, "I thank Newman for allowing me to be a footnote. I'd hate to have been a chapter." Most of the Establishment figures I had profiled said nothing, even if they cringed at my descriptions. Others sued.

It had taken me three years to persuade Montreal's Paul Desmarais, head of the giant Power Corporation, to talk to me, and he had done so only when I told him that Bud McDougald (whose company he had tried to take over) had said some nasty things about him that needed answering. Desmarais had never before given an extended interview. He fit no stereotypes. He was like some rare breed of mountain cat, prowling the corporate jungles. Free of the timidity that held back would-be challengers, he was fearless, and this, more than intellect or moxie, was his secret. It allowed him to dismiss the Calvinistic sense of guilt that haunted accredited WASPs. He had drawn his most useful experience from hanging round the garages, community rinks, drug stores, and pool halls in Sudbury, where he was born. He moved up in Canada's post-war business hierarchy so quickly and so quietly that only a few top insiders knew him or even heard his footsteps. As he grew in influence, members of English Canada's Establishment regarded him as their unofficial ambassador to contemporary Quebec, while they tried to understand a militant part of the country they viewed with only slightly less comprehension than some distant Transylvania.

We had spent several days together, and I found Desmarais to be a living testament to the proposition that you can be powerful and remain human. His appearance was not simple to capture. He seemed to invent himself for each occasion, changing his demeanour according to the impression he wanted to create. Yet whatever role he happened to be playing, the stern centre of the man remained inviolate: his natural grace; the six-foot, two-inch frame, bent like a parenthesis, moving with a deliberately slowed stride; the brown eyes disengaged from whatever might be occupying his mind; the shrug, so elusive that it could be carefree or serious, confirming a joke or a promise; the elegance of his vented three-piece suits; his grey cowlick; his barely discernible stutter; the thumbs that curved outward; the hot temper, which I felt at least twice.

I detected a streak of unrest in Desmarais, the existential dread of a vacuum in his affairs that he would take any risk to fill. Breaking my rule of never quoting anyone's thoughts, I ended my chapter on him with an imagined interior monologue: *"I've made all this money, but what else can I do? I'm not yet fifty. I'm the richest French Canadian there ever was. I have an office full of Krieghoffs and Chippendale chairs, an ambassador's son as my assistant. Cabinet ministers come and play poker with me. I own the O'Connells' place in the Laurentians and the old Timmins mansion at Murray Bay. E.P. Taylor's daughter did my Montreal house. The governor general throws special receptions for me. My wife is beautiful and I can entertain eighty relatives at a time. I don't have to bow to anybody. Here I am, done up in my gorgeous three-piece dark blue cashmere suit with a Patek Philippe gold watch and custom-made, valet-shined shoes. What else can I do? There must be something I can turn my wits to . . .*

What Paul Desmarais turned his wits to was getting me. He instructed J.J. Robinette, Canada's premier legal counsel, to block my book from being published. I had written about one of his stock deals, which two governors of the Montreal Stock Exchange had described in less than flattering terms. Once they discovered that Paul was unhappy about the item, they stopped taking my phone calls. Jack McClelland had 75,000 copies in his warehouse, ready to be shipped but Ontario's Supreme Court, prompted by Robinette, had granted an injunction on their sale. Jack hired twenty people over a weekend to glue a new version over the offending paragraph on page seventy-four, and the crisis was averted. But the next time I saw Desmarais at a Montreal function, he came right over and said in mock anger: "Your damn sticker comes off!" He told me that when he put the book in his freezer for a week, the sticker could be removed. I shrugged and we had a good laugh about it.

I received half a dozen legal threats over some of my other books in the series, including a nasty letter from Emmett Cardinal Carter (about the ceremony I had described of Conrad Black's conversion to Catholicism) in which His Eminence wrote, "even for you this reaches a new low in journalistic smears." That didn't sound like a reference letter I could use in Purgatory.

When *The Acquisitors* came out, Doug Creighton, publisher of the *Toronto Sun*, decided to sue me because I had reported that his expense account at Winston's, an Establishment restaurant, equalled Albania's national debt. The threat vanished when I produced his actual bill and sent him a hand-lettered dispatch, pretending to come from Tirana, claiming that his bar bill was actually *greater* than the Albanian Socialist Republic's debt. But then things got serious. In my listing of the extremes of bad taste enjoyed by the nouveaux riches I had included by way of example the story that Carol Rapp, the wife of a wealthy Toronto businessman, had ordered her chauffeur's uniforms to match the bright blue at the bottom of her swimming pool. This information came from my lawyer, Michael Levine, whose father claimed to have made them, which I confirmed with a phone call. Right after publication, Mrs. Rapp contacted her own lawyer, the redoubtable Aubrey Golden, and assured him that it wasn't true. She accused me of having ridiculed and trivialized her, which indeed I had, and demanded that the books be removed from circulation. Julian Porter, who was the capable libel lawyer for most of my books and for *Maclean's* while I was editor, began to worry when Golden produced the chauffeur's uniform. It was black. I phoned Levine's father and was told that he had left town, by amazing coincidence, just two hours before the court hearings started, heading for Florida, where he was booked into a hotel with an unlisted phone number. Not many of those, I figured, but I was stuck. I was guilty as charged and Mrs. Rapp could have held up the book forever.

Julian came up with the solution. Since most of the books were already in the stores, it was impractical to either ship them back or destroy them, so why not have the booksellers cross out the offending passage with a black felt pen? Mr. Justice W.D. Griffiths of the Ontario Supreme Court fortunately agreed, and the book was home free. Still, we might not have made it if Jack McClelland had carried out his threat to attend the court hearings flaunting a white toga, which he planned to loudly justify by explaining that it matched the bottom of his bathtub. Instead, to satisfy his taste for the dramatic, when he heard that my book was sold out in western Canada, he filled several eighteen-wheelers with fresh copies and dressed their drivers in rented tuxedos, as befitting Establishment couriers. I never did understand the purpose of that manoeuvre since no one except Jack himself, who waved off the convoy with exaggerated formality, paid the slightest attention to the strange caravan snaking its way across the country.

When it was published in fall 1975, *The Canadian Establishment* set off a publishing frenzy. Sales were astronomical (nearly a million books for the whole series plus their hefty distribution as main selections at the Book of the Month Club and alternates of the Fortune Book Club). Separate editions were published in the United States, Quebec, and Russia. At 350,000, the first volume set the sales record for any Canadian non-fiction book published up to that point. Like *Renegade*, most of my Establishment volumes earned the ultimate accolade of people walking into stores, asking for "the book," and automatically being handed mine. I recall one incredible Saturday afternoon autographing *The Canadian Establishment* at the David Mirvish bookstore in Toronto, which was very small at the time, with not much room for display copies. Clerks brought cartons up from the basement, but customers kept grabbing the book out of the boxes, so that they were empty by the time they reached my autographing desk. *The Canadian Establishment* stayed on the bestseller list for fifty-seven weeks. At one point, I had autographed so many books that *unsigned* copies became collectors' items.

The sales bonanza started all over again with the airing, three years after the first book was published, of a seven-hour television version. It was masterminded by CBC director of public affairs Peter Herndorf, produced by Cameron Graham, organized by Ron Graham, narrated by Patrick Watson, and buttressed by Ron Harrison's magnificent soundtrack. Its programs highlighted by directors Michael Gerard (on Conrad Black) and Peter Pearson (on Paul Desmarais), were seen by a cumulative sixteen million viewers, drawing individual audiences nearly as large as hockey games. Although at first they had been dismissive of the possibility of allowing television cameras into their homes and offices, the

Establishment's big names soon rallied to the cause. When the crew filming Sinclair asked to be allowed into a CPR directors' meeting, he welcomed them, and after a board member pointed out that this was against security regulations, Ian swore them in as "insiders."

In his review, novelist Ian Adams suggested that from now on "you could situate other journalists by whether they were far enough up the posterior of the Establishment to glimpse Newman's heels." Others took the opposite view. John Gray, the playwright-novelist, commented: "You really have a subversive streak which is just far enough under the surface that you can pass yourself off as a chronicler of the poo-bahs. A neat trick." Allan Fotheringham wrote: "Newman's book could be used as a Communist Manifesto. Everything that the Marxist conspiratorial theorists maintain — that the system is fixed — is confirmed by the massive evidence he has compiled." Writing for the political Left, NDP Leader David Lewis agreed: "Newman succeeds in revealing the autocratic structure of the modern corporation and the class-conscious arrogance of the ruling junta. The moral emerges naturally from his full and accurate reporting of people and events." Nick Hills, then with Southam News, went even further: "In earlier times this book might well have been burned as a dangerous revolutionary tract. Given the recent history of the business community, some might describe the performance of certain characters in these pages as self-immolation."

The critic Robert Fulford took a different tack: "Business writing in Canada now is generally in a condition resembling that of political writing when Newman wrote *Renegade in Power*. It's dominated by shy, hesitant, over-polite journalists who would rather rewrite press releases than find out what their subjects are actually doing. Newman's book proves otherwise and if he inspires a generation of business writers as he inspired a generation of political writers, then he'll have accomplished the remarkable feat of creating two small revolutions in one lifetime. This might not be enormous accomplishment in England or America but in Canada it's little short of a miracle." The only literary personages totally unimpressed by my efforts were the judges of the Governor General Awards, who gave that year's prize to *Hallowed Walls*, a picture book about early eastern Ontario church architecture – a choice that William French, the *Globe and Mail* literary critic, wrote, "reveals a quirkiness bordering on the bizarre." My fellow author and business writer Rod McQueen later wrote in the *National Post*: "Here's the thing. Newman the outsider has embraced the country and gets it right, but the country fails to embrace him and that's all wrong. Fusty scholars dismiss his history because his books sell better than theirs. Lazy business journalists rob from his research without so much as a footnote. Big-time awards have eluded him. Maybe he should have himself Newmanized."

THE EXISTENCE OF AN ESTABLISHMENT offended Canadian sensibilities. It negated the popular notion of the country as a land of universally accessible opportunities symbolized by its wide-open spaces and Imax horizons. This egalitarian ideal was reinforced by the strenuous disavowals of the power-wielders themselves that any self-serving effects resulted from their Establishment credentials; there was no plot; the fix was not in. Innocence is always relative, but theirs had some validity: they thought – and acted – the same way *naturally*. They didn't *need* to conspire; their ideas meshed without consultation. They recognized so few conflicts of interest because their interests so seldom conflicted. That's why they were an Establishment.

Most Canadians tended – and they still do – to view the class system as referring mainly to lifestyles and levels of sophistication. It was as though nearly everyone belonged to the same class – a class that could help give its offspring the advantages of education but not much in the way of inherited wealth or social position. Yet the elegant footprints of Canada's Establishment were everywhere. In the days of its great dynasties, they shared indulgences and attitudes, such as treating servants as mobile furniture. They cultivated British country house styles of dress and decor, plummy accents, and other subtleties that identified members of the core group to one another. Automatic accreditation was gained through discreet signals that spoke of shared experiences.

The country's founding WASP Establishment suffered from a fatal shortcoming: its members always chose family loyalty over commercial expediency. They believed in good breeding as an activity instead of a process. The reason for their rapid decline was the same as the reason for their long ascendancy – they treated everyone with equestrian condescension. Their search for understanding began not in wonder but in determinedly reducing an increasingly confusing world to safe, conventional values. They continued clinging to the notion that somehow in the not too distant future, society would return to what they considered normal. As unlikely a thought as it was, it fed their souls and protected them from the wind, but it also accelerated their demise.

FOLLOWING PUBLICATION of the original *Establishment* in 1975, I began researching another volume, in which I meant to feature the Jewish community. The notion of Jewish power had always intrigued me. Although they wielded tremendous collective influence, individually their wounded eyes and fragile egos reflected profound vulnerability, their feeling of being under siege by the society that surrounded them. Theirs was a kind of cousinhood: men and women who still regarded survival as a contest, and in self-defence, had formed the most vital and effective Establishment of them all. I watched their elders attend election rallies, sipping their flat ginger ale, nodding like wise old turtles as some hapless politician tried to explain why his government hadn't done more for Israel lately. Some of their best friends might be WASPs, but they acted as though their next supper might be their last. And I knew how they felt.

As I probed more deeply into their curious power structure, my lines of inquiry inevitably led to various branches of the Bronfman family, Montreal's distilling dynasty, who had become, as I later described them in the subtitle of my book, with only a pinch of hyperbole: "The Rothschilds of the New World." I interviewed Sam's son, Charles Bronfman, who was in charge of the Canadian branch, and quickly realized that this remarkable tribe deserved a book of its own. Even among that small group of pre-eminent families who dominated world commerce, the Bronfmans were unique. By devoting a separate volume to them, I could draw a clinical portrait of how international power was exercised, diffused, hoarded, and camouflaged, all within the cloak of a fiercely proud (and constantly feuding) Jewish family that rose from being peddlers of firewood and frozen whitefish in Brandon, Manitoba, to selling some of the best vintage liquor in an operation worth $2 billion a year, all in one generation. My initial session with Charles, who was such a proud son that he had seven pictures of his father, Sam, decorating his office, also made it very clear that the family was not about to share the secrets of its origins.

Another Canadian author, Terence Robertson, had written a commissioned biography of Sam Bronfman in 1970 but took his own life after completing a rough draft of the manuscript. When McClelland and Stewart sued Mutual Life to collect the $100,000 policy on Robertson's life, Roderick Goodman of the *Toronto Star* editorial department testified that the author had telephoned him from his New York hotel room to report that he had "found out things they don't want me to write about." Graham Caney, another *Star* editor, testified that Robertson had told him his life had been threatened and that "we would know who was doing the threatening but that he would do the job himself." While he was still on the telephone, Caney had the call traced, and he alerted the New York Police Department. Detectives burst into Robertson's hotel room just minutes before he died of self-administered barbiturate poisoning. That was not a promising start for the *unauthorized* book I intended to write.

There was another problem. I was editor of *Maclean's* at the time, and Seagrams (the main Bronfman company) were our lead advertisers. Yet Lloyd Hodgkinson, the magazine's publisher, stood squarely behind me, providing I made damn sure I got everything right. That was the attitude of Jack McClelland as well, because his company was shaky enough without having to entertain a hefty libel suit. He placed his faith in Doug Laidlaw, a top libel lawyer, who warned me that before I published any controversial material he would examine me in his office as if I were a witness in a court of law and he, the prosecutor.

The mystery that had been deliberately created to shroud the Bronfmans' early careers as bootleggers in the Prairie provinces (mostly smuggling booze into the United States during the Prohibition period) was not simple to dispel. Fortunately, the Royal Canadian Mounted Police came to my rescue. Cliff Harvison had been a young corporal in Manitoba and Saskatchewan, constantly on their tail, finally arresting the four brothers on criminal conspiracy charges in 1934 and leading Sam out of his office in handcuffs. He eventually rose to become commissioner of the RCMP but he kept his early Bronfman records. When his widow, Doris, heard I was writing the book, she gave me his files.

In a rented car I spent part of a summer visiting the dusty one-elevator towns along the Saskatchewan–North Dakota boundary – Oxbow, Bienfait, Carnduff, and Torquay, among others. I haunted retirement homes on their outskirts and finally managed to track down several surviving drivers who had been behind the wheels of some hyped-up Studebakers. With reinforced springs, stripped down with their upholstery removed, they could carry forty cases of whisky, worth $2,000. Once across the border, these speeding boozemobiles eluded American federal agents by disappearing into clouds of dust stirred up by thirty-foot chains dragged behind them. At night, miniature searchlights mounted on rear windows would direct fierce beams into the eyes of police pursuers. Now in their nodding eighties, these young speedsters remembered vividly how they used to "run the booze for the Bronfmans," and shared their memories with me. Among them was Ken John, a hale and articulate retired Estevan accountant who in 1922 had been in Bienfait, one memorable night. That was when Paul Matoff, Sam

Bronfman's brother-in-law and operator of one of Saskatchewan's busiest "boozoriums," was killed by the blast from a sawed-off shotgun poked through the railway station window. There were many other first-hand sources who had never been tapped before.[6]

My other advantage was that the Bronfmans had been *Canadian* bootleggers. Unlike their American counterparts, who settled arguments with gang warfare, Sam and his brothers, being otherwise law-abiding citizens, went to court. I spent many a day in dusty archives, reading up on their numerous legal challenges, and eventually was able to piece together what had really happened. As supporting documentation, I managed to acquire a bootleg (!) copy of an unpublished diary written by Harry Bronfman, Sam's older brother, detailing his days in the liquor trade. No one in the family had even seen it before.

In the three years it took to complete *The Bronfman Dynasty*, I interviewed a dozen Bronfmans, several dozen of their critics, competitors, and friends, plus the usual retinue of hangers-on and camp followers that a fiscal galaxy of this magnitude inevitably attracts. It was my toughest assignment. The group profile that emerged was of restless men in Gucci loafers, still in search of themselves. The warring members of this unusual and impassioned tribe lived behind the tightest curtain of privacy money could buy. Away from the glare of public concern and attention – through tier upon tier of private holding subsidiaries listed only in the offices of the many lawyers they retained on full-time standby – the Bronfmans had amassed assets worth more than $7 billion, which in 1978 was one of the largest capital pools remaining in the non-Arab world.

---

[6] They even revealed to me the secret of the formula used to make the early batches of the Bronfman hooch: the sixty-five-overproof white alcohol was reduced to the required bottling strength by mixing it with water, then a bit of real Scotch was added, plus a dash of burnt sugar (caramel) for colouring and sulphuric acid for aging. When the caramel ran out, iodine was used; after that some of the distilling crew just spat their chewing tobacco remnants into the vat.

For all his business acumen and boundless success, Sam was never able to fit harmoniously into the society that enriched him, and that he himself enriched as a generous philanthropist in his later years. A Russian by background, a Canadian by adoption, a Texan by temperament, and an upper-class Englishman by aspiration, he was not the easiest man to please. Haunted by his past, too full of passion to hide his feelings, he spent the final three decades of his life in a tumultuous struggle to join the Canadian Establishment. He never made it. He longed to be named a governor of McGill University, elected a member of Montreal's Mount Royal Club, appointed a director of the Bank of Montreal, and summoned to the Senate of Canada. As these distinctions kept eluding him, he began to retreat into himself, defining his life by its exclusions instead of by his remarkable commercial achievements.

Except for their fear of publicity, the Bronfmans demonstrated little compunction about enjoying their riches, although some members of the family's fourth generation were raised in a very different tradition. To teach his children the value of money, Gerald Bronfman (son of Harry) gave his teenaged daughters a weekly cash allowance of thirty-seven and a half cents. He accomplished this by paying out thirty-eight cents one week and thirty-seven the next. Peter, a thoughtful introvert who became my favourite Bronfman, hated to spend money. I was once relaxing with him in a Vancouver hotel room when he took off his shoes and started darning his socks. When I had dinner with him and his then wife, Dora, at Toronto's Hyatt Regency Hotel, which he half owned, she ordered half a lobster, the most expensive appetizer. He became so agitated about its cost that he started fidgeting with his wedding ring and finally dropped it on the pewter serving plate with a loud, symbolic clang.

Their affections often wore boxing gloves. In the early morning hours of May 30, 1970, when a squad of radical Quebec separatists threw four sticks of dynamite into the foyer of Peter Bronfman's house, it was front-page news in Montreal. But the only comment that Sam's wife Saidye made about it next time they met, was

"Why *you*?" implying that he was hardly an important enough member of the clan to have been singled out for special treatment.

Mr. Sam was not an impressive-looking man – five feet five, with a paunch and thinning hair – but the expressive eyes, flickering out at the world, gave off precise barometric readings of the weathers of his soul. They could change in an instant from cold Arctic fury to the delighted sparkle of a child's first glimpse of Santa Claus. His staff treated him like a killer whale. Whenever he appeared, they scattered like pilot fish darting behind protective barriers. Any given group of Seagram executives attending a meeting in his office would be shifting about constantly, each man craning to keep the boss in direct sight, monitoring his thoughts and words, trying to guess what Mr. Sam wanted them to think and comment. He alone could say and do exactly as he pleased, treating his underlings with the faintly forgiving air of an Albert Schweitzer among the incurables. He made Frank Marshall, who was director of export sales during the early 1950s, so nervous that the executive arranged to be away from Montreal whenever Sam was in town. In case Bronfman should return unexpectedly, Marshall kept a packed suitcase in his office so that he could immediately drive to Dorval Airport, where he'd buy a ticket to one of Seagram's world operations. The system worked fine for a while because overseas sales were booming, but eventually Bronfman realized that he hardly ever saw his export manager, and the word went out: "Find Marshall. Mr. Sam wants to see him."

The hunted man kept moving around the globe for a few more months, but Mr. Sam's sixtieth birthday party was coming up, and that was an obligatory occasion for head-office executives. The staff mounted an elaborate film presentation, complete with soundtrack, depicting highlights of Seagram's sales campaigns during the past year. Sam was sitting in the front row of the ballroom at the Windsor Hotel, laughing as he watched scenes of slightly tipsy Egyptian army officers toasting one another with Crown Royal on the terrace of Shepheard's Hotel in Cairo. This was followed by a long shot of a Bedouin riding a camel toward the Pyramids, a bottle tucked into his burnoose. The camel approached the camera. Sam suddenly sat up, peering at its swaying rider. The focus was much tighter now, and the "Bedouin," it became clear, was none other than Frank Marshall in a long nightshirt with a fez on his head, brandishing a bottle of V.O.

Sam leaped out of his chair, bellowing at the screen, "There's the son of a bitch! That's where he's been spending his time! Riding a goddamn camel!"

Once Bronfman had calmed down a little, Marshall, who had slunk into the hall after the lights were turned out, came up behind him, tapped him lightly on the shoulder, and pleadingly whispered, "That film was taken on a Sunday, Mr. Sam." The reply went unrecorded.

The senior Bronfman felt that elevation to the Canadian Senate would crown his name with the mark of legitimacy, a sure sign of acceptance into the upper strata of his country's society. Having set his sights on the upper chamber, he decided to buy his way into it. His chief agent in these transactions was Maxwell Henderson, who later served as Canada's auditor general. Ever the methodical accountant, Henderson not only kept records of his boss's donations but, to Sam's amazement, obtained signed receipts for the bribes as they were changing hands. At one point, Bronfman became so frustrated that he confronted C.D. Howe with a direct threat: if he wasn't made a senator, he would cut off all contributions to the Liberal Party. The great C.D. fixed Bronfman with a steely gaze through the foliage of his magnificent eyebrows, smiled a sweet smile, and said, "It doesn't matter, Sam. We'll just raise the excise tax on liquor another ten per cent and get it that way." Then he asked the distiller to leave his office.

Sam Bronfman's problem was that he never learned to appreciate the subtlety of the process in which he was involved. Any number of senators had purchased their appointments by contributing to party coffers. Senatorships might be for sale, but they could not appear to have been purchased. Worst of all, when Sam briefly tried to lobby on his own behalf by joining the Ottawa cocktail circuit, he found himself the object of some unwanted attention. Wherever he appeared, Clifford Harvison, then the RCMP's assistant commissioner, who had once arrested him, would noiselessly join any group of people that included the distiller and stand there quizzically staring at him. When Bronfman moved on, Harvison would follow, and repeat the treatment.

Sam and a caucus of his senior executives were conferring in Seagram's boardroom on the morning of July 28, 1955, when his secretary brought in the bad news that David Croll had been appointed Canada's first Jewish senator. Henderson remembered Sam exploding, parading about the room in a kind of military mourner's slow march, wailing, "I'm the King of the Jews! It should have been mine . . . I bought it! I paid for it! Those treacherous bastards did me in!"

AS PUBLICATION of *The Bronfman Dynasty* approached, in the summer of 1978 I started to receive warnings from Leo Kolber. He was the non-Bronfman Bronfman, so close to the family that Sam treated him as a son, while Leo worshipped Sam as a father. He brought to the table a shrewd, street-smart understanding of Canadian society, and the family used him to do some of the things they preferred not to have done with their names attached to them, such as stopping my book. He was a tough cookie and surprisingly shy in public, though he was always honest and had a sense of humour about himself.

"We're too smart to try and stop publication or withhold our advertising from *Maclean's*," Kolber told me, in a way that made me realize these options were on the table. Then he suggested I show him the manuscript, so that he and Charles could read it in a locked room. When I politely refused, he invited me to a Harry Belafonte concert and a private party with the star afterwards. On another, less hospitable occasion, he took me aside and whispered,

"You better bloody well be kind to us in your book, or I'll cut your balls off." When I pointed out that all my writings were objective, he shot back, "I didn't say objective, I said kind."

Except for one copy that had gone off to the Book of the Month Club, Jack McClelland kept the manuscript and galleys in a company safe because we feared an injunction. But on the evening of August 25, I received a call from a mutual friend informing me that Charles had received a copy "from an unsolicited source" (how were we to know that the Bronfmans were silent partners in the Book of the Month Club?). He was furious, informing my friend: "McClelland and Newman may make a lot of money on the book, but they'll spend the rest of their lives in court."

The two of us were invited to meet with Charles and Leo at their private office (graced by a gorgeous Joyce Wieland tapestry) on the fifty-fifth floor of the main TD Tower, which everyone thought had only fifty-four floors. We met for seven hours, seated around a small rectangular table in the middle of the room, like negotiators for the ceasefire line between North and South Korea. I was nervous because they had me on one central issue. I had originally gone to them with the idea that they would be part of my book on the Jewish Establishment, which indeed was my intention. But I had become so intrigued that they ended up as the entire book. I hadn't told them, because I didn't want to scare them off, though I would have thought that to have me hanging around their homes and offices for three years might have provided a clue.

They began the conversation by stating that they had a list of seven hundred errors, and what the hell were we going to do about it? I said that I was interested in accuracy and that if I had indeed made errors of fact, as opposed to interpretation, I would be glad to correct them.

The bulk of the "errors" were trivial; they complained that Mr. Sam had chubby cheeks, not "leathery folds" in his face. Worse, when I described Leo Kolber's Montreal house, a building so huge that neighbours thought it was an elementary school, I had been inaccurate in pointing out that during a party his bedroom had accommodated sixty of his friends and a six-piece band; it was only a three-piece band. They accused me of downplaying Mr. Sam's pivotal role in the support of Israel and his truly impressive philanthropic activities. What it came down to was Charles's emotional outburst that he didn't recognize his loving father in my portrait. To that I pleaded guilty, gently pointing out that he was not *my* father, and that I could only write about him as a successful businessman. He replied that if we were fair-minded people concerned with our integrity we would not publish such a book, and that if we delayed it six months they would supply us with enough information to turn it into a balanced piece of work. He accused me of hating his father, though I had never met him (he died in 1971), but he confirmed my story about trying to buy the senatorship.

We were getting nowhere. At the end of his mournful soliloquy, Charles sat back grieving, and Leo took over. At one point he leaned over and threatened McClelland, "Jack, if you publish this goddamn book, we'll buy out your company!" Jack, whose firm was going through one of its comatose financial phases, jumped up as if shot from a cannon, almost leaping over the table. With a relieved smile on his face he exclaimed, "Leo! Leo! Would you really do that?"

"That was pretty well the end of the conversation," McClelland noted in a memo to himself about the meeting. "There were no threats except by implication, but it was clear that the matter is a subject of a family conclave. And it is also clear that they are going to do everything they can to destroy the book."

We made the factual corrections they had requested, but the bulk of the book, including its tone, remained inviolate. After publication, Charles's brother Edgar labelled my work "a cheap collection of gossip-column trivia, anecdotes, caricatures and amateur psychologizing." And of course the historian Michael Bliss chimed in on schedule, with his usual venom, calling it "part Harlequin romance, part encyclopedia . . . a wretched, trashy book." My faith in Canadian reviewers was further devalued when Larry Zolf turned down a request from *Saturday Night* to review it. I thought he would have been the perfect choice because he was from Manitoba, where many of the incidents I described had occurred, and would know how difficult it had been for me to document them. When I met him at a party later and asked him why he had rejected the assignment, he looked quite indignant. "I couldn't review your book," he said. "I *liked* it." Others hailed it as "a masterpiece of investigative journalism," and stuff like that. Meanwhile, *Bronfman Dynasty* was outselling *The Happy Hooker*, with eighty thousand copies sold in the first three weeks.

Surprisingly, my best reception was in the United States, where the book (retitled *King of the Castle*) went into three printings, got on bestseller lists, and received a big boost by being chosen as a main selection of the Fortune Book Club. Robert Sherrill, White House correspondent for *The Nation*, wrote in his *Washington Post* review: "Newman has been so devastatingly, cruelly fair as to portray the Bronfmans in the very fashion, I'm sure, they see themselves. I call that a masterful knife job. If I were trying to stir up a nice Trotskyish revolution, *King of the Castle* would be my chief ammunition."

I was interviewed by Mike Wallace of *Sixty Minutes* and Gene Shalit of NBC's then top-rated *Today Show*. There and elsewhere I was asked what brands of liquor the Bronfmans sold. There were six hundred, but I had memorized a short list that included Wolfschmidt Vodka. Unfortunately this brand became lodged in my mind as Wolfshit Vodka, and try as I might, I would always say it wrong. Canadian interviewers corrected me, but in the United States, I could almost hear them thinking, "*Who knows? Maybe that's what they use up there in Canada for making Vodka.*" I was never asked to explain the formula.

The Bronfmans never did try to destroy my book, though one of their subordinates launched a harassment-type lawsuit that cost me half my royalties. Instead, in typical Bronfman style, they had a book written for them. Michael R. Marrus, a respected university professor, took on their commission and followed their editorial advice. It was a good book, but it left out most of the juicy bits.

There was one final coda to my Bronfman story. Two distinguished filmmakers, Fil Fraser of Edmonton and John McGreevey of Toronto, optioned the book, laid out real money, commissioned a fine script by Charles Israel, and even cast Mr. Sam (either Dustin Hoffman or Saul Rubinek). But the cameras never rolled. Most of the production funds came from Calgary and they mysteriously dried up after Leo Kolber swept through town. I remain firmly convinced this must have been a coincidence.

WITHIN FIVE YEARS of the appearance of my first volume, many of the once-powerful Establishment figures had died, retired, or been stripped of their authority. At the same time, the centre of economic gravity had shifted from the commercial and industrial heartland to the new petro-rich West. The Establishment managed to reinvent itself in mutations to fit the times, and this was the theme of my next volume, *The Acquisitors*. Many of the new breed welcomed risk, practised U-turn ethics, and combined their macho approach to business with gonzo lifestyles, acting out their fantasies with other people's money. They gambled on real estate, chanced the possibilities of space-age technology, capitalized on the whims and desires of a consumer society on a spending spree, and spun off government subsidies into everything from offshore oil to horror films. "As an anthropologist of this weird cult and its rites, Newman is matchless," wrote Margaret Wente in her review of *The Acquisitors*. But the highlight of my promotional tour was appearing on Jack Webster's BC-TV interview show. For his opening, he summoned up his most guttural Scottish accent, held my book up to the camera, and bellowed: "I am holding in my hand a SKARRRALOUS book, a most scurrilous book. If I were in it, I'd sue right NOW!" No author could ask for more than that.

Closer in touch with the pleasure syndrome than their patrician predecessors, the Acquisitors were constantly in flight and in flux, perpetually trading up, whether it was cars, houses, yachts, or wives, convinced beyond redemption that some women and some driving machines were more *ultimate* than others. They considered themselves citizens of their age as much as of their country or province. No matter what their birth certificates stated, they were perpetually just shy of forty, the most outrageous of them sporting dyed chest hair and constantly discussing their goddamn biceps. The boldest of the Acquisitors' architectural fantasies was the 100,000-square-foot house built on his private Caribbean island off the Bahamas by Peter Nygard. Guests required golf carts to get from the football-field-sized living room to their bedrooms, while Peter himself lived in a treehouse with mirrored ceilings. His fortune, built on his Winnipeg-based fashion house, fed construction of his hangar-sized dwelling, which included a sauna for his twenty-five best naked friends. When I asked him what his peers thought about his creation, he sensibly answered, "I have no peers."

The Acquisitors tended to love and marry (not necessarily at the same time) spunky women with great bods, clenched dimples, and surfs of shampoo-ad hair who wore labels instead of clothes. The women lived by the same jungle ethic as their men. When a reasonably minor Vancouver acquisitor named Barry Tobler jilted his live-in, Sylvia Lewis, she waited until he was asleep, doused him with Grand Marnier, then set him on fire. That cooled their relationship.

The making of fast deals provided the Acquisitors with the essential rhythm of their lives. The gathering and display of material goods became their most creative art form. "What's the point of making money if you're not going to spend it?" demanded Nelson Skalbania, the British Columbia real estate flipper who was their prototype. A rhinestone in the rough, Skalbania, at the height of his intuitive powers during the 1970s, did six to seven hundred deals a year, flipping real estate so rapidly that he usually sold buildings before the first down payment was due. With his beseeching eyes, messianic beard, and charismatic bearing, he looked like the lead in a travelling company of *Jesus Christ, Superstar*. At one point, he owned a $2.7-million private jet, a pair of

Mercedes-Benz 450s, and four Rolls-Royces, including the 1928 phaeton convertible used in the motion picture *The Great Gatsby*. He also acquired John David Eaton's luxurious fifty-three-metre diesel yacht, *Chimon*; after paying $1.5 million to modernize the vessel, he went on a three-day cruise before putting the ship back on the market. The last time I saw Nelson, who faded into near obscurity after a questionable trust deal, he assured me that he had changed his ways and had, in fact, become a conservative investor. When I asked for an example, he explained that only the previous week a group of entrepreneurs had asked him to finance the raising of the *Titanic* by filling it with ping pong balls. He had firmly resisted the opportunity. With that change of heart the Acquisitors passed into history, like mayflies at dusk.

Except in Calgary.

"If you've paid your debts in this town, you're Establishment," I was told by Ron Coleman, an Oil Patch guru I befriended. The city's most colourful local character was Jack Gallagher, who had read too many Ferrari ads ("What Can Be Conceived, Can Be Created") and believed them. During his thirty-year run he transformed Dome into Canada's most important energy consortium, and managed to do it entirely with other people's money, not paying a dollar in taxes or dividends. He was never very interested in making money for himself or for his shareholders, preferring the less mundane pursuit of altering the Canadian North's geography. Convinced that the Beaufort Sea was another Persian Gulf, bursting with ninety billion barrels of cold, crude oil, he took gambles that made corporate responsibility seem banal, winkling entire treasuries out of the feds, divining oil out of ice, and amassing loans that exceeded bank reserves. Gallagher understood that the real conflict in Canada was between those who are cowed by authority and those who are not. He wasn't. Without actually lying, he enlisted investors' imaginations, so that a board lot of one hundred Dome shares that could have been bought for $380 in 1951 was worth $120,000 three decades later – though in the interval the company had not proven out a major new oil or natural gas strike. He could move the market with a smile. On September 7, 1979, when Gallagher was asked on TV about rumours of a major strike in the Beaufort Sea, he said nothing, but his answering Cheshire smile not only drove his own stock to a new high but moved the entire TSE Energy Index up 186 points.

Long before Dome's bankruptcy, I asked him what he was planning to do, once the Beaufort had become the new Middle East. "Hell, that's easy," he said. "Gonna irrigate the Sinai. I've already written to the secretary-general of the UN describing the technology involved. Much of the sand is really silt, so the eastern third of the desert, running from El Arish to Aqaba, would be set aside for nuclear-powered desalination units to turn seawater into irrigation systems that would transform it into a green belt and a new home for the Palestinians."

I backed out of his office as fast as I could, found the nearest broker, and sold my Dome stock. Just in time. What was left of Dome eventually was absorbed by an American multinational.

A very different character was Arthur Child, who turned Calgary's insolvent Burns Foods into a $2-billion food-processing giant that became Alberta's largest private employer. He maintained no public profile outside his company, yet was the most interesting Canadian businessman I knew. He was a skilful flyer, performing impressive aerobatics in his own vintage Tiger Moth. He captained his thirty-ton motor yacht, *Cybele III*, on some hair-raising voyages off British Columbia's west coast. The vessel, which he designed himself, was typical of Child, toughly built but functional, its white-carpeted engine room as neat and innocent of bric-a-brac as the desk in his Calgary office. (It was typical of him that when he purchased his boat, he also bought the company that made it.) He was extraordinarily sensitive to the ways of the sea. When he lent me his ship's log, it read like Joseph Conrad.

He was also a learned man, having graduated from Queen's University in commerce, read French literature at Laval, taught himself German, Spanish, and Russian, as well as writing his Ph.D. for the Harvard Business School. During the Cold War he was regularly flown to the Pentagon for top-secret briefings. His only vanity was to wear a red toupee that fitted him so awkwardly it looked like a skewed beret. At eighty-three, a few months before he died, he took the controls of a Top Gun F-16 fighter jet at Nellis Air Force Base, outside Las Vegas, and flew it at 1,550 miles an hour. Before takeoff, when an instructor started to lecture the octogenarian on how the ejection seat worked, Child gently interrupted him. "I won't be needing that," he said. "At my age, if I get into trouble, I'll just ride her down . . ."

During the mid 1980s, I spent a few days at Jimmy Pattison's retreat in Palm Springs, California. What I remember most from that long weekend was our departure. Pattison drove me to the airport where his private jet, a $40-million Challenger, was standing by to whisk us back to Vancouver. As Jimmy and I were ambling toward the gates, he veered away and I found myself walking beside him as we passed a long row of pay phones. In a ritual obviously evolved from long practice, Jimmy pulled open the change slot of every telephone. He scooped out whatever coins had been forgotten and never missed a beat as he continued toward the runway. I was speechless. Was this the ultimate capitalist – a man so money-minded that he felt compelled to collect pay phone leftovers on the way to his $40-million jet?

I asked why he had done it.

"Habit," he deadpanned. "My first job was as a bellhop at the old Hotel Georgia, and I made more money from forgotten telephone change than from tips. So even now, whenever I see a phone, I go for it."

There have been a lot of pay phones in Jimmy's life. His private empire – no partners, no shareholders, no annual reports – enjoyed revenues of $6 billion per year, and the net profit was all his. Jimmy made it easy for people to supply their own reasons for liking him and had surprisingly few enemies or even critics.

Of all the Establishment's inheritors, I found young David Thomson to be the most impressive. As head of Thomson Corporation, a multinational electronic information provider, its stock

73 per cent owned by his family (worth $48 billion), he was the richest Canadian, in charge of the country's largest privately controlled enterprise. David invited me to his Rosedale mansion just before he took over. The house was really a magnificent art gallery, with kitchen, bathroom, and bedrooms attached.

Although I know nothing about art I was anxious to make a good impression. Of all the many art objects the young Thomson showed me that day, the most memorable was a magnificent depiction in gnarled, almost petrified wood of the Crucifixion, with a suffering, near-life-sized Jesus mounted on its original cross. The carving had been the worship-point of an unidentified church in southern Germany during the last quarter of the twelfth century, and it was priceless.

"The agony of Christ is pronounced with the hips slightly tilted," he explained. "The profile of Jesus's head is quite spectacular. In this piece, one confronts the beginnings of Gothic carving and the tremendous expressionism of the northern world . . ."

He went on, praising the creative genius of the holy sculpture in his living room, speaking in a monotone, his throat muscles stretched by the force of his concentration. Overcome by the intensity of his emotions, I reacted with my own passionate, Mel Gibson moment.

"Yes, oh yes, and look at those nails," I offered helpfully, "how honest and embryonic they are . . ."

"Yeah, well actually, I put them there myself," he shot back, looking at me as if I had just thrown up on his magnificent carpet. "They're what the cross is hanging on." Bad start. But then, David operated so far outside the box he was not even in the warehouse. That's the trouble with being burdened by an original mind – not mine, his.

BY THE MID 1990s I knew it was time to write another Establishment volume; a sea change had taken place since my 1981 dissection of the Acquisitors, most of whom had disappeared under water as quickly as they had bubbled up. The great dynasties of my first volume were suffering a crisis of nerve and faith, a loss of the easy self-confidence that had once marked their passage. They knew that their world was no longer their own. The best of them realized that they ought to have perpetuated their power more purposefully, instead of relying on surrogate managers, distant cousins, and spoiled first sons.

As I looked around and started to resurrect my contacts, I quickly became aware that a new posse of corporate raiders had ridden into town – or rather, out of town. The digital revolution had made it possible for these upstarts to operate their fledgling empires on an international scale, while approval of the North American Free Trade Agreement made it mandatory. I decided to name them Titans, and was captivated by their self-confidence, which separated them from both sets of predecessors. Global adventurers. Canada to them was but a dot on their virtual maps of the mind.

Still, there was an air of gamesmanship about them that any court jester could appreciate. They believed implicitly that it was never too late to have a happy childhood, and that you should die young as late as possible. They lived as much for the fun as the money, and pursued both to the ends of the earth. If the old Establishment was a club, they were a network, linked by cellphones and mutual self-interest. Seldom did they follow a game plan, let alone a set of rules; long-term planning meant next Wednesday's power breakfast. This new Establishment was a floating crap game – anybody could join. You were judged not by who you were, but by what you had done – and might achieve tomorrow.

Instead of the coalitions of power brokers who had once dominated Toronto, Montreal, Winnipeg, Halifax, or Vancouver, now there were mainly mercenary individuals in heat. They might hook up for specific projects, but those alliances seldom evolved into enduring structures. "Reputation is character, minus what you've been caught doing," emphasized Seymour Schulich, a Toronto investment specialist. Lured to Nevada by the quality of its poker games, he struck it rich there and returned to live in a non-descript Toronto highrise, and keep a six-shooter in his office desk.

The rough and ready Schulich inadvertently became one of Canada's most successful university fundraisers. In the early 1990s he decided to grab himself a bit of *civitas* by endowing a new business school that would bear his name. His two-year odyssey into the minefield of university philanthropy is not a subject he will happily discuss, but I persuaded him to tell me the story, providing I didn't quote him directly. Because he had gone to McGill, he originally planned to donate $15 million to the university's mining school, with the understanding that it would be named after him. That wasn't possible, he was told, unless he donated $25 million. McGill eventually received $35 million from several other donors and named its new mining building after former engineering student Man Hung (Jimmy) Wong, who left McGill $8 million in his will.

Meanwhile, Schulich took his offer to Rob Prichard, then president of the University of Toronto, who said, well, no, he was hoping to get more from Joe Rotman, the Toronto merchant banker. Having been made aware of the competition, Rotman promptly wrote cheques totalling $18 million, and the Joseph L. Rotman School of Management was created. (Schulich still refers to the University of Toronto as "Prichard's Palace.") Undaunted, Schulich drove to London, Ontario, and tried to get the business school at the University of Western Ontario to accept his $15 mil. No dice. When Richard Ivey, heir of the family that founded London's Empire Brass Ltd., heard of the possibility of his alma mater accepting the out-of-towner's option, he donated $11 million to UWO's swiftly renamed Richard Ivey School of Business. Increasingly exasperated, Schulich called on Dean Horvath, York University's Hungarian-born business dean, and York's Schulich School of Business was born. Seymour never expected to raise $54 million more in the process.

These were the voices of the new *meritocracy*, an awkward term coined by Thomas Jefferson, who described it as "a natural aristocracy, based on virtue and talent." Virtue? Not as Jefferson would have defined it, but the new Establishment's major players did share a loose set of character traits that helped make them who they were. Their highest "virtues" were cunning, competitive fire, greased-lightning decisiveness, and a passion for their quests. This, plus talent and muscle, was what separated them from their predecessors, who belonged to an aristocracy based on inheritance, clubs, private schools, and family connections. By definition, that elite depended for its authority on different sets of assumptions. The meritocracy's power came from its brass knuckles. That was why, when the hungry newcomers appeared on the scene, wielding their razor-edged assets, nothing like a war ensued. The Old Establishment wasn't murdered; it surrendered, in a distracted stupor.

It was only when I began researching *Titans* that I realized the Establishment had at last, hesitantly, begun to cross gender lines. Women were gaining power and wealth, as was their just reward in any society that operated on merit: Maureen Kempston Darkes, president of General Motors of Canada; Diane McGarry, CEO of Xerox of Canada; Sheelagh Whittaker, head of Electronic Data Systems Canada; Annette Verschuren, president of Home Depot Canada; Bobbie Gaunt, CEO of Ford Canada; and others, notably Heather Reisman, who had become the country's leading bookseller. Whittaker once aptly summed up the state of play. "We'll have true equality," she declared, "when we have as many incompetent women in positions of power as we have incompetent men." That won't be easy.

When *Titans* was published in the fall of 1998, I was astounded to read Sandra Gwyn's review in the *Globe and Mail*. An evocative chronicler of Ottawa's early social history, she had never shown the slightest interest in contemporary business or any of my subject matter, yet she labelled the book "a major disaster . . . not a book at all, but a mass of undigested research," and so on. After that, she got nasty, accusing me of recycling the book's contents from my previous volumes. Now, that was just plain silly, since I hadn't written about the mainstream Establishment for the past twenty-three years, and my material was not only new but had to be fresh by definition, because the Establishment had almost totally renewed itself. (It was true that in about a dozen of the book's 652 pages I had reconstructed, in the same words, the original Establishment – as I have in this volume – to retrace its several incarnations. I saw nothing wrong with that.) Only one person bridged the first and last volumes, and that was Paul Desmarais, though his chapter in *Titans* was based on completely new information.

In the spring of 1998, a quarter century after I had first written about him, I went back to interview Desmarais at his home in Palm Beach, Florida. He was in a class of his own, the only major Establishment figure whose hold on power had bridged all of my books. We reminisced as we sat on his front porch. Since the assets he controlled by then added up to $100 billion and his annual income was more than $33 million, the "porch" where we sat was actually the marble terrace of a 12,000-square-foot neoclassical manor house designed by the kid from Sudbury himself, so that he could live in comfort where the climate was nothing like home. An amateur architect, Desmarais controlled every detail of the building and its site, even throwing up an artificial hill precisely high enough to cut off views of the road, so that from the house you could see, without distraction, straight out to the heaving Atlantic.

Because my original volume included a long chapter on him, after he had heard that the manuscript was locked up but before he had seen its contents, he had scribbled me a note: "If it's good, I'll buy five hundred copies. If it's no good, I'll buy all the copies." He never made good on his promise, which was too bad, because we were ready to keep the presses rolling. I hadn't seen him since. He had suffered several heart attacks and survived two major bypass operations, but his sense of fun had hardly diminished.

About halfway through our interview sessions, he launched into the previously untold story of how, in the late 1970s, he had saved Power Corp. from being taken over. Desmarais knew he couldn't defend himself against an onslaught by Ian Sinclair's CPR, then Canada's mightiest corporate giant, run by its fiercest CEO. The two men decided to spend the Montreal evening sparring and they started to drink. They went to the Château Champlain and guzzled their way through a meal, then went up to the hotel's roof, where there was a private club to which Sinclair belonged, and drank many more toasts. It was three o'clock in the morning by the time they finished, and they were very drunk. They went to Desmarais's house, but he couldn't find his key — or even his pocket — and when he finally did, couldn't locate the keyhole. So the pair of staggering corporate heavies used their shoulders to break down the front door. A startled Jacqueline Desmarais threw Sinclair out on the street.

The next morning, Desmarais, feeling very hungover, reserved a room at the Queen Elizabeth Hotel and slept for most of eight hours, but not before asking his secretary to call Sinclair and tell him that he was at a business conference all day, that Power Corp. was definitely not for sale, and that he'd get back to him later in the afternoon. Finally, at five o'clock, Desmarais went over to Windsor Station to see Sinclair, who was sitting behind his giant desk, looking green, the sweat pouring off him. He had worked all day, and was so upset when his eyes focused on the smiling and vibrant-looking Desmarais that he gave up the whole takeover scheme and Power Corp. was saved.

A small story, but that was the kind of shared confidence that made the Establishment books readable, because it revealed the character of my host. We talked for most of two days and I ended up with seventeen hours of tape that produced a definitive chapter. "I've been like a fisherman who goes out and puts out a net, and if he's lucky, he gets a good catch," Desmarais concluded. "But sometimes, even if he's a good fisherman, he gets nothing. Well, I spent a lot of time putting out nets and finally, I've been lucky. You've got to expose yourself to the fish precisely when circumstances are favourable. . . . We have a lot of capital now, much more than I ever dreamed possible. There are many things I'd like to accomplish still. I sometimes ask myself, why don't you stop?

With everything you have, there is a corresponding responsibility – and after a while it becomes a heavy burden. But the fascination to go on never stops . . ."

"My enemy now is time," Desmarais said as we parted. I climbed into my rented Chevy and drove back to my Days Inn special, past the darkened Palm Beach mansions, and thought to myself that there would never be another Establishment giant like this one. He was the forerunner. He showed the way. His competitors studied him and tried to copy him, like apprentice hunters of the plains, learning how to shadow a great buffalo. But he wasn't about to be brought to ground.

THE CANADIAN ESTABLISHMENT exerts its veto powers stealthily, far below the radar. Such incidents are difficult to document, and impossible to prove. Yet they must be brought to light if accountability – let alone a genuine open free market – is to mean anything. In *Titans* I had described the irrational exuberance of the stock market in the mid 1990s, especially its high-tech sector. It was a topsy-turvy world with wealth creation no longer flowing from savings, investments, or lucky mineral strikes, but from the human imagination. The New Economy was new because it created its own rules. In high-tech's heyday companies no longer required consecutive profitable quarters before they offered their stock to the public. It was *potential* growth that mattered, not established earnings. Possibility had won out over reality – which eventually caused the bubble to burst. Most high-techers were sculptors in snow; the empires they built vanished with the market thaw. But for that frantic half-decade the red-hot high-tech market spawned a highly creative and lucrative group of innovators in both technology and financing. Its most imaginative animator was a charismatic and precocious Bay Street genius named G. Scott Paterson, who became the unwilling victim of his own success.

In a way, Paterson's story was at the heart of my book because I devoted a full chapter to him, the first time his astonishing story had been told. As chairman and CEO of Yorkton Securities, the country's largest non-bank Canadian investment house, he represented a novel, multidimensional prototype that qualified him as a role model for the twenty-first-century money-movers who were taking command of Bay Street, and therefore Canada. While stock-trading volumes and prices rose to frenetic levels of activity, there were more hands on the levers of financial power than ever before. Some left no fingerprints. His did. Paterson was the rashest and loudest member of the new group of men and women in their bursting thirties who took over Canada's financial markets. Unlike Old Money, which passed on its legacy in a slow turning of generations, Scott Paterson waited for no man, seized power, ran with it, and revolutionized Canada's fiscal universe.

What set Paterson apart was his remarkable negotiating skill. He had a knack for exploiting the electric moment. During the closed-door discussions that priced initial public offerings or decided the size and terms of new issues, he would often break the impasse by grabbing the deal through a combination of intuitive leaps and invented logic – or waltzing away with Brownie points for the next time around. He moved half a dozen start-ups into the billion-dollar market capitalization range. "At the end of the day," he liked to preach, "finance is an art, not a science, as the kids who come out of MBA schools are taught. The vast majority of opportunities are ignited by putting together exactly the right players at precisely the right moment. It's managing the art of timing that creates the greatest plays."

Paterson's biggest problem in challenging the Bay Street Establishment was his impatience. He became Yorkton's CEO at only thirty-three, while looking at least ten years younger. (That meant he was being toilet-trained during Expo 67 and earned his first million before he had to shave.) Kiki Delaney, the legendary Bay Street money manager whose investment firm transacted significant business with him, once told me, "I'm very high on Scotty. I'm a big cheerleader for people like that," then leaned forward, impishly adding, "And he's only twelve years old!"

He became too rich too quickly and made sure that everybody knew about it. Certainly he was high-spirited to the point of recklessness, not a disciple of the deferential humility that is supposed to be the hallmark of success in this Presbyterian curse of a country. He stepped over the fine line between being important enough to attract notice and appearing too pushy. It wasn't his ambition that the Establishment frowned on, it was his rapid ascent to success on brains alone. Industry whispers claimed that Paterson's 1997 earnings added up to $7 million, double the compensation received by the best paid of the Big Five bank chairmen, and if true (and it was), it was deemed to be too much too fast. But that's what innovators do; their mantra is not so much to destroy the status quo as to move it into a more contemporary and lucrative dimension.

This was no theoretical exercise. Paterson and his search-and-destroy squad bypassed the Establishment channels and precedents, barging into Bay Street's tranquil assumptions about its divine right to commissions, upsetting not just a few apple carts but the whole cozy market. During Paterson's half-decade as head of Yorkton, the firm raised $3 billion as lead underwriter and a further $6 billion co-managing transactions, ranking ahead of all the bank dealers in financing technology, biotech, film, and entertainment companies. In the process, Yorkton's revenues quadrupled; its return on equity shot up to an annual average of 74 per cent, which was unmatched on Bay Street. His secret was to finance start-ups with private placements, so that when it came time to do an initial public offering, the clients were already in his pocket, and the bank-owned houses were mostly left out in the cold.

Something had to be done. And here the story becomes murky. Prompted by adverse newspaper stories, the Ontario Securities Commission launched a massive investigation into his activities, either on its own or, more likely, because of complaints from fellow brokers who resented Paterson taking away their business and realized he was only at the beginning of his run. For eighteen months, employing a multitude of its best lawyers at any one time, the OSC went at him, requiring Yorkton to publicly declare in all of its client communications that it was under investigation. That drove the firm close to bankruptcy, finally prompting some of its executives to a desperate tactic: they decided to sacrifice Paterson, who had been their main asset. The only way to get the OSC order lifted was to agree with its charges – in other words, jettison him, and move on.

Apart from its dubious ethics, there turned out to be one small problem: despite one of the most intensive investigations in its history, the OSC turned up no evidence that any securities laws had been breached. Leading Bay Street broker Gene McBurney told me that Scott never did anything that the rest of them weren't doing. Brian Butler, the commission's manager of investigations, gave the game away when he publicly declared: "We're prepared to take on high-profile people because they are the best way to send a message of deterrence." Paterson fit all the requirements except one, so the OSC settled on levelling the rarely-used, esoteric charge that he had engaged in "conduct contrary to the public interest." That harsh verdict (which in its broadest context ought to have included all of Bay Street) had the advantage of not requiring any troublesome further proof or explanations. On a much different scale it was reminiscent of George Bush's war on Iraq, which was based on nonexistent weapons of mass destruction but went ahead anyway.

What gave the accusation credibility was its quick acceptance by Yorkton's pragmatic executives, who recognized that sacrificing Scotty was the only way to save the firm, and agreed that they had indeed acted in a manner contrary to the public interest, and were probably responsible for the plague of locusts that had descended on northern Saskatchewan's canola crop as well.

And that was that. Scott Paterson had to pay a personal penalty of $1 million and agree not to manage a brokerage firm for two years. Served him right. He was, of course, guilty as charged. Those who challenge the Establishment in this country leave its members with only two alternatives: to take them in and co-opt their energies, or to destroy their effectiveness. They ought to have done the former because they'll never succeed in the latter. The Canadian Establishment never learns.

CLASS TREASON BEGINS IN HERESY. The decline in the Canadian Establishment's influence had its genesis in its enthusiastic support of Brian Mulroney's 1988 campaign that sealed the free trade agreement with the Americans. It may have boosted our exports, but the pact also reduced our elite to a colonial and irrelevant offshoot of the American empire. The Canadian Establishment scattered. Peter Munk sold all his Canadian real estate (except the CN Tower, which attracted no bids). Izzy Sharp was down to two hotels in Canada, compared to seventy-three abroad. Conrad Black moved away, abandoning his citizenship and, as it turned out, his reputation. At the same time, the combined defeats of the Meech and Charlottetown constitutional agreements turned out to be the Vietnam (or Iraq) of the Canadian Establishment, which had not only supported both initiatives but urged the people to follow them. With the decisive rejection of both accords, the tranquil possession of power that had characterized the Establishment's members had finally been shattered. The dirty little secret was out: our betters didn't know better; the Canadian Establishment could no longer impose its agenda on a nation reaching for the digital realities of the twenty-first century. It dealt in nostalgia now; the power had moved elsewhere, mostly beyond our borders.

By the turn of the century I realized that with the Internet now automatically providing the connecting links I had so painfully traced in the past, there was no longer much purpose in continuing to track the Canadian Establishment's networks. Besides, I had grown tired of the hunt. After the last book, I had been warned that I would never eat lunch at the Toronto Club again if I continued to harass certain gentlemen members. "Is that a promise?" I replied, causing much consternation to my interlocutor. I had always regarded the Toronto Club and its branches across the country as depositories of human trophies, celebrations of the art of taxidermy at its finest. Good breeding was for horses. Besides, most of the clubs still treated women and Jews with about as much enlightenment as your average Islamic state. Members belonged only, as one of them put it, because it took the guesswork out of friendships, but it removed the spontaneity as well. The club adherents' unspoken fear was that hooligans (anyone not wearing ties) would one day burst through the doors and grab all those trophy cups with names of past recipients engraved on them, and throw them into rivers, or melt them down for coin, like the silver goblets and golden angels in the cathedrals of pre-revolutionary France. That was the nightmare. It never happened. Nobody bothered to take the trouble to storm these islands of bygone privilege. The little silver cups are still there, untouched, and no one any longer bothers to polish or even dust them.

The Establishment's grandees had talked at me for almost thirty years. I felt like the disillusioned camp follower of an exhausted repertory company, as I dragged myself from one of my books to the next. They knew I was different and never felt truly comfortable with me; there was a part of me they couldn't buy. They submitted to being "Newmanized" because it became a rite of passage on the way to being recognized as one of the big boys. But the game had played itself out. It was when I visited their homes that I recognized how surprisingly interchangeable and, in the end, uninspiring they were. Most of them weren't families, just collections of people with the same last names. I quietly resigned as the Establishment's gatekeeper and turned in my court jester's outfit, substituting my Greek fisherman's cap.

What might have been the final act was played out at Montreal's Mount Royal Club, the most snobbish of the exclusive luncheon clubs, in the fall of 1993. Red Wilson, then chairman of BCE Inc. and the club's president, had gathered four dozen of his friends for a cigar evening. Who better to invite than Ray Hnatyshyn – one of the few Canadian governors general to openly enjoy lighting up cigars – and Marvin Shanken, publisher and editor of *Cigar Aficionado*, the glossy international publication devoted to the pleasures of cigar smoking?

The Brooklyn-born Shanken had never heard of anyone calling himself a governor general, and kept addressing Hnatyshyn as "Your Admirable" instead of "Your Excellency," but the evening proceeded smoothly until the question period, when the G.G. asked which size of cigar Marvin preferred at different times of day, citing his own evolutionary approach of starting with a cigarillo in the morning and working his way up.

"Personally, Your Admirable," Shanken replied, gazing pointedly at Canada's head of state, "I light up one big mother-fucker at seven-thirty in the morning, and that keeps me going all day."

The room was stunned. Quickly and silently the smokers dispersed into the cool of the evening. But something happened that night that forever devalued the country's elitist culture, and connected it with the real world. Thus died the Canadian Establishment.

PASSIONS: WRITER OF THE PURPLE SAGE

–⟨⟨◎

I wanted to make the facts dance.
My style of creative non-fiction was literary choreography,
often savaged by the very critics who secretly enjoyed it.

A ll of that writing – the scores of columns, the hundreds of news articles, the weighty magazine pieces, the thousands of pages between the covers of all those books, the humorous notes for Federal Express drivers, the billets-doux left on lovers' pillows, the apologies and explanations, the lively exchanges of correspondence with trusted friends and misguided critics, the *aides-mémoire* following too-long literary lunches, the how–high–the–moon promises to literary agents, the inventive excuses later offered to publishers, the millions of letters of the alphabet that I scattered to the winds in a lifetime as a man of letters – all shared one elusive object of desire. I wanted to invent an individual prose style that fused the best of creative writing with the hard-headed habits of journalism.

At first I imagined journalists were self-anointed watchdogs. I sniffed out whiffs of authenticity behind the pillared Establishment façades lodged at the end of those long, curving driveways. I hounded the pale masters of power who inhabited these castles-in-the-air for facts and follies that could be constructed into door-stopping books that deconstructed their lives in the process. But that was an enervating enterprise. They regarded me as part black-guard at their keyholes, part father-confessor, part annoying intruder. I was intrigued by the combination of character traits required to wield power but quickly realized that simply telling and retelling how they earned mountains of cash, or more often amassed fortunes through inadvertence, was as repetitious and uninspiring as watching the sex act instead of experiencing it.

An impulse to find a more alluring way of describing their vir-tually unlimited authority, both political and economic, led me to formulate (or, more accurately, borrow) a style of writing that was then fresh to Canada, and certainly new to the pages of the popular press and the conventional book publisher for whom I wrote.

I became a Writer of the Purple Sage.

"Purple" was the adjective my critics most frequently attached to my prose, and that was fair enough. I took it as a badge of honour. To me, "purple sage" hinted at some exotic prose style set loose in the world of feelings. I came up with my own literary mantra: to paint is to see; to compose is to hear; to write is to *feel*.

Before I disappeared into the hinterland and jammed my trade-mark Greek fisherman's cap on my bald head, I scampered around the redoubts of Canada's various establishments, taking notes and wearing out my tape recorders. I had no secret agenda beyond that of any other campfire storyteller who wants to sell two million books.[1] Unlike novelists, who can create their own worlds, I was limited by the facts of each situation, or their reasonable facsimile. I became a storyteller, not a story inventor. "A story that matters to us becomes a bundle in which we wrap truth, hope, and dread,"

---

[1] The Australian-born journalist Clive James once attended the Monaco Grand Prix and was invited to watch the races from the quarterdeck of a Greek ship-ping tycoon's personal yacht. Although merely a poor, wretched scribe, he rev-elled in the luxury of the ringside view, the liveried attendants, and the yacht's helicopter tethered to the deck. When the German owner of a 108-foot yacht docked beside them, James leaned over and shouted, "Where's your helicopter, then?" This became my ultimate defence against my critics: "Where's your two million sold copies, then?"

wrote the noted Canadian critic Robert Fulford. "Stories are how we explain, how we teach, how we entertain ourselves, and how we often do all three at once. They are the juncture where facts and feelings meet."

If some of my stories turned out not to be totally true (as opposed to as accurate as I could make them), it was because I don't believe that truth is the sum of all the ascertainable facts. Instead, I've always tried to achieve maximum authenticity, which adds up to the ring of truth. Willa Cather, the American novelist/writer, wisely advised: "Let your writing grow out of the land beneath your feet."

I wanted to make the facts dance. My style of creative non-fiction was literary choreography, often savaged by the very critics who secretly enjoyed it. Unlike the imaginary people who populate novels, my characters had the special power of being real. My friend Canadian poet Doug Beardsley, who uses and teaches the technique, once aptly described the format as: "A full description of the facts of the matter, fused with the literary techniques of prose fiction: narration, figurative language, dramatic scene-by-scene construction, dialogue, character development, interior monologue, the use of voice, and highly symbolic detail. At best, it seeks a larger truth and has the ability to penetrate beyond the obvious, to circle in on the heart of a subject, to make the hidden visible."

That approach parades under many guises: literary journalism, New Journalism, or most aptly, in Henry James's evocative phrase, "felt life." "Creative non-fiction," which I have chosen to call it, is a lousy, negative label, a bit like referring to Canadians as "invented non-Americans," but it does describe the process. The genre perceives the world with the sensibility of a novelist or poet, yet deals strictly with things as they are, not as they might be, could have been, or should be.

To apply the Beardsley formula, I first had to develop a strong sense of audience, a clear notion of who I was writing for, and why. I quickly realized that this meant competing for my readers' time. No longer does the *cost* of reading material alone determine its purchase; for many, the *time* they invest in reading is the deciding factor. Trying to hold my readers' interest implied being entertaining as well as informative, and writing in a fresh style that would connect with their emotions as well as their intellects. Anything to keep them turning pages.

The aim of storytelling – to portray what's really happening, behind what appears to be going on – is far more important than any categorization. The genre was most famously pioneered by Tom Wolfe in his experimental articles published by the long-defunct *New York Herald-Tribune* and his books about the 1960s, with their wigged-out titles like *The Kandy-Kolored Tangerine-Flake Streamline Baby*, *Radical Chic and Mau-Mauing the Flak Catchers*, and *The Electric Kool-Aid Acid Test*. (Sample: "A stewardess is walking to the back of the plane to buckle herself for takeoff. Under a Lifebuoy blue skirt, her fireproof legs are clicking out her Pinki-Kinki-Panti Fantasy . . .") "One of the points I wanted to prove," Wolfe told me when I interviewed him in Vancouver in 1972, "was that novels and non-fiction should be written the same way. You are bringing some news to the reader, and you have a solid grounding in fact and detail. It ascends from there." His boyish, preppy head incongruously sticking out of his signature white suit and stiff-necked collars, Wolfe kept asking me polite questions about Canada and Marshall McLuhan.

The art form arrived with the shock of the new in the United States during the 1960s and 1970s, perfected by such writers as Norman Mailer, Joan Didion, Truman Capote, Sara Davidson, John Gregory Dunne, Jimmy Breslin, Tracy Kidder, Gay Talese, Tom Morgan, and the most outrageous of them all, "Dr. Gonzo" Hunter S. Thompson.

The "Old Journalism" it replaced, designed to accomplish widespread palatability through the bleaching of meaning and emotion from its prose, was boring. Tom Kent, asked to chair a royal commission into the newspaper industry, concluded that no Canadian city could possibly be as boring as the newspaper that served it. He was right. The mass-market dailies that force-fed most Canadian and U.S. cities their daily diet of news pablum, owned by a handful of media barons who faced neither competition nor oversight, had the feel of McDonald's processed, preservative-laden, profit-generating pap. They represented, if not a crime against humanity, then certainly a crime against the vividness, diversity, and meaning of human experience.

That slide into sameness was best captured by the English writer Michael Frayn in *The Tin Men*, a novel about a research institute where a computer is programmed to publish daily newspapers that will satisfy the readers without actually having to report on anything that happened on the day in question. The computer's programmers consult public opinion surveys to find out how often readers want a specific news event to recur – a fire, say – and then whether they want the victims to die, or the young girl to be saved by a valiant firefighter. Should there be an air-crash story every month, or more frequently? Did it provide the right blend of anxiety and comfort if these crashes happened in places far away, such as the Peruvian Andes, and if only foreign carriers were involved? This way, the "product" (which is what far too many owners and editors call newspapers these days) could be guaranteed to satisfy the customers. Proprietors loved the scheme, since it not only sold newspapers but also prevented them from having to spend money on the messy business of hiring reporters to gather the news. Written as a satire, Frayn's work is closer to the truth than many of us would like to believe, though Canada is blessed with a few superior exceptions.

Creative non-fiction has actually been around since man first put quill to parchment. It reaches as far back as Tacitus, Thucydides, Julius Caesar, and Pliny the Younger. It was practised by Daniel Defoe, and later by Stephen Crane, Mark Twain, and George Orwell. But it was Tom Morgan who first broke the barrier in the modern era, when, in a 1960 *Esquire* magazine profile, he quoted CBC interviewer Joyce Davidson, then married to famed Broadway producer David Susskind, as hissing at her husband: "What have you got? No money, bad shows, no guts, no integrity, and Diana

Lynn in *Philadelphia Story*." Susskind later told Morgan that his use of that devastating retort ruined his life, but he never denied the quote. Suddenly, everything was permissible.

The best Canadian practitioners of this black art include Ted Allan, Doug Beardsley, Ian Brown, Barry Callaghan, Christina McCall Clarkson, Allan Fotheringham, William Kilbourn, Jack Ludwig, Lawrence Martin, Robert Mason Lee, Roy MacGregor, Rod McQueen, Heather Robertson, Sandy Ross, Norman Snider, Mark Steyn, and Patrick Watson. Diane Francis is in a category all her own: the best. "Since non-fiction emerged as a clearly recognized genre in Canadian literature, it has been enormously popular and influential," wrote Heather Robertson. "Yet it is shunned by the literary and academic establishments as uncreative or unscholarly, a bastard defined by what it is not. Negative definition and second-class status have encouraged a prejudice that it is second-rate hack work we publish to make money, while we create our 'real' books. But non-fiction is not failed fiction, ñor is it random jottings . . . scribbled hastily over coffee, although journalism . . . is where it begins. George Grant and Marshall McLuhan were both academics, and for all their differences of discipline and subject, they share with Peter Newman a biblical prophetic style, the legacy of another great seminal root of Canadian literature, the sermon." Hallelujah, sister!

We may be dismissed as heretics by our old-fashioned rivals, but our approach – true stories artfully told – sprang into life as a necessary evolution of the printed word that would more accurately reflect modern reality. It was no longer acceptable for journalists to write prose devoid of colour or emotion. Instead, along with my fellow converts, I attempted to turn myself into an omnipresent video camera, moving in and out of situations and recording the action. The idea was not only to divine what was being said, but to describe gestures, backdrops, habits, manners, glances, poses, furniture, clothes, modes of treating wives or husbands, children, servants, superiors, and inferiors, the ambiance that dominated whatever situation I was describing. My writing style changed drastically as I tried to obliterate the distance between my verbal outpourings and my readers' perceptions, so that they wouldn't sense they were watching me watch them, but instead feel themselves involved in the action.

Observed reality requires a style that is visual, something that the readers can picture and identify with. To evoke the mood of an event is as vital to understanding it as its substance. The trick is to illuminate without casting distorting shadows, or creating a counteracting mood of my own, instead of the mood of the subject under scrutiny. This is where all too many practitioners of the art stumble, and where too many documentary filmmakers lead us astray. It may be necessary for me to inject myself as the reader's proxy into a story, for it to make sense. But the story is never *about* me. It is legitimate, however, to bring to an article a certain sensibility, which is the proper and unavoidable job of the writer. The comment that best captured my particular take on events was noted by Walter Young, then chairman of the University of Victoria's political science department: "There is an autumnal and slightly melancholy flavour to Newman's writing that seems to fit into an Atwood category."

THE VISUAL VERSION of creative non-fiction seems like a natural extension, but except for some early cinéma-vérité experiments and a few Canadian innovators like Patrick Watson, John McGreevey, Doug Leiterman, and Bill McAdam, television has remained mostly what FCC chairman Mark Fowler once described as "just another appliance; a toaster with pictures." The blow-dried sameness, the capped-tooth Sahara of all those vapid Kens and Barbies who currently dominate television's public affairs airtime has destroyed the medium as a creative force. Television at its most affecting is the raw footage: the courageous Chinese youth standing up to a tank in Beijing's Tiananmen Square, the explosion of the space shuttle *Challenger*, the collapse of the Twin Towers. At such moments, television reveals its unique power to convey raw emotion to global audiences. But just as quickly, the Kens and Barbies (lots of hair and echo-chamber voices) are called in to mediate our experience for us, and the magic is lost.

I made brief forays into television and wrote half a dozen documentaries, but quickly realized that print was my natural format. Mood writing became essential to my art. In *The Bronfman Dynasty*, while documenting that aggressive clan's early bootlegging adventures in Saskatchewan, I came across the little-known fact that a family member had been shot to death by American bootleggers, in a border community called Bienfait (its name came from a French-speaking CP railway worker and was quickly reduced by the locals to the pronunciation *Beanfate*). To reconstruct the place and the event, I first had to capture its small-town atmosphere:

Main Street runs one dusty block south from Highway 18 to its dead end at the CPR tracks, and the only reason the little town doesn't give off an air of abandoned hope is that it is impossible to imagine any sense of promise or enchantment *ever* having been conjured up in this bleak moonscape. Old men with their good, wind-reddened faces spend hours allowing countless cups of bitter coffee to grow cold between them in the Kopper Kettle Café, trading those shattering small quips that can burn away the scrub of a hidebound life. Something has leaked out from them into the dun-coloured walls, the toll of small-town life gone sour.

Outside, the wind is howling in, rainless, across the great plains of North Dakota, whipping Bienfait's unpaved main street into dust storms, or screaming down from Lac la Ronge, carrying angry clouds of rain that turn the town into gumbo. The farmers who drive in from the surrounding countryside walk with a practised lean to compensate for the winds that make tiny jibs in the vents of their jackets and tear at their nostrils. Their wives, dressed up in small crowns of afternoon hats, sit impatiently in the pick-ups, waiting for their husbands to finish their man-talk so they can go shopping in Estevan, nine miles west.

Bienfait is a one-elevator town nestled into Saskatchewan's bleak southeast corner, a bare ten miles north of the international boundary, its modest skyline limited to a large Ukrainian Catholic church, the Plainsman Hotel, a branch of the Royal Canadian Legion, two cafés, a general store, and the CPR station guarded by a large grey cat. Less than a hundred farmers live in and around Bienfait now. And what little nightlife exists is transacted in the cramped beverage room of the Plainsman Hotel, which boasts eleven bedrooms at nine dollars a night. Back in the 1920s, when it was the King Edward Hotel but more widely known as White's, this was the centre of the booze trade, the place where American bootleggers stayed while picking up their loads from Harry Bronfman's boozorium around the corner.

The legend of the rum-running days still recounted by old-timers is the story of a week-long visit by Harry's best known customer, the infamous American bootlegger Arthur Flegenheimer – better known as Dutch Schultz. He was later taken by surprise while dining in the Palace Bar, a Newark, N.J., chop house. Two hoods came through the door firing .38s, killed three of his bodyguards and ventilated Dutch so thoroughly that he expired twenty-four hours later. His last words were: "Mother is the best bet."

I chose this book fragment because it illustrates one of the first lessons learned by Canadian writers: landscape is always one of the dominant characters. The setting of a story is as important as what happens. How does the classic children's tale begin? "A long, long time ago, in a country far, far away . . ." The elements of time and place take precedence. It's a lesson taught to us in childhood but forgotten in everyday journalism, where all too often a dateline on a story will evoke some foreign, mystical locale – the Khyber Pass, or Baghdad, or Kathmandu – yet the story that follows might have taken place in central Detroit or the outskirts of Orillia for all the local colour it contains.

MY EVERY INSTINCT as a young journalist had been centrifugal – to spin myself out to the sidelines and watch. As I grew in experience, I realized that I had to become centripetal instead – swirling into the vortex at the centre of the story. It is only through the dogged and patient pursuit of the core of things that telling details and revealing thoughts are captured. I attempted to create books and articles that possessed enough compelling material and emotional heft to touch my readers' consciousness, yet tried to endow the experience with the extra dimension of humour, or at least irony. To defuse the possibility of readers being intimidated by my 652-page opus *Titans*, for example, I opened the book with a quote from the Toronto society hostess at a Rosedale cocktail party I attended. When I asked her for a glass of water, she replied, paraphrasing W.C. Fields: "Sorry, we never serve the stuff. Fish fuck in it." That was followed by another offbeat non sequitur I overheard at the same gathering as two debutantes debated their wedding plans: "Do I believe in sex before marriage? Well no, not if it holds up the ceremony."

An integral part of my "purple" style, often disparaged, is my generous use of footnotes. These often appear to be off topic, but I believe that providing readers with a break from the persistent beat of the story, giving them instead an oblique observation or random thought, actually assists the process of revelation. After all, we do not think like microchip processors, relentlessly grinding data to an inevitable conclusion. Our thoughts are creative, stray, will-o'-the-wisps that arrive at their destinations through an organic process of synthesis. Footnotes are my way of opening up readers to this mysterious experience, inviting them along on my creative journey, rather than force-feeding their thoughts.[1]

MORE THAN ANY OTHER EVENT, the Vietnam War of the 1960s and 1970s transformed my craft. "Conventional journalism could no more reveal the harsh realities of this guerrilla encounter, than conventional military power could win it," wrote Michael Herr, its most evocative chronicler. "The War had a surreal quality, with no linear front line; it was everywhere." Herr's *Dispatches*, a collection of disconnected conversations, unexplained acronyms, and fragments of hard reporting, gave expression to his stunningly effective voice. (Francis Ford Coppola in his seminal film of that conflict, *Apocalypse Now*, drew on two sources of inspiration: Joseph Conrad's *Heart of Darkness* and Michael Herr's *Dispatches*.)

Since Vietnam, the everyday landscape of our lives has been shifting too rapidly and too fundamentally to be authentically captured in standard prose. The classic journalistic lead paragraph is an historical anachronism, designed for efficient transmission in the event that the telegraph line unexpectedly went down. It presumes that the story can be told in a "nutshell," usually based on verbatim quotes from Jurassic "official spokespersons," military, political, or corporate. In reality, the truth of any situation is a miasma of impressions, memories, contradictory facts, and conflicting emotions. Anyone who has ever reported from the scene of an important news event will confirm this, yet reporters spend their entire careers denying this fundamental truth in their tidy twenty-five-word leads. "The World Trade Center twin towers collapsed yesterday after being struck by terrorist-hijacked aircraft, with the loss of three thousand lives." Does that come close to

---

[1] In his review of one of my books Arthur Johnson, a former editor of *Canadian Business*, noted: "Rather than imparting some worthy statistic that causes a reader's eyelids to become heavy, Newman's footnotes become a nudge in the ribs, a whispered aside. But these flourishes do not make Newman's story trivial."

conveying anything remotely like what happened on that horrific, history-shaking morning?

Nietzsche argued that language was originally developed to shield mankind from the bewildering welter of reality in which everything – every stone, tree, and individual animal – was unique, a drain on comprehension. So mankind invented category words, like "stone," "tree," and "animal" to generalize experience and somehow contain it. But this gain entailed a loss, in that every "category word" in some sense shrouds reality. In daily journalism, "category words" have become the stock-in-trade, sheltering us from the intolerable truth of the world.

Herr's notion that writers should possess their own individual voices, instead of hiding behind the institutionalized anonymity of their newspapers or magazines, is the most essential element in any written as well as spoken communication. Realizing that the prime animating force in the process is the validity and originality of the author's voice, I fashioned a tone of my own. It was wry yet biting, intimate yet unintimidating, tough yet ironic, discomforting yet compassionate, forever emphasizing feelings over facts.

The best creative non-fiction, to my way of thinking, has the cadence of improvised hangdog blues on a steel guitar. "Although it is not necessary for a writer to be a prick, neither does it hurt," claimed Los Angeles novelist John Gregory Dunne, a master of the form. "Resentment sharpens his eye; hostility hones his killer instinct. . . . I am especially interested in overheard conversations, in the mosaic of petty treason that decorates small lives." Certainly the creative non-fiction style is aggressive in its intent. It deconstructs events and personalities. "Words are loaded pistols," warned Jean-Paul Sartre.

ANOTHER LOADED PISTOL is the interview, a long-lost art form revived by creative non-fiction. If there was any talent that kept tofu in my larder during my career as a writer, it was the ability to draw out from my subjects the sort of revealing anecdotes that would otherwise have gone no farther than the family dinner table. This talent was built on the skill of conducting interviews, which is about much more than mere conversation. Everything matters, including dress and stage settings. When I was interviewing for my half-dozen Establishment chronicles, I was careful not to dress like a wharf rat, which is my favourite disguise. It was white shirts and three-piece dark suits all the way, except when I was writing about the fast-flying Acquisitors. Since I didn't have enough hair to have it blow-dried, I interviewed those hotshots in my black Dockers and turtlenecks, though I never worked up the nerve to hang gold chains around my neck or wear pinkie rings. The idea was to appear utterly non-threatening. I would have put on wallpaper to blend in, if I could have. This wasn't whoopee-cushion time.

While I lack theatrical good looks, I am armed with a pair of expressive brows, and eyes that can register sympathy, astonishment, or a sense of wonder. I have the ability to transfix my interviewees with such intense concentration that they are convinced I believe them to be the world's most fascinating creatures – even when their canned dialogue bores me out of my skull. To grease the wheels a little, the information highway seldom flows one way. I learned long ago that to get, you've got to give. I offered tidbits of information in return for theirs. The idea is always to establish a link, become what Gay Talese, the American non-fiction ace, called "a curious confidant, a collaborator, a trustworthy fellow traveller searching in their interior, seeking to discover, clarify, and finally to describe what they personify and how they think."

My readers must have wondered how I could publish fairly exact figures about the wealth of the Canadian Establishment's adherents, and how I found out who belonged to the local elite and who didn't. It was easy. Establishments are self-selected, operating as much by exclusion as inclusion. Before going to Vancouver, for example, I would look up the directors of its poster corporations, the memberships of its leading yacht, golf, and downtown lunching clubs, and debrief my friendly banking contacts. Then I would ask everyone I saw to go over the lists and identify members of the city's core Establishment and how they had earned that distinction. They invariably took extraordinary trouble to do so, and at the end of the process, I had a valid list. (Of course, they were unaware that in some other corner office elsewhere in the glass tower jungle I would be asking another bigwig to similarly assess them.) Arriving at estimates of individual wealth worked the same way. To ask rich Canadians how much money they have is like suggesting they describe their favourite sex positions. They clam up. But ask rich Canadians what their rivals and competitors are worth, and they immediately spout the details, almost to the penny. By using this technique, I learned more about the country's distribution of wealth than the tax department. In my first Establishment volume I broke down the country's rich into eighteen individuals worth more than $100 million and 239 other high riders worth more than $20 million, and I was right on the button.

I found that the most essential talent in interviewing is to have the skill of a hunter, or better still, the warning systems of a hunted animal, ears on the alert, snout up to smell danger — or opportunity. It's the unexpected nuances that give people away. It's not what they mean to say, it's what they reveal inadvertently. That's why my voice-activated tape recorder is so valuable; it picks up the words, allowing me to concentrate on the essential sidelights, which I scribble in my notebook while the machine whirrs away. When I started to interview influential power brokers who had never talked to a journalist, they seemed hypnotized by my tape recorder. Instead of paying attention to my questions, they would watch its wheels going around. The sight of the mechanism froze their responses, reminding them that every word was being preserved and would be judged, which made them much more reticent. I found that removing the sight of the recording mechanism eased their fears, and so I obliterated the tape recorder's glass window with hockey tape.

Heavy breathing, a slight rise in the pitch of the voice, a slowing of limb movements, a change of rhythm in hand gestures, an accelerated blink rate or tendency to look away were sure giveaways that my interview subject was lying (to me or to himself), or at least inventing a more acceptable version of events several steps removed from the truth. Body language is always the first to answer difficult questions, and it *never* lies. Anyone who spoke in perfectly parsed sentences – plural predicates for plural subjects, no dangling participles, the perfect usage of *that* and *which* – was highly suspect in my book, because his answers were so obviously rehearsed. Also falling under suspicion was any overreliance on Latin-based words: events that were *unanticipated* rather than a shock, people who were *exemplars of probity* rather than straight, *fiscal resources* rather than cash. These choices gave me reason to squint at them – to *regard them askance*.

As with any interview technique, a little bluff can go a long way. One obstinate backstage influence-wielder put me off with clouds of words that said nothing. But I happened to have my sailboat docked near his at Toronto's Royal Canadian Yacht Club, and got to know the friendly Norwegian shipwright who looked after it. He proudly confided in me that he was one of only two people who had the boss's private phone number, the other being his mistress. When I mentioned the shipwright's name to the tycoon, said that I had already interviewed him, and thought it might be interesting to talk to his other private telephone contact, my reluctant interview subject's body language went crazy. He started to rub his ears, blink at five-second intervals, clasp and unclasp his elbows, and refused to make eye contact. Then he gave me the straight goods.

Particularly at the start of an interview, charming small talk is essential. That picture of your subject's sailboat: "That's the prettiest Hinckley-51 I've seen. Bet she goes upwind like stink." Or: "How about those (Argonauts, Habs, Broncos)?" – even though I've been to only one sporting event in my life. I always felt if there was anything disingenuous about sucking up, it was a flaw in the receiver, not the giver. "Flattery hurts no one," remarked U.S. presidential candidate Adlai Stevenson. "That is, if he doesn't inhale."

I always let the subjects think they were in control of the interview, while subtly steering them back to the storyline. By the conclusion of most interviews I had built up a sense of sympathy and obligation that could be parlayed into "just a few questions to wrap up." I played as dumb as I could, pretending to be delighted by my subject's early revelations, although they were often obvious, seldom thought-provoking, and always self-serving. I usually didn't bother transcribing the first half hour of any interview, and most times didn't even turn on the tape recorder.

Problems arose when an interview flagged, as most do at some point. While I was debriefing Canada's richest man, Lord Ken Thomson of Fleet, I resorted to my ultimate weapon. He was droning on about his paintings and favourite music while I wanted to talk about the Hudson's Bay Company, which he then owned. But I couldn't move him from discussing the artist Cornelius Krieghoff, and Hank Snow, his favourite country singer. So I allowed myself to fall asleep.

Being a kindly person, he finally realized that he was being a bore, and by the time I woke up, he had switched subjects. I have often fallen asleep during interviews since, sometimes without actually wanting to. It has never failed to produce the desired effect. Silences are also useful and must not be interrupted. I find there is nothing more valuable during an interview than a shared silence. The subject almost invariably feels he should fill the void with something interesting, and usually does.

The choice of venue can be helpful. It's always preferable to interview in the subjects' homes or offices, because their different essences are on display in both places. That allows me to take field notes about dress, decor, art and photos, off-beat traits, and defining habits. The most unusual locale for a serious interview was one I used in 1997 when I was profiling Terry Hui, the youthful Hong Kong entrepreneur then in charge of drastically altering Vancouver's downtown skyline by riding herd over Li Ka-shing's $3-billion redevelopment of False Creek. Shy and secretive, he had never before granted an interview. We talked several times, mainly in Chinese restaurants, but his machine-gun staccato English, combined with a natural diffidence, produced no worthwhile quotes. He did tell me that he owned a motorboat and wanted to learn sailing. So I invited him out on the *Raven*, and after a while we started to talk. It was no better than before. Then, I noticed the sky had turned menacing. The seas started to kick up, and Hui began to look worried. I decided to use the situation to my advantage.

"This is looking really bad, Terry," I told him. His face registered some alarm, and I nodded gravely. "Really bad. Why don't you take this tape recorder and interview yourself below? Your hopes, dreams, and stuff like that." I left unsaid, but implied, that this might be his last chance. "Here, this is the button that turns it on."

Hui went below and spilled the beans in the confessional of the ship's tossing galley. It turned out that what he really wanted to do with his life was to be responsible for one of those pivotal ideas that change how things work. "If I could invent something like Kleenex or Xerox that became a household world, I would be really happy," he confided to my machine, among other intimate details, while I was wrestling with the steering wheel. The world is still waiting for a Hui, but I had my interview.

Almost always, as I snap my notebook shut and turn off the recorder, my subjects relax. They feel free to reveal, if not the inner demons that haunt them, at least their telltale presence. That's the moment I go into my exit mode. The only way to rescue and accurately recall those final, invaluable snippets, I have found, is to excuse myself, run to the bathroom, and write down what they said while it's still fresh in my mind. Come to think of it, I must have an undeserved but justified reputation among Establishment folk for chronic diarrhoea. Whatever works.

IN MY BOOKS, the ideal is to use the first person while writing for third-person effect. This can be tricky because it involves use of the word "I," which inevitably borders on the self-indulgent. (You can't get into anybody's head except your own, which doesn't guarantee being in touch with an original mind.) The ego too often intrudes. Ideally, the first person singular should serve merely as an orienting point of entry, nothing more, though that alone can be a powerful device. The distinguished anthologist Alberto Manguel has noted how many experienced Canadian writers use the first person singular with diffidence and anxiety, "as if making themselves visible on the page was not much different from streaking." But he has also pointed out the shortcomings of more conventional techniques. "When writing in the third person," he maintains, "journalists don't need to justify themselves. Anonymity excuses them from introspection or self-knowledge: the given facts assume all responsibility."

The worst kind of journalist is the unquestioning transmission-machine style of reporter who delivers the lies and damn lies pronounced daily by politicians and CEOs as though they were fact. This isn't reporting; it's embalming. Just because an article or book is *written* as if it reverberates with universal truth, that doesn't make it so. Even the sweaty business of politics becomes boring if described too dryly.

To encapsulate the differences between the two styles of writing, I made up this table:

JOURNALISM:	CREATIVE NON-FICTION:
Truth as Passion	Passion as Truth
Personality	Character
Thought	Feelings
News	Drama
Facts	Verities
Politics	Prophesy
Experience	Innocence
Scoops	Curiosity
The World	The Self
Simplicity	Complexity

Maturity	Adolescence
Synthesis	Exploration
Quotes	Sensations
Certainty	Quest
Celebrity	Achievement
Story Repeating	Storytelling

Sometimes the first person singular becomes essential to the story. When I flew with the Ottawa press corps to report on Prime Minister Pierre Trudeau's first Commonwealth conference in London, during the fall of 1968, I unexpectedly seized the opportunity to witness the action first-hand. This was my dispatch to the *Toronto Star*, which managed to steer entirely clear of a single fact about the conference:

The meeting of Commonwealth leaders opened here yesterday with most of the participants acting about as interested as a road company preparing to give *HMS Pinafore* for the hundredth time, with everybody properly costumed but no one prepared to put much heart into the performance. By some wild chance and wilder inefficiency, I was herded into the delegate's lounge with the prime ministers and their advisers. I had edged up the steps of Marlborough House to escape the crush of demonstrators and the frenzy that accompanied the arriving prime ministers. The doorway to the historic building was ringed by policemen and Guardsmen in ceremonial uniform, all bent on inspecting credentials. Somehow (mainly, I suspect, because I was wearing a dark three-piece suit and carried a leather briefcase) I was shoved through the doors without any checks. I stood uncertainly for a moment in the main hall and was approached by a functionary in a morning coat who asked me with intense courtesy whether he might take my coat and then direct me "to the delegates' lounge, sir?"

Since the press is being treated with bare tolerance and is strictly forbidden any close contact with delegates, the enormity of the guide's mistake very nearly unnerved me but I followed his decorous figure across the marble hall and found myself standing beside the Right Honourable Harold Wilson, Prime Minister of Great Britain.

Wilson stared at me sourly for five seconds, turned his back, irritably issuing an order to Michael Stewart, his foreign secretary, while glowering about the room at the assembled statesmen, disenchanted with his role as the villain of this conference at a time when he was plagued with an avalanche of domestic political problems. Everywhere PMs and their deferential advisers were whispering to each other, sounding like a group of professors forming up an academic procession just before a university prize-giving.

Close up, I overheard them discussing the UK's failures and omissions. London ought to have taken a firm stand on Rhodesia; the British had no business supplying arms to Nigeria; the sanctions against Rhodesia have been disappointingly ineffective, and so on. The speakers glanced at me for confirmation. I tried to appear puzzled yet sympathetic.

The most colourful delegates were the African statesmen in long grey, blue, and white gowns, earnestly reading documents stamped "Secret" produced by their assistants out of official-looking dispatch cases. Archbishop Makarios, the prime minister of Cyprus, gloomed by, wearing his familiar four-cornered hat, with long jewelled medallions under his beard. He gave me a nasty look, which I hastily returned, just in case he might have thought I was a delegate soft on whatever cause he was espousing. Most of the prime ministers looked at me in puzzlement, as though they suspected I might be part of a recent *coup d'état* in some distant corner of the Commonwealth.

I exchanged pleasantries with Indian PM Indira Gandhi and Tunku Abdul Rahman of Malaysia, and was winked at by

Uganda's Milton Obote. But I could tell from the gathering hush that the business of the Conference was about to begin, and I wasn't sure where I could hide. The problem was resolved when I spotted a familiar figure at my shoulder.

"How did you get in here?" Pierre Trudeau demanded incredulously.

"What will you do this morning?" I casually asked, ignoring his question.

"Oh, I don't know. What would you do?" he replied.

We shrugged eloquently at one another, and Trudeau went off, shaking his head, to seek the company of his peers, and get me thrown the hell out of there.

Meanwhile, Dudley Senanayake, the prime minister of Ceylon, had sidled up to express the hope that Rhodesia would not be at the top of the agenda and I said that I certainly hoped it wouldn't be. Overhearing us, the president of Zambia gave us both a dirty look. As far as I could tell, this conference was going to be a contest of dirty looks. My money was on Harold Wilson. He couldn't afford the economic generosity to give the Commonwealth much concrete meaning, except as a ceremonial safety valve, and would find himself at the receiving end of much lively criticism.

My reverie was interrupted when I found myself levitated between two guards, literally carried out the door, my feet barely touching the ground. Luckily they grabbed me by the armpits, so I was free to wave a fond farewell to my fellow delegates. No one waved back.

What passion was evident at the Conference's opening session was out on the street, where I quickly found myself. Mobs of pickets, most of them black, lined the sidewalk. It was cold and wet and the place was jammed with angry Africans, mostly Biafrans protesting the Nigerian war, straining against an impregnable line of London Bobbies. A group of South African freedom fighters, carrying lighted torches, were badgering a woman in a green feather hat who was stolidly holding up a sign that read: "Britain stands by our kinsmen in Rhodesia."

Then, I spotted a forlorn picket who looked across the line of policemen out of great wet dark eyes, his dignity unimpaired by a deerstalker, Sherlock Holmes hat. He was holding up a piece of cardboard on which was hand-lettered the urgent message, "We Yorubas demand an independent Oduduwaland." I walked over to him in my capacity as an ex-delegate. "Jolly good, old boy," I said, or words to that effect . . .

THE RULES OF CREATIVE NON-FICTION are still being invented. "They are like flagpoles in a slalom race," commented the American novelist Katherine Neville, astutely. "You observe their presence religiously, skirt around them as closely as possible but never let them cut your speed." Only one guideline is not negotiable: practitioners enter into a contract with their readers that they will not bend facts, invent dialogue, attribute thoughts, or distort reality. We can, however, choose which facts and quotes to use or discard, and how to play them to greatest advantage in order to reveal the character of our victims . . . oops, I mean *subjects*. The bridge we must cross runs between what we intend and what the reader understands. Truth might be elusive; authenticity is not. We must bear witness to our experience, but the credibility of what we write flows directly from its fairness and accuracy. Everything else is window dressing.

American publisher Joseph Pulitzer once boasted that "accuracy is to a newspaper what virtue is to a lady." (To which one of his more cynical reporters shot back, "That may be, but we can print retractions.") The problem is in defining accuracy. When a military official describes a bomb gone astray as causing "collateral damage," is it accurate to report his remarks verbatim, even with the knowledge that he really means "civilian deaths"? Hunter S. Thompson, the wildest of the gonzo journalists, always claimed to be accurate in his reportage. His problem, which made him so delightful to read, was that his "facts" had to be filtered through the perceptions of drug-induced hallucinations, which were probably a closer approximation of the American reality of his day than the sober pronouncements of White House officials. Nonetheless, he insisted in an interview with *Rolling Stone*: "I'm a great fan of reality. Truth is easier, and weirder, and funnier. I'm lazy. I like facts."

Creative non-fiction is the antithesis of objectivity, a quality that is highly overrated. When Abe Rosenthal was managing editor of the *New York Times*, his lecture on objectivity was reduced to 16 words: "I don't care if you fuck elephants, as long as you're not covering the circus." Stripped of theory and pretence, readers tend to regard as objective that part of any writer's argument with which they agree. True objectivity resides only beyond the grave. Any exercise in this new style of journalism is bound to be subjective. The presentation of nearly every so-called fact depends on the reporter's memory, mood, alcohol consumption, honesty, and vocabulary. The difficulty is not that so many journalists distort truth; the problem is that most of them reach professional maturity without harbouring much of a notion of what, if anything, they believe in – except deadlines and a high degree of ego satisfaction. Their perceptions inevitably reflect personal values. The best writers are loners who survive on anger and animal cunning. I didn't always agree with Mordecai, but loved it when he was sounding off at 7.5 on the Richler scale.

In *Acquisitors*, my book about the wilder shores of Canadian capitalism, its circus mentality, and gambling ethic, I set the atmosphere by describing a racquetball match at Vancouver's YMCA. There's hardly an objective word in the piece, yet it captures the spirit of the event:

> Herb Capozzi, a playboy-entrepreneur whose idea of throwing a great party was to helicopter in a side of beef for the barbecue and a string quartet to play Mozart for a bash at the top of Grouse Mountain's best ski run, was out to prove

his prowess as a racquetball player. How better to establish his credentials than to challenge Nelson Skalbania to a public match?

Skalbania, then Canada's leading real-estate flipper, had recently donated $100,000 to the Vancouver YMCA for two extra courts, with the stipulation that they be made available exclusively to him at 5:00 p.m. daily for the rest of his life. Capozzi felt the gesture had somehow threatened his unofficial status as godfather to Vancouver's middle-aged jocks. So the two men agreed to the match and, just to make things interesting, bet $5,000 on the outcome.

A dazzle of the city's Beautiful People gathered behind the court's glass walls to watch, exchanging $30,000 in wagers. There were pom-pom girls, a Dixieland band, official handlers wearing togas and throwing bunches of grapes, while a gloomy Doberman slouched around in a T-shirt proclaiming, "Skalbania is a poor country in the Balkans."

Striding through this rowdy assembly were the lean young lionesses of the Vancouver scene, zipped up in their Frye boots and raw silk tunics, revealing there were no tan lines on their artificially bronzed bodies.

The players split their first two sets, but Skalbania slowed the third set down to a walk and Herb, playing in a "Wops Are Tops" sweatshirt, finally packed it in at 21-18. "I bet on Capozzi to win," bitched one of the cheerleaders. "I should have bet on him to survive."

The sequel to the match is less well known.

Capozzi, who had been a pro football lineman with the Montreal Alouettes and the Calgary Stampeders, was determined to get revenge. Capozzi had an attitude where women were concerned. Once questioned about his view of monogamy, he replied: "I think it's a wonderful wood, but I wouldn't want a whole house made of it." He was recently separated from his wife and living with a spunky young beauty named Ellen Brown. At the time, nobody knew about her outstanding tennis record. One sunny afternoon about a year after their racquetball match, Capozzi casually suggested that Skalbania have a friendly game with Ellen on the tennis court.

She waxed him, 6–2, 6–3.

Smiling her sweet smile, Ellen walked up to the net and said, "Hope I didn't embarrass you, Nelson."

Skalbania graciously replied, "Fuck off," and walked away.

Creative non-fiction at its best captures people and events in their compelling interactions, while "objective" journalism turns them into colourless statistics that breathe no life. "I'm always on the lookout for the tiny moment or fact that crystallizes the subject," Sandy Ross, the editor of *Canadian Business*, once told me. Good writing captures character, bad writing bleaches it out. During my research for *Titans*, the last of my Establishment books, published in 1998, I was looking for a small event that might capture the ethic of the global economy. During a visit to Phoenix, where many of the big players hang out, I found it while attending an early Easter prayer breakfast:

Don Hannah, CEO of U.S. Properties Inc. and the father of the actress Daryl, has invited me to a non-denominational service on his impressive spread. We are here to toast the dawn on Easter Sunday. It's all very spiritual. A turbocharged Bible-thumper keeps yelling, "He is risen! He is risen! He is risen *indeed!*" My host reminds me that we live for love, and I keep trying to forget that these guys are all developers. They greet the sun by holding their arms out to the cloudless sky, while attending gurus and gurettes chant that getting in touch with your "spatial boundaries" will expand your "emotional pastures." Or perhaps it was the other way round, but an urban cowboy standing beside me, Stetson pushed back on his head, fails to clue in to the message. "Hell," he says, raising his glass to the sky in a perfect *non sequitur*, "life is too short to drink bad wine." Among this crowd, a radical is anyone who frequents bookstores. Their cropped hair leaves their ears exposed and that lends them a deceptive air of friendly candour, but inside they're crude and unforgiving. Conversation is as strong as horseradish and gets straight to the point. "Burglar alarm? You betcha. Keeps the house shut tighter than a bull's ass in fly time."

Personalities are proclaimed loudly and make bold statements, but characters are revealed in small gestures and their throwaway remarks.

WRITERS OF CREATIVE NON-FICTION must also pay attention to cadence, the sequence of words that appeal to the reader's inner ear – writing that possesses lilt and symmetry, a sense of rhythm, its own melody. Proper cadence makes prose so accessible that it can almost be sung.

For me, jazz supplies this missing element. It is the only music that depends for its high energy on inspired improvisation, the same impulse that fuels creative non-fiction. Musicians call it "jammin'," the spontaneous sounds they make when they gather in late-night sessions to express their feelings. It's the only time they play for themselves, which is why these are toe-tapping, finger-snapping odes to joy. "We play life," Louis Armstrong replied when asked to define jazz. No one has coined a better explanation. While jammin', musicians remain true to a tune's rhythmic impulses but dismember its core, pass it around, turn it over, play it forwards, backwards, and sideways, blow it out of sight, then bring it on home, transforming standards into a fresh and alluring experience. That's how jazz regenerates itself. The best of my creative non-fiction applies the fundamentals of jazz to writing: everything is negotiable, the story elements are shaken up and put together again in unexpected, imaginative ways. Jazz musicians, the good ones, are non-repetitive existentialist poets, just like the great non-fiction writers. The story, like the music, is spontaneous, but both operate within limits: in the former, it's the facts that create the boundaries; in the latter, it's the originating melody, the harmonics and time signatures — in other words, its "facts." Neither jazz nor creative non-fiction flows from tested formulas or conventional wisdom. Reading sheet music gets you nowhere.

I never write anything without jazz pulsating through my earphones. While I jam on my computer, I am accompanied by the cannonade of Stan Kenton's nineteen-piece orchestra, his *Artistry in Rhythm*, supplying the energy I need and the cadence I want. It's an impossible process to define. All I know is that this music transforms the task of writing into bursts of ecstasy: hours sweep by like minutes, paragraphs flow, not from thoughts or even feelings, but from the entrancing, almost hypnotizing sounds that I groove to. When I explained my obsession to Stan Kenton himself, he looked at me very seriously for a long moment then delivered a verdict that few would dispute. "Peter," he said, as kindly as he could, "you're nuts." I prefer to call it a state of grace, seldom granted.

One reason I found his music so gripping was that Kenton seldom used standard jazz time signatures (4/4 or 3/4 time), moving his music into such unheard of cadences as alternating 7/4 and 14/8 time, or 5/4 mixed with a 20/16 tempo. That scoring produced a dramatic imbalance that kept his listeners (and musicians) constantly on the edge of about-to-be-fulfilled promises, which is exactly what I seek in creative non-fiction. Every age has the good fortune to produce musicians who work against the grain, and Kenton was a contrarian devoted to his art. He could swing with the hard beat of an army on the march, but his best charts owed as much to the polytonal inventions of Bartok and Ravel as to the harmonic conventions of Lunceford and Hines. London's Sadler's Wells ballet company choreographed his arrangements; Princess Grace of Monaco had him score her wedding theme; his repertoire encompassed every rhythm known to man, including belly-dance Egyptian, passacaglia and fugues, spirituals, Christmas carols, and Richard Wagner's *Lohengrin* — all played as inventions in jazz.

His many orchestras projected his unique theory of collective improvisation, an oxymoron that's difficult to score and even more impossible to play. His broad, vibrant voicing, staccato phrasing, the showers of open scalding notes that engulfed the listener with a sense of shared loneliness were what Kenton's music was all about. I cherish it and have played it, with my own band and at two sold-out concerts at the Shaw Festival's main theatre in Niagara-on-the-Lake. It has inspired all I have written.

I grew particularly close to Stan during the last decade of his life when he commissioned me to write liner notes for his albums, and I even spent some time on his band bus in that hectic final period. He had been on the road for thirty-eight years, careening around the continent, still making converts but now reduced to playing one-night stands at shopping centre openings, musty nightclubs, and other neon snakepits of the American highway. He never stopped experimenting, inspiring his musicians to dredge up new sounds from their exhausted psyches. The best of them would grope for a melodic line, pursue it, then explore and soar with it, like astronauts dangling in the starlight. A lion in winter who died in 1979, Stan Kenton became my last mentor.

Any creative artist can understand how one art form can influence another, although the process is impossible to define. All I can say is that my writing has been informed by the affinity I felt for Kenton and his music. In my own way, I tried to capture its lustre, its eloquence, its rage and unfulfilled promise. If I could achieve one goal in my own writing it would be to leave a similar artistic legacy, and I only hope that I will, like him, end my days in full command of my worth.

A sense of cadence can illuminate a thorny subject with an inner spirit. In *Caesars of the Wilderness*, in my description of the Hudson's Bay Company voyageurs who paddled heavily laden birchbark canoes deep into the fur country from Montreal, I wanted to convey a sense of the unimaginable toil that cracked their backs and ruptured their intestines but never broke their spirits:

No smear of their sweat or echo of their lives reaches out to us, yet in their time they were cockleshell heroes on seas of sweet water. Unsung, unlettered, and uncouth, the early fur trade voyageurs first gave substance to the unformed notion of Canada as a transcontinental state. The traditional postcard pastiche of slap-happy buffoons with sly moustaches and scarlet sashes, bellowing dirty *chansons* about pliant maidens, that was *not* who they were. Their eighteen-hour paddling days were more wretched than most men then or now could survive. They were galley slaves, their only reward being the defiant pride in their courage and endurance; they could boast of their exploits to no one but themselves, concocting their own sustaining myths.

No voyageur ever reported meeting a small bear, a tame moose, or a wolf that wasn't snarling with blood lust. Running through mosquito clouds along boggy portages with 180 pounds or more on their shoulders, strong-arming four tons of cargo through icy rapids while, as one trader told it, not only hanging on by their hands and feet but by their eyebrows, the canoe men cherished those small daily victories which became grist for the self-justifying legends that kept them going.

The tally of their hardships was most clearly visible at the steepest of the killing portages: The plain wooden crosses, sometimes thirty in a group, marking the spot where drowning, stroke, heart attacks, or strangulated hernias had finally claimed their victims. Out in that witches' brew of a wilderness, they outran their souls and maimed their bodies, yet nobody was there to salute them or mark their passage.

I am not the first writer of non-fiction to be concerned with writing's musicality, I am not even anywhere near the best. I am simply aware of it. Many non-fiction writers obsessed with their own "voice" or unique "point of view" ought to concern themselves with how their writing *sounds*. John McPhee, among the most accomplished practitioners of literary journalism, keeps a quotation by Albert Einstein on the music of Schubert: "But in his larger works I am disturbed by a lack of architectonics." The term architectonics refers to the structural design that gives order, balance, and unity to a work, the element of form that relates each part to another and all the parts to the whole. In his writings, McPhee sets out to accomplish this symphonic quality. He assembles the facts and passages that form the orchestra's parts, but as a writer he is the conductor of the whole. "The kind of architectonic structures that you have to build, that nobody ever teaches or talks about, are crucial to writing and have little to do with verbal abilities," he says. "They have to do with pattern ability – generalship, if you will. Writers don't talk about it much, unfortunately." Mark Kramer, another accomplished writer of non-fiction, uses a musical metaphor to explain his approach to the craft. "It's like a Steinway piano," he has written. "It's good enough for all the art I can put into it. You can put Glenn Gould on a Steinway and the Steinway is still better than Glenn Gould. It's good enough to hold *all* the art I can bring to it. And then some."

ANY STYLE IS SUBJECT TO SATIRE, especially mine, which so often borders on the absurd. My worst blunder was to describe Joe Clark, when he proved to be so astonishingly ineffective as prime minister, as acting "like a fawn caught eating broccoli." Even I couldn't fathom the meaning of that one, though Joe immediately dropped me a line promising to stop munching the green stuff. Another blooper was my description of Charles Bronfman: "His sweet brown eyes reflect that quality of living at a distance from the centre of things sometimes possessed by folk singers, gaitered Anglican bishops, and pet reindeer." Nothing much wrong with that, except that Charles is smart, not sweet; he identifies with folk singers about as much as with Formula One race car drivers; he is an Orthodox Jew who wouldn't know a gaitered Anglican bishop if he ran over one; and he probably knows that reindeer don't make pets.

Mostly the takeoffs on my hip-hop prose were cruel, but at least one was witty and wonderful. Alison Gordon, the novelist and sportswriter who was assigned to write a profile of me in 1987 for the *Toronto Star*, began her story with this description:

> Peter C. Newman's got these big bushy eyebrows.
>
> No, wait a minute. That won't do. We're talking about the master of metaphor here, the sultan of simile, the high priest of hyperbole. We can't just say he's got these big bushy eyebrows.
>
> Peter C. Newman's eyebrows are like dense thickets in the countryside of his face.
>
> Not good enough. The man who described a character in *Caesars of the Wilderness*, his twelfth book, as having "a long nose that swung around menacingly like a compass needle" deserves a better description than that.
>
> Peter C. Newman's eyebrows are like a pair of woolly caterpillars curled up for the winter on the egg of his forehead.
>
> No, too grotesque.
>
> Larks could nest in Peter C. Newman's eyebrows.
>
> Better. Almost worthy of the man.

THE CAPITAL CHARGE brought against me was that my books were gossip. Of course I wrote gossip, at least in its dictionary meaning, which is "the repetition of what one knows about other people and their affairs." Without such intimate glimpses into the elites' private lives, history – and my books – would be boring and incomplete. The *Globe and Mail* dismissed my studies of the country's power structures as having been written by "the Hedda Hopper of Canadian business," referring to a long-expired, airhead Hollywood tittle-tattle-monger. Hardly.

The stories and anecdotes I dig up help to preserve the true flavour of the history that is being made. Consider the gutsy and emotionally informative diaries of Samuel Pepys — some three million words describing court, London, and the personal gossip of the seventeenth century — which provide us with the liveliest depiction of his life and times. Of course I became the subject of much gossip myself, and I never cared for the experience. The experience of being the subject of gossip could be a flattering one, however, as Allan Fotheringham demonstrated in one of his books:

> When a small group of Toronto's media heavies were gathered at the cottage home of Peter Gzowski, the host proudly showed a guest around the beautiful landscape of the old mill town and, on returning to the house to pour drinks, heard a familiar strain of conversation. "Oh my God," he cried in mock despair. "Are we into Newman stories *already?*"
>
> Gather three journalists together and within a few quaffs there will be new Newman gossip, some imagined, some real. I've seen little book-representative girls reduced to tears at lunches when they can't get the author they are nervously escorting to quit swapping Newman stories with the reporter who is supposed to be enquiring about the *book*, while the expense-account gin flows.
>
> Peter C. Newman is without doubt the most eccentric journalist around. The stories are legend about how he falls asleep at 9:05 at 9:00 movies. His painful inability at small talk, chitchat, and what is now called interpersonal relationships fuel a thousand anecdotes. He seldom drinks, claims to have invented Perrier water, and has the appetite of a hummingbird. His personal affairs are sometimes tempestuous. And he makes — oh, sin — too much money. History will better judge the most controversial editor of his day. What is overlooked in the most gossipy trade of all is that Newman refashioned journalism in this country and is in large part responsible for reviving Canadian magazines. He cares about what he believes in.

My chief tormentor was Professor Michael Bliss, the University of Toronto historian who didn't so much write bitchy comments about my works as proclaim his determination to squash me like a bug. He could discover not a single redeeming value in anything I have ever written, and kept publishing the same verdict ("a wretched, gossipy, trashy book"), savaging me to the point of banishment, hoping I would never write another lousy word. Bliss never let up. When I wrote my history of the Hudson's Bay Company, which was praised by such academic heavyweights as Northrop Frye in Canada and A.L. Rowse in England, Bliss spun out of control. He called my books "artless, sloppy, and cardboard rehashings," condemning my prose as "indigestible, irrelevant, and a crime against the uses of literacy" – all this vitriol, without citing a single factual error.

I'd like to say that I was cool and that his poison darts didn't hit home, but they did. Possibly Bliss's motive was tied up with his loathing of anyone who stood for Canadian independence, as I did, in opposition to his declaration of surrender. "We stand for the same values as the Americans," Bliss repeatedly declared. He wrote about "the end of English Canada," describing the border between the two countries as being "not so much a fence as a lawn-marker," and joyfully predicted an eventual "U.S.-Canada Confederation."

I can't imagine that his hostility was personal. We never met. He didn't know me well enough to hate me.[2] But unlike coal miners, deep-sea fishermen, and high-wire acrobats, who take care of each other because their lives depend on it, writers tend to envy success and glorify failure, living out Woody Allen's quip: "Intellectuals are like the Mafia. They only kill their own."

---

[2] There was a wonderful footnote to Michael Bliss's persecution. One Saturday afternoon, after one of his unguided missiles was published in the *Globe*, my daughter Ashley and I were walking through a park in Toronto's Beaches neighbourhood. As a middle-aged couple passed by us, the man turned to his wife, winked at me, and, loudly enough for me to overhear, whispered: "Ignorance is Bliss." Bless you, Brother . . .

WRITING IS THE WORST LIFE (because you're always competing with yourself and are only as good as your most recent book) and the best life (because there is nothing more exhilarating than fashioning a sentence or paragraph that glows). We writers live out our days isolated between the misdemeanours of the past and the terrors of the future. In the end it comes down to novelist Margaret Laurence's description of the process: "I begin to write when the torture of writing becomes less than the torture of not writing." The magnificent Ms. Laurence was a proud professional, offended by anyone who didn't adequately respect her craft. Once at a Montreal reception, a distinguished gentleman came up to her and gushed, "Oh, I'm so glad to meet you. I've read everything you've written. I'm a brain surgeon, and when I retire, I'm going to do novels too!" She looked at him with pretend enthusiasm, grabbed him by the elbow, and bellowed, "WHAT A COINCIDENCE! When I retire, I'm going to be a brain surgeon."

"In my mind is a picture of Kipling's itinerant storyteller of India, with his rice bowl, who tells tales of ancient romance and legend to a circle of villagers by firelight," wrote noted popular U.S. historian Barbara Tuchman in a collection of essays titled *Practising History*. "If he sees figures drifting away from the edge of the circle in the darkness, and his audience thinning out, he knows his rice bowl will be meagerly filled. I feel just as urgent a connection with the reader." So do I.

The Chinese have an expression, "iron rice bowl," referring to a sure thing, steady employment that will provide the means of existence through good times and bad. Writing has been my iron rice bowl, and, like Tuchman, I wanted it always to be filled. An unorthodox approach to storytelling ensured that my bowl was never empty, although the rice was heavily spiced with purple sage.

CHAPTER SEVENTEEN

THE COMPANY THAT BECAME A COUNTRY

⁓⁂

*Because I had been an immigrant and had studied the
country as a subject, I felt that my Canada had been built
on dreams as well as appetites.*

I t was 1983 and we had spent an early Christmas with Camilla's
parents in Tsawwassen, reaching the B.C. Ferry dock to
Vancouver Island, just as Lane 16 was filling up. We had just
missed the five o'clock sailing, which meant a two-hour delay. We
grinned at each other and settled in for the wait. That was when
the difference really struck us.

In Toronto, two hours of downtime had meant holding a one-
way ticket to Purgatory. Now, a leisurely sojourn in Lane 16
seemed no big deal. Like deep-sea divers approaching the surface,
we were becoming acclimatized to our new life aboard the *Indra*,
our sailboat that was tethered at Marina Park Marina, at the foot
of White Birch Road in Tsehum Harbour, on the southeast side of
Vancouver Island. We were snug there, planning some prime time
together inside the compact sanctuary of our thirty-five-foot sloop.

Anyway, here we were, waiting for the 7 o'clock ferry, happily
heading back to the Island.

When we reached Sidney, the small sea-town on the Saanich
Peninsula near our marina, we decided to hit Hannigan's, the best
fast-food outlet, which served the most delicious fish burgers in

the universe. We had not been to Hannigan's for months. It was jammed with holiday shoppers and pouting toddlers awake past their bedtimes.

Camilla, who was allergic to cheese but loved it, decided to celebrate with a full-fledged fish burger. I went up to the counter and ordered, "Two with the works."

We claimed one of the booths and enviously eyed the customers who had placed their orders ahead of us. Our chit number was called and I sauntered up to collect our meal. One of the fish burgers had a decorative slice of cucumber on top of it. "That's the one without the cheese," explained the young woman behind the cash register. "Alison, the cook, says your wife shouldn't have it."

That would never have happened in Toronto. But then, we had chosen to abandon the rat race. Or so I claimed.

My version of dropping out was, as I look back on it, plainly ridiculous; it required monthly return visits to Toronto for research to write my weekly business columns in *Maclean's*, broadcast my weekly interview show on the Global television network, and complete my monthly column in *City & Country Home* magazine. I also had two new books out that season: *True North, Not Strong and Free* (a highly critical analysis of our stumblebum defence policies) and *Debrett's Illustrated Guide to the Canadian Establishment* (commissioned by the official scorekeepers of the British aristocracy, sponsoring their first colonial venture).

We had trucked our floating home from Toronto to Vancouver and sailed it across to Sidney. The *Indra* was more suitable for navigating lakes than fighting ocean swells, but it was just large enough for us both to pursue our assignments – Camilla, her freelance editing, and me, my new book projects. She worked in our miniature dining area, while I tucked myself into the forepeak, a tiny space right up at the bow barely the width of my body, with just room enough for my typewriter, a pile of notes, and a wall-mounted stereo. Outside, the setting of the miniature marina was fetching, with its resident blue heron, a proud bird with an eight-foot wing span and spindly legs that arrived at low tide to feed on the local fish, and a mustachioed harbour seal attracted by the noise of my typing reverberating through the fibreglass hull. We were regularly visited by a pair of swans, and when I heard the rustle of wings above me, I would look up to watch a squadron of Canada geese flap by in perfect *V* formation. The politics of the marina were vicious, with everyone vying for a berth at the outer docks, where you could shrimp and crab over the side and literally catch your dinner in a bucket. The talk was never concerned with politicians or any of my Establishment players; it was about the time the cutter next to us beat the typhoon off Australia, or how the boat that snagged the outer slip had hit a deadhead coming out of False Creek. Sidney itself had Tanners, the best newsstand west of the CN Tower, not to mention Scandinavian and Dutch restaurants and the world's largest Safeway.

Occasionally, we took time off to go sailing, nosing around Haro Strait, reaching across to Saltspring or Lopez islands or even all the way out to the wild shores of the west coast, where rugged slashes of rock elbowed into the Pacific surf. The eighteen months we spent aboard the *Indra* overloaded our senses. Despite my crazy timetable, there was an opportunity to savour the sights, the scents, and the sounds of the turning seasons. Our days were measured, not by the acts of cursing aggression required to grab a place in the passing lanes on the Don Valley Parkway or the Gardiner Expressway, but by the gentle tides that lifted our boat and occasionally left it stranded on a mudbank. Larger than Texas, British Columbia seceded from reality a long time ago, but living on the edge of the country and the continent had its advantages: the province's isolation fed self-sufficiency, which in turn tested inner resolve. We loved it.

But eventually we longed to feel solid ground under our feet again, and one Sunday afternoon we went real estate hunting. Our first stop was at an open house on Major Road, a dead-end lane in Cordova Bay, a dent in the coastline northeast of Victoria with a population of maybe two thousand. It took us about ten minutes to decide to buy it, and the family joke ever afterwards was: "Why did you wait ten minutes?" One reason for our haste was that if I had lingered any longer Randy Bachman, the rock musician (who was also in the bidding), would have snagged it. The better reason was that it ideally suited our purpose. With 130 feet of seashore frontage overlooking the San Juan Islands, it was a garden of houses on a magical hillside. As well as a free-standing study for Camilla, it had a separate guest cottage, storage shed, and a main house that included a large deck, hanging over the ocean, and two fireplaces. There was a bit of a hill overlooking the ocean at the other end of the property on which I chose to build my first study that wasn't a spare bedroom. I had heard that Hank Shubart, who was Frank Lloyd Wright's last student, was living on Saltspring Island and asked him to be my architect. The results were stunning: a two-storey structure, with room for my ten file drawers and drum set and a fireplace, all jutting over our cliff that ran to the sea. There was a meadow around the studio that I kept blooming with wild-flowers and we even installed a tiny, self-reversing waterfall.

"Luminous place, this," Camilla wrote as we moved in. "Sun fills the mist flowing up the cliff, and when the middle-branches are still half-white, there's no far shore." She loved the garden and almost made peace with having to do housework. "With a sense of achievement equal to that when Kant's *Foundations of the Meta-physics of Morals* became clear, I have waxed a floor, my first," read a note on my desk one morning. We learned the hardships of life in Victoria: how you have to wear high boots in late February to wade through the daffodils, and how the bills for sunblock can get fierce by mid March. I had done my research and discovered that tiny Cordova Bay must boast the country's best climate, since more meteorologists have retired there than any other Canadian loca-tion. Although Vancouver Island is famous for its winter rains, the summers were so dry I had to install an irrigation system to keep our garden growing. Local stores sold only the bare necessities, but the village centre was McMorran's Seaview Ballroom, an old-fashioned dance hall built to accommodate the big bands, which still performed on Saturday nights. I dreamed that one week the drummer wouldn't show up and I'd be called in as a replacement. It never happened. When my ankles gave out after a farewell concert with a pickup band in downtown Victoria, I donated my drum set to the Port Alberni Big Band.

We loved Victoria, which is not, as we had feared, an old folks' retreat. Instead, it may well be the world's most attractive city, combining the maritime culture of a sailors' paradise with a lively and varied intellectual life. I renewed my friendship with Arthur Irwin, the former (and in a way, founding) editor of *Maclean's* and the man who turned it into a serious publication. And a bonus was the chance to get to know his wonderful wife, P.K. Page. I had sought refuge in their living room during twenty years of crossing the country to promote my books and other enterprises. Now we could visit often and exchange vile assessments of whatever politician was bold enough to pretend to be governing the country we loved. By fortunate coincidence I met Doug Beardsley, who became my closest buddy and fellow inventor of the creative non-fiction genre that became our trademark.

I joined the University of Victoria's faculty club, gave a few lectures, and, thanks to Murray Fraser, then VP-Academic, was invited to join its creative writing department as a full professor. I took no pay but was amply rewarded by the talents of my students, who took my breath away. This was not a graduate course and it forced me to examine the many complaints about the writing capabilities of the average university students. It turned out that they were splendid to begin with, and by the end of each of my years of weekly seminars I would proudly have matched their talents against any group of professional writers in the country. It was here also that I began to fashion theories for the new art form that I had been championing. The excitement we felt, especially while sharing post-session glasses of draft beer, was palpable.

Unlike my fellow professors, I took my students into the field, including a memorable visit to one of B.C. Premier Bill Vander Zalm's meetings. Just four frantic days before British Columbians gave free rein to their gambling instincts by entrusting their future to the Dutch gardener-turned-politician, we went to one of the premier's final rallies. This event, at the Macaulay Elementary School gymnasium in Esquimalt, a sleepy suburb of Victoria, turned out to be one of only three brief appearances that the Social Credit leader made in the provincial capital, but the political voodoo that made his remarkable victory possible was on full display.

The audience was made up mostly of decent, middle-aged, middle-class citizens, confused and troubled by a world they never made. There were a few yuppie bungaloids looking for a cause to follow, the odd leftover sixties hippie with hair tied back Willie Nelson–style, a quartet of loud loggers with room-temperature IQs, a few stray dogs and mutual fund salesmen – in other words, your typical Social Credit gathering. A few backroom Socred functionaries were cruising the hall, taking soundings of the crowd that numbered something less than two hundred. Big men with cruel mouths (scars in bloodless faces), they strutted about, obviously proud of their new boy.

When he arrived, leaping off his tour bus, Vander Zalm's smooth handling of what must have been the 419th stop on his four-week campaign, totally indistinguishable from all the others, was impressive. He had the rugged good looks of a safari guide in an old-fashioned jungle movie, with bronzed face, chestnut hair, and restless limbs. Much has been written about his smile, and it certainly is no ordinary grin. The choreography of arched eyebrows, flashing dimples, pulled-back lips, sparkling cuspids, and crinkled eyes produced a glow that enveloped his audience. Wife Lillian had a heart-shaped face (not much chin, lots of forehead for her obligatory headband) and a perky, cheerleading manner. Most noticeable was *her* smile, which seemed wired to her husband's, so that they flashed their ivories simultaneously, even when they were on opposite sides of the room and out of sight of one another. They seemed to be not so much political cronies as lovers with an almost palpable flow of affection between them. Nice.

Their campaign appearance had little to do with platform or policy. In fact, the party leader's mind hardly seemed to be engaged with his vocal cords. But his nervous system was going full tilt. Suddenly the source of Vander Zalm's political magic became clear: he was the first Canadian politician to transmit his essential message entirely through body language. And it worked. Before and after the election, Vander Zalm was accused of being vague. Yet the message, at least that Saturday afternoon in Esquimalt, was as plain as the caps on his teeth: *Elect me and I'll worry for you. Sure, British Columbia may be on the verge of becoming the ravaged Manchuria of the Pacific Rim, but at least we'll all go down smiling.* Somehow the notion was passed along that with Smilin' Billy and Smilin' Lillian safely ensconced in the Walt Disney pile of stones that passes for Victoria's parliament buildings, neither Ottawa, Washington, nor God would deal the province any more karate chops.

Vander Zalm's greatest asset – and the reason he won such a resounding mandate – was his fresh way of approaching the province's problems. Instead of attempting to preach specific options or pretending that he had all the answers, he limited himself to the pledge of changing the climate in which solutions might be negotiated. "We're open about what we propose to do for the people," he said in Esquimalt that afternoon. In British Columbia during that election campaign, this amounted to a major policy statement. There were many misconceptions about the nature of the Social Credit movement, none more prevalent than the belief that it was composed largely of marginal misfits, former and future talk-show hosts, used up used-car dealers, and rednecks from bumper-sticker country who subscribed to the dotty dogmas of the party's official founder, Major C.H. Douglas. The meeting displaced none of those stereotypes but did explain how Vander Zalm, who would become known as "the kamikaze premier," won his inaugural campaign – and it produced deliciously nasty papers from my class.

Many of the students kept in touch with me after graduation, and among them they have written, at the last count, thirteen books. A typical example was Jane Seyd, who produced two good books and later edited the weekly newspaper on the Sunshine

Coast. They were a grand crew who restored my faith in my profession and their future.

MY PLEASANT ROUTINE was disrupted by the arrival in Victoria of the awkwardly named Special Joint Committee on the Government's Proposal for a Renewed Canada, charged with rewriting the Canadian constitution. The location for their hearings was a cold, marble-lined chamber in the local conference centre. But the occasion was inexplicably moving, and I was anxious to be a small part of it. Hardly anyone had bothered to show up. The tiny audience, which through the day was often outnumbered by the thirty members of the committee, consisted mostly of the sort of middle-aged, middle-class citizens who wrote request letters to CBC-FM disc jockeys, read consciousness-raising books by Joseph Campbell, grew alfalfa, and protested against the system by cutting their own hair. Now they just sat there in quiet disbelief.

Their mood of incredulity was understandable. Here we were, a country celebrating its 125th birthday, seriously debating the proposition of whether we should split apart or stay together – whether we could devise a constitution that would save the country from becoming a burnt-out residue of warring provinces, with Quebec leading the charge to battle. That the burden of coming up with a formula to prevent this tragedy had come to rest with this creaky committee seemed the ultimate insult. Not that its members lacked dedication; the co-chairman, Senator Gérald Beaudoin, was the Wayne Gretzky of constitutional law, turning his Gallic charm on a subject that defied levity. But the petitioners to the committee, myself included, felt that history had bypassed these well-meaning legislators and that the decisions that counted would be taken in some civil-service-green futuristic office of some Ottawa mandarin, far from sunlight and enlightenment.

The Victoria hearings had all the trappings associated with constitutional conferences. There was an accompanying press corps bored out of its skull, praying for some bigot to propose that we get "the frogs to speak white" or "tow Newfoundland out to sea." There were consultants who collected fat fees for standing around looking glum and raising the odd eyebrow whenever someone mentioned the BNA Act. And, of course, there was the inevitable bevy of simultaneous translators.[1]

Watching the proceedings, I felt that they should have been held in a public market or a legion hall, some place that breathed energy and commotion, instead of this sterile conference centre, whose most recent occupants had probably been detergent marketers or mutual fund hucksters. My conviction was growing that the once-smug citizens of our once-smug nation were in the process of staging a quiet revolution against the idea of having decisions made for them by self-selected hierarchies like this one.

In my own testimony to the committee I speculated about the roots of the country's problems: that most Canadians believed we were born without having been properly conceived – that we were, in effect, a residual state with no economic logic or reason for being except to fill the void between Detroit and the North Pole. I didn't quarrel with the notion that we might be a loose federation of wildly diverse regions on the very margin of the civilized world, but it was my contention that, despite their self-absorption, most citizens still shared a commitment to preserving Canada as an entity, washed by three oceans. Because I had been an immigrant and had studied the country as a subject, I felt that my Canada had been built on dreams as well as appetites, put together not only by bloodlines, kin, or tradition, but by waves of newcomers of every seed and stock, determined to create new lives. Being Canadian was still too new to be considered a nationality; it remained a condition, an act of faith, a matter of permissions, potential, and possibilities that would take generations to

---

[1] During any televised political conference, when a participating male speaks in French, chances are his words will appear to come out of his mouth in English, spoken by a female translator – and vice versa. Surely this unique trans-sexual, trans-linguistic phenomenon is among the things that really define Canada.

complete. Still, I thought it was time we began to sing some songs in praise of ourselves, that we had got this far. It was time to recognize that if a nation is a body of people who have done great things together, we qualified. From the hearings that day, I realized that a new constitution was not the answer. But I felt better for having waved the flag and given Canada a hug.

IT WAS BOOK WRITING TIME AGAIN. Having more or less abandoned my pursuit of the political scene and the Canadian Establishment, I decided to try something very different. With the continuing existence of Canada being questioned, it seemed to me the ideal moment to reconstruct some of the country's essential history, specifically the chronicles of the Hudson's Bay Company, the seventeenth-century royal fur trade partnership that explored and conquered a subcontinent, ruling over a slab of territory ten times the size of the Holy Roman Empire. It was truly the company that became a nation: Canada.

I had been toying with the idea for years, in fact had made a deal with Pierre Berton to save the writing of that great institution's popular history for myself. Before starting *Renegade in Power* I had considered writing a book on the Canadian Pacific Railway, which had, after all, saved my life. All I had was a title, *Steal of Empire* (referring to its generous subsidies and land grants), which was a take-off on its officially sanctioned corporate history, *Empire of Steel*. When Berton heard about it, he phoned me and pointed out that he was halfway through *The National Dream*, his own book on the subject, and that it was pointless for both of us to do it. I agreed but asked him to stay away from the Hudson's Bay Company, which I intended to chronicle some day. He agreed, warning me that it would be a tough gig.

First I had to find the financing.

My Hudson's Bay Company series was originally planned as a continuation of my McClelland & Stewart publishing program, but Jack's firm was yet again in a downward fiscal spiral and I desperately wanted to link up with a publisher who would provide not only stability but also international exposure. I asked my friend Moses Znaimer for advice and he suggested I consult his lawyer, Michael Levine, who was also distantly connected with the Bronfman family and could probably also help me with research on that book. I first met Levine on the rooftop bar of the Sheraton Hotel and immediately began to grill him about the Bronfmans. He turned frosty, indicated that he would not talk about any topic that involved his law practice, and left the restaurant with a haughty don't-call-me-because-I-won't-call-you expression.

"A few days later," Levine later remembered, "it was a Jewish holiday and I was secretly in my office when I should have been somewhere else, when Peter called and I asked rather icily why he was phoning me on such a sacred day, knowing his own background. He replied that he wanted to retain me as his lawyer. I backpedalled so fast I almost fell out the window. Peter and I met to discuss his dissatisfaction with the $50,000 contract he had signed with Jack McClelland for the first of his Hudson's Bay books. I had done only one book contract before, for Bruce Kidd and Earl Rosen for *China: An Introduction For Canadians*, which I think sold three copies. I phoned a friend of mine, Michael Frankfurt, a New York lawyer, and asked him for an introduction to a British publisher. He told me that he was the international counsel to Viking/Penguin and that I would really enjoy meeting a transplanted New Yorker by the name of Peter Mayer, who was World Head of Penguin and worked out of London.

"Before I left for the Cannes Film Festival, I conspired with Anna Porter, who was then working with McClelland, and asked her how I could get Newman out of the contract. She suggested inviting her boss to share a large bottle of vodka in my den. I asked McClelland over to the house and told him that the book would never be delivered unless he paid Peter ten times more than he had offered. He laughed and told me I was an arrogant son-of-a-bitch and drank the whole bottle. Somehow, we got him to the subway platform at Bloor and Yonge Street and, in a fit of pique, he turned and again called me an arrogant son-of-a-bitch, but said that if I could deliver Peter half a million dollars, he would rip up his contract. I ask him to put it in writing, which he did. I later saw a number of secret memos in Jack's biography in which 'son-of-a-bitch' was the kindest description of me."

Jack and Michael exchanged many, increasingly ill-tempered letters at this time, with Levine putting a bold WITHOUT PREJUDICE label at the top of his correspondence. McClelland finally put a stop to that when he wrote: "Please, no more 'without prejudice' letters. All my letters are laden with prejudice."

Levine went off to London, walked into Peter Mayer's office, sang my praises, and, to his surprise, discovered that such a project would fit precisely into Penguin's strategy, since their Canadian subsidiary had until then been merely a reprint operation and they were at that very moment actively searching for a lead hardcover book to launch their conversion to an originating publishing house. The two men sized one another up, decided they could probably do business, and made a date to meet with me at Toronto's Winston's restaurant in June.

That lunch certainly ranked as my most memorable meal. Mayer turned out to be a refined mullah with an impressive nimbus of silver hair who arrived with a vintage leather bag slung over his shoulder. Born in Britain and educated at Oxford, he had the manner of a posh British gentleman but spoke with a barely detectable Bronx accent. We quickly got down to business. I was my usual tongue-tied self. I muttered a few rehearsed phrases about the economic and social significance of the Hudson's Bay Company in British and Canadian history, a recital to which neither of my luncheon companions paid the slightest attention, then settled down to watch the bargaining. It was a bit like witnessing a Wimbledon tennis match, since I was sitting between them, but when Levine started off by pegging his bottom-of-the-barrel, aw-shucks-we're-in-a-benevolent-mood-today demand for an advance of a million dollars, I wanted to slide under the table.

"Michael," Mayer replied with a look of Hasidic *weltschmertz*, "I thought you were a serious person. Do you really believe that I crossed the Atlantic Ocean and half a continent to indulge in some sort of silly game? So please. Be serious."

"Peter," Levine replied, "I am just a simple man of God but I believe in a making-love-under-the-train style of bargaining. What paltry amount did you have in mind?"

"Well, at the very most, we might possibly be able to pay something close to $250,000 for all rights, including the paperback, French edition, and whatever else. But that would be stretching it."

I was desperately trying to find Levine's leg under the table, so that I could kick it while I nodded my head, sending him the urgent signal: "For God's sake grab it, before he changes his mind."

"Mr. Mayer." My legal eagle swooped down from his imaginary mountaintop, and went on in his most ingratiating tone. "You must not think of us as deferential colonials. We are offering you the chance to participate in one of the great transatlantic literary ventures of all time. Newman here has already sold more than a million books. This is not a gamble. *Blah, blah, blah . . .*"

That was all I could take. I got up and dashed to the washroom so that I could catch my breath, cursing my lawyer for the opportunity he had missed.

I returned to the plush hum of the dining room, expecting the two literary studs to be locking horns, possibly even yelling at one another. Instead I found Mayer and Levine perfectly chummy, quietly toasting the deal they had just wrapped up, at a cool $500,000. (That was at a time when even the Canadian authors of prospective bestsellers accepted advances of $20,000.)

I was stunned. To me, that meant deliverance from the sweatshop pressures of running *Maclean's*. It meant the life I had always longed for, the luxury granted so few Canadian authors of being able to write books as an occupation instead of a sideline. I thanked Peter Mayer with a Buddhist prayer handclasp and, since I knew he had a free afternoon until he was due to speak to the

Canadian Booksellers Association that evening, invited him to spend a few hours on my sailboat. He accepted, and because Jack McClelland had yet to be advised, the three of us solemnly pledged to keep the deal absolutely secret. Since the book world in Canada lived on envy I nervously felt my neck, knowing that as soon as news of my advance leaked out, my fellow authors would organize a lynching party. We agreed that Mayer and I ought not to be seen together until Jack had been informed and the contract had actually been signed.

As soon as Mayer boarded my boat, he stretched out in the cockpit and promptly went to sleep. I put it down to jet lag, though he later told me that it was the largest commitment he had negotiated since joining Penguin four years earlier, "except for authors like Frederick Forsyth, and those kinds of writers, in the U.S. market." It was an extraordinary leap of faith for him, and a high-jump through the window of opportunity for me.

There was little wind, so we drifted along and I was able to come down from that exhilarating but testicle-wrenching lunch. Pretty soon it was five o'clock and I realized that my guest ought to be on his way. I headed for Centre Island, where the Booksellers convention was in full swing. Then it hit me. That part of the island had no docks except for one tiny cement-block landing, where I would have to deposit the Big Kahuna from Penguin, and that landing was located slap in the middle of the convention. Even as I considered the awkwardness of my position, I was approaching the shore, which I could see was lined with booksellers watching my boat come in. I knew most of them by sight and they all knew me as a McClelland & Stewart author. Standing in the stern, blissfully unaware of our dilemma, was the highly recognizable figure of my secret new publisher. I kept shrugging, spreading my hands as a gesture of puzzlement trying to get across the message that I had no idea how this elegant stowaway had boarded my boat. But I could spot the whispering and see the pointing, and knew we had blown our cover.

Not much later Robert Fulford blew the whistle on the deal itself, with a column headed: "The day the world changed for Canadian publishing." He postulated that the day I signed my Penguin contract (September 29, 1982) had altered the nature of the country's publishing industry: "Any future history of publishing in modern Canada will likely be divided into two periods, pre-1982 and post-1982," he wrote. "It was typical of Newman that he stood at the centre of this transformation. Newman is now mainly a writer of popular history, but he's also been a maker of publishing history. No other writer, except perhaps Pierre Berton, has had such an influence on the books that are written in Canada. In 1963, with *Renegade in Power*, he demonstrated for the first time that a book on current Canadian politics could sell large numbers; scores of books followed in his wake over the next two decades. In 1975, with the first volume of *The Canadian Establishment*, he proved that Canadian business could be the subject of a bestseller. Again, scores of imitators followed, more of them each year. Those two titles changed the content of Canadian non-fiction books. But the events surrounding Newman's Penguin contract of 1982 altered the economy of publishing and authorship, and the relationship of author to publisher."

The sad aspect of that incident was abandoning Jack McClelland as my publisher. But as I expected he was gracious and wished me well. He also turned out to be prescient in advising caution about getting too excited about the international potential of my contract.

I SPENT THE HALF-DECADE after leaving *Maclean's* and moving west completing the first volume in my Hudson's Bay Company project, which proved to be the largest and most complicated literary undertaking of my life. It took me almost a decade to complete my chronicles, and during that time I often wondered if it was worth my energy and the time of my readers to resurrect the lives of anonymous fur traders who had huddled under the polar moon in centuries past, with no great adventures to relate except their survival.

Yet the more I dug into the project, the fiercer grew my conviction that in a precarious country like Canada, which has so much more geography than history, it is essential to illuminate the past, not backlit by hindsight but as it really was. My books set out to measure the impact of the HBC on the evolution of the nation and its state of mind: to chronicle the half-remembered genesis of English Canada's corporate and psychic beginnings on the bleak shores of Hudson Bay.

More than any of my other books, this project enveloped me, kidnapping my emotions and channelling my thoughts backwards through time to the birth of the Company of Adventurers in 1670. My first discovery was that its founder was a fellow Czech, Prince Rupert of the Rhine, born in Prague's Hradcany Castle to royal parents whose lineage reached back to Charlemagne. The Bohemian prince was a Renaissance man, having been an admiral, freebooting pirate, erotic painter, metallurgist, inventor of the torpedo, and the field marshal who restored Charles II to the British throne. His reward was the royal charter that established "The Governor and Company of Adventurers of England Trading into Hudson's Bay" with Prince Rupert as its founding governor. The second governor, the Duke of York, gave it up only to become king of England as James II. The Company's minute books record his apology for not being at a subsequent board meeting because he had just ascended to the throne. He was followed in due course by John Churchill, the Duke of Marlborough, whose epic military victories helped lead to two centuries of British imperialism. The Duke's direct descendant, nine generations removed, was Sir Winston Churchill, Britain's great wartime prime minister. When he retired from politics in 1955, Churchill accepted only one post in any commercial enterprise, though many were offered. He became Grand Seigneur of the Hudson's Bay Company and remained so until his death. Another early HBC director was the famed architect Sir Christopher Wren, builder of St. Paul's Cathedral, who chaired the Company's meetings when Prince Rupert was otherwise engaged. No commercial outfit had a grander history and I intended to make the most of it.

In the course of our research, Camilla and I eventually interviewed five hundred men and women who had either worked for the Company or were touched by its activities. We ranged the country like a bureau of missing persons, coaxing memories out of aloof Highlanders who had given the best of their lives to the Bay and suddenly found a couple of eager listeners for the tall tales they had almost forgotten. Out of that research plus the HBC archives, I eventually wrote the three thick volumes of text and an illustrated version of my Hudson's Bay histories, which eventually totalled 1,588 pages, or more than 700,000 words, just short of Leo Tolstoy's *War and Peace*.

I never ceased to wonder about the hold that the HBC exercised over its "servants," as it was pleased to call its employees. Some of its bachelor officers willed it their life savings; one woman executive confided to me that she loved the HBC more than either of her husbands. I even heard the grumblers, fed up with their long, slow lives in dreary wilderness postings, vow that they were "damn well going to retire early" – after only thirty-eight years in the service. Serving under the crimson ensign of the HBC (the only commercial banner permitted to include the Union Jack) became a fever in the blood.

The one emotion the HBC never engendered was neutrality. In Canada's North, the Inuit and Indians, touched by its inevitable presence but feeling exploited by the steep prices at its local stores, insisted that the initials ought to signify the Hungry Belly Company, while the women, speaking from experience, denounced it as the Horny Boys' Club. Equally appropriate, because it seemed to have been there forever, was the claim that the initials stood for Here Before Christ, or more appropriately, Here Before Canada. (Edmonton, which became one of the Company's most important inland depots, proclaimed that HBC really meant Here Before Calgary.) No one touched by the Hudson's Bay Company's

Darwinian will to survive remained unaffected. No wonder that being a Bay man throughout most of Canadian history was tantamount to having joined a quasi-religious order, one that might in modern times have been reduced to selling socks and underwear – but once had touched the hand of God.

I BECAME CAUGHT UP in the Company's history, and my interest in the subject began to take on the quality of an obsession. My conversations in London with its past governors and directors altered my preconceived notions of the British business mentality. I understood at last how the Company's huge domain could have been run with such enduring results for three centuries by men who seldom set foot in it.

As I made my appointed rounds through the City, London's bustling financial district, meeting the dozen remarkable men who had been the Company's last British overlords, it occurred to me that in few former seats of empire was there so much to occupy the eye, the imagination, and the memory. The men who built London's magnificent office structures, and whose descendants still occupied them, brought a touch of civility to the rough-and-tumble world of commerce. Former U.S. secretary of state Dean Acheson, who knew his history, once remarked that he could think of no more delightful period or place in which to have lived than mid-nineteenth-century England, when the country was run by a small group of highly intelligent and largely disinterested individuals. I knew precisely what he meant, even if the merchant adventurers I met were anything but disinterested. Their involvement with the Hudson's Bay Company had been a magical moment in their already distinguished professional lives.

Interviewing them was no simple task. Steeped in discretion, they pleaded everything except ignorance to avoid my questions, and it took several visits before they felt at ease with me and my tape recorder. That impression of reticence stayed with me as I visited a Royal Bank of Canada safe-house near Buckingham

Palace for a meeting with the principals. The site was so historic that I vaguely wondered what century I had blundered into, until I caught the glimpse of a 747 in a holding pattern above Hyde Park. Inside, the assembled, tight-lipped guests included Lord Adeane, financial adviser to the Queen of England; Jocelyn Hambro, a leading merchant banker and chairman of the Phoenix Assurance Company; Hugh Dwan, managing director in London for the HBC; Geoff Styles, in charge of the Royal Bank's British operations; and Lord Tweedsmuir, who had once been an HBC trader.

I had heard rumours that the Royal Family still owned the Company stock that their ancestors had acquired more than three centuries earlier, so I asked Lord Adeane whether they had a special interest in the firm. "Yes," was the discreet reply. That, and not another word.[2]

The most interesting guest turned out to be Lord Tweedsmuir, son of John Buchan, first Baron Tweedsmuir of Elsfield and Canada's fifteenth governor general. He had spent fourteen months as a trader with the Hudson's Bay Company at Cape Dorset on the southwestern tip of Baffin Island. That had been forty-one years earlier, but when he spoke about "our flag" he still meant not the Union Jack but the HBC's house pennant. "I am a Scottish adventurer, and we do not change much with the centuries," he told me, recalling that his years at Dorset had been the happiest of his life, that the Company had been a great link of empire, and that the Scots were its perfect servants.

My final visit was to Beaver House, the HBC's London headquarters, to lunch at the Strathcona restaurant with Arthur Frayling. The last head of the HBC's fur auction house – the world's largest – he had spent fifty-eight years with the Company, yet could still muster the enthusiasm of a boy on the first day of summer camp. Munching his delicious "Trout Cleopatra," he described his obsession with

---

[2] The Royals' investment was confirmed more directly during one of their Canadian tours, when Prince Philip sidled up to HBC governor Don McGiverin and whispered, "How are we doing?"

the Bay. "It's not a job, it's a calling," said he. "To be a Bay man has always caused me to feel that one is working for a Company with a fairly big foot in history. Where is the value commercially in such a feeling? There is none. But I always felt, as did most old-time Hudson's Bay employees, that I was contributing to something a little outside the ordinary commercial run. I can't really put it into words, because I can't see too much sense in it. But that's the way I feel."

I knew what he meant because I was beginning to feel like a Blues Brother myself, on a mission from God, charged with safe-keeping of the Company's heritage and the memories of the men who had lived it. That was a foolish presumption, to be sure, but typing away, hacking at the story to the accompaniment of Stan Kenton's music, late at night or long before dawn, I swore I could hear voices whispering: "Turn off that awful music and make sure you get it right."

The closest I came to these ghostly reminders of my mission was during the few days I spent at the Company's primitive out-post in Moose Factory, at the south end of James Bay (and guess who named the Bay). First scouted in 1671 by Pierre Radisson, it was populated by ghosts. I devoted most of my time to the ceme-tery, walking among the tombstones and the crosses that were twisted into crazy angles by the heaving permafrost. It was begin-ning to snow a little and as I stood in front of a tilted marker that proclaimed "Sacred to the Memory of Peter McKenzie of Assynt, Scotland, a Chief Trader in the Service of the Honourable Com-pany," I sensed the spiritual presence of the Bay men who had lived and died here, their deeds and misdeeds long ago consigned to the dustbin where Canadians store their history.

Yet, walking among their graves, some of the markers weath-ered beyond recognition, I felt them silently watching me, with faces like those haunting slashes of pigment Vincent van Gogh used to portray the Borinage miners: flat eyes, prominent cheek-bones, and looks of profound accusation. "Why?" they seemed to be demanding. "Why have our lives prompted so little attention?

Why have our names been ignored even in that crowded corner of obscurity reserved for Canada's heroes? After all, we did everything expected of us and more, expending our lives in a cold, bitter land, being eaten alive by blackflies, cut off from our loved ones, exploring the virgin forests, buried where we fell, unknown and unappreciated through eternity." I wanted to reassure them that my books would at least resurrect an echo of their existence, but the phantoms were in no mood for literary debates and, with an audible "*Och*, away with ye," vanished into the gathering blizzard.

I walked back through the snowstorm to the Hudson's Bay store. There the shopkeeper showed me a twenty-dollar bill with a note attached to it: "This is to cover the cost of 2 knives stolen from your store 13 years ago." That was typical of the Bay ethic, which applied to merchants and customers alike.

That evening I joined a Scotch burr of veteran Bay men who were trading yarns: drinking to remember the good old days, then drinking some more to forget them. They and their predecessors would gladly have bartered or given away the Bay blankets off their beds to maintain the Company's reputation. They missed the fur trade because it had been less a business than a way of life, an escape from the restrictive codes of civilization. Now it was virtually finished, and so were they.[3]

Somebody mentioned George Simpson McTavish, an HBC factor who had spent forty years at the Company's most isolated posts. To break his seclusion, he had domesticated a mouse and discussed in great earnestness each day's events with the friendly rodent. McTavish always travelled with a loaded pistol, not to ward

---

[3] I wrote my books at the height of the anti-fur crusades of the environmental lobbies. An imposing and spunky New York hostess (a friend of mine) loved her fur coat and kept wearing it throughout the militant protests. As she emerged from the Waldorf-Astoria Hotel one wintry evening, sporting her full-length beaver, a protestor ran up to her and, almost spitting, shouted: "Lady, do you know that twenty-seven animals died to make that goddamn coat you're wearing?" She grabbed him by the windbreaker, pulled his face close to hers, and hissed through a vicious smile: "Do you want to make that twenty-eight?"

off attackers but to shoot himself in case he broke a leg on the trail and couldn't get back to his post. That's lonely. Nothing ever happened, except that McTavish's mouse died. But I couldn't get him out of my mind, trekking across those screaming stretches of empty wilderness, wondering when he might have to put the gun in his mouth.

Canada's backcountry, where the HBC held sway, was populated by many such "ordinary" individuals. They expended their lives in that obscure killing ground of the soul that the poet Al Purdy called "north of summer." Thinking and writing about these "ordinary men" I grew to admire so much, I remembered a line in William Shakespeare's *Henry V*, after the battle of Agincourt, when the King requests a list of England's many dead. "Edward the Duke of York, the Earl of Suffolk, Sir Richard Ketly, Davy Gam, Esquire; none else of name," replied the King's herald. Surely history's most devastating epitaph – and yet "none else of name" was the most appropriate obituary for the hard cases who lived and died here in the service of the Company of Adventurers.

Defining the gravitational pull of that compelling enterprise became my compulsion, even after my first book in the series was published in 1985. It wasn't difficult to prove that the Hudson's Bay Company was permanently woven into the marrow of this country. Its land holdings, after all, became western and northern Canada in 1870 when Ottawa purchased the territories for £300,000 cash, plus title to seven million acres. What I hoped to add to the mix was my theory that the Company's frontier presence had spawned the new nation's founding ethic. All those early forts and trading posts (and there were as many as a thousand at different times) were really company towns, demanding deference to corporate authority from inhabitants inside their ramparts, and deference to nature beyond them. That subservient attitude, stressing collective survival instead of individual excellence, became the tiny communities' – and later, I would argue, the country's – prevailing ideology. It determines what Canadians do and especially what they don't do, even to this day. That deferential mentality made Canada very different from the American frontier, where authority was challenged rather than obeyed, and where the quest was on for a nation that would value "life, liberty, and the pursuit of happiness" instead of the more muted Canadian ideal of "peace, order, and good government."

One expression of those dissimilar approaches was the treatment of aboriginals. The Americans conquered their frontier, sharpshooters against tomahawks, first with the mountain men slaughtering First Nations tribes for their furs, then the U.S. Cavalry, which fought sixty-nine deadly Indian wars, often killing "Injuns, just to watch 'em spin." In contrast, the HBC carefully established long-term commercial relationships with the First Nations. At the core of this partnership was the trade of furs in exchange for goods manufactured in England. Beaver became the breathing equivalent of gold. What made the animals so valuable was not the fur but its fine, thick under-hair, which was made into the felt used to make the beaver hats that became a high fashion item in England and on the Continent for several generations.[4] Before the invention of the umbrella, beaver headgear provided an elegant way to keep dry, but more to the point, men and women could be instantly placed within the social structure according to their hats.

In obtaining the valuable pelts, local factors imposed a strict caution on their frontline traders: never shoot your customers. It was meant less in benevolence than as a sensible precaution against losing business. The terms of trade were never fair compared to the prices the pelts fetched on the London market, but being exploited was better than being shot. In a curious way, it was a form of mutual exploitation, because the Indians and Inuit were able to

---

[4] The lead fumes inhaled during the felt-making drove its practitioners into early senility; thus the saying "mad as a hatter." Another part of the beaver that sparked dreams of fortune in men's eyes were the pear-shaped glands located in the anal region of both sexes. They contained an orange-brown, alkaloid, aspirin-like substance that proved to be surprisingly effective in curing headaches.

capitalize on what they considered to be a near-worthless commodity. They killed animals for food, with the fur, except for the odd robe and blanket, used mainly as bum-wipes. By trading it for axes, hunting guns, blankets, tea kettles, and the other desirable goods that made their wilderness life easier, they thought they were getting the best of the exchange.

Over time mutual exploitation slowly turned into mutual dependence. As the trade developed, the Indians lost their ability to hunt and thus their self-sufficiency. They became trappers instead of hunters, which devastated their self-image because they, in effect, became wards of the Company. That was the unintended yet irreversible psychological damage that the HBC inflicted on the First Nations. Yet keeping in mind that they ruled a twelfth of the earth's land surface for nearly a dozen generations with virtually no accountability, I found that the HBC's governors, officers, and servants did not deserve to be charged with any great burden of shame. Its traders were mostly good men, some better than others, who did the best they could and lived to tell the tale.

Professor Jennifer Brown, a leading fur trade historian at the University of Winnipeg, and others argued that white traders were moved mainly by economic motives to entwine their private lives with First Nations women during their temporary sojourns in the Canadian wilderness. While this was certainly true, I suggested in my books that such liaisons were based as much on loneliness and human nature as on purely economic considerations. "The men were mostly dewy-faced boys torn from their home turf, who found themselves living in a strange and wild territory that had its own rules and obeyed few sanctions," I wrote twenty years ago in the passage that caused most of the commotion.

> Liberated from Presbyterian mothers who would not allow them even to play cards on Sundays and stern fathers who equated sensuality with sinfulness, the young HBC clerks suddenly found themselves surrounded by attractive tawny-skinned women willing and proud to express their uninhibited

sexuality. Love-making on the frontier did not carry much emotional baggage, being routinely offered and casually accepted. The lure of these "bits of brown" or "smoked bacon" – as the women were then crudely called – demurely asking some lonely fur trader to dry his breeches in front of their tepee fire must have been difficult to resist. The women were there, every day and every night, within sight and sound of the forts, an overpowering presence, causing yearnings that erupted into mad dark evenings of ecstasy and pain. By guttering candlelight in a trader's wood-gathering camp and by firelight among the country-family members, the rough or sweet enchantments of intimate moments became a phenomenon that pervaded HBC life through the centuries.

This was more Harlequin than *Hustler*, but having spent part of my own youth, at about the same age, in a desolate mining camp in northern Quebec, I knew those feelings firsthand, and even if politically incorrect, they were poignant and very real. It was the odd Bay men, not me, who used those derogatory descriptions, which was why I placed them in quotation marks.[5] The Native women may indeed have been coopted into casual sexual relationships, though many liaisons resulted in "country marriages," some lasting lifetimes. But First Nations society operated along kinship lines, and it was often advantageous for a family or tribe to be represented inside the white man's world.

Most of the storm that raged around the sexual references in my books was connected with the reign of Sir George Simpson, between 1821 and 1860, when he ran the HBC as his private domain. Acting with the hauteur of a man in charge of his own universe, Simpson did any damn thing he pleased. Darting across his empire

---

[5] One bit of stray evidence of just how solitary the HBC men felt were letters I found sent to the Company's mail-order catalogue division. Enthralled by the layouts featuring women's underwear, one lonely soul wrote away to order, "the lady on the right corner of page 59."

in a fleet of express canoes, he cheered up local factors by announcing his arrival with the loud help of an accompanying bagpiper
named Colin Fraser. The most puzzled observers of these musical
interludes were the aboriginals, who had never seen or heard such
an instrument. They shared the mixture of delight and dismay that
characterized the response of most non-Scottish listeners to its
mournful wail. "One white man was dressed like a woman, in a
skirt of many colours," one puzzled Cree reportedly told his chief,
after hearing an impromptu bagpipe recital at Norway House, north
of Winnipeg. "He had whiskers growing from his belt and fancy
leggings. He carried a black swan which had many legs with ribbons
tied to them. The swan's body he put under his arm upside down
then put its head in his mouth and bit it. At the same time, he
pinched its neck with his fingers and squeezed the body under his
arm . . . until it made a terrible noise." It rang true to me.

Simpson, who was a bastard by birth and by persuasion, had a
nasty habit of keeping a "country wife" in many forts along his
cross-country tours. He referred to these Native women in his
journal as his "bit of brown." When he was described as "the father
of the fur trade," it was more than a figure of speech. The historian Grant MacEwen estimated that he fathered seventy sons
between the Red River and the Rocky Mountains, though the
accuracy of that census is questionable.

In my first volume, *Company of Adventurers*, only 6 of 413 pages
dealt with sex in the wilderness and none of it was explicit, though
the auctioning of female slaves and the tale of an Indian woman
suckling a baby bear were mentioned. Yet those few pages ignited
a firestorm of academic criticism. Fur trade historian Lyle Dick
challenged me to fight a duel on the ramparts of Prince of Wales
Fort, complete with seconds and beaver pistols. "For your sake," he
wrote me, "I hope that your aim is more accurate than your book."
We later substituted a civilized dinner in Winnipeg. No shots were
fired, but no agreement was reached.

My references to Simpson and his mistresses caused something
close to riots on my book tour, with aboriginal women picketing

my every appearance in Winnipeg, Regina, and Edmonton, all accusing me of sexism and racism. My explanation that it was Simpson who had been racist and sexist, not me, carried little weight, especially when Jennifer Brown spearheaded the attack by organizing a special colloquium of the Rupert's Land Research Centre to rip my books apart. The titles of the debates indicated their bias: "Newman's treatment of history: fact or fiction?" "To what degree can a pop historian be footloose and fancy-free with the facts?" and "Is Newman's book Canadian history's answer to *Raiders of the Lost Ark?*" They then issued a press release which, as they might have said, terminally disrespected me, charging me with every crime except spreading the plague of locusts that devastated prairie crops in the Dirty Thirties.

This was all good fun, I suppose, but there was a serious issue at the core of the confrontation. It was my contention that academics should recognize the relevance of popular history, since, as Professor Ramsay Cook has pointed out, "it is the popularizers, more than the professionals, who provide this country with whatever tenuous historical conscience it has."[6] I believe that both approaches to the writing of history – mine and Jennifer Brown's – are equally valid; one is as incomplete as the other.

The trouble with the scholarly community is that there are so few successors to Donald Creighton, W.L. Morton, Chester Martin, A.R.M. Lower, Ramsay Cook, and Richard Glover, master historians who combined academic integrity with an ability to weave evocative prose. The writing of history – both academic and popular – comes down to a process of selection. Once an event has happened, it can never be replayed. It is the character of

---

[6] The official history of the HBC was written by a Cambridge savant named Professor E.E. Rich, whose three volumes were so impossible to read that I managed to get through them only by taking every scrap of reading matter off my boat (including cereal boxes), anchoring it in the middle of the Bay of Quinte, and vowing that I would not leave until I had ploughed through the texts. As a print addict I had no choice, but it was one of life's most masochistic assignments.

the evidence that historians pick that establishes the framework in which they write. In that context, the popular historian will inevitably choose character over circumstance, while academics remain convinced that truth is the sum of all the ascertainable facts. The professors tend to regard us outsiders as uninformed infidels and maintain the cozy assumption that the passage of time somehow purifies their prose.

Another essential difference is that, unlike their sombre university mentors, popular historians use writing techniques once employed exclusively by novelists and poets: narrative, symbolism, irony, and so on. The essence of the popular historian's craft is to recreate the event itself, conveying the authenticity of the moment. Vast piles of statistics, so dear to the academics, seldom fit into such imaginative forays. The popular historian imbues his tale with bounce and bravado, so that readers find their emotions as well as their intellect activated by his prose. We nose about in the chaotic welter of information, defining our themes, harpooning arche-typal characters, dramatizing conflicts, and squeezing metaphors out of our tired brains. There are strict limits to invention in this process, but there need be no limits to insights. A story's narrative thrust is what counts, not the number of annotations. Instead of a straight, sequential narrative, I structured the HBC books as a sequence of vignettes about the Company's dominant personalities, each the length of a novella.

Writing in the *Winnipeg Free Press*, Professor Brown spent nearly an entire page describing *Company of Adventurers* as "history's junk food" but apparently found only one factual error. She then went on to lay waste to my book in the *Canadian Historical Review*, which fortunately allowed me the right of reply, in which I again advocated a truce. "Perhaps the moral of this exchange," I wrote, "is that Canadian history should be made up of bits of Newman as well as bits of Brown."

The professor was not amused.

While radical Native women took public exception to my description of their ancestors' sexual liaisons, this did not affect the

mainstream of First Nations opinion. After *Company* was published, I was appointed an adjunct professor at the Saskatchewan
Indian Federated College in Regina, Canada's only Indian university. I briefly lectured there and was delighted with their reception
and detailed discussions of my work, which was listed as required
reading for several courses.

One of the academics' accusations did stick – namely that I had
not spent enough time at the HBC's archives in Winnipeg. When
they were moved from London in 1974, they were weighed for
insurance purposes and came in at 68 tons. Since I was fairly busy
as a journalist during the time I was writing the HBC volumes, I
indeed did not spend much time in the archives. If I had made it
my goal to go through them in detail, I would be there still. I was
fortunate that Shirlee Anne Smith, keeper of the archives, enthusiastically approved of my project and not only opened her magnificent collection but guided the work of my chief researcher, Allan
Levine, a talented Ph.D. who later taught Canadian history at
Winnipeg's St. John's Ravenscourt School, and has become an
author himself. It was he who spent more than two years digging
through the raw material, passing it on to me, and it was from the
copies of these documents (plus the many original interviews) that
my books took root. At the end of the project, I donated to the
archives the tapes and transcripts of the nearly one thousand interviews we recorded with contemporary Bay employees. The men
and women I interviewed, who formed the core of the twentieth-
century fur trade, were elderly and most have since died. Not one
of them had ever been interviewed by an academic historian, who
presumably all had their noses buried in ancient documents. I
found that a delicious irony, because when they or their successors
write the history of the twentieth century fur trade, the primary
research they will have to rely on will be mine.

Any author of a corporate history owes a debt to his sponsors.
Mine was unusual in that HBC governor Donald S. McGiverin and
corporate vice-president Rolph Huband never even tried to influence my judgments. They had no financial or editorial involvement

in the project, but it was the unimpeded freedom they granted me that made it possible. (My only debt to the Company was a slightly overdue department store bill, but as I kept telling them, the cheque was in the mail.) McGiverin and Huband understood that I was setting out to popularize the Company without adorning it. The characters who populated its annals spoke eloquently enough for themselves, though I kept in mind Abbé Raynal's stern admonition that "the murmurs of the nation have been excited against this Company." I discovered plenty of good reasons why.

Knowing that the academics would inevitably be out to scalp me (good luck) as soon as my books hit the stores, I tried to preempt their criticism by consulting their writings, in some cases supplemented by personal interviews. Their contributions to my three volumes were credited in 103 pages of bibliography and annotated chapter notes. At the same time, I recruited a distinguished clutch of academics to vet my manuscript prior to publication. They included: Professor Glyndwr Williams, head of the department and professor of history at Queen Mary College, University of London, who spent a decade as general editor of the Hudson's Bay Record Society; Professor Richard Glover, distinguished British military historian, who edited many of the original volumes of the Hudson's Bay Record Society and later headed the National Museum of Man in Ottawa;[7] Professor John Galbraith, a Bay historian at the University of California in San Diego; Professor Abraham Rotstein, the University of Toronto political economist and my loyal friend, who allowed me to read and discuss with him at length his unpublished thesis *Fur Trade and Empire*; Alastair Sweeny, the diligent author of Sir George Étienne Cartier's biography, who scouted the Public Archives of Canada for me;

---

[7] Professor Glover patiently helped me follow Samuel Hearne's epic trek down the Coppermine River and became my friend as well as my tutor. I still recall the moment when his Gothic features lit up as he confided to me during lunch at Rattenbury's restaurant in Victoria, B.C. (after first looking around to make sure no one could overhear), that "Hearne might have had a *mistress!*" Samuel Hearne died in 1792.

Professor Timothy Ball, the University of Winnipeg geographer and climatologist who launched the Rupertsland Society and may well be the most militant guardian of HBC history in the country; Dr. Al Hochbaum, an artist/naturalist living in Delta, Manitoba, who had been poking around marshes and forests all his life and had made twenty-eight camping trips into the Arctic – a free spirit who made a fetish of being beholden to no one, he turned out to be my most valuable editor.

My guardian angel and chief mentor throughout the project was George Whitman, a former Hurricane fighter pilot during the Battle of Britain; his was the first Allied fighter to fly over the beaches of Normandy on D-Day. Like most great teachers, he never stopped learning, but he treated book-knowledge as decidedly inferior to the knowhow he had picked up test-flying exotic jets, as a bush pilot, fighting drug wars when he was chief social planner for Vancouver, setting up federal community development plans for the First Nations, and latterly as vice-president of public affairs for the Bay. He was a lousy PR man; armed with a wry sense of humour and no respect for institutional authority, the only thing he held sacred was the truth.

My glittering panel of in-house experts ought to have kept me out of harm's way. No such luck. While the academics who condemned my work found few factual errors in my text, it was its *existence* they resented. Their almost manic reaction left me feeling doubtful if the two distinct approaches to history, academic and popular, could ever be reconciled, or could even peacefully coexist. As the Natives felt about the whites, they just wanted me to go away.

APART FROM THE DEFERENCE to authority that the Company's presence engendered, the most significant strain it injected into the character of the Canadian frontier was the Presbyterian notion of stressing life's sombre virtues. There was no Wild West in Canada; everybody was too busy working and surviving. The Bay traders set the mood. Nearly all dour Scots, they were gentle Orkney carpenters, ambitious Aberdeen clerks, and the black-sheep progeny of Highland clergy. Sparse of speech but swift of action, these tight-lipped characters had a temperament that was ideal for the fur trade: a meld of persistence and self-sufficiency. While the concealment of feelings was their chief article of faith, they made up in loyalty and moral fibre what they lacked in imagination and exuberance. Their wintry stoicism and the notion that a hard day's work well done was the Lord's eleventh commandment contrasted sharply with the swaggering individualism of the American frontier. The idea on our side of the forty-ninth parallel was to be plainly dressed and plain spoken, and never too free with one's money or emotions.[8]

Within its North American domain, the HBC became a significant instrument of empire, its explorers probing the West and North, planting the necklace of forts that kept the American annexationists at bay. The Bank of England coddled its treasury, lending credit and occasional governors, while the Royal Navy defended its forts against French incursions. By birchbark canoes, York boats, steamships, and Red River carts, on snowshoes and aboard pack-ponies, the HBC's rag-tag mercenary army was the first to establish the glimmerings of the economic viability of a transcontinental Canadian economy, and eventually a Canadian state.

In its operations, the Hudson's Bay Company suffered from three

---

[8] The best illustration of just how Scottish the Company really was – from its lowest-rung apprentices to its haughty governors – came up during my interview with Joe Links, then official furrier to the Queen of England by royal warrant. Links ran a luxury fur salon opposite Harrods. A distinguished and compassionate individual, he was the first Jew to be named a director of the HBC. When I asked him with great hesitation, whether that created a problem, he laughed and said: "Not at all, my boy. It wasn't so much that I was the first and only Jewish member of the board, but that I was the only Englishman among six Scots or sons of Scots!" Links, who was one of my most valuable sources, paid me a rare compliment when the job was done: "From the beginning I felt that I could talk to you frankly and trust you completely," he wrote. "I have often misjudged people, but not on this occasion. I am proud to have had even a tiny part in your books' realization."

centuries of being run on a part-time basis by well-connected and well-meaning London financiers who didn't know the going rate for stamina in the Canadian bush. They were the ultimate absentee landlords. It was 264 years before any HBC Governor – Sir Patrick Ashley Cooper, the thirtieth man to hold the office – actually visited Hudson Bay. In 1934, comfortably lodged with his wife and retinue aboard the Company steamer, *Nascopie*, Cooper toured the Bay, announcing his arrivals and departures to the gathered aboriginal hunters and trappers over the ship's radio system. Sitting in front of a large microphone, he would drone on about how glad he was to be there, how it had taken "many moons travelling" to reach the Eskimos and their land, how they should be more diligent in trapping foxes and how they must always be loyal subjects of the King. Then, straining even his own considerable limits of condescension, the governor would conclude with the admonition: "We leave you with confidence that you will work with our post manager as one large, happy family, you following his advice as if he were your father, for he does the things which I tell him and I want you to do the things which he tells you."

There were three problems with the governor's broadcasts. First, each settlement had only one radio receiver, usually in the store manager's staff house, so that the chances of an Inuk actually hearing Cooper were next to nil. Second, since he spoke English, the few aboriginals who actually heard him did not understand a word he was saying. Third, and most important, when Ottawa objected to an HBC official speaking to Canadian subjects on behalf of the King, the plug was pulled on Cooper's microphone amplifier. As a result, his carefully rehearsed speeches were never heard outside the little shipboard radio studio.

As I began reading the factors' private journals (as opposed to the accounts they sent to their London managers) I was astounded by their almost canine loyalty to the Company, even in their private musings. It was as if signing on with the Bay included an unspoken contract that, in return for accepting low pay and pathetic working conditions, they could enter the faith.

The first duty of any faith is to perpetuate itself. Ironically, it was this creed that paralyzed the HBC's policy planners. They took occasional risks, but never bet the Company. Whenever an intuitive leap was required to advance the HBC into fresh and lucrative jurisdictions, its distant decision-makers inevitably opted for safety and survival. While survivors are the winners in any contest, standing by is not enough. The problem with concentrating on merely surviving is that it too often produces an over-respectful, timorous mentality. Hypnotized by the extraordinary history of the institution they represented, the Bay men turned inward and became marginal to the country growing up around them. Their obsessive concern with durability dominated every stage of the Company's evolution from a one-fort trading operation on Hudson Bay to its modern incarnation as a $5-billion merchandising conglomerate. The Bay men's journals glowed with their overwhelming sense of the obligation they felt to those who had gone before and would come after, as if one wrong step might wipe out the HBC's glorious history. They didn't realize that history is not a disposable commodity, that the future cannot erase the past.

I had intended to glorify the Company's exploits because its early physical presence kept western Canada out of the hands of the land-grabbing Yanks, but as I moved deeper into my research, I found myself questioning its achievements – not so much for what it did as for what it failed to do. Sir Henry Benson (later Lord Benson), who resigned in a huff as the HBC's deputy governor in 1962 to become senior adviser to the governor of the Bank of England, told me: "I remember giving enormous offence to the Canadians when I said it was extraordinary how little the Company had achieved, bearing in mind that it had by then been in existence for nearly three hundred years. It was asleep."

He was right. Although the HBC owned the world's most valuable land monopoly – a third of the still-to-be-explored northern part of the American continent – it did nothing to take advantage of its position, allowing others to profit from that magnificent hunk of real estate. Here was a company that dominated the world's fur trade for most of three hundred years, yet never made a fur coat. Here was a company that pioneered Canada's transportation arteries (much of the TransCanada Highway runs along its canoe routes) and for two centuries exercised a transportation monopoly over western Canada, yet when it came time to build a transcontinental railway across that same territory, it opted out of this nation-building venture. Here was a company that had the only functioning infrastructure in the Canadian plains and owned seven million acres of prime land along the new railway route, yet did little to capitalize on that invaluable asset. Here was a company that established a worldwide market for its "Best Procurable" scotch, high-quality gin and rye, but instead of continuing to distil its popular house brands turned the business over to Seagrams, harvesting no advantage from its great reputation in this high-mark-up industry.

The HBC's most obvious dereliction of opportunity was the failure to capitalize on its potential oil and gas reserves. In the mid 1920s the Company still held mineral rights on 4.5 million acres checkered across the Prairies. Rather than exploit that invaluable asset, described by *Fortune* as "an oilman's dream," the HBC leased the entire package to Marland Oil of Ponca City, Oklahoma (and its successor, Continental), retaining only a 21 per cent interest. By the late 1960s, the joint venture ranked as Canada's third-largest oil and gas producer, with 1,606 wells in production; its earnings were twice as high as those of the HBC itself, and its equity was worth four times as much, with the Company receiving less than a quarter of the royalties.

Even in its modern retailing phase, the HBC, having had the money and opportunity to snare most of the desirable shopping centre sites across western Canada, concentrated instead on the miniature versions of Harrods, the London department store, it had built in provincial capitals, nurturing these masonry mausoleums even when they became as obsolete as transatlantic ocean liners. While other department-store chains became anchor-tenants in the suburban shopping malls that quickly captured the bulk of the retail business, the proud but misguided HBC executives were frozen in their notion that the customers would come to them, and threw up grand concrete parking garages next to their downtown retail palaces. Throughout its history, the Hudson's Bay Company shuttled between unstoppable momentum and impending collapse.

THE HIGHLIGHTS of researching the HBC story were the two journeys Camilla and I took across the Canadian North. She had provided a healthy chunk of the research, plus the essential day-to-day structural editing for the project, and was an invaluable companion during the creative wrangling over the right words and phrases.[9]

The HBC then operated a string of 173 stores and fur-trading posts across the top of Canada. In a series of airborne sweeps – into Baffin Island, up to Resolute, and around the great arcs of James and Hudson bays – we interviewed many of the Bay men and their aboriginal customers. Durable Scottish mercenaries (also including representatives from Newfoundland, Nova Scotia, and New Brunswick), their time-worn faces were permanently leathered from lifetimes spent outdoors. Even if the Company's glory days were long gone, it still meant something to be a Bay man in the land of the midnight sun.

The outrageous dimensions of Arctic geography – 1.3 million square miles, spread over five time zones – dwarfed yet enchanted the fur traders.[10] Most of the HBC field hands we met viewed the

---

[9] Other members of the production team included Martin and Jane Lynch, Janet Craig, and Penguin's Cynthia Good, whose spirited and enlightened editing much lightened my load, as well as the company president Morty Mint, sales manager Brad Martin, and promotion genius Sara Thring.

[10] The prize here was mostly arctic fox plus polar bear, wolf, and weasel skins, instead of beaver. Fox prices plunged after prostitutes in Paris and London decided their profession was enhanced by walking the streets decked out in silver fox stoles. When the furs became the tarts' badge of office, the bottom, as it were, dropped out of the market, and it never really recovered.

North as a place with its own natural laws, where they got to know their inner devils on a first-name basis. "Hell," I was told by James Deyell, then head of the HBC's Ungava District, who had arrived in 1965 from the Shetlands, "I was born the equivalent of three hundred miles *north* of here. I came right out of grammar school at seventeen because the only other choice I had at home was joining the merchant navy or living off my father. I was getting $2,500 a year, which I thought was marvellous – an unheard-of salary in the Shetlands for a trainee. Since I arrived here, I've never had time for an identity crisis. When you're surrounded by silence, you find out in a hurry who you are. Once the life grabs you, it never lets you go."

The Canadian Arctic has only two seasons, winter and August, its weather varying from clear, scorching heat waves to white-outs that reduce visibility to zero and the human comfort zone to the immediate vicinity of kitchen stoves. The cold is unimaginable. Temperatures drop below -55°F, causing steel to snap like celery stalks and tires to detonate. Human senses are stretched to their limits as the moisture in the atmosphere freezes, breaking down into countless ice particles that attack exposed skin. Ptarmigans make the sound of tearing silk as they painfully propel themselves through the frigid atmosphere. One HBC trader told me how he and his companion managed to survive a typical winter in their Company house: "The weather grew colder and colder and, at Jim's suggestion, I moved from my room upstairs down to the kitchen, where I slept on top of the table. Then came the day when even Jim was forced to leave his bedroom to sleep with me in the kitchen. Then the living room, and finally the office, became uninhabitable. . . . If I had to go only to the store I would dress as though I was going on a hunting trip." Another HBC factor, W.O. Douglas at Baker Lake, loved eggs and imported a few chickens every summer. In winter, he not only had to bring them indoors, but ended up having to knit little duffel coats for them.

The resident Bay traders lived and worked in a strange world. In summer, the northern sun never sets; for the next eight months it seldom rises. During most of the winter the moon remains below the horizon, with the main natural light source being the shimmering aurora borealis, hanging over the horizon like a spangled theatre curtain.

The first stop on our journey was Norway House, near the top of Lake Winnipeg, once the inland rallying point for the HBC canoe brigades on their way to tidewater at York Factory on Hudson Bay. The Company's Northern Council met here intermittently between 1821 and 1860, and the ghost of Sir George Simpson still haunted the place. I met Adam Dick, chief of the War Lake Indian band, who had been born in a teepee seven miles northwest of Split Lake in 1897. He had started trapping beaver and snaring rabbits at the age of eight. "My dad made me a bow and arrow and snowshoes, and my mum made me a bag," he recalled. "When I began hunting by myself, I caught one rabbit and four prairie chickens. Later, I worked twenty-three years for the Bay as a cribber, freighting supplies by dog team or canoe to twelve trappers' camps. They paid me sixty-five dollars a month. I never got a raise and never got a pension." The chief, who was eighty-seven and had yet to acquire his first grey hair, had only one kind thought about the Company. "There was never any room in the sled for me because they piled all the space up with supplies. So I had to run behind it. I guess that's why I feel so healthy."

At Fort Severn, I spent a long afternoon with Manasseh Munzie Albany, aged ninety-seven, a hunter and ship's pilot who used to lug seven bags of mail to York Factory and back every winter. His friends, the Reverend Jeremiah Albany and Abel Bluecoat, told me about life at Fort Severn: gasoline cost $6 a gallon, there was no electricity, and the bill for a four-litre can of naphtha that would light a cabin for three nights was $9. Nearly everybody was on welfare, barely getting by. Only 270 people live at Severn, but the Bay store's annual sales topped $350,000, with average mark-ups of 40 per cent. Not long before we got there, a ninety-foot freighter loaded with eighty tons of foodstuffs for the Bay, operated by an Inuk named Lewis Voisey, had run aground nearby, and the weather had turned so nasty that the ship had been abandoned for the winter. We later learned that the following spring, when she was refloated, not a single item of the vessel's cargo was missing – except half a dozen cans of pop, consumed by the captain while cleaning out the bilge. He paid the HBC for the six-pack.

Rupert House, where we spent a fascinating two days, was the oldest of the Bay settlements, built by Médard Chouart, Sieur Des Groseilliers, who led the first trading expedition into the Bay in 1668. There was palpable tension here between the HBC and its captive customers. The Cree measured their feelings for the Company by the price it paid for skins. Only twenty whites and a thousand Cree lived there, yet there was enough traffic to fill a DC-3 four times a week.

Cape Dorset, our next stop, was where the artist James Houston spent a decade developing the trade in Inuit sculpture before introducing the Inuit to printmaking. I had always been mystified by how such luminous artistry could flourish in a climate that a local factor described as being so cold that "people are born with jumper cables as umbilical cords." Houston, who took a year off from the North to learn the graceful alchemy of printmaking in Japan, inspired the local stone-carvers to try this new art form, which quickly brought the best of them world fame. I remembered Houston's wonderful story about the time he gathered his artists for an early-morning pep-talk because he wanted them not only to produce prints of great originality but to support their families by bringing the concept of money into what was then a cashless society. He made his point by slapping down several types of dollar bills on the print-room table and explaining that some were bigger, more valuable, than others. "When I returned to the shop later," he recalled, "I found one of our most talented print-makers just completing a stone-cut of his version of a Canadian dollar bill. He had made it oversize, he said, to increase its value."

On Broughton Island, where we landed next, the going rate for marijuana joints was $50, and I heard that the market was brisk. The HBC had once bought 30,000 sealskins a season there, but

Brigitte Bardot's protests had killed that trade. The only remaining cash crop was selling hunting tags to American tourists who wanted to shoot polar bears; the local quota was twenty-two tags, and they fetched $3,000 each. When I cornered an Inuk and asked how fair the HBC's prices really were, he was lost for an answer because there was no alternative outlet to match quotes against. Head lettuce was selling at $2.98, which didn't seem unreasonable. Dog teams had all but disappeared; teenaged Inuit with mirrored sunglasses raced their snowmobiles in endless circuits of the settlement's one short street.

Resolute Bay, Canada's second-most-northern community, had lost its horizon when we arrived; the sky was the same pitted-pewter hue as the land. Hugging the seventy-fourth parallel and about a thousand miles from the North Pole, Resolute has the worst climate and the worst economy in Canada. I couldn't interview Mayor George Eckalook because he was busy; one of the few people with a job, he was driving the settlement's only garbage truck. The place was dotted with snowmobile skeletons and boarded-up houses, including a complex of Ottawa-sponsored apartment buildings that had to be abandoned because the plumbing was embedded in the north walls, where it froze for good. An earlier bureaucratic initiative moved Inuit families here from Port Harrison and Pond Inlet. They were told the hunting would be better, but nobody notified the animals. The Resolute Inuit were proud and independent. In 1982, the Bay store burned to the ground and its credit records were destroyed. Within hours, every Inuit family had reported its outstanding debts and credit to the local manager. A quick check with head office confirmed that the total tallied precisely with the Company's figures.

In our travels into the high Arctic I tried to discover the truth about the sexual relationships of HBC traders with the Inuit. The Bay men's perceptions of these sensual assignations varied according to their own experiences. "It was the accepted thing to do when I was up there as a kid," I was told by veteran northern navigator Scotty Gall. "You went to the husband and asked for the wife, and you paid him in goods or ammunition and her in so many yards of calico or whatever she wanted."

No Bay man was more explicit in his sexual confessions than the author Duncan Pryde, whose exploits once prompted him to boast that "every community should have a little Pryde." NWT commissioner Stu Hodgson vouched for his reputation. "Duncan took on all comers," he told me. "One time, I had a party travelling with me and arranged to pick him up at one of the far northern settlements. I couldn't find him. There were thirteen houses near the beach. Suddenly Duncan came running out of the twelfth and said – 'Wait a minute – I have only one more to go,' and he dashed into the thirteenth. The local missionary came along, wringing his hands, unhappy with his position. When we left, I am sure it was the first peaceful night he'd had in three weeks."

Each tale of sexual liaisons under the northern moon may have tallied with specific moments and circumstances, but the overriding notion that Inuit women could be bought and couldn't wait to climb into the white men's beds cruelly distorted the rigid Inuit code of sexual ethics. Marriage was, and is, at the core of Inuit society. Men and women depended on one another not only for love and moral support but to carry out the division of labour so essential to the functioning of the Arctic family. "Wife-trading was a very serious matter to the Eskimos," observed the American sociologist Ernest S. Burch, Jr. "It was an integral part of their system of marriage, which also included polygamous as well as monogamous forms of union." An exception was "putting out the lamp" – a game like "musical chairs" played to relieve the tension of long winter nights. Nude couples shuffled about in their host's igloo until, at the given signal, they embraced the nearest person of the opposite sex.

EACH OF MY FOUR Hudson's Bay books was published to considerable fanfare and controversy, garnering glowing reviews from non-academic critics and devastating putdowns from the profs.

Happiest was the Penguin Big Kahuna. Peter Mayer's gamble had paid off. Because I couldn't cram everything into one volume, his $500,000 advance was spread into a second (*Caesars of the Wilderness*), and between them the two books sold just under 400,000 copies, earning me $775,642, which more than covered his advance. Those books were followed by a third volume, *Merchant Princes*, and the illustrated edition, *Empire of the Bay*, which sold another 100,000 copies between them. (Those figures included revenues from each of the four books having been chosen as main selections by the American Book of the Month Club.)

Penguin Canada was magnificent, performing daily miracles in producing the books from my tardy manuscripts and marketing them against stiff competition. However, despite near-hysterical appeals by my lawyer and hysterical threats from me, the London and New York branches of the firm did next to nothing. Jack McClelland had been right. Penguin was a publishing empire affected by complicated literary politics, and since I was neither an English nor an American author, the book was simply published and left to fend for itself. *Company of Adventurers*, which told a story as British as it was Canadian, sold exactly 926 copies within the United Kingdom. This despite favourable notice in the *Times Literary Supplement*, a review by British novelist Alan Sillitoe in the *New Statesman*, who described it as "a sort of companion volume to Chekhov," and most surprising of all, two glowing articles in London's *Financial Times* by A.L. Rowse, the fabled Oxford historian: "I cannot conceal my enthusiasm for the story of the Hudson's Bay Company, here very well told. Much of Newman's monumental but lively story is a hair-raising tale of clashes, fights, murders – like a Western film, amounting almost to guerilla warfare in the wild."

American reviews were even more enthusiastic. The *Washington Post* flatly declared that "Newman's trilogy is surely the most enjoyable history of a business ever written. His supple prose and knowledge of humanity infuse the narrative with such warmth and depth that you almost forget he's got a corporation for a protagonist."

The *Milwaukee Journal* compared me to Francis Parkman, the best chronicler of the American frontier, and the reviewer for the *New York Times* exclaimed: "What a story these rogues who shaped Canada's destiny have to tell! Peter Newman has told it with unmitigated rawness instead of awe." The most unusual aspect of this Hallelujah Chorus was that both the *Chicago Tribune* and the *Washington Post* considered the subject significant enough within an American context to lead their Sunday book sections off with reviews of my HBC volumes. There must have been thirty welcoming reviews across the United States; somehow, the American branch of Penguin managed to ignore this unexpected bonanza.

In Canada, the non-academic reviewers were equally generous, notably David Olive in *Quill & Quire*: "Newman's special talent and his three years of research have produced that rarest of things: a corporate history that is both authoritative and shamelessly populist – and thus thoroughly engrossing." Victoria poet/essayist Charles Lillard ignored the books' minutiae and went straight to the grand purpose of my literary enterprise: "Peter Newman is certainly our finest historian, if we agree that a historian is one who writes it, not one who teaches it. His narrative is a warming sun, bringing our ancestral voices to life. Taken together, the three volumes may be the epic that has eluded Canadian novelists and poets."

The *Toronto Star*'s wonderful Susan Kastner saw right through me: "Newman meets interviewers with a twinkling array of succulent statistics, bite-sized quotes, HBC maps and souvenirs – very like one of the original Company traders deftly disarming potentially hostile natives. It's the familiar defensive charm of a Canadian artist who makes money, and knows he is always going to have to apologize for it."

The book tours – which meant becoming Canadian Content on the hoof, an expandable and expendable commodity jammed between leftover Humane Society cats and local guitar twangers – were enlivened by stops to visit Brenlee Carrington, who had the only talk show on CFRW and Q-94-FM, uptown country stations in downtown Winnipeg. Authors would arrive expecting the usual once-over-lightly interview, only to find that this feisty lady had all but memorized their books. More than once, I had to beg Brenlee to stop the tape so I could puzzle out a contradiction she had discovered in my text. Winnipeg was also memorable as the city where Cara Foods had purchased the airport bookstore and transferred some of its employees to run their acquisition. It was, for a time, the world's only bookstore whose clerks wore hairnets, constantly wiped the counters, and were rumoured to take stock of the books every Friday evening just in case they went bad over the weekend.

I remembered the tours when I had first started and interviewers actually read an author's book. I also recalled the in-between stage, when they glanced at its jacket. From the mid 1980s on, however, the interviewers were whiz kids whose main qualifications were teased (or blow-dried) hair and gleaming molars. The give-away came when they settled in for "the interview," and I would hear that awful crack as the book's binding was stretched for the first time. It is the most brutal sound a travelling author can hear.

When I had begun to read up on the HBC's history in 1980, the CBC had optioned my yet unwritten books for what I was told would be the public network's most elaborate and expensive dramatic series: four two-hour extravaganzas budgeted at $8.4 million. (It amazed me how these leviathans of TV could set a precise budget for an unscripted series based on an unwritten book.) I was told that the project was such a sure thing that the CBC had killed its planned dramatization of Pierre Berton's *War of 1812* and was shelving two other series then in pre-production, with all the funds diverted to the HBC series. Michael Levine had negotiated my deal with John Kennedy, then head of CBC drama, and they had hired Charles Israel, a veteran TV writer who had done the *Marcus Welby, M.D.* series, *The Bold Ones*, and so on. Israel was a capable professional, but I found his approach far too simplistic. His script read like a shoot 'em up Western that had no connection with the Bay or my books. Who should come to my rescue but Professor Jennifer Brown. She had somehow seen the prospectus and rightly objected to its "historical fallacies and Hollywood stereotypes." Her critique of the "fabricated and implausible plot" was similar to mine, and I like to think that between us we squashed that bizarre approach.

The project was then moved under the wing of Peter Kelly, the executive producer of CBC TV who reported directly to Denis Harvey, the head of English TV. The Walt Disney organization expressed serious interest and Levine made five trips to Britain, negotiating a tentative commitment from the Scottish wing of the BBC. By this time it was the summer of 1984, but except for endless meetings nothing had been accomplished. Whoever was in charge at that point (and I've lost track) decided to farm out the project to Ralph Thomas and Vivian Leebosh, who owned an independent production house. I had done a seventy-seven-page outline at the CBC's request but no one asked to see it, and suddenly, after five years of inaction, Charles Wood appeared on the scene. He was, everyone assured me, "a *numero uno* British playwright." His film credits included the Beatles' film *Help!*, but he did have experience with historical drama also, having written the screenplay for *The Charge of the Light Brigade*. Wood called me about six months later and with undisguised pride asked me to read his draft for the first two episodes. Soon I was in shock. He had cast no fewer than 144 characters, which would have escalated costs into the heavens and left confused viewers wondering who was who – particularly since much of the dialogue was in Gaelic. A typical exchange:

GLENNAQUOICH: *Seot! Seot! Da tha seo? Sud!*
MILES: *Tha e lan stilean!*

From the little I could make out, Wood had written a haggis of a script about feuding clans that might be understood only by the six muscular Scotsmen who still toss the caber in Cape Breton and curse in Gaelic. When I complained to the CBC bosses, they kept assuring me that Wood was "a *numero uno* playwright," politely pointing out that I was commenting on an area outside my expertise. I wish I had known how to say "Screw you" in Gaelic, but I didn't. Still, I disrupted one extended gabfest of CBC's top brass, which as usual had no agenda and no critical path, by pointedly quoting that delicate lady of song, Grace Slick of Jefferson Airplane, when she told a concert crowd after a rough night: "You know, it's goddamn hard to sing and throw up at the same time." My feelings exactly.

By now it was 1987 and I had researched, written, and published my first two massive volumes of HBC history, while not a foot of film had been shot. Keeping Charles Wood on tap, the CBC suddenly decided they would farm out the whole guacamole to that Hungarian fireball Robert Lantos at Alliance Entertainment. He took one look at it and passed it on to a fellow Hungarian, Andras Hamori, who hired a Maltese filmmaker, Mario Azzopardi, to direct the shooting. I only had one conversation with the pride of Malta, and if memory serves, he asked me how I thought we could stage the sea battles. I passed on that one, but speculated that some of the fur traders must have hailed from Malta, so perhaps we could salt the dialogue with touches of Maltese. By this time, eight years had elapsed since the project's glorious launch, with no results. I was told that the CBC had wasted close to $5 million, but somewhere between Budapest and Malta the project mercifully expired from negligence and the CBC's dysfunctional bureaucracy.[11]

THE EFFORT OF COMPLETING and defending my HBC history exhausted me. Unfortunately, it also exhausted my marriage to the

---

[11] It was finally completed by the British-Canadian filmmaker John McGreevey efficiently, brilliantly, and cheaply, and was broadcast in 2000 over CTV, the History Channel, and PBS in the United States, with Robert MacNeil doing a masterful narration and Gordon Pinsent (who also recorded a talking book of *Company of Adventurers*) playing one of the main characters.

beautiful Camilla. We had turned into work machines. The schedule had become everything. A deadness had grown up between us, and we began to doubt whether the marriage was salvageable. There was as much laughter as tears as we tried negotiating various improvements in our lifestyle, but somehow the changes never translated into mutual happiness. Camilla understood that "fullness of life" had nothing to do with quantity; I had yet to learn that lesson. For most of our dozen years together we had enjoyed a powerful interlock. How tragic to find it loosening. This would be my third divorce, and the threads of our faded affection mocked me and made me ashamed and bitter.

We sold our coastal haven in Cordova Bay, the most beautiful house I had ever called home. Camilla stayed in Victoria, where she followed a successful editing career. I moved across the Gulf of Georgia to Deep Cove, a tiny village at the far end of Burrard Inlet, which is really Vancouver Harbour. I purchased a spectacularly situated house on Panorama Drive, which had a dozen different levels and a sea view from most of them. I came to Deep Cove as an exile, at the end of my third marriage, feeling hurt and confused, spending the arid days and brooding nights remembering the happiness we had enjoyed and how it had escaped us. I wanted so much to live there, in the tongue of the wind, in the shade of my trees, to take a sabbatical from life as I had known it.

I needed a "time out" but instead I went back to work, completing the third volume of the Bay series and drawing up plans for my biography of Brian Mulroney. He and I had met in 1961 at a one-day symposium on Quebec's Quiet Revolution at Laval University, where he was a law student, chasing nurses and quaffing beers at the Aux Délices tavern. Sitting at his boardinghouse on Rue St. Louis, I found it difficult to take seriously this kid from a small mill town up on the North Shore who matter-of-factly told me that he would one day be prime minister – until the phone rang and it was Prime Minister John Diefenbaker asking for his advice on how to hold Quebec.

We kept in close touch because I found him a journalist's dream: once ensconced in his Montreal law office, he got to know everybody and was willing to discuss, off the record, the backstage whispers that made Canadian politics our drug of choice. When he purchased his first car, a Pontiac convertible, he drove it to Ottawa and took Ashley and me out for a spin. I introduced him to my political buddies and was one of the first outside his personal clique to meet Mila, his fiancée, as well as his mother, Irene.

During his first run for the Tory leadership in 1976, I went to Magog where he was preparing his convention appearance. It was there, while we were enjoying a sunset view over the lake, that he suggested I should become Canadian ambassador to Austria if he won office. I laughed and shook my head, explaining that while it might be my birthplace and I knew the language, being an ambassador and having to lie for my country was not my preferred career option. But since he had brought up the subject of some sort of collaboration, I told him that I wanted to write a book about his time in office, should he be elected, providing it was not a commissioned effort.

Eight years later when he became prime minister, that arrangement was formalized. His only proviso was that nothing be published while he remained in office. I interviewed him and his retinue frequently, always asking for documentary proof of what I was being told. Since it was to be an objective assessment, I wanted independent sources, not merely Brian's word. That was ultimately denied, and I had to move on to other projects.

Prevented from doing my Mulroney book, I wrote instead about the Mulroney period which I believed had fundamentally transformed the Canadian psyche, so that its customary deference evolved into a new defiance of authority. *The Canadian Revolution* turned out to be a brave rant. My thesis was that between 1985 and 1995, Canada became theatre, performing a sub-Arctic update of Pirandello – thirty million characters in search of an author. The prerequisite for Canadian citizenship – inner silence, a form of emotional detachment so profound that nothing could reach or touch it – was shattered. The move from deference to defiance was not based, like most revolutions, on a shock troop of rebels grabbing power from authority. In our case it grew out of the much more sensible notion that the time had come to stop pretending that being Canadian was some kind of malady. While it was still better to be Canadian than to be anything else, and while our country remained one of the most envied places on the planet, our ingrained ethic came unglued.

Because he was prime minister for most of the revolutionary decade, Brian Mulroney bore the brunt of the public's disdain. The Progressive Conservative government further risked unpopularity by sponsoring a series of measures required to modernize Canada's economy for the twenty-first century. That was as difficult as it was necessary, but instead of being hailed as a radical reformer the prime minister aroused more fear and loathing than any previous Canadian head of government. Bob Bossin, the singer-satirist based on Gabriola Island, spoke for most of his country folk when he described the situation as being unique. "It's the first time in history," he proclaimed, "that a government has overthrown a country."

National in scope and unforgiving in nature, the shared sense of affront moved far beyond the rational boundaries that had traditionally held Canadian tempers in check. If the country weren't so damn big – or if the airlines had posted a seat sale for the occasion – Ottawa's parliament buildings would have been stormed in the style of a Latin American uprising. When Elijah Harper rejected the Meech Lake Accord – which, along with the sinking of the Charlottetown agreement, ranked among the decade's most significant acts of defiance – his weapon of choice was a feather. You can't get a revolution more Canadian than that.

The absence of mayhem didn't mean that not much happened. What ultimately decided the authenticity of the revolution was that the animating ideas and most of the institutions that had reflected the Canadian reality were weakened to the point of being discarded. That included such touchstones as believing in God, the monarchy, the wisdom of bankers, the Grey Cup, and the sense of entitlement that was at the core of being Canadian.

October 26, 1992, was the day when the energy of a generation reached its flash point of dissent. It was the day of the Great Referendum, when the majority of Canadians went against the advice of the country's elites by rejecting the Charlottetown compromises. Here was a proposition unanimously endorsed by the ruling classes, including corporate CEOs, the leaders of every national political party, most unions, aboriginal organizations, mainstream journalists (including me), cultural groups, and those observers who counted themselves among the enlightened. Yet in the referendum that followed, the carefully crafted deal unravelled like a poorly knit sweater. Nearly eight million Canadians rose up and cried "No!" defiantly overturning the constitutional smorgasbord prepared by their best and their brightest. This turned out to be the Vietnam of the Canadian Establishment. It had been a long time coming, but the imperturbable possession of power that had characterized Canada's elites had finally been shattered. The dirty little secret was out: the policies of the elites no longer reflected the public will. The elites had failed to impose their political agenda.

The Canadian Revolution must have hit a nerve, because the week after its publication it shot directly to the top of the bestseller lists, toppling Bill Gates's *The Road Ahead*.

AT THE SAME TIME, I was becoming part of life in Vancouver, a twenty-minute drive from Deep Cove. When I had been preparing to leave Ontario and move to the West Coast, I had asked Christopher Newton, artistic director of the Shaw Festival, about living in British Columbia. Newton had spent his early years directing experimental plays in the Pacific city and knew the scene very well. His reply surprised me. "It's stunningly beautiful," he told me, "but it makes for lousy theatre. No matter what you do, you're always competing with God." It was true. However you occupied your days, God was always out there, tempting you to ski, sail, hike, golf, surf, bat a few tennis balls, or jog around Stanley Park.

Like most newcomers who arrive in British Columbia I came as a refugee, not from Victoria or even Toronto, but from a marriage that had sadly self-destructed. Having cut myself off from past lives, at first I thought of the city as my last stop, the end of the line. While I didn't feel particularly at home, I loved the scenery and found it surprisingly easy to live in harmony with the seasons: there were none – the rain was either warm or cold. The eco-activists, pan-flutists, skateboarders, and street chess champions who gathered at Robson Square represented the city's leisure class, but I spent few evenings in town, preferring to hibernate in my seaside nest. I was a bachelor again and took full advantage of it. I quickly got back in the dating game, which was difficult, since I was working full out on my books. A spirited Slovenian beauty named Diane Rajh took me to her villa in Spain and we set several personal records. She was funny yet compassionate and we enjoyed each other's company with few limits. A gorgeous sales rep for a drug company followed, her beauty enhanced by her talented piano playing by candlelight. But when we decided to part company it was not a pleasant sight, or so the police claimed when they were called in to calm her down. My longest relationship, amidst a dozen casual encounters, was with Marjatta Ritva Karajadja, an unusual and striking Finnish woman who had spent twenty years as a policewoman, had shot the largest moose in the history of Prince George, and had recently received her master's degree in anthropology from the University of British Columbia. She was even more intense than me, and we grew inordinately fond of each other, but it was not to be. My most alluring dates were with Joanie Carlisle-Irving, who had married into two of Canada's richest families, had a luxury hangout on the island of Mystique, and let me drive her Excalibur convertible.

In some of my other incarnations, I was invited to join the board of St. Paul's Hospital Foundation, chaired by the charismatic Terry Salman, a former sergeant in the American army who had fought in Vietnam and now headed his own investment house. I also became a director of the newly privatized Vancouver Airport Authority and was one of the initiators of its purchase (for $3 million) of one of Bill Reid's five-ton *Spirit of Haida Gwaii* sculptures, which still decorates its main lobby. Unexpected honours came my way: I was promoted (along with Yousuf Karsh) to Companion rank in the Order of Canada; named to the Canadian News Hall of Fame; was sued for $6 million by Jeannette Walsh, the widow of the swindler whose Bre-X Corporation foisted a mountain of mud on a gullible public, for a story I did revealing their tactics (a badge of honour, to be sure); was given lifetime achievement awards by the Canadian Journalism Foundation and the Magazine Association of Canada; and was invited to give a summer lecture at the main theatre of the Stratford Festival. Since it is a theatre-in-the round, I had to give my talk walking around the stage, which meant having a portable microphone tucked into my back pocket. When they fitted it nobody warned me that it was live, and just before walking on I went to the bathroom. My flush was still echoing in the theatre as I walked on to discuss Canada's inferiority complex. It was the first time I got a laugh without saying a word.

I sampled the usual West Coast cures: getting Brian Finney to balance my *chakras*, trying to interest my inner child in a game of stud poker, and attending seminars on levitation to make sure I was properly grounded. Like most citizens of my Pacific paradise, I was convinced that I inhabited a field of dreams – that if I cleaned up my spiritual life, the love of my life would magically appear.

CHAPTER EIGHTEEN

PASSIONS: SAILING

Child of a Discontented Earth

*The Pacific Ocean, where I have sailed in recent years,
is an empty space filled with wonders. And it is only when I traverse
that great sea's heaving surface that I realize there is nothing on God's
Earth that equals the excitement of sleigh riding down its waves
under a full moon. Nothing.*

In our hectic workaday world during the early 1980s in Toronto, a nano-minute wait between floors on the office elevator ruined our whole day. In the steam-pressure jobs we held at that time, in my position as editor of *Maclean's* and Camilla's as managing editor of *Flare* magazine, our lives were so minutely programmed that if anyone stopped the elevator to get on or off before we reached our offices, that extra split-second endangered our day's congested work schedule.

It was time to leave Dodge City.

When we first decided to buck-and-wing our way off the corporate stage into the vaudeville of self-employment, we had great trouble persuading our friends and acquaintances that we were truly planning to abandon the sophisticated playgrounds of Toronto for the "cultural wasteland" of Vancouver Island, and were doing so voluntarily. "You're actually going to live on a houseboat in Vancouver?" one superannuated yuppie chirped when we proudly announced our intention to live in a sailboat on Vancouver Island.

To be fair, some Torontonians had heard of Vancouver Island ("Isn't that near Stanley's Park?"), but no matter how often we repeated our new coordinates, they could never get them straight. Even after we gave up trying to correct these otherwise well-travelled folks' geography and resignedly let them believe that we did indeed intend to live on a houseboat in Stanley Park, the occasional well-wisher would take us aside and bend our ears with such helpful suggestions as, "Make sure you take plenty of razor blades . . . warm socks . . . pastrami . . ." hinting that such mundane necessities of life might not be available west of Toronto's Humber River, unless we had some beaver pelts to trade.

A few months later, aboard our thirty-five-foot sloop, *Indra*, we dropped anchor at Whaletown, a tiny notch in the rocky southwest coast of Cortes Island, three days' hard sail north of Vancouver. Once home to the Dawson Whaling Company and its daring harpoon masters, the tiny settlement had been rehearsing to become a ghost town ever since. We spent a long afternoon sitting in the cockpit watching the intertidal duck ballet and the alternating sequence of their multi-hued backs and upturned bums; listening to the whiskered snort of a curious harbour seal; and watching seagulls bleating their derision at a preening eagle.

There was another vessel anchored on our stern quarter. We watched its owner, who looked as though he surfed for a living, washing its decks. He, in turn, watched us. He said nothing for a long while, studying the white letters of our hail port, *Toronto*, which I had left on the transom, under our boat's name, even after we had changed our home base to Sidney, B.C. Bemused, he finally shook his head and quipped, "You must have had a hell of a time getting through Rogers' Pass."[1]

---

[1] We had, of course, trucked the *Indra* across the country, but the remark was not so outlandish as it seemed. By then, I was deep into research for my history of the Hudson's Bay Company and had discovered that, except for Rogers' Pass, it was indeed possible to cross most of Canada by boat, if not aboard the *Indra*, then certainly in a birchbark canoe. While the three-thousand-mile journey entailed many portages around rapids, waterfalls, and beaver dams, the largest land bridge was twelve miles at Methy Portage in northern Saskatchewan.

I have owned a boat since 1960, when Christina and I were in Ottawa and purchased the *Tina*, a twenty-four-foot runabout with a tiny cabin. She was homemade of plywood construction, but I was assured (I swear) that the boat had only been used on Sundays by a kindly retired optometrist. If this were true, it must have been because he spent the rest of the week pumping her out – she leaked like Mike Pearson's Cabinet. We switched to a more professional vessel (built at a small yard in Merrickville, Ontario), called the *Foxglove,* which took us down the Rideau Canal, through Kingston, and into the Thousand Islands resort area of the St. Lawrence River. There really are more than a thousand islands (1,864), and I often wished they had signposts; from the water they appear interchangeable.

When we returned to Toronto, we bought a twenty-five-foot Shepperd motor launch called the *Pelican* and spent most of our spare summer days in the Kawarthas, particularly on Balsam Lake. Our home port was the charming pioneer village of Bobcaygeon, Ontario, which holds the best autumn fair in the region. It was a good time, with our daughter Ashley at her sweetest, and Christina and I at our happiest.

At one point, I had the *Pelican* parked at the Trenton municipal dock when a sleek sailboat appeared and asked permission to raft off, tying alongside our vessel. My dormant WASP pretensions were reawakened by the sailboat's crew, who wore white ducks and the navy-blue blazers of the Royal Canadian Yacht Club. The men had a decidedly Gatsby-esque air of self-possession and that elitist upper-lip curl I had so envied at Upper Canada College. The women sported crowns of waving golden hair, their elegance conveyed in throwaway gestures that WASPs alone can carry off. "*I got to get me one of those,*" I thought – meaning the boat, of course.

I was motivated by this encounter to take proper sailing lessons in a seventeen-foot Grampion dinghy off Toronto's Centre Island. Soon afterward, I purchased a Niagara-35 I named *Indra*, after a Stan Kenton tune that derived its title from the Hindu god of wind.[2] Designed by Mark Ellis (who also did the Nonsuch fleet) and built by George Hinterhoeller (one of the founding partners of C&C Yachts) in St. Catharines, Ontario, she was a standard cruising boat, with one exception. Her bow did not house the usual, crowded V-berth; instead, there was a tiny workshop, which I quickly converted into an office just big enough to hold my type-writer and sound system. I have had a writing station in every boat since, and have composed my best prose on the water.

Every summer, for a few stolen weeks, we climbed aboard *Indra* and headed for rural Ontario and Prince Edward County, or, as its natives preferred, "The County." Three days' boating from Toronto, The County is a sailor's paradise, weaving a spell of coves, bays, and islands. It was then a little-known corner of eastern Ontario, having first been settled by United Empire Loyalists in 1783. The mood it created was less nostalgic than calming. County folks welcomed visitors, while land-buying newcomers were tolerated but carefully watched for a generation or two before being accepted.

Our favourite haunt was Picton, The County's largest settle-ment, where we joined the Prince Edward Yacht Club, as friendly and informal a sanctuary for "boaties" as any I've yet encountered. A PEYC member for a decade, I was taken aback only once, when the club's mimeographed newsletter contained an item preten-tiously headlined "PROTOCOL." Not having been aware the club had any, I was much relieved to read the text that followed: "Effec-tive immediately, no one will be admitted to the Saturday night dances without shoes on."

Here, in the peaceable kingdom of Quinte's Isle, I sailed my sloop, annually rediscovering a postcard paradise inhabited by rural philosophers such as Bob Davis, who spent four years handcrafting

---

[2] One evening Christina and I were tied to the seawall overnight at Oakville, relaxing after dinner with only a coal miner's lamp to illuminate the cockpit. Two small boys came out to inspect the boat, which had a dark, midnight-green hull. Misreading her name, one explained to the other: "They sail for India in the morning . . ."

an exquisite thirty-six-foot ketch called *Kindly Light*. The County had some fabled fishing holes, with pickerel, rainbow trout, and bass in abundance; nearby Milford boasted one of the few cheese factories in the universe not owned by Kraft, and it made wonderful, crumbly cheddar. The greatest treat was sneaking off to the Maple Inn at Bloomfield for one of their succulent chicken dinners.

Just how quintessentially Canadian was The County became particularly noticeable one summer when we crossed Lake Ontario to spend July 4 at Sodus Bay, a tiny resort in northern New York State. A squad of Legionnaires presented arms as the assembled picnickers sang "America The Beautiful." Frank Horton, the local congressman, delivered a rousing harangue, ending with the assurance that, "People are strong. If we can just get the government off our backs!" Picton's July 1 celebration had been much more subdued, including such traditional country pastimes as a taffy pull and a strawberry festival, inviting everyone to eat all they could pick.

We often dropped our hook after running up Hay Bay past Ram Island, or spent the day sliding down Adolphus Reach past Glenora to Prinyers Cove. When the day finally cooled, we would head for our berth at the yacht club, crew members hugging themselves against the early evening chill. Blue herons and terns patrolled the luminous dusk as we tied up for the night.

I vowed always to have a sailboat.

THE PACIFIC OCEAN, where I have sailed in recent years, is an empty space filled with wonders. And it is only when I traverse that great sea's heaving surface that I realize there is nothing on God's Earth that equals the excitement of sleigh riding down its waves under a full moon. Nothing. Those precious moments affirm Joseph Conrad's claim that sailors are "the grown-up children of a discontented earth." To sail at night is to inhabit another world. Unable to steer by sight, I navigate by sound. Unexpected whitecaps that don't merit a second look in daylight take on an ominous authority, in case they're heralding rocks or a rising wind. On cloudy evenings, I can feel the boat speed up, getting away from me, and pray for the illumination of a late moon. As the sunrise begins to divide earth from sky, the morning spreads like a benediction across the sea, and I head for land.

Once anchored, the boat is still alive to the winds, yet tethered to Earth. Its mast sweeps the sky in slow arcs, waiting to be released. When freed, the bow shudders, the breeze balloons the great triangle of the jenny, and the vessel bites the wind, like a dolphin at play.

Having spent my happiest moments on this planet in various shapes and sizes of wind-driven craft, I've always considered sailing more of an art form than a sport. At the practical level, it consists of adrenaline panics slotted into eternities of dumb slogging, a process that somehow adds up to ecstasy. The wind is always on the nose, lighthouses are never where they're supposed to be, and salt-water spray eats away the fittings that hold your flimsy craft together. No mode of transportation is more ritualized than a sailboat. Its parts obey their own musical score; the tuned rigging hums in the wind, halyards beat an uneven tattoo on the mast. "Owning a boat," an old salt warned me when I started nosing around the docks, "is the equivalent of tearing up hundred-dollar bills while standing in a cold shower." He was wrong. Thousand-dollar bills, maybe. But then, owning a boat is not a rational act. It plays to the romantic side in us all. My rationalization is that the succession of vessels I have owned since 1960 were not so much toys as floating therapy labs. Messing about in boats heals.

Sailing is a spiritual experience, a proving ground for the soul. To sail is to ride on the tongue of the wind; under taut canvas the boat dispenses catharsis. Contentment has as much to do with intensity of feeling as banishment of alienation, and that's where the sea comes in. Life on the water is unpredictable and dangerous, full of thrust and power, and a sky that feeds your sixth sense and projects a fourth dimension to experience.

Navigation, as someone once said, is like fencing – everything turns on keeping your adversaries (rocks, shallows, riptides) at a distance. Nowadays it is accomplished by satellite, but every salt also knows how to juggle the speed and direction of wind, tides, and currents, to fix the ship's position by ded (as in deduced) reckoning.[3] Radars and warning bells can tell of a pending collision, but any sailor worthy of the name knows a constant bearing on an object closing in range indicates a collision course. This "feel" for navigation, like the ability to "feel" the wind and tides, cannot be taught; it is the graduate diploma of seamanship granted only by years before the mast.

While crossing the Gulf Stream from the Florida Keys to New Providence Island, aboard deep-sea diver Joe MacInnis's *Spirit of Apollo*, I asked him why water had become so important in both our lives. "Because its mirrored surface gives the best view of those great elements, space and time," he said. "Urban living chops them up into what we like to think of as manageable units. But when we're next to the water, we are reminded of their cyclical and infinite qualities."[4]

I find grace in every landfall and sunset. After a few days at sea, a rhythm develops between me and my boat, so that the slightest shift in winds or cloud formations becomes important. Altered sea states or the eternal faring of tides and currents – even bird flights – take on definite meanings. Ocean crossings are such endurance tests that no one but a lunatic or a long-distance sailor (the difference is marginal) would attempt them. Passage making ("doing extraordinary maintenance in exotic locations") is the way to go. "Away from the sea, I would wither and perish like a jellyfish on dry land," wrote David Conover in his classic, *One Man's Island*. "The sea spawned life and it spawned life in me. I love its ebb

---

[3] The surest way to spot a non-sailor, or an ignorant one, writing on nautical themes is to spot the all-too-frequent non sequitur, "dead" reckoning.

[4] Two less esoteric moments of that wonderful expedition: Once we arrived in the Caribbean, our fridge packed up, so at night we raided nearby hotels and liberated the contents of their ice-cube dispensers, dumping the cubes into garbage bags and eluding the prowling security guards. And when I had to leave ship and was wafted off to the nearest airport aboard a rubber dinghy, the entire *Apollo* crew mooned me – a sight that I would not soon forget.

and flow, its tang and its glitter, its anger and its calm, its mystery and boundless life."

Sailing has no absolutes. The frantic big-city players who want it all (missing the opportunity to be excited by anything less) earn no berths in a cockpit being drenched by waves crashing over the bow. The sea has its own rhythms that must be obeyed; emotional detachment may make it in an office downtown, but it will sink a ship. "Seamanship," my friend the champion Vancouver sailor Vlad Plavsic contends, "is measured by how profoundly you respect the ocean. It does not respect you. The longer you sail, the less you know about the sea, but the more you learn about your boat, and about yourself." Sailors recognize this as the true path to contentment: bet the farm every time you shove off, and sail toward the horizon.

DURING THE LATE 1980s I sailed with three others part of the way around Vancouver Island, a journey touching some of Canada's most wonderful shoreline. Late one evening, after night had fallen, we sought shelter in a tiny cove just past Meares Island on Clayoquot Sound, north of Tofino on the west coast of the island. We were exhausted from the day's long slog, and anxious to drop anchor and be done for the day.

We felt as if we had drifted into a cloistered cathedral – until the next morning. Dawn revealed that the shores of the cove we had so gently entered in darkness had been stripped of vegetation. Our cathedral had been desecrated. We found ourselves anchored in a barren, ugly clear-cut that resembled the cone of a burnt-out volcano. It was because of this experience that I became engaged in the controversy over forestry company efforts to clear-cut the world's largest remaining temperate rain forest at Clayoquot Sound, which raged during the summer of 1992 and was to smoulder for years afterward.

I proudly became a tree-hugger, and can think of few gestures more comforting than embracing one of those first-growth giants that still stand tall in the distant pockets of British Columbia's dwindling coastal forests. Sailing to the Queen Charlotte Islands two years later, I was part of a human chain at the edge of an unnamed inlet on the east side of Moresby Island, where it took seventeen of us to link hands around a single stately cedar. Old-timers like that deserve all the hugs they can get.

On the sun-washed morning of May 31, 1986, a fleet of fifty-six boats, the *Indra* among them, gathered at the inner harbour outside Victoria's Parliament Buildings to begin a month-long counter-clockwise odyssey around Vancouver Island. It would be the first major sea venture for Camilla and me since moving to the West Coast. Like nearly everyone else who had signed up for "Island Odyssey," we had been nervous about tackling the journey by ourselves; the island's stormy west coast has earned its reputation as the "Graveyard of the Pacific." I later discovered that surprisingly few B.C. boat owners had actually made the trip around Vancouver Island, or done much long-distance sailing of any kind.

Except for the two of us, we alternated crews on the circumnavigation, including my Toronto pals Fred Soyka and Vic Koby; my legal compatriot, Michael Levine; and my favourite sailing companions, Tony and Kitty Griffin, whose forty-ninth wedding anniversary we celebrated at Winter Harbour with a homemade cake.

At each of the twenty-one communities we and the rest of the Island Odyssey fleet visited, nearly everyone turned out to greet us, inspect our boats, visit with us, and feast us with steamed crab, barbecued chicken and ribs, and other delicacies. Our tour became one long feast. The scattered inhabitants of the inlets and fjords along Vancouver Island's rugged west shore think of themselves as a breed apart, referring to the snug townspeople on the more populous southern and eastern shores as "down islanders." They are the "up islanders," gutsy and brave enough to endure the isolation and perpetual downpours of the rain forests. They live "on the edge," psychologically and geographically, inhabiting the outer rim of the country and the continent.

To catch the slack tide through the dangerous Seymour Narrows, where currents run up to fourteen knots, our flotilla pulled out of

Campbell River at 4:00 a.m. in single file, our red, white, and green running lights stretching a mile or more in the darkness. On the way through the deceptively benign Johnstone Strait, we passed much history. Kamano Island was once inhabited by Hawaiians who had drifted across the Pacific; Harbledown Island once housed a mighty Buddhist temple; on Cracroft Island an adventurer named Charles Cavanaugh had built a tavern for loggers, inviting them to wear their spiked climbing boots and compete how far up its walls they could run. (If they didn't land on their feet, they bought a round for the house.) The aboriginal history was no less interesting, although more tongue-twisting: pictographs, burial sites, and shell middens abound in such places as Mamalilaculla, an abandoned Kwakwaka'waka village. On our way into Port Hardy, Camilla spotted the flick of a killer whale's dorsal fin off our bow. We cut the engine and drifted into a pod of six Orcas lying just below the surface, their black-and-white markings clearly visible through the cold, clear water. Caught up in the reverence of the moment, we spoke in whispers for most of an hour afterward. Sailing into Robson Bight near Port McNeill, we saw four Orca pods rubbing themselves on the pebbled beach, a practice observed there and nowhere else.

With some apprehension we picked our way into Bull Harbour, the jumping-off point for the boiling Pacific and the long reach down Vancouver Island's west coast. It is a small, private community, the only place where no one came out to watch us arrive or leave. At dusk, I walked alone past the abandoned Coast Guard station, then across the narrow isthmus to Rolling Beach, and watched the sun set across the wide ocean directly en route to Japan. The huge rollers pounded into the small rocky bay, grinding its granite stones into tiny perfect spheres.

Next morning, the long line of running lights dotted the darkness once again as we slipped carefully through the winding channel to tackle Cape Scott, the northernmost tip of Vancouver Island. The wind was twenty knots and rising, just what we needed to skim around the slash of rock that has sunk so many of our predecessors. (The winds can be so fierce here that a lighthouse keeper's cows were once blown over a cliff into the sea.) It was an unforgettable sight to look back and see dozens of spinnakers glowing in the sunrise.

Cape Scott is abandoned now, but there have been two attempts to colonize it by immigrants of Scandinavian stock. In 1897, Rasmus Hansen led a group of about a thousand Danes, mostly from Minnesota, Iowa, Nebraska, and North Dakota, looking to establish an ethnic community around Hansen Lagoon and Fisherman Bay. The colony hoped to subsist on fishing until the government delivered on its promise to build a road from their settlement to San Josef River and on to Holberg. They even dragged in their own sawmill, schoolhouse, and post office, and published their own newspaper, *The Sandfly*. The problem was that the road never materialized. The first settlement petered out about 1907, but another wave of Scandinavian immigrants, mostly from the prairie provinces, swelled its population to one thousand again by 1913, occupying the homes left by the first wave. It, too, was doomed to failure – even though they grew some impressive crops. With no road or harbour access they couldn't export their produce, and finally grew only subsistence crops, yielding no cash for anything else. Some hardy souls lasted into the 1930s, but all that remains are a few of their homestead foundations and Rasmus Hansen's grave.

After a pleasant rest in Winter Harbour, a community that is reduced to four self-reliant families in winter, we sailed past Cape Cook on the forbidding Brooks Peninsula, appropriately known as the Cape Horn of the west coast. The groundswell creates waves off nearby Solander Island that frequently rise ten storeys high, the mighty equal of the monster waves in the film *The Perfect Storm*. There is no lighthouse. Neither has there been any attempt to tame this inaccessible wilderness that has dealt cruelly with any sailors unfortunate enough to survive their shipwrecks.

Docking eleven hours later in Kyuquot, a First Nations village tucked into a chain of twisty waterways and islands, we found ourselves among an array of brightly painted fishing boats laid up by rows of tidy, if weathered, houses, some of them on stilts. This gave the proud little community the aspect of an African river village. Its streets are canals and its traffic lights are buoys. Kyuquot has about 140 Native people and thirty non-Natives. There is no road access, although the hardy little coastal steamer *Uchuck III* out of Gold River brings in weekly supplies.

When I asked one of locals how much it rained on an average year, he replied, "Oh, I dunno. Maybe sixteen, seventeen . . ."

"Now come on, it feels as though it's rained seventeen inches since we got here."

"No, man," he shot back, with a tinge of annoyance. "Not inches. *Feet*! Last year we had 16.6 feet, and it wasn't even a record." I looked to see if he had gills.

The next evening we were invited to witness the rain dance of the Kyuquot Natives; considering the downpour, it was either highly effective or completely redundant. Accompanied by the mesmerizing chant of men pounding their eight-sided drums, eighteen young women stepped and swayed in their button-beaded black capes to the powerful beat. Adding to the mystical moment, rain swept over the cove, bringing the smell of wet cedar drifting into the hall like incense. Outside it was blowing stink, gusting winds of fifty knots with waves reaching twenty feet high in open water. We stayed tucked in for the day, marvelling at the rain that came down in streams so thick it bounced a foot off the decks.

We slogged in heavy weather around Estevan Point on the Hesquiat Peninsula, where I was at long last able to see its fabled 125-foot-tall lighthouse. Estevan Point is the site where the First Nations peoples of Vancouver Island initially laid eyes on a European ship, in 1774, and made their first contact with European peoples. The lighthouse was built in 1909, the best example of designer William P. Anderson's flying-buttress design. It is also the only part of Canada to have been attacked by enemy gunfire in the Second World War. In 1942, it was shelled by a Japanese submarine lying two miles off the coast. It lobbed a few dozen rounds, but the gunner's aim was poor and no damage was done. The keeper ended the duel by turning off his light. Although there were no casualties, the incident had serious repercussions for mariners, as all the other outer coast stations were subsequently turned off to prevent a similar attack, paralyzing shipping off the coast for the remaining war years. Lightkeepers were also issued with rifles, to repel the enemy, which I doubt would have discouraged too many Japanese submarine commanders.

Sailing seventy nautical miles or more a day was not cruising as most of us had experienced it, skipping off for a lazy meander inshore or spending a couple of weeks gently gunkholing through islands and coves. The long, hard days were measured by the beat of the diesels and tacks required to reach new harbours. We eventually anchored at Hot Springs Cove, and walked in through thick and twisted vegetation to enjoy a sulphurous soak. "We had a boat running contraband drugs seized here a few years ago," the Hot Springs shopkeeper told me. "Two crew members escaped ashore and disappeared. The police calmly settled in to wait and, sure enough, a few days later the smugglers stumbled out." They were glad to face prison instead of the wet, twisted confusion of the Openit Peninsula. "This," as he put it, "is tough country."

Returning "down island," we anchored on a sandy ledge off Port Renfrew (a ghost town except for one surprisingly cheerful pub) and the next day, our last, heading around Point No Point past Sooke to home, we had to contend with our first serious fog bank. Back in Victoria, we were welcomed by fireboats pumping great arcs of water, pipers playing, and lavender-gowned and bonneted hostesses pinning roses onto sailing sweaters. Looking back on our month-long sequence of fetes and private moments, what remained most vivid was that this scarcely known corner of Canada had proved so visually sensual; it had overloaded our existing senses and suggested the possibility of one or two more. "This island is more than an eyeful – it seeps through every pore directly into your soul," summed up Camilla. "A trip like this sharpens your perceptions because it's so rare to spend a month in a state of high mental and physical alert without being afraid."

THAT WASN'T MY FIRST deep-sea voyage, or my only memorable one. Four years earlier, I had joined the delivery crew of a forty-two-foot Whitby sailboat, owned by Jim Domville, then chairman of the National Film Board, who wanted to place his new boat into the Caribbean charter fleet. That entailed sailing from Moorehead City in North Carolina to Tortola in the British Virgin Islands, a journey of more than 1,200 miles. On the way, we had to cross the Gulf Stream and the horse latitudes and some of the stormiest patches off America's east coast where, just the previous week, a sailboat larger than ours had sunk with all hands. The trick was to complete the passage between the hurricane season and the winter gales. It is a narrow window.

We divided the watches, four hours on and eight hours off. The crew consisted of the owner; his girlfriend, Pat Michel; a young Montreal sailor named Jono Howson; the navigator, Kitty Griffin (who was Walter Gordon's sister); and myself as deckhand. Our skipper was A.G.S. "Tony" Griffin, one of the Canadian Establishment totems I have written about. The first Canadian naval reserve officer to take command of a major warship during the Second World War, he later became a diplomat, a British merchant banker, and the director of fifteen senior Canadian companies. Unlike his peers, he regularly spoke out against the "dehumanizing and desensitizing" effects of acquiring too much wealth. He knew exactly when to be civilized and when to be tough, and had the intellectual resources to be both. His grandfather, Sir William Mackenzie, had been Canada's most prolific railway builder, while his son, Scott, established the world's richest poetry prize – the Griffin Prize, worth $80,000.

When we were way out in the Atlantic, about eighty miles west of Bermuda, and motoring through a patch of the doldrums, we altered course southeast to Tortola. At that precise moment the engine stopped and could not be started again. For a sailboat, this was no big problem in terms of motion, but it meant we had no electric power, no refrigeration, no running lights, no electronic instruments, and no radio to call for help. Worst of all, the electric pumps were inoperable and the bilges began to overflow, which usually means a hull punctured below the waterline. That problem was solved when Tony tasted the bilge liquid and discovered it was fresh water, leaking out of our tank. That meant going on strict rations, with little water left to drink and none for showers. We were on our own.

As we moved farther south, bucking the wind all the way, the heat became unbearable, and we threw what little fresh food was left (now rotten) overboard. To relieve the tension we decided to go for a swim, and hove to, pointing the ship's bow into the wind. In hindsight, this was not a good idea. I was first in – and first out, setting a world speed record for climbing a ship's ladder. The garbage had attracted a shark, whose black fin followed us for the rest of the journey.

The highlight of the sail for me was watching Kitty's skilful navigation. When our electronic mapping devices failed, she brought out her sextant and "shot the sun" every day at noon. She was seventy-seven years old at the time and none of us knew how steady her grip might be, but we did know that we were supposed to be in the Atlantic's main shipping lanes and never saw a ship. We woke up one morning beside a grey cliff, which turned out to be an American aircraft carrier.

A booming voice came down from the bridge: "Can we help you?"

None of us said a word, watching Kitty at the navigation table as she worked out our position. Our unspoken prayer was for Kitty to say, "Ask him where we are." But, being good Canadians, we kept quiet.

The voice came down again: "Can we help you?"

Kitty finally looked up and deadpanned: "Ask him if he needs a fix." She brought us exactly where she had predicted we would land.

In the summer of 1988, I traded the *Indra* for a forty-foot Tashiba, designed by the legendary Robert Perry. Based on a stock production model by Ta Shing yard in Taiwan, and outfitted by Bent Jespersen in Sidney, B.C., she incorporated all I had learned about boats. Built to sail anywhere in the world, or around it, the *Raven*, as I called her, was nineteen tons and rigged as a cutter with a staysail and jib. She had a roomy pilothouse that replicated the cockpit's steering instruments, but within a dry cabin affixed to a solid, hand-laid fibreglass mono-hull. But the vessel's overwhelming advantage was the strength and design of her hull. Out in the open Pacific, braving often mountainous swells originating off Japan, she dug into a slot and stayed there. Heavy, yet easy to manage when her rigging was properly tuned, she would stay on course even when I took my hands off the wheel. *Raven* was the boat of my dreams, but in the end I knew that she had outgrown me; I wasn't ready to follow her across the Pacific and around the world, where she wanted to lead. I also couldn't afford her upkeep.

For our maiden voyage, Camilla and I boarded with David and Silk Questo and headed for the Queen Charlotte Islands, the wind-swept domain of the Haida nation, 425 miles northwest of Vancouver at the very edge of the continental shelf. It would be a month-long expedition into a strange world, the only part of North America unscathed by the last ice age. Its botany and biology are unique, making up the most concentrated biomass of living material on the planet. The Haida were the Mayans of the north, except that, prior to European contact, their artisans carved in cedar instead of gold. Anyone who had been there brought back tales of a supernatural place that did not welcome strangers. "The place breathes differently," wrote the poet Susan Musgrave, who has spent much time on the Charlottes. "There's an intangible quality that many people find frightening and vaguely hostile. It is easy to remember you're a foreigner here."

Camilla was a highly competent navigator and all-round boon companion. We sailed through Fitz Hugh Sound to Bella Bella, then past Athlone Island into Hecate Strait – Hecate is the Greek goddess of the ghost-world, and her namesake strait resembles the River Styx. It is as treacherous a body of water as exists on the Pacific coast, mainly because it's as shallow as a bathtub and can blow up teeth-clenching storms in minutes.

We found the shores of the Charlottes' 150 islands littered with giant starfish, herds of sea lions, colonies of puffins, sand hoppers, and jellyfish the size of floating life-rings. Offshore lurked ten species of whales and a profusion of salmon, so thick you could almost walk on them. The forests, populated by thousand-year-old Sitka spruce up to two hundred feet tall, concealed a unique breed of caribou, hairy woodpeckers, nests of peregrine falcons, and the world's largest black bear population. This is a temperate rain forest, though tropical jungle would be a better description. Moresby Island National Park was virtually impenetrable. We dared not step off the few short, rough trails that had been slashed through the undergrowth; massive fallen trunks formed tunnels that dwarfed hikers. The moss-covered ground is as soft to the touch as plush broadloom carpet. Sunlight barely pierces the overhead canopy of moss-laden branches, infusing the forest with emerald light.

The most unexpected aspect of the Charlottes was its people. On the one hand were a few thousand non-Native woods workers, fishers, missionaries, and miners; on the other, when we were there in the summer of 1989, was the nation of Haidas on the warpath to reclaim the islands as Haida Gwaai, seldom mixing and always angry. They treated us, and other visitors, as unnecessary evils; they were willing to sell fuel, groceries, and the odd souvenir, but offered no local knowledge or sailing directions.

Our charts and maps showed a place called Rose Harbour on Kunghit Island, which intrigued me because it had been one of

Canada's final whaling stations.[5] When we sailed into the bay that had been home to its fleet of killer ships, there was not a trace of evidence that anything had ever happened there. As we proceeded deeper into the islands, we found that mines, canneries, and lumber camps had been similarly reclaimed by nature. Vegetation in the Queen Charlottes does not tolerate man-made artifacts of former efforts to exploit its resources. One guidebook lists thirty abandoned sites, including a gold mine and a Royal Canadian Air Force base at Alliford Bay; not a recognizable remnant remains to be seen. Near Windy Bay, there used to be a community called Jedway that had hotels, schools, streets, and a functioning mine. Not a rusted nail is to be found. "The Charlottes are not really at the edge of civilization, but beyond it," I wrote in my boat journal. "No amenities, no grace, no raison d'être. Nature is supreme; man irrelevant. This wild land will always triumph over its interlopers. No humans need apply."

From Rose Harbour, we sailed north to Anthony Island and a precarious anchorage from which we rowed our dinghy into the long-abandoned village of Ninstints, which was once the Haidas' largest and most spiritual settlement. Many of the bleached and leaning totem poles still guard the skeletons of longhouses. Here the grandeur of the Haida civilization is most visible, and most impressive. Also on view is evidence of the plunder by marauding souvenir-seekers, who invaded this site and stole most of its artifacts, towing away the carved totem poles behind their boats.

We anchored off Cape St. James, the jumping-off spot for our return journey. Overhead, the wheeling eagles outnumbered the yawing gulls, and the spindly silhouettes of great blue herons were a common diversion. As we settled down for the night, dozens of small seabirds staged an aerial ballet, swooping in white arcs close

---

[5] B.C.'s last whaling station was located at Coal Harbour in Quatsino Sound, on Vancouver Island. As late as 1911, the industry harvested 1,623 whales, mainly for use as fertilizer. It closed in 1967.

to the mirror-surface of the water and upward to the tip of the mast. The still evening bade us an almost audible *Amen*.

IN 2002, AFTER A BRIEF FLIRTATION with a tug (named *Titan* after the book that paid for her), which was perfect at dockside but rolled like a drunken sailor in any kind of weather, I returned to sailing. I found a Baba-35 Pilothouse in Seattle, one of only four ever built. She is a smaller Bob Perry version of the *Raven*, which had been the favourite of all my vessels. I was going to call her *My Last Damn Boat IV*, but decided to honour her vintage by christening her *Windrose*, paying tribute to the earliest navigators who, before they could read longitudes, used wind roses instead of compass roses to plot their way. I loved her old-fashioned lines and wooden construction, which separate her from the plastic Tupperware that passes for modern boating. She became a true Newman boat when I removed her galley stove and substituted a teak writing desk.

Every May the Royal Vancouver Yacht Club stages its "Sailpast," a naval tradition that gives the commodore a chance to inspect his fleet. It's a time honoured and traditional affair, with the boats spiffied up and dressed in flags for the occasion, their crews encased in navy blazers with proper crests, white shirts, white pants, white shoes, and the skipper wearing a captain's hat. The women opt for skirts, white berets, and black ribbon ties. The boats line up according to class and size and take their turn circling the commodore's anchored vessel, saluting him and lowering their ensigns as they go by. An official club photo is taken and there is a competition for the best dressed boat and most seaworthy crew. It's a delightful tradition, but one season we got honourable mention in the club newsletter for "Most Interesting Manoeuvre While Saluting the Commodore."

It had been a windy twenty-five knots and I had made the mistake of trying to circle the inspection boat under sail, instead of adding the manoeuvrability of my engine. Then I lost my hat overboard. Determined to retrieve it, I executed three tight U-turns in front of a stunned crowd, very nearly crashing into the commodore's boat and coming within inches of bouncing off the seawall. The following May we won second prize for our seamanship, but the previous season has been much more fun to remember.

My favourite part of any journey comes when the day folds into itself and I'm heading toward home port. Crew members hug themselves against the cold, holding mugs of steaming coffee or sticky rum, like Crusaders bearing chalices. It is only when my boat is tied firmly at its dock that I realize why sailing means so much to me. I return from even the briefest outing with heightened sensitivity, the way you feel when you first step outdoors at the end of a rainy spell. I see the world anew, freshly and vividly, with a surge of inner excitement that the best of urban experiences can never rival. I feel nearer my God to thee.

CHAPTER NINETEEN

FOR THE LOVE OF ALVY

—⚭—

Having become indispensable,
each to the other's life,
Alvy and I made a pact, both vowing:
"If you ever leave me, I'm coming with you."

I had been single for six agonizingly long years when on June 29, 1995, in what can only be described as a winning hand in the luck of the draw, I met the woman of my dreams. That entirely unexpected encounter would change the course of my life.

Alvy Jaan Bjorklund was born to a family that had left Sweden for Minnesota in the early 1800s and moved north over time. She was raised in Alberta's Peace River Valley. She had spent her adult life in Calgary and breezed into Vancouver in August 1990, about the same time I did. Fate had stepped in to prevent our meeting earlier. In 1993, she had placed an ad in the singles column of the Vancouver *Sun*, and I had responded, using the code name "Paul Neilson." Shyness, not modesty, caused me to employ a pseudonym, but the ploy worked to my disadvantage. Alvy's mother read my letter and advised her: "Answer this one." But I'd declared a love of jazz, which did not interest her.

The following summer, in the Stanley Park Fish House restaurant, she caught my eye just as she was leaving. I ogled her so intensely that her friend, then Taiwan Ambassador Ron Berlet, commented on my obvious rapture. But one quick glance at the rascally full beard I was sporting in those days, and she marched on.

The following year saw me hosting a private *Maclean's* reception when, wonder of wonders, the mystery woman reappeared. Ostensibly representing the Board of Trade while my friend managing director Darcy Rezac was out of town,[1] she chatted with Patti Mair (producer of Rafe Mair's radio call-in show),[2] whom I'd known for years. My confidence bolstered by knowing Patti, I realized that I had to make my move this time, so I didn't hesitate to approach her. I sidled up to this gorgeous, statuesque creature with what I hoped was a charming expression. At the same time, I was saying to myself: *Newman, give your head a shake, this woman looks to be in her thirties.* When she mentioned being a grandmother – a legitimate status for an old fogey like me – I moved in for the kill. The details of that first evening are misty now because I was so captivated by her company. Seemingly unaware that I already had designs on her, as we said goodbye, she devastated me with a firm handshake and an equally firm, "Goodnight, sir."

I was not daunted. I asked for her card, explaining that, as a writer, I found it easier to put certain things down on paper than to express them aloud. I then raced home and composed for a readership of one the most important letter of my life. "I was absolutely bowled over by you tonight," I began, having decided that faint heart never won fair lady. "If eyes are indeed the window of the soul, you are a goddamn miracle, and I hope to get to know

---

[1] Darcy had tried to set us up before. When he first met Alvy he told her, "I want you to meet Peter Newman, he will love you."

[2] Since it was Patti who facilitated our introduction that night, we figured we owed her big time. She was divorced from Rafe and so I introduced her to one of my best friends, architect Gerald Hamilton. The ultimate Tristan and Isolde story, he was suffering from terminal lung cancer, while she developed the most lethal type of breast cancer shortly after their meeting. But they married and packed as much love as they could into his remaining years.

you better, much better . . ."[3] I concluded by saying that I wasn't doing anything for the rest of my life and requested her company at dinner the following evening.

Although surprised by the intensity of my declarations, for Alvy my letter merely confirmed what she had already known to be true. After she'd coolly sent me on my way with a handshake the previous evening, she had swept through the door of her apartment and announced to her daughters: "I have just met the man I am going to marry."

WE SPENT THE FOLLOWING evenings drenched in each other's memories, as we told of the pains and pleasures that had marked our lives. We spoke freely and intimately. There was no air of hostage-taking in our confessions of past intimacies, only the joy of deliverance from the horrors of dating. We formed the sort of mutual trust that only men and women who know themselves, and feel comfortable in that knowledge, instinctively develop. I felt drawn to her with the strength of a homing pigeon with a thousand miles to fly. In those first weeks, we never kissed; never even held hands. "I've always maintained that physical involvement too early in a relationship presupposes an intimacy that doesn't exist," declared my intended. "Someone invariably gets hurt. It won't be me." I realized early on that I was becoming involved with a sensible and sensitive woman, who would not be wooed in a day. She would require a long courting, or, to be more precise, she would always need to be courted, and I was about to apply for that position.

"Whatever other compatibilities we might share, a rage to live, the existential streak of constantly expanding experience is at the top of our list," I told her. "Maybe it's time for me to stop acting

---

[3] One of the oil patch's less poetically inclined paladins had once winked at Alvy and whispered, "Honey, you got pipe wrench eyes. I look into 'em, and my nuts tighten." He said it in his way, I said it in mine.

like a goddamn writer with a notebook, to stop editing my life, and start giving it away. I've spent most of my days immersed in – no, drowning in – the world of ideas, now I need a guide to the world of feelings." She responded: "People forget what you write; people forget what you do; but they never forget how you make them feel." I knew what she meant, because I was feeling the same passion. And we have been together from that day forward.

At that point Alvy was forty-two, which was a good midway point between how young she looked and how wise she sounded. I found her looks deceiving. Alvy was vivacious in a highly infectious way. Ideas flickered across her face like strobe lights and emotions mobilized an array of lively expressions, mostly of barely concealed bemusement. She still retained that innocent (or was it mischievous) gleam in her eyes as she smiled at me, but she could smell bullshit a mile away – a family trait, as I later discovered.

She tested at the Mensa level, yet did not parade the fact. She was a captivating charmer, but beneath that empires-have-fallen-for-less smile ticked an implacable determination to remain true to herself. She could name anything in Latin, having been schooled at the master's level in the medical sciences, could explain how the body parts interacted and were susceptible to diseases, but could never find her house keys. She was a false extrovert in that, although socially adept, she valued her privacy above all else. She was delightful, spirited, but seemed genuinely bemused by the compliments that came her way. She used a lot of air behind her Ws, as in: "You did WWWWWHAT?"

There was no way to express the strength of my feelings without sounding silly. So I tackled my thorniest issue, the difference in our ages. "There's a little known traffic law, referred to as 'the last clear chance,' that has always intrigued me," I began, being as roundabout as I could. "It maintains that, other evidence to the contrary, the driver who had the last clear chance to avoid an accident is responsible. I feel that way about us – at least about me, exercising my last clear chance for happiness. After all, I'm sixty-six, for God's sake, a time when society thinks I am beyond the chronological boundaries of love."

But my age wasn't an issue for Alvy. She had waited eighteen years to find someone she could feel completely comfortable and comforting with, and during that time the responsibility of raising two children as a single parent and sole provider had fostered a maturity that meant she had little in common with men her own age. With age no psychological barrier, we've discovered that we are one another's brain mates, soul mates, and body mates. We're glorious remnants of an outdated style of romanticism, each with a million miles on our meters.

We never forget the headiness of falling in love, but we do forget some details of that magical time. Two exchanges in particular tickle the memory, from the morning after we had finally consummated our desire for one another. "It was Anton Chekhov," I said, "who described a moment like this in *The Seagull*: 'The angel of silence has flown over us.'" The next morning she sent me one of her favourite poems by Maxine Kumin:

Nothing is changed, except
there was a moment when

the wolf, the mongering wolf
who stands outside the self

lay lightly down, and slept.

Living together without the sanctity of marriage was not an option for us as we needed a deeper level of commitment. We never uttered that ambivalent word "relationship" that people use when they aren't really in love but are merely practising at it. We were meant to be together, and so we planned our life that way. After four months, we got engaged at a beachfront cottage at the El Conquistador Resort in Puerto Rico.

We had literally planned our home and life together from week one, but I wanted the actual engagement to be a romantic surprise. The resort was perched on a cliff and its waterfront condos were accessible only by gondola, and therefore lacked room service, so, in order to plan my moonlight performance on our balcony, I had to hire the catering department of the hotel. The staff was abuzz for days with the secret plans, assuring me at every encounter that "de lady" would say yes.

The next morning we arrived for breakfast. Unaware that the whole hotel staff had been anticipating our momentous occasion, Alvy was shocked as they swarmed her to see the ring.

The divine incongruity of the wedding ceremony that followed two months later, my fourth, was not lost on me, so that it wasn't easy to feel the presence of any legitimizing deity, however permissive. To stack the odds in our favour, we were married twice the same day. I had invited an old friend from Los Angeles, Rabbi Jamie Weinstein, to conduct the wedding service. He had discovered only that morning that he was not licensed to perform the ceremony in Canada, so our marriage would not be legally valid. This was no problem, as the intrepid rabbi arrived with his own solution in the form of a justice of the peace, Ken Dong, who whisked Alvy and me through the civil ceremony before we went upstairs to meet our guests. There, Rabbi Weinstein married us in the religious ceremony with none of our guests any the wiser. Afterwards we played our favourite absurd song, by Steve Goodman, with the infectious chorus, "You don't have to call me darlin', darlin'," and I dedicated to Alvy the Kris Kristofferson tune "Loving Her Was Easier (Than Anything I'll Ever Do Again)."

We held both the service and reception in our new home in Vancouver, which was fitting for two confirmed homebodies who had found their nest at last. Although our guest list included a century of Canada's media, political, and business elites, the highlights for me were the speeches by Alvy's two daughters. Dana raised her champagne glass and said, "Welcome to the family,

Captain. And Mom — it's about time!" Eighteen-year-old Brandi gave a delightful dissertation on unconditional love that had many people in tears.

WHEN I MARRIED ALVY, a real sailor joined the family, because she had crewed in races for her previous boyfriend, Brian Moorhouse, a Flying Dutchman champion who owned sailboats in Vancouver and also in Europe. Our honeymoon trip was three weeks aboard an ancient chartered Morgan-44 (named *Heartbeat*) in the British Virgin Islands. She was comfortable and vaguely seaworthy (and as well as *being* an old tub, actually *had* a small bathtub off the master cabin). We had no trouble sailing her double-handed, especially in those kindly waters. The BVIs form a natural circle of islands that keeps out the steepest of the transatlantic rollers, yet allows in the daily, twenty-knot prevailing northeasterlies, which ensure ideal sailing conditions. It was a double treat because we had not had nearly enough time alone together, and as we capably managed our first expedition, it was clear we had yet another reason to become more closely linked.

We were interrupted only once. Somehow, the *Toronto Star* had found my cellphone number and called for my comment on a lawsuit that Joe Clark was launching against me for something I'd written about him in *The Canadian Revolution*. The *Star* wanted to know if I was going to apologize and retract. Being on the best of my honeymoons, I was feeling particularly mellow, so I came back with something un-Canadian, like, "Hell, no. Publish and be damned!" The paper quoted my comment accurately, but my setting was identified as "aboard a chartered yacht in the Caribbean, with his fourth wife," which made me sound like some international playboy installed in my luxury yacht ordering the white-liveried crew to refill my mai tai while pointing the captain to our next destination. But after I mixed myself a couple of strong rum-and-Cokes, it made no difference.

We returned to the British Virgins with Dana and Brandi for a Christmas sailing holiday in 1997, this time moving up to a forty-foot Beneteau, and vaguely wondered why ours was one of the few boats out on charter. Then we found out. On our third day, while on a leisurely morning sail, the wind suddenly whipped itself into a whiteout so fierce that it threw up a barrier of water obliterating my view of the bow. Brandi and Alvy managed to pound the sail down while Dana fetched the lifejackets, but even with engine forward at full throttle we were being rapidly blown backwards toward rocky Gordon Island, and I could do nothing to stop us. Luckily the miniature hurricane lasted only half an hour, and we later found out that this was one of the typical "Christmas Winds" that kept sensible charters at home.

DANA AND BRANDI have become an indispensable element of my happiness because they treat me like a true father. I not only gained two daughters through my marriage but also, through Dana, a young grandson. I dedicated one of my books to them with the comment that my stepdaughters light up my life, which they continue to do. They inherited a love of irreverent humour from their mother, but the trait must have expanded exponentially while passing through the gene pool. Alvy summed up this state of benign teasing in one of her letters to me: "You embraced my children and grandchild with love, guidance, and humour (a much-needed quality as they attempt to strip you of all dignity and reduce you to a mere mortal), but I know you are smugly confident, knowing that these little darlings would fiercely defend you to the ends of the world." True, but they're hardly "little darlings," being close to six feet tall and drop-dead gorgeous.

The younger (twenty-eight as of this writing) and the most independent, Brandi is a delightfully intriguing woman, surpassing even her mother's wit. She is loyal and terminally funky, never hesitating to puncture anyone's (especially my) pretensions. Dana, the elder, shares some of my qualities in that she is a temperamental loner who needs a lot of loving. She is smart and observant; her heart is an open city. At thirty-two, she has raised on her own a spirited and talented boy, Adon Kerr, now twelve, who is the family darling.

In the nine years since the wedding and honeymoon, our lives have spilled into each other, and we revel in the mix. There's no distance left between us. We feel incomplete when we're alone and have become each other's sixth sense. Having become indispensable each to the other, Alvy and I made a pact, both vowing: "If you ever leave me, I'm coming with you." The longer we're together, the more our love becomes like a garden that draws its natural increase from the seasons. "We have come to love each other with all the open-eyed certitude of two mature, capable adults who recognized quality and comfort when they saw it," Alvy wrote me.

We lament that we have limited time left together, but are determined to make the most of our union. For that reason we observe our anniversaries on the twenty-ninth of every month, the date of our first meeting. By the time this book is published, we will be celebrating our 112th anniversary, which isn't bad for any couple. We love to recall old memories together, while at the same time planning new adventures.

"I only regret, in fact he only regrets, that I wasn't there for the whole ride," Alvy wrote to a friend at one point. "What a life we could've had together, if I had only met him sooner. No one imagines just how compatible we are. *We* can't imagine it. We spend 24/7 together and want more. We wake up holding hands. If I touch him in his sleep, he reaches for my hand and kisses it, not even aware that he is doing it. The depth of our love is that profound. I treasure it, and for once, can make up for all of the lonely years when I thought I'd never find this contentment, this excitement, this absolute state of grace."

So great is my fortune that I have often asked myself: why had I never before been able to enjoy this depth of content and domestic harmony, which others seem to find so easy to achieve? Part of the answer, of course, lies in Alvy. Her powers of deductive reasoning astound me. She seems possessed of a rare incandescence; she is a proud and accomplished woman who knows what's truly important. But part of the answer lies with me. There lurks deep inside my psyche a dragon that has been hard to propitiate and harder still to hold back from wrecking my life. Now that dragon has finally been slain. Here Be Dragons no more.

I had spent much of my adulthood as a refugee from the marital wars, which was scarcely an improvement from my previous status as a childhood refugee from the martial wars. I longed to belong. I was always on the hunt for the security of love and allegiance. Emotional surfing became a way of life. It wasn't until I met Alvy that I finally realized that for fairy tales to work, you've got to believe in them. Ours took me by storm. I had become a dragonmaster.

Alvy was different because she fell in love with Peter Newman, not Peter C. Newman. The former is the man I really am; the latter is the persona I created. Alvy neither knew nor cared about Peter C. Newman. Yes, she had vaguely heard of me, but she is one of those rare people (thank God there aren't too many) who, when she reads, pays not the slightest attention to the name of the author; it's only the content that she finds important. For example, she subscribed to *Maclean's* for a dozen years, mainly because she liked my editorials – she could even quote some of my thoughts back to me – but she wasn't aware that I had written them, except that when she read what was identified as my last editorial, she cancelled her subscription.

By the time we met, I was ready to abandon Peter C. Newman myself. If I was going to grab a life (as opposed to remaining satisfied with all that self-generated tumult), I figured I had this one "last clear chance" to do so. How quaint and unusual, I thought, for this wondrous creature to fall in love with me, instead of my carefully cultivated and nurtured image. I'd used the P.C.N. persona as a sexual lure for years. Most of the women wanted P.C.N., they didn't want plain old Peter Newman.

Her timing was equally opportune. After the collapse of her teenage marriage, she had spent nearly two decades alone, raising two daughters with no financial support. She was wooed by Oil Patch chiefs who showered her with red roses and luxurious outings, when what she really needed was groceries for the family. She tried a few serious relationships, which always fell apart on the grounds of her partners' infidelities – a disappointment to her and an affront to her high moral standards.

So we were both ready. Somehow we recognized in one another that last clear chance, and we grabbed it. This does not mean it was a union born of loneliness and desperation; rather it was a marriage of values and aspirations. Alvy was smart enough to figure out my large ration of complexities and neuroses, but regarded me as a safe bet all the same, because I lived the values that she believed in. Meanwhile, I had never experienced unconditional love – or, more accurately, been prepared to offer it. I had tired of having to prove myself over and over again, and that was the point at which I met the one woman who didn't expect me to prove myself at all. As a friend noted: "She doesn't expect you to *do* Peter, just to *be* Peter."

What a treat. For once, I didn't have to be a "good boy so the nanny would stay," or prove my love of Canada, or write a big book. I just had to be myself – a trick, as it turned out, that I had seldom performed, and that sounded easier than it was. Alvy saw the sleight-of-hand behind the department store magician who made himself disappear. She looked behind the court jester's costume and makeup. Her gaze penetrated beyond the fisherman's cap and the unkempt beard that made me look like a dispossessed rabbi. And she saw the man she wanted to love.

During our courtship, when she realized there was a Peter C. Newman, Alvy kept asking me, "You could have any woman you want. Why me?" And my answer was always the same: "Because not only do I get you, but I also get the family I need." Most of my relatives were killed by the Nazis. My parents were dead, and I had been an only child. What I needed most, besides a love of my own, was to experience the warmth of hearth and family, even more as I grew older. Another benefit, I realized only as I grew to know her, was that mothers are naturally better at nurturing than single women. On top of which, Alvy is a trained nurse — *oy vey*!

I found a family of beautiful Amazons to share my life. My commitment is total, and it runs both ways. We never tire of one another; we're too exhausted dealing with each other's lives. Brandi and Dana keep us constantly on edge. I never know what the answer will be when I ask, "So, what's new?" Neither do they.

As a family, we often disagree but never fight. There are no hidden agendas; everybody's business is out in the open. We understand that human frailty is not a sign of weakness, and that none of us is perfect. We respect each other's values, thrill as we watch grandson Adon grow from a boy into a man, and, if we ever get him off video games, we expect him to conquer the world.

The truth is, our time together has not been without its jolts of reality. But we get past these human foibles and draw a line underneath them, because we feel instinctively that one sure road to disappointment and defeat would be to take our love for granted. So we may have our moments, but those are unintended; we concentrate on pampering each other and cherishing what we have. That is the reason for celebrating monthly the anniversary of our meeting and why we shower each other with gifts and take delightful vacations. In the words of the old jazz standard: "If not you, who? If not now, when?"

The hinge of fate that put us together was the time in our lives when we met, being finally ready to appreciate another's company and to surrender to the delights and complexity of love. It has been almost ten years now, and the lust and longing is still there, along with the accompanying commitment and responsibility. We recognized in one another a paradoxical combination of beatitude and exhilaration that we both missed in previous pairings. Instead of a sequence of discontinuities, the rhythm of our days has become our guiding light. We have come to realize that the power of enchantment is life's only true mercy, and that we are possessed by it. We are a heady mixture of hedonism and paranoia living on the precipice of time: the perfect marriage, if you ask me.

CHAPTER TWENTY

GREEN MONKEYS, GNOMES, AND GUV'NORS

You cannot discover new oceans
until you lose sight of the shore.

lvy had long dreamed of living in Europe, not just briefly as a tourist but as a resident, and was actively planning to do so, now that her children were launched. When I came on the scene in 1995, her eldest, Dana, was divorced and living in Ladner, and Brandi was off at college. The time was ripe for her dreams to finally be realized. She declared that she'd paid her dues, and the future was now hers. I agreed, with one caveat – I must be part of it. As our love blossomed and we both saw home in each other's eyes, she was fearful that her lifelong dream of living in foreign lands would be curtailed.

She needn't have worried, because I had been entertaining similar thoughts. I felt that when the time came to write my auto-biography, that introspective exercise ought to be done with the objectivity of distance, preferably from Europe, my original home. Breaking free would be no simple process. Nietzsche got it right (for once) when he postulated that it is less difficult to abandon a powerful fatherland than a country still in its formative stages, which needs its people. I realized that any exile, however pleasant, was bound to be an exile *to*, not *from*. I knew I would return to a Europe that was strange and unpredictable, bereft of familiar markings – out of reach and out of mind. Yet I would always remain Canadian. As Mavis Gallant, a resident of Paris for fifty years, so wisely affirmed: "It is not a thing you can escape from. It's like having blue eyes."

Changing continents would not be that different from my previous cross-continental leap. In 1982, after spending more than forty years claiming pride of place as the serial chronicler and occasional shit-disturber among the Central-Canadian elite who determined and implemented the country's Perrier agenda, I had found a romantic coastal British Columbia village that followed no agendas and consumed no mineral water. It required serious reorientation of my values and priorities. Each day was measured by the rushing tides, with the angular silhouettes of blue herons providing its grace notes. This was a place where people lacked social affectations and still happily ordered coffee *before* the meal.

That migration to the Pacific coast had made me realize that Canada's psychic energy was increasingly originating from its geographical margins. With Ottawa bankrupt, spiritually as well as financially, the country was in a crisis of public confidence. I needed distance to recognize its seriousness. During the two sweet decades I spent in British Columbia, I got a feel for the natural wisdom of its people. They knew little (and cared less) about the subtleties of Ottawa's power games. But earlier than me or the other so-called pundits, they had recognized Pierre Trudeau as an emotional gypsy, Brian Mulroney as an artificial construct, Kim Campbell as a ditzy dame, and Jean Chrétien as a ruthless mother.

My switch of venues turned out to be professionally productive and personally inspiring. In the same way, I could now see much advantage in becoming an expatriate. Distance would expose me to a more balanced assessment of my homeland as I viewed Canada from a nomadic, contrapuntal existence on the wilder shores of the global village. As the poster says: you cannot discover new oceans without first losing sight of the shore.

After decades of faithful servitude in the country's literary and journalistic vineyards, I needed a respite. In Alvy, who held the original patent on creative discontinuity, I had found the ideal catalyst to recharge my energies. I knew, too, that we would expand our horizons. "Don't discount the quest for betterment; it's the hallmark of the intelligent being," she wrote in an anniversary card I found at the breakfast table one morning. "Without the intellectual elite who always strive for Utopia, the world stagnates. Enjoy your enthusiastic nature and capacity for change. You and I are part of a small minority, with our nomadic tendencies and striving for the 'lived experience.' You are an exciting man, full of dreams, ambitions, ideas, absurdities, and most of all passions. Passions for life, passions for women, for the sea, for thoughts, for love . . . I am the same and we found each other. Let's enjoy that and let it take us where it may."

While the glories of Europe dangled before our noses, it took us most of six years to disentangle ourselves from the lives we led, the obligations, real and imagined, we had assumed. But once the wind was behind us we set off on an odyssey that took us to a tropical island, then to the home of the gnomes who control world finance, and finally to the world's most glorious imperial city. It was, and continues to be, a great adventure, made even more alluring by being together 24/7. We have almost (but never quite) satisfied the insatiable appetite we nurture for one another's company.

But first, I was committed to producing *Titans*, the third volume in my *Canadian Establishment* series, for Penguin Books. That would require four years of intensive research plus fourteen months of writing. Although I was chronologically past my productive period, I never for a moment considered not working. For most people, retirement is like stepping off a pier. If you've achieved anything, you go overnight from *Who's Who* to "Who's That?" Yet no one reaches statutory senility at sixty-five. This might be the only clear advantage to being a writer: we have no preordained expiry date, except the speed at which our works move off the shelves at bookstores.

We decided to fill the time before embarking on our European journey by returning to school. Alvy had switched from clinical health care to consulting, and enrolled in the University of British Columbia to complete an MBA in health education. As a conceptual thinker, she could envision combining clinical and theoretical knowledge to build her reputation as a leader in patient education and advocacy, especially in the burgeoning field of obesity. At UBC she found a mentor in the department head, Dr. Robert Modrow. "Dr. Bob" became a champion for her cause, providing wise direction and friendly support.

I joined UBC's recently established graduate School of Journalism to teach courses in creative non-fiction. Even more than my previous experiences lecturing at McMaster, York, and Victoria universities, this turned out to be a blessing. Donna Logan, who had previously been deputy managing editor of the *Montreal Star* and head of CBC Radio, was an effective and inspirational founding dean of the enterprise. We had fun negotiating the gap between the lively imperatives of a professional journalism school and its tame academic environment.

The unexpected bonus was the students' glittering writing talents. They took my breath away. I decided early on that there was no point pretending I could teach anyone to write, especially within the highly provisional parameters of creative non-fiction. I set down a few boundaries and we took it from there, making up the rules as we went along. Weekly assignments were critiqued (sometimes far more brutally than I would have done) by the students themselves, who encouraged each other with constructive suggestions and pointed comments. Instead of standard top-down classes, our sessions became lively seminars with few taboos. Within a few weeks the essays, confessions, investigative and advocacy articles being discussed were far more exhilarating than most of the staff-written copy I had edited at *Maclean's*. It was an important time for me because I could pass on my techniques, perceptions, and insights, perpetuating my chosen art form. At the same time, the students told me they found the courses profoundly liberating, a way of discovering their own path through the minefields of personal experience. "When I was a child," a graduate wrote in the anonymous teaching evaluation questionnaire at the end of one course, "I used to dream of flying down the stairs beyond the confines of my parents' home. Peter Newman has given me wings – given us all wings. But what's better, more marvellous, is that he's given us no trajectory, only a destination. He believes in us and his faith is contagious. He stresses drippy, sappy, gut-wrenching feeling, and I trust him entirely. He lavishes praise and criticism with equal weights and pushes everyone to reach higher, deeper and further."

THE INSPIRATION I GAINED from five years of these inspiring seminars was in sharp contrast to what I saw happening in Ottawa. Many songs ago, the American folk artist Don McLean had swept the boards with his strangely affecting lament "American Pie," which became the anthem for a generation. That was the message and melody that haunted me as I observed, with growing horror, the decade-long stewardship of Jean Chrétien. No other politician in my experience had changed character so abruptly. The benign and charming political lightweight I had interviewed frequently during his Cabinet days had transformed himself into a sub-Arctic Manuel Noriega, the Panamanian dictator. This was not because he headed an elected dictatorship better known as the Liberal Party of Canada; we had long since become used to One-Party rule. Chrétien corrupted that political monopoly and turned it into One-Man rule, which was something even most loyal Liberals could not stomach. He ran the country without feeling accountable to anyone, least of all the lapdog ethics commissioner who approved his every transgression.

This was not the man I had first met on July 22, 1965, the day he was picked out of the Liberal backbenches to become parliamentary secretary to Prime Minister Lester Pearson. At thirty-one, his Gallic charm was irresistible, a stir-fry of homespun humility, self-deprecating humour, and upfront decency. I remember thinking how comfortable he seemed in his skin, one of those rare politicians

who didn't need adoring crowds or genuflecting flunkies to legitimize his worth. When I asked him a question, he would hesitate,
like a dutiful child who wanted to get it right, then give me an
honest answer.

Chrétien had entered federal politics in 1963, when John F.
Kennedy was still canoodling in the White House, and for three
long decades successfully scuffled in the vestibules of Liberal
power, blessed by his apparent inability to make enemies and the
two most valuable elements in any political success: impeccable
timing and the quality of always being underestimated. (The only
election he lost was to John Turner in the 1984 Liberal leadership
contest; if he had won it, it would have made him the sacrificial
lamb in the Mulroney sweep that followed.) Chrétien was elected
to the House of Commons a dozen times, treating the political wars
not as a science or an art but as a game. "Politics," he specified, "is
a game of friends." And so it was. No other Canadian prime minister, including Brian Mulroney, was so cynically personal in his
distribution of patronage. His appointments required only one
qualification: blood-oath loyalty to Jean Chrétien. (Being a faithful Liberal was no longer enough.)

He was one tough mother, unable or unwilling to demonstrate
grace under pressure, or in any other circumstance. He treated his
parliamentary caucus like a servile retinue instead of the source of
his power, and it was Paul Martin's recognition of the difference
that allowed him to steal the party from under its leader.

I saw Chrétien several times when he ventured to the west coast,
and realized what had changed in him: nothing danced in his eyes.
That was why that song about how "the music died" haunted me
so, whenever I saw or thought about him. There was no music in
him. It wasn't the quality of his grin, which by now had more to
do with cheek muscles than mirth, or his face, which had begun
to look as though some amateur taxidermist had been practising
on it. It was the absence of that twinkle in his gaze that had been
so characteristic of the man. Instead of the fuzzy, self-deprecating

humour he had once projected, he now gave off a distant, lunar chill. "I'm De King of De Castle" was his only message.

This once kindly politician was at his most insensitive in dealing with University of British Columbia students who protested the 1997 visit to Vancouver of the Indonesian dictator Suharto, soon afterwards overthrown by his own people and charged with massive corruption. As the subsequent investigation documented, the RCMP had discarded the rule of law and embraced a direct order sent from Chrétien's office to protect the visiting despot, not just from harm but from embarrassment. When the students involved in the peaceful demonstration were pepper-sprayed into submission by the Mounties, Chrétien quipped that, for him, pepper was something he used on his steaks. (Later he admonished the protestors, saying they were lucky the RCMP hadn't used baseball bats.)[1] Chrétien's mindless comments and behaviour demonstrated how profoundly he had lost touch with his gentler, more thoughtful former self.

Much was made of his weird pronouncements, since it was virtually impossible to follow his train of thought, which was always on the point of derailing itself. He turned incoherence into an art form. During a debate about proof of the presence of weapons of mass destruction in pre-war Iraq, he clarified the situation by telling Parliament: "The proof is the proof. And when you have a good proof, it's proven."[2]

His critics constantly condemned Chrétien for not having had a single original thought. Not me. I always believed that, on the contrary, his most daring epiphany was the audacious notion that he was qualified to be prime minister. This outrageous idea took

---

[1] There is nothing amusing about pepper spray, as some of its victims, who were in my writing classes, can attest. It is more powerful than tear gas or mace, causing bronchial spasms, eyes that swell shut, and extreme nausea.

[2] To a female Vancouver high school student advocating athletic scholarships, he said: "I tend to incline with you."

wings without any conversion in his character or expanded view of the country. His greatest boast – that he had won majorities in three general elections – was dubious at best. He did win those campaigns, not because he was Jean Chrétien but because he *wasn't* Brian Mulroney (or his surrogate, Kim Campbell, in 1993), Preston Manning (1997), or Stockwell Day (2000). "For a decade our country was governed by a schoolyard bully who ruthlessly abused his power and sought the ruin of those who stood in his way," concluded the Montreal *Gazette*'s L. Ian MacDonald.

Exactly. That was why Don McLean's evocative refrain reflected the rueful mood of most Canadians at the frigid and long-overdue end of Jean Chrétien's tenure.

The real tragedy of Chrétien's term was his inaction on every front, especially repatriation of the Canadian economy. By the butt end of the twentieth century – the century that was supposed to have belonged to Canada – the country belonged to strangers. With our dollar at a 40 per cent discount and an administration in Ottawa oblivious to its implications, the sellout of the country's corporate assets resembled nothing so much as the liquidation of Eaton's on a national scale. By my calculations, the economy had stepped over an invisible line in the mid 1990s, when we actually controlled a smaller portion of our productive wealth than the citizens of any other industrialized country. America's global traders had moved in and grabbed nearly everything that wasn't nailed down, except Cape Breton (although shoreline properties there are going fast to long-distance vacationers from Germany) and the terminally unprofitable B.C. ferry fleet. Globalization had been advertised as a natural marketing phenomenon, promising to increase business and multiply profits for all concerned. Instead, it meant Americanization. Pure and simple. (Well, neither pure nor simple, really.) Willy-nilly, we became less the citizens of a proud country than the drones of a homogeneous continent.

This happened because, at that crucial juncture in our history, we were led by a politician without vision or priorities. That he might be presiding over a hollowed-out nation-state, no longer in

charge of itself, never entered his mind. Grieving for my country
– left with little more than the fugitive souvenirs of a misspent
century – I decided that I had no choice but to surrender my long
and exhausting struggle to make Canadians aware of the price that
the American takeover would ultimately exact. That fate was
brought home to me by the exuberant (off-the-record) outburst
by chief American trade representative, Clayton Yeutter, at the
1989 White House signing ceremony of the Canada-U.S. Free
Trade Agreement. "We've signed a stunning new trade pact with
Canada," he gloated. "The Canadians don't know what they've
signed. In twenty years they'll be sucked into the U.S. economy."
 Yeutter was wrong. It didn't take twenty years.
 I felt it was time to leave my benighted home country and find
solace in alternative pursuits, such as reconstructing my own life as
a cautionary tale to any surviving idealists still dreaming of Canada
as a proudly independent homeland. Perhaps in Europe, the fountainhead of western civilization, I would discover solace or at least
a historical perspective for my failed quest.
 In spring 2001 I had one final opportunity to bear witness to
what I regarded, then and now, as the ultimate threat of Americanization: Canada's cultural genocide. That turned out to be the
pivotal issue at the Summit of the Americas held in Quebec City.
Defence of indigenous cultures was the key battleground for the
rowdy protestors, though it was seldom given specific voice at the
galvanized-wire barricades. It was an ambiguous concept at best,
depending as it did on individual interpretations of collective
nationality. To Americans, culture is a commodity, their most profitable commercial export; to Canadians, and to most of the thirty-
two other countries in our hemisphere, it is the fragile essence of
their nationhood. What "culture" does not mean is the limiting
concept most people endow it with, such as a country's literature,
visual arts, music, and so on. Bernard Ostry, the most intellectual
of our bureaucrats, once defined the slippery word as "central to
everything we do. It's our environment and our adaptation to it.
It's the way we know ourselves and each other. It's the image and

abstractions that allow us to live together in communities and nations – the element in which we live."

Watching the brave protests of the Quebec City rioters, it seemed to me that our goal ought to be straightforward: the economy was negotiable; our culture was not. Preserving our distinctive identity ought to have been our highest calling. Yet we were giving it away.

I had a brief diversion in the spring of 1997 when I was scheduled to interview Fidel Castro. The Cuban visit was arranged through Wally Berukoff, a Canadian entrepreneur who had tried every trade except piracy and believed that taking risks was fun and taking bigger risks was even more fun. He was busy opening mines and building resort hotels in Cuba and had forged an easy rapport with the local dictator because they shared a common language (Russian – Wally is a Doukhobor). Canada's ambassador in Cuba, Mark Entwistle, supported the project and I had agreed to *El Comandante*'s surprisingly commercial conditions (that he retain Spanish publication rights to our interview and use his own photographer). I received final approval through Carlos Lage Davila, vice-president of the council of state and Cuba's second-highest-ranking government official. We were all set. Then the project abruptly collapsed. As a courtesy, Cuba's ambassador to Canada had informed Ottawa's PMO about the scheduled interview. It was instantly vetoed by Jean Pelletier, then Chrétien's chief of staff, who presumably feared I might prefer the Latin American dictator to our domestic variety.

BY THE FOLLOWING SPRING I had much more serious problems. In November 1997, though I didn't realize it at the time, I suffered a heart attack. I took to my bed with what I thought was flu. I was extremely fatigued but had no chest pains, none of what I thought of as "heart attack symptoms," so I rested for a day and resumed work the next. Termed a "silent heart attack," it was the kind that is accompanied by flu-like sweats, nausea, exhaustion, and anxiety. I learned that it usually kills the second time around. The damage it caused was picked up the following April on an ECG by Dr. Jim Paupst, my trusted GP, who suggested I get an immediate stress test to determine its severity. Because Canada's medical system operates on waiting, I couldn't get that examination until June. That was a deadly interval. Neither Alvy nor I could concentrate on work. Being relative newlyweds – and nine years later we still act it – we wanted to spend every minute together in case it was our last.

When the test showed hints of damage, Dr. David Hilton, my cardiologist, performed an angiogram which showed that my left-main artery (ominously known as "the widow-maker"), the one that feeds blood to most of the heart muscle, was more than 90 per cent blocked. The obstruction was high up in that one-inch area before the artery splits to become the left anterior and circumflex arteries. My situation was declared urgent in the extreme; I needed immediate bypass surgery to have any chance of survival. As the angiogram was taking place, and Alvy was pacing the hallways of the Royal Jubilee Hospital, she overheard someone trying to assemble a cardiac team for that night, declaring, "We've got an emergency situation here, this guy is in serious trouble, with over 95 per cent blockage." She figured it was the fellow in the room next to me and remembers thinking, "*Oh, that poor bugger.*" Then Dr. Hilton emerged from my room with an ominous face. "Let's go for a walk," he told her. "I can't save him," he warned, "even if he has a heart attack right here, in the hospital, if his heart closes off any more, whether from stress, from lifting, from laughing. I couldn't save him. We're trying for a team tonight." It turned out that I was that "poor bugger."

That night Alvy sugarcoated the news to me, afraid that learning about its severity might trigger another constriction of the arteries. Not realizing the full seriousness of my plight, I asked Dr. Hilton next morning to postpone the operation until I had completed my book. At that point, they had to tell me the stone-cold truth. I was appalled. I had worked for too many years and shed too many tears to reach this state of contentment, and now I saw this dream life and this dream wife being swept away.

Hilton was adamant. Not only could I not postpone the operation to finish the book, he wouldn't even grant me one day's leave to settle my affairs. He did advise me to get them in order the best I could by phone.

The surgical team was not forthcoming that night, and so the delays began. Hilton shrewdly realized that it would be more stressful for me to lie there doing nothing than writing my book, and he gave me special dispensation to use my laptop. In the United States, anyone with a left main blocked by more than 75 per cent is guaranteed a bypass within twenty-four hours. That's also the recognized medical standard in Canada, and my blockage was more serious. Hilton even asked me to consider having the operation done at the Cleveland Clinic. British Columbia's medical system was in the grip of one of its frequent rotating strikes, and it was six long days before I was wheeled into the operating room. I could have died at any moment. And still can.

Alvy, Dana, and Brandi moved into the Oak Bay Beach Hotel nearby and held loving vigils, which included nightly servings of schnitzel and sauerkraut from the Rathskeller, Victoria's premier central European restaurant. I figured if I had one week to live, it had to include soul food for a Vienna boy like me. Alvy had recently read an emotionally charged short story in *Chatelaine* by Betty Jane Wylie, which told the story of how a widow (at a time when pay-phone calls cost only five cents) had succeeded in placing a call to her dead husband. When I was wheeled away for the operation, I pressed a nickel into Alvy's hand and asked her to call. Just in case. I'd been sedated enough to mute the panic I felt, but knew that if I survived, the rest of my life would be a gift.

My only previous experience with operating rooms had been from watching re-runs of *M*A*S*H*, on which surgeons enjoyed cutting up patients to music. So when Dr. Dick Brownlee appeared at my bedside, I had only one question: did he take musical requests? I handed him a tape of my favourite Stan Kenton tunes. He obliged, and the OR staff was boogying to a hopped-up version of "Lush Life" as I went under. It was the usual brutal procedure. My sternum was split from top to bottom with an electric saw. Heavy-duty retractors were fitted against the jutting edge of the rib cage, then cranked apart until a nine-inch opening was achieved, through which the open-heart operation proceeded.

I made Alvy promise that if I made it through, she'd give me the news by mentioning a Stan Kenton tune, so when she whispered "does 'Intermission Riff' mean anything to you?" I struggled to the surface from the depths of anaesthesia. But they were still keeping my body temperature low to reduce my rising blood pressure so that it wouldn't blow off those recently attached bypasses. Seven hours later, I woke up, hurting but alive. It had been a close call. The left main blockage had been even more severe than the angiogram indicated, and my left ventricle had started fibrillating before the operating crew could properly attach the heart-lung machine that temporarily replaced my heart function.

Coming back to life was a bizarre experience. I felt as though I were on a teeter-totter, swinging between life and death, floating through blindingly white nothingness, not sure whether I would, could, or wanted ever to awaken, listening to "the soft, enticing rustle of angel feathers."

The concern and kindness of my family and my friends, notably the Victoria poet Doug Beardsley (who snuck into the family-only ward by pretending to be my brother, Stan), carried me through the next two months. "I don't think I blinked or swallowed for ten hours," Alvy said afterwards. The bypass had been successful. My heart now pumps through its newly installed veins, one of them taken from my leg.

The recommended post-operative procedure required two months of stress-free recuperation. It was now the end of June and Penguin had already scheduled a first printing of sixty thousand copies of *Titans* for October publication. I still had seven chapters to write.

Our home in Vancouver had seven levels with what seemed like a hundred stairs. My office was at the very top. There was no way I could go home. So, to find a sanctuary where I could work and heal, Alvy arranged for Kurt Frost, my favourite shipwright, to bring our sailboat over from Vancouver. For three months, we lived aboard the *Pacific Mystic*, parked in the Oak Bay Marina, near the hospital.

It was in the cutter's tiny, triangular forepeak that I completed the book. I told no one of my dilemma except Cynthia Good, the publisher at Penguin, because I needed a deadline extension, which would compress the publication schedule from six to three months. She was particularly anxious to get the completed manuscript because this was her first season as head of the company and *Titans* was scheduled to be her lead book.

What made it all bearable was Alvy. Her nursing background was a godsend; she also became my in-boat editor and interlocutor. I talked to virtually no one during that unique recuperation. The blessed Dr. Hilton made weekly boat calls to see if my premature return to writing was causing any permanent damage, one time calling upon a neighbouring skipper who was shocked to find Victoria's finest cardiologist asking to borrow a wrench to fix his blood-pressure machine.

"How long do I need to wait to have sex again?" I quizzed him one sunny afternoon. Man to man, he knew the question foremost on every bypass-stud's mind even when his breastbone is held together with chicken wire, which a sneeze can tear apart.

"The rule of thumb is that you must climb a flight of stairs unassisted first," he replied.

"Good call, Doc," I said, nodding toward the three companion-way steps into the pilothouse. I was a man on a mission, ready to celebrate being alive. He howled with laughter, but being a man understood full well where my priorities lay, and I counted that easy climb as credible evidence of my recovery.

In the ensuing weeks, I had a major scare when I was rushed back into the emergency ward with a suspected blood clot that could have been the end of me. Lying aboard the boat in our bunk at night with my chest still aflame, usually passed out with the exhaustion of working while skipping the obligatory recuperation period, I realized that living the passion of their times, as journalists do, is not enough. Life is much too transient and much too precious. I also knew, finally, that Newman was human.

I never abandoned Stan Kenton but experienced a temporary post-operative flurry of interest in country and western music. My favourite band was Kinky Friedman and his Texas Jew Boys, which specialized in such off-the-map tunes as "They Don't Make Jews like Jesus Any More" and "If Your Phone Don't Ring, You'll Know It's Me." Friedman visited Vancouver while I was there. When Max Wyman, then entertainment editor of the Vancouver *Sun*, asked him why he had quit the band to write satiric detective novels, the outrageous Kinky replied, "Yeah, well, we were doing a gig near Austin. I went for a walk one day and began thinking that I really felt ambivalent about my music. Then I realized that anybody who used the word 'ambivalent' had no business being a country singer."

Kinky was crude and funny. He wrote an unusual acknowledgement section in one book in which he has himself in a hotel room making love when a maid enters and begins picking up crumpled notes from the floor, reading them aloud to inquire about the importance of each. Kinky is not pleased by the intrusion, complaining, "Can't you see I'm in the middle of somebody?" Not surprisingly, Bill Clinton was one of his biggest fans. He was especially grateful, during his Lewinsky period, for Kinky's dedication to him of the down-and-dirty ditty "Eatin' Ain't Cheatin'."

In the summer of 2003, I temporarily lent my talents to that musical genre to MC the wedding reception of Duane Steele (Alvy's brother) when he married the perky Shauna Taylor of Red Deer, Alberta. Duane is the hot Canadian star who was the first country artist signed to Mercury Canada, with an unprecedented five-album contract. Duane had spent six years in Nashville, so I appeared on stage as a mystery guest from Tennessee. I dressed up as Willie Nelson, complete with ponytail, cowboy hat, red bandana, and too many shots of Southern Comfort, then sang that Julio Iglesias hit, the lament of married men everywhere, "To All the

Girls I've Loved Before," to the amusement of the bridegroom. I exited to strains of "On the Road Again," in full character and having the time of my life. No one had asked for my autograph as Peter Newman, but as Willie Nelson I was mobbed. The hall was packed, and some from the back pressed forward, certain I was the real McCoy. I signed "Keep on Truckin' – Willie" on many a girl's wrist. That brief incarnation made me realize I was an ardent disciple of Willie's motto: "Sometimes I take it all the way, and sometimes I don't even go there." (It became our family motto.)

Just before my heart operation, we had decided to move forward with our European travel plans by selling the Kitsilano townhouse to settle in a much more modest country dwelling. We chose an obscure chunk of territory, an hour by ferry from West Vancouver, on what is known as the Sunshine Coast.[3] The string of villages that made up that area, located on the eastern shore of Georgia Strait, backed on an impenetrable mountain range, assuring the Sunshine Coast the geographical and psychological isolation most of its inhabitants wanted. From my renovated study I could watch eagles hunger through space, their talons knotting as they hunted for prey along the wild vegetation of the shoreside cliffs. It was a Land of Oz, surrounded by reality. And we loved it.

Our three-storey house was in Hopkins Landing, on the lower marine drive from the ferry into Gibsons. It was on a slight rise, which afforded us a clear view of the Strait, but also, I discovered, classified our home as a hazard to navigation. We were located in direct line of sight of the ferries steaming from Vancouver. I had decorated the house with antique red and green ship's lanterns. One day we received official notification from the RCMP that on foggy evenings ferry captains reported our navigation lights confused them because they made the house resemble an approaching freighter.

---

[3] There had been so many oil spills along the coastline that whenever I purchased fish sticks, I would ask the puzzled cashier: "Are these leaded or unleaded?"

Nearby Gibsons was renowned as the fishing village setting of *The Beachcombers*, the very popular TV series starring Bruno Gerussi that ran for nineteen years. Nothing much had changed, except that real-life beachcombers were now known as "log salvers." We often dined at Molly's Reach, still frequented by Gerussi's sidekicks, but also feasted on spring rolls at Rat Pack Louis', enjoyed the best homemade pea soup from Trudy's and Mexican tortillas[4] from Howl At The Moon, bought fresh sourdough bread daily from The Flying Cow, and had weekly feasts of the crab legs at Grandma's Pub, which was right out of Jack Kerouac, slumming on the waterfront. The regulars fondly recalled that one time strippers had livened up Grandma's but left when the crowd threw lit cigarette butts at them instead of money. It was a charming place. When we arrived on the coast we felt as though the weight of the world had been lifted. The air was clean and crisp. We felt like farmers on the homestead; whenever a car drove by at night, we'd wonder who they were and why they were out past 10:00 p.m.

The most fascinating characters I encountered on the coast were Peter Aelbers, the Granthams Landing postmaster, and his partner, Lindy. A Dutch Buddhist who had spent most of his career working aboard luxury cruise liners and being a maitre d' for fancy restaurants, Aelbers radiated humanity, humour, and wisdom, all delivered in the guise of teasing and pretending that I knew everything while he knew nothing. He called me "Your Highness" and poked fun at our hilltop perch, calling it our mansion on the hill. He is one of the wisest men I have ever met.

Another highlight was the selection of *Titans* for the 1999 B.C. Book Prize. It was my first (and only) literary award. I had by then lived in British Columbia for seventeen years, but was still considered a Toronto writer. Now I certifiably belonged to the Pacific coast. That status was confirmed when Rafe Mair signed one of his

---

[4] My Spanish is unskilled and in my first draft, I'd erroneously written this as having chinchillas at Howl at the Moon, until Alvy's editing eye caught it and she asked, "Didn't the fur balls kinda stop you cold?"

books to me, declaring that I had earned honorary B.C. citizenship. My prize was somewhat dimmed when Cynthia Good, the Penguin publisher at whose behest I had risked my life to finish the book, flatly refused to pay the fifty dollars (tax deductible) to invite my daughters Dana and Brandi to the ceremony. I was, of course, happy to buy the tickets, but having written eight books that produced revenues of close to $10 million for Penguin, I was stunned by her tight-fisted attitude. I decided to seek a different publisher for my next work – this autobiography, which saw me happily return to McClelland & Stewart, where I had started.

My distressing heart problems and the two emergency room visits that followed convinced me that our time on the Sunshine Coast had run out. The closest hospital was in Sechelt, miles away along what could be a dark and treacherous winding road for a car in a hurry at night if I had another heart attack. I knew a medical emergency helicopter could not reach me in time, due to the fog that frequently socked in the coast. I needed to be near a hospital, and so we abandoned our country living and bought from Patti Mair Hamilton the English Bay beachfront home of her recently deceased husband, the architect Gerald Hamilton. We walked along the beach nightly and fed the ducks and turtles at the Lost Lagoon, and thrilled to the sight of beavers, before they were euphemistically "relocated."

Alvy was fortunate enough to have been raised out of the city; she spent her childhood riding horses bareback in strawberry-filled pastures past clear brooks and beaver dams, nuzzling new batches of puppies each year, excitedly naming newly hatched chicks as they emerged each spring, only to be overwhelmed by the end of first day when the numbers rose dramatically. Home to her was the Peace River country of Alberta, where one could see glorious yellow rape fields march past the horizons and roadsides lined with fragrant clover. And so, on our nightly walks to the pond, she pretended we were walking on our acreage. Our stay there would be short-lived, however, as it was time to honour our intention of whizzing off to Europe.

CELEBRATING THE BAY: Raising the Governor's flag with Camilla and HBC Governor Donald McGiverin.

Launching *Caesars of the Wilderness* at Fort Edmonton in 1987.

MY BAND: Peter Newman and his Bouncing Czechs.

MY GUARDIAN ANGEL: and the musical accompanist to all my scribbling, Stan Kenton.

PLAYING A SOLO: for Leonard Cohen, and others. (*Toronto Star*)

MY ALTER EGO: On the road again as Willie Nelson celebrating my brother-in-law Duane Steele's wedding in Lacombe, Alberta.

CAPTAIN NEWMAN, C.D.
Breaking the barrier as one of
the very few Jewish Captains
in the Canadian Navy.

THE FAMILY: Posing with Alvy and daughters Dana and Brandi, who light up my life.

Going over Niagara Falls together.

NEWMAN FLEET: From *Indra* (Niagara – 35) to *Pacific Mystic* (Sea Bird – 37) and *Windrose* (Baba – 35) plus my dream boat, *Raven* (Tashiba – 40), in which I explored the Queen Charlottes and circumnavigated Vancouver Island.

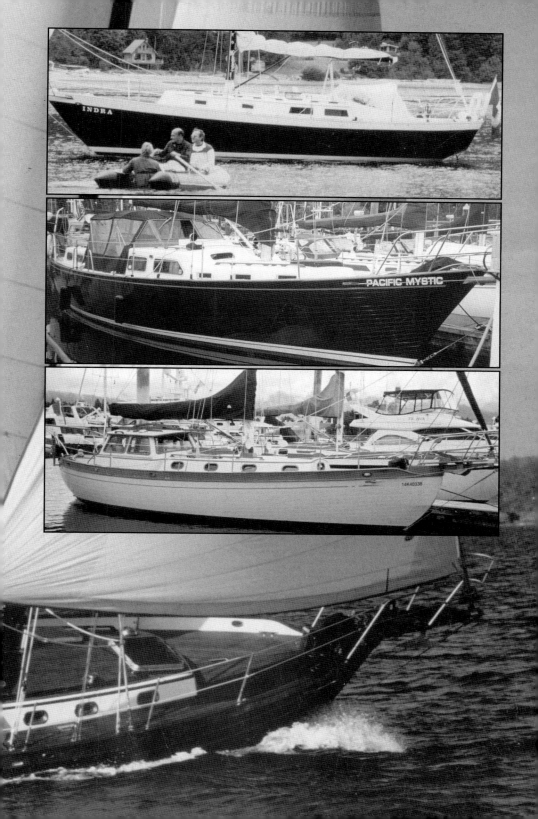

MY LAST DAMN WIFE: The love of my life – Alvy Jaan (Bjorklund). If she ever leaves me, I go with her.

In 1996, in preparation for our move abroad, we began to spend six weeks each spring travelling the Continent. Our plan was to find the places where we wanted to spend more time. We traced Alvy's roots in Sweden and were pleased to discover that everyone spoke Swedish to her automatically, their eyes registering betrayal when she answered in English. She identified strongly with her Scandinavian roots, being a statuesque, five-foot, nine-inch glowing picture of health, with the trademark heart-shaped face, high cheekbones, and deep-set sparkling blue eyes – eyes that would grow moist at the haunting strains of "Santa Lucia." She grew up loving the traditional delicacies of gingersnaps and pickled herring on rye, but turned away from her father's favourite, that glutinous creation known as *Lutefisk*.

The roots issue was abruptly raised in Vienna the following year. We weren't in the Austrian capital more than a day before I ran into an unmistakable example of anti-Semitism. I was hoping to buy a music box that played the "Blue Danube Waltz" (they didn't carry anything by Willie) for my dear friend Tidy Neubauer of Hamilton, but was stymied by a shopkeeper who flatly refused to acknowledge my presence in her store. I went next door to find Alvy, complaining to her that the woman was deliberately rude and wouldn't get off the phone to serve me. Alvy suspected what was happening and walked in by herself. She was greeted with a big smile and shown the music boxes. When I came back in, Alvy turned to me, smiling. "Was this the one you wanted, dear?" The shopkeeper was furious, slamming things down on the glass countertop. She completed the sale, glaring at me, and never said another word. We didn't let that silly woman spoil our travels that summer, but it did prevent me from fulfilling my original dream of writing this book in Vienna.

We fell in love with Spain and especially with Tossa de Mar on the Costa Brava, vowing we would someday return to the Antonio Gaudí–designed beachfront Hotel Diana outside the old fortress. One memorable summer we sailed a Jeaneau 45 around Majorca for three weeks piloted by good friend David Margerison of

Vancouver, who knew the waters. Over the years we divided our time among Norway, Denmark, Holland, Belgium, Germany, southern France, and Switzerland. On one trip, we drove from Vienna through Austria to my hometown, Břeclav, on the Czech border. There we found my father's former sugar factory being converted into condos. The property developer took us into his office, where we saw photos of the factory in its original glory. It stretched along the river for a distance of five blocks. I found my old school but didn't want to find my house, because under the Communists it had been converted to a shabby apartment building.

Because she grew up on fresh cow's milk still warm from the separator and homemade butter from the churn, Alvy felt a Heidi-like romanticism about Switzerland, so we spent a brief interval in Zurich and fell in love with this quiet, elegant town. It seemed like the most civilized city we had ever seen: the only lake pollution was from swan feathers and the only noise pollution from the tolling of church bells. Not too shabby, we decided, and vowed some day to return.

Two unusual events marked our Canadian departure. I was invited to speak at a mess dinner of the Seaforth Highlanders of Canada, the only naval officer ever to do so. I used the occasion to ream out the federal government for unilaterally disarming Canada through stupidity and neglect. "Our loyalty is beyond question, our equipment is beyond salvage," I concluded, feeling an overwhelming sense of shame.

Shortly after that, in June 1999 the editor of *Maclean's*, Bob Lewis, hosted a small dinner for Alvy and me to mark my final weekly column in the magazine. *Maclean's* had been the fulcrum of my professional life; I had published at least two million words between its covers over five decades. It had been a glorious gig, but it was time to say *adieu*. (At Lewis's behest and that of his successor Tony Wilson-Smith, I have since continued to contribute monthly columns to the magazine.)

With typical thoughtfulness, Lewis presented me with an engraved pewter mug, such as the one I had missed receiving when

I had left the Parliamentary Press Gallery three decades earlier. His other gift was a mock-up of a *Maclean's* cover, declaring: "NEWMAN IS HUMAN: The Captain Asks for Shore Leave."

I had expressed a similar sentiment at a previous *Maclean's* anniversary party where I had given a speech celebrating the magazine, pointing out to the crowd gathered on the former Toronto Stock Exchange floor that, regardless of any rumours they might have heard, "Newman really is human." There was standing room only at the event, and Alvy, who was then my fiancée, found herself along the outside wall. As I ended my speech and walked off stage, she turned to the lady beside her and asked, "Do you know Peter?"

"Oh yes, very well," the woman laughed.

Alvy pressed, without identifying herself. "Is it true what he is saying, that Newman is human?"

"He certainly is," the lady replied. "He's had three and half wives and God knows what else!"

Safely off stage, I now made my way along the wall to Alvy. As the embarrassed woman realized that she had just been talking to the "half," she tried skittering away along the wall, but Alvy quickly grabbed her arm and pulled her back, demurely saying, "Darling, this woman says she knows you." Dorothy Sangster (the wife of Sidney Katz, who'd worked with me at *Maclean's*) was beet-faced. I love the old adage "Keep your words soft and sweet, there may be some you'll have to eat," and this could have been one of those times. But I must admit that Dorothy was correct in her assessment of me. With twelve years of bachelorhood between two divorces, there were some great ladies and a lot more "God knows what else"s.

A few weeks later, I attended a $22,000 dinner at the $17-million Rosedale home of Steve Hudson, the founding chairman of Newcourt Credit Group. I was the prize. Bay Street tycoon Gene McBurney had donated that sum to the Toronto Hospital in return for my promise to tell him and his guests (including John Cassaday, CEO of Corus Entertainment, and Michael McMillan, CEO of Alliance-Atlantis) the inside gossip I had left out of *Titans*.

There we sat with our wives, and as I looked around the room, its glittering chandeliers, arcane paintings, and Adam tables, I thought that this moment, this meal, was as good a time as any to make my exit, figuring no one would pay $22,000 to have dinner with me ever again.

We decided to winter in Barbados, to begin our adventure.

BARBADOS WAS ABOUT WIND. Our writers' hut stood alone on Westmoreland Ridge, a hillock due east of Holetown on the west coast, the island's second-largest settlement. We enjoyed a 160-degree view of the turquoise Caribbean Sea, caressed by the Atlantic Ocean breezes blowing in from the island's east coast. This provided natural air conditioning and endowed the grove of mahogany trees that nestled close to our rented house with a permanent westward lean. The islanders believe that the winds tell stories, and they do if you know how to listen. Such legendary winds as the mistrals of the Mediterranean, the *hamsins* of Israel, the *foehns* of Switzerland, and the *Santa Anas* of Los Angeles all carry consequences. "On nights like this," Raymond Chandler wrote about the *Santa Ana*, "every booze party ends in a fight. Meek little wives feel the edge of the carving knife and study their husbands' necks."

The Barbados winds provide the backdrop to everything that happens on this small island in the sun, planted nearly a quarter of the way across the Atlantic. The weather is hot and windy, except for the days when it is windy and hot. The island lives with the threat of devastating hurricanes, which we were told occur only every fifty years or so. That made us feel comfortably smug until we discovered that the last major storm, which had devastated the island, was 1955's Hurricane Janet, which had killed thirty-nine people and left twenty-five thousand homeless. We were clearly within the time range for another big blow.

Only thirteen degrees north of the Equator, Barbados floats at the southern end of the West Indies chain. At one level, it is a living postcard with miles of public beaches, painters' sunsets, friendly locals, and an annual million sun-blistered tourists. My previous experience of Barbados was having spent several wonderful holidays there with Christina in the 1970s, when we were taken sailing by Pat Toppin and met the island's colourful attorney general, who went by the wonderful name of "Sleepy" Smith.

Now, I quickly discovered that wintering at a luxury resort was not the same as living in a house on the edge of the jungle. Our rented dwelling was isolated from its neighbours by wild stretches of impassable bush. Especially at night, when we were the only lighted oasis in sight, we came under constant siege by the lower orders of the animal kingdom. Cane toads that looked like giant hopping warts would arrive with each sunset, gurgling and shooting their poison tongues at us. Colonies of green monkeys peered from the trees lining our driveway, venturing ever closer and closer. We had a family of ten in and out of the garden. The monkeys looked cute but they were famous biters, and whenever I was tempted to sleep on our deck, the only cool spot available, I debated whether to take the chance. The island's monkeys made the mistake of eating bananas and pineapples fresh off the plantations' trees. Angry farmers put through a bounty system to decimate their numbers by paying for each tail turned in to local police stations. We adored their cute quizzical faces and the antics of their babies, so the bounty was a heartbreaking thought. But we didn't sleep outside.

Then there were the giant blue death-watch beetles that flipped themselves on their backs and performed a suicide dance accompanied by an eerie whine, which was agony to hear and watch. A spider the size of a catamaran – oh, all right a soup plate – which Alvy killed by dropping a large dictionary on it, had legs as thick as a frog's. Centipedes were found curled in the dryer lint, and on the nights we ventured out for dinner we had to run a gauntlet to our front door, with Alvy throwing her sandals at the creatures drawn to our porch lights.

For the first six weeks this was fun. I was the Great White Hunter, defending the family homestead from the invaders. But after a while I came to realize that I was on the wrong side of this siege. The island belonged to them, not us.

The pace of life varied from Slow to Very Slow, except for people driving the coastal highway. The buses literally swayed from side to side to miss the potholes, careening to a near stop with long-limbed Rastas jumping off while they were still moving. There was only something like 3 per cent unemployment on the island, but that was achieved by having three workers for every job. It was not uncommon to find half a dozen employees behind the counter of a gas station – one manning the till, the others chattering away in their soft Bajan voices. With the house came a crew to tend the swimming pool; it included two pool guys who came twice a week, one to remove the leaves and the other, it seemed, to watch him. A third fellow came on alternate days to flip a big white disinfectant pill into the pool. Alvy suggested that all these functions could be done by one person, which prompted their supervisor to decide that her services were also required to monitor the situation, so we ended up with almost daily visits.

The island's main problem is traffic. Most of the roads follow winding sugar plantation trails and are too narrow for one car, never mind two. Street names and numbers are rationed in a bizarre fashion: you get one or the other but seldom both. There is no accurate street map of the place. Whenever we asked directions, we were told some variation of: "Now, there's a Shell station up the road, and you might want to turn left there, then go as far as a field on the right that usually has a brown cow on it, which will take you to another road where there is a row of abandoned telephone poles, and if you follow them, you're bound to arrive near where you want to be." It all depended on that brown cow still being there.

When a Canadian company mapped potential Barbados mineral deposits from the air, its chief pilot was so pleased with the project that he took his crew up and produced a faultless digital map of the island, showing every house and every street. When the job was done, he went to see the minister responsible to present him with a free, definitive map of Barbados. The politician was shocked, and pushed it away. "No, no," he said, "that would be far too expensive!"

The puzzled pilot insisted, "You don't understand. There is no charge. We want to give you this map to show our appreciation."

"*You* don't understand," the minister replied, stepping away from the unwanted object as if he were frightened of it. "If we had a map like that, we'd have to name all our streets, and *that* would be too expensive."[5]

Alone at last, Alvy and I enjoyed our seclusion, afloat on the sea of love that evolves outside the marriage bed, even if it is most ardently expressed in it. We grew ever closer, experiencing the release of the senses that accompanied our transformation from big-city sophisticates to desert-island sensualists. We felt as snug as a bug in a rug – an unfortunate metaphor, since members of the nocturnal menagerie regularly invaded our house.

In this primitive and unspoiled place, we awoke one morning to discover that there had been a robbery at the Royal Bank branch in Holetown, just down the road. Nothing unusual about that, except that this robber had been armed with a cutlass. He leapt over the counter and shovelled the contents of the tellers' drawers into a bag, yelling "Money! Money! Money!" then escaped on foot and was never caught. The cutlass disappeared too. There was something wild and untamed about Barbados that gave it charac-ter, despite its relatively advanced infrastructure. I used to drive inland past the ruined windmills and great tamarind trees to inspect the chattel houses where slaves had once lived. "Chattel" meant moveable possessions, and the one-room shacks (which could be taken apart and reassembled in one day) originated when slaves were required to provide their own shelters while following jobs at various sugar plantations. Walking under the Caribbean sun, past the sour remains of derelict sugar refineries, I watched shirtless kids

---

[5] We got around the problem by making up our own address: 3 Westmoreland Ridge, St. James Parish, and without skipping a beat the local post office began delivering our mail.

kicking around soccer balls or practising cricket. We visited the Morgan Lewis sugar windmill, the largest and lone intact sugar windmill in the Caribbean, now on the World Monuments Fund's list of 100 Most Endangered Sites.

We drank raw cane juice straight off the press, and watched with amazement as a wizened cane picker in her late eighties, dressed in demure high-necked clothes and white protective gloves that made her look decked out in her Sunday best, fed cut cane into the crusher. She had worked the mills all of her life and was in her glory. On the receiving end of the machine, where workers fed in the plants, there was a hand-lettered sign next to a huge machete knife, that read:

SAFETY EQUIPMENT:
The cutlass is to cut off hand/arm.
If they are caught in mill rollers apply
strong downward chopping motion
QUICKLY!

AS WE SETTLED into Barbados, we recognized its qualities of tranquility and natural beauty, as well as the honesty and sweet disposition of its permanent residents. My best friend was my lawyer, Trevor Carmichael, who had written widely on Canadian-Caribbean relations and was one of those wise men who know as much about life as the law. We spent many happy lunches at Daphne's (a beachside bar that wouldn't allow me to wear my Greek Fisherman's cap), debating the world's joys and dilemmas. Other friends included Peter and Katy Hermant, late of Toronto's Imperial Optical; David and Lynda Csumrik, formerly of Vancouver; Nigel Browne, the hemisphere's most honest car dealer; and Roger Carmichael, a Bajan who'd spent many years in New York. He'd returned to the island at his grandma's behest and ran a taxi out of Holetown, quickly establishing himself as trusty family friend and my buddy. During an extended visit by my mother-in-law, Cathy

Bjorklund, Roger squired her around the island in elegant Bajan style and called her "Mom."

Our time in Barbados had been fabulous, but I wanted to complete my autobiography, and Alvy her Ph.D. in medical psychology. We decided to move on and try our luck in Zurich, the spot we had years earlier designated a favoured port of call.

"YOU'RE NOT *the* Peter Newman, are you?" the slightly accented Swiss voice was asking.

"Well, I'm *a* Peter Newman, though in Canada I guess I might be considered *the* Peter Newman. But how do you know about me?" I asked. I had called the Zurich Yacht Club with a view to joining, and here was Rolf Greter, one of its chief animators, recognizing my name.

"I learned English from you – I delivered your papers!" Greter excitedly replied, explaining that when he was starting out his father had sent him to teach himself English in Canada. His first job had been driving *Toronto Star* delivery trucks when I was the paper's editor. To kill the monotony and learn the language, he had read my columns, and he even remembered some of them.

I got lucky. A few weeks after we had arrived and settled into a small apartment in Zurich's majestic Old Town, I connected with Greter and he became a fast friend. He had grown up in the city's elegant Enge district within an ethnically mixed community that included some Jewish families, whose sons became his playmates. "Every Saturday," he told me, "I acted as their broker at the local pastry shop, where they picked out their favourite sweets but weren't permitted to pay for them because it was the Sabbath. I laid out the money, which they paid me back the following Monday." He won their respect by charging them 20 per cent interest over the weekend.

When Greter joined the Zurich Yacht Club crowd as a youngster, he promised himself that he would be a millionaire by thirty and retire by fifty. He attained the first goal by becoming

Switzerland's busiest ship broker, and later operated a major over-seas shipping company. His position made him a fortune and brought him into contact with the European and Arab money crowds. He grew particularly close to the powerful Baron Hans Heinrich "Heini" Thyssen-Bornemisza, who became his patron. By the time we met, Greter's impeccable ethics and web of con-tacts had paid off to rank him near the top of Europe's mega-yacht and executive aircraft brokers, dealing in the biggest toys for the biggest boys. We had lots to gossip about.

On August 21, 2002, he introduced Alvy and me to the Zurich Yacht Club (ZYC) at a special luncheon, hosted by Jörg Hotz, its president. The ZYC enjoyed more prestige than elegance. It was in reality a miniature barge tied up to pilings, off a downtown Zurich park. The club's quarters consisted of a small bar on the main deck with a tiny dining room and smaller kitchen on its upper floor. But I was eager to join because the club would open a window for me into Swiss society, the access to local sailors with whom I would at least have a hobby in common, and it would give me a place to tie up the dinghy I intended to purchase so I could sail the thirty-mile-long Lake Zurich, surrounded by snow-capped Alps.

Rolf and the club president warmly welcomed Alvy and me and made it sound as if joining their club would be merely a pleasant formality. They suggested I attend their Wednesday luncheons to meet the members who would eventually vote on my application. I did just that, enjoying their company but very early on realizing that my idea of immersing myself in my former Czech-Austrian culture by coming to Switzerland had been impractical. In Europe you are what you speak. The prevailing tongue-twister spoken in Zurich was Schwyzerdütsch, a guttural dialect that made its speak-ers sound like Joe Cocker with a fatal cold. They understood my Viennese German, but I couldn't comprehend more than word or two of their regional lingo.

One ZYC member came up to me at a Wednesday lunch and, realizing that I couldn't follow the conversation, solicitously asked, "Does it bother you that we speak German?"

"Not at all," I replied. "It bothers me that you *don't* speak German."

Because Switzerland has four official languages (German, French, Italian, and Romansh, a descendant of Latin spoken by only 0.5 per cent of its citizens) everyday phrases are often a mixture. Instead of the German "*danke*" for "thank you" they use the French "*merci,*" but then add "*vielmal,*" which is part of the German for "very much." (They leave out the *s* which is added by so-called High Germans.) Their speech reflects the Swiss character. Because everything in Switzerland runs on schedule (you really can set your watch by train arrivals), the assumption is that if you have to ask the time, you're already late. "How late is it please?" they ask when they want to know the time.

Social reforms have been slow in coming. The year we arrived, gays and lesbians were finally allowed to visit their partners in hospitals, a privilege previously limited to heterosexuals. Yet Zurich pioneered a scheme that offered free sexual services to the handicapped; the municipality picked up the tab for prostitutes and volunteers. The Swiss are not simple believers. They need proof. When the chef at a Zurich hotel lost a finger in a meat-cutting machine and submitted a claim, the insurance company, suspecting negligence, sent out an agent to investigate. He tried the machine and also lost a finger. The claim was promptly paid.

Garbage collection is a weekly production. We had been living in Switzerland for most of a year when we flew to London on a Sunday morning. That meant having to put the garbage, which is usually collected Tuesday mornings, out early. And that, in turn, resulted in our only run-in with the Swiss police. By putting out the garbage too early we had committed a faux pas serious enough that we were warned one more such misdemeanour would bring a police summons.

Zurich is the world's best-kept secret: grandiose and classy, tranquil and organized, it is the epitome of everything that is orderly in the world. The Swiss are right to jealously safeguard the utopia they have created; with over half of the country covered by uninhabitable mountain ranges and no natural resources, they must carefully preserve their lifestyle. Street beggars are given a one-way ticket home. Environmental misdeeds of any magnitude – like throwing a cigarette butt into a river – are high on their list of serious infractions, and rightly so. When you are a guest, whether in their homes or their country, you conduct yourself accordingly, with dignity and decorum. Anything short of that and you don't get, or deserve, a second chance. We lived across the canal from the city's main police station but hardly ever saw a cop; the jewellery stores, some of Europe's fanciest, leave their display windows filled overnight; young girls and boys walk to school unattended. Switzerland may be as close as any urban space gets to Utopia: comfortable, peaceful, and civilized. When the trouble in Iraq began, a London TV station announced that the safest position in the world was to have your money in cash and a one-way train ticket to Switzerland in your pocket.

In the winter of 2003, I was invited to chair a panel on Culture and Governments at the World Economic Forum conference in Davos, a mountain village two hours by train from Zurich. The meeting took place just days before the Americans invaded Iraq and the war was the flashpoint of heated debate everywhere during the six-day gathering, which included the world's top CEOs, academics, and innumerable heads of state. (I became so jaded that by the third day I was greeting people by asking, "And you are the king of . . .?")

I wandered around the heavily guarded complex, searching for diversions, and found a few. The Mongolian prime minister, Nambar Enkhbayar, told the story of being invited to North Korea. When he had inquired what an appropriate gift for the country's dictator might be, it was suggested that he bring a leather coat, but when he asked for the size he was told that this was secret information. Criticizing American farm subsidies, the Swiss head of Nestlé calculated that for the same cost, each American cow could be flown first class round the world, while three cows could take a bull along in the economy section.

My Davos visit was an enlightening experience. Listening to the after-hours thoughts of global leaders, I realized that the Iraqi war was only the symptom of a much more profound clash of civilizations. That made me even more content to be in neutral Switzerland.

Swiss neutrality dates back to 1515, when its armies were decisively beaten by the French and they decided that such pro bono fighting was a waste of time. During parts of the Middle Ages they had marched into battle as mercenaries in support of whichever side paid the highest retainers. In modern times, Switzerland declared its armed neutrality and fielded one of Europe's most effective armies to enforce it. Military service remains compulsory, and about 10 per cent of the population is enrolled at any one time. (The same proportion would mean that Canada would have an armed force of three million, instead of the puny 60,000 who are currently enrolled.) Draftees, who later in life must update their skills annually, take their kits and guns home so they can be mobilized faster. No details of the Swiss army's weapons and communications capabilities are published.[6] Switzerland belongs to no alliances, and its only peacekeeping venture was to send a dozen civilian plumbers to Kosovo. There exists a capable officer corps, but generals are appointed only in times of national emergency. (In five centuries of neutrality, the country has needed only five generals, though none of them declared war.)

"Switzerland does not have an army," John McPhee wrote in *The New Yorker*. "Switzerland *is* an army." He was referring to the country's regimented mentality, but the army also represents one of the diminutive nation's few uniting institutions. It's the only time in most citizens' lives when they mix with their ethnic counterparts from other cantons across the mountains. This works as a social leveller and a splendid networking opportunity.

---

[6] There was one indication in 1995 that Switzerland's military capability might not all be rocket science and satellite hookups. That was the year the Swiss army finally pensioned off its corps of thirty thousand carrier pigeons.

I personally found the constant speculation about the strength of the Swiss army irrelevant. No power-crazed dictator has ever attacked the country, but not, I contend, out of fear of Switzerland's armed might. Rather because, if the idea occurred to him, he would slap his forehead and say to himself: "Why should I attack the country where all my illegal millions are stashed?"

And they are. More than a third of the world's offshore assets — the equivalent of about $2.3 trillion — is hidden in the numbered accounts of Zurich banks alone. Most Swiss bankers either perpetuate a fraternal air of mystery or insist on treating their profession as a holy order, so I was surprised when I met Marcel Ospel, chairman of UBS, largest of the country's 369 banks. Instead of appearing in the formal three-piece suit that most Swiss bankers hide behind, when he welcomed me into his private office, just off Zurich's fabled Bahnhoffstrasse, he was wearing a brown corduroy jacket on top of a grey turtleneck sweater, his feet comfortably encased in black leather moccasins. He chain-smoked throughout my visit, sipped Diet Coke, quoted the Czech existential novelist Milan Kundera, and punctuated his sentences with laughter instead of frowns. "I like diversity of opinions and style," he told me. "If I dress and talk differently it's to show that we focus on substance over form."

A former windsurfer who left school at fifteen, Ospel is Europe's highest-paid banker ($21 million in 2003). Despite his enlightened views concerning most aspects of his trade, he is an unrepentant advocate of Switzerland's banking secrecy laws. He has wrapped the issue in the banner of human rights, claiming that taxes negate the freedom of individuals to maximize their earnings. "The secrecy combined with our tough anti-laundering standards allows us to protect people's privacy with determination and ethical conviction," he told me. Yet UBS was reprimanded (and fined 750,000 Swiss francs, which translates to a similar amount in Canadian dollars) for its lack of due diligence in accepting a $200-million deposit from Nigerian dictator Sani Abacha. Saddam Hussein is still supposed to have $40 billion hidden abroad, most of it in

Switzerland. Lately, however, money is pouring in not so much to escape taxes as for safekeeping. The UBS branch at Zurich's Paradeplatz had 13,000 safety deposit boxes, some of them in vaults dug several storeys below ground.

The British prime minister, Harold Wilson, liked to blame his country's financial troubles on Swiss bankers, whom he called "the gnomes of Zurich." Local gnomes have a saying: "If you see a Swiss banker jump out the window, jump after him. There's bound to be money in it." There may well be gnomes in Zurich but I never met one. The closest I came was walking up Uraniastrasse one day and seeing this dwarf-like figure approaching me dressed in a tiny suit, carrying what looked like a toy briefcase. I put on my best "I'm a journalist about to ask you an embarrassing question" smile, desperately trying to remember the German word for gnome (*zwerg*). Before I could say anything, the little man looked up at me and, in perfect Oxford English, said, "Don't even go there, old boy," then walked away on little feet.

OUR APARTMENT on Schwanengasse (the Lane of Swans), only one block from the city's main canal (the straightened Limmat River), was the third floor of a hostel originally built in 1155. We lived in a virtual stage setting, with narrow cobblestone streets (just wide enough for a bicycle) and Jack-the-Ripper street lanterns. Not a creepy-crawly in sight. The flat was small (I had my office in the spare bedroom, Alvy in the living room) but cozy. We would work full out for four weeks and take four-day holiday trips to nearby cities. We didn't have a car, but the Zurich railway station had overnight trains to thirty-one European destinations.

We lived around the corner from the famous Augustinerstrasse, with its seventeenth-century houses and exquisitely decorated window boxes. The pub where James Joyce wrote much of *Ulysses* was nearby, and our apartment was halfway between St. Peter's Church, which has the continent's largest clock face and dates back to 857, and Fraumünster Cathedral, founded four years earlier as a convent for noble ladies. The stained-glass windows installed in the cathedral's Romanesque chancel were completed by Marc Chagall when he was in his eighties. Alvy, whose calling, second to health care, was architecture, thought she had gone to heaven. We walked the city for hours. It was a feast for the eyes. Every morning we awoke to the evocative peal of church bells, clanging the time of day, the death of a parishioner, lunchtime, or just that it was Tuesday morning, sunny, and Zurich. We made the best of our time together. We were giddily in love and hated every minute we spent apart.

By the spring of 2003, my probationary period at the Zurich Yacht Club was coming to an end. I had happily attended the weekly luncheons, met nice people, participated in regattas, and made friends. At the club's annual sailpast we had been invited to crew with Julius Minder, a wonderfully droll and worldly Swiss industrialist whose sailboat, the *Aquila*, was the oldest and prettiest in the club. It was one of those perfect sailing days when the wind locks your boat into a slot and drives it home. We came in second and drank a toast to the skipper.

The first hint of trouble came unexpectedly from an executive committee meeting on May 22 when my two sponsors, Rolf Greter and marine artist Hans Rudolf Hugentobler, were informed that my membership would not be approved. This decision was based squarely on the anti-Semitic attitude of some ZYC executives. In an open letter to club members, Greter asked them to reconsider: "Who would like to be connected with the membership of a sporting club of which it is said that racially tinted criteria are applied as a pretext for the rejection of candidates of Jewish descent?" He also pointed out that the club's geographical location was granted on sufferance and that "this tolerance might change to the detriment of the club if word spreads that it is kicking freedom of religion with its bare feet." No dice. The move to have me rejected had been spearheaded by a few elderly members who had previously voiced their virulent anti-Semitism to Jörg Hotz, the club president, who didn't lift a finger to defend me.

Shortly afterwards, Rolf Greter resigned from the ZYC's active list. "I simply could no longer eat at a table together with others who practise not only small-talk but double-talk and display a silly aura of racism with a stiff upper lip," he wrote me. "If this club didn't want you, it does not need me either. I enjoyed half a century of leisure time and fostered many friendships which will live on for long into the future without the floating platform of the yacht club, and I wish to keep my good memories of the past without poisoning them with those of recent events."

My own reaction was more muted. I was sitting in a Toronto restaurant when I received the news and immediately sensed my nose morphing into a Shylock hook. In a flash I was back on the beaches of Biarritz, reliving the memory of another assault on my soul sixty-three years earlier. Despite all my travels and travails, I had not come very far.[7]

While Alvy had accumulated a string of impressive credentials – a B.Sc. in biological psychology, focusing on the study of the correlation between stress and disease, called psychoneuroimmunology; an MBA in health education and preventive medicine from the University of British Columbia; plus professional development courses at the Harvard School of Public Health – she had hoped to complete her doctorate in Zurich. To her disappointment, the regulations governing the Ph.D. courses at the University of Zurich were changed and now required five compulsory classes that were taught only in German. Fortunately, she was able to connect with Dr. Jane Ogden, a lively and superbly qualified clinical health

---

[7] The Canadian record is no better. There have been many recent cases of anti-Semitism but none more blatant than the statements made by David Ahenakew, the Saskatchewan aboriginal leader, who twice publicly defended – in fact praised – Hitler's Holocaust. Along with other members of the Order of Canada I lobbied to have him removed from its roster, since that honour is dedicated to "creating a better country." They dismissed our concern with bureaucratic double-talk and did nothing.

psychologist specializing in the problems of obesity at Guy's, King's & St. Thomas' School of Medicine at the University of London, who agreed to supervise her thesis. That meant weekly commutes to London as she set up her research protocol, although she was active in the Professional Women's Group of Zurich and senior consultant to the Swiss branch of the pan-European obesity organization Eurobesitas.

I accompanied her as often as I could. It was not difficult to convince me to spend a few days there. London was an old and familiar face, a welcoming friend I had visited often over the years as an author and naval officer, since my first stay in the capital during the wartime Blitz in 1940, when I slept on Underground train platforms during the nightly Nazi bombings. I should say London was *several* friends, since its many parishes and boroughs are as distinctive, yet as distinctly "London," as members of the same family. Stately Mayfair and Belgravia, with their white-columned Georgian terraces, reminded me of the family's comfortable maiden aunts; the red-brick shops of Knightsbridge, from Harrods to the designers' row along Sloane Street, were to my mind London's stylish matriarch; while the City and its satellite Pall Mall clubs (with their ever-flowering window boxes) were the family's dignified and prosperous patriarchs. As for charming Chelsea and fragrant Kensington, both literary and fashionable enclaves, they were the family's heir and heiress. London is a city of villages, each with its own character and pace of life, and this alone makes it the world's most habitable metropolis. I welcomed the chance to return to its leafy squares, its musty libraries and even mustier jazz clubs, and the magnificent, poky bookstores – that and the many other attractions that had made me an unabashed admirer of this magnificent imperial metropolis.

Hotels were proving too expensive, so Alvy found a furnished basement studio in the parish of Pimlico, on the north bank of the Thames River, wedged between the fashionable precinct of Chelsea and the majestic Houses of Parliament. We took to the area right away, because, while it had no grand distinguishing landmarks, it dripped with wonderful glimpses of decorative architecture without being the least bit pretentious.

It was a new district to me, as my knowledge of London had been built around a regular circuit of favourite haunts during my frequent visits. The epicentre of my London pilgrimages was Jermyn Street, such an ever-fixed symbol of elegant London that a society lady in one of the West End's most popular plays, upon seeing a man relieving himself there, asks: "Is this the end of civilization as we know it, or is it just a man pissing in Jermyn Street?" I would often stop there and ogle the turtlenecks I love en route to a fish luncheon at Wheeler's on Duke of York Street. An institution since 1856 (and reputedly haunted by the ghost of a nineteenth-century fishmonger), Wheeler's is spread vertically over five impossibly narrow storeys. Each floor (which has space for only five tables along one wall) is redolent of burnished oak and forest-green baize. My favourite is the top landing, which narrows to a single table that seats four. The atmosphere is one of controlled and joyous chaos, with waiters shouting orders up and down the stairwell, and the sound of footsteps stamping up from the kitchens in the basement to the dining rooms above. The bartender has been there since birth, and the liveried waiters never fail to remember which of the ten varieties of Dover sole on the menu I favour. Being a man of habit I always order Dover Sole Capri, the house specialty, served with chutney-dipped bananas.

For a taste of traditional London at its finest, I treat visiting Canadians (and they come through monthly, sometimes weekly) to dinner at the Carlton Club, the extra-parliamentary home of the Conservative Party, which offered me reciprocal privileges as a member of the Rideau Club in Ottawa. It is the very picture of a London gentleman's habitat, rebuilt by architect Sir Sidney Smirke in 1857 and modelled on the library of St. Mark's in Venice. It boasts a massive cupola in the Classic Revival style and sweeping Tory-blue carpeted staircases of patterned marble with wrought-iron balustrades and oak banisters, overlooked by oil paintings of its most celebrated members, from Benjamin Disraeli to Sir Winston

Churchill to Baroness Margaret Thatcher. Disraeli, the favourite of Queen Victoria, was the founder of modern British conservatism and a Jew, yet he had no difficulty in being welcomed through its doors, and neither (the Zurich Yacht Club notwithstanding) did I.

Most of my time in London was spent with my laptop but I ventured out as often as possible. A perfect London day for me is rounded off with a visit to Foyles book shop along Charing Cross Road. Foyles has been tidied up and looks very much like any other big-box retailer now, but the store I fell in love with was an untidy place, with jumbles of books falling off tables, real dust on the dust jackets, and mice scurrying between shelves. Each department – BUTTERFLIES, say, or LAOS – was run as a separate fiefdom, with typical British anarchy. To purchase a book, you first had to find the department through mazes of faded hand-lettered signs, seeking directions from the bewildered and dust-mite-afflicted staff. There was no guarantee that Beth, working in WAR on the first floor, would have any idea how to reach DISARMAMENT on the fourth. Once you were in the right place, an aging retainer in belt and braces would know exactly where to locate an obscure Bernard Crick book of essays on parliamentary reform or Doug Beardsley's first collection of poetry. Actually *buying* the book became another exercise in logistics, as you would be handed a slip to take to the cashier, who would issue a receipt, which could then be exchanged for the book. It was madly inefficient, and I loved it.

No evening is complete without a visit to Ronnie Scott's at 47 Frith Street. A tenor sax player who lived as hard as he played, Scott died in 1998, but his legend lives on. He got the idea of starting the jazz club with fellow tenor saxophonist Pete King after a visit to New York, where he played with Dizzy Gillespie. His club was the only place in London to hear such big bands as those of Woody Herman, Buddy Rich, or my muse, Stan Kenton. It was part of its charm that the facilities fell so far below its reputation. I was present one night when Rich began a set with the sarcastic benediction: "We don't play too many condemned buildings, but here we are, glad to be back at Ronnie's!"

In the years since, London had become a much more cosmopolitan, complex, and above all costly city: it has the costliest housing, priciest restaurants, highest property taxes, world's busiest airport (Heathrow) – all of them confirming, in the basest terms of supply and demand, that London had become the most desirable place in the world in which to live. It is also the largest: Greater London is now home to twenty million souls. It can safely be called the capital of the world, since its time zones allow access to most of the money centres, and the city itself is home to forty billionaires, compared to thirty-one in New York and five in Toronto. They deal in new, active money and are mostly foreigners, particularly from Russia and the Indian subcontinent. Their reason for living in London is the same as mine – it may lack efficiency, but it is still the most civilized of communities and, incidentally, the only one where the rich can buy a home in the middle of town with a garden and servants' quarters, as opposed to, say, a steamy New York condo. For most of the past fifty years, London's richest man was Gerald Grosvenor, the Duke of Westminster, inheritor of the largest privately owned swaths of luxury property in the city core. He was supplanted in 2004 by Roman Abramovich, a thirty-seven-year-old self-made billionaire from Ukhta, near the Arctic Circle, who made his fortune in oil and gas during the privatization gold rush in the wake of Russian perestroika.

Nearly as high on the list is Anglo-Indian steel magnate Lakshmi Mittal, another member of London's new moneyed elite, who purchased a £70-million property in Kensington, the most expensive home ever, anywhere. The twelve-bedroom mansion, a mere stone's throw from the darkened residence of Conrad Black, features a jewel-encrusted pool and marble pillars hewn from the Indian quarries that built the Taj Mahal. (It has garage space for twenty cars, compared to Lord Black's paltry dozen.)

PIMLICO HAS TRADITIONALLY been a working-class district dedicated to servicing travellers' needs. Row upon row of its terraced

housing is given over to budget hotels, but in most of the row residences where we live (on the corner of a square that runs along
Grosvenor Road, which parallels the Thames River) Pimlico is
still, if not exactly a bargain, then certainly the last remaining
affordable district in central London.

The basement flat is within easy walking distance of such
marvels as the Tate Gallery and the Palace of Westminster to the
east (not to mention the Victorian pub patronized by the late
Queen Mum, who was amused rather than repelled by its name,
The Spread Eagle). To the west is another London treasure that
serves up works of art and features both lord and commoner, and
that is Pomegranates restaurant. Its owner, Patrick Gwynn-Jones,
MBE, is a host who is nearly as famous and eclectic as his menu. He
cures his own gravlax (I didn't know it was unwell) and carves his
own steak tartare out of beef from Scotland's Glenbervie Angus
herd, more flavoursome than anything on the hoof in Texas,
Alberta, or Argentina. On top of which, he is the resident head of
the British Tabasco Society, ensuring that his establishment serves
the tangiest Bloody Mary in all of London, so hot that I am sure
it can be used as fuel for rocket-boosters.

On the other end of the street there is a Mary Poppins hut,
surrounded by a wrought-iron fence protecting the nondescript
Young England Daycare, where Lady Diana Spencer worked before
she became engaged to Prince Charles. (Alvy and I walk past it
daily and cannot help but imagine the scene during her first
betrothed day at work, when the paparazzi arrived to photograph
her in that winsome picture – carrying a child and wearing her
sheer skirt – that made her famous.)

Behind our flat, encompassing an entire block and containing
three and a half acres of garden, is the notorious and monstrous
block of flats known as Dolphin Square, home to fifty members of
Parliament. The building is within the sound of Big Ben's chimes
and has always been popular with MPs, who at one time dispatched
servants on their behalf when the division bells calling them to
a vote rang out from the clock tower. (An amendment to the

Commons rules now requires the MPs to lift their faces when voting, which put an end to this subterfuge.) Among the residence's many notorious tenants were Christine Keeler and Mandy Rice-Davies, the high-priced prostitutes who were central in the Profumo scandal; William Vassall, the Admiralty clerk convicted of spying; and Oswald Mosley, the wartime Fascist leader, who was arrested in the block. More recent guests have included William Hague, the former Tory leader, while Princess Anne and her husband Timothy Lawrence had a seven-room flat on the premises. As a result of our illustrious neighbours, the streets are guarded by dark-glassed vans while the sky above thunders with the sound of black "security gunship" helicopters that have infrared sights. I haven't decided whether this makes me feel more or less secure, but I know that couples who work at Westminster take separate trains home to ensure that one parent has a better chance of surviving any terrorist attacks.

Our landlords are the cultured Tony and Tashira Hambro, of the merchant banking family. Tony is a prolific artist with a "Group of Seven" bent, while neighbours include art dealer Grenville Collins and his wife Sue. Grenville was a colleague and friend of Canadian art dealer Anne Fotheringham, Allan's wife. He is a delightful luncheon companion and one of nature's true gentlemen.

Entering the flat, we walk into the most eccentric home Alvy and I have yet occupied: it descends two levels below the street, with the lower platform built into a series of connected underground vaults, or "caves." In actuality they are the coal bins into which the coal carts wheeling along the streets dumped their wares. Rumour has it, though, and I much prefer this version, that the vaults were used as holding pens before convicts were moved onto waiting ships moored near the Vauxhall docks for transport to Australia. The ghosts of these convicts still haunt the place, although the only cool draughts I have felt in my new home have been the result of the legendary British central heating. Quentin Crisp noted that "the English think incompetence is the same thing as sincerity." In which case, they have the most sincere boilers in the world.

Though Alvy delights in earning the doctorate she always coveted from a first-rank university and we both thrive on the civilized tumult of London town, we love returning to the orderly universe of Zurich.

When I am in London I take daily delight in the English love of incongruity, wordplay, and sense of fun, not to mention the little civilities that make life here so much less bruising than elsewhere. Rolf Dahrendorf, another London immigrant and the erudite former chancellor of the London School of Economics, put it succinctly when he said, "I have a feeling that this island is uninhabitable, and therefore people have tried to make it habitable by being reasonable with one another." I also find intriguing the fact that the English can at one and the same time be the most civil and insular of peoples to be found anywhere. "Your extrovert Englishman or woman of the supposedly privileged classes," wrote the novelist John Le Carré, "can have a Force Twelve nervous breakdown while he stands next to you in the bus queue. You may be his best friend, but you'll never be the wiser."

The tolerance – even embrace – of eccentricity is close to my heart; the English define themselves by the unusual and the bizarre, encouraged by their profound admiration for the absurd. To cite one example: Jeremy Bentham, who died in 1832, was the pioneer of "utilitarianism" (a philosophical precept also known as the "greatest happiness principle"), which influenced John Stuart Mill and most modern politicians since. He was also a delightful eccentric who designed harpsichords, invented jogging, and coined two words without which modern life would be impossible: "international" and "monetary." Despite his seminal contribution to the modern system of thought, he is remembered less for his accomplishments than for the peculiar disposal of his remains. He despised long meetings and willed that his body be stuffed and wheeled into committee considerations, assuming that his otherworldly presence would drastically reduce their tedium by cutting them short. He is now kept behind a glass case at University College on Gower Street, in London's bookish Bloomsbury area, and regularly wheeled out to attend committee deliberations, where his presence is noted: "Mr. Bentham attended but declined to speak." He wears dapper suits of clothes, their fashion unchanged by the altering tastes of time: frock coat, wide-brimmed straw hat, walking stick crooked over his knee. His face is fixed in a pleasant expression, his eyes are bright and clear. He looks good for a man his age (he died at eighty-four), and for a man who has been dead for nearly two centuries he looks surprisingly cheerful.

He is not the only eccentric in town. My favourite London judge recently sentenced offenders who played rap music much too loudly on their car stereos to a night at the opera. At the same time, a football fan went to the High Court to defend his right to sleep at a boring football game, after having his season ticket removed for snoring during a 4-0 drubbing of Aston Villa. (The judge restored his ticket.)

While these and other lovable aspects of the "old Britain" remain, the country survives and prospers through its admirable ability to absorb and co-opt new trends without so much as a raised eyebrow. Eton College, training ground of the country's elites, recently appointed an imam to deal with the influx of its newly rich Muslim students.[8] British undergraduates are now a minority at Oxford. It remains a testament to the British character that the countries once colonized by its Empire now are returning in droves – the biggest audience in the world for the annual Oxford-Cambridge boat race is in India, not England. Historically, the British are admired for conquering half the world and not feeling guilty about it, then losing their empire without any sense of failure.

At the same time, one attitude of the past ("no sex please, we're British") has lost its sting. In keeping with its role as leader of the world's cultural and social trends, Britain has ventured into

---

[8] Indian restaurants now employ more workers than the United Kingdom's mining and shipbuilding industries combined, while chicken tikka marsala has replaced roast beef as the country's most popular dish.

sensuality with a long-repressed vengeance. As for the idea that England is the nation of the stiff upper lip, anyone who witnessed its World Cup victories in rugby, or the response to the death of Princess Diana, can put that notion to rest.

It is hard not to admire a country that gave us both Winston Churchill and the Beatles; that reached its height of gastronomic achievement with bitter beers and roast beef so rare it is merely carried past the stove. To borrow from George Bernard Shaw, all of a man's pleasures bar smoking and gambling can be, and mostly are, shared with his dog. The French may have a reputation for *joie de vivre*, but it is the English, to my way of thinking, who really know how to live – cozily, unpretentiously, and with a constant hint of amusement at themselves.

Edward R. Murrow, the fabled U.S. journalist broadcast from London during the Blitz ("I speak to you from a city in flames . . .") described the English character most accurately during a broadcast over the BBC at the war's end: "I am persuaded that the most important thing that happened in Britain during the last six years was that this nation chose to win or lose this war under the established rules of parliamentary procedure. It feared Nazism but did not choose to imitate it. The government was given dictatorial power but it was used with restraint, and the House of Commons was ever-vigilant. While London was being bombed in the daylight, the House devoted two days to discussing conditions under which enemy aliens were detained on the Isle of Man. . . . There was still law in the land, regardless of race or nationality. Representative government, equality before the law, survived. Future generations who bother to read the official record of the proceedings in the Commons will discover that British armies retreated from many places, but that there was no retreat from the principles for which your ancestors fought. The record is massive evidence of the flexibility and toughness of the principles you profess . . . I have been privileged to see an entire people give the reply to tyranny that their history demanded of them."

George W. Bush, please copy.

The city does not work at the technical level, as Londoners are the first to admit. It took us two months to have a telephone line installed in our flat, while train lines have been halted when the "wrong type of leaves" fell on the tracks. Commuting passengers on the London Underground suffer through conditions of heat and overcrowding during the summer months that would be illegal under EU regulations, if they were livestock. Yet Londoners show a great tolerance for these inefficiencies. It is not the technical, but the human, at which London specifically and Britain in general excels.

Every once in a while I call on Jeremy Bentham. I pay my respects to the man's spirit. Since he would not be needing his body, he bequeathed it to some useful purpose. That's how I think of London. It is a marvellously complex and beguiling metropolis, filled with wonders. The spirit of this great Empire City is in the lives and ideas it allows to flourish, including – and for this, I am truly grateful – my own.

As I write this, I am ensconced in my cave in the London flat, just as I always dreamed of it, on the Thames Embankment. In a miraculously short time, as usual, Alvy has transformed it into a welcoming, if tiny, home. She is chatting to her daughters on the telephone, making plans for Christmas in Zurich. I know that our home will be echoing to their laughter, the barbs of their teasing, the joys of watching what grandson Adon will get up to next. We will talk about our daughters' recent experiences, their love lives, their plans for the future. I will be happy knowing that I have found something that long eluded me – complete belonging. My family is the snuggest of ships, and one that will carry me to home port.

EPILOGUE: CHILD OF THE CENTURY

—⟡—

I am a child of the century,
a child of disbelief and doubt,
and will remain so until the grave.
How much terrible torture this thirst for faith has cost me,
which is all the stronger in my soul
the more arguments I can find against it.
— Fyodor Dostoevsky

All memoirs are an exercise in plea bargaining, but this one is an exception. I can be accused of much foolishness and many misdemeanours, but failing to inhabit my life isn't one of them. Each experience produced a bounce that led me to the next. If, during some uncharacteristic down times, my life wasn't apocalyptic, it didn't take me long to make it so.

I never did find that pole star in the sheltering sky that I longed for to guide me. I just followed my ambition and curiosity, and allowed myself to be carried along on the rising and falling tides. Shelley Wood, a first-year student in one of my University of British Columbia graduate writing classes, caught the pattern of my existence perfectly when she wrote (about herself): "I've often thought of my life as an unfurling flag in an unpredictable wind, snapping off in different directions, as if I had little to say in the deciding."

As noted in the prologue, my life became an odyssey, tiny in scope but mighty in keeping at bay the contentment it was supposed to deliver. To the readers of my overheated prose, I became the ultimate insider, their snickering guide to the bacchanalian smorgasbord of the rich, the famous, and the powerful. I thrived in the role, but it was only a handy disguise, a passport to my own wealth, fame, and influence, however modest they were compared to those of the people I wrote about. Journalists are perennial visitors, bound to disillusion our hosts. Anyone who has gained any measure of success practising my mad craft thrives on pretend intimacy and ultimate betrayal.

I might not have learned much in my event-filled life, except how to survive. But that was something. Charles Darwin never did proclaim the truism so often credited to him about "survival of the fittest." That was a pithy refinement promulgated later by Herbert Spencer, one of his disciples. Instead, Darwin opted for the more practical (and useful) maxim that postulated survival for the most adaptable: "It is not the strongest of the species that survive, nor the most intelligent, but the one most responsive to change."

And that has been my game. I could thrive doing anything, anywhere, anytime, with almost anybody. From mining gold to performing magic, to mastering economics, to becoming a naval captain, to co-founding an ardent Canadian nationalist movement, to editing the country's largest newspaper and its most influential magazine, to writing two dozen books in three disparate genres, to crossing oceans in sailboats, to leading a jazz band, to turning myself into a marrying fool with a happy ending. I have been loved and I have been hated, but never simply tolerated, and I never gave up the dream of becoming true to myself. If I obeyed any guiding maxim, it was Norman Mailer's evocative lament: "There is a law of life, so cruel and so just, that one must grow or else pay more for remaining the same."

Divorce might be the ultimate indulgence, fame and ambition the ultimate madness, terminal immaturity the ultimate flaw. But they were all weapons against a status quo that I could not or would not abide. Nobody's life is a sequence of great leaps forward. Everyone makes mistakes they later regret. They become the rocky waltz of life. Mine was a full dance card.

In *Cousins*, a minor but insightful 1989 film, Ted Danson (of *Cheers* fame) is courting a woman (touchingly played by Isabella Rossellini) who is at a loss to understand her man. He is charming, funny, and good-hearted, with no bad qualities, yet he drifts from job to job, his most recent teaching the cha-cha to pensioners in a decrepit dance studio. At a family picnic, she corners her lover's favourite uncle and asks what he is really like, and why he doesn't try to be more successful. "He is a failure," the uncle replies, "at everything except life."

That answer stabbed me to the quick. Had I been a *success* at everything except life? Had I spent my days desperately reaching for something already in my grasp? Sounds about right. Too often, I have lived and behaved as a fugitive on the lam – but running away from what? From myself, I recognize in retrospect. Certainly I championed my rage to live. Life is not hard; I made it hard. My problem was my unquiet spirit, boiling like water on a stove to no great purpose. When one of the kinder ladies I briefly wooed decided to dump me, she bade me a memorable adieu. "I'm reluctant to leave, I really am," she said, "but I can no longer reconcile the gentle, caring, and considerate Peter I know with the bitter, angry man on television, encased in his light blue shirt and three-piece suit, barking at bewildered politicians. As I watched that TV debate you were on the other night, I cried. Not for myself. But for you." Then I cried too.

I AM STRETCHED OUT in the cockpit of my auxiliary cutter, the *Windrose*, anchored in Tsehum Harbour, a notch in the shore of the lee side of Vancouver Island, still wondering whether I have written this extended memoir for my so-called "public" or to cleanse my soul. If it was for my readers, then I should have tried harder to keep alive the Peter C. Newman myth. I should have concentrated on the illusions we all need to get through life, the internal screenplay we believe ourselves to be living, the mythologies we create for ourselves to lend order and meaning to existence.

The story in a nutshell: Having Lost All in the cauldron of war, immigrant Jew-boy comes to foreign country, penniless and tongue-tied, yet overcomes all obstacles to reach the pinnacle of his profession and his adopted nation's esteem. Having been of great – nay, defining – service to his compatriots, he retires to another country with his dearly beloved. The Theme that animates this life is his search for a Land and Heroes so that he will never again feel so threatened. But at the twilight of his life, he realizes that this security is only to be found within and through the redeeming power of love.

Well, there's nothing wrong with that. It's a noble story, and I have worked damn hard and done a lot, and deserve kudos, even if they come from me. Unfortunately, that sanitized version of events is not entirely true; it is incomplete and needs sorting out.

Now, at the end of that long process, I know that I must grace this long volume with a little more than that: to leave behind my rationale for taking such exotic detours, venturing on so many existential errands, challenging myself at every turn instead of staying on the farm, maybe selling tractors, marrying the first babushka-in-training who came along, and having a few affairs that nobody noticed.

What moved me to make all those risky – public – choices? Why so many books, and almost as many marriages? Why such a mixture of rage at and adulation for Canada's elites? What was I seeking besides fame and fortune, those double-edged swords, as elusive and transient as they deserve to be? Why the perpetual quest for security and safety when no one was really threatening me? What was I trying to make myself safe *from*, since the Nazis had not conquered Canada, and never would?

I was safe the moment I landed here. I didn't have to search for a land, I had just been allowed into one. That little piece of paper they gave me at Pier 21 in Halifax meant they couldn't kick me out. Having reached sanctuary, why did I persist in my quest for heroes when they were all around me? My father was certainly one – but for his brave efforts we would have been cremated in one of Hitler's concentration camps. How lucky to have connected with all those people who mentored me: Ralph Allen, Doug Beardsley, Doug Gibson, Stan Kenton, Robert Mason Lee, Martin Lynch, Christina McCall, Jack McClelland, Joe MacInnis, Ron McEachern, Jim Paupst, Vlad Plavsic, William Strange, George Whitman, and so many others.

And it was while I contemplated these verities that it finally came to me. I was in search of a hero, all right. But the hero, I blush to admit, was me. True, I was also in search of a home country. *My* land. I'd had a land once, and a father who was as much a hero figure as any to be found in Greek mythology: all-powerful, rich, majestic beyond belief. The lesson of Biarritz was that all could be taken away in the blink of a well-aimed eye. So, like the other Jews who survived that terrible period, I swore to myself: *Never Again.* The not inconsiderable task I set for myself was not only to search for heroes in my adopted Canada, but to become one of them. The moment I set foot in Canada and realized the evil forces threatening my life were behind me, I resolved to seize control of my own. It was a fierce, burning need to control my destiny, born of not knowing unconditional love, but of experiencing first-hand unconditional surrender. I had an agenda. We all do, but few are brave or stupid enough to admit it – and even fewer are sufficiently foolhardy to follow it.

The need to control my destiny led me to try and exert some slight degree of influence over Canada's prevailing attitudes, at least in my determination to prompt its citizens not to take their magical home country for granted, or to allow the Yanks to swallow it up, reducing Canadians to squatters on their own land. It's far too much to claim that I set out to fashion the country in my own image, but I harboured a much stronger sense of priority than I admitted to myself. Why all those big fat books? Because I thought that if I could steer the head, the rest of the body would follow. I was no passive player, no deferential nomad begging for refuge. I set out to make my adopted land the sort of place I could trust – a liberal, tolerant, and independent Canada where Peťa could be safe.

I don't really know what got me so interested in low politics and high finance, but I suspect my wind rose was not set to any ideology. I was not drawn to liberalism, socialism, or conservatism per se. The regional battles of my adopted country meant little to me. They were merely there to be studied and mastered, but they did not command my loyalty. Only one thing demanded my allegiance, because it is what makes the world turn. My internal compass was set to achieving personal power, though I could realistically only claim a small measure of influence. The only thing that power cannot control, which is why it is holy, is love.

There was little I set out to gain that I did not achieve. Yet the succession of failed relationships – professional, personal, romantic – left my heart weary. Those that worked best for me were hierarchical, well defined, the ones where everyone played an assigned role. What mystified me were the loosey-goosey ones, the connections-without-rules that come and go with the spirit. Chief among those, of course, is love. Love became my perpetual quest, because I knew there was personal protection there. I thought I had found it at least three times before Alvy, and yet I couldn't make it stick. Was I really the passive player in all this, the eternal romantic smelling the roses and drowning in nectar? Or is the real explanation that true love involves a considerable degree of surrender of personal will, and surrender is the last thing I wanted to consider? That meant having to be quick on both feet, able to duck and dive, compromise, make amends, give in. Finally, at retirement age, I decided to surrender to myself. And then Alvy waltzed in. She didn't need to be conquered. She loved me already. She loved me even before I loved myself.

"THE HERO COMES HOME AGAIN." Five words that sum up much of the western literature of the past 2,500 years. In all the great odysseys, from Homer to Joyce, the hero ends up . . . at the beginning. It is archetypal, because the greatest lesson in life is that we venture outward to journey inward; we seek new continents to discover ourselves. I certainly did. And I might still be running, but now I'm running for home.

That's the legend. And what of the man? I have learned that the love of a country is nothing compared to the love of a good woman, that surrender is as important as control, that the world can be a frightening place, but it can also be safe and splendid. I have learned that love is freely given; it is neither earned nor demanded.

Every life is a soul's journey to somewhere, often to recapture something lost early on: a mother's love, a father's security, an eternity's wisdom. In the preceding chapters I have tried to invent a thread that sews together everything I did.

I sit here in the cockpit of my boat and experience a glimpse of light, then a shaft, and then feel illuminated with self-discovery. After all, every life should have meaning. It's our purpose on earth. The journey must possess what one memoirist (Tim Lott, writing in the *Sunday Times*) has called "the intangible quality of resonance, so that each event follows the next inexorably, with a kind of mysterious, almost symbolic rather than chronological logic." Easier said than done, because it amounts to a living quest for meaning in which the writer substitutes self-knowledge for embroidery.

I do not pretend that I have managed to achieve that state of grace in this book, because I'm no genius with an original mind who rolls out golden epiphanies with the same ease as my purple metaphors. But having spent three-quarters of a century on the journey, I believe that my chronicle extends beyond timetables and anecdotes. I was a child of the last half of the twentieth century. Dostoevsky left only one letter dealing with the nature of his inner struggle. "I am a child of the century," he wrote," a child of disbelief and doubt, and will remain so until the grave. How much terrible torture this thirst for faith has cost me, which is all the stronger in my soul, the more arguments I can find against it." Ditto.

While I sought external validation through my search for personal heroes and my quest for Canada's identity, there was another agenda, unknown only to myself: the search for Peťa, the spoiled little boy who was happiest, and felt safest, in his childhood home. If only the nannies had stayed. Being a successful journalist brought me a measure of protection, but in the process I found myself caught in the inevitable trap of having to live through others.

Despite every effort to sabotage myself, I finally got it right. I am now more at peace with myself than I have ever been, certainly more than I was at the height of my glory years. The wealth and fame I earned might have been useful tools in getting me to this point, but they are not the reason for it. I am much more contented, now that I have been released from the struggle for greater notoriety, in pursuit of my own star, rather than following the unrealized expectation that a grateful nation might salute my having been "a good boy" on its behalf. I feel at home at last, and my refuge is not in company of the Establishment's Titans, whose exploits I chronicled, but in the loving company of Alvy and her family. I still need to jet off to Davos or Bay Street, cultivate the yachting circles. I always want to be "in the know," to remain "connected." But these diversions are no longer my lifeblood. They are just as much a part of me as my Greek fisherman's cap.[1] But that is no longer the essence of me. The essence of me now feels at home, and this time the nanny stays.

Against inevitable death there is no defence, but the human spirit is fortified by two things only: love and faith. I have the former, but lack the latter, and wouldn't be too surprised if life turned out to be an inside joke dreamed up by a bored Deity with a highly developed sense of the absurd. Still, I try to live my life with a modicum of grace, and if I'm convinced of anything, it is that the inner circle of Dante's Inferno is reserved not for those who failed, but for those who did not try. To repeat my credo, first

---

[1] My final disillusionment: I received a letter from a retired naval officer whose friend had gone on a bareboat charter to sail the Greek Islands. "Feeling he would be less conspicuous as a tourist," he wrote, "my friend bought a hat just like yours, only to find that the only natives wearing them were donkey drivers." Is nothing sacred?

published thirty years ago in *Home Country*: "What I've learned is not to believe in magical leaders any more, that character and compassion are much more important than ideology and prayer. That even if it's absurd to think you can change things, it's even more absurd to believe that it is foolish and unimportant to try."

BEING AT SEA ON Canada's west coast is like waking inside a diamond. The tang and glitter of the Pacific connect you to the universe and activate your dream machine. Settling into *Windrose*'s comforting perch for the evening, I feel the breath of the only God I can claim to know. The sun will soon go down; it has begun to drizzle. I hear a dog barking. It is a tentative sound, as though it is rehearsing, the way a singer at a party flexes his voice as someone removes the tasselled runner from the grand piano.

Silhouetted against a meadow on Coal Island, just where Iroquois Passage sneaks through to Swartz Bay, I spot a woman with a red umbrella walking in the twilight, as luminous as a figure in a Renoir canvas. And even if the connection is oblique, that tableau flashes me back to Biarritz and our escape from Europe, more than half a century ago, where I spotted a similar sundown image of that aristocratic lady with her scarlet parasol, walking the beach that was about to be strafed by machine-gun fire.

Dreams of our escape in turn remind me of *Arrival and Departure*, a novel by Arthur Koestler about precisely that week when we were in and around Bordeaux as he was. His protagonist, a Russian escapee, imagines that he's on trial. He stands before the judge, silent but alert.

"What's he doing?" asks the judge.

"He's tuning his heart," explains his defence attorney. "When he succeeds, his self will expand and become dissolved in the universal spirit."

The exasperated prosecutor, his bloodless lips curved by bitterness and disappointment, wearily announces the charges: "I accuse this man of complicity in murder and crimes of the present, past, and future."

"He never killed a fly!" his astonished defender angrily protests.

"The flies he did not kill brought pestilence to a whole province," the prosecutor replies.

"Condemned because of the presence of doubt," rules the judge, and he later sentences the prisoner to "Purgatory, on probation."

Koestler wrote the scene to ridicule and condemn the Communist regime's justice system, following his classic *Darkness at Noon*, but as I thought about this fragment of that imaginary trial in the context of my career, it hit home. The opinions I didn't publish brought pestilence to the provinces. I had been too subtle for my own good. My assumption that readers would grasp my message – that Canada had been fatally weakened by the blatant inadequacies of its political and economic elite – never hit home as it should have. I was being too damn Canadian, too respectful of those twin traits that sink us every time: our affinity for ambiguity and our deference in the face of authority. That is our national plague, and I thought I was immune, stirring up trouble for those in authority. Not trouble enough to have displaced the Establishment, or reformed its operational code, which amounts, as I have written here, to equating their self-worth with their net worth. They know that this country takes a lot of killing (and if nothing else, my writings have at least documented that dubious distinction). Theirs is a selfish ethic that will ultimately kill the Canadian dream.

MOVING HESITANTLY, with the touch of an inexperienced lover, I go below and prepare the *Windrose* for the coming of the night, checking the ride of the anchor, making sure the anchor light is on, the bilge pumps are at the ready, and the cabin lights have been doused to save battery juice. The darkened houses visible on shore slip by as the boat swings on her anchor. The night grows darker.

I feel enough of my Jewish heritage to realize I am sitting shiva, not only for me, but also for a way of life and a way of looking at the world.

Robert Mason Lee, who helped to edit this memoir, wrote to me when we began: "Of the men and women of letters in this country, you are the last of the learned elders who remains politically relevant. It is a blessing, and like all blessings it contains a curse. The blessing is that the readers will approach you expectantly and willingly; the curse is that the critics will approach you looking for a fault. Professional jealousies will reign supreme. They will think they could have done a better job themselves. There will be one defining difference, however: you wrote the book and they didn't."

He was being too kind. My thinking is more in line with that of John Updike, the American novelist of similar vintage to mine, who concluded: "That a negative review might be a fallible verdict, delivered in haste, against a deadline, for a few dollars, by a writer with problems and limitations of his own, is a reasonable and weaselling supposition that I can no longer, in the dignity of my years, entertain."

Nor can I.

Spiritual man will always be in conflict with natural man. Religion explains everything – except *why*. I know it is possible that there is a Heaven and a Hell in which the souls of men and women spend eternity. It is possible, but I doubt it. To me, jettisoning the melancholy burden of sanity – the life force – is the most profound moral option of our time, and while I sometimes find the mysteries of life as impenetrable as a *Globe and Mail* editorial, I am not afraid to die.

I also agree with Woody Allen, who was asked by a hesitant interviewer whether he intended to achieve immortality through his work. "Hell no," he shot back. "I want to achieve immortality through not dying."

We'll see. I currently occupy the uncomfortable no man's land between being neither an extinct volcano nor an erupting one. I still write columns for *Maclean's* and anyone else who'll ask me. I am working on at least two more books, and plotting new adventures aboard my sailboat.

Apart for being granted an Italian afterlife, I have one final wish: that as I am laid out in my coffin being inspected by the caring and the curious, I overhear a whispered: "I thought I saw him move."

ACKNOWLEDGEMENTS: NEWMAN'S ARMY

One day, in the blustery fall of 1998, I was walking on the lower, grungy part of Vancouver's Granville Street when I heard the sounds of jazz guitar emanating from a street person, huddled in a doorway. I went over, dropped a pair of loonies in his battered cap, and started to walk away when I heard him say: "Well, if it ain't the Bard himself . . ." That was the moment I knew I had arrived.

The recognition factor doesn't get any better than that. And I promised myself that when I got around to writing my memoirs, I would pay proper tribute to all those blessed individuals who helped me along the way.

Looking back on my life, I realize that I have been extraordinarily fortunate in my mentors, my friends, and even my enemies, who spurred me on to greater effort. Like most lives, mine has been constructed from bits of other people, a shifting, remarkable contingent of compelling men and beguiling women who enlisted in my various causes over the years, leaving their indelible mark on my life, my writing, and my character. Call them Newman's Army. Well, platoon.

These compatriots and friends (which is a mundane word for the most prized of human kinships) contributed to who I was and what I became. I am not their composite, but they made me – they, and many others not named here, for had I done so, this chapter would have overwhelmed this book's already considerable heft. All too often we appreciate mentorships, friendships, and relationships (and sailboats, for that matter) only after they have vanished from our lives. We underestimate how intense the experience of knowing them was until we look back on the time we shared in bittersweet remembrance. (It's the same way with countries; homelands are seldom appreciated until you lose them. I know.)

I have, of course, paid tribute to most of my professional and personal *compadres* in the preceding pages, but that was in specific situations and events. Most of these other benefactors have pervaded my lifetime.

Dr. Jim Paupst must lead any parade of Newman's Army, because without him there would no longer be a Newman. He has been my GP and confidant for more than three decades, and has saved my scrawny neck not once but twice. It was his early diagnoses that kept me out of harm's way, keeping at bay the fatal diseases that threatened my life.

When I asked Paupst, who is Irish enough to believe that God created human beings in order to hear their stories, to describe himself, he shrugged and said, "Early on, I embraced the doctrine of unconditional joy. I came to learn that life is scar tissue and happiness can be a learned trait. I am a Sagittarian, an ironist, an irresistible raconteur, Jesuit, and a thoroughly bad ass, proud of my patients."

As I discovered in the fall of 2001, they are just as proud of him. Allan Rock (then Health minister in the Chrétien government) and I were relaxing aboard my tug, *Titan*, one summer afternoon, comparing notes on how the good doctor had saved our lives. It occurred to us that we must be just two of many others, and that it would be appropriate if a few of us could gather to pay tribute to our healer. We organized a dinner for Paupst at Hart House in Toronto on October 19, and we had to cut the list off at 350, because its largest hall would accommodate no more.

His intuitive diagnosis requires that Paupst take the time to assess his patients as profoundly as their illnesses. The only reason he can afford to invest such concentration is that he earns much of his income outside his practice. How he does this I discovered one evening when he took me to dinner at a Church Street restaurant called Bigliardi's, a hangout favoured by Ontario Cabinet ministers. Our meal was constantly interrupted as Jim excused himself and disappeared into a back room. Each time he mumbled something like, "Brave Heart – thirty to one," and by the end of the meal his horses had won him – and his patients – six thousand dollars. That's excellence in Canadian medicine, twenty-first-century style.

In a similar aura of excellence, I acknowledge the contributions to my writing life of the late Martin Lynch and his wife, Jane. Dating back to *Flame of Power*, and continuing through the dozen books that followed, Martin was the fountainhead of the countless historical details that endowed these texts with authority. A self-educated savant (who instead of attending university ran away to sea at fourteen), he knew everything worth knowing, or where to find it. He became easily recognizable in the *Globe*'s newsroom, where he spent thirty years, because he carried a large set of copy-editor's shears, attached to his waist with a bathtub chain. He would occasionally use the instrument to cut off the ties of reporters with insufficient respect for factual reporting. In 1982, Martin decided to take early retirement from the *Globe* and he and Jane moved to Kaslo, British Columbia, where he died in 2000. In combination with the very professional copy-editor Janet Craig, the Lynches were the essential architects of my first dozen books, keeping me out of harm's way and allowing me to sound as authoritative as their wall-to-wall research.

Another essential influence, not so much in keeping me out of harm's way as making the risks of being in harm's way worth-while, has been Michael Levine, the country's leading entertainment lawyer, whose first literary client I became in 1980. CBC broadcaster Hana Gartner once described his manner as being non-confrontational, "But when he calls it's, 'My God, Levine's on the line, and he's sounding intimidatingly friendly.'" Michael prefers to describe his method as exercising the "making-love-under-a-train aspect of negotiations." When confronted, he describes himself as "a simple man of God," which may be the worst case of misrepresentation since Joe Clark tried to govern the country.

It has been Levine's skill in negotiating the publishing and TV rights for the last ten of my books that has allowed me to prosper as a freelance writer for the past two decades. We have become fast friends – fast in the sense that I can get him on his cellphone any time, and occasionally manage to stay on the line a full three minutes before another client cuts in.

A mentor of a different genre (who taught Levine, Pierre Trudeau, and Prince Charles how to scuba dive) is Joe MacInnis, the medical doctor who switched to undersea research in 1960 and has since led an exhilarating life as one of Canada's few full-time adventurers. A sailing buddy who shares my love of the sea, and comprehends its mysteries, he is drawn to risking his life in deep-sea dives to discover sunken vessels and live in another dimension. He is a friend for life who, as the British used to say of such comrades, is a good man to go tiger hunting with, even if the tigers turn out to be sharks. "Explorers are curious and want to test themselves," he told me when we were crossing the Gulf Stream in his sailboat. "You do it with words, pushing the limits in terms of getting inside people's heads and trying to understand who they really are, beyond the stage on which they perform and the costumes they wear. That's exploration too." Joe flatters me. His half dozen remarkable books bear witness to his tremendous talent.

A fellow poet and soulmate is Doug Beardsley, the sage from Victoria, B.C., whose creative non-fiction masterpiece *Country on Ice* turned Canada's national game into a metaphor. The author of eighteen books, mostly poetry of a rare calibre that compresses yet expands modern realities, Doug is my alter ego. An English professor at the University of Victoria and the hub of several literary networks, he is one of those rare individuals who excel in fostering and nurturing intensive friendships. Doug has counted among his friends fellow poets Leonard Cohen, Irving Layton, and the late Al Purdy. As well as analyzing sports as a serious social phenomenon, he is an expert in regional First Nations history. He is also keeper of the flame for Holocaust studies on the west coast, making him perhaps the only freckled WASP in whose honour several clumps of trees have been planted in Israel. When we meet, we can pick up at the exact point our previous discussion ended.

My other Victoria guru, sadly missed, was the late Bruce Hutchison, the crusty former editor of the *Victoria Times* and a famed columnist for the Vancouver *Sun*. He first came into prominence as author of *The Unknown Country*, the 1943 bestseller that, along with his many other books, came as close as any text to defining the Canadian identity. Bruce and I knew one another casually for most of forty years, but it was only when I moved to his hometown in 1982 that we became close. We would lunch at the Union Club, tear apart whatever politician was bold enough to pretend to be running the country, and settle Canada's problems between the vichyssoise and the Stilton. I would then return to my computer and Bruce to his loyal Underwood upright.

Jack McClelland was very much more than a fabulous promoter and superb book person. To those of us who were privileged to be his authors, Jack (nobody ever called him Mr. McClelland) was, above all, a sensitive and shrewd editor, spotting a book's weaknesses and dictating casual fix-notes that magically resolved writer's block. He would do anything for his writers, not excluding arrangements for bail or abortions, though I didn't have to avail myself of either. It's tempting to call him our father figure, but in truth he was our father, offering unconditional approbation. Jack's fundamental strength, and the reason those of us who were his wards swore by him, was the fact that he cared a great deal more about his authors, than about his books or his company. He was the grand ringmaster of the most exciting publishing house that ever drew breath in this benighted country of ours. He turned a faltering business into a faltering cultural institution, essential to documenting the nation's purpose and identity.

The agent of my most valuable education was Abraham Rotstein, the University of Toronto political economist who was the first to provide a solid academic grounding for Canadian nationalism. Before we met, I had felt instinctively that America's accelerating takeover of corporate Canada was undercutting our ability to remain independent, but had no theoretical basis to defend my beliefs. Abe, who initially became my mentor and later my close friend, taught me the fundamentals of our entrepreneurial ethic, noting that "Canada has a business class unique to the western world, in that its most dramatic achievement has been to preside over its own liquidation." I enjoyed his one-person seminars, developing respect and affection for his wry, McLuhanesque humour ("Canada will have to change a great deal to stay the same"), and we began to play off each other in our hunt for prescriptions that might allow our homeland to develop according to its own, instead of imported values.

Two other nationalists became important in my life: Mel Hurtig and Jerry Goodis. A successful bookseller, imaginative publisher, and vocal polemicist on behalf of Canadian independence, Mel was content (as I was) to remain a reformer instead of trying to become a revolutionary, but he did more than any of us to legitimize and propagate the cause. A decent, fun-loving gentle man who taught me not to abandon the crusade for Canadians to appreciate their country, he remains one of my defining heroes.

A nice Jewish boy in a bad trade, the late Jerry Goodis rose to the top of Canada's advertising business, often speculating that he should have taken up "a decent occupation like debt collecting, or running a chain of franchised bawdy houses." He was very good at what he did, loved his country, and became a key figure in the Committee for an Independent Canada, never flinching from controversial crusades. His madcap adventures reminded me of an exploding Mexican flag, its colours and emotions bursting in great, periodic detonations. We had fun, enjoying the same music, and what I admired most about him was a trait I shared: he never hesitated to exploit his communicable passions to the full.

Another brother-in-arms is Vlad Plavsic, a Serbo-Montenegrin immigrant who arrived here when he defected from the 1951 Yugoslav Olympic water polo team. He became one of the west coast's leading architects and turned himself into a Renaissance man. When I invited him to my housewarming party at Deep Cove, I found him examining a Stan Kenton poster in my living room and I patronizingly explained that Kenton used to lead a great jazz orchestra. "I know who he is, for Christ's sake," Plavsic exploded. "I used to be in his trumpet section." We putter around the B.C. coast together, playing Kenton and comparing our heart problems. He is the toughest friend I have, his Serbian legacy asserting itself when we once discussed the boundaries of our friendship: "You're my friend – I kill for you. You cross me – I kill you," he told me. "But don't worry. I say the same to my mother."

Another architect within my orbit was the late Gerald Hamilton, of whom I was inordinately fond. He called me "chum," and it was a good word for our relationship. We chummed around and learned much from each other, mostly about endurance, love, and courage (he had been told that he would die of cancer eleven years before he did, and seldom gave it a thought). There is an old gypsy saying that we are all kings when we die. Gerald, whose dreams included the founding of the new island country of Taluga, for which he had completed a blueprint, on a rocky outcrop 113 miles off the California coast, held that regal title in life.

Other good friends who have enriched my life have included: Fred Augerman (the jazz connoisseur supreme); Senator Jack Austin (the most enlightened politician in the country who knows enough to treat his calling both as a science and as an art); Michael Benedict of *Maclean's* (who edits my column with patience, inspiration, and chutzpah); Graham Clarke (Vancouver's waterfront king who became a great pal); the late Eddie Cogan (the unique huckster with a heart and tongue of gold); John Fraser (the most scholarly and articulate of Canadian journalists); Ray Heard (the knowledgeable political genius who became the country's leading media guru while managing to keep his soul intact); John Gray (the Vancouver playwright/novelist and freelance intellectual who became my most erudite luncheon companion); Al Johnson (who demonstrated that Ottawa mandarins can operate on conscience); Lyall Knott and Darcy Resac (the linchpins of the Vancouver Establishment); Vic Koby (fellow sailor and my comrade from *Financial Post* days); Sherrill and Woody MacLaren (my favourite couple, who along with Alvy and me – and a quartet of St. Bernards –

make up the world's most exclusive club); Leon Major (the Toronto theatrical genius who declared his street, Rathnelly Avenue, an independent republic); Scotty McIntyre (the west coast publisher whose hobby is performing miracles); Ed and Theresa Odishaw (whose loyalty and friendship delight me); Bobbi Newson (who became my guardian angel); Fred Soyka (a boon companion of many years, who sadly found life too great a burden); Hebron Shyng (my accounting genius); Patrick Watson (the broadcasting genius whose talent and friendship I value); Ken Whyte (the founding editor-in-chief of the *National Post*, whose journalistic skills and integrity won my respect, admiration, and affection); Patrick MacAdam (who did much of my historical Ottawa research); and Fran McNeely (who has been my loyal and patient assistant since I hired her at *Maclean's* in 1978.)

MY GOOD FORTUNE in attempting this autobiography was to team up with Robert Mason Lee as its editor, at least for the book's first half, after which illness sadly halted his participation. I acknowledge his generous contribution with profound gratitude. I grew to admire Lee even before we met, when I reviewed his marvellous *100 Monkeys*, the best book written about Canadian political manipulation of the 1980s, and certainly the most aptly titled. He then rode herd on *The Canadian Revolution*, which I published in 1995, and which I believe to have been my second-best book. (The current offering always tops the list.) It was Robert who imposed the narrative literary form that propels this memoir.

Here Be Dragons was originally contracted for by that jewel of a publishing house run by Jan Walter, John McFarlane, and Gary Ross, and I grieve that their worthy venture was a victim of Canadian publishing's lethal economics. At the same time, I am delighted to be returning to the firm where I started to make my name, McClelland & Stewart. My great good fortune is to be part of the Douglas Gibson imprint that includes Alistair MacLeod and Alice Munro. He is as enlightened and inspiring a publisher as remains in the perilous trade's jungle. A salute also to Terri Nimmo for her inspired art direction.

My wife Alvy edited this book with her incisive instinct for recognizing what's real and what's artsy-fartsy. She improved the former and eliminated the latter. Her main contribution was to provide its author with a loving and happy home and family, which is beyond price and was, for me, beyond hope.

All my previous volumes have ended with the prissy little disclaimer, "This book owes its existence to many others not mentioned here: only the responsibility for its imperfections is fully my own."

Not this time. The whole damn thing is my fault.

Peter C. Newman
May 2000 – August 2004

PAPERBACK EDITION AFTERWORD

I've always believed that authors are the ultimate entrepreneurs. Every few years, after a painful interval of intense, lonely, and bum-numbing labour, they turn out a product that nobody needs. In my case, it took four years to write this damn book, and it was the most bewildering and elusive literary task I ever set myself. The fact that it ballooned to 733 pages, and was all about *moi*, turned the tough odds against its success into an impossible dream, bodacious presumption of the worst sort. I figured most potential purchasers would snort and walk away. They surely had better ways of spending their time and their money.

They did. But that didn't stop them from buying *Here Be Dragons: Telling Tales of People, Passion and Power*. During its initial six-week publishing run last fall, it sold almost thirty thousand copies; it then stayed on the bestseller list for twenty weeks, four in the coveted top slot. And that wasn't all. For the first time in my forty-seven years of authoring, I actually won a national literary award: the Drainie-Taylor Biography Prize. Since I couldn't attend the ceremony, my prize was accepted by my editor, Doug Gibson, who runs his own imprint at McClelland & Stewart and had much to do with the book's merit. He phoned to ask what I wanted him to say at the prize-giving ceremony if the book were to win. "Demand a recount," I replied. (Still reeling at my good fortune, I thank the judges – Suanne Kelman, Ken McGoogan, and John Porter – and salute their impeccable taste.)

The writing of *Dragons* provided a welcome catharsis; its publication was a cross-country hootenanny, the most joyful literary launch I've ever experienced. Except for two reviews that I won't mention, the critics seemed favourably impressed. (Authors are constantly accused of being thin-skinned. It's not true. We have *no* skin.) I've always thought that the great advantage of the Internet was that authors could secretly review their own books, but there was no need for Plan B this time around.[1]

Equally exhilarating was the unexpected show of respect by my peers. In the process of reviewing my book, they were really reviewing me: my rusty psyche, my residual lapses of taste and courage, my hidden strengths, and the sweetness and loss that I experienced in my quest for love – and the renewal of finding it with Alvy, which has been my happy lot. They assessed my record of the expenditure of my days, and particularly of my nights, and judged it to be worth recording. They discovered, along with me, that I wasn't a nice, gentle guy, doing nice, gentle things. Instead, I adopted a hard-assed approach that made facts dance to the music of history. I took no prisoners as I told my tales: everything from the intimate details of how Barbara Amiel seduced Conrad Black, to the secrets of Pierre Trudeau's pre-Margaret love life, and the Toronto debutante whom I overheard telling a friend, "Do I believe in sex before marriage? Well, not if it holds up the ceremony."

One of the most heartening consequences of *Dragons*'s notoriety was the sequence of events it produced at the Zurich Yacht Club, which had banned me from membership. Their anti-Semitism was exposed in an article about my book by Dr. Reinhard Meier, in the *Neuer Zuricher Zeitung* and several other publications. "It is easier to push a camel through the eye of a needle," Meier concluded, "than for a Jew to become a member of the ZYC." Although club president Jorg Holtz had instructed Rolf Greter, my brave and elegant sponsor, to brief me of his board's decision to have my candidacy removed from the membership election list because of my religion, he denied ever having done so. It was a

---

[1] The press was uncharacteristically generous. The *Globe and Mail*, for example, published a highly positive cover review by Rex Murphy in its book section, carried news reports, and even published a hilarious feature by Judith Timson in its career section. At one point I feigned bafflement and asked Pat Cairns, my wonderful publicist, why there had been no story on my book in the paper's car section. This left her baffled in turn, until I pointed out, "Hell, it's an *auto*biography!"

mess, but as this edition goes to press, it looks as if the club (which, in reality, is just a floating barge, moored off downtown Zurich) is cleaning up its act, and may soon join the twentieth century – perhaps, eventually, even be a part of the century we're in.

I was often asked why I wrote the memoir, and why now? I am seventy-six years old, I count it a special day if nothing drops off, and when I boast that I got lucky, it means that I remembered where I parked the car. Why the memoir? At some point late in our careers we all become aware of the need to set down remembrances of our haphazard lives. It's an essential summing up, closure with the coffin still open. Given that how we put in our time makes only partial sense to us and no sense at all to anyone else, we need some kind of sustaining gospel for our expected sojourn in purgatory.

As I reconstructed my life, I realized that I could be accused of sins of omission and commission, but failing to live my life to the fullest wasn't one of them. During my dozen years in Ottawa, I switched from dissecting the political mayhem triggered by John Diefenbaker's tenuous hold on reality and Pierre Trudeau's tendency to govern with an icicle for a heart, to writing about Canada's business Establishment, which moved from a sleepy pseudoaristocracy to a bushy-tailed meritocracy. I became its Robin Leach without his glass-shattering seal honk. Most members of the Establishment consented to being Newmanized, only because I pointedly explained that I would do it with them or without them. Luckily, Establishments in this country are movable feasts. They evolve like snakes: new skins but the same animal. What intrigued me, more than their wealth and lifestyles, was their disposable power and that, with a few exceptions, they treat their servants, assistants, and secretaries as mobile furniture.

We warblers of non-fiction are vulnerable romantics, always on the quest for that perfect profile that will crack open our subject's character – as opposed to his personality, which changes with his company's quarterly earnings, or the weather. I have been lucky in that I arrived on the scene before the smooth and homogeneous M.B.A. crowd, when every bigwig was a character, proud to be different. Insider trading was their favourite indoor sport, their offices resembled British merchant banks, and I was usually the first "blackguard journalist" allowed into their sanctums. They had a certain Episcopalian grace that I tried to capture; they didn't bother denying that they ran the country, and they gleefully forced competitors out of their misery.

They were my involuntary mentors, and this book was my last chance to pay them tribute. Near the end of my days, I cannot pretend to be blessed with an original mind that rolls out epiphanies with the same topspin as my purple metaphors. But by telling the true tales of my life, I freed myself, to *be* myself. As my sweatshirt proclaims, I am able, perhaps alone among Jews of my vintage, to convincingly believe its embroidered message: "SCREW GUILT."

When I undertook this weighty autobiography, I was determined to deal in truth, not only about the times and events I experienced, but about myself. About how I felt at every station of the cross, from being machine-gunned on the beaches of Biarritz, to abandoning my daughter Laureen; from marrying Alvy, the love of my life, to going under the knife for a quadruple bypass. From being born Peťa Karel Neumann, a rich man's son in pre-war Europe, to becoming the public Peter C. Newman, and now relaxing into my final incarnation as Peter Newman, a part-time writer and full-time wharf rat.

Onslow Village, Surrey, England, 2005

1929
Born in Vienna, Austria, May 10

1939–40
Flight to Canada, resettlement in Freeman, Ontario

1945–47
Attended Upper Canada College

1947
Enlisted as Ordinary Seaman, Royal Canadian Navy (Reserve)

1950–55
B.A. and M. Com., University of Toronto

1951
Promoted to sub-lieutenant, RCN (Reserve)
Married, Patricia McKee, Toronto

1951–54
Assistant editor, *The Financial Post*, Toronto

1954–55
Montreal bureau, *The Financial Post*

1955–56
Production editor, *The Financial Post*

1956–59
Assistant editor, *Maclean's* magazine

1957
Daughter Laureen, born on June 26

1958
Divorced, Patricia McKee

1959
Author, *Flame of Power*
Married, Christina McCall, Ottawa, October 22

1959–63
Ottawa editor, *Maclean's* magazine

1963
Author, *Renegade in Power: The Diefenbaker Years*

1963–64
National editor, *Maclean's* magazine

1964
Daughter, Jennifer Ashley, born on June 13

1964–69
Ottawa editor, the *Toronto Daily Star*
Syndicated column in 29 newspapers, 2 million circulation

1966
National Newspaper Award, Feature Writing

1967
CBC Wilderness Award, Best Television Documentary

1968
Author, *The Distemper of Our Times: Canadian Politics in Transition*

1968–72
Director, National Youth Orchestra

1969
Author, *A Nation Divided: Canada and the Coming of Pierre Trudeau*

1969–71
Editor-in-chief, the *Toronto Daily Star*
Visiting professor, Political Science, McMaster University
Deputy governor, International Press Institute

1970–73
Member, Board of Governors, University of Toronto

1971
Michener Award for CBC-TV series, *The Tenth Decade*
Co-founder, Committee for an Independent Canada

1971–82
Editor, *Maclean's* magazine

1972–83
Director, Maclean Hunter Publishing, Inc.

1973
Author, *Home Country*
President's Medal, University of Western Ontario

1974
LL.D. (Hon.), Brock University

1975
Author, *The Canadian Establishment – Volume I: The Great Dynasties*
D.Lit. (Hon.), York University

1976
Divorced, Christina McCall

1977
Quill Award for Excellence in Canadian Journalism
Achievements in Life Award, Encyclopaedia Britannica
Married, Camilla Turner, Toronto

1978
Author, *Bronfman Dynasty: The Rothschilds of the New World*
Installed, Officer, Order of Canada

1980
Author, *The Canadian Establishment* (Russian Edition)
The Canadian Establishment (CBC-TV series)

1981
Author, *The Canadian Establishment – Volume II: The Acquisitors*
1981–87
Host, *Everybody's Business*, Global Television Network

1982
Author, *The Establishment Man: A Portrait of Power* (Conrad Black)

1982–present
Contributing editor and columnist, *Maclean's* magazine

1983
Author, *True North: Not Strong and Free – Defending the Peaceable Kingdom in the Nuclear Age*
Author, *Debrett's Illustrated Guide to the Canadian Establishment*
LL.D. (Hon.), Wilfrid Laurier University
Installed, Knight of Grace, Order of St. Lazarus

1984–90
Governor, Shaw Festival, Niagara-on-the-Lake

1985
Author, *Company of Adventurers: An Unauthorized History of the Hudson's Bay Company, Volume I*
Director, Canadian Council for Native Business
Director, Canadian Council for Economic Education
Fellow, Royal Society of the Arts, London

1985–87
Adjunct professor, Saskatchewan Indian Federated College, Regina

1986
LL.D. (Hon.), Queen's University
LL.D. (Hon.), Royal Military College
Northwest Territories Royal Life Saving Society Medal

1986–90
Professor, Creative Writing, University of Victoria

1987

Author, *Caesars of the Wilderness: Volume II, Hudson's Bay Company*
Book of the Year, Canadian Authors Association

1988

Author, *Sometimes a Great Nation: Will Canada Belong to the 21st Century?*

1989

Author, *Empire of the Bay: Illustrated History of the Hudson's Bay Company*
Author, *Canada: The Great Lone Land*

1989–91

President, Maritime Defence Association of Canada

1989–97

Director, St. Paul's Hospital Foundation, Vancouver

1990

Elevated, Companion, Order of Canada
Divorced, Camilla Turner

1991

Author, *Merchant Princes: Volume III, Hudson's Bay Company*

1992

Author, *Canada 1892: Portrait of a Promised Land*
Elected to the Canadian News Hall of Fame
Director, Vancouver Airport Authority

1995

Author, *The Canadian Revolution: From Deference to Defiance*

1996

Author, *Vancouver: The Art of Living Well*
Married Alvy Bjorklund, Vancouver, January 27; Stepdaughters,
  Dana Rae Doll and Brandi Paulayne Doll

1997
Author, *Defining Moments: Dispatches from An Unfinished Revolution*

1998
Author, *The Canadian Establishment – Volume III: Titans: How the New Canadian Establishment Seized Power*
Lifetime Achievement Award, Canadian Journalism Foundation
Director, Lions Gate Entertainment Inc.

1998–2002
Visiting professor, Graduate School of Journalism, University of British Columbia

1999
LL.D. (Hon.), University of British Columbia
B.C. Book Prize for Non-Fiction

1999–2003
Columnist, *National Post*

2000
Outstanding Achievement Award, National Magazine Association

2002
Author, *Continental Reach*
LL.D. (Hon.), University of Victoria

OTHER TITLES FROM
DOUGLAS GIBSON BOOKS

PUBLISHED BY McCLELLAND & STEWART LTD.

ROLLERCOASTER: My Hectic Years as Jean Chrétien's Diplomatic Adviser 1994–1998 *by* James Bartleman
"Frank and uncensored insider tales of the daily grind at the highest reaches of the Canadian government. . . . It gives the reader a front row seat at the performance of Jean Chrétien and his top officials." Ottawa *Hill Times*
Autobiography, 6 × 9, 358 pages, hardcover

ON SIX CONTINENTS: A Life in Canada's Foreign Service 1966-2002 *by* James K. Bartleman
A hilarious, revealing look at what our diplomats actually do, by a master storyteller who is a legend in the service. "Delightful and valuable." *Globe and Mail*
Autobiography, 6 × 9, 256 pages, trade paperback

WORTH FIGHTING FOR *by* Sheila Copps
The former Deputy Prime Minister and life-long Liberal tells all in this revealing look at what really goes on behind the scenes in Ottawa. "Copps gives readers a blunt, no-holds-barred glimpse into the seamy backrooms of Canadian politics." Montreal *Gazette*   *Autobiography, 6 × 9, 224 pages, hardcover*

TO EVERY THING THERE IS A SEASON: A Cape Breton Christmas Story *by* Alistair MacLeod, with illustrations *by* Peter Rankin
A "winsome tale of Yuletide past" (*Toronto Star*), almost every page of this beautiful little book is enriched by a perfect illustration, making this touching story of a farm family waiting for Christmas into a classic for every home.
Fiction, illustrations, 4⅝ × 7¼, 48 pages, hardcover

CRAZY ABOUT LILI: A Novel *by* William Weintraub
The author of *City Unique* takes us back to wicked old Montreal in 1948 in this fine, funny novel, where an innocent young McGill student falls for a stripper.
Fiction, 5½ × 8½, 272 pages, hardcover

THE QUOTABLE ROBERTSON DAVIES: The Wit and Wisdom of the Master *selected by* James Channing Shaw
More than eight hundred quotable aphorisms, opinions, and general advice for living selected from all of Davies' works. A hypnotic little book.
Non-fiction, 5¼ × 7, 176 pages, hardcover

ALICE MUNRO: Writing Her Lives. A Biography *by* Robert Thacker
The literary biography about one of the world's great authors, which shows how her life and her stories intertwine.
Non-fiction, 6½ × 9⅜, 604 pages plus photographs, hardcover

MITCHELL: The Life of W.O. Mitchell, The Years of Fame 1948–1998 *by* Barbara and Ormond Mitchell
From *Who Has Seen the Wind* on through *Jake and the Kid* and beyond, this is a fine biography of Canada's wildest – and best-loved – literary figure.
Non-fiction, 6½ × 9⅜, 462 pages plus photographs, hardcover

RUNAWAY *by* Alice Munro
The 2004 Giller Prize-winning collection of short stories by "the best fiction writer now working in North America. . . . Runaway is a marvel." *The New York Times Book Review*   *Fiction, 6 × 9, 352 pages, hardcover*

DAMAGE DONE BY THE STORM *by* Jack Hodgins
The author's passion for narrative glows through this wonderful collection of ten new stories that are both "powerful and challenging." *Quill & Quire*
Fiction, 5⅜ × 8⅜, 224 pages, hardcover

DISTANCE: A novel *by* Jack Hodgins
"Without equivocation, *Distance* is the best novel of the year, an intimate tale of fathers and sons with epic scope and mythic resonances. . . . A masterwork from one of Canada's too-little-appreciated literary giants." *Vancouver Sun*
Fiction, 5⅜ × 8⅜, 392 pages, trade paperback

BROKEN GROUND: A novel *by* Jack Hodgins
It's 1922 and the shadow of the First World War hangs over a struggling Soldier's Settlement on Vancouver Island. This powerful novel with its flashbacks to the trenches is "a richly, deeply human book – a joy to read." W.J. Keith
Fiction, 5⅜ × 8⅜, 368 page

THE MACKEN CHARM: A novel *by* Jack Hodgins
When the rowdy Mackens gather for a family funeral on Vancouver Island in the 1950s, the result is "fine, funny, sad and readable, a great yarn, the kind only an expert storyteller can produce." *Ottawa Citizen*
Fiction, 5⅜ × 8⅜, 320 pages, trade paperback

RAVEN'S END: A novel of the Canadian Rockies *by* Ben Gadd
This astonishing book, snapped up by publishers around the world, is like a *Watership Down* set among a flock of ravens managing to survive in the Rockies. "A real classic." Andy Russell
Fiction, 6 × 9, map, 5 drawings, 336 pages, trade paperback

THE SELECTED STORIES OF MAVIS GALLANT *by* Mavis Gallant
"A volume to hold and to treasure" said the *Globe and Mail* of the 52 marvellous stories selected from Mavis Gallant's life's work. "It should be in every reader's library."   *Fiction, 6⅛ × 9¼ , 900 pages, trade paperback*

AT THE COTTAGE: A Fearless Look at Canada's Summer Obsession *by* Charles Gordon *illustrated by* Graham Pilsworth
This perennial best-selling book of gentle humour is "a delightful reminder of why none of us addicted to cottage life will ever give it up." *Hamilton Spectator*
Humour, 6 × 9, 224 pages, illustrations, trade paperback

A PASSION FOR NARRATIVE: A Guide for Writing Fiction *by* Jack Hodgins
"One excellent path from original to marketable manuscript. . . . It would take a beginning writer years to work her way through all the goodies Hodgins offers." *Globe and Mail* The Canadian classic guide to writing fiction.
Non-fiction / Writing guide, 5¼ × 8½, 216 pages,
updated with a new Afterword, trade paperback

TEN LOST YEARS: Memories of Canadians Who Survived the Depression *by* Barry Broadfoot
Filled with unforgettable true stories, this uplifting classic of oral history, first published in 1973, is "a moving chronicle of human tragedy and moral triumph during the hardest of times." *Time*
Non-fiction, 5⅞ × 9, 442 pages, 24 pages of photographs, trade paperback

HOW I SPENT MY SUMMER HOLIDAYS *by* W.O.Mitchell
A novel that rivals *Who Has Seen the Wind*. "Astonishing . . . Mitchell turns the pastoral myth of prairie boyhood inside out." *Toronto Star*
Fiction, 5½ × 8½, 276 pages, trade paperback

JAKE AND THE KID *by* W.O. Mitchell
W.O.'s most popular characters spring from the pages of this classic, which won the Stephen Leacock Award for Humour.
Fiction, 5½ × 8½, 211 pages, trade paperback